The International Institute for Strategic Studies

THE
MILITARY
BALANCE
1998/99

Published by **Oxford University Press** for
The International Institute for Strategic Studies
23 Tavistock Street, London WC2E 7NQ

The Military Balance 1998/99

Published by Oxford University Press for
The International Institute for Strategic Studies
23 Tavistock Street, London WC2E 7NQ
http://www.isn.ethz.ch/iiss

Director	Dr John Chipman
Assistant Director and Editor	Colonel Terence Taylor
Defence Analysts	
Ground Forces	Phillip Mitchell
Aerospace	Wg Cdr Kenneth Petrie RAF
Naval Forces	Lt Cdr John Downing RN
Defence Economist	Digby Waller
Editorial	Susan Bevan
Design and Production	Mark Taylor
Production Assistant	Anna Clarke
Research Assistants	Marc DeVore
	Hilary Kivitz

This publication has been prepared by the Director of the Institute and his staff, who accept full responsibility for its contents. These do not, and indeed cannot, represent a consensus of views among the world-wide membership of the Institute.

First published October 1998

ISBN 0-19-922372-6
ISSN 0459-7222

The Military Balance (ISSN 0459-7222) is published annually in October by Oxford University Press, Great Clarendon Street, Oxford OX2 6DP, UK. The 1998 annual subscription rate is: UK£58; overseas US$102.

Payment is required with all orders and subscriptions are accepted and entered by the volume (one issue). Please add sales tax to the prices quoted. Prices include air-speeded delivery to Australia, Canada, India, Japan, New Zealand and the USA. Delivery elsewhere is by surface mail. Air-mail rates are available on request. Payment may be made by cheque or Eurocheque (payable to Oxford University Press), National Girobank (account 500 1056), credit card (Mastercard, Visa, American Express, Diners', JCB), direct debit (please send for details) or UNESCO coupons. Bankers: Barclays Bank plc, PO Box 333, Oxford, UK, code 20-65-18, account 00715654. Claims for non-receipt must be made within four months of dispatch/order (whichever is later).

Please send subscription orders to the Journals Subscription Department, Oxford University Press, Great Clarendon Street, Oxford, OX2 6DP, UK *tel* +44 (0) 1865 267907 *fax* +44 (0) 1865 267485.

In North America, *The Military Balance* is distributed by M.A.I.L. America, 2323 Randolph Avenue, New Jersey, NJ 07001, USA. Periodical postage paid at Rahway, NJ, and additional entry points.

US POSTMASTER: Send address corrections to *The Military Balance*, c/o M.A.I.L. America, 2323 Randolph Avenue, New Jersey, NJ 07001, USA.

Printed in Great Britain by Bell & Bain Ltd, Glasgow.

Contents

United States

NATO and Non-NATO Europe

Russia

Middle East and North Africa

Central and South Asia

East Asia and Australasia

Carribean and Latin America

Sub-Saharan Africa

Analyses and Tables

The Military Balance is updated each year to provide an accurate assessment of the military forces and defence expenditures of 168 countries. The current edition contains data as at 1 August 1998.

The regional groupings of countries are unchanged from last year's edition, except that Myanmar is now shown in the East Asia and Australasia region and not Central and South Asia as previously. Countries are listed alphabetically within each region.

GENERAL ARRANGEMENT

Part I of *The Military Balance* comprises country entries grouped by region. Regional groupings are preceded by a short introduction describing the military issues facing the region, and significant changes in the defence economics, weapons and other military equipment holdings and acquisitions of the countries concerned. Inclusion of a country or state in *The Military Balance* does not imply legal recognition or indicate support for a particular government.

Part II contains analyses and tables. New elements in this edition include an analysis of mergers and acquisitions in the US and Western European defence industries; an account of the global arms trade; and tables on light weapons and small arms, armed helicopters and warships. The loose wall-map showing data on recent and current armed conflicts is updated from last year and a new feature is the inclusion of data on the cost of conflict.

USING THE MILITARY BALANCE

The Military Balance is a quantitative assessment of the personnel strengths and equipment holdings of the world's armed forces. It does not attempt to evaluate the quality of units or equipment, nor the impact of geography, doctrine, military technology, deployment, training, logistic support, morale, leadership, tactical or strategic initiative, terrain, weather, political will or support from alliance partners. *The Military Balance* does not evaluate and compare directly the performance of items of equipment. Those who wish to do so can use the data provided to construct their own force comparisons.

The strengths of forces and numbers of weapons held are based on the most accurate data available, or, failing that, on the best estimate that can be made with a reasonable degree of confidence. The data presented each year reflect judgements based on information available to the Director and staff of the IISS at the time the book is compiled. Information may differ from previous editions for a variety of reasons, generally as a result of substantive changes in national forces, but in some cases because of IISS reassessment of the evidence supporting past entries. Hence, care has to be taken in constructing time-series comparisons from information given in successive editions, although an attempt is made to distinguish between new holdings and revised assessments in the text that introduces each regional section.

In order to interpret the data in the country entries correctly, it is essential to read the explanatory notes beginning on page 5.

ATTRIBUTION AND ACKNOWLEDGEMENTS

The International Institute for Strategic Studies owes no allegiance to any government, group of governments, or any political or other organisation. Its assessments are its own, based on the material available to it from a wide variety of sources. The cooperation of governments has been sought and, in many cases, received. However, some data in *The Military Balance* are estimates. Care is taken to ensure that these are as accurate and free from bias as possible. The Institute owes a considerable debt to a number of its own Members, consultants and all those who helped compile and check material. The Director and staff of the Institute assume full responsibility for the data and judgements in this book. Comments and suggestions on the data presented are welcomed. Suggestions on the style and method of presentation are also much appreciated.

Readers may use data from *The Military Balance*, without applying for permission from the Institute, on condition that the IISS and *The Military Balance* are cited as the source in any published work. However, applications to reproduce portions of text, complete country entries or complete tables of *The Military Balance* must be addressed, with a copy of the request to the Editor of *The Military Balance*, to: Journals Rights and Permissions, Oxford University Press, Great Clarendon Street, Oxford OX2 6DP, UK, prior to publication.

Explanatory Notes

ABBREVIATIONS AND DEFINITIONS

Abbreviations are used throughout to save space and avoid repetition. The abbreviations may have both singular or plural meanings; for example, 'elm' = 'element' or 'elements'. The qualification 'some' means *up to*, while 'about' means *the total could be higher than given*. In financial data, '$' refers to US dollars unless otherwise stated; billion (bn) signifies 1,000 million (m). Footnotes particular to a country entry or table are indicated by letters, while those that apply throughout the book are marked by symbols (* for training aircraft counted by the IISS as combat-capable, and † where serviceability of equipment is in doubt). A full list of abbreviations appears on pp. 319–20.

COUNTRY ENTRIES

Information on each country is shown in a standard format, although the differing availability of information results in some variations. Each entry includes economic, demographic and military data. Military data include manpower, length of conscript service, outline organisation, number of formations and units and an inventory of the major equipment of each service. This is followed, where applicable, by a description of the deployment of each service. Details of national forces stationed abroad and of foreign stationed forces are also given.

GENERAL MILITARY DATA

Manpower

The 'Active' total comprises all servicemen and women on full-time duty (including conscripts and long-term assignments from the Reserves). Under the heading 'Terms of Service', only the length of conscript service is shown; where service is voluntary there is no entry. 'Reserve' describes formations and units not fully manned or operational in peacetime, but that can be mobilised by recalling reservists in an emergency. Unless otherwise indicated, the 'Reserves' entry includes all reservists committed to rejoining the armed forces in an emergency, except when national reserve service obligations following conscription last almost a lifetime. *The Military Balance* bases its estimates of effective reservist strengths on the numbers available within five years of completing full-time service, unless there is good evidence that obligations are enforced for longer. Some countries have more than one category of 'Reserves', often kept at varying degrees of readiness. Where possible, these differences are denoted using the national descriptive title, but always under the heading of 'Reserves' to distinguish them from full-time active forces.

Other Forces

Many countries maintain paramilitary forces whose training, organisation, equipment and control suggest they may be used to support, or in place of, regular military forces. These are listed, and their roles described, after the military forces of each country. Their manpower is not normally included in the Armed Forces totals at the start of each entry. Home Guard units are counted as paramilitary. Where paramilitary groups are not on full-time active duty, '(R)' is added after the title to indicate that they have reserve status. When internal opposition forces are armed and appear to pose a significant threat to a state's security, their details are listed separately after national paramilitary forces.

Equipment

Quantities are shown by function and type and represent what are believed to be total holdings, including active and reserve operational and training units and 'in store' stocks. Inventory totals for missile systems (such as surface-to-surface missiles (SSM), surface-to-air missiles (SAM) and anti-tank guided weapons (ATGW)) relate to launchers and not to missiles.

Stocks of equipment held in reserve and not assigned to either active or reserve units are listed as 'in store'. However, aircraft in excess of unit establishment holdings, held to allow for repair and modification or immediate replacement, are not shown 'in store'. This accounts for apparent disparities between unit strengths and aircraft inventory strengths.

Operational Deployments

Where deployments are overseas, *The Military Balance* lists permanent bases and does not normally list short-term operational deployments, particularly where military operations are in progress. An exception is made in the case of peacekeeping operations. The contribution or deployment of forces to peacekeeping operations is shown on pp. 284–91. Recent changes and developments are also described in the text for each regional section.

GROUND FORCES

The national designation is normally used for army formations. The term 'regiment' can be misleading. It can mean essentially a brigade of all arms; a grouping of battalions of a single arm; or (as in the UK) a battalion-sized unit. The sense intended is indicated in each case. Where there is no standard organisation, the intermediate levels of command are shown as headquarters (HQs), followed by the total numbers of units that could be allocated to them. Where a unit's title overstates its real capability, the title is given in inverted commas, with an estimate given in parentheses of the comparable unit size typical of countries with substantial armed forces. Guidelines for unit and formation strengths are: **Company** 100–200 • **Battalion** 500–800 • **Brigade (Regiment)** 3,000–5,000 • **Division** 15,000–20,000 • **Corps (Army)** 60,000–80,000.

Equipment

The Military Balance uses the following definitions of equipment:

Main Battle Tank (MBT) An armoured, tracked combat vehicle, weighing at least 16.5 metric tonnes unladen, that may be armed with a 360° traverse gun of at least 75mm calibre. Any new wheeled combat vehicles that meet the latter two criteria will be considered MBTs.

Armoured Combat Vehicles (ACV) A self-propelled vehicle with armoured protection and cross-country capability. ACVs include:

Heavy Armoured Combat Vehicle (HACV) An armoured combat vehicle weighing more than six metric tonnes unladen, with an integral/organic direct-fire gun of at least 75mm (which does not fall within the definitions of APC, AIFV or MBT). *The Military Balance* does not list HACVs separately, but under their equipment type (light tank, reconnaissance or assault gun), and where appropriate annotates them as HACV.

Armoured Infantry Fighting Vehicle (AIFV) An armoured combat vehicle designed and equipped to transport an infantry squad, armed with an integral/organic cannon of at least 20mm calibre. Variants of AIFVs are also included and indicated as such.

Artillery A weapon with a calibre of 100mm and above, capable of engaging ground targets by delivering primarily indirect fire. The definition covers guns, howitzers, gun/howitzers, multiple-rocket launchers and mortars.

Armoured Personnel Carrier (APC) A lightly armoured combat vehicle, designed and equipped to transport an infantry squad, armed with integral/organic weapons of less than 20mm calibre. Variants of APCs converted for other uses (such as weapons platforms, command posts and communications vehicles) are included and indicated as such.

Military Formation Strengths

The manpower strength, equipment holdings and organisation of formations such as brigades and divisions differ widely from country to country. Where possible, the normal composition of formations is given in parentheses. It should be noted that where both divisions and brigades are listed, only separate brigades are counted and not those included in divisions.

NAVAL FORCES

Categorisation is based on operational role, weapon fit and displacement. Ship classes are identified by the name of the first ship of that class, except where a class is recognised by another name (such as *Udalay*, *Petya*). Where the class is based on a foreign design or has been acquired from another country, the original class name is added in parentheses. Each class is given an acronym. All such designators are included in the list of abbreviations at the end of the book.

The term 'ship' refers to vessels with over 1,000 tonnes full-load displacement that are more than 60 metres in overall length; vessels of lesser displacement, but of 16m or more overall length, are termed 'craft'. Vessels of less than 16m overall length are not included. The term 'commissioning' of a ship is used to mean the ship has completed fitting out and initial sea trials, and has a naval crew; operational training may not have been completed, but otherwise the ship is available for service. 'Decommissioning' means that a ship has been removed from operational duty and the bulk of its naval crew transferred. Removing equipment and stores and dismantling weapons, however, may not have started. Where known, ships in long-term refit are shown as such.

Definitions

To aid comparison between fleets, the following definitions, which do not necessarily conform to national definitions, are used:

Submarines All vessels equipped for military operations and designed to operate primarily below the surface. Those vessels with submarine-launched ballistic missiles are listed separately under 'Strategic Nuclear Forces'.

Principal Surface Combatant This term includes all surface ships with both 1,000 tonnes full-load displacement and a weapons system for other than self-protection. All such ships are assumed to have an anti-surface ship capability. They comprise: aircraft carriers (defined below), cruisers (over 8,000 tonnes) and destroyers (less than 8,000 tonnes), both of which normally have an anti-air role and may also have an anti-submarine capability, and frigates (less than 8,000 tonnes) which normally have an anti-submarine role. Only ships with a flight deck that extends beyond two-thirds of the vessel's length are classified as aircraft carriers. Ships with shorter flight decks are shown as helicopter carriers.

Patrol and Coastal Combatants These are ships and craft whose primary role is protecting a state's sea approaches and coastline. Included are corvettes (600–1,000 tonnes carrying weapons systems for other than self-protection); missile craft (with permanently fitted missile-launcher ramps and control equipment); and torpedo craft (with an anti-surface ship capability). Ships and craft that fall outside these definitions are classified as 'patrol'.

Mine Warfare This term covers surface vessels configured primarily for mine-laying or mine countermeasures (such as mine-hunters, mine-sweepers or dual-capable vessels). A further classification divides both coastal and patrol combatants and mine-warfare vessels into offshore (over 600 tonnes); coastal (300–600 tonnes); and inshore (less than 300 tonnes).

Amphibious This term includes ships specifically procured and employed to disembark troops and their equipment over unprepared beachheads and by helicopter or directly to support amphibious operations. The term 'Landing Ship' (as opposed to 'Landing Craft') refers to vessels capable of an ocean passage that can deliver their troops and equipment in a fit state to fight. Vessels with an amphibious capability, but which are known not to be assigned to amphibious duties are not included. Amphibious craft are listed at the end of each entry.

Support and Miscellaneous This term covers essentially non-military support and the inclusion of these vessels provides an indication of the operational capability of naval forces in terms of range and the ability to sustain operations.

Weapons Systems Weapons are listed in the order in which they contribute to a ship's primary operational role. Significant weapons relating to the ship's secondary role are added after the word 'plus'. Short-range self-defence weapons are not listed. To merit inclusion, a surface-to-air missile system must have an anti-missile range of 10km or more and guns must be of 100mm bore or greater. Exceptions may be made in the case of some minor combatants with a primary gun armament of a lesser calibre.

Aircraft All armed aircraft, including anti-submarine warfare and maritime-reconnaissance aircraft, are included as combat aircraft in naval inventories.

Organisations Naval groupings such as fleets and squadrons frequently change and are often temporary; organisations are shown only where it is meaningful.

AIR FORCES

The term 'combat aircraft' refers to aircraft normally equipped to deliver air-to-air or air-to-surface ordnance. The 'combat' totals include aircraft in operational conversion units whose main role is weapons training, and training aircraft of the same type as those in front-line squadrons that are assumed to be available for operations at short notice. Training aircraft considered to be combat-capable are marked *. Armed maritime aircraft are included in combat aircraft totals. Air force operational groupings are shown where known. Squadron aircraft strengths vary with aircraft types and from country to country.

Definitions

Different countries often use the same basic aircraft in different roles; the key to determining these roles lies mainly in air-crew training. In *The Military Balance* the following definitions are used as a guide:

Fixed Wing Aircraft

Fighter This term is used to describe aircraft with the weapons, avionics and performance capacity for aerial combat. Multi-role aircraft are shown as fighter ground attack (FGA), fighter, reconnaissance and so on, according to the role in which they are deployed.

Bombers These aircraft are categorised according to their designed range and payload as follows:

   Long-range Capable of delivering a weapons payload of more than 10,000kg over an unrefuelled radius of action of over 5,000km;

   Medium-range Capable of delivering a weapons payload of more than 10,000kg over an unrefuelled radius of action of between 1,000km and 5,000km;

   Short-range Capable of delivering a weapons payload of more than 10,000kg over an unrefuelled radius of action of less than 1,000km.

A few bombers with the radius of action described above but designed to deliver a payload of less than 10,000kg, and which do not fall into the category of FGA, are described as **light bombers**.

Helicopters

Armed Helicopters This term is used to cover helicopters equipped to deliver ordnance, including for anti-submarine warfare. They may be further defined as:

   Attack Helicopters with an integrated fire control and aiming system designed to deliver anti-armour, air-to-ground or air-to-air weapons;

   Combat Support Helicopters equipped with area supression or self-defence weapons, but without an integrated fire control and aiming system;

   Assault Armed helicopters designed to deliver troops to the battlefield.

Transport Helicopters The term describes unarmed helicopters designed to transport personnel or cargo in support of military operations.

ARMS ORDERS AND DELIVERIES

Tables in the regional texts show arms orders and deliveries listed by country buyer for the past and current years, together with country supplier and delivery dates, if known. Every effort has been made to ensure accuracy but some transactions may not be fulfilled or may differ from those reported.

DEFENCE ECONOMICS

Country entries in **Part I** show defence expenditure, selected economic performance indicators and demographic aggregates. **Part II**, *Analyses and Tables*, contains an international comparison of defence expenditure and military manpower giving expenditure figures for the last two years against a bench-mark year in constant US dollars. The aim is to provide an accurate measure of military expenditure and of the allocation of economic resources to defence. All country entries are subject to revision each year as new information, particularly regarding defence expenditure, becomes available. The information is necessarily selective. A wider range of statistics is available to IISS members on request.

In **Part I**, individual country entries typically show economic performance over the past two years, and current-year demographic data. Where these data are unavailable, information from the last available year is provided. Defence expenditure is generally shown for the past two years where official outlays are available, or sufficient data for reliable estimates exist. Current-year defence budgets and, where available, defence budgets for the following year are also listed. Foreign Military Assistance (FMA) data cover outlays for the past year, and budgetary estimates for the current and subsequent years. Unless otherwise indicated, the US is the donor country. All financial data in the country entries are shown in both national currency and US dollars at current-year, not constant, prices. US dollar conversions are generally, but not invariably, calculated from the exchange rates listed in the entry. In a few cases, notably Russia and China, purchasing-power-parity (PPP) rates are used in preference to official or market-exchange rates.

Definitions of terms

To avoid errors in interpretation an understanding of the definition of defence expenditure is important. Both the UN and NATO have developed standardised definitions, but in many cases countries prefer to use their own definitions (which are not in the public domain). For consistency, the IISS uses the NATO definition (which is also the most comprehensive) throughout.

In *The Military Balance*, military expenditure is defined as the cash outlays of central or federal government to meet the costs of national armed forces. The term 'armed forces' includes strategic, land, naval, air, command, administration and support forces. It also includes paramilitary forces such as the *gendarmerie*, customs service and border guard if these are trained in military tactics, equipped as a military force and operate under military authority in the event of war. Defence expenditures are reported in four categories: Operating Costs; Procurement and Construction; Research and Development (R&D); and Other Expenditure. Operating costs include: salaries and pensions for military and civilian personnel; the cost of maintaining and training units, service organisations, headquarters and support elements; and the cost of servicing and repairing military equipment and infrastructure. Procurement and construction expenditure covers national equipment and infrastructure spending, as well as common infrastructure programmes. It also includes financial contributions to multinational military organisations, host-nation support in cash and in kind, and payments made to other countries under bilateral agreements. FMA counts as expenditure by the donor, and not the recipient, government. R&D is defence expenditure up to the point at which new equipment can be put in service, regardless of whether new equipment is actually procured. The fact that the IISS definitions of military expenditure are generally more inclusive than those applied by national governments and the standardised UN format means that our calculated expenditure figures may be higher than national and UN equivalents.

The issue of transparency in reporting military expenditures is a fundamental one. Only a minority of the governments of UN member-states report defence expenditures to their electorates, the UN, the International Monetary Fund (IMF) and other multilateral organisations. In the case of governments with a proven record of transparency, official figures generally conform to a standardised definition of defence expenditure, and consistency problems are not usually a major issue. Where these conditions of transparency and consistency are met, the IISS cites official defence budgets and outlays as reported by national governments, NATO, the UN, the Organisation for Security and Cooperation in Europe (OSCE) and the IMF. On the other hand, some governments do not report defence expenditures until several years have elapsed, while others understate the figures they report. Where these reporting conditions exist, *The Military Balance* gives IISS estimates of military expenditures for the country concerned. Official defence budgets are also shown, in order to provide a measure of the discrepancy between official figures and what the IISS estimates real defence outlays to be. In these cases *The Military Balance* does not cite official defence expenditures (actual outlays), as these rarely differ significantly from official budgetary data. The IISS defence-expenditure estimates are based on information from several sources, and are marked 'ε'. The most frequent instances of budgetary manipulation or falsification typically involve equipment procurement, R&D, defence-industrial investment, covert weapons programmes, pensions for retired military and civilian personnel, paramilitary forces, and non-budgetary sources of revenue for the military arising from ownership of industrial, property and land assets. The principal sources for economic statistics cited in the country entries are the IMF, the Organisation for Economic Cooperation and Development (OECD), the World Bank and three regional banks (the Inter-American, Asian and African Development Banks). For some countries basic economic data are difficult to obtain, for example a few former command economies in transition and countries currently or recently involved in armed conflict.

The Gross Domestic Product (GDP) figures are nominal (current) values at market prices, but GDP per capita figures are nominal values at PPP prices. GDP growth is real not nominal growth, and inflation is the year-on-year change in consumer prices. Two different measures of debt are used to distinguish between OECD and non-OECD countries: for OECD countries, debt is gross public debt (or, more exactly, general government gross financial liabilities) expressed as a proportion of GDP. For all other countries, debt is gross foreign debt denominated in current US dollars. Dollar exchange rates relate to the last two years plus the current year. Values for the past two years are annual averages while current values are the latest monthly value.

Calculating exchange rates

Typically, but not invariably, the exchange rates shown in the country entries are also used to calculate GDP and defence-expenditure dollar conversions. Where they are not used, it is because the use of exchange rate dollar conversions can misrepresent both GDP and defence expenditure. This may arise under the following conditions: when the official exchange rate is overvalued (as with some Latin American and African countries); whenever relatively large currency apprecia-tions or depreciations occur over the short to medium term; and whenever a substantial medium-to-long-term discrepancy between the exchange rate and the dollar PPP exists. Where exchange rate fluctuations are the problem, dollar values are converted using lagged exchange rates (generally by no more than six months). The GDP estimates of the Inter-American Development Bank, usually lower than those derived from official exchange rates, are used for Latin American countries. For former communist countries, PPP rather than market exchange rates are sometimes used for dollar conversions of both GDP and defence expenditures, and this is marked.

The arguments for using PPP are strongest for Russia and China. Both the UN and IMF have issued caveats concerning the reliability of official economic statistics on transitional economies, particularly those of Russia and the former Soviet republics. Non-reporting, lags in the publica-tion of current statistics and frequent revisions of recent data (not always accompanied by timely revision of previously published figures in the same series) pose transparency and consistency problems. Another problem arises with certain transitional economies whose productive capabili-ties are similar to those of developed economies, but where cost and price structures are often much lower than world levels. PPP dollar values are used in preference to market exchange rates in cases where using such exchange rates may result in excessively low dollar-conversion values for GDP and defence expenditure.

Demographic data

Population aggregates are based on the most recent official census data or, in their absence, demographic statistics taken from *World Population Projections* published annually by the World Bank. Data on ethnic and religious minorities are also provided under country entries where a related security issue exists.

MILITARY CAPABILITY

The implementation of the 1997 Quadrennial Defense Review (QDR) plan for transforming US defence strategy and military forces is well underway. An important element is 'Joint Vision 2010', the new conceptual framework for the way future US forces will fight and achieve what is described as 'full spectrum dominance' on the battlefield. At the heart of full spectrum dominance is the ability to collect, process and disseminate information essential to US forces, while denying opponents the opportunity to gain and use intelligence. The 1999 defence budget supports 'Joint Vision 2010' primarily by funding relevant new technologies. It accelerates the acquisition of new command, control, communications, computers, intelligence, surveillance and reconnaissance (C4ISR) capabilities. For example, the fielding of the Army's first digitised division and corps is brought forward by two years. Such advances will enable military commanders to direct forces and transfer information more effectively.

Also funded by the 1999 budget are:

- Key surveillance assets, such as unmanned aerial vehicles (UAV) and more widespread use of navigation aids such as the global positioning system (GPS).
- Upgrades of primary combat platforms like the Army's *Abrams* tank, *Bradley* fighting vehicle and *Apache Longbow* helicopter, with major development efforts including the *Comanche* helicopter and *Crusader* artillery system.
- Restructuring of the 'Heavy' combat divisions into the Army XXI division, with personnel cut by some 3,000 to 15,719. This new organisation, which includes over 400 reservists, is designed for operations to the year 2010.
- Marine Corps modernisation, including the *Osprey* (MV-22) tilt-rotor aircraft, the Advanced Amphibious Assault Vehicle, and the upgrading of *Cobra* (AH-1W) and *Iroquois* (UH1N) helicopters.
- Modernisation of naval forces including procurement of the DDG-51 destroyer, LPD-17 amphibious transport dock ship and New Attack Submarine (NSSN) and full funding of the tenth and final *Nimitz*-class carrier (CVN-77) in 2001 – a cost-saving acceleration of one year. The budget also supports development of the next generation aircraft carrier (CVX) and destroyer. However, the CVX is unlikely to be in service before 2015.
- Major programmes for modernising combat aircraft. However, the budget plans reduce and delay some planned procurement of the Joint Strike Fighter (JSF), the F-22 and the Navy's F/A-18E/F. The JSF will continue in its concept demonstration phase into 2001, in preparation for procurement to commence in 2005. The first two production F-22s are requested for 1999, leading to a gradual build-up to procurement of 36 aircraft per year by 2004. Production should soon increase for the F/A-18E/F, which has greater survivability and weapons payloads than earlier F/A-18 models. In the longer term, the date for Navy plans to make the transition to the JSF from the F/A-18E/F depends on the pace of JSF development.
- Substantial provision for improvements in precision-guided munitions for all services, including the Anti-Tank Army Tactical Missile System/ *Brilliant* (ATACMS/BAT), *Longbow Hellfire*, Search and Destroy Armour Munition (SADARM) and *Javelin* for the Army; the Sensor Fused Weapon for the Air Force; and the Joint Stand-off Weapon (JSOW), Joint Direct Attack Munition (JDAM) and Advanced Medium Range Air-to-Air Missile (AMRAAM) for both the Air Force and Navy. The Navy will continue to improve its inventory of *Tomahawk* missiles and convert anti-ship *Harpoon* missiles to SLAM-ER land attack missiles.

- Continued development of the ability to project forces over long distances, including the continuation of the airlift and sealift improvements from previous years. Some 120 C-17 long-range transport aircraft are expected to be in service by 2003 and all KC-135 air-to-air refuelling tankers will receive major avionics upgrades. Sealift procurement in 1999 includes the last of the transport ships needed to move early-deploying Army divisions.

The scale of the modernisation programme is illustrated in the table below.

Table 1 Procurement for major defence modernisation programmes, 1999–2003

Army	US$bn	Navy	US$bn	Air Force	US$bn
Ammunition	6.6	F/A-18E/F ac	15.0	C-17 tpt ac	13.4
Trucks/spt veh	5.5	DDG-51	14.1	F-22 FGA	11.7
M1A2 tk upgrade	3.2	NSSN	7.5	C-22 tilt-rotor ac	1.7
Apache Longbow hel	2.8	LPD-17 amph tpt dock ship	6.5		
		MV-22 tilt-rotor ac	5.8		

As Table 1 shows, there is more investment in modernisation and upgrades than in research, development, testing and evaluation (RDT&E) for new weapons platforms (see Table 3 below).

Strategic Weapons

While the Strategic Arms Reduction Treaty (START) II has yet to be ratified by the Russian parliament, reductions under the terms of START I continue in the US. The reduction timetable is shown in Table 2 below.

Table 2 Planned reductions in the US strategic arsenal, 1990–2007

	1990	1998	START I (5 Dec 2001)	START II (31 Dec 2007)
ICBMs	1,000	550	550	500
Attributed Warheads on ICBMs	2,450	2,000	Not over 2,000	500
SLBMs	568	432	432	336
Attributed Warheads on SLBMs	4,864	3,456	Not over 3,456	Not over 1,750
SSBs	31	18	18	14
Attributed Warheads on SSBs	7,314	5,456	Not over 4,900	Not over 2,250
Heavy Bombers	324	115	92	92

Notes [1] 1990 figures exclude 5 decommissioned SS (and associated msl and warheads) that were still START accountable.

[2] 1998 figures exclude two *Poseidon* SSBNs, which have been re-designated as SSNs and converted for Special Operations Forces, but are still technically START accountable.

[3] 1990 figures exclude FB-111s.

[4] For 1998 and beyond, figures exclude 94 B-1s that are designated entirely for conventional missions.

Countering NBC Weapons and Missile Threats

The 1999 budget plan bolsters existing US defences against chemical and biological threats. The bulk of the increased funding is for improved protective suits and masks and better detection and decontamination systems. The remainder will enhance capabilities for destroying or neutralising nuclear, biological and chemical (NBC) weapons and materials. The missile defence programmes continue, with greatest emphasis on theatre-missile defence. The primary goal is to develop, procure and deploy systems that can protect forward-deployed US forces. To defend against short-range missiles, the key lower-tier programmes include the *Patriot* PAC-3 and Navy Area systems. Key upper-tier programmes are the Theater High Altitude Area Defense (THAAD) and the Navy Theater Wide systems. The Airborne Laser development programme, for defence against theatre-range missiles during their boost phase, continues, as does the National Missile Defence (NMD) programme, which is now purely for developing and testing a system which protects against a limited strategic ballistic missile attack. Defense Secretary William Cohen, in his 1999 budget statement in February 1998, said the programme would only progress to deployment when 'such a strategic threat (to the US) begins to emerge'. The 1999 budget includes $4 billion for missile defence programmes, with an additional $12.8bn planned for 2000–2003. The total $16.8bn includes funds added as a result of the QDR.

Contingency Operations and the Reserves

The extended mission in Bosnia, instability elsewhere in the Balkans and the tensions in the Gulf region, arising from Iraq's obstruction of UN weapons inspections, severely tested the US ability to maintain forces at a high state of readiness in overseas theatres. Increasing reliance has been placed on the reserve component, both in carrying out missions and in maintaining forces on station for protracted periods. The reserves have provided substantial support to peacekeeping missions and exercises, particularly in specialised areas such as aerial refuelling, strategic lift, counter-drug operations and civil–military affairs. While there are plans to reduce their numbers from a 1998 total of 892,000 to a target of 835,000, the 1999 budget provides substantial funding to improve their current readiness and future capabilities. It also includes plans to create reserve teams to respond to domestic incidents involving weapons of mass destruction (WMD) and efforts are being made to integrate reserve forces more directly with the active forces. For example, work has begun on creating two army divisions, each integrating three National Guard brigades into a regular army formation. This is part of what is termed the 'total force' policy.

DEFENCE SPENDING

The Clinton administration's budget request for the 1998 fiscal year (FY), released on 6 February 1997, was $265.3bn and Congress increased the proposed spend by $2.3bn to $267.6bn. By comparison, in FY1996 and FY1997, Congress added over $8bn and $15bn respectively to the budget request. Much of the additional funding in FY1998 went to Ballistic Missile Defense (BMD). Pressure from Congress succeeded in adding $474 million to National Missile Defense (NMD) and $803m to BMD overall.

The administration is requesting $270.6bn for FY1999 – a real decline of 1% over the 1998 Budget Authority. The request conforms to the $270bn spending cap imposed on the 1999 defence budget under the August 1997 Balanced Budget Act, supported by both parties in Congress,

[1] Early in each calendar year, the US government presents its defence budget to Congress for the next fiscal year which begins on 1 October. It also presents its Future Years' Defense Program (FYDP), which covers the next fiscal year plus the following five. Until approved by Congress, the Budget is called the Budget Request; after approval, it becomes the Budget Authority.

[2] Definitions of US budget terms: *Authorisation* establishes or maintains a government programme or agency by defining its scope. Authorising legislation is normally a prerequisite for appropriations and may set specific limits on the amount that may be appropriated. An authorisation, however, does not make money available. *Budget Authority* is the legal authority for an agency to enter into obligations for the provision of goods or services. It may be available for one or more years. *Appropriation* is one form of Budget Authority provided by Congress for funding an agency, department or programme for a given length of time and for specific purposes. Funds will not necessarily all be spent in the year in which they are initially provided. *Obligation* is an order placed, contract awarded, service agreement undertaken or other commitment made by federal agencies during a given period which will require outlays during the same or some future period. *Outlays* are money spent by a federal agency from funds provided by Congress. Outlays in a given fiscal year are a result of obligations that in turn follow the provision of Budget Authority.

under which the federal budget is meant to be deficit-free by 2002. For its part, Congress has not sought to change the budget's top-line, but will probably succeed in adding to the procurement budget at the expense of other functions in the course of the 1998 budget process.

Table 3 National Defense Budget Authority, 1998–2003

(US$m)	1998	1999 Request	2000 Projection	2001 Projection	2002 Projection	2003 Projection
Military Personnel	69,966	70,777	70,715	71,639	73,024	74,884
Operations & Maintenance	94,385	94,802	95,852	97,838	99,623	101,885
Procurement	44,824	48,708	54,122	61,267	60,661	63,523
RDT&E	36,600	36,079	33,920	32,993	33,531	34,344
Military Construction	5,089	4,302	4,874	4,378	3,702	3,967
Family Housing	3,807	3,477	3,910	3,923	3,866	4,151
Revolving and Management Funds	1,892	400				
Other, including DoD Net Receipts	-1,655	-1,287	-527	-946	-112	1,214
Total DoD	**254,908**	**257,258**	**262,866**	**271,092**	**274,295**	**283,968**
Department of Energy (defense-related)	11,665	12,283	11,944	11,540	11,703	11,993
Other defense-related	987	1,090	1,122	1,140	1,088	1,112
Total National Defense	**267,560**	**270,631**	**275,932**	**283,772**	**287,086**	**297,073**

Table 4 US National Defense Budget Function and other selected budgets, 1992–2003

(US$bn)	National Defense Budget Function		Department of Defense		Atomic Energy Defense Activities	International Security Assistance	Veterans Administration	Total Federal Government Expenditure	Total Federal Budget Deficit
FY	(BA)	(outlay)	(BA)	(outlay)	(outlay)	(outlay)	(outlay)	(outlay)	(outlay)
1992	295.1	298.4	282.1	274.7	10.6	7.5	34.1	1,042.7	386.4
1993	281.1	291.1	267.2	271.4	11.0	7.6	35.7	1,060.9	355.4
1994	263.3	281.4	251.4	265.8	11.9	6.6	37.6	1,073.5	298.5
1995	266.3	272.1	255.7	258.4	11.8	5.3	37.9	1,102.0	263.2
1996	266.0	265.7	254.4	253.2	11.6	4.6	37.0	1,139.2	222.1
1997	270.3	270.5	258.0	258.3	11.3	4.6	39.3	1,158.2	147.9
1998	267.6	264.1	254.9	251.4	11.6	5.2	43.1	1,209.1	158.7
1999[R]	270.6	265.5	257.3	252.6	11.8	5.4	43.3	1,255.1	161.5
2000[P]	275.9	268.7	262.9	255.8	11.7	5.5	44.0	1,286.3	164.6
2001[P]	283.8	269.8	271.1	257.1	11.5	5.6	44.8	1,313.0	148.4
2002[P]	287.1	272.1	274.3	259.7	11.3	5.6	45.4	1,331.2	111.3
2003[P]	297.1	288.5	284.0	275.8	11.6	5.7	47.5	1,389.6	119.7

FY = Fiscal Year (1 October–30 September), [R] = Request, [P] = Projection

Notes [1] The National Defense Budget Function subsumes funding for the DoD, the DoE Atomic Energy Defense Activities and some smaller support agencies (including Federal Emergency Management and Selective Service System). It does not include funding for International Security Assistance (under International Affairs), the Veterans Administration, the US Coast Guard (Department of Transport), nor for the National Aeronautics and Space Administration (NASA). Funding for civil projects administered by the DoD is excluded from the figures cited here.
[2] The figures for Federal Government Expenditure and Federal Budget Deficit differ from previous figures cited in *The Military Balance* because US Government Trust Funds are no longer included. If Trust Funds were included, net US Government expenditure would show a surplus rather than deficit from 1999 [+$9.5bn] through to 2003 [+$82.8bn].

Table 5 Department of Defense Total Obligational Authority, 1985–2003

(constant 1998 US$m)		Army	Navy	Air Force	Defense-wide	Total
1985		108,200	135,767	138,716	20,595	403,278
1990		99,816	122,778	115,825	25,015	363,434
1997		67,720	82,647	76,341	38,570	265,278
1998		62,472	82,834	76,300	40,413	262,019
1999		64,265	81,455	77,097	35,793	258,610
2003		64,891	80,286	78,568	36,992	260,737
% change	1985–1990	-7.7	-9.6	-16.5	21.5	-9.9
	1990–1998	-37.4	-32.5	-34.1	61.6	-27.9
	1985–1998	-42.3	-39.0	-45.0	96.2	-35.0
	1998–2003	3.9	-3.1	3.0	-8.5	-0.5

US defence spending has declined by some 35% since 1985, with most of the fall since 1990. Over the same period, the Department of Defense (DoD)'s military and civilian workforce has fallen by around a third, as has employment in the US defence industry.

Table 6 US military employment, 1985–1999

(thousands)	Active Military	DoD Civilian	Total DoD	Defence Industry	Total Military Related	US Manu-facturing	Total US
1985	2,206	1,043	3,249	2,980	6,229	19,248	108,349
1990	2,143	997	3,140	3,150	6,290	19,076	119,650
1995	1,583	807	2,390	2,350	4,740	18,524	126,298
1996	1,537	779	2,316	2,260	4,576	18,457	127,603
1997	1,504	746	2,250	2,180	4,430	n.a.	130,416
1998	1,483	731	2,214	2,050	4,264	n.a.	132,100
1999	1,459	709	2,168	2,030	4,198	n.a.	133,300
% change 1985–99	-33.9	-32.0	-33.3	-31.9	-32.6	n.a.	23.0

The spending decline has now levelled off and plans are for spending to be much the same each year to 2003. This reflects the compromise reached between the White House and Democratic and Republican leaders in Congress under the 1997 Bi-Partisan Agreement leading to the Balanced Budget legislation. In return, Congress is being asked by the DoD to end the practice of adding substantial spending to the defence budget beyond that requested by the administration. According to the DoD, unrequested funding is especially damaging when it fails to take account of the future expenditure obligations it generates.

Procurement is planned to reach the DoD's target level of $60bn in FY2001 and stay at this level to 2003, while there is some reduction in R&D funding over the next five years.

Funding for Contingency Operations

The incremental net cost of US operations in and around Bosnia from 1996 to June 1998 amounted to $6.4bn – somewhat lower than earlier estimates after taking into account savings elsewhere in the operations and maintenance budget arising from the troop presence in Bosnia. The Implementation Force (IFOR) cost the US $2.5bn in 1996. The subsequent Stabilisation Force (SFOR) cost $2.3bn in 1997 and a further $1.6bn up to the original mission termination date in June 1998. The administration has obtained FY1998 supplementary funding of $487m to sustain extended SFOR operations from June to September 1998, while the FY1999 budget request contains $1.9bn for continuing operations related to Bosnia.

Operations in the Gulf region were budgeted at around $700m in FY1997 and 1998, of which maintaining the no-fly zone (Operations *South Watch* and *Provide Comfort*) accounts for some $400m. The administration has secured a supplementary FY1998 allocation of $1.4bn to cover the costs of deploying large additional US forces to the Persian Gulf in November 1997.

Non-proliferation

Some $1bn is requested in FY1999 for activities related to WMD non-proliferation. Of this, the request for the DoD's 'Nunn–Lugar' Cooperative Threat Reduction Programme accounts for $442m (an increase of $60m over FY1998), while the Department of Energy's Non-Proliferation and National Security Programme contains a funded request for $676m, an increase of $6m.

Foreign Military Assistance

Foreign military and economic assistance appears in the foreign affairs budget, not that of the DoD, and its FY1999 budget request includes $6.4bn for this purpose. The major change from previous years is the absence of aid for Greece and Turkey. Israel (receiving $3bn) and Egypt ($2.1bn) continue to take the bulk of Foreign Military Financing (FMF) and the Economic Support Fund.

Table 7 **US foreign military and security assistance, FY1999**					
Programme	**Foreign Military Financing ($m)**	**Programme**	**Economic Support Fund ($m)**	**Programme**	**International Narcotics Control ($m)**
Israel	1,800	Israel	1,200	Latin America	166
Egypt	1,300	Egypt	815	Asia/Africa/Europe	13
Jordan	45	Jordan	150	Aviation Support	41
Partnership for Peace	80	Haiti	140	Systems Support	10
Central Europe	20	Guatemala	25	Training	8
African Crisis Response	5	Cambodia	20	Organisations	8
East Africa	5	Lebanon	12	Programme	29
Caribbean	3	Albania	10		
Peacekeeping	8	Crime	10		
Other	30	Other	132		
Total	**3,296**	**Total**	**2,514**	**Total**	**275**

Note The FY1999 budget requests $50m for International Military Education and Training (IMET).

Table 8 Major US Research and Development programmes, FY1999

Type	Model	FY1999 Request ($m)	Units	Order date	Delivery date	Comment
Joint						
BMD	BMD	4,002		1983		FY1999 budget: $2.4bn for TBMD, $963m for NMD $12.8bn FY2000–03 including 1997 QDR additions FY1998 expenditure of $3,479m. 1998 FYDP for $21.5bn including NMD at $6.6bn
SAM	*Patriot*	343		1999		Under BMD, advanced *Patriot* development
FGA	JSF	919	2,852	1994	2010	Development programme with earliest production start in 2007 1998 FYDP expenditure of $10,131m
hel	V-22	1,070	410	1982	2001	Programme cost: $36bn including over $10bn for development
Air Force						
FGA	F-22	2,393	785	1989	2006	First two production aircraft ordered in FY1999 339 units under 1997 QDR. Costs: $19bn development, $48bn production
Navy						
DD	DD-21	84	30	1998	2008	Feasibility study in 1998. Detail design contract in 2001. $84m in FY1999. $25bn programme
Army						
cbt hel	RAH-66	368	1,292	1981	2007	1998 FYDP expenditure of $3,712m. Programme plan: 1,292 units for $34bn including $5.4bn development
SPA	*Crusader*	310	824	1994	2005	FY1998 expenditure of $322m. Total development contract value to 2000 over $1bn Replacement of US Army's M-109 155mm series and derivatives. FY1998 expenditure of $322m Total development contract value to 2000 over $1bn. 2 prototypes for delivery by 2000
lt tk	TRACER			1998	2007	With UK. PD phase. Programme worth up to $4.8bn
BMD						FY1998 exp $3.5bn, FYDP projection $21.5bn

Table 9 Major US equipment orders, FY1999

Type	Model	Units	Value ($m)	Comment
Joint				
SAM	*Patriot* PAC-3	60	103	First full year of procurement in 1998 (52 ordered)
sat	NAVSTAR	6	258	GPS sat with FY1998 cost of $363m
sat	*Milstar*	4	550	Comms sat with FYDP expenditure of $3,290m
UAV	UAV	15	620	Various models: TUAV, *Predator, Global Hawk, Darkstar*
trg	JPATS	19	152	Total of 711 planned for USAF and USN
Air Force				
JSTARS	E-8	2	654	Total procurement of 13
ASM	JSOW	100	52	

Type	Model	Units	Value ($m)	Comment
PGM	JDAM	2,187	53	
FGA	F-22	2	785	First two production ac. 339 units required under 1997 QDR
tpt	C-17	13	3,207	120 on order up to 2003
bbr	B-2	21	376	Continuing upgrade. FY1998 expenditure of $331m on procurement and R&D
bbr	B-1	43	34	Upgrade
AEW	E-3	5	42	Upgrade
AAM	AMRAAM	180	115	
HLV	*Titan* IV		579	
Army				
ATGW	*Javelin*	3,316	320	
arty	SADARM	550	57	Sense and Destroy Armor Munition
arty	ATACMS	126	142	
MRL	MLRS	24	129	For 24 launchers ($85m) and 522 rockets ($17m)
MBT	M-1	120	692	Upgrade. To date 68 new-build M1A2 have been purchased and 368 M1AI remanufactured to A2 standard. 1996 five-year order for an additional 580 upgrades. Total of 998 upgrades planned
AIFV	M-2	73	361	Upgrade. 1,603 M-2s to be remanufactured to A3 standard
ATGW	*Longbow Hellfire*	2,000	361	For AH-64D
hel	UH-60	22	221	
hel	AH-64	66	634	Total requirement for 758 AH-64D
Navy				
DD	DDG-51	3	2,904	FY1999–2003: 15 DDG-51-class to bring total procurement to 57 units.
SLCM	*Tomahawk*	114	200	
LPD	LPD-17	1	634	
SSN	NSSN	1	2,303	4 units planned for 1998–2003
SLBM	*Trident*	5	386	
AAM	AMRAAM	115	63	
FGA	AV-8	12	378	Upgrade. 72 remanufactured AV-8Bs on order up to 2001
FGA	F/A-18	30	3,275	Requirement reduced to 548 – 785 under 1997 QDR
AEW	E-2	3	457	Upgrade
PGM	JDAM	898	41	
ASM	JSOW	328	125	
trg	T-45	15	364	
ATGW	*Javelin*	741	83	
hel	V-22	7	665	USMC requirement for 360 under 1997 QDR. USAF (50) and USN also expected to purchase V-22
IT	IT-21		612	'Information Technology for the 21st century'
Other				
arty	155mm	190		1997 order from UK. Total USMC and Army requirement: 799.

United States

	1996	1997	1998	1999
GDP	$7.6tr	$8.1tr		
per capita	$27,900	$29,300		
Growth	2.8%	3.8%		
Inflation	2.9%	2.4%		
Publ debt	63.1%	61.5%		
Def bdgt				
BA	$266.0bn	$270.3bn		
Outlay	$265.7bn	$270.5bn		
Request				
BA			$267.6bn	$270.6bn
Outlay			$264.1bn	$265.5bn
Population			270,629,000	
Age	*13–17*	*18–22*	*23–32*	
Men	9,422,000	9,253,000	19,776,000	
Women	8,973,000	8,819,000	19,010,000	

Total Armed Forces

ACTIVE 1,401,600

(200,200 women, excl Coast Guard)

RESERVES 1,350,550

(total incl Stand-by Reserve)

READY RESERVE 1,323,000

Selected Reserve and Individual Ready Reserve to augment active units and provide reserve formations and units

NATIONAL GUARD 473,700

Army (ARNG) 364,000 **Air Force** (ANG) 109,700

RESERVE 849,300

Army 461,100 **Navy** 220,300 **Marines** 97,800 **Air Force** 70,100

STAND-BY RESERVE 27,550

Trained individuals for mob **Army** 1,100 **Navy** 12,700 **Marines** 850 **Air Force** 12,900

US Strategic Command (US STRATCOM)

HQ: Offutt AFB, NE (manpower incl in Navy and Air Force totals)

NAVY up to 432 SLBM in 18 SSBN

(Plus 16 *Poseidon* C-3 launchers in each of 2 op ex SSBN redesignated SSN (32 msl) both START accountable)

SSBN 18 *Ohio*

10 (SSBN-734) with up to 24 UGM-133A *Trident* D-5 (240 msl)

8 (SSBN-726) with up to 24 UGM-93A *Trident* C-4 (192 msl)

AIR FORCE

ICBM (Air Force Space Command (AFSPC)) 680

2 strategic msl wg, 2 gp (1 test wg with 13 test silo launchers)

590 *Minuteman* III (LGM-30G)

50 *Peacekeeper* (MX; LGM-118A) in mod *Minuteman* silos (Excluded from the above are 115 *Minuteman* II which remain START-accountable)

AC (Air Combat Command (ACC)): 174 active hy bbr (329 START-accountable)

13 bbr sqn (6 B-1B, 2 B-2A, 5 B-52)

6 sqn (2 ANG (not yet op)) with 95 B-1B

5 sqn (1 AFR) with 66 B-52H (with AGM-86B ALCM)

2 sqn with 13 B-2A (plus 2 at production site)

FLIGHT TEST CENTRE 9

1 B-52, 2 B-1, 6 B-2A (not START-accountable)

Strategic Recce/Intelligence Collection (Satellites)

IMAGERY Improved *Crystal* (advanced **KH-11**) visible and infra-red imagery (perhaps 3 op, resolution 6in)

Lacrosse (formerly *Indigo*) radar-imaging satellite (resolution 1–2m)

ELECTRONIC OCEAN RECCE SATELLITE (EORSAT) to detect ships by infra-red and radar

NAVIGATIONAL SATELLITE TIMING AND RANGING (NAVSTAR) 24 satellites, components of Global Positioning System (GPS); block 2R system with accuracy to 1m replacing expired satellites

ELINT/SIGINT 2 *Orion* (formerly *Magnum*), 2 *Trumpet* (successor to *Jumpseat*), 3 name unknown, launched, August 1994, May 1995, April 1996

NUCLEAR DETONATION DETECTION SYSTEM detects and evaluates nuclear detonations; sensors to be deployed in NAVSTAR satellites

Strategic Defences

US Space Command (HQ: Peterson AFB, CO)

North American Aerospace Defense Command (NORAD), a combined US–Canadian org (HQ: Peterson AFB, CO)

US Strategic Command (HQ: Offutt AFB, NE)

EARLY WARNING

DEFENSE SUPPORT PROGRAM (DSP) infra-red surveillance and warning system. Detects missile launches, nuclear detonations, aircraft in after burner, spacecraft and terrestrial infra-red events. Approved constellation: 3 op satellites and 1 op on-orbit spare

BALLISTIC-MISSILE EARLY-WARNING SYSTEM (BMEWS) 3 stations: Clear (AK), Thule (Greenland), Fylingdales Moor (UK). Primary mission to track ICBM and SLBM; also used to track satellites

SPACETRACK USAF radars at Incirlik (Turkey), Eglin (FL), Cavalier AFS (ND), Clear, Thule, Fylingdales Moor, Beale AFB (CA), Cape Cod (MA); optical tracking systems in Socorro (NM), Maui (HI), Diego Garcia (Indian Ocean)

USN SPACE SURVEILLANCE SYSTEM (NAVSPASUR) 3 transmitting, 6 receiving-site field stations in south-east US

PERIMETER ACQUISITION RADAR ATTACK CHARACTERISATION SYSTEM (PARCS) 1 north-facing phased-array system at Cavalier AFS (ND); 2,800km range

PAVE PAWS phased-array radars in Massachusetts, GA; 5,500km range

MISCELLANEOUS DETECTION AND TRACK-ING RADARS US Army Kwajalein Atoll (Pacific) **USAF** Ascension Island (Atlantic), Antigua (Caribbean), Kaena Point (HI), MIT Lincoln Laboratory (MA)

GROUND-BASED ELECTRO-OPTICAL DEEP SPACE SURVEILLANCE SYSTEM (GEODSS) Socorro, Maui, Diego Garcia

AIR DEFENCE

RADARS

OVER-THE-HORIZON-BACKSCATTER RADAR (OTH-B) 1 in Maine (mothballed), 1 in Mountain Home AFB (mothballed); range 500nm (mini-mum) to 3,000nm

NORTH WARNING SYSTEM to replace DEW line 15 automated long-range (200nm) radar stations 40 short-range (110–150km) stations

DEW LINE system deactivated

AC ANG 90
6 sqn: 3 with 45 F-15A/B, 3 with 45 F-16A/B ac also on call from Navy, Marine Corps and Air Force
AAM *Sidewinder*, *Sparrow*, AMRAAM

Army 479,400

(72,400 women)
3 Army HQ, 4 Corps HQ (1 AB)
2 armd div (3 bde HQ, 5 tk, 4 mech inf, 3 SP arty bn; 1 MLRS bty, 1 AD bn; 1 avn bde)
2 mech div (3 bde HQ, 5 tk, 4 mech inf, 3 SP arty bn; 1 MLRS bty, 1 ADA bn; 1 avn bde)
1 mech div (3 bde HQ, 4 tk, 5 mech inf, 3 SP arty bn; 1 MLRS bty, 1 ADA bn; 1 avn bde)
1 mech div (3 bde HQ, 4 tk, 3 mech inf, 2 lt inf, 3 SP arty bn; 1 ADA bn; 1 avn bde)
2 lt inf div (3 bde HQ, 9 inf, 3 arty, 1 AD bn; 1 avn bde)
1 air aslt div (3 bde HQ, 9 air aslt, 3 arty bn; avn bde (7 hel bn: 3 ATK, 2 aslt, 1 comd, 1 med tpt))
1 AB div (3 bde HQ, 9 AB, 1 lt tk, 3 arty, 1 AD, 1 cbt avn bn)

5 avn bde (1 army, 3 corps, 1 trg)
3 armd cav regt (1 hy, 1 lt, 1 trg)
6 arty bde (3 with 1 SP arty, 2 MLRS bn; 1 with 3 arty, 1 MLRS bn; 1 with 3 MLRS bn; 1 with 1 MLRS bn)
3 indep inf bn, 1 AB Task Force
9 *Patriot* SAM bn (5 with 6 bty, 2 with 4 bty, 2 with 3 bty)
2 *Avenger* SAM bn

READY RESERVE

ARMY NATIONAL GUARD (ARNG) 364,000 (35,100 women): capable after mob of manning 8 div (1 armd, 4 mech, 2 inf, 1 lt inf) • 18 indep bde, incl 15 enhanced (2 armd, 5 mech, 5 inf, 2 lt inf, 1 armd cav), 1 armd, 1 lt inf, 1 inf scout (3 bn) • 16 fd arty bde HQ • Indep bn: 3 inf, 36 arty, 18 avn, 9 AD (1 *Patriot*, 8 *Avenger*), 37 engr

ARMY RESERVE (AR) 461,100 (51,400 women): 7 trg div, 5 exercise div, 13 AR/Regional Spt Cmd (Of these, 206,200 Standing Reservists receive regular trg and have mob assignment; the remain-der receive no trg, but as former active-duty soldiers could be recalled in an emergency)

EQUIPMENT

MBT some 7,836: 192 M-60A3, 7,644 M-1 *Abrams* incl M-1A1, M-1A2
LT TK 130 M-551 *Sheridan*
RECCE 113 Tpz-1 *Fuchs*
AIFV 6,720 M-2/-3 *Bradley*
APC 17,800 M-113A2/A3 incl variants
TOTAL ARTY 5,680
  TOWED 1,308: **105mm**: 413 M-102, 417 M-119; **155mm**: 478 M-198
  SP 2,601: **155mm**: 2,572 M-109A1/A2/A6; **203mm**: 29 M-110A1/A2
  MRL 227mm: 840 MLRS (all ATACMS-capable)
  MOR 931: **107mm**: 152 M-30 (incl SP); **120mm**: 879 M-120/121; plus **81mm**: 679 M-251
ATGW 8,457 TOW (1,237 HMMWV, 500 M-901, 6,720 M-2/M-3 *Bradley*), 24,400 *Dragon*, 500 *Javelin*
RL 84mm: AT-4
SAM FIM-92A *Stinger*, 767 *Avenger* (veh-mounted *Stinger*), 485 *Patriot*
SURV Ground 75 AN/TPQ-36 (arty), 40 AN/TPQ-37 (arty), 65 AN/TRQ-32 (COMINT), 40 AN/TSQ-138 (COMINT), 54 AN/TLQ-17A (EW)
  Airborne 4 *Guardrail* (RC-12D/H/K, 3 RU-21H ac), 6 EO-5ARL (DHC-7), 35 OV/RV-1D
AMPH 58 ships:
  6 *Frank Besson* LST: capacity 32 tk
  35 LCU-2000, 17 LCU-1600
  Plus craft: some 107 LCM
UAV 7 *Hunter* (5 in store)
AC some 269: 51 **C-12C/R**, 89 **C-12D/-F/J**, 48 **C-23A/B**, 11 **C-26**, 2 **C-182**, 2 **O-2**, 55 **RC-12D/G/H/K**, 2 **T-34**, 4 **U-21**, 3 **UV-18A**, 2 **UV-20A**
HEL some 4,990 (1,489 armed): 483 **AH-1S**, 753 **AH-64A/D** (710/43), 59 **AH-6/MH-6**, 907 **UH-1H/V**,

1,363 **UH-60A/L**, 60 **MH-60L/K**, 66 **EH-60A (ECM)**, 468 **CH/MH-47D/E**, 386 **OH-58A/C**, 370 **OH-58D** (incl 194 armed), 135 **TH-67** *Creek*

Navy (USN) 380,600

(52,800 women)

5 Fleets: **2nd** Atlantic, **3rd** Pacific, **5th** Indian Ocean, Persian Gulf, Red Sea, **6th** Mediterranean, **7th** W. Pacific; plus Military Sealift Command, Naval Reserve Force (NRF)

SUBMARINES 84

STRATEGIC SUBMARINES 18 (see p. 20)
TACTICAL SUBMARINES 66 (incl about 8 in refit)
  SSGN 32
  1 *Seawolf* (SSN-21) with up to 45 *Tomahawk* SLCM plus 660mm TT; about 50 tube-launched msl and torp
  23 imp *Los Angeles* (SSN-751) with 12 *Tomahawk* SLCM (VLS), 533mm TT (Mk 48 HWT, *Harpoon, Tomahawk*)
  8 mod *Los Angeles* (SSN-719) with 12 *Tomahawk* SLCM (VLS); plus 533mm TT (Mk 48 HWT, *Harpoon, Tomahawk*)
  SSN 34
  22 *Los Angeles* (SSN-688) with Mk 48 HWT, plus *Harpoon, Tomahawk* SLCM
  11 *Sturgeon* (SSN-637) with Mk 48 HWT; plus *Harpoon*, 21 with *Tomahawk* SLCM (incl 10 capable of special ops)
  1 *Narwhal* (SSN-671) with Mk 48 HWT, *Harpoon, Tomahawk*
OTHER ROLES 2 ex-SSBN (SSBN 642 and 645) (special ops, included in the START-accountable launcher figures)

PRINCIPAL SURFACE COMBATANTS 138

AIRCRAFT CARRIERS 12
  CVN 8 *Nimitz* (CVN-68)
  CV 4
  2 *Kitty Hawk* (CV-63)
  1 *J. F. Kennedy* (CV-67) (NRF but op)
  1 *Enterprise* (CVN-65)
  AIR WING 11 (10 active, 1 reserve); average Air Wing comprises 9 sqn
    3 with 12 F/A-18C, 1 with 14 F-14, 1 with 8 S-3B and 2 ES-3, 1 with 6 SH-60, 1 with 4 EA-6B, 1 with 4 E-2C, 1 spt with C-2
CRUISERS 29
  CGN 2
  2 *California* (CGN-36) with 2 SM-2 MR; plus 2 x 4 *Harpoon*, 1 x 8 ASROC, 2 x 3 ASTT, 2 127mm guns
  CG 27 *Ticonderoga* (CG-47 *Aegis*)
  5 *Baseline* 1 (CG-47–51) with 2 x 2 SM-2 MR/ASROC; plus 2 x 4 *Harpoon*, 2 127mm guns, 2 x 3 ASTT, 2 SH-2F or SH-60B hel
  22 *Baseline* 2/3 (CG-52) with 2 VLS Mk 41 (61 tubes

each) for combination of SM-2 ER, and *Tomahawk*; other weapons as *Baseline* 1
DESTROYERS 57 (incl some 6 in refit)
  DDG 26
  24 *Arleigh Burke* (DDG-51 *Aegis*) with 2 VLS Mk 41 (32 tubes fwd, 64 tubes aft) for combination of *Tomahawk*, SM-2 ER and ASROC; plus 2 x 4 *Harpoon*, 1 127mm gun, 2 x 3 ASTT, 1 SH-60B hel
  2 *Kidd* (DDG-993) with 2 x 2 SM-2 MR/ASROC; plus 2 x 3 ASTT, 2 SH-2F hel, 2 x 4 *Harpoon*, 2 127mm guns
  DD 31 *Spruance* (DD-963) (ASW)
  7 with 1 x 8 ASROC, 2 x 3 ASTT, 1 SH-2F hel; plus 2 x 4 *Harpoon*, 1 with 2 RAM, 2 127mm guns, 2 x 4 *Tomahawk*
  24 with 1 VLS Mk 41 (*Tomahawk*), 2 x 3 ASTT, 1 SH-60B hel; plus 2 127mm guns, 2 x 4 *Harpoon*
FRIGATES 40 (incl some 5 in refit)
  FFG 40 *Oliver Hazard Perry* (FFG-7) (10 in NRF) all with 2 x 3 ASTT; 24 with 2 SH-60B hel; 27 with 2 SH-2F hel; all plus 1 SM-1 MR/*Harpoon*

PATROL AND COASTAL COMBATANTS 21

(mainly responsibility of Coast Guard)
PATROL, COASTAL 13 *Cyclone* PFC with SEAL team
PATROL, INSHORE 8<

MINE WARFARE 26

MINELAYERS none dedicated, but mines can be laid from attack submarines, aircraft and surface ships.
MCM 26
  1 *Inchon* MCMCS
  11 *Osprey* (MHC-51) MHC
  14 *Avenger* (MCM-1) MCO

AMPHIBIOUS 43

COMD 2 *Blue Ridge*, capacity 700 tps
LHA 11
  6 *Wasp*, capacity 1,892 tps, 60 tk; with 6 AV-8B ac, 12 CH-46E, 4 CH-53E, 4 UH-1N, 4 AH-1W hel; plus 3 LCAC, 2 RAM
  5 *Tarawa*, capacity 1,713 tps, 100 tk, 4 LCU or 1 LCAC, 6 AV-8B ac, 12 CH-46E, 4 CH-53E, 4 UH-1N, 4 AH-1T/W hel, 2 RAM
LPH 1 *Iwo Jima*, capacity 1,489 tps, 12 CH-46E, 4 CH-53E, 4 UH-1N hel, 4 AH-1T/W hel
LPD 11 *Austin*, capacity 788 tps, 4 tk
LSD 16
  8 *Whidbey Island* with 4 LCAC, capacity 450 tps, 40 tk, 1 with 2 x RAM
  4 *Harpers Ferry* with 4 LCAC, capacity 500 tps, 40tk
  4 *Anchorage* with 3 LCAC, capacity 302 tps, 38 tk
LST 2 *Newport*, capacity 347 tps, 10 tk

CRAFT 210

90 LCAC, capacity 1 MBT; about 37 LCU-1610, capacity 3 MBT; 8 LCVP; 75 LCM; plus numerous LCU

SUPPORT AND MISCELLANEOUS 99

UNDER WAY SPT 39

AO 17
  5 *Cimarron*, 12 *Henry Kaiser* (MSC)
AOE 7
  3 *Supply*, 4 *Sacramento*
AE 7 *Kilauea* (MSC)
T-AFS 8
  5 *Mars* (MSC), 3 *Sirius* (MSC)
MAINT AND LOG 28
  9 AS, 7 AT (MSC), 8 TAO-T (MSC), 2 T-AH (MSC), 2
  T-AVB
SPECIAL PURPOSES 8
  2 LCC, 6 AGS (4 MSC)
SURVEY AND RESEARCH 24
  10 AGOS (towed array) (MSC), 5 AGOR, 9 AGS

MILITARY SEALIFT

Military Sealift Command (MSC) operates 123 ships, incl 53 Naval Fleet Auxiliary Force ships deployed in direct fleet spt and special mission ships for survey, range and research activities incl in Spt and Misc. Other assets are:

MSC Active Force 52

Operating Vessels 18
8 dry cargo (3 ro-ro, 1 *Combo*, 2 freighters, 2 other) 10 tkr

Afloat Prepositioning Force 34
13 maritime prepositioning ships (MPS) (in 3 sqn each to spt an MEB)
21 prepositioned ships (7 ro-ro, 5 LASH, 1 tac, 1 flo-flo, 1 flt, AH, 3 tkr, 3 container)
Based in Diego Garcia, Guam and the Mediterranean

MSC Strategic Sealift Force 10

1 sqn of 8 fast sealift ships (30 KT ro-ro at 4 days' readiness), 2 hosp ships

Additional Military Sealift

Ready Reserve Force 82
32 breakbulk, 29 ro-ro, 4 LASH, 3 'Seebee', 4 tkr, 2 tps, 8 tac (at 4–20 days' readiness, maintained by Department of Transport)

National Defence Reserve Fleet (NDRF) 62
30 dry cargo, 9 tkr, 4 tps, 4 container, 1 crane, 3 ro-ro, 2 hy lift, 7 research, 2 Maritime Academy

Naval Reserve Surface Forces 20
1 CV (*J. F. Kennedy*) fully op with assigned air wg, 10 FFG, 4 MCM, 2 MHC, 2 LST, 1 mine-control ship (*Inchon*) generally crewed by 70% active and 30% reserve

Augment Forces
28 MIUW units and 12 cargo handling bn

NAVAL INACTIVE FLEET about 123

includes about 25 'mothballed' USN ships, 3 CV, about 25 dry cargo ships, 10 tkr and some 60 *Victory* Second World War cargo ships (60–90 days' reactivation, but many ships are of doubtful serviceability). 89 awaiting scrap/sale

COMMERCIAL SEALIFT about 303

US-flag and effective US-controlled (EUSC) ships potentially available to augment military sealift

NAVAL AVIATION 63,200

(5,700 women), incl 12 carriers, 11 air wg (10 active, 1 reserve) **Flying hours** F-14: 216; F-18: 252
Average air wg comprises 9 sqn
  3 with 12 F/A-18C, 1 with 14 F-14, 1 with 8 S-3B and 2 ES-3, 1 with 6 SH-60, 1 with 4 EA-6B, 1 with 4 E-2C, 1 spt with C-2

AIRCRAFT

FTR 12 sqn
  5 with F-14A, 4 with F-14B, 3 with F-14D
FGA/ATTACK 24 sqn with F/A-18C/D
  3 with A-6E
ELINT 4 sqn
  2 with EP-3, 2 with ES-3A
ECM 13 sqn with EA-6B
MR 12 land-based sqn
  1 with P-3CII, 11 with P-3CIII
ASW 10 sqn with S-3B
AEW 10 sqn with E-2C
COMD 2 sqn with E-6A (TACAMO)
OTHER 4 sqn
  2 with C-2A, 2 with C-130T
TRG 11 sqn
  2 'Aggressor' with F/A-18
  9 trg with T-2C, T-34C, T-44, T-45A

HELICOPTERS

ASW 20 sqn
  10 with SH-60B (LAMPS Mk III)
  10 with SH-60F/HH-60H
MCM 2 sqn with MH-53E
MISC 6 sqn
  5 with CH-46, 1 with MH-53E
TRG 2 sqn with TH-57B/C

NAVY RESERVE 23,480

(3,840 women)
FTR ATTACK 2 sqn with F-18
FTR 1 sqn with F-14 (transition to F-18 FY 99)
AEW 2 sqn with E-2C
ECM 1 sqn with EA-6B
MPA 9 sqn: 1 with P-3C, 1 with EP-3J
FLEET LOG SPT 1 wg
  8 sqn with C-9B/DC-9, 4 sqn with C-130T
TRG 2 aggressor sqn (1 with F/A-18, 1 with F-5E/F)
HEL 1 wg
  ASW 3 sqn: 2 with SH-2G, 1 with SH-3H
  MSC 3 sqn: 2 with HH-60H, 1 with UH-3H

AIRCRAFT

(Naval Inventory includes Marine Corps ac and hel)

1,510 cbt ac; 506 armed hel

235* **F-14** (112 **-A** (ftr, incl 14 NR) plus 30 in store, 77 **-B** (ftr), 46 **-D** (ftr)) • 771* **F/A-18** (194 **-A** (FGA, incl 34 NR, 80 MC (48 MCR)), 28 **-B** (FGA, incl 2 NR (5 TACAMO MC)), 413 **-C** (FGA, incl 81 MC), 129 **-D** (FGA, incl 95 MC), 5 **-E**, 2 **-F**) • 35* **F-5E/F** (trg, incl 13 MCR) • 57* **TA-4J** (trg) plus 3 in store • 116 **EA-6B** (ECM, incl 4 NR, 22 MC) plus 80 in store • 16 **E-6B**, 167* **AV-8B** (FGA) plus 5 in store • 14* **TAV-8B** (trg) plus 1 in store • 74 **E-2** (72 **-C** (AEW, incl 11 NR) plus 3 in store, 2 **TE-2C** (trg) • 272 **P-3** (3 **-B**, 231* **-C** (MR, incl 70, NR), 13 **EP-3** (ELINT), 13 **NP-3D** (trials), 10 **U/VP-3A** (utl/VIP), 2 **TP-3A** (trg) plus 42 **P-3** in store) • 132 **S-3** plus 21 in store (116 **-B** (ASW), 16 **ES-3A** (ECM)) • 105 **C-130** (20 **-T** (tpt NR), 80 **-KC-130F/R/T** (incl 79 MC (28 MCR)), 1 **-TC-130G/Q** (tpt/trg), 4 **LC-130** (Antarctic)) • 3 **CT-39G** (misc, MC incl 1 MCR) • 38 **C-2A** (tpt), 17 **C-9B** (tpt, 15 NR, 2 MC), 12 **DC-9** (tpt), 7 **C-20**, 2 **-D** (VIP/ NR), 5 **-G** (tpt/4 NR, 1 MC)) • 59 **UC-12** (utl) 39 **-B** (incl 14 MC, 3 MCR), 10 **-F** (incl 4 MC), 10 **-M** • 1 **NU-1B** (utl) • 2 **U-6A** (utl) • 107 **T-2C** (trg) plus 16 in store • 1 **T-39D** (trg) • 55 **T-44** (trg) • 71 **T-45** (trg) • 313 **T-34C** (incl 2 MC) • 11 **T-38A/B** (trg) • 20 **TC-12B** • 2 **TC-18F** (trg)

HELICOPTERS

106 **UH-1N** (utl, incl 103 MC (20 MCR)) • 26 **HH-1H** (utl, incl 7 MC) • 148 **CH-53E** (tpt, incl 16 MCR) • 47 **CH-53D** (tpt MC) • 43 **MH-53E** (tpt, incl 12 NR, 5 MC) • 241 **SH-60**: 166 **-B**, 75 **-F** • 38 **HH-60H** (cbt spt, incl 16 NR) • 14 **SH-2G** (ASW, 14 NR) plus 3 in store • 8 **VH-60** (ASW/SAR MC) • 7 **SH-3H** (ASW/ SAR incl 6 NR) • 53 **UH-3H** (ASW/SAR incl 10 NR) • 27 **CH-46D** (tpt, trg) • 232 **CH-46E** (tpt, incl 231 MC (25 MCR)) • 53 **UH/HH-46D** (utl incl 9 MC) • 118 **TH-57** (45 **-B** (trg), 73 **-C** (trg) (plus B-2, C-12 in store)) • 14 **VH-3A/D** (VIP, 11 MC) • 182 **AH-1W** (atk, incl 175 MC (37 MCR)) • 47 **CH-53D** (tpt, incl 37 MC) plus 25 in store

TILT ROTOR 12 **MV-22B** (MC)

MISSILES

AAM AIM-120 AMRAAM, AIM-7 *Sparrow*, AIM-54A/C *Phoenix*, AIM-9 *Sidewinder*

ASM AGM-45 *Shrike*, AGM-88A HARM; AGM-84 *Harpoon*, AGM-119 *Penguin* Mk-3, AGM-114 *Hellfire*

Marine Corps 171,300

(9,300 women)

GROUND

3 div

1 with 3 inf regt (10bn), 1 tk, 2 lt armd recce (LAV-25), 1 aslt amph, 1 cbt engr bn, 1 arty regt (4 bn), 1 recce coy

1 with 3 inf regt (9 bn), 1 tk, 1 lt armd recce (LAV-25), 1 aslt amph, 1 cbt engr bn, 1 arty regt (4 bn), 1 recce bn

1 with 2 inf regt (6 bn), 1 cbt aslt bn (1 AAV, 1 LAR coy), 1 arty regt (2 bn), 1 cbt engr, 1 recce coy

3 Force Service Spt Gp

1 bn Marine Corps Security Force (Atlantic and Pacific)

Marine Security Guard bn (1 HQ, 7 region coy)

RESERVES (MCR)

1 div (3 inf (9 bn), 1 arty regt (5 bn); 2 tk, 1 lt armd recce (LAV-25), 1 aslt amph, 1 recce, 1 cbt engr bn)

1 Force Service Spt Gp

EQUIPMENT

MBT 403 M-1A1 *Abrams*

LAV 401 LAV-25 (**25mm gun**) plus 334 variants incl 50 Mor, 95 ATGW (see below)

AAV 1,322 AAV-7A1 (all roles)

TOWED ARTY 105mm: 355 M-101A1; **155mm**: 599 M-198

MOR 81mm: 600 (incl 50 LAV-M)

ATGW 1,157 TOW, 1,121 *Dragon*, 95 LAV-TOW

RL 83mm: 1,659 SMAW; **84mm**: 1,300 AT-4

SURV 22 AN/TPQ-36 (arty)

AVIATION 36,500

(1,270 women)

Flying hours 264

3 active air wg and 1 MCR air wg

Flying hours cbt aircrew: 264

AIR WING no standard org, but a notional wg comprises

AC 130 fixed-wing: 48 **F/A-18A/C/D**, 60 **AV-8B**, 10 **EA-6B**, 12 **KC-130**

HEL 167: 12 **CH-53D**, 32 **CH-53E**, 36 **AH-1W**, 27 **UH-1N**, 60 **CH-46E**

1 MC C² system, wg support gp

AIRCRAFT

FTR/ATTACK 18 sqn with 216 F/A-18A/C/D (4 MCR sqn)

FGA 7 sqn with 112 AV-8B

ECM 4 sqn with 22 EA-6B

TKR 6 sqn with 79 KC-130F/R/T (4 MCR sqn)

TRG 4 sqn

1 with 14 AV-8B, 8 TAV-8B

1 with 41 F/A-18A/B/C/D, 3 T-34C

1 with 12 F-5E, 1 F-5F

1 with 8 KC-130F

HELICOPTERS

ARMED 6 lt attack/utl with 108 AH-1W and 54 UH-1N

TPT 15 **med** sqn with 180 CH-46E, 4 sqn with 32 CH-53D; 6 **hy** sqn with 96 CH-53E

TRG 4 sqn

1 with 20 AH-1W, 10 UH-1N, 4 HH-1N

1 with 20 CH-46

1 with 6 CH-53D

1 with 15 CH-53E, 5 MH-53E

SAM 3+ bn

2 (1 MCR) with phase III I HAWK (will be phased out January 1999)

3 bn, 1 bty + (1 bty, 1 MCR) with *Stinger* and
  Avenger
UAV 2 sqn with *Pioneer*

RESERVES 6,600

(500 women); 1 air wg

AIRCRAFT
  FTR/ATTACK 4 sqn with 48 F-18A
    1 *Aggressor* sqn with 13 F5-E/F
  TKR 2 tkr/tpt sqn with 28 KC-130T

HELICOPTERS
  ARMED 2 attack/utl sqn with 36 AH-1W, 18 UH-
  1N
  TPT 4 sqn
    2 **med** with 24 CH-46E, 2 **hy** with 16 CH-53E
  SAM 1 bn (3 bty) with I HAWK, 1 bn (2 bty) with
    Stinger and *Avenger*

EQUIPMENT (incl MCR): 442 cbt ac; 175 armed hel
Totals included in the Navy inventory

AIRCRAFT
  259 **F-18A/-B/-C/-D** (FGA incl 48 MCR) • 154 **AV-8B**,
  14* **TAV-8B** (trg) • 21 **EA-6B** (ECM) • 13* **F-5E/F**
  (trg, MCR) • 79 **KC-130F/R/T** (tkr, incl 28 MCR) • 2
  C-9B (tpt) • 1 **C-20G** (MCR) (tpt) • 3 **CT-39G** (1
  MCR) • 18 **UC-12B/F** (utl, incl 3 MCR) • 3 **T-34C**
  (trg)

HELICOPTERS
  175 **AH-1W** (GA, incl 37 MCR) • 103 **UH-1N** (utl,
  incl 20 MCR) • 7 **HH-1H** (utl) • 231 **CH-46E** (tpt incl
  25 MCR) • 9 **UH/HH-46D** (utl) • 149 **CH-53-E** (tpt,
  incl 16 MCR) • 5 **MH-53E**, 47 **CH-53D** (tpt) • 8 **VH-
  60** (VIP tpt) • 11 **VH-3A/D** (VIP tpt)
  TILT ROTOR 12 MV-22B

MISSILES
  SAM 60 phase III I HAWK launcher, 1,929 *Stinger*,
  235 *Avenger*
  AAM *Sparrow* AMRAAM, *Sidewinder*
  ASM *Maverick*, *Hellfire*, TOW

Coast Guard (active duty) 36,000 military, 6,000 civilian

(includes 3,300 women)
By law a branch of the Armed Forces; in peacetime
operates under, and is funded by, the Department of
Transport

	Bdgt Authority		
	1994	$3.7bn	1997	$3.8bn
	1995	$3.7bn	1998	$4.0bn
	1996	$3.7bn	1999	request $4.1bn

PATROL VESSELS 175

OFFSHORE 78
  12 *Hamilton* high-endurance with HH-60J LAMPS
    HU-65A *Dolphin* hel, all with 76mm gun
  13 *Bear* med-endurance with 76mm gun, HH-65A hel

16 *Reliance* med-endurance with 25mm gun, hel
  deck
2 *Vindicator* (USN *Stalwart*) med-endurance cutter
3 other med-endurance cutters (inactive status)
32 buoy tenders

INSHORE 86
  49 *Farallon*, 37 *Point Hope*<

SPT AND OTHER 11
  2 icebreakers, 8 icebreaking tugs, 1 trg

AVIATION
  AC 20 HU-25 (plus 21 in store), 26 HC-130H (plus 4
  in store), 2 RU-38A, 35 HH-60J (plus 7 in store), 80
  HH-65A (plus 14 in store), 1 VC-4A, 1 C-20B

RESERVES 14,400

Air Force 370,300

(65,700 women) **Flying hours** ftr 232, bbr 238
Air Combat Comd (ACC) 5 air force (incl 1 ICBM), 23
ac wg **Air Mobility Comd** (AMC) 2 air force, 13 ac wg

TACTICAL 52 ftr sqn
incl active duty sqn ACC, USAFE and PACAF (sqn
may be 12 to 24 ac)
  14 with F-15, 6 with F-15E, 23 with F-16C/D (incl
  3 AD), 7 with A-10/OA-10, 2 with F-117

SUPPORT
  RECCE 3 sqn with U-2R and RC-135
  AEW 1 Airborne Warning and Control wg, 6 sqn
    (incl 1 trg) with E-3
  EW 2 sqn with EC-130
  FAC 7 tac air control sqn, mixed A-10A/OA-10A
  TRG 36 sqn
    1 *Aggressor* with F-16
    35 trg with **ac** F-15, F-16, A-10/OA-10, T-37, T-38,
    AT-38, T-1A, -3A, C-5, -130, -141 **hel** HH-60,
    U/TH-1
  TPT 28 sqn
    17 strategic: 5 with C-5 (1 trg), 9 with C-141 (2 trg),
    3 with C-17
    11 tac airlift with C-130
    Units with C-135, VC-137, C-9, C-12, C-20, C-21
  TKR 23 sqn
    19 with KC-135 (1 trg), 4 with KC-10A
  SAR 8 sqn (incl STRATCOM msl spt), HH-60, HC-
  130N/P
  MEDICAL 3 medical evacuation sqn with C-9A
  WEATHER RECCE WC-135
  TRIALS weapons trg units with **ac** A-10, F-4, F-15,
  F-16, F-111, T-38, C-141 **hel** UH-1
  UAV 2 sqn with *Predators*

RESERVES

AIR NATIONAL GUARD (ANG) 109,700
(17,000 women)
  BBR 2 sqn with B-1B

FTR 6 AD sqn with F-15, F-16
FGA 43 sqn
  6 with A-10/ OA-10
  31 with F-16 (incl 3 AD)
  6 with F-15A/B (incl 3 AD)
TPT 27 sqn
  24 tac (1 trg) with C-130E/H
  3 strategic: 1 with C-5, 2 with C-141B
TKR 23 sqn with KC-135E/R (11 with KC-135E, 12 with KC-135R)
SPECIAL OPS 1 sqn (AFSOC) with EC-130E
SAR 3 sqn with **ac** HC-130 **hel** HH-60
TRG 7 sqn

AIR FORCE RESERVE (AFR) 70,100

(14,500 women), 35 wg
BBR 1 sqn with B-52H
FGA 7 sqn
  4 with F-16C/D, 3 with A-10/OA-10 (incl 1 trg)
TPT 19 sqn
  7 strategic: 2 with C-5A, 5 with C-141B
  11 tac with 8 C-130H, 3 C-130E
  1 weather recce with WC-130E/H
TKR 7 sqn with KC-135E/R (5 KC-135R, 2 KC-135E)
SAR 3 sqn (ACC) with **ac** HC-130N/P **hel** HH-60
ASSOCIATE 20 sqn (personnel only)
  4 for C-5, 8 for C-141, 1 aero-medical for C-9, 2 C-17A, 4 for KC-10, 1 for KC-135

AIRCRAFT

LONG-RANGE STRIKE/ATTACK 206 cbt ac
  93 **B-52H** (with AGM-86 ALCM, 1 test) • 94 **B-1B** (2 test) • 19 **B-2A**
RECCE 31 **U-2R/S** • 4 TU-2 R/S • 20 RC-135 • SR-71 (6 in store)
COMD 32 **E-3B/C** • 4 E-4B • 12 EC-135
TAC 2,398 cbt ac (incl ANG, AFR plus 1,004 in store); no armed hel
  14 F-4E (FGA plus 309 -D, -E, -G models in store) • 707 **F-15** (506 -**A/B/C/D** (ftr incl 90 ANG, 14 test), 201 -**E** (FGA) (plus 101 F-15A/B in store)) • 1,237 **F-16** (105 -**A** (incl 102 ANG), 44 -**B** (incl 26 ANG), 963 -**C** (incl 340 ANG, 56 AFR), 125 -**D** (incl 29 ANG, 8 AFR) (plus 410 F-16A/B in store)) • 53 F-117 (42 (FGA), 10* (trg), plus 1 test) • 232 A-10A (FGA, incl 78 ANG, 27 AFR), plus 184 in store • 134* OA-10A (FAC incl 18 ANG, 27 AFR) • 4 EC-18B/D (Advanced Range Instrumentation) • 5 E-8C (JSTARS) • 1 TE-8A • 2 E-9A • 2 WC-135H/J (AFR) • 3 WC-135W • 3 OC-135 ('Open Skies' Treaty) • 21* AC-130H/U (special ops, USAF) • 31 HC-130N/P • 30 EC-130E/H (special ops incl 8 SOF) • 66 MC-130E/H/P (special ops) • 13 WC-130H/J/W (weather recce, 10 AFR) • 12 EC-135-C/E/N/Y, 20 RC-135S/U/V/W, 3 WC-135H/J/W
TPT 126 C-5 (74 -A (strategic tpt, incl 14 ANG, 32 AFR), 50 -B, 2 -C) • 41 C-17A • 2 C-38 (ANG) • 155 C-141B (incl 16 ANG, 44 AFR) • 513 C-130B/

D/E/H/J (tac tpt, incl 215 ANG, 112 AFR), plus 71 in store • 7 C-135A/B/C/E • 6 C-137B/C (VIP tpt) • 23 C-9A/C • 36 **C-12C/-D/-J** (liaison) • 12 **C-20** (2 -A, 5 -B, 3 -C, 2 -H) • 79 **C-21A** • 3 **C-22B** (ANG) • 3 **C-23A** • 2 **VC-25A** • 11 **C-26A/B** (ANG) • 10 **C-27A** (tpt)
TKR 549 KC-135 (225 ANG, 75 AFR) • 59 **KC-10A** tkr/tpt
TRG 183 **T-1A** • 111 **T-3A** • 415 **T-37B** • 414 **T-38** • 3 **T-41** • 10 **T-43A** • 2 TC-135S/W • 2 UV-18B • 78 AT-38B • 2 TC-18E • 1 CT-43A

HELICOPTERS

40 **MH-53-J** *Pave Low* (special ops) • 10 **MH-60G** (incl 10 SOC) • 8 **HH-1H** • 92 **HH-60G** (incl 21 AFR, 17 ANG) • 64 **UH-1N**, 6 TH-53A
UAV 6 **RQ-1A** (*Predator*)

MISSILES

AAM AIM-9P/L/M *Sidewinder*, AIM-7E/F/M *Sparrow*, AIM 120, A/B AMRAAM
ASM AGM-86B/C ALCM, AGM-65A/B/D/G *Maverick*, AGM-69A, AGM-88A/B HARM, AGM-84B *Harpoon*, AGM-86C ALCM, AGM-129A, AGM-130A, AGM-142A/B/C/D

CIVIL RESERVE AIR FLEET (CRAF) 683

commercial ac (numbers fluctuate)
LONG-RANGE 501
  passenger 271 (A-310, B-747, B -757, B-767, DC-10, L-1011, MD-11)
  cargo 230 (B-747, DC-8, DC-10, L-1011, MD-11)
SHORT-RANGE 95
  passenger 81 (A-300, B-727, B-737, MD-80/83)
  cargo 14 (L-100, B-727, DC-9)
DOMESTIC AND AERO-MEDICAL 34 (B-767)

Special Operations Forces (SOF)

Units only listed
ARMY (15,500)

5 SF gp (each 3 bn) • 1 Ranger inf regt (3 bn) • 1 special ops avn regt (3 bn) • 1 Psychological Ops gp (5 bn) • 1 Civil Affairs bn (5 coy) • 1 sigs, 1 spt bn
  RESERVES (2,800 ARNG, 7,800 AR)
  2 ARNG SF gp (3 bn) • 12 AR Civil Affairs HQ (3 comd, 9 bde) • 2 AR Psychological Ops gp • 36 AR Civil Affairs 'bn' (coy)
NAVY (4,000)

1 Naval Special Warfare Comd • 1 Naval Special Warfare Centre • 3 Naval Special Warfare gp • 6 Naval Special Warfare units • 6 SEAL teams • 2 SEAL delivery veh teams • 2 Special Boat sqn • 6 DDS
  RESERVES (1,400)
  1 Naval Special Warfare Comd det • 6 Naval Special Warfare gp det • 3 Naval Special Warfare unit det • 5 SEAL team det • 2 Special Boat unit • 2 Special Boat sqn • 1 SEAL delivery veh det • 1 CINCSOC det

AIR FORCE (9,320): (AFRES 1,260) (ANG 750)

1 air force HQ, 1 wg, 14 sqn with
    7 AC-130H, 12 AC-130U, 5 MC-130E, 21 MC-130H,
      19 MC-130P, 34 MH53J
    7 MH-60G, 5 C-130E. AETC (Air Education and
      Training Command) 1 wg, 2 sqn: 3 MC-130H, 4
      MC-130P, 5 MH-53J, 4 TH-53A

RESERVES

1 wg, 2 sqn:
8 MC-130E, 4 MC-130P, 2 C-130E
ANG
1 wg, 2 sqn:
5 EC-130E

Deployment

Commanders' NATO appointments also shown
(e.g., COMEUCOM is also SACEUR)

EUROPEAN COMMAND (EUCOM)

some 102,500 incl 20,500 in HQ and centrally control-
led formations/units. Plus 14,000 Mediterranean 6th
Fleet: HQ Stuttgart-Vaihingen (Commander is
SACEUR)
ARMY (54,600) HQ US Army Europe (USAREUR),
Heidelberg
NAVY HQ US Navy Europe (USNAVEUR), London
    (Commander is also CINCAFSOUTH)
AIR FORCE (27,400) HQ US Air Force Europe
    (USAFE), Ramstein (Commander is
    COMAIRCENT)

GERMANY

ARMY (42,600)
V Corps with 1 armd(-), 1 mech inf div(-), 1 arty, 1
    AD (1 *Patriot* (6 bty), 1 *Avenger* bn), 1 engr, 1 avn
    bde
Army Prepositioned Stocks (APS) for 4 armd/mech
    bde, approx 57% stored in Ge
    EQPT (incl APS in Ge, Be, Lux and Nl)
    some 805 MBT, 738 AIFV, 857 APC, 441 arty/
    MRL/mor, 138 ATK hel
AIR FORCE (15,140), 72 cbt ac
1 air force HQ: USAFE
1 ftr wg: 4 sqn (2 with 42 F-16C/D, 1 with 22 F-15C/
    D, 1 with 12 A-10 and 6 OA-10)
1 airlift wg: incl 16 C-130E and 4 C-9A, 9C-21, 2C-20,
    1CT-43

BELGIUM

ARMY 200; approx 22% of POMCUS
NAVY 100
AIR FORCE 500

GREECE

NAVY 250; base facilities at Soudha Bay, Makri
    (Crete)
AIR FORCE 170; air base gp. Facilities at Iraklion

(Crete)

ITALY

ARMY 1,750; HQ: Vicenza. 1 inf bn gp, 1 arty bty
    EQPT for Theater Reserve Unit/Army Readiness
    Package South (TRU/ARPS), incl 122 MBT, 133
    AIFV, 81 APC, 56 arty/MLRS/mor
NAVY 4,600; HQ: Gaeta; bases at Naples, La
    Maddalena, 1 MR sqn with 9 P-3C at Sigonella
AIR FORCE 4,230; 1 AF HQ (16th Air Force), 1 ftr
    wg, 2 sqn with 36 F-16C/D
    SFOR Air Element 6 F-16, 1 AC-130, 3 EC-130, 1
    MC-130P, 5 KC-135, 4 C-12, 6 EA-6B, 2 MH-53J

LUXEMBOURG

ARMY approx 21% of APS

MEDITERRANEAN

NAVY some 14,000 (incl 2,200 Marines). 6th Fleet
    (HQ Gaeta, Italy): typically 4 SSN, 1 CVBG (1 CV,
    5 surface combatants, 1 fast spt ship), 1 T-AO.
    MPS-1 (4 ships with equipment for 1 MEF (fwd)).
    Marine personnel: some 2,000. MEU (SOC)
    embarked aboard Amphibious Ready Group
    ships

NETHERLANDS

ARMY 200; approx 7% of APS
AIR FORCE 290

NORWAY

prepositioning incl 24 M-109, 8 M-198 arty, no
aviation assets
AIR FORCE 60

PORTUGAL

(for Azores, see Atlantic Command)
NAVY 65
AIR FORCE 950

SPAIN

NAVY 2,200; base at Rota
AIR FORCE 240

TURKEY

NAVY 20, spt facilities at Izmir and Ankara
AIR FORCE 2,410; facilities at Incirlik. 1 wg (ac on
    det only), numbers vary (incl F-15, F-16, EA-6B,
    KC-135, E-3B/C, C-12, HC-130, HH-60)
Installations for SIGINT, space tracking and seismic
    monitoring

UNITED KINGDOM

NAVY 1,540; HQ: London, admin and spt facilities,
    1 SEAL det
AIR FORCE 9,000
1 air force HQ (3rd Air Force): 1 ftr wg, 66 cbt ac, 2
    sqn with 48 F-15E, 1 sqn with 18 F-15C/D
1 special ops gp with 3 sqn: 1 with 5 MH-53J, 1 with
    4 HC-130, 1 with 4 MC-130H
1 air refuelling wg with 9 KC-135

PACIFIC COMMAND (USPACOM)

HQ: Hawaii

ALASKA

ARMY 6,600; 1 lt inf bde

AIR FORCE 9,350; 1 air force HQ (11th Air Force) 1 ftr wg with 2 sqn (1 with 18 F-16, 1 with 6 A-10, 6 OA-10), 1 wg with 2 sqn with 36 F-15C/D, with 18 F-15E, 1 sqn with 10 C-130H, 2 E-3B, 3 C-12, 1 air tkr wg with 8 KC-135R

HAWAII

ARMY 15,400; HQ: US Army Pacific (USARPAC) 1 lt inf div (2 lt inf bde)

AIR FORCE 4,530; HQ: Pacific Air Forces (PACAF) 1 wg with 2 C-135B/C, 1 wg (ANG) with 15 F-15A/B, 4 C-130H and 8 KC-135R

NAVY 19,500; HQ: US Pacific Fleet
Homeport for some 7 SS, 16 PSC and 10 spt and misc ships

MARINES 6,300; HQ: Marine Forces Pacific

SINGAPORE

NAVY about 100; log facilities

AIR FORCE 40 det spt sqn

JAPAN

ARMY 1,800; 1 corps HQ, base and spt units

AIR FORCE 14,030; 1 air force HQ (5th Air Force): 90 cbt ac
1 ftr wg, 2 sqn with 36 F-16 • 1 wg, 3 sqn with 54 F-15C/D • 1 sqn with 15 KC-135 • 1 SAR sqn with 8 HH-60 • 1 sqn with 2 E-3 AWACS • 1 Airlift Wg with 16 C-130 E/H, 4 C-21, 3 C-9 • 1 special ops gp with 4 MC-130P and 4 MC-130E

NAVY 6,750; bases: **Yokosuka** (HQ 7th Fleet) homeport for 1 CV, 8 surface combatants **Sasebo** homeport for 4 amph ships, 2 MCM

MARINES 16,600; 1 MEF

SOUTH KOREA

ARMY 27,460; 1 Army HQ (UN command), 1 inf div with 2 bde (6 bn), 2 SP arty, 1 MLRS, 1 AD bn, 1 avn, 1 engr bde plus 1 avn bde, 1 air cav bde (2 ATK hel bn), 1 *Patriot* SAM bn (Army tps)

EQPT incl 116 MBT, 126 AIFV, 111 APC, 45 arty/MRL/mor

AIR FORCE 8,660; 1 air force HQ (7th Air Force): 2 ftr wg, 90 cbt ac; 3 sqn with 72 F-16, 1 sqn with 6 A-10, 12 OA-10, 1 special ops sqn, 5 MH-53J

GUAM

AIR FORCE 1,980; 1 air force HQ (13th Air Force)

NAVY 4,600; MPS-3 (4 ships with eqpt for 1 MEB) Naval air station, comms and spt facilities

AUSTRALIA

NAVY some 35; comms facility at NW Cape, SEWS/SIGINT station at Pine Gap, and SEWS station at Nurrungar

DIEGO GARCIA

NAVY 900; MPS-2 (5 ships with eqpt for 1 MEB)

Naval air station, spt facilities

US WEST COAST

MARINES 1 MEF

AT SEA

PACIFIC FLEET (HQ: Pearl Harbor) **Main base** Pearl Harbor **Other bases** Bangor, Everett, Bremerton (WA), San Diego (CA)

Submarines 7 *Ohio* SSBN, 5 SSGN, 27 SSN

Surface Combatants 6 CV/CVN, 29 CG/CGN, 2 DDG, 15 DD, 12 FFG

Amph 1 comd, 3 LHA, 3 LPH, 7 LPD, 6 LSD, 2 LST

Surface Combatants divided between two fleets

3rd Fleet (HQ: San Diego) covers Eastern and Central Pacific, Aleutian Islands, Bering Sea; typically 4 CVBG, 4 URG, amph gp

7th Fleet (HQ: Yokosuka) covers Western Pacific, Japan, Philippines, ANZUS responsibilities, Indian Ocean; typically 1 CVBG, 1 URG, amph ready gp (1 MEU embarked)

CENTRAL COMMAND (USCENTCOM)

commands all deployed forces in its region; HQ: MacDill AFB, FL

ARMY 2,070

AT SEA

5th Fleet, HQ Manama. Average US Naval Forces deployed in Indian Ocean, Persian Gulf, Red Sea: 1 CVBG (1 CV/CVN, 2 CG/CGN, 2 DD/DDG, 1-2 AO/AOE/AE, 2 SSN) (forces provided from Atlantic and Pacific)

KUWAIT

ARMY 1,200; prepositioned eqpt for 1 armd bde (2 tk, 1 mech bn, 1 arty bn)

NAVY 1,000

AIR FORCE 25 (force structure varies)

QATAR

ARMY 13; prepositioned eqpt for 1 armd bde (forming)

AIR FORCE 2 (force structure varies)

SAUDI ARABIA

ARMY 1,400; 1 *Patriot* SAM, 1 sigs unit incl those on short-term (6 months) duty

AIR FORCE 1,820. Units on rotational detachment, **ac** numbers vary (incl F-15, F-16, F-117, C-130, KC-135, U-2, E-3)

SOUTHERN COMMAND (USSOUTHCOM)

HQ: Miami, FL

PANAMA

ARMY 820; HQ: US Army South, Fort Clayton, Panama; 1 inf, 1 avn bn

NAVY HQ: US Naval Forces Southern Command, Howard AFB: 700 personnel. Special boat unit, fleet support

MARINES 180

AIR FORCE 1,800; 1 wg (1 C-21, 9 C-27, 1 CT-43)

HONDURAS
ARMY 619
AIR FORCE 100

ATLANTIC COMMAND (USACOM)

HQ: Norfolk, VA (CINC has op control of all CONUS-based army and air forces)

US EAST COAST

MARINES 1 MEF

BERMUDA

NAVY 800

CUBA

NAVY 1,000 (Guantánamo)
MARINES 420 (Guantánamo)

HAITI

ARMY 189

ICELAND

NAVY 1,800; 1 MR sqn with 6 P-3, 1 UP-3
MARINES 80
AIR FORCE 600; 6 F-15C/D, 1 KC-135, 1 HC-130, 4 HH-60G

PORTUGAL (AZORES)

NAVY 10; limited facilities at Lajes
AIR FORCE 950; periodic SAR detachments to spt space shuttle ops

UNITED KINGDOM

NAVY 150; comms and int facilities, Edzell, Thurso

AT SEA

ATLANTIC FLEET (HQ: Norfolk, VA) **Other main bases** Groton (CT), King's Bay (GA), Mayport (FL)
Submarines 7 *Ohio*, 3 SSBN, 16 SSGN, 35 SSN
Surface Combatants 6 CV/CVN, 23 CG/CGN, 5 DDG, 16 DD, 23 FFG. Amph: 1 LCC, 2 LHA, 4 LPH, 6 LPD, 5 LSD, 6 LST, 1 LKA
Surface Forces divided into 2 fleets:
2nd Fleet (HQ: Norfolk) covers Atlantic; typically 4–5 CVBG, amph gp, 4 URG
6th Fleet (HQ: Gaeta, Italy) under op comd of EUCOM

Continental United States (CONUS)

major units/formations only listed

ARMY (USACOM)

200,500 provides general reserve of cbt-ready ground forces for other comd
Active 1 Army HQ, 3 Corps HQ (1 AB), 1 armd, 2 mech, 1 lt inf, 1 AB, 1 air aslt div; 6 arty bde; 3 armd cav regt, 6 AD bn (1 *Avenger*, 5 *Patriot*)
Reserve (ARNG): 3 armd, 1 mech, 3 inf, 1 lt inf div;18 indep bde

US STRATEGIC COMMAND (USSTRATCOM)

HQ: Offutt AFB, NE
See entry on p. 20

AIR COMBAT COMMAND (ACC)

HQ: Langley AFB, VA. Provides strategic AD units and cbt-ready Air Force units for rapid deployment

SPACE COMMAND (AFSPACECOM)

HQ: Peterson AFB, CO. Provides ballistic-missile warning, space control, satellite operations around the world, and maintains ICBM force

US SPECIAL OPERATIONS COMMAND (USSOCOM)

HQ: MacDill AFB, FL. Comd all active, reserve and National Guard special ops forces of all services based in CONUS. See p. 26

US TRANSPORTATION COMMAND (USTRANSCOM)

HQ: Scott AFB, IL. Provides all common-user airlift, sealift and land transport to deploy and maintain US forces on a global basis

AIR MOBILITY COMMAND (AMC)

HQ: Scott AFB, IL. Provides strategic, tac and special op airlift, aero-medical evacuation, SAR and weather recce

Forces Abroad

UN AND PEACEKEEPING

BOSNIA (SFOR II): up to 7,400; 1 inf bde plus spt tps
CROATIA (SFOR): 650. SFOR AIR ELEMENT (OP JOINT GUARD) 3,200. Forces are deployed to **Bosnia, Croatia, Hungary, Italy, France, Germany** and the **United Kingdom**. Aircraft include F/A-16, A-10, AC-130, MC-130, C-130, E-3, U-2, EC-130, RC-135, EA-6B, MH-53J and *Predator* UAV. EGYPT (MFO): 917; 1 inf bn. FYROM (UNPREDEP): 338; 1 inf bn, incl 3 UH-60 hel. GEORGIA (UNOMIG): 2 Obs. HUNGARY (SFOR): 1,560. 230 Air Force *Predator* UAV. IRAQ/KUWAIT (UNIKOM): 10 Obs. MIDDLE EAST (UNTSO): 2 Obs. WESTERN SAHARA (MINURSO): 15 Obs. SAUDI ARABIA (*Southern Watch*) **Air Force** units on rotation, numbers vary (incl F-15, F-16, F-117, C-130, KC-135, E-3). TURKEY (*Northern Watch*) **Army** 22 **Air Force** 1,400; 1 tac, 1 Air Base gp (ac on det only), numbers vary but include F-16, F-15, EA-6B, KC-135, E3B/C, C-12, HC-130

Paramilitary

CIVIL AIR PATROL (CAP) 53,000

(1,900 cadets); HQ, 8 geographical regions, 52 wg, 1,700 units, 535 CAP ac, plus 4,700 private ac

MILITARY DEVELOPMENTS

Regional Trends

The NATO-led Stabilisation Force (SFOR) in **Bosnia-Herzegovina** remains the largest military deployment in the region. While hostilities have been contained there, a new conflict erupted in early 1998 in the mainly ethnic-Albanian province of Kosovo in **Serbia**. There continue to be tensions in the Transcaucasus region. In particular, there was renewed fighting in the Georgian province of Abkhazia in May 1998. The potential for conflict between **Greece** and **Turkey** over the **Cyprus** issue also increased during the year.

SFOR

SFOR II came into effect on 20 June 1998 with a similar mandate to its predecessor, this time without a set expiry date (see p. 290). The SFOR Follow-on Force (FOF) is slightly reduced from an SFOR I strength of 34,900 to between 32,400 and 33,200, reflecting its success in averting large-scale conflict and reinforcing the implementation of the 1995 General Framework for Peace in Bosnia and Hertzegovina (the Dayton Accords) and the civil reconstruction process. SFOR (FOF) II is composed of contingents from 29 countries. The biggest troop contributors are the US, whose contingent numbers between 6,900 and 7,400, and the **United Kingdom**, which provides 4,900 personnel. The military have now become much more directly involved in arresting suspected war criminals, although two key accused, the former President of the Bosnian Serb Republic Radovan Karadic and the former Army commander, General Ratko Mladic, have not yet been apprehended.

Instabilities

The escalating battle between the ethnic-Albanian Kosovo Liberation Army (KLA) and the Serbian security forces backed by the Yugoslav Army had resulted in some 500 fatalities and the displacement of over 150,000 people by August 1998, when the KLA, which lacks firm central direction and coordination, was under intense pressure. Agreement by NATO and Partner countries on action to contain the conflict extended only as far as demonstration exercises by air and ground troops in neighbouring **Albania** and Former Yugoslav Republic of **Macedonia**. Elsewhere, peacekeeping missions are maintained in Cyprus, Nagorno-Karabakh and **Georgia**. The lack of progress in negotiations between the Greek and Turkish communities in Cyprus has contributed to increased military tensions. In particular, Turkey reacted strongly to the Greek Cypriot decision to purchase S-300 surface-to-air missiles (SAMs) from Russia, which became widely known in March 1998. Delivery, originally planned for August 1998, has been postponed until November. Greek-Cypriot National Guard personnel have been reported on demonstration and training visits in Russia, so it seems highly likely that the deal will go ahead. The S-300 version being supplied is reported to be the PMU-1 model (otherwise known as the SA-10D), with a maximum effective range of 150 kilometres. This puts airspace over the Turkish mainland in reach from Cyprus, although the launchers, supporting radars and other elements, would be highly vulnerable to the Turkish Air Force once deployed. It is not certain that, if the missiles were delivered in November 1998, they would be deployed immediately. The Greek Cypriots will exploit deployment as a bargaining lever, in particular to try to block military flights over the southern part of the island. Both Greece and Turkey have practised deploying naval and air force reinforcements to the island during 1998.

NATO *and*
Non-NATO Europe

Zagreb

Logistic
Support
HQ
(Comm
Z HQ)

H U N G A R Y

C R O A T I A

Divisional
HQ
MND (SW)
(UK)

Nordic
Brigade
HQ

Divisional
HQ
MND (N)
(US)

S
E
R
B
I
A

N

Russian
Brigade
HQ

Coralici

Bos
Gradiska

Orasje

Bihac

Brcko

Banja Luka

Doboj

Ugljevik

SW **XX** N

**BOSNIA
AND
HERZEGOVINA**

Maglaj

Tuzla

Kljuc

Dubrave

Zvornik

Mrkonjic Grad

Vlasenica

Sipovo

Zenica

Srebrenica

C
R
O
A
T
I
A

Kiseljak

N
XX
SE

Zepa

Turkish
Brigade
HQ

Gornji
Vakuf

Sarajevo

SW
X
SE

Visegrad

Gorazde

Foca

Medugorje

Mostar

F
R
Y

Main
SFOR
HQ

Spanish
Brigade
HQ

Blieca

French/
German
Brigade
HQ at
Rajlovac

Divisional
HQ
MND (SE)
(France)

Trebinje

M O N T E N E G R O

*A d r i a t i c
S e a*

Dayton Agreement line
Bosnian Croat–Muslim Federation
Republika Srpska
military sector boundary
N   Sector North
SW Sector South-west
SE Sector South-east
international boundary
capital city

All data as at 6 August 1998

0   100km

0   50 miles

As in previous years, the military have been drawn into counter-terrorism activity and periodic support for the police in their battle against large-scale organised crime. In the UK, despite the 'Good Friday' agreement between the communities of Northern Ireland and the British and Irish governments, terrorist splinter groups persist in carrying out attacks in an attempt to derail the peace process. This means that UK forces will still be required to support the civil authorities in Ulster for some time. Troops were finally withdrawn from southern Italy, where for nearly two years they supported the police in their campaign against organised crime.

NATO Enlargement

The **Czech Republic**, **Hungary** and **Poland** signed protocols of accession to NATO in December 1997 and they seem virtually certain to join the Alliance in 1999 as planned. The enlargement process is subject to ratification in accordance with legislation in each of the NATO member-states; 13 out of the 16 had ratified the protocols by August 1998 and the **Netherlands** and **Portugal** were due to complete their processes soon. There was some delay in Turkey approving the enlargement process, but the Defence and Foreign Affairs Committee of the Turkish parliament had approved a draft law to ratify the protocols by August 1998 and this was likely to be submitted to the Turkish General Assembly in its September 1998 session.

Euro-Atlantic Partnership Council

The 44-member Euro-Atlantic Partnership Council (EAPC) deepened and widened its activities in 1998. It proved to be a valuable forum for consultations on the future of SFOR in Bosnia and NATO's response to the situation in Kosovo. In the latter case, EAPC consultation eased the path to Russian, Lithuanian and Albanian participation along with 11 NATO members in activities such as Exercise 'Co-operative Assembly' held in Albania on 17–22 August 1998. More than 1,300 soldiers, sailors, airmen and marines and nearly 70 fixed wing and rotary aircraft participated in this Partnership for Peace (PfP) exercise.

In June 1998, the EAPC set up the Euro-Atlantic Disaster Response Co-ordination Centre (EADRCC) in Brussels as part of a move to broaden its focus to deal with non-military aspects of security. The new organisation builds on NATO's longstanding Civil Emergency Planning activities for mutual assistance among NATO members in large-scale disasters. The EADRCC's task is to coordinate the response capabilities of EAPC members to ensure a prompt and effective offer of disaster assistance to the United Nations. The organisation institutionalises a third link between NATO and the UN, adding to the two existing working links in the political and security areas. This demonstrates not only NATO's broadening activities but also the extent to which the Alliance is developing and institutionalising its connections with other bodies and countries. Other examples include the Mediterranean Co-operation Group, set up in August 1997, which has resulted in exchanges on a range of issues relevant to security in the Mediterranean with the Southern Mediterranean Dialogue Partners – Egypt, Israel, Jordan, Mauritania, Morocco and Tunisia. Activities in the fields of science and information include the designation of NATO contact-point embassies in the Dialogue countries and the opening of NATO schools to their officers. Another example of NATO's broadening activities was the announcement in May 1998 that it would pursue regular exchanges on peacekeeping operations with African countries.

DEFENCE SPENDING

NATO Europe

Defence expenditure by NATO's European member-states fell by 9% in 1997, to $173bn from $191bn in 1996, measured in constant US dollars. The reduced dollar value of European defence outlays reflected depreciation against the US dollar of around 15% by most currencies in the European Monetary System during 1997. Sustaining defence budgets, even at these reduced levels, requires an act of political will for the majority of NATO's European governments, particularly those which are committed to European Monetary Union (EMU) and under pressure to meet the Maastricht Treaty criteria for fiscal deficits and government debt. At the same time, many governments have to balance costly priorities, such as professionalisation (as in **Belgium**, **France**, the Netherlands and **Spain**) and equipment modernisation, within static or shrinking defence budgets. As a result, while partner governments approved production orders for the first batch of *Eurofighter* combat aircraft in January 1998, there is considerable uncertainty surrounding the timing, unit quantities and future status of several other expensive European programmes. These include the Future Large Aircraft (FLA), the *Horizon* frigate and the NH-90 and EH-101 helicopters.

The UK's 1998 defence budget is £22.2bn ($37bn). The government released its Strategic Defence Review (SDR) in July 1998, which set out a three-year spending plan of £22.3bn in 1999, £22.8bn in 2000, and £23bn in 2001. According to UK government calculations, these figures mean an annual saving of £915m ($1.5bn) in the defence budget by 2001. Over the same period, asset sales of £700m over four years are expected to result in a net saving of £685m by 2001 and the UK's defence expenditure as a proportion of gross domestic product (GDP) is expected to fall from 2.7% to 2.4%. The SDR endorses existing procurement programmes, and provides for two new aircraft carriers to be acquired from 2012. The major savings are expected to come from the reorganisation of defence logistics and procurement. In France, the new government has not altered the six-year 1997–2002 defence plan (*Loi de Programmation*), introduced by its predecessor in June 1996, which fixed the annual defence budget at an average level of FF185bn and the equipment allocation at FF86bn (in constant 1995 francs) over the six years. However, while the 1998 defence budget is set at FF185bn ($30bn), the equipment allocation has been cut to FF81bn. In **Germany**, the 1998 defence budget is DM46.7bn ($26bn), while the 1999–2002 plan sets the 1999 defence budget at DM47.6bn ($26bn) rising to DM49.4bn in 2002. In Italy, the 1998 defence budget is L31tr ($17bn) rising to L31.9tr ($18bn) in 1999.

Elsewhere in NATO Europe, spending levels are, in real terms, either static or in slight decline. The exceptions are Greece and Turkey, where real spending increases have been sustained since the end of the Cold War in contrast to the general trend in NATO Europe of reductions of up to a third and sometimes more. In Turkey, 1997 defence outlays are estimated at TL1,232tr ($8.1bn), compared to TL612tr ($7.5bn) in 1996, with the 1998 budget increasing to $8.2bn. In Greece, the 1998 defence budget is dr1,166bn ($3.8bn) compared with dr984bn ($3.6bn) in 1997.

NATO European countries have budgeted some $40bn between them for spending on equipment in 1998, down from $41bn in 1997. This contrasts with the US spend of $80bn ($79bn in 1997). Production funding of some $30bn in NATO Europe is about two-thirds the US total of $44bn in 1998, whereas NATO Europe's spending on research and development (R&D) is, at $10bn, less than one-third that of the $36bn spent in the US. This disparity in R&D effort has existed for some time, and the gap shows no sign of closing, nor is there any significant reduction in the duplication and fragmentation that remains a feature of NATO Europe's R&D activities. Moreover, several large European cooperative programmes are now reaching the production phase, which entails a larger proportion of equipment funding for production. This not only raises questions about whether production programmes can be afforded under current spending plans, but also reinforces the tendency for NATO European countries to under-spend on R&D. There have been few new European cooperative development programmes for major conventional weapon systems since the Cold War, and a marked absence of substantial cooperative commitments in a number of increasingly relevant areas such as ballistic missile defence, unmanned aerial vehicles (UAVs), and command and control systems

Most of NATO Europe's major current equipment programmes have their genesis in the Cold War. After two years of uncertainty surrounding Germany's commitment, Europe's largest co-operative programme, *Eurofighter*, was finally approved for production by the four partner governments (UK, Germany, Italy and Spain) in December 1997. The aircraft is expected to enter service in 2002 and approval for the first batch of 148 out of a planned 620 was authorised in January 1998. According to the UK National Audit Office (NAO), *Eurofighter* development has cost around $7bn since 1984, while the production cost of 232 aircraft is estimated at $15–16bn. The unit cost of each *Eurofighter* to the UK is about $98m, including R&D. By comparison, France's *Rafale* fighter has cost an estimated $7–8bn to develop as a national venture, while the last production cost estimates (made by the previous government in 1996) were FF17bn ($2.8bn) for the first batch of 48. At these prices, the unit cost for 234 *Rafales* for the French Air Force and 60 variants for the French Navy is estimated at about $75m. The Navy variant of the *Rafale* is expected to enter service in 2001 and the Air Force variant in 2005.

Despite escalating costs and shrinking demand, Europe's helicopter programmes have escaped outright cancellation, but are vulnerable to funding cuts under current spending plans. The Anglo-Italian EH-101 helicopter has cost the British government about $8.3bn for the 44 naval and 22 utility variants on order. This represents a unit cost of $126m, including R&D since 1979, according to the NAO. By comparison, the 1996 purchase from the US of 67 AH-64D attack helicopters for the British Army entails a unit cost of $66m, while the unit cost of 14 CH-47D support helicopters ordered from the US in 1995 is $35m. The NH-90 helicopter involving France, Germany, Italy and the Netherlands, and, like the EH-101, designed for naval and utility roles, has been the subject of disagreement among the four partners, and a production decision has been delayed pending a satisfactory price. The total requirement of the four partner nations remains at 647 for entry into service in 2003, but some partners seem to lack full commitment to this programme. In the meantime, Germany ordered seven new naval *Lynx* helicopters from the UK in 1996 and contracted to modernise its entire fleet of 17 naval *Lynxes* in June 1998. Some doubt remains over the viability of the NH-90 programme, given the availability of the Franco-German AS-532 *Cougar* and US UH-60 *Black Hawk* for transport roles and the EH-101 *Lynx* and SH-60 *Sea Hawk* for naval applications. In May 1998, the French and German governments approved production of the first batch of 160 Franco-German *Tiger* attack helicopters. France withdrew from the *Trigat* long-range anti-tank missile programme in May 1998, leaving Germany with leadership for the missile destined for the *Tiger*. Production of the planned 427 helicopters is expected to stretch to 2025, with entry into service planned for 2003. France retains its leadership in the *Hélios* 1 and 2 satellite programmes, which also involve Germany, Italy and Spain, but withdrew its commitment to the *Horus* satellite in May 1998, leaving Germany as the sole provider of funds for this programme. Commitment to develop the (FLA) has still not been achieved by the seven partner nations. Germany's insistence on evaluating the joint Ukrainian-Russian An-70 has raised further uncertainties about the future status of the FLA programme. The UK is to take late delivery in 1999 of 25 C-130J *Hercules*, ordered from the US in 1994. Italy has also ordered 18 of the type for 1999 delivery. In July 1998, the UK announced that it was intending to lease four C-17 *Globemasters* from the US. The largest cooperative warship programme is the *Horizon* frigate initiated in 1994 after the NATO Frigate NFR-90 programme collapsed. It involves the UK (with a requirement for 12) France (2) and Italy (4). An associated programme is the Principal Anti-Air Missile System (PAAMS). Entry into service is planned for 2004, but, while there is no doubting the UK commitment, its status as a cooperative programme is far from secure. Meanwhile, former

European partners of the defunct NFR-90 programme have opted for national programmes, albeit with some commonality. Germany is building three F-124 frigates for delivery from 2002, the Netherlands four F-870 frigates for delivery from 2001, and Spain 4 F-100 frigates for delivery from 2001.

The future of the joint Anglo-French-German armoured vehicle (MRAV/VBCI/GTK) remains uncertain after the April 1998 decision on contractor choice failed to win French approval. Meanwhile, the UK and the US signed a July 1998 memorandum of understanding on the Tactical Reconnaissance Armoured Combat Requirement (TRACER) for about 1,600 with entry into service planned for 2007. Project definition including an advanced technology demonstrator is expected to be contracted in December 1998 and will last for 42 months. Potentially the largest co-operative programme to 2010, the US Joint Strike Fighter (JSF) replacing the F-16 and *Harrier*, is at the project-definition phase. Development is expected to begin in 2001, with first deliveries planned for 2007–10. The UK joined as a full collaborative partner in 1995, since when Norway, Denmark and the Netherlands have joined as a single associate partner. Canada is an observer and Italy and Australia are in the process of deciding whether or not to take observer status. The US-led Medium Extended Air Defence System (MEADS) – a BMD programme also involving Germany and Italy remains in the feasibility phase. The US FY1999 budget request seeks $43m for MEADS.

Non-NATO Europe

Defence spending in non-NATO Europe declined in real terms to some $27bn in 1997 from $30bn in 1996. Cuts in countries with relatively large defence budgets, mainly non-NATO EU states, accounted for most of the decline. At a sub-regional level, military spending increased in the Transcaucasus, the Baltic States and Cyprus. Although there were nominal increases in the defence budgets of the three prospective new NATO member-states in 1997, currency depre-ciation meant that real defence spending declined in Poland, Hungary and the Czech Republic. The 1998 defence budget in Cyprus remains high, and there are large increases in the defence budgets of **Azerbaijan** and **Lithuania**. Procurement of major conventional weapons from domestic sources remains at comparatively low levels outside Western Europe. Elsewhere in the region, most supplier countries appear to be focusing their productive efforts on export markets for conventional weapons, light weapons and surplus equipment.

In the non-NATO EU countries and **Switzerland**, 1998 defence budgets are mainly static or slightly down on 1997 both in national currency and dollar terms, with the dollar trend exag-gerated by the continuing weakness of most European currencies against the US dollar. Large fighter procurement – the JAS-39 *Gripen* in **Sweden** and the F-18C/D in **Finland** and Switzerland, account for a large proportion of the equipment budgets of these countries in 1998. Finland's defence imports, largely 64 F-18C/D for assembly in Finland, amounted to $610m in 1996 and $660m in 1997. The government approved a supplementary budget of m1bn ($180m) for the year in February 1998. Later, in April 1998, the Finnish parliament approved a multi-year supple-mentary budget of m6.1bn ($1.1bn) to fund the purchase of transport helicopters and the formation of a rapid-reaction force. In Cyprus, defence spending accounted for 5.8% of GDP in 1996 and 1997. The 1998 defence budget is C£265m ($507m), compared to C£259m ($505m) in 1997. Delivery of the Russian S-300PMU1 (SA-10D) SAM is expected in November 1998. Another batch of 40 T-80 main battle tanks (MBTs) are on order for the National Guard, following delivery of 41 of the type (costing $172m) in 1996–97.

Defence budgets for 1998 in the prospective new NATO countries show real increases over 1997 in the case of Poland and the Czech Republic. In Poland, the 1998 budget is z11.6bn ($3bn) against z9.8bn ($2.9bn) in 1997, and rises to z12.1bn ($3.4bn) in 1999. According to Poland's Ministry of National Defence in February 1998, defence spending is intended to remain at current levels of around 2.4% of GDP until 2002. Over the longer term, the proportion of the budget spent on equipment is expected to rise from some 16% in 1997 to 37% in 2012, while spending on personnel is expected to fall from 51% to 34%. In the Czech Republic, the 1998 defence budget rose to k35.6bn ($1.1bn) from k31.3bn ($1bn) in 1996, rising to k42.3bn ($1.3bn) in 1999. The target level for defence spending by 2001 is around 2% of GDP. Czech arms exports increased in 1997 to $183m from $120m in 1996. In Hungary, the 1998 defence budget is f142bn ($643m), compared to f124bn ($666m) in 1997, and rises to f168bn ($701m) in 1999 and f237bn in 2001. The target level for defence spending by 2001 is 1.8% of GDP. All three countries are introducing a higher level of professionalisation into the armed forces in order to phase out conscription gradually. Poland and Hungary aim to have 60% professional personnel and the Czech Republic 50%. Equipment modernisation in all three countries is mostly at the planning stage until NATO membership is assured in 1999. Concern about the cost of NATO membership, to both prospective and existing member-states, has been allayed by the moderation of initially exaggerated estimates of what the costs will be. It has become evident that neither unilateral (US) nor multilateral (NATO common-funded) contributions will be substantial. It has also become clear that incremental costs will be carried mainly by the new member states. According to Polish government estimates in February 1998, the direct costs of joining NATO will amount to some $3bn in the period 1998–2010, or about 5% of the annual defence budget. The indirect costs (achieving inter-operability with NATO armed forces and equipment modernisation) are expected to be some $8.3bn over 15 years. These estimates are comparable with figures at the low end of the range published last year in *The Military Balance 1997/98* (see Costs of NATO Enlargement, pp. 268–273).

In the Baltic States, there is much interest in the possibility of joining NATO at some stage. Although large increases in defence budgets are planned, the changes reflect the adoption of NATO definitions of defence spending (specifically the separation of paramilitary from police allocations) rather than a rise in real spending. In Lithuania, the 1998 defence budget is L462m ($116m), up from L314m ($79m) in 1997 and rising to L730m ($183m) in 1999. In **Latvia**, the 1998 defence budget of L23m ($39m), compares with L22m ($38m) in 1997. The budget will rise to L43m ($72m) in 1999. In **Estonia**, the 1998 defence budget is kn825m ($57m), compared to kn736m ($53m) in 1997.

In the Balkans, **Slovenia**'s 1998 defence budget has risen to t41.4bn ($241m) from t35bn ($219m) in 1997. In Bosnia, military-related spending accounts for two-thirds of the entire government budget, excluding funding for economic reconstruction. The 1998 defence budget is cm343m ($188m) of which cm257m goes to war veterans and their families. In **Croatia**, the 1998 budget is k7.5bn ($1.1bn), compared to k7bn ($1.1bn) in 1997. In the **Federal Republic of Yugoslavia** (Serbia and Montenegro), the official 1998 budget is d6.6bn ($1.1bn at the exchange rate used for the budget, falling to some $600m after the April 1998 devaluation). The 1998 police budget (under the Ministry of Internal Affairs) is d3.3bn ($550m). In addition, some d3bn is allocated under the heading President of the Republic. Real military outlays are estimated to have been some 8% of GDP in 1997.

In **Ukraine**, the 1997 defence budget was h1.4bn ($769m) and the security budget, including Defence and the National Guard, Border Guard, Interior Troops and Civil Defence, h2.5bn ($1.3bn). The 1998 budget is h1.7bn ($813m) and the security budget including defence h3.3bn ($1.6bn). Since 1992, Ukraine has received some $520m from the US Cooperative Threat Reduction Programme to implement nuclear disarmament under START I. According to a Ukrainian parliamentary commission investigating Ukrainian arms sales in 1998, Ukrainian arms exports were worth around $760m for deliveries between 1995 and 1997. In May 1998, Ukrainian membership of the Missile Technology Control Regime (MTCR) was approved after four years of negotiations to overcome, in particular, US resistance to Ukrainian membership. In **Belarus**, official defence outlays in 1997 were r5.7tr ($185m). This figure reflected the halving in value of the rubel during 1997; the 1997 defence budget amounted to r2.4bn. A further r8.8tr goes to the Law Enforcement and Security budget in 1998. In **Bulgaria**, national currency depreciation has reduced the dollar value of the 1998 defence budget from $339m to $270m. In **Romania**, the 1998 defence budget increases to $782m from $764m in 1997, while in **Slovakia** the 1998 allocation of $416m is down from $427m in 1997.

In the Transcaucasus, military expenditure is difficult to judge and probably higher than official figures suggest. In **Armenia**, official figures for 1997 show that defence received an allocation of d30.5bn ($62m), about 18% of the government budget and 4% of forecast GDP. Among recent arms transfers from Russia were as many as 32 *Scud*-B missiles and eight associated launchers. In **Azerbaijan**, official figures gave the defence budget in 1996 as m502bn ($117m), being nearly 20% of government spending and some 3.5% of GDP.

Table 10 Arms orders and deliveries in NATO Europe and Canada, 1996–1998

Supplier	Classification	Designation	Units	Order Date	Delivery Date	Comment
Belgium						
US	FGA	F-16	48	1993	1998	Upgrade. Option for 24 more
Collab.	tpt	A-310	2	1997	1998	
Fr	arty	105mm	14	1996	1997	
A	APC	*Pandur*	54	1997	1998	
US	hel	MD-900	2	1994	1996	
Canada						
US	hel	Bell 412EP	100	1992	1994	Deliveries 1994–98. Built in Ca
Collab.	hel	EH-101	15	1998	2001	Deliveries 2001–2002
UK	SSK	*Upholder*	4	1999	2001	Leased from UK
Domestic	FFG	*Halifax*	12	1983	1992	Deliveries 1992–1996
Domestic	MCMV	*Kingston*	12	1992	1996	Deliveries continue to 1999
UK	hovercraft	API-88/400	2	1996	1998	Delivery May 1998. For Coast Guard
Ge	MBT	*Leopard 1*	114	1997		Upgrade of existing inventory to C1A5
US	APC	M-113	400	1997	1998	Life extension update
Domestic	APC	LAV-25	240	1996	1998	
CH	AD Guns	GDF-005	20	1996	1997	Upgrade
Domestic	C4I	LFCS	1	1997		Land Force Command System
Fr	arty	105mm	28	1995	1996	Eight in 1996, 20 in 1997
Denmark						
US	FGA	F-16	4	1995	1997	Used
US	FGA	F-16	63	1993	1998	Mid-life update
US	AAM	AMRAAM	44	1993	1997	
Ca	tpt	*Challenger*	1	1998	1999	Option for 2 more
UK	hel	*Lynx*	8	1998	2001	Upgrade to *Super Lynx* standard
Domestic	PCI	MHV-800	6	1997	1997	Follow-on order
Ge	MBT	*Leopard* 2A4	51	1998	1999	Ex-Ge Army
Domestic	AFV	*Hydrema*	12	1996	1997	Mine-clearing AFV. Deliveries to 1998
CH	APC	*Piranha* III	2	1998	2000	Option for 20 more. For UN peacekeeping

Supplier	Classification	Designation	Units	Order Date	Delivery Date	Comment
France						
Collab.	Sat	SKYNET 5	4	1998	2005	With Ge
Collab.	Sat	Helios 1A	1	1994	1996	With Ge, It, Sp
Collab.	Sat	Helios 2	1	1994	2002	Development with Ge
Collab.	Sat	Horus	1	1994	2005	With Ge. Fr participation ended 1998
Domestic	FGA	Mirage 2000	86	1991	1994	Deliveries 1994 to 2000
Domestic	FGA	Mirage 2000	37	1993	1998	Upgrade deliveries 1998 to 2002
Domestic	FGA	Rafale	234	1984	2005	
Collab.	ALCM	Scalp	500	1998	2003	Delivery starting in 2003
Collab.	ALCM	Apache	100	1997	2000	
Collab.	AAM	MICA	225	1998	1999	
Collab.	ASM	Vesta		1997	2005	In development
Sp	tpt	CN 235	7	1996	1998	
Collab.	tpt	FLA	52	1989		Predevelopment. Status uncertain
Collab.	hel	AS-532	4	1995	1998	Combat SAR, requirement for 6
Domestic	SSBN	Triomphant	3	1986	1996	Deliveries 1996–2007
Domestic	SLBM	M-45		1986	1996	For Triomphant SSBN class
Domestic	SLBM	M-51		1996	2010	To replace M-45.
Domestic	CVN	Charles De Gaulle	1	1986	1999	Sea trials mid-1998. To commission 1999
Domestic	FGA	Rafale	60	1984	2002	For Charles De Gaulle CV
US	AEW	E-2C	3	1995	1998	Unit 3 to be ordered in 2001
Domestic	FF	Lafayette	6	1990	1996	Lafayette class. Deliveries to 2003
Collab.	FF	Horizon	2	1994	2003	In development with UK, It. See UK
Collab.	torpedo	MU-90	150	1991	2000	With It and Ge. Deliveries 2000–2002
Collab.	ASSM	ANNG			2005	Development with Ge
Collab.	hel	AS-565	15	1990	1993	Deliveries 1994-96
Collab.	SAM	PAAMS	60	1994	2003	Anti-Air Missile System, with UK, It
Be	MHC	Tripartite	3	1996	1997	
Domestic	LSD	TCD 90	2	1994	1998	
Domestic	OPV	Flamant	3	1992	1996	
Domestic	recce	Falcon-50	4	1997	1998	Deliveries 1998–2000
Domestic	MBT	Leclerc	406	1985	1992	Deliveries 1992–2002
Collab.	APC	VBCI		1998	2004	MARV. In development with Ge, UK
Domestic	SAM	Mistral	1,130	1996	1997	Deliveries 1997–2002
Collab.	hel	Tiger	215	1984	2003	With Ge, requirement may be reduced
Collab.	hel	NH-90	160	1987	2003	With Ge, It, Nl. Numbers may reduce
Collab.	hel	AS-532	4	1992	1996	Battlefield radar system Horizon
Collab.	hel	BK-117	32	1997	1999	Paramilitary
Collab.	ATGW	Trigat		1988	2004	In development with Ge, UK
Domestic	ATGW	Eryx	6,400	1997	1997	Deliveries 1997–2002
Germany						
Collab.	BMD	MEADS		1995		With US and It. Feasibility study
US	SAM	Patriot		1998		Upgrade to Phase Three configuration
Collab.	sat	Skynet 5	4	1997	2005	With Fr
Collab.	Sat	Helios 1A	0	1994	1996	With France, It, Sp
Collab.	Sat	Helios 2	0	1994	2001	Development programme, with Fr, It
Collab.	Sat	Horus	1	1994	2005	Development programme was with Fr
Collab.	FGA	EF-2000	180	1985	2001	With UK, It, Sp
Collab.	AAM	IRIS-T		1997	2003	Development with It, Swe, Gr, Ca and No
Collab.	tpt	FLA	75	1989	2004	Pre-development phase

Supplier	Classification	Designation	Units	Order Date	Delivery Date	Comment
Collab.	tpt hel	AS-532U2	3	1994	1997	
Domestic	SSK	Type 212	4	1994	2003	Development
Collab.	torpedo	MU-90	600	1998	2000	With Fr and It
Domestic	FFG	Type 124	3	1996	2002	Deliveries 2002–06. Option for one more
Domestic	FFG	Type 123	4	1989	1994	Deliveries completed in 1996
Collab.	ASM	Taurus	350	1997	2002	Development with Swe
Collab.	hel	Lynx	7	1996	1999	
Collab.	hel	Lynx	17	1998	2001	Upgrade to Super Lynx standard
Domestic	MHC	Type 332	2	1995	1998	
Domestic	AOE	Type 702	1	1996	2001	Option for 3 more
Domestic	MBT	Leopard 2	225	1994	1995	Upgrade
US	APC	M-113	270	1997	1998	Ex-US
Domestic	APC	TPz KRK	50	1998	1999	
Collab.	LAV	GTK	200	1998	1905	MRAV. Contract awarded
Collab.	recce	Fennek	164	1994	2000	DP with Nl. Production of 2000
Domestic	arty	PzH 2000	186	1986	1998	Requirement for 594
Domestic	AAA	Gepard	147	1996	1998	Upgrade
Domestic	AIFV	Wiesel 2	50	1998	1999	With 17 command/co-ordination posts
Collab.	hel	Tiger	212	1984	2003	With Fr
Collab.	ATGW	Trigat		1988	2000	For Tiger
Collab.	hel	EC-135	15	1997	1998	Trg. Deliveries to start in mid-1998
Domestic	hel	BO-105	17	1996	1996	Deliveries completed in 1997
Greece						
US	ftr	F-16C/D	40	1992	1997	16 in 1997
Fr	ASSM	AM-39		1997	1998	For Mirage 2000.
US	ftr	F-4	40	1997		Upgrade in Ge
US	MPA	P-3 Orion	20	1991	1995	Three in 1997
US	tpt	C-130	8	1992	1995	
Nl	FFG	Kortenaer	1	1997	1997	Will bring class total to 6
Domestic	FFG	Meko	2	1988	1997	Deliveries end of 1997 and 1998
US	hel	SH-60B	7	1992	1994	Deliveries 1994–99
Domestic	LST	Jason-class	5	1986	1996	Deliveries 1996–98
Ge	MBT	Leopard 1A5	170	1997	1998	
Ge	APC	M-113	100	1993	1995	Ex-US Army
US	MRL	MLRS	9	1994	1997	
US	MRL	ATACM	71	1996	1997	
US	arty	M-109A5	12	1997	1998	155mm. Option for further 12
US	hel	AH-64	20	1991	1995	Deliveries 1995–98
US	hel	CH-47D	7	1995	1998	
Italy						
Collab.	BMD	MEADS		1995		With US and Ge. In feasibility phase
Collab.	sat	Helios 1A		1994	1996	With Fr, Ge, Sp
Collab.	FGA	AMX	136	1980	1989	
Collab.	FGA	EF-2000	121	1985	2002	With UK, Ge, Sp, option for nine more
Collab.	FGA	Tornado		1994	1997	Upgrade. 16 completed to date
Collab.	FGA	Tornado F-3	24	1993	1996	Deliveries 1996–97
US	MSL	AMRAAM	246	1990	1995	
US	tpt	C-130J	18	1997	1999	Options for 14 more
Collab.	tpt	FLA	44	1989	2004	Status uncertain
Domestic	tpt	P-180	12	1997	1999	
Fr	tpt	Falcon	2	1997	1999	
Domestic	trg	MB-339CD	15	1990	1996	Deliveries 1996–98

Supplier	Classification	Designation	Units	Order Date	Delivery Date	Comment
Ge	SSK	Type 212	2	1997	2004	Built in It under licence
Collab.	FGA	AV-8B	18	1990	1994	Deliveries to 1997
Domestic	FF	*Artigliere*	4	1992	1994	Commissioned by Feb 1996. Built for Irq
Collab.	FF	*Horizon*	4	1994	2003	In development with UK, Fr
Collab.	SAM	PAAMS		1994	2003	For *Horizon* use, with UK, Fr
Collab.	hel	EH101	16	1993	1999	With UK
Domestic	PCO	P-405	4	1993	1998	Deliveries May 1997 to Jul 1998
Domestic	AO	*Etna*	1	1994	1998	Launched Jul 1997, commission Jan 1998
Domestic	PCI	*Zara*	1	1995	1998	Third of class delivered in 1998
Domestic	MBT	C1 *Ariete*	200	1984	1996	Deliveries 1995–2001
Domestic	lt tk	*Centauro* B1	400	1984	1991	Deliveries 1991–96
Domestic	AIFV	VCC-80	150	1982	1999	Deliveries 1999–2010
Domestic	hel	A-129	66	1978	1990	Deliveries 1990–98
Collab.	hel	NH90	214	1987	2003	With Fr, Ge, Nl
US	hel	AH-500	5	1994	1996	Licensed production
US	hel	AB-412	80	1988	1990	Deliveries 1990–97. Licensed production
Netherlands						
US	FGA	F-16	136	1993	1997	Update programme continues to 2001
Domestic	tpt	F-50	4	1993	1996	
US	hel	AH-64	12	1995	1997	Lease until arrival of AH-64D
US	hel	AH-64D	30	1995	1998	
Collab.	hel	AS-532	17	1993	1996	Deliveries 1996–97
Domestic	FFG	LCF	4	1995	2001	
Domestic	LPD	L 800	1	1993	1997	
Collab.	hel	NH-90	20	1987	2003	With Fr, Ge, It
Domestic	LCU	LCU	4	1996	1997	Option on fifth
Domestic	OPV		3	1997	1997	
Ge	MBT	*Leopard* 2A5	330	1994	1996	Upgrade programme, first in 1996
SF	APC	XA-188	90	1997	1998	
Ge	AD guns	*Gepard*	60	1995	1998	Upgrade
Norway						
US	FGA	F-16	58	1993	1997	Mid-life update programme to 2001
US	AAM	AMRAAM	500	1993	1995	Deliveries to 2000. 66 delivered in 1997
Domestic	FAC	*Skjold*-class	8	1996	2004	Unit 1 trials. Contract for rest 1999
Swe	LCA	90 H	16	1995	1997	Deliveries 1997–98
Domestic	MCMV	M-350	5	1989	1996	Deliveries 1996–97
UK	hel	*Sea King*	2	1994	1996	
Ge	AFV	*Leopard* 1	73	1996	1999	Deliveries to 2000
Swe	AIFV	CV-90	104	1990	1996	Option for 70 more. Deliveries 1996–99
US	MRL	MLRS	12	1995	1997	Deliveries to 1998. Six in 1997
Fr	ATGW	*Eryx*	424	1996	1997	
US	APC	M-113	205	1995	1997	Surplus from US, Ge, Nl
Portugal						
US	AGOS	*Stalwart*	1	1995	1997	Towed array removed
UK	arty	105mm	21	1997	1998	
Spain						
Collab.	Sat	*Helios* 1A	1	1994	1996	With Fr, Ge, It
Collab.	FGA	EF-2000	87	1994	2001	With Ge, It, UK
US	FGA	F/A-18A	30	1994	1995	EX-USN, deliveries 1995–98
US	tpt	C-130	12	1995	1999	Upgrade programme
Collab.	tpt	FLA	36	1989	2004	In PD phase. Fr, Ge, It, UK, others

Supplier	Classification	Designation	Units	Order Date	Delivery Date	Comment
Fr	hel	AS-532	18	1995	1996	Deliveries 1996–2002.
US	ftr	*Harrier*	8	1992	1997	
Domestic	FFG	F-100	4	1992	2001	
Domestic	LPD	L 51	2	1994	1998	Second ordered in 1997
Domestic	OPV	P-62	1	1993	1996	
Collab.	MHC	M-31	4	1989	1998	
Ge	MBT	*Leopard* 2A4	108	1993	1995	Leased from Ge. Deliveries 1995–96
Ge	MBT	*Leopard* 2A5	235	1998	2000	Built in Sp
A	AIFV	*Pizarro*	144	1996	1997	Manufactured in Sp
Domestic	arty	SBT-1		1998	2000	155mm 52 cal artillery piece
UK	arty	105mm	25	1995	1997	
Turkey						
US	FGA	F-16	80	1994	1996	Deliveries 1996–99. Follow-on order
US	AAM	AMRAAM	138	1997	2000	
Il	ftr	F-4	54	1996	1997	Upgrade. Deliveries 1997–2002
Il	AGM	*Popeye* 1	50	1997	1997	For use with upgraded F-4 aircraft
Il	FGA	F-5	48	1998	1999	Upgrade programme
Sp	tpt	CN-235	52	1991	1993	48 delivered by early 1998
US	TKR AC	KC-135R	9	1994	1995	Deliveries 1995–98
Ge	SSK	Type 209	4	1998	2003	Deliveries 2003–06
US	FFG	OH *Perry*	3	1995	1998	Two grant transfer, one lease transfer
Ge	FFH	MEKO	4	1990	1995	Deliveries in 1995–2000
US	asw hel	SH-60B	8	1997	2000	
Ge	corvette	P-330	3	1993	1998	Deliveries 1998–99
Fr	MHC	*Circe*	5	1997	1998	Ex-Fr Navy. Delivery 1998
Domestic	PGG	*Dogan*	3	1993	1998	Last 3 of class of 13
Sp	MPA	CN-235	6	1998	2001	Licensed assembly. For Navy
Sp	MPA	CN-235	3	1998	2001	Licensed assembly. For Coast Guard
It	sar hel	AB-412	5	1998	2000	
US	APC	M-113	1,698	1988	1992	Manufactured under licence
US	MRL	ATACM	72	1996	1998	36 missiles delivered in June 1998
US	tpt hel	CH-47	4	1996	1999	
RF	hel	Mi-17	19	1994	1996	16 delivered by April 1996
Collab.	hel	AS-532	50	1994	1995	Deliveries through 1999
It	hel	AB-206	23	1994	1995	Deliveries 1995–96. 3 for Coast Guard
US	APC	M-1064	179	1995	1997	
UK						
US	C4I	JTIDS		1988	1998	
Collab.	sat	*Skynet* 5	4	1997	2005	With Fr and Ger
Collab.	bbr	FOAS		1997	2020	Pre-feasibility phase, with Fr
Collab.	FGA	EF-2000	232	1984	2002	With Ge, It, Sp. Option for 65 more
Collab.	FGA	JSF		1995	2010	With US and No. In early development
Collab.	FGA	*Tornado* GR4	142	1994	1998	Upgrade from GR-1 to GR-4 IDS
Domestic	ASM	*Brimstone*		1996	2002	
Collab.	ASM	*Storm Shadow*	900	1997	2001	With Fr. Deliveries start 2001
Collab.	Ftr	*Tornado* F-3	100	1996	1998	Upgrade
Domestic	AAM	ASRAAM		1980	1998	
Domestic	trg	*Harrier*	13	1990	1994	Deliveries complete in 1996
UK	MPA	*Nimrod* 2000	21	1996	2001	Upgrade
US	tpt	C-130J	25	1994	1999	

Supplier	Classification Designation		Units	Order Date	Delivery Date	Comment
Collab.	tpt	FLA	45	1993	2004	Status uncertain
Domestic	hel	*Sea King*	6	1993	1996	
US	hel	CH-47	14	1995	1998	Deliveries to 2000
Collab.	hel	EH-101	22	1995	2000	Utility hel
Domestic	SSN	*Astute*	3	1997	2006	
Domestic	SSBN	*Vanguard*	4	1986	1993	Deliveries 1993-99 *Vanguard*-class
US	SLBM	*Trident* D-5	7	1997	2000	Follow on order
US	SLCM	*Tomahawk*	65	1995	1998	SSN-launched Block 3 variant
Domestic	FFG	Type-23	3	1996	2000	Last 3 of 16. Deliveries 2001–2002
Collab.	FFG	*Horizon*	12	1996	2003	In development with Fr, It
Collab.	SAM	PAAMS	0	1994	2003	In development with Fr, It
Domestic	AO	AO	2	1997	2000	
Domestic	AK	*Sea Chieftain*	1	1997	1998	18 month lease. Heavy sea lift
Domestic	AGOS	A-131	1	1995	1997	
Domestic	LCU	Mk 10	10	1998	2000	
Domestic	LPD	*Albion*	2	1996	2000	Deliveries 2000–2002
Domestic	LPH	*Ocean*	1	1993	1998	
Collab.	hel	*Lynx*	50	1992	1995	Upgrade. Completion in 1998–99
Collab.	hel	EH101	44	1992	2000	Primarily for ASW. With It
Domestic	MHC	*Sandown*	7	1994	1997	Deliveries to 2001
J	roro	*Sea Crusader*	1	1996	1996	Chartered from J
Domestic	FGA	*Sea Harrier*	18	1990	1995	Deliveries 1995–99
Domestic	FGA	*Sea Harrier*	35	1985	1994	Upgrade programme
Domestic	PCI	*Archer*	2	1997	1998	
Domestic	MBT	*Challenger* 2	408	1993	1996	Deliveries to units started in 1998
Collab.	lt tk	TRACER	200	1998	2007	With US. Development commencing 2002
Collab.	APC	MRAV	200	1998	2002	Development with Fr, Ge
Collab.	radar	*Cobra*		1986	1999	Counter-battery radar
Domestic	arty	AS90	179	1989	1992	Deliveries 1992–96
US	hel	AH-64D	67	1995	2000	A further 20 may be purchased
Collab.	ATGW	*Trigat*		1988	2000	With Fr and Ge
Collab.	hel	AS-550	12	1996	1997	
NATO						
US	AWACS	E3-A	18	1997	2000	NATO fleet upgrade
UK	trg	*Hawk*	18	1997	1999	Option for 8 more
US	trg	T-6	24	1997	1999	Deliveries to 2000

Table 11 Arms orders and deliveries in Non-NATO Europe, 1996–1998

Supplier	Classification Designation		Units	Order Date	Delivery Date	Comment
Albania						
US	PFC	PB Mk-III	3	1996	1997	Ex-US
US	PFC	*Sea Ark*	2	1996	1997	
Austria						
Ge	MBT	*Leopard* 2	114	1997	1997	Ex-Nl. 35 in 1997
Domestic	AIFV	ASCOD	112	1998	1999	
Domestic	APC	*Pandur*	68	1995	1996	
Domestic	APC	*Pandur*	269	1997	1998	Follow-on order
Ge	ATGW	*Jaguar*	90	1997	1997	87 delivered in 1997

Supplier	Classification Designation		Units	Order Date	Delivery Date	Comment
US	SPA	M-109	42	1996	1997	
Bosnia-Herzegovina						
US	MBT	M-60	45	1995	1996	Ex-US
Fr	MBT	AMX-30	36	1996		Ex-UAE
US	APC	M-113	80	1995	1996	Ex-US
US	arty	M-114	126	1995	1997	155mm
RF	arty	M-46	12	1995	1996	130mm. Ex-Et
RF	arty	D-30	12	1995	1996	122mm. Ex-Et
US	arty	M-59	36	1996		105mm. Ex-US
RF	AAA	ZU-23-4	18	1997		Ex-Et
US	hel	UH-1H	15	1995	1997	Ex-US
R	MRL	122mm	18	1997	1997	
Bulgaria						
RF	ftr	MiG-29	14	1997		Delivery cancelled
RF	trg	Yak-18T	6	1996	1996	
RF	MBT	T-72	100	1995	1996	Arms-for-debt deal
RF	AIFV	BMP-1/2	100	1995	1996	Arms-for-debt deal
Croatia						
CH	trg	PC-9	20	1997	1997	
US	hel	Bell-206	10	1996	1997	
Domestic	FAC	FAC	4	1992	1992	*Kralj Petar Kresimir*-class, 2nd building
Domestic	LCT	*Silba*	3	1992	1993	Unit 3 under construction
Cyprus						
RF	MBT	T-80	81	1996	1996	Deliveries to 1998
Gr	MBT	AMX-30	27	1997	1997	
RF	AIFV	BMP-3	43	1995	1995	Deliveries 1995–96
RF	SAM	S-300 PMU1	48	1997	1998	Also known as SA-10D. Delivery Nov 1998
Gr	APC	*Leonidas*	39	1997	1997	
Czech Republic						
Domestic	trg	L-39	27	1997		Delivery withheld pending payment
Domestic	FGA	L-159	72	1997	1999	Deliveries to 2002
Domestic	MBT	T-72	250	1995	1998	Upgrade programme
Estonia						
Ge	MCI	Type 394	2	1997	1997	Ge donation
Domestic	PCI	*Pikker*	1	1995	1996	
SF	arty	M61/37	18	1997	1997	105mm. Deliveries 1997–98. Six in 1997
Finland						
US	FGA	F/A-18C/D	64	1992	1995	Deliveries to 2000. 13 in 1997
US	AAM	AMRAAM		1993	1997	For F/A-18C/D
Domestic	PFM	*Rauma*	5	1987	1990	*Rauma*-class, deliveries 1990–1997
Domestic	PFM	*Rauma* 2000	1	1997	1997	Upgrade to 5th boat of *Rauma* class
Domestic	AFV	SISU RA-140	10	1997	1998	
SF	arty	K-98	24	1996	1998	155mm 52 cal. Deliveries to continue
RF	SAM	BuK-M1	6	1996	1997	SA-11, arms-for-debt deal
It	hel	AB-412	4	1992	1995	Deliveries 1995–96
Hungary						
Bel	MBT	T-72	100	1995	1996	Ex-Bel. 31 delivered in 1996.
RF	APC	BTR-80	309	1995	1996	119 in 1996, 190 in 1997
Fr	SAM	*Mistral*-2		1995	1998	Deliveries 1998–99
Macedonia, Former Yugoslav Republic of						
Tu	ftr	F-5A/B	20	1998	1999	Ex-Tu

Supplier	Classification	Designation	Units	Order Date	Delivery Date	Comment
RF	APC	BTR-80	12	1997	1997	
US	arty	M-101	14	1997	1998	105mm
Moldova						
Bel	APC	BTR-80	20	1997	1998	
Poland						
Domestic	recce	Su-22M4		1996	1997	Upgrade for reconnaissance duties
US	tpt	PZL M-20	2	1995	1996	Licensed variant of Piper *Seneca* II
Domestic	trg	I-22	17	1995	1997	
Domestic	hel	W-3	10	1995	1998	For Air Force
Domestic	hel	W-3	1	1995	1998	For Navy
Domestic	hel	W-3WB	100	1997	1999	Upgrade with Il cooperation
Domestic	SAR	PZL M-28	3	1998	2000	
Romania						
Domestic	FGA	MiG-21	110	1995	1997	Upgrade with Il cooperation
US	tpt	C-130B	4	1995	1996	Ex-US
US	hel	AH-1RO	96	1997		Licensed production, status uncertain
Domestic	hel	IAR-330L	26	1997	1998	Upgrade
Il	UAV	*Shadow*-600	6	1997	1998	
Slovakia						
RF	FGA	MiG-29	8	1995	1996	
Collab.	hel	EC-135	12	1997	2000	
Collab.	hel	AS-532	5	1997	2000	
Collab.	hel	AS-350B2	2	1997	1999	
RF	trg	*Yak*-130/131	12	1997	1998	
Domestic	MBT	T-72	200	1997	2000	T-72 upgrade programme
Domestic	arty	*Zuzana* 2000	8	1997	1998	155mm. Deliveries 1998–99
RF	SAM	S-300		1998	1999	
Slovenia						
CH	tpt	PC-6	2	1997	1998	Delivered May 1998
Il	trg	PC-9 mk2	9	1997	1998	Upgrade
Domestic	MBT	M-55 S1		1998	2000	T-55 upgrade involving 105mm gun
Il	arty	M-845	18	1996	1997	155mm. Towed arty
Il	PCI	*Super Dvora*	1	1995	1996	
Sweden						
Domestic	FGA	JAS-39	204	1981	1995	Deliveries continue to 2004
Collab.	AAM	IRIS-T		1997	2003	With Ge, Gr, Ca and No
Collab.	ASM	*Taurus*	250	1997	2002	With Ge
US	AAM	AMRAAM	110	1994	1998	Option for a further 700
Domestic	AWACS	Saab-340	6	1993	1997	Deliveries 1997–1998
Domestic	EW	*Gulfstream* IV	2	1996	1998	S 102B, SIGINT aircraft
Collab.	hel	AS-532	12	1993	1996	
Collab.	hel	AS-532	12	1998	2001	Deliveries 2001–2002
It	hel	AB-412	9	1993	1995	Deliveries 1995–1996
Domestic	SSK	A-19 *Gotland*	3	1986	1996	First commissioned in 1998
Domestic	corvette	YS-2000	4	1995	2003	
Domestic	LCA	SRC-90E	72	1995	1998	20 delivered by Jan 1998
Domestic	LCA	SRC-90H	93	1997	1997	Follow-on order
Domestic	LCA	LCA	2	1997	2001	Transport. Planned total of 30
Domestic	MCM	YSB	4	1994	1997	All 4 for delivery 1997–1998
Ge	MBT	*Leopard* 2	120	1994	1998	Licence built deliveries 1998–2001
Ge	MBT	*Leopard* 2	160	1994	1997	Deliveries 1997–2000. 26 in 1997
Domestic	AIFV	CV-90	600	1984	1993	Deliveries to 2000

Supplier	Classification	Designation	Units	Order Date	Delivery Date	Comment
CH	APC	*Piranha* III	5	1996	1998	Command variant. Option for 30
Domestic	SPA	*Karelin*	50	1998		155mm development. 50 required
Switzerland						
US	FGA	F/A-18C/D	34	1993	1997	Assembly in CH 1997–99. 19 in 1997
US	AAM	AMRAAM		1993	1997	Deliveries to 1999
Fr	hel	AS-532	12	1998	2000	Deliveries between 2000 and 2002
US	arty	M-109	456	1997	2000	Upgrade, deliveries in 2000–2002
Domestic	recce	*Eagle* II	175	1998	1999	Follow-on order. Deliveries to 2001
Il	UAV	*Ranger*	4	1995	1998	Licensed production in 1998–1999
Domestic	AAA	*Skyguard*	100	1997	1999	Upgrade
Yugoslavia						
Domestic	MCM	S-25 *Nestin*	1	1994	1996	

Belgium

	1996	1997	1998	1999
GDP	fr8.3tr	fr8.7tr		
	($242bn)	($242bn)		
per capita	$21,900	$23,000		
Growth	1.4%	3.0%		
Inflation	2.1%	1.6%		
Publ debt	121.2%	118.4%		
Def exp	fr131.3bn	fr134.8bn		
	($4.2bn)	($3.8bn)		
Def bdgt			fr102.5bn	fr100.8bn
			($2.8bn)	($2.7bn)
$1 = franc	31.0	35.8	37.5	
Population		10,104,000		
Age	*13–17*	*18–22*	*23–32*	
Men	309,000	320,000	722,000	
Women	295,000	308,000	700,000	

Total Armed Forces

ACTIVE 43,700
(incl 1,250 Medical Service, 2,650 women)

RESERVES 152,050 (to be 62,000)
Army 105,200 **Navy** 6,250 **Air Force** 20,700 **Medical Service** 19,900

Army 28,250

(1,500 women)
1 joint service territorial comd (incl 2 engr, 2 sigs bn)
1 op comd HQ
1 mech inf div with 3 mech inf bde (each 1 tk, 2 mech inf, 1 SP arty bn) (2 bde at 70%, 1 bde at 50% cbt str), 1 AD arty bn, 2 recce coy (Eurocorps); 1 recce bn (MNDC)
1 cbt spt div (11 mil schools forming, 1 arty, 1 engr bn – augment mech inf div, plus 1 inf, 1 tk bn for bde at 50% cbt str)
1 para-cdo bde (3 para-cdo, 1 ATK/recce bn, 1 arty, 1 AD bty, 1 engr coy)
1 lt avn gp (2 ATK, 1 obs bn)

RESERVES
Territorial Defence 11 lt inf bn (9 province, 1 gd, 1 reserve)

EQUIPMENT
MBT 155: 132 *Leopard* 1A5, 23 *Leopard* 1A1
RECCE 141 *Scimitar* (29 in store)
AIFV 230 YPR-765 (plus 278 'look-alikes')
APC 190 M-113 (plus 127 'look-alikes'), 115 *Spartan*, 4 YPR-765
TOTAL ARTY 243
TOWED 19: **105mm**: 5 M-101, 14 LG Mk II
SP 132: **105mm**: 19 M-108 (trg); **155mm**: 112 M-

109A2, plus 1A3 (trials)
MOR 107mm: 90 M-30; **120mm**: 2 (for sale), plus **81mm**: 100
ATGW 476: 420 *Milan* (incl 218 YPR-765 (24 in store), 56 M-113 (4 in store))
AD GUNS 35mm: 51 *Gepard* SP (all for sale)
SAM 118 *Mistral*
AC 10 BN-2A *Islander*
HELICOPTERS 78
ASLT 28 A-109BA
OBS 18 A-109A
SPT 32 SA-318 (5 in store)
UAV 28 *Epervier*

Navy 2,600

(incl 270 women)
BASES Ostend, Zeebrugge. Be and Nl Navies under joint op comd based at Den Helder (Nl)
FRIGATES 3
3 *Wielingen* with 2 dual role (Fr L-5 HWT), 1 x 6 ASW mor; plus 4 MM-38 *Exocet* SSM, 1 100mm gun and 1 x 8 *Sea Sparrow* SAM
MINE COUNTERMEASURES 11
4 *Van Haverbeke* (US *Aggressive* MSO) (incl 1 used for trials)
7 *Aster* (tripartite) MHC
SUPPORT AND MISCELLANEOUS 4
2 log spt/comd with hel deck, 1 research/survey, 1 sail trg **hel** 3 SA-316B
ADDITIONAL IN STORE 1 FF for sale

Air Force 11,600

(incl 800 women)
Flying hours 165
FGA 2 sqn with F-16A/B
FGA/RECCE 1 sqn with F-16A/B
FTR 3 sqn with F-16A/B
TPT 2 sqn
1 with 11 C-130H
1 with 2 Airbus A310-200, 3 HS-748, 5 *Merlin* IIIA, 2 *Falcon* 20, 1 *Falcon* 900
TRG 4 sqn
2 with *Alpha Jet*
1 with SF-260
1 with CM-170
SAR 1 sqn with *Sea King* Mk 48
EQUIPMENT
100 cbt ac (plus 59 in store), no armed hel
AC 100 F-16 (81 **-A**, 19 **-B** (plus 32 in store)) • 11 C-130 (tpt) • 2 **Airbus** A310-200 (tpt) • 3 HS-748 (tpt) • 2 *Falcon* 20 (VIP) • 1 *Falcon* 900B • 5 SW 111 *Merlin* (VIP, photo, cal) • 11 **CM-170** (trg, liaison) • 34 **SF-260** (trg) • 31 *Alpha Jet* (trg)
HEL 5 (SAR) *Sea King*
IN STORE 27 *Mirage* 5 (12 -BA, 12 -BR, 3 -BD)

MISSILES
AAM AIM-9 *Sidewinder*, AIM-120 AMRAAM
ASM AGM-65G *Maverick*
SAM 24 *Mistral*

Forces Abroad

GERMANY 2,000; 1 mech inf bde (1 inf, 1 arty bn, 1 recce coy)

STANAVFORLANT/STANAVFORMED

1 FF (part time basis)
1 MHC

UN AND PEACEKEEPING

BOSNIA/CROATIA (SFOR II): up to 550. SFOR **Air Component** 3 F-16. (UNMOP): 1 obs. **FYROM** (UNPREDEP): 1 obs. **INDIA/PAKISTAN** (UNMOGIP): 2 obs. SFOR **Air Component** 3 F-16. **MIDDLE EAST** (UNTSO): 6 obs

Foreign Forces

NATO HQ NATO Brussels; HQ SHAPE Mons
WEU Military Planning Cell
US 800: **Army** 200 **Navy** 100 **Air Force** 500

Canada

	1996	1997	1998	1999
GDP	C$820bn	C$856bn		
	($602bn)	($618bn)		
per capita	$21,200	$22,300		
Growth	1.2%	3.8%		
Inflation	1.5%	1.7%		
Publ debt	97.5%	93.8%		
Def exp	C$11.5bn	C$10.7bn		
	($8.4bn)	($7.8bn)		
Def bdgt			C$9.4bn	C$9.7bn
			($6.4bn)	($7.1bn)
US$1 = C$	1.36	1.38	1.47	
Population		28,959,000		
Age	*13–17*	*18–22*	*23–32*	
Men	983,000	972,000	2,121,000	
Women	939,000	938,000	2,075,000	

Canadian Armed Forces are unified and org in functional comds. Land Force Comd has op control of TAG. Maritime Comd has op control of maritime air. This entry is set out in traditional single-service manner

Total Armed Forces

ACTIVE 60,600

(6,500 women). Some 15,700 are not identified by service

RESERVES

Primary 28,600 **Army** (Militia) (incl comms) 22,200
Navy 4,000 **Air Force** 2,100 **Primary Reserve List** 300
Supplementary **Ready Reserve** 14,700

Army (Land Forces) 20,900

(1,600 women)
1 Task Force HQ • 3 mech inf bde gp, each with 1 armd regt, 3 inf bn (1 lt), 1 arty, 1 engr regt, 1 AD bty • 1 indep AD regt • 1 indep engr spt regt

RESERVES

Militia 20,100 (excl comms); 18 armd, 19 arty, 51 inf, 12 engr, 20 log bn level units, 14 med coy
Canadian Rangers 3,250; 127 patrols

EQUIPMENT

MBT 114 *Leopard* C-1
RECCE 5 *Lynx* (in store), 195 *Cougar*, 170 *Coyote*
APC 1,858: 1,329 M-113 A2 (1,247 to be upgraded, 82 in store), 61 M-577, 269 *Grizzly*, 199 *Bison*
TOWED ARTY 196: **105mm**: 185 C1/C3 (M-101), 11 LG1 Mk II
SP ARTY 155mm: 76 M-109A4
MOR 81mm: 167
ATGW 150 TOW (incl 72 TUA M-113 SP), 425 *Eryx*
RL 66mm: M-72
RCL 84mm: 1,040 *Carl Gustav*; **106mm**: 111
AD GUNS 35mm: 34 GDF-005 with *Skyguard*; **40mm**: 57 L40/60 (in store)
SAM 22 ADATS, 96 *Javelin*, Starburst

Navy (Maritime Command) 9,000

(incl 2800 women)
SUBMARINES 3

3 *Ojibwa* (UK *Oberon*) SS with Mk 48 HWT (equipped for, but not with, *Harpoon* USGW)
PRINCIPAL SURFACE COMBATANTS 16
DESTROYERS 4

DDG 4 *Iroquois* (incl 1 in conversion refit) with 1 Mk-41 VLS for 29 SM-2 MR, 2 CH-124 *Sea King* ASW hel (Mk 46 LWT), 2 x 3 ASTT, plus 1 76mm gun
FRIGATES 12

FFH 12

12 *Halifax* with 1 CH-124A *Sea King* ASW hel (Mk 46 LWT), 2 x 2 ASTT; plus 2 x 4 *Harpoon* and 2 x 8 *Sea Sparrow* SAM
PATROL AND COASTAL COMBATANTS 14

12 *Kingston* MCDV, 2 *Fundy* PCC (trg)
MINE COUNTERMEASURES 2

2 *Anticosti* MSO (converted offshore spt vessels)
SUPPORT AND MISCELLANEOUS 7

2 *Protecteur* AO with 3 *Sea King*, 1 AOT, 2 AGOR, 1 diving spt, 1 *Riverton* spt

DEPLOYMENT AND BASES

NATIONAL Ottawa (Chief of Maritime Staff)
ATLANTIC Halifax (National and Marlant HQ; Commander Marlant is also OMCANLANT): 3 SS, 2 DDH, 7 FFH, 2 FF, 1 AOR, 1 AGOR, 6 MCDV, 1 MSO; 2 MR plus 1 MR (trg) sqn with CP-140 and 3 CP-140A, 1 ASW and 1 ASW (trg) hel sqn with 26 CH-125 hel
PACIFIC Esquimalt (HQ): 2 DDH, 3 FHH, 1 AOR, 4 MCDV, 1 MSO, 2 PBL; 1 MR sqn with 4 CP-140 and 1 ASW hel sqn with 6 CH-124 hel

RESERVES

4,000 in 24 div: patrol craft, coastal def, MCM, Naval Control of Shipping, augmentation of regular units

Air Force (Air Command) 15,000

(1,700 women)
Flying hours 210
1 Air Div with 13 wg responsible for operational readiness, combat air-support, air tpt, SAR, MR and trg
EARLY WARNING Canadian NORAD Regional HQ at North Bay; 47 North Warning radar sites: 11 long-range, 36 short-range; Regional Op Control Centre (ROCC) (2 Sector Op Control Centres (SOCC)). 4 Coastal Radars and 2 Transportable Radars. Canadian Component – NATO Airborne Early Warning (NAEW)

EQUIPMENT

140 (incl 18 MR) cbt **ac**
AC 122 **CF-18** (83 **-A**, 39 **-B**) • 18 **CP-140** (MR) • 3 **CP-140A** (environmental patrol) • 32 **CC-130E/H** (tpt) • 5 **KCC-130** (tkr) • 5 **CC-150** (Airbus A-310) • 7 **CC-109** (tpt) • 11 **CC-144** (EW trg, coastal patrol, VIP/tpt) • 4 **CC-138** (SAR/tpt) • 6 **CC-115** (SAR/tpt) • 45 **CT-133** (EW trg/tpt plus 9 in store) • 121 **CT-114** (trg) • 6 **CT-142** (2 tpt, 4 trg)
HEL 13 **CH-113** (SAR/tpt) • 30 **CH-124** (ASW, afloat) • 100 **CH-146** (tpt, SAR)

Forces Abroad

UN AND PEACEKEEPING

BOSNIA (SFOR II): 960; 1 inf bn, 1 armd recce, 1 engr sqn; **SFOR Air Component** 6 CF-18; (UNMIBH): 1. **CAR** (MINURCA): 29. **CROATIA** (UNMOP): 1 obs. **CYPRUS** (UNFICYP): 4. **EGYPT** (MFO): 28. **FYROM** (UNPREDEP): 1 obs. **IRAQ/KUWAIT** (UNIKOM): 5 obs. **MIDDLE EAST** (UNTSO): 11 obs. **SYRIA/ ISRAEL** (UNDOF): 182; log unit

Paramilitary 9,350

Canadian Coast Guard has merged with **Department of Fisheries and Oceans**. Both are civilian-manned.
CANADIAN COAST GUARD (CCG) 4,700

some 137 vessels incl 19 navaids/tender, 23 survey/research, 17 icebreaker, 39 cutter, 22 lifeboat, 10 utility, 4 ACV, 3 trg; plus **hel** 1 S-61, 6 Bell-206L, 5 Bell-212, 16 BO-105

DEPARTMENT OF FISHERIES AND OCEANS (DFO) 4,650

some 67 vessels incl 23 survey and research, 44 patrol

Denmark

	1996	1997	1998	1999
GDP	kr1,066bn	kr1,121bn		
	($165bn)	($170bn)		
per capita	$22,000	$23,200		
Growth	3.5%	3.4%		
Inflation	2.2%	2.1%		
Publ debt	67.3%	62.7%		
Def exp	kr17.9bn	kr18.6bn		
	($3.1bn)	($2.8bn)		
Def bdgt			kr18.1bn	kr17.9bn
			($2.6bn)	($2.6bn)
$1 = kroner	5.80	6.60	6.89	
Population		5,246,000		
Age	*13–17*	*18–22*	*23–32*	
Men	147,000	164,000	390,000	
Women	142,000	158,000	377,000	

Total Armed Forces

ACTIVE 32,100

(about 7,900 conscripts; 940 women)
Terms of service 4–12 months (up to 24 months in certain ranks)

RESERVES 100,000

Army 72,000 **Navy** 10,000 **Air Force** 18,000
Home Guard (*Hjemmevaernet*) (volunteers to age 50)
Army 51,100 **Navy** 4,700 **Air Force** 8,500

Army 22,900

(6,900 conscripts, 420 women)
1 op comd, 1 land comd (east) • 1 mech inf div (3 mech inf bde (1 reserve) each 2 mech, inf, 1 tk, 1 arty bn), 1 recce, 1 mech inf, 1 AD, 1 engr bn (reserve), div arty (reserve)) • 1 rapid-reaction bde with 2 mech inf, 1 tk, 1 SP arty bn (20% active cbt str) • 1 mech inf bde with 2 mech inf, 1 tk, 1 arty bn • 1 recce, 1 indep AD, 1 indep engr bn • Army avn (1 attack hel coy, 1 recce hel det) • 1 SF unit

RESERVES

7 mil region (regt cbt gp or 1–2 inf bn), 4 regt cbt gp HQ, 1 mech inf, 4 mot inf, 2 inf • 1 arty comd, 1 arty, 1 AD, 2 engr bn

EQUIPMENT

MBT 337: 230 *Leopard* 1A5 (58 in store), 54 *Centurion*, 53 M-41DK-1
RECCE 10 Mowag *Eagle*
AIFV 50 M-113A2 (with **25mm** gun)
APC 592 M-113 (incl 'look-alikes')
TOTAL ARTY 503
  TOWED 105mm: 134 M-101; **155mm:** 24 M-59, 97 M-114/39; **203mm:** 12 M-115
  SP 155mm: 76 M-109
  MOR 120mm: 160 Brandt; plus **81mm:** 313 (incl 53 SP)
ATGW 140 TOW (incl 56 SP)
RL 84mm: AT-4
RCL 1,151: **84mm:** 1,131 *Carl Gustav*; **106mm:** 20 M-40
SAM *Stinger*
SURV *Green Archer*
ATTACK HEL 12 AS-550C2
SPT HEL 13 Hughes 500M/OH-6

Navy 3,700

(incl 500 conscripts, 200 women)
BASES Korsør, Frederikshavn
SUBMARINES 5
  3 *Tumleren* (mod No *Kobben*) SSC with Swe FFV Type 61 HWT
  2 *Narhvalen*, SSC with FFV Type 61 HWT
FRIGATES 3
  3 *Niels Juel* with 2 x 4 *Harpoon* SSM and 1 x 8 *Sea Sparrow* SAM, 1 76mm gun
PATROL AND COASTAL COMBATANTS 41
MISSILE CRAFT 10 *Willemoes* PFM with 2 x 4 *Harpoon*, 2 or 4 533mm TT, 1 76mm gun
PATROL CRAFT 31
  OFFSHORE 5
  1 *Beskytteren*, 4 *Thetis* PCO all with 1 *Lynx* hel
  COASTAL 17
  14 *Flyvefisken* (Stanflex 300) PFC, 3 *Agdlek* PCC
  INSHORE 9
  9 *Barsø*
MINE WARFARE 9
(All units of *Flyvefisken* class can also lay up to 60 mines)
MINELAYERS 6
  4 *Falster* (400 mines), 2 *Lindormen* (50 mines)
MINE COUNTERMEASURES 3
  1 *Sund* (US MSC-128)
  2 *Flyvefisken* (SF300) MHC
SUPPORT AND MISCELLANEOUS 14
  2 AOT (small), 4 icebreakers (civilian-manned), 1 tpt, 6 environmental protection, 1 Royal Yacht
HEL 8 *Lynx* (up to 4 embarked)

COASTAL DEFENCE

1 coastal fortress; **150mm** guns, coastal radar
2 mobile coastal missile batteries: 2 x 8 *Harpoon*

RESERVES (Home Guard)
37 inshore patrol craft

Air Force 5,500

(545 conscripts, 320 women)
Flying hours 180
TACTICAL AIR COMD
FGA/FTR 4 sqn with F-16A/B
TPT 1 sqn with C-130H, *Challenger*-604
SAR 1 sqn with S-61A hel
TRG 1 flying school with SAAB T-17
AIR DEFENCE GROUP
2 SAM bn: 8 bty with 36 I HAWK, 32 **40mm**/L70
CONTROL/REPORTING GROUP
5 radar stations, one in the Faroe Islands
EQUIPMENT
  69 cbt ac, no armed hel
  AC 69 **F-16A/B** (FGA/ftr) • 3 **C-130H** (tpt) • 2 *Challenger*-604 (tpt) • 28 **SAAB T-17**
  HEL 8 **S-61** (SAR)
MISSILES
  ASM AGM-12 *Bullpup*
  AAM AIM-9 *Sidewinder*
  SAM 36 I HAWK

Forces Abroad

UN AND PEACEKEEPING
BOSNIA (SFOR II): up to 600; 1 inf bn gp incl 1 tk sqn (10 *Leopard* MBT); aircrew with NATO E-3A operations; Air Force personnel in tac air-control parties (TACP); (UNMIBH): 1 plus 37 civ pol. **CROATIA** (UNMOP): 1 obs. **FYROM** (UNPREDEP): 47 plus 1 obs. **GEORGIA** (UNOMIG): 3 obs. **INDIA/PAKISTAN** (UNMOGIP): 6 obs. **IRAQ/KUWAIT** (UNIKOM): 5 obs. **MIDDLE EAST** (UNTSO): 10 obs. **TAJIKISTAN** (UNMOT): 5 obs

Foreign Forces

NATO HQ Allied Forces Baltic Approaches (BALTAP)
US 1,360: **Army** 740 **Navy** 100 **Air Force** 520

France

	1996	1997	1998	1999
GDP	fr7.9tr	fr8.1tr		
	($1.4tr)	($1.4tr)		
per capita	$21,100	$22,000		
Growth	1.6%	2.3%		
Inflation	2.1%	1.1%		
Publ debt	63.0%	64.6%		

contd	1996	1997	1998	1999
Def exp	fr237bn	fr242bn		
	($46.4bn)	($41.5bn)		
Def bdgt			fr184.8bn	
			($30.4bn)	
$1 = franc	5.12	5.84	6.07	
Population		58,905,000		
Age	_13–17_	_18–22_	_23–32_	
Men	1,960,000	1,998,000	4,342,000	
Women	1,872,000	1,910,000	4,184,000	

Total Armed Forces

ACTIVE 358,800

(19,200 women, 129,250 conscripts; incl 5,200 **Central Staff**, 8,600 (2,300 conscripts) _Service de santé_, 400 _Service des essences_ not listed)
Terms of service 10 months (can be voluntarily extended to 12–24 months)

RESERVES 292,500

Army 195,500 **Navy** 27,000 **Air Force** 70,000
Potential 1,096,500 **Army** 782,000 **Navy** 135,000 **Air Force** 179,500

Strategic Nuclear Forces (8,700)

(**Navy** 5,000 **Air Force** 3,100 _Gendarmerie_ 600)
NAVY 64 SLBM in 4 SSBN
   SSBN 4
   3 _L'Inflexible_ with 16 M-4/TN-75 or -71; plus SM-39 _Exocet_ USGW and 4 533mm HWT
   1 _Le Triomphant_ with 16 M-45/TN-75 SLBM; plus SM-39 _Exocet_ and 4 533mm HWT
AIR FORCE
   TRG 1 _Mystère-Falcon_ 20P, 1 _Alpha Jet_
   TKR 1 sqn with 11 C-135FR, 3 KC-135
   RECCE 1 sqn with 5 _Mirage_ IV P

'FINAL WARNING' NUCLEAR FORCES

NAVY 36 _Super Etendard_ strike **ac** (ASMP); plus 16 in store
AIR FORCE 3 sqn with 60 _Mirage_ 2000 N(ASMP)
   TRG 3 _Mystère-Falcon_ 20 SNA

Army 203,200

(9,100 women, 89,800 conscripts) regt normally bn size
1 Int and EW bde
1 corps with 2 armd, 1 mtn inf div (48,200)
Summary of div cbt units
   5 armd regt • 6 arty regt • 4 mech inf regt • 3 recce sqn • 4 mot inf regt • 2 ATK sqn • 3 mtn inf regt
Corps units: 1 armd recce, 1 mot inf, 1 arty bde (1 MLRS, 2 _Roland_ SAM (each of 4 bty), 1 HAWK SAM regt • 1 air mobile bde with 2 cbt hel regt (**hel** 26 SA-330, 48 SA-342 HOT ATK, 20 SA-341 gunships) • 1

engr bde (4 regt)
1 armd div (in Eurocorps): 2 armd, 1 mech inf, 2 arty regt
1 Fr/Ge bde (2,500): Fr units incl 1 lt armd, 1 mot inf regt; 1 recce sqn
Rapid Action Force (FAR) (41,500)
   1 para div: 6 para inf, 1 armd cavalry, 1 arty, 1 engr regt • 1 lt armd marine div: 2 APC inf, 2 lt armd, 1 arty, 1 engr regt • 1 lt armd div: 2 armd cavalry, 2 APC inf, 1 arty, 1 engr regt • 1 air-mobile div: 1 inf, 3 cbt hel, 1 spt hel regt (245 **hel** 63 SA-330, 90 SA-342/HOT, 20 AS-532, 72 SA-341 (30 gun, 42 recce/liaison))
Corps units: 1 arty bde (1 MLRS, 1 _Roland_ SAM, 1 HAWK SAM regt) • 1 engr regt
Territorial def forces incl spt of UN missions: 7 regt

FOREIGN LEGION (8,200)

1 armd, 1 para, 6 inf, 1 engr regt (incl in units listed above)

MARINES (31,000)

(incl 12,000 conscripts, mainly overseas enlisted)
1 div (see FAR), 4 regt in France (see div cbt units above), 11 regt overseas

SPECIAL OPERATIONS FORCES

(see also above) 1 Marine para regt, 1 para regt, 2 hel units (EW, special ops)

RESERVES

Indiv reinforcements for 1 corps (incl Eurocorps) and FAR (75,000)
Territorial def forces: 10 regt, 75 coy (all arms), 12 coy (engr, tpt, log)

EQUIPMENT

MBT 1,210: 1,071 AMX-30B2 (incl 662 in store), 139 _Leclerc_
RECCE 337 AMX-10RC, 192 ERC-90F4 _Sagaie_, 155 AML-60/-90, 899 VBL M-11
AIFV 713 AMX-10P/PC
APC 3,820 VAB (incl variants)
TOTAL ARTY 1,055
   TOWED 155mm: 113 BF-50, 105 TR-F-1
   SP 155mm: 272 AU-F-1
   MRL 380mm: 58 MLRS
   MOR 507: **120mm**: 361 RT-F1, 146 M-51
ATGW 660 _Eryx_, 1,405 _Milan_, HOT (incl 125 VAB SP)
RL 19,540: **89mm**: 9,850; **112mm**: 9,690 APILAS
AD GUNS 20mm: 774 53T2
SAM 570: 69 HAWK, 156 _Roland_ I/II, 345 _Mistral_
SURV RASIT-B/-E (veh, arty), RATAC (veh, arty)
AC 2 Cessna _Caravan_ II , 5 PC-6
HELICOPTERS 518
   ATTACK 342: 157 SA-341F, 155 SA-342M, 30 SA-342AATCP
   RECCE 4 AS-532 _Horizon_
   SPT 172: 24 AS-532, 18 AS-555, 130 SA-330
UAV 6 CL-289 (AN/USD-502), 2 _Crecerelle_, 4 _Hunter_

Navy 63,300

(incl 9,400 Naval Air, 2,900 Marines, 3,800 women, 17,250 conscripts)

COMMANDS SSBN (ALFOST) HQ Paris **Atlantic** (CECLANT) HQ Brest **North Sea/Channel** (COMAR CHERBOURG) HQ Cherbourg **Mediterranean** (CECMED) HQ Toulon **Indian Ocean** (ALINDIEN) HQ afloat **Pacific Ocean** (ALPACI) HQ Papeete

ORGANIC COMMANDS ALFAN (Surface Ships) **ALGASAM** (Surface Ships ASW) **ALMINES** (mine warfare) **ALAVIA** (naval aviation) **COFUSCO** (Marines) **ALFOST** (Submarines)

BASES France Cherbourg, Brest (HQ), Lorient, Toulon (HQ) **Overseas** Papeete (HQ) (Tahiti), La Réunion, Noumea (New Caledonia), Fort de France (Martinique), Cayenne (French Guinea)

SUBMARINES 14

STRATEGIC SUBMARINES 4 SSBN (see p. 50)

TACTICAL SUBMARINES 8

SSN 6 *Rubis* ASW/ASUW with F-17 HWT, L-5 LWT and SM-39 *Exocet* USGW

SS 2 *Agosta* with F-17 HWT and L-5 LWT; plus *Exocet* USGW (plus special reserve 2)

PRINCIPAL SURFACE COMBATANTS 41

CARRIERS 1 *Clémenceau* CVS (33,300t), capacity 40 ac (typically 2 flt with 16 *Super Etendard*, 1 with 6 *Alizé*; 1 det with 2 *Etendard* IVP, 8 *Crusader* F8/P, 2 *Super Frelon*, 2 *Dauphin* hel)

CRUISERS 1 *Jeanne d'Arc* CCH (trg/ASW) with 6 MM-38 *Exocet* SSM, 2 x 2 100mm guns, capacity 8 SA-319B hel

DDG 4

2 *Cassard* with 1 x 1 *Standard* SM-1 MR; plus 8 MM-40 *Exocet*, 1 100mm gun, 2 ASTT, 1 *Panther* hel (ASW/OTHT)

2 *Suffren* with 1 x 2 *Masurca* SAM; plus 1 *Malafon* SUGW, 4 ASTT, 4 MM-38 *Exocet*, 2 100mm guns

FRIGATES 35

6 *Floréal* with 2 MM-38 *Exocet*, 1 AS-365 hel and 1 100mm gun

7 *Georges Leygues* with 2 *Lynx* hel (Mk 46 LWT), 2 ASTT; plus 5 with 8 MM-40, 2 with 4 MM-38 *Exocet*, all with 1 100mm gun and CN SAM

3 *Tourville* with 2 *Lynx* hel, 1 *Malafon* SUGW, 2 ASTT; plus 6 MM-38 *Exocet*, 2 100mm guns, CN SAM

16 *D'Estienne d'Orves* with 4 ASTT, 1 x 6 ASW mor; plus 10 with 2 MM-38, 6 with 4 MM-40 *Exocet*, all with 1 100mm gun

3 *La Fayette* with 8 MM-40 *Exocet*, CN-2 SAM, 1 100mm gun, 1 *Panther* hel

PATROL AND COASTAL COMBATANTS 40

PATROL, OFFSHORE 1 *Albatross* PCO (Public Service Force)

PATROL, COASTAL 23

10 *L'Audacieuse*, 8 *Léopard* PCC (trg), 3 *Flamant* PCC, 1 *Sterne* PCC, 1 *Grebe* PCC (Public Service Force)

PATROL, INSHORE 16

2 *Athos* PCI, 2 *Patra* PCI, 1 *La Combattante* PCI, 6 *Stellis* PCI, 5 PCI< (manned by *Gendarmarie Maritime*)

MINE WARFARE 21

COMMAND AND SUPPORT 1 *Loire* MCCS

MINELAYERS 0, but submarines and *Thetis* (trials ship) have capability

MINE COUNTERMEASURES 20

13 *Eridan* MHC, 4 *Vulcain* MCM diver spt, 3 *Antares* (route survey/trg)

AMPHIBIOUS 9

2 *Foudre* LPD, capacity 450 tps, 30 tk, 4 *Super Puma* hel, 2 CDIC LCT or 10 LCM

2 *Ouragan* LPD: capacity 350 tps, 25 tk, 2 *Super Frelon* hel

5 *Champlain* LSM: capacity 140 tps, tk

Plus craft: 5 LCT, 21 LCM

SUPPORT AND MISCELLANEOUS 36

UNDER WAY SUPPORT 5 *Durance* AO with 1 SA-319 hel

MAINTENANCE AND LOGISTIC 18

1 AOT, 1 *Jules Verne* AR with 2 SA-319 hel, 2 *Rhin* depot/spt, with hel; 8 tpt, 6 ocean tugs (3 civil charter)

SPECIAL PURPOSES 7

5 trial ships, 2 *Glycine* trg

SURVEY/RESEARCH 6

5 AGHS, 1 AGOR

DEPLOYMENT

CECLAND (HQ, Brest): 4 SSBN, 2 SS, 1 CCH, 5 DDH, 9 FFG, 3 MCMV, 1 MCCS, 10 MHC, 1 diver spt, 3 AGS, 1 AGOR

COMAR CHERBOURG (HQ, Cherbourg): 1 clearance diving ship

CECMED (HQ, Toulon): 6 SSN, 1 CV, 5 DDH, 4 DDG, 4 FFH, 7 FFA, 3 LSD, 3 AOR, 1 LSM, 4 LCT, 2 diver spt, 3 MHC, 1 AR

NAVAL AIR (9,400)

(incl 700 women, 450 conscripts)

Flying hours *Etendard* and *Crusader*: 180–220 (night qualified pilots)

NUCLEAR STRIKE 2 flt with *Super Etendard* (ASMP nuc ASM)

FTR 1 sqn with F-8E (FN) *Crusader*

RECCE 1 sqn with *Etendard* IV P

AEW 2 flt with *Alizé*

MR 2 flt with N-262 *Frégate*

MP 2 sqn with *Atlantique*

ASW 2 sqn with *Lynx*

AEW 2 E-2C

TRG 3 units with N-262 *Frégate*, *Rallye* 880, CAP 10, 1 unit with SA-316B

COMMANDOS 1 aslt sqn with SA-321

MISC 1 SAR unit with SA-321, SA-365, 1 unit with SA-365F, SA-319, 2 liaison units with EMB-121

EQUIPMENT

61 cbt ac (plus 35 in store); 25 armed hel (plus 9 in store)

AC 29* *Super Etendard* plus 23 in store (52 to be mod for ASMP) • 9* *Crusader* plus 2 in store • 5* *Etandard* IV P • 6 *Alizé* (AEW) plus 2 in store • 18* *Atlantique* 2 (MP) plus 10 in store • 13 *Nord 262* (MR/trg) • 8 *Xingu* (misc) • 7 *Rallye 880* • 8 **CAP-10** (trg) • 5 *Falcon* **10MER** (trg)

HEL 25 *Lynx* (ASW) plus 9 in store • 10 **SA-321** (SAR, trg) plus 4 in store • 13 **AS-565SA** (SAR, trg) plus 2 in store

MISSILES

ASM *Exocet* AM-39
AAM R-550 *Magic* 2

MARINES (2,900)

COMMANDO UNITS (400) 4 aslt gp
1 attack swimmer unit
FUSILIERS-MARIN (2,500) 14 naval-base protection gp
PUBLIC SERVICE FORCE naval personnel, performing general coast guard, fishery, SAR, anti-pollution and traffic surv duties: 1 *Albatross*, 1 *Sterne*, 1 *Grebe*, 1 *Flamant* PCC; **ac** 4 N-262 **hel** 4 SA-365 (ships incl in naval patrol and coastal totals). Comd exercised through *Maritime Préfectures* (Premar): *Manche* (Cherbourg), *Atlantique* (Brest), *Méditerranée* (Toulon)

Air Force 78,100

(6,300 women, 19,900 conscripts, incl strategic and 'final warning' NUC forces)
Flying hours 180

AIR SIGNALS AND GROUND ENVIRONMENT COMMAND

CONTROL automatic *STRIDA* II, 10 radar stations, 1 sqn with 4 E3F
SAM 10 sqn (1 trg) with 24 *Crotale* bty (48 fire, 30 radar units), 36 *Mistral*
AA GUNS 12 sections with 170 AA gun bty (**20mm**)

AIR COMBAT COMMAND

FTR 5 sqn with *Mirage* 2000C/B
FGA 7 sqn
   3 with *Mirage* 2000D • 2 with *Jaguar* A • 2 with *Mirage* F1-CT
RECCE 2 sqn with *Mirage* F-1CR
TRG 3 OCU sqn
   1 with *Jaguar* A/E • 1 with F1-C/B • 1 with *Mirage* 2000/BC
EW 1 sqn with C-160 ELINT/ESM

AIR MOBILITY COMMAND (CFAP)

TPT 13 sqn
   1 hy with DC-8F, A310-300
   5 tac with C-160/-160NG, C-130H
   7 lt tpt/trg/SAR/misc with C-160, DHC-6, CN235,

Falcon 20, *Falcon* 50, *Falcon* 900, TBM-700, N-262, AS-555
EW 1 sqn with DC-8 ELINT
HEL 6 sqn with AS-332, SA-330, AS-555, AS-355, SA-319
TRG 1 OCU with C-160, N-262, 1 OCU with SA-319, AS-555, SA-330

AIR TRAINING COMMAND

TRG *Alpha Jet*, EMB-121, TB-30, EMB-312, CAP-10/-20/-231, CR-100, N262

EQUIPMENT

505 cbt ac, no armed hel

AC 345 *Mirage* (10 **F-1B** (OCU), 10 **F-1C** (OCU plus 6 in Djibouti), 40 **F-1CR** (recce),• 40 **F-1CT** (FGA), 5 **MIVP** (recce), 120 **-M-2000B/C** (95 **-C** (ftr), 25 **-B** (OCU)), 60 **-M-2000N** (strike, FGA), 60 **-M-2000D** (FGA) • 50 *Jaguar* (30 **-A**, 20* **-E** (strike, FGA)) • 110* *Alpha Jet* (trg, 6 test plus 39 in store) • 4 **E-3F** (AEW) • 2 **A** 310-300 (tpt) • 3 **DC-8F** (tpt) • 14 **C-130** (5 **-H** (tpt), 9 **-H-30** (tpt)) • 11 **C-135FR** (tkr) • 60 **C-160** (40 **-AG**, 20 **-NG** (tpt of which 14 tkr)) • 3 **KC-135** • 8 **CN-235M** (tpt) • 22 **N-262** (14 lt tpt, 3 OCU, 5 trg, plus 2 in store) • 17 *Falcon* (11 **-20** (4 tpt, 7 misc plus 3 in store), 4 **-50** (VIP), 2 **-900** (VIP)) • 12 **TBM-700** (tpt) • 24 **MS-760** (misc) • 11 **CM-170** (*Fouga*) (misc) • 10 **DHC-6** (tpt) • 49 **EMB-121** (trg) • 97 **TB-30** (trg plus 50 in store) • 4 **CAP-10/20/231** (trg) • 48 **EMB-312** (trg) • 2 **CR-100** (trg)

HEL 14 **SA-319** (12 tpt, 2 OCU) (*Alouette* III) • 28 **SA-330** (25 tpt, SAR, 3 OCU) (*Puma*) • 7 **AS-332** (tpt/VIP) (*Super Puma*) • 3 **AS-532** (tpt) (*Cougar*) • 6 **AS-355** (*Ecureuil*) • 39 **AS-555** (30 tpt, 9 OCU) (*Fennec*)

MISSILES

ASM AS-30/-30L
AAM *Super* 530F/D, R-550 *Magic* 1/II

Forces Abroad

GERMANY 11,700; Eurocorps with 1 armd div (div returns to Fr 1 July 1998) *Gendarmerie* 260
ANTILLES (HQ Fort de France) 5,000; 3 marine inf regt (incl 2 SMA), 1 marine inf bn, 1 air tpt unit **ac** 2 C-160 **hel** 2 SA-330, 2 SA-319, 1 FFH (1 AS-365 hel), 2 PCI, 1 LSM, 1 spt
FRENCH GUIANA (HQ Cayenne) 3,600; 2 marine inf (incl 1 SMA), 1 Foreign Legion regt, 2 PCI 1 *Atlantic* **ac**, 1 air tpt unit **hel** 4 SA-330, 3 AS-555 *Gendarmerie* 1,400
INDIAN OCEAN (Mayotte, La Réunion) 4,000; 2 Marine inf (incl 1 SMA) regt, 1 spt bn, 1 Foreign Legion coy, 1 air tpt unit **ac** 2 C-160 **hel** 2 AS 555, 1 LSM, 1 spt; *Gendarmerie* 700 **Navy** Indian Ocean Squadron, Comd ALINDIEN (HQ afloat): 1 FFA (2 AS-365 hel), 2 PCI, 1 AOR (comd), reinforcement 2 FF, 1 *Atlantic* ac

NEW CALEDONIA (HQ Nouméa) 3,900; 1 Marine inf regt; some 12 AML recce, 5 **120mm** mor; 1 air tpt unit, det **ac** 2 CN-235 **hel** 2 AS-555, 5 SA-330 **Navy** 2 FFH (2 AS-365 hel), 2 PCI, 1 LSM, 1 AGS, 1 spt **ac** 2 *Guardian* MR *Gendarmerie* 1,100

POLYNESIA (HQ Papeete) 3,800 (incl *Centre d'Expérimentation du Pacifique*); 1 Marine inf regt, 1 Foreign Legion bn, 1 air tpt unit, 2 CN-235, 3 AS-332 *Gendarmerie* 350 **Navy** 1 FF, 3 patrol combatants, 1 amph, 1 survey, 5 spt **ac** 3 *Guardian* MR

CHAD 800; 2 inf coy, 1 AML sqn (-) **ac** 2 C-160, 1 C-130, 3 *Mirage* FICT, 2 *Mirage* FICR

CÔTE D'IVOIRE 500; 1 marine inf bn (18 AML-60/-90) **hel** 1 AS-555

DJIBOUTI 1,500; 1 marine inf(-), 1 Foreign Legion regt(-); 26 ERC-90 recce, 6 **155mm** arty, 16 AA arty; 3 amph craft, 1 sqn with **ac** 6 *Mirage* F-1C (plus 4 in store), 1 C-160 **hel** 1 SA-319, 2 SA-330

GABON 600; 1 marine inf bn (4 AML-60) **ac** 1 C-160 **hel** 1 AS-555

SENEGAL 1,300; 1 marine inf bn (14 AML-60/-90) **ac** 1 *Atlantic* MR, 1 C-160 tpt **hel** 1 SA-319

UN AND PEACEKEEPING

ANGOLA (UNOMA): 3 obs. BOSNIA (SFOR II): 3,300: 2 mech inf bde, 1 N-262; (UNMIBH): 1. CAR (MINURCA): 201. CROATIA: SFOR Air Component 11 *Jaguar*, 10 Mirage 2000C/D, 1 E-3F, 1 KC-135, 1 N-262. EGYPT (MFO): 17; incl 1 DHC-6. GEORGIA (UNOMIG): 4 obs. IRAQ/KUWAIT (UNIKOM): 11 obs. ITALY (SFOR Air Component): 10 *Mirage* 2000C/D, 1 C-135, 1 E-3F, 11 *Jaguar*, 1 N-262, 3 SA-330 (*Puma*). LEBANON (UNIFIL): 246; elm 1 log bn. MIDDLE EAST (UNTSO): 4 obs. SAUDI ARABIA (*Southern Watch*): 170; 5 *Mirage* 2000C, 3 F-1CR, 1 C-135. WESTERN SAHARA (MINURSO): 24 obs (*Gendarmerie*)

Paramilitary 93,400

GENDARMERIE 93,400

(3,500 women, 13,000 conscripts, 1,600 civilians); incl **Territorial** 60,000 **Mobile** 17,000 **Schools** 5,500 **Overseas** 3,100 **Maritime, Air** (personnel drawn from other Dept.) **Republican Guard, Air tpt, Arsenals** 4,800 **Administration** 3,000 **Reserves** 139,000

    EQPT 121 AML, 28 VBC-90 armd cars; 155 VBRG-170 APC; 813 **60mm, 81mm** mor; 5 PCIs (listed under Navy), plus 11 other patrol craft and 4 tugs, **hel** 12 SA-319, 30 AS-350

Foreign Forces

SINGAPORE AIR FORCE 400: 10 TA-4SU *Skyhawks* (Cazaux AFB)

Germany

	1996	1997	1998	1999
GDP	DM3.5tr	DM3.6tr		
	($2.1tr)	($2.1tr)		
per capita	$21,100	$21,900		
Growth	1.3%	2.0%		
Inflation	1.5%	1.8%		
Publ debt	64.9%	65.0%		
Def exp	DM58.7bn	DM58.0bn		
	($39.0bn)	($33.4bn)		
Def bdgt			DM46.7bn	DM47.5bn
			($25.8bn)	($26.4bn)
$1 = DM	1.50	1.73	1.81	
Population		81,102,000		
Age	*13–17*	*18–22*	*23–32*	
Men	2,309,000	2,278,000	5,909,000	
Women	2,187,000	2,181,000	5,685,000	

Total Armed Forces

ACTIVE some 333,500

(137,500 conscripts; incl 2,500 active Reserve trg posts, all services)
Terms of service 10 months; 12–23 months voluntary

RESERVES 315,000

(men to age 45, officers/NCO to 60) **Army** 258,000 **Navy** 10,200 **Air Force** 46,800

Army 230,600

(110,700 conscripts)

ARMY FORCES COMMAND

1 air-mobile force comd (div HQ) with 2 AB (1 Crisis Reaction Force (CRF)) • 1 cdo SF bde • 1 army avn bde with 5 regt • 1 SIGINT/ELINT bde • 1 spt bde

ARMY SUPPORT COMMAND

3 log, 1 medical bde

CORPS COMMANDS

I Ge/Nl Corps 2 MDC/armd div
II Corps 2 MDC/armd div; 1 MDC/mtn div
IV Corps 1 MDC/armd inf div; 1 armd inf div; 1 MDC
Corps Units 2 spt bde and Ge elm of Ge/Nl Corps, 1 air mech bde (CRF), 1 ATGW hel regt

Military District Commands (MDC)/Divisions

6 MDC/div; 1 div; 1 MDC comd and control 8 armd bde, 9 armd inf and the Ge elm of the Ge/Fr bde, 2 armd (not active), 2 armd inf (not active), 1 inf, 1 mtn bde. Bde differ in their basic org, peacetime str, eqpt and mob capability; 4 (2 armd, 1 inf and Ge/Fr bde) are allocated to the CRF, the remainder to the Main Defence Forces (MDF). The MDC also comd and control 27 Military Region Commands (MRC). One armd div earmarked for Eurocorps, another for Allied Rapid Reaction Corps (ARRC). 7 recce

bn, 7 arty regt, 7 engr bde and 7 AD regt available for cbt spt

EQUIPMENT

MBT 2,716: 888 *Leopard* 1A1/A3/A4/A5, 1,828 *Leopard* 2 (350 to be upgraded to A5)
RECCE 523: 409 SPz-2 *Luchs*, 114 TPz-1 *Fuchs* (NBC)
AIFV 2,121 *Marder* A2/A3, 343 *Wiesel* (210 TOW, 133 **20mm** gun)
APC 814 TPz-1 *Fuchs* (incl 87 EW plus variants), 2,641 M-113 (incl variants, 320 arty obs)
TOTAL ARTY 2,040
  TOWED 325: **105mm**: 19 Geb H, 114 M-101; **155mm**: 192 FH-70
  SP 155mm: 573 M-109A3G
  MRL 234: **110mm**: 80 LARS; **227mm**: 154 MLRS
  MOR 908: **120mm**: 393 Brandt, 515 Tampella
ATGW 2,367: 1,907 *Milan*, 98 TOW, 226 RJPz-(HOT) *Jaguar* 1, 136 RJPz-(TOW) *Jaguar* 2
AD GUNS 1,529: **20mm**: 1,150 Rh 202 towed; **35mm**: 379 *Gepard* SP
SAM 143 *Roland* SP, *Stinger*
SURV 22 *Green Archer* (mor), 110 RASIT (veh, arty), 77 RATAC (veh, arty)
HELICOPTERS 624
  ATTACK 204 PAH-1 (BO-105 with HOT)
  SPT 420: 174 UH-1D, 108 CH-53G, 96 BO-105M, 42 *Alouette* II
UAV CL-289 (AN/USD-502)
MARINE (River Engineers) 14 LCM

Navy 26,700

(incl 4,500 Naval Air, 4,700 conscripts and 450 women)
FLEET COMMAND Type comds Frigate, Patrol Boat, MCMV, Submarine, Support Flotillas, Naval Air **Spt comds** Naval Comms, Electronics
BASES Glücksburg (Maritime HQ), Wilhelmshaven, Kiel, Olpenitz, Eckernförde, Warnemünde. Bases with limited spt facilities **Baltic** Flensburg, Neustadt **North Sea** Emden

SUBMARINES 14

12 Type 206/206A SSC with *Seeaal* DM2 533mm HWT (12 conversions to T-206A complete, plus 2 in store)
2 Type 205 SSC with DM3 HWT

PRINCIPAL SURFACE COMBATANTS 15

DESTROYERS 3

DDG 3 *Lütjens* (mod US *Adams*) with 1 x 1 SM-1 MR SAM/*Harpoon* SSM launcher, 2 127mm guns; plus 1 x 8 ASROC (Mk 46 LWT), 2 x 3 ASTT

FRIGATES 12

FF 8 *Bremen* with 2 *Lynx* hel (ASW/OTHT), 2 x 2 ASTT; plus 2 x 4 *Harpoon*
FFG 4 *Brandenburg* with 4 MM-38 *Exocet*, 1 VLS Mk-41 SAM, 2 RAM, 21 Mk-49 SAM, 1 76mm gun, 4 324mm TT, 2 *Lynx* hel

PATROL AND COASTAL COMBATANTS 30

MISSILE CRAFT 30

10 *Albatross* (Type 143) PFM with 2 x 2 *Exocet*, and 2 533mm TT
10 *Gepard* (T-143A) PFM with 2 x 2 *Exocet*
10 *Tiger* (Type 148) PFM with 2 x 2 *Exocet*

MINE COUNTERMEASURES 38

10 *Hameln* (T-343) comb ML/MCC
6 *Lindau Troika* MSC control and guidance, each with 3 unmanned sweep craft
5 converted *Lindau* (T-331) MHC
11 *Frankenthal* (T-332) MHC
5 *Frauenlob* MSI
1 MCM diver spt ship

AMPHIBIOUS craft only

some 13 LCU/LCM

SUPPORT AND MISCELLANEOUS 42

UNDER WAY SUPPORT 2 *Spessart* AO
MAINTENANCE AND LOGISTIC 26
  6 *Elbe* spt, 4 small (2,000t) AOT, 4 *Lüneburg* log spt, 2 AE, 8 tugs, 2 icebreakers (civil)
SPECIAL PURPOSE 10
  3 AGI, 2 trials, 3 multi-purpose (T-748), 2 trg
RESEARCH AND SURVEY 4
  1 AGOR, 3 AGHS (civil-manned for Ministry of Transport)

NAVAL AIR (4,100)

Flying hours *Tornado*: 160
3 wg, 7 sqn
  1 wg with *Tornado*, 2 sqn FGA/recce, 1 sqn trg
  1 wg with ASW/SIGINT/SAR/pollution control/ tpt, 1 sqn with *Atlantic* (MPA/SIGINT), 1 sqn with *Atlantic* (pollution control/tpt) and Do-228, 1 sqn with *Lynx* (ASW)
  1 SAR/tpt wg with 1 sqn *Sea King* Mk 41 hel

EQUIPMENT

52 cbt ac, 17 armed hel
AC 52 *Tornado* • **18** *Atlantic* (14 MR, 4 ELINT) • 2 **Do-228** (pollution control) • 2 **Do-228** (tpt)
HEL 17 *Sea Lynx* Mk 88 (ASW) • 22 *Sea King* **Mk 41** (SAR/tpt)

MISSILES

ASM *Kormoran*, *Sea Skua*, HARM
AAM AIM-9 *Sidewinder*

Air Force 76,200

(22,100 conscripts, 930 women)
Flying hours 150

AIR FORCE COMMAND

2 TAC cmds, 4 air div
FGA 4 wg with 8 sqn *Tornado*
FTR 4 wg (with F-4F (7 sqn); MiG-29 1 sqn)
RECCE 1 wg with 2 sqn *Tornado*
ECR 1 wg with 2 sqn *Tornado*

SAM 6 mixed wg (each 1 gp *Patriot* (6 sqn) plus 1 gp HAWK (4 sqn plus 2 reserve sqn)); 14 sqn *Roland*
RADAR 2 tac Air Control regts, 7 sites; 10 remote radar posts

TRANSPORT COMMAND (GAFTC)

TPT 3 wg, 4 sqn with *Transall* C-160, incl 1 (OCU) with C-160, 4 sqn (incl 1 OCU) with Bell UH-1D, 1 special air mission wg with Boeing 707-320C, Tu-154, Airbus A-310, VFW-614, CL-601, L-410S (VIP), 3 AS-532U2 (VIP)

TRAINING

FGA OCU 1 det (Cottesmore, UK) with 18 *Tornado*, OCU (Holloman AFB, NM) with 14 *Tornado*
FTR OCU (Holloman AFB, NM) with 24 F-4F
NATO joint jet pilot trg (Sheppard AFB, TX) with 35 T-37B, 40 T-38A; primary trg sqn with Beech *Bonanza* (Goodyear AFB, AZ), GAF Air Defence School (Fort Bliss TX)

EQUIPMENT

451 cbt ac (36 trg (overseas)) (plus 106 in store); no attack hel
AC 152 **F-4** (145 -F (FGA, ftr), 7 -E (OCU, in US being wfs) • 276 *Tornado* (169 FGA, 35* ECR, 40 Recce, 14* OCU, 18* in tri-national trg sqn (in UK)) • 23 **MiG-29** (19 (ftr), 4* -UB (trg)) • *Alpha Jet* (106 in store) • 84 *Transall* **C-160** (tpt, trg) • 2 **Boeing 707** (VIP) • 5 **A-310** (VIP, tpt) • 1 **Tu-154** • 7 **CL-601** (VIP) • 4 **L-410-S** (VIP) • 35 **T-37B** • 40 **T-38A** • 2 **VFW-614** (VIP)
HEL 99 **UH-1D** (95 SAR, tpt, liaison; 4 VIP) • 3 **AS-532U2** (VIP)

MISSILES

ASM AGM-65 *Maverick*, AGM-88A HARM
AAM AIM-9 *Sidewinder*, AA-8 *Aphid*, AA-10 *Alamo*, AA-11 *Archer*
SAM 72 HAWK launchers, 84 *Roland* launchers, 36 *Patriot* launchers

Forces Abroad

NAVY 1 DD/FF with STANAVFORLANT, 1 DD/FF with STANAVFORMED, 1 MCMV with STANAVFORCHAN, 3 MPA in ELMAS/Sardinia
US Army trg unit with 40 *Leopard* 2 MBT, 32 *Marder* AIFV, 12 M-109A3G **155mm** SP arty. **Air Force** 812 flying trg at Goodyear, Sheppard, Holloman AFBs, NAS Pensacola, Fort Rucker AFBs with 35 T-37, 40 T-38, 24 F-4F; 14 *Tornado*, missile trg at Fort Bliss
UK 65 OCU at RAF Cottesmore with 18 *Tornado*

UN AND PEACEKEEPING

BOSNIA (SFOR II): 2,600; 56 SPz-2 *Luchs* recce, 98 TPz-1 *Fuchs* APC, 7 CH-53 hel, 1 CL-289 UAV. **SFOR Air Component** 14 *Tornado* 2 C-160. **GEORGIA** (UNOMIG): 10 obs. **IRAQ/KUWAIT** (UNIKOM): 13

Foreign Forces

NATO HQ Allied Land Forces Central Europe (LANDCENT), HQ Allied Rapid Reaction Corps (ARRC), HQ Allied Air Forces Central Europe (AIRCENT), HQ Allied Land Forces Jutland and Schleswig-Holstein (LANDJUT), HQ Multi-National Division (Central) (MND(C)), HQ Allied Command Europe Mobile Force (AMF), Airborne Early Warning Force: 17 E-3A *Sentry*, 2 Boeing-707 (trg)
BELGIUM 2,000: 1 mech inf bde(-)
FRANCE 11,700: 1 armd div (Eurocorps)
NETHERLANDS 3,000: 1 lt bde
UK 28,167: **Army** 23,600: 1 corps HQ (multinational), 1 armd div, 2 armd recce, 4 fd arty, 2 AD regt **Air Force** 4,567: 2 air bases, 4 sqn with **ac** 52 *Tornado* GR1, 2 sqn with 33 *Harrier*, RAF regt, 1 *Rapier* SAM sqn, 2 fd sqn
US 57,700: **Army** 42,600: 1 army HQ, 1 corps HQ; 1 armd (-), 1 mech inf div (-) **Air Force** 15,138: HQ USAFE, (HQ 17th Air Force), 1 tac ftr wg with 4 sqn FGA/ftr, 1 cbt spt wg, 1 air-control wg, 1 tac airlift wg; 1 air base wg, 54 F-16C/D, 12 A-10, 6 OA-10, 16 C-130E, 9 C-9A, 9 C-21, 2 C-20, 1 CT-43

Greece

	1996	1997	1998	1999
GDP	dr29.9tr	dr33.0tr		
	($119bn)	($121bn)		
per capita	$11,900	$12,500		
Growth	2.7%	3.5%		
Inflation	8.2%	5.5%		
Publ debt	111.5%	108.4%		
Def exp	dr1.3tr	dr1.5tr		
	($5.6bn)	($5.5bn)		
Def bdgt			dr1,166bn	
			($3.8bn)	
FMA (US)	$225m	$123m	$15m	$0.025m
$1 = drachma	241	273	306	
Population	10,597,000 (Muslim 1%)			
Age	*13–17*	*18–22*	*23–32*	
Men	351,000	383,000	826,000	
Women	330,000	364,000	786,000	

Total Armed Forces

ACTIVE 168,500

(112,700 conscripts, 5,100 women)
Terms of service **Army** up to 19 months **Navy** up to 21 months **Air Force** up to 21 months

RESERVES some 291,000

(to age 50) **Army** some 235,000 (Field Army 200,000, Territorial Army/National Guard 35,000) **Navy** about 24,000 **Air Force** about 32,000

Army 116,000

(88,500 conscripts, 2,700 women)

FIELD ARMY

3 Mil Regions • 1 Army, 5 corps HQ • 5 div HQ (1 armd, 3 mech, 1 inf) • 4 inf div (3 inf, 1 arty regt, 1 armd bn) • 5 indep armd bde (each 2 armd, 1 mech inf, 1 SP arty bn) • 7 mech bde (2 mech, 1 armd, 1 SP arty bn) • 5 inf bde • 1 army avn bde with 5 avn bn (incl 1 ATK) • 1 amph bn • 4 recce bn • 5 fd arty bn • 1 indep avn coy • 10 AD arty bn • 2 SAM bn with I HAWK
Units are manned at 3 different levels
  Cat A 85% fully ready **Cat B** 60% ready in 24 hours
  Cat C 20% ready in 48 hours

TERRITORIAL DEFENCE

Higher Mil Comd of Interior and Islands HQ
4 Mil Comd HQ (incl Athens) • 1 inf div • 4 AD arty bn • 2 inf regt • 1 army avn bn • 1 para regt • 8 fd arty bn

RESERVES 34,000

National Guard internal security role

EQUIPMENT

  MBT 1,735: 714 M-48 (15 A3, 699 A5), 669 M-60 (357 A1, 312 A3), 352 *Leopard* (105 -1CR, 170 -1V, 77 -1A5)
  RECCE 130 M-8, 13 VBL
  AIFV 500 BMP-1
  APC 308 *Leonidas* Mk1/Mk2, 1,669 M-113A1/A2
  TOTAL ARTY 1,886
    TOWED 730: **105mm:** 18 M-56, 445 M-101; **155mm:** 267 M-114
    SP 398: **105mm:** 72 M-52A1; **155mm:** 133 M-109A1/A2, **175mm:** 12 M-107; **203mm:** 181 M-110A2
    MRL 122mm: 116 RM-70; **227mm:** 18 MLRS (incl ATACMS)
    MOR 107mm: 624 M-30 (incl 191 SP); plus **81mm:** 2,800
  ATGW 290 *Milan*, 336 TOW (incl 212 M-901), 262 AT-4 *Spigot*
  RL 64mm: 21,625 RPG-18; **66mm:** 12,000 M-72
  RCL 84mm: 2000 *Carl Gustav*; **90mm:** 1,314 EM-67; **106mm:** 1,291 M-40A1
  AD GUNS 23mm: 506 ZU-23-2
  SAM 838 *Stinger*, 42 I HAWK, 12 SA-8B
  SURV AN/TPQ-36 (arty, mor)
  AC 43 U-17A
  HELICOPTERS
    ATTACK 20 AH-64A
    SPT 9 CH-47D (1 in store), 76 UH-1H, 30 AB-205A, 14 AB-206

Navy 19,500

(incl 9,800 conscripts, 1,300 women)
BASES Salamis, Patras, Soudha Bay

SUBMARINES 7

  3 *Glavkos* (Ge T-209/1100) with 533mm TT, and *Harpoon* USGW (1 in refit)
  4 *Poseidon* (Ge T-209/1200) with 533mm TT and *Harpoon* USGW

PRINCIPAL SURFACE COMBATANTS 16

DESTROYERS 4 *Kimon* (US *Adams*) (US lease) with 1 SM-1; plus 1 x 8 ASROC, 2 x 3 ASTT, 2 127mm guns, 6 *Harpoon* SSM
FRIGATES 12
  3 *Hydra* (Ge MEKO 200) with 2 x 3 ASTT; plus 2 x 4 *Harpoon* SSM and 1 127mm gun (1 SH-60 hel, 1 DC)
  6 *Elli* (Nl *Kortenaer*) with 2 AB-212 hel, 2 x 2 ASTT; plus 2 x 4 *Harpoon*
  3 *Makedonia* (ex-US *Knox*) (US lease) with 1 x 8 ASROC, 4 ASTT; plus *Harpoon* (from ASROC launcher), 1 127mm gun

PATROL AND COASTAL COMBATANTS 42

CORVETTES 5 *Niki* (ex-Ge *Thetis*) (ASW) with 1 x 4 ASW RL, 4 533mm TT
MISSILE CRAFT 19
  13 *Laskos* (Fr *La Combattante* II, III, IIIB) PFM, 8 with 4 MM-38 *Exocet*, 5 with 6 *Penguin* SSM, all with 2 533mm TT
  4 *Votis* (Fr *La Combattante* IIA) PFM 2 with 4 MM-38 *Exocet*, 2 with *Harpoon*
  2 *Stamou* with 4 SS-12 SSM
TORPEDO CRAFT 8
  4 *Hesperos* (Ge *Jaguar*) PFT with 4 533mm TT
  4 *Andromeda* (No *Nasty*) PFT with 4 533mm TT
PATROL CRAFT 10
  COASTAL 4
  2 *Armatolos* (Dk *Osprey*) PCC, 2 *Pirpolitis* PCC
  INSHORE 6
  2 *Tolmi*, 4 PCI

MINE WARFARE 16

MINELAYERS 2 *Aktion* (US LSM-1) (100–130 mines)
MINE COUNTERMEASURES 14
  8 *Alkyon* (US MSC-294) MSC
  6 *Atalanti* (US *Adjutant*) MSC, plus 4 MSR

AMPHIBIOUS 10

  2 *Chios* LST with hel deck: capacity 300 tps, 4 LCVP plus veh
  1 *Nafkratoussa* (US *Cabildo*) LSD: capacity 200 tps, 18 tk, 1 hel
  2 *Inouse* (US *County*) LST: capacity 400 tps, 18 tk
  3 *Ikaria* (US LST-510): capacity 200 tps, 16 tk
  2 *Roussen* (US LSM-1) LSM, capacity 50 tps, 4 tk
  Plus about 57 craft: 2 LCT, 6 LCU, 11 LCM, some 31 LCVP, 7 LCA

SUPPORT AND MISCELLANEOUS 14

  2 AOT, 4 AOT (small), 1 *Axios* (ex-Ge *Lüneburg*) log spt, 1 AE, 5 AGHS, 1 trg

NAVAL AIR (250)

6 cbt ac, 15 armed hel

AC 6 P-3B (MR)
HEL 2 sqn with 8 AB-212 (ASW), 2 AB-212 (EW), 2 SA-319 (ASW), 5 S-70B (ASW)

Air Force 33,000

(14,400 conscripts, 1,500 women)
TACTICAL AIR FORCE
8 cbt wg, 1 tpt wg
FGA 10 sqn
2 with A-7H, 2 with A-7E, 2 with F-16C/D, 1 with F-4E, 3 with F-5A/B, NF-5A/B, RF-5A
FTR 8 sqn
2 with *Mirage* F-1CG, 2 with *Mirage* 2000 EG/BG, 2 with F-4E, 2 with F-16 C/D
RECCE 1 sqn with RF-4E
TPT 3 sqn with C-130H/B, YS-11, C-47, Do-28, *Gulfstream*
LIAISON 4 T-33A
HEL 1 sqn with AB-205A, AB-212, Bell 47G
AD 1 bn with *Nike Hercules* SAM (36 launchers), 12 bty with *Skyguard/Sparrow* SAM, twin **35mm** guns
AIR TRAINING COMMAND
TRG 4 sqn
1 with T-41A, 1 with T-37B/C, 2 with T-2E
EQUIPMENT
402 cbt ac, no armed hel
AC 92 **A-7** (42 -H (FGA), 4 TA-7H (FGA), 40 A-7E (plus 15 in store), 6 **A-7C**) • 83 **F-5** (60 -A/B, 6 -B, 10 NF-5A, 1 NF-5B, 6 RF-5A) • 66 F-4E/RF-4E • 64 **F-16** (50 -C (FGA/ftr), 14 -D) • 26 *Mirage* F-1 **CG** (ftr) • 35 *Mirage* 2000 (31 -EG, 4* BG (trg)) • 4 **C-47** (tpt) • 11 **C-130H** (tpt) • 2 C-130B (tpt) • 10 **CL-215** (tpt, fire-fighting) • 4 **Do-28** (lt tpt) • 1 *Gulfstream* I (VIP tpt) • 36* **T-2** (trg) • 30 **T-33A** (liaison) • 34 **T-37B/C** (trg) • 19 **T-41D** (trg) • 3 **YS-11-200** (tpt)
HEL 12 AB-205A (SAR) • 1 **AB-206** • 4 **AB-212** (VIP, tpt) • 5 **Bell 47G** (liaison)
MISSILES
ASM AGM-65 *Maverick*, AGM-88 HARM
AAM AIM-7 *Sparrow*, AIM-9 *Sidewinder* L/P, R-550 *Magic* 2, AIM 120 AMRAAM, *Super* 530D
SAM 1 bn with 36 *Nike Hercules*, 12 bty with *Skyguard*, 40 *Sparrow*, 35mm guns

Forces Abroad

CYPRUS 1,250; incl 1 mech bde and officers/NCO seconded to Greek-Cypriot forces
UN AND PEACEKEEPING
ADRIATIC (*Sharp Guard* if re-implemented): 2 MSC.
BOSNIA (SFOR II): 250. **SFOR Air Component** 1 C-130. **GEORGIA** (UNOMIG): 4 Obs. **IRAQ/KUWAIT** (UNIKOM): 5 obs. **WESTERN SAHARA** (MINURSO): 1 obs

Paramilitary 4,000

COAST GUARD AND CUSTOMS 4,000
some 100 patrol craft, **ac** 2 Cessna *Cutlass*, 2 TB-20 *Trinidad*

Foreign Forces

US 419: **Navy** 250; facilities at Soudha Bay **Air Force** 169; air base gp; facilities at Iraklion

Iceland

	1996	1997	1998	1999
GDP	K485bn	K527bn		
	($7.3bn)	($7.4bn)		
per capita	$21,100	$22,400		
Growth	5.5%	5.0%		
Inflation	2.3%	1.8%		
Publ debt	56.4%	52.7%		
Sy exp[a]	K6.3bn	K6.5bn		
	($95m)	($92m)		
Sy bdgt[a]			K7.6bn	
			($106m)	
$1 = kronur	66.5	70.9	71.9	

[a] Iceland has no Armed Forces. Sy bdgt is public order and safety bdgt

Population		278,000		
Age	*13–17*	*18–22*	*23–32*	
Men	11,000	11,000	22,000	
Women	10,000	10,000	20,000	

Total Armed Forces

ACTIVE Nil

Paramilitary 120

COAST GUARD 120
BASE Reykjavik
PATROL CRAFT 4
2 *Aegir* PCO with hel, 1 *Odinn* PCO with hel deck, 1 PCI<
AVN 1 F-27 **ac** 1 SA-360 **hel**

Foreign Forces

NATO Island Commander Iceland (ISCOMICE, responsible to CINCEASTLANT)
US 1,871: **Navy** 1,180; MR: 1 sqn with 6 P-3C, 1 UP-3 **Marines** 91 **Air Force** 600; 4 F-15C/D, 1 HC-130, 1 KC-135, 4 HH-60G
NETHERLANDS 30: **Navy** 1 P-3C

Italy

	1996	1997	1998	1999
GDP	L1,874tr	L1,951tr		
	($1.1tr)	($1.1tr)		
per capita	$20,000	$20,700		
Growth	0.7%	1.5%		
Inflation	3.9%	2.0%		
Publ debt	123.7%	121.7%		
Def exp	L36.2tr	L37.2tr		
	($23.4bn)	($21.8bn)		
Def bdgt			L31.0tr	L31.9tr
			($17.4bn)	($17.8bn)
$1 = lira	1,543	1,703	1,783	
Population		57,90,000		
Age	*13–17*	*18–22*	*23–32*	
Men	1,616,000	1,891,000	4,574,000	
Women	1,536,000	1,806,000	4,429,000	

Total Armed Forces

ACTIVE 298,400

(134,100 conscripts; incl 29,200 Central Staff and centrally controlled formations/units)
Terms of service all services 10 months

RESERVES 304,000 (immediate mobilisation)
Army 500,000 (obligation to age 45) (immediate mob 240,000) **Navy** 36,000 (to age 39 for men, variable for officers to 73) **Air Force** 28,000 (to age 25 or 45 (specialists))

Army 165,600

(99,100 conscripts)
1 Op Comd HQ, 3 mil region HQ
1 Projection Force with 1 mech, 1 airmobile, 1 AB bde, 1 amph, 1 engr, 1 avn regt
1 mtn force with 3 mtn bde, 1 engr, 1 avn regt, 1 alpine AB bn
2 defence force
 1 with 1 armd, 1 mech, 1 armd cav bde, 1 engr regt
 1 with 3 mech, 1 armd bde, 1 engr, 1 avn regt
1 spt comd with
 1 AD div: 3 HAWK SAM, 2 AAA regt
 1 arty bde: 1 hy arty, 4 arty regt
 1 avn div: 2 avn regt, 2 avn bn
EQUIPMENT
 MBT 1,299: 823 *Leopard* (incl 120 -1A5), 400 *Centauro* B-1, 76 *Ariete*
 APC 738 M-113, 1,794 VCC1/-2, 157 Fiat 6614, 14 LVTP-7
 TOTAL ARTY 1,567
  TOWED 485: **105mm**: 267 Model 56 pack (233 in store); **155mm**: 164 FH-70, 54 M-114 (in store)
  SP 286: **155mm**: 260 M-109G/-L; **203mm**: 26 M-

 110A2 (in store)
 MRL 227mm: 22 MLRS
 MOR 120mm: 774; plus **81mm**: 1,205 (381 in store)
 ATGW 426 TOW 2B (incl 270 SP), 1,000 *Milan*
 RL 2,000 *Panzerfaust* 3
 RCL 80mm: 720 *Folgore*
 AD GUNS 25mm: 275 SIDAM SP
 SAM 66 HAWK, 128 *Stinger*, 24 *Skyguard/Aspide*
 AC 30 SM-1019, 3 Do-228
 HELICOPTERS
  ATTACK 45 A-129
  ASLT 27 A-109, 62 AB-206
 SPT 86 AB-205A, 68 AB-206 (obs), 15 AB-212, 23 AB-412, 38 CH-47C
 UAV CL-89 (AN/USD-501), *Mirach* 20/-150

Navy 40,000

(incl 2,500 Naval Air, 1,000 Marines and 16,000 conscripts)
COMMANDS 1 Fleet Commander CINCNAV (also NATO COMEDCENT) **Area Commands** Upper Tyrrhenian, Adriatic, Lower Tyrrhenian, Ionian and Strait of Otranto, Sicily, Sardinia
BASES La Spezia (HQ), Taranto (HQ), Ancona (HQ), Brindisi, Augusta, Messina (HQ), La Maddalena (HQ), Cagliari, Naples (HQ), Venice
SUBMARINES 8
 4 *Pelosi* (imp *Sauro*) with Type 184 HWT
 4 *Sauro* with Type 184 HWT (includes 2 non-op, undergoing mod)
PRINCIPAL SURFACE COMBATANTS 30
CARRIERS 1 *G. Garibaldi* CVV. Total ac capacity 16 AV-8B *Harrier* V/STOL or 18 SH-3 *Sea Kings* hel. Usually a mix
CRUISERS 1 *Vittorio Veneto* CGH with 1 x 2 SM-1 ER SAM, 6 AB-212 ASW hel (Mk 46 LWT); plus 4 *Teseo* SSM, 2 x 3 ASTT
DESTROYERS 4
 2 *Luigi Durand de la Penne* (ex-*Animoso*) DDGH with 1 SM-1 MR SAM, 2 x 4 *Teseo* SSM, plus 2 AB-312 hel, 1 127mm gun, 2 x 3 ASTT
 2 *Audace* DDGH, with 1 SM-1 MR SAM, 4 *Teseo* SSM, plus 2 AB-212 hel, 1 127mm gun, 2 x 3 ASTT
FRIGATES 24
 8 *Maestrale* FFH with 2 AB-212 hel, 2 533mm DP TT; plus 4 *Teseo* SSM, 1 127mm gun
 4 *Lupo* FFH with 1 AB-212 hel, 2 x 3 ASTT; plus 8 *Teseo* SSM, 1 127mm gun
 4 *Artigliere* FFG (ex-*Lupo* for Iraq) with 8 *Tesco* SSM, 8 *Aspide* SAM, 1 127mm gun, 1 AB-212 hel
 8 *Minerva* FF with 2 x 3 ASTT
PATROL AND COASTAL COMBATANTS 17
MISSILE CRAFT 4 *Sparviero* PHM with 2 *Teseo* SSM
PATROL, OFFSHORE 6
 4 *Cassiopea* with 1 AB-212 hel
 2 *Storione* (US *Aggressive*) ex-MSO

PATROL, COASTAL 7

3 *Bambu* (ex-MSC) PCC

4 *Esplatore* PCO

MINE COUNTERMEASURES 13

1 MHC (ex *Alpino*)

4 *Lerici* MHC

8 *Gaeta* MSC

AMPHIBIOUS 3

3 *San Giorgio* LPD: capacity 350 tps, 30 trucks, 2 SH-3D or CH-47 hel, 7 craft

Plus some 33 craft: about 3 LCU, 10 LCM and 20 LCVP

SUPPORT AND MISCELLANEOUS 44

2 *Stromboli* AO, 8 tugs, 9 coastal tugs, 6 water tkr, 4 trials, 2 trg, 3 AGOR, 6 tpt, 2 salvage, 1 research, 1 *Etna* AOR

SPECIAL FORCES (Special Forces Command – COMSUBIN)

3 gp; 1 underwater ops; 1 school; 1 research

MARINES (San Marco gp) (1,000)

1 bn gp, 1 trg gp, 1 log gp

EQUIPMENT

30 VCC-1, 10 LVTP-7 APC, 16 **81mm** mor, 8 **106mm** RCL, 6 *Milan* ATGW

NAVAL AIR (2,500)

18 cbt ac, 80 armed hel

FGA 1 sqn with 16 AV-8B plus and 2*TAV-8B plus

ASW 5 hel sqn with 21 SH-3D, 45 AB-212

HEL 8* SH-3D (amph aslt), 6* AB-212 (amph aslt)

AAM AIM-9L *Sidewinder*

ASM *Marte* Mk 2, AS-12

Air Force 63,600

(20,300 conscripts)

FGA 8 sqn

4 with *Tornado* • 4 with AMX

FTR 7 sqn

5 with F-104 ASA • 2 with *Tornado* F-3

RECCE 2 sqn with AMX

MR 2 sqn with *Atlantic* (OPCON to Navy)

EW 1 ECM/recce sqn with G-222VS, PD-808

CAL 1 navigation-aid calibration sqn with G-222RM, PD-808

TPT 3 sqn

2 with G-222 • 1 with C-130H

TKR/TPT 1 sqn with B707-320

LIAISON 3 sqn with **ac** *Gulfstream* III, *Falcon* 50, DC-9, P-166, P-180 **hel** SH-3D

TRG 1 OCU with TF-104G; 1 det (Cottesmore, UK) with *Tornado*; 4 sqn with **ac** AMX-T, MB-339A, SF-260M, 1 sqn with MB-339 (Aerobatic Team) **hel** 1 sqn with NH-500

SAR 1 sqn and 3 det with HH-3F

6 det with AB-212

AD 6 SAM sqn with *Nike Hercules*, 14 SAM sqn with *Spada*

EQUIPMENT

253 cbt ac (plus 92 in store), no armed hel

AC 77 *Tornado* (58 FGA (4* in tri-national sqn), 19 F-3 (plus 36 FGA and 5 F-3 in store)) • 65 **F-104 ASA** (plus 35 in store) • 6 **TF-104G** (plus 12 in store) • 80 **AMX** (60 (FGA), 20 **-T** (trg)) (plus 21 FGA and 2 T in store) • 75 **MB-339** (13 tac, 62 trg Acrobatic Team) (plus 16 in store) • 11* **MB-339CD** • 14* *Atlantic* (MR) (plus 4 in store) • 4 **Boeing-707-320** (tkr/tpt) • 9 **C-130H** (tpt) • 39 **G-222** (34 tpt, 4 cal), 1 **-GE** (ECM) • 2 **DC9-32** (VIP) • 2 *Gulfstream* III (VIP) • 3 *Falcon* 50 (VIP) • 7 **P-166** (2 **-M**, 5 **-DL3** (liaison and trg)) • 5 **P-180** (liaison) • 7 **PD-808** (ECM, cal, VIP tpt) • 26 **SF-260M** (trg) • 30 **SIAI-208** (liaison)

HEL 21 **HH-3F** (SAR) • 1 **SH-3D** (liaison) • 27 **AB-212** (SAR) • 51 **NH-500D** (trg)

MISSILES

ASM AGM-88 HARM, *Kormoran*

AAM AIM-9L *Sidewinder*, *Aspide*

SAM *Nike Hercules*, *Aspide*

Forces Abroad

GERMANY 92: **Air Force, NAEW Force**

MALTA 16: **Air Force** with 2 AB-212

UK 21: **Air Force** tri-national *Tornado* sqn with 4 ac

US 33: **Air Force** flying trg

UN AND PEACEKEEPING

BOSNIA (SFOR II): 2,500; 1 mech inf bde gp; **EGYPT** (MFO): 81; 3 PCC. **INDIA/PAKISTAN** (UNMOGIP): 7 obs. **ITALY** (SFOR Air Component): 8 *Tornado*, 6 AMX, 1 B-707 (tkr). **IRAQ** (UNSCOM): 1 obs. **IRAQ/KUWAIT** (UNIKOM): 5 obs. **LEBANON** (UNIFIL): 46; hel unit. **MIDDLE EAST** (UNTSO): 7 obs. **WESTERN SAHARA** (MINURSO): 5 obs

Paramilitary 255,700

CARABINIERI (Ministry of Defence) 113,200

Territorial 5 bde, 18 regt, 94 gp **Trg** 1 bde **Mobile def** 1 div, 2 bde, 1 cav regt, 1 special ops gp, 13 mobile bn, 1 AB bn, avn and naval units

EQPT 40 Fiat 6616 armd cars; 40 VCC2, 91 M-113 APC **hel** 24 A-109, 4 AB-205, 39 AB-206, 24 AB-412

PUBLIC SECURITY GUARD (Ministry of Interior) 79,000

11 mobile units; 40 Fiat 6614 APC **ac** 5 P-68 **hel** 12 A-109, 20 AB-206, 9 AB-212

FINANCE GUARDS (Treasury Department) 63,500

14 Zones, 20 Legions, 128 gps **ac** 5 P-166-DL3 **hel** 15 A-109, 65 Breda-Nardi NH-500M/MC/MD; 3 PCI;

plus about 300 boats

HARBOUR CONTROL (*Capitanerie di Porto*)
(subordinated to Navy in emergencies): some 12 PCI,
130+ boats and 4 AB-412 (SAR)

Foreign Forces

NATO HQ Allied Forces Southern Europe
(AFSOUTH), HQ 5 Allied Tactical Air Force (5 ATAF)
US 10,580: **Army** 1,750; 1 inf bn gp **Navy** 4,600 **Air
Force** 4,200; 2 ftr sqn with 36 F-16C/D
SFOR AIR COMPONENT: Be (3 F-16A), **Fr** (10 *Mirage*
2000C/D, 11 *Jaguar*, 1 E-3F, 1 KC-135, 1 N-262), **Ge** (14
Tornado ECR/recce, 2 C-160), **Gr** (1 C-130), **It** (6 *Tornado*,
8 AMX, 1 B-707 (tkr)), **NATO** (4 E-3A), **Nl** (9 F-16, 1 C-
130, 1 F-60, 1 KDC-10 (tkr)), **Sp** (8 F/A -18, 2 KC-130
(tkr), 1 CASA 212 (spt ac)), **Tu** (18 F-16C), **UK** (8 *Harrier*
GR-7, 1 K-1 *Tristar* (tkr), 2 E-3D *Sentry*), **US** 6 F-16C
(USAF), 1 AC-130 (USAF), 3 EC-130 (USAF), 1 MC-
130P (USAF), 3 EA-6B (USMC), 5 KC-135 (USAF), 4 C-
12

Luxembourg

	1996	1997	1998	1999
GDP	fr531bn	fr556bn		
	($15bn)	($16bn)		
per capita	$24,000	$25,300		
Growth	3.0%	3.7%		
Inflation	1.4%	1.4%		
Publ debt	6.5%	6.5%		
Def exp	fr4.4bn	fr4.6bn		
	($141m)	($129m)		
Def bdgt			fr3.9bn	
			($105m)	
$1 = franc	31.0	35.8	37.3	
Population	414,000 (ε123,000 foreign citizens)			
Age	*13–17*	*18–22*	*23–32*	
Men	12,000	12,000	29,000	
Women	12,000	12,200	29,000	

Total Armed Forces

ACTIVE 811

Army 811

1 lt inf bn (recce coy to Eurocorps/BE div)
EQUIPMENT
  APC 5 *Commando*
  MOR 81mm: 6
  ATGW TOW some 6 SP
  RL LAW

Air Force

(none, but for legal purposes NATO's E-3A AEW ac
have Lu registration)
1 sqn with 17 E-3A *Sentry* (NATO standard), 2 Boeing
707 (trg)

Forces Abroad

UN AND PEACEKEEPING
BOSNIA (SFOR II): 25; **SFOR Air Component** 4 E-3A

Paramilitary 560

GENDARMERIE 560

Netherlands

	1996	1997	1998	1999
GDP	gld662bn	gld703bn		
	($356bn)	($360bn)		
per capita	$20,600	$21,700		
Growth	3.5%	3.7%		
Inflation	2.1%	2.1%		
Publ debt	76.6%	71.4%		
Def exp	gld13.2bn	gld13.4bn		
	($7.9bn)	($6.9bn)		
Def bdgt			gld13.9bn	gld13.9bn
			($7.0bn)	($6.8bn)
$1 = guilder	1.69	1.95	2.04	
Population		15,655,000		
Age	*13–17*	*18–22*	*23–32*	
Men	446,000	475,000	1,197,000	
Women	427,000	454,000	1,134,000	

Total Armed Forces

ACTIVE 57,180
(incl 3,600 Royal Military Constabulary, 800 Inter-
Service Organisation; 2,600 women)

RESERVES 75,000
(men to age 35, NCO to 40, officers to 45) **Army** 60,000
Navy some 5,000 **Air Force** 10,000 (immediate recall)

Army 27,000

1 Corps HQ (Ge/Nl), 1 mech div HQ • 3 mech inf bde
(2 cadre) • 1 lt bde • 1 air-mobile bde (3 inf bn) • 1 fd
arty, 1 AD gp • 1 engr gp
Summary of cbt arm units
  7 tk bn • 7 armd inf bn • 3 air-mobile bn • 3 recce bn
  • 7 arty bn • 1 AD bn • 2 MLRS bty

RESERVES

(cadre bde and corps tps completed by call-up of reservists)

National Command (incl Territorial Comd): 3 inf, 1 SF, 2 engr bn spt units, could be mob for territorial defence

Home Guard 3 sectors; lt inf weapons

EQUIPMENT

MBT 600: 270 *Leopard* 1A4 (in store; for sale), 330 *Leopard* 2 (180 to be A5)

AIFV 383 YPR-765, 65 M-113C/-R all with **25mm**

APC 269 YPR-765 (plus 491 look-a-likes)

TOTAL ARTY 439

TOWED 125: **105mm**: 1 M-101 (in store); **155mm**: 27 M-114/23, 82 M-114/39, 15 FH-70 (trg)

SP 159: **155mm**: 129 M-109A3; **203mm**: 30 M-110 (in store; for sale)

MRL 227mm: 22 MLRS

MOR 81mm: 40; **120mm**: 133

ATGW 753 (incl 135 in store): 427 *Dragon*, 326 (incl 90 YPR-765) TOW

RL 84mm: *Carl Gustav*, AT-4

RCL 106mm: 185 M-40 (in store)

AD GUNS 35mm: 77 *Gepard* SP (60 to be up-graded); **40mm**: 60 L/70 towed

SAM 312 *Stinger*

SURV AN/TPQ-36 (arty, mor)

MARINE 1 tk tpt, 3 coastal, 3 river patrol boats

Navy 13,800

(incl 950 Naval Air, 2,800 Marines, 1,200 women)

BASES Netherlands Den Helder (HQ). Nl and Be Navies under joint op comd based Den Helder

Overseas Willemstad (Curaçao)

SUBMARINES 4

4 *Walrus* with Mk 48 HWT; plus provision for *Harpoon* USGW

PRINCIPAL SURFACE COMBATANTS 16

DESTROYERS 4

DDG (Nl desig = FFG)

2 *Tromp* with 1 SM-1 MR SAM; plus 2 x 4 *Harpoon* SSM, 1 x 2 120mm guns, 1 *Lynx* hel (ASW/OTHT), 2 x 3 ASTT (Mk 46 LWT)

2 *Van Heemskerck* with 1 SM-1 MR SAM; plus 2 x 4 *Harpoon*, 2 x 2 ASTT

FRIGATES 12

8 *Karel Doorman* FF with 2 x 4 *Harpoon* SSM, plus 2 x 2 ASTT; 1 *Lynx* (ASW/OTHT) hel

4 *Kortenaer* FF with 2 *Lynx* (ASW/OTHT) hel, 2 x 2 ASTT; plus 2 x 4 *Harpoon*

MINE WARFARE 17

MINELAYERS none, but *Mercuur*, listed under spt and misc, has capability

MINE COUNTERMEASURES 17

15 *Alkmaar* (tripartite) MHC

2 *Dokkum* MSC

AMPHIBIOUS 1

1 *Rotterdam* LPD: capacity 4 LCU or 6 LCA, 600 troops

SUPPORT AND MISCELLANEOUS 10

1 *Amsterdam* AOR (4 *Lynx* or 3 NH-90 or 2 EH-101 hel), 1 *Mercuur* torpedo tender, 2 trg, 4 *Cerberus* div spt, 1 *Zuideruis* AOR (2 *Lynx* hel), 1 *Pelikaan* spt

NAVAL AIR (950)

MR 1 sqn with F-27M (see Air Force)

MR/ASW 2 sqn with P-3C

ASW/SAR 2 sqn with *Lynx* hel

EQPT 13 cbt ac, 22 armed hel

AC 13 P-3C (MR)

HEL 22 *Lynx* (ASW, SAR)

MARINES (2,800)

3 Marine bn (1 cadre); 1 spt bn

RESERVES

1 Marine bn

EQUIPMENT

TOWED ARTY 105mm: 16 lt

MOR 81mm: 18; **120mm**: 28 (2 in store)

ATGW *Dragon*

RL AT-4

SAM *Stinger*

Air Force 11,980

(720 women)

Flying hours 180

FTR/FGA 6 sqn with F-16A/B (1 sqn is tac trg, evaluation and standardisation sqn)

FTR/RECCE 1 sqn with F-16A

MR 2 F-27M (assigned to Navy)

TPT 1 sqn with F-50, F-60, C-130H-30, DC-10-30

TRG 1 sqn with PC-7

HEL

1 sqn with AH-64A

2 sqn with AH-64D

1 sqn with BO-105, SA-316

1 sqn with AS-532U2

SAR 1 sqn with AB-412 SP

AD 8 bty with HAWK SAM (4 in Ge), 4 bty with *Patriot* SAM (in Ge)

EQUIPMENT

170 cbt ac (plus 11 in store), 42 armed hel

AC 170 **F-16A/B** (plus 11 in store) • 2 F-27M (MR) • 2 **F-50** • 4 **F-60** • 2 **C-130H-30** • 2 **DC-10-30** (tkr/tpt) • 1 *Gulfstream* III • 10 **PC-7** (trg)

HEL 3 **AB-412 SP** (SAR) • 9 **SA-316** • 27 **BO-105** • 12* **AH-64A** • 30* **AH-64D** (deliveries start April 1998) • 13 **CH-47D** • 17 **AS-532U2**

MISSILES

AAM AIM-9/L/N *Sidewinder*, AGM-88 HARM

SAM 48 HAWK, 5 *Patriot*, 100 *Stinger*

AD GUNS 25 VL 4/41 *Flycatcher* radar, 75 L/70
    40mm systems

Forces Abroad

GERMANY 3,000; 1 lt bde (1 armd inf, 1 tk bn), plus
spt elms
ICELAND 30: **Navy** 1 P-3C
NETHERLANDS ANTILLES Netherlands, Aruba
and the Netherlands Antilles operate a Coast Guard
Force to combat org crime and drug smuggling. Comd
by Netherlands Commander Caribbean. HQ Curaçao,
bases Aruba and St Maarten **Navy** 20 (to expand); 1
frigate, 1 amph cbt det, 2 P-3C **Air Force** 25; 2 F-27MPA
UN AND PEACEKEEPING
BOSNIA (SFOR II): 1,220; 1 mech inf bn gp. CYPRUS
(UNFICYP): 102. ITALY: 155 (SFOR Air Component) 9
F-16, 1 C-130, 1 F-60, 1 KDC-10. MIDDLE EAST
(UNTSO): 11 obs

Paramilitary 3,600

ROYAL MILITARY CONSTABULARY (*Koninklijke
Marechaussee*) 3,600
(500 conscripts); 3 'div' comprising 10 districts with 72
    'bde'

Foreign Forces

NATO HQ Allied Forces Central Europe
US 490: **Army** 200 **Air Force** 290

Norway

	1996	1997	1998	1999
GDP	kr1,108bn	kr1,085bn		
	($143bn)	($153bn)		
per capita	$22,900	$24,100		
Growth	5.3%	3.5%		
Inflation	1.2%	2.6%		
Publ debt	40.7%	40.6%		
Def exp	kr24.3bn	kr25.4bn		
	($3.8bn)	($3.6bn)		
Def bdgt			kr23.9bn	
			($3.2bn)	
$1 = kroner	6.45	7.07	7.60	
Population		4,407,000		
Age	*13–17*	*18–22*	*23–32*	
Men	138,000	145,000	337,000	
Women	130,000	137,000	317,000	

Total Armed Forces

ACTIVE 28,900

(incl 16,500 conscripts; 400 Joint Services org, 500
Home Guard permanent staff)
Terms of service **Army**, **Navy**, **Air Force**, 12 months, plus
4–5 refresher trg periods

RESERVES

234,000 mobilisable in 24–72 hours; obligation to 44
(conscripts remain with fd army units to age 35,
officers to age 55, regulars to age 60)
Army 101,000 **Navy** 25,000 **Air Force** 25,000 **Home
Guard** some 83,000 on mob

Army 15,200

(incl 10,000 conscripts, 665 recalled reservists)
2 Comd, 4 district comd, 14 territorial regt
North Norway 1 inf/ranger bn, border gd, cadre and
trg units for 1 div (1 armd, 2 inf bde) and 1 indep mech
inf bde
South Norway 2 inf bn (incl Royal Guard), indep units
plus cadre units for 1 mech inf and 1 armd bde

RESERVES

17 inf, 3 ranger plus some indep coy and spt units. 1
arty bn; 10 inf coy, engr coy, sigs units

LAND HOME GUARD 77,000

18 districts each divided into 2–6 sub-districts and
some 465 sub-units (pl)

EQUIPMENT

MBT 170 *Leopard* (111 -1A5NO, 59 -1A1NO)
AIFV 53 NM-135 (M-113/**20mm**), 18 CV 9030N
APC 194 M-113 (incl variants), 18 XA-186 *Sisu*
TOTAL ARTY 222
    TOWED 84: **105mm**: 36 M-101; **155mm**: 48 M-114
    SP **155mm**: 126 M-109A3GN SP
    MRL **227mm**: 12 MLRS
MOR **81mm**: 454 (40 SP incl 28 M-106A1, 12 M-
    125A2)
ATGW 320 TOW-1/-2 incl 126 NM-142 (M-901), 424
    Eryx
RCL **84mm**: 2,517 *Carl Gustav*
AD GUNS **20mm**: 252 Rh-202 (192 in store)
SAM 300 RBS-70 (120 in store)
SURV *Cymberline* (mor)

Navy 6,100

(incl 160 Coastal Defence, 270 Coast Guard and 3,300
conscripts)
OPERATIONAL COMMANDS: 2 JOINT OPERA-
TIONAL COMMANDS, COMNAVSONOR and
COMNAVNON with regional naval commanders and
7 regional Naval districts
BASES Horten, Haakonsvern (Bergen), Olavsvern
(Tromsø)
SUBMARINES 12
    6 *Ula* SS with 8 533mm TT

6 *Kobben* SSC with 8 533mm TT

FRIGATES 4

4 *Oslo* with 2 x 3 ASTT, 1 x 6 *Terne* ASW RL; plus 4 *Penguin* 1 SSM, *Sea Sparrow*

PATROL AND COASTAL COMBATANTS 22

MISSILE CRAFT 24

14 *Hauk* PFM with 6 *Penguin* 1, 2 (Swe TP-613) HWT, 8 *Storm* PFM with 6 *Penguin* 1

MINE WARFARE 14

MINELAYERS 3

2 *Vidar*, coastal (300–400 mines), 1 *Tyr* (amph craft also fitted for minelaying)

MINE COUNTERMEASURES 11

4 *Oskøy* MHC, 5 *Alta* MSC, 2 diver spt

AMPHIBIOUS craft only

5 LCT, 8 S90N LCA

SUPPORT AND MISCELLANEOUS 7

1 *Horten* sub/patrol craft depot ship, 1 *Mariata* AGOR (civ manned), 1 *Valkyrien Torpedo* recovery, 1 *Sverdrup* II, 1 Royal Yacht, 2 *Hessa* trg

ADDITIONAL IN STORE 1 *Sauda* MSC

NAVAL HOME GUARD 5,000

on mob assigned to 10 sub-districts incl 33 areas. Some 400 fishing craft

COASTAL DEFENCE

FORTRESS 17 **75mm**: 6; **120mm**: 3; **127mm**: 6; **150mm**: 2 guns; 6 cable mine and 4 torpedo bty

COAST GUARD (270)

PATROL AND COASTAL COMBATANTS 20

PATROL, OFFSHORE 13

3 *Nordkapp* with 1 *Lynx* hel (SAR/recce), fitted for 6 *Penguin* Mk 2 SSM, 1 *Nornen*, 7 chartered (partly civ manned), 2 *Chartered* (Coast Guard spec)

PATROL INSHSORE 7 PCI

AVN ac 2 P-3N *Orion* **hel** 6 *Lynx* Mk 86 (Air Force-manned)

Air Force 6,700

(incl 3,200 conscripts, 185 women)

Flying hours 180

OPERATIONAL COMMANDS 2 joint with COMSONOR and COMNON

FGA 4 sqn with F-16A/B

FTR 1 trg sqn with F-5A/B

MR 1 sqn with 6 P-3D/N *Orion* (2 assigned to Coast Guard)

TPT 3 sqn

1 with C-130, 1 with DHC-6, 1 with *Falcon* 20C (CAL, ECM)

TRG MFI-15

SAR 1 sqn with *Sea King* Mk 43B

TAC HEL 2 sqn with Bell-412SP

SAM 6 bty NASAMS, 6 bty RB-70

AAA 10 bty L70 (with Fire-Control System 2000) org into 5 gps

EQUIPMENT

79 cbt ac (incl 4 MR), no armed hel

AC 15 F-5A/B (ftr/trg) • 58 F-16A/B • 6* P-3 (4 -D (MR), 2 -N (Coast Guard)) • 6 C-130H (tpt) • 3 *Falcon* 20C (EW/tpt Cal) • 3 DHC-6 (tpt) • 15 MFI-15 (trg)

HEL 18 Bell 412 SP (tpt) • 12 *Sea King* Mk 43B (SAR) • 6 *Lynx* Mk 86 (Coast Guard)

MISSILES

ASM CRV-7, *Penguin* Mk-3, AGM-88 HARM

AAM AIM-9L/N *Sidewinder*, AIM 120 AMRAAM

AA HOME GUARD

(on mob under comd of Air Force): 2,500; 2 bn (9 bty) AA **20mm** NM45

Forces Abroad

UN AND PEACEKEEPING

ANGOLA (UNOMA): 3 obs. **BOSNIA** (SFOR II): up to 700; 1 inf bn. **CROATIA** (UNMOP): 1 obs. **EGYPT** (MFO): 4 Staff Officers. **FYROM** (UNPREDEP): 43 (elm Nordic bn) plus 2 obs. **LEBANON** (UNIFIL): 627; 1 inf bn, 1 service coy, plus HQ personnel. **MIDDLE EAST** (UNTSO): 12 obs

Foreign Forces

US prepositioned eqpt for **Marines**: 1 MEB. **Army**: 1 arty bn. **Air Force**: ground handling eqpt

Ge prepositioned eqpt for 1 arty bn

NATO HQ Allied Forces North Europe (HQ North)

Portugal

	1996	1997	1998	1999
GDP	esc16.5tr	esc17.4tr		
	($93bn)	($99bn)		
per capita	$13,100	$13,900		
Growth	3.0%	3.5%		
Inflation	3.2%	2.1%		
Publ debt	68.7%	65.3%		
Def exp	esc401bn	esc449bn		
	($2.6bn)	($2.6bn)		
Def bdgt			esc286bn	
			($1.5bn)	
FMA (US)	$0.5m	$0.8m	$0.8m	$0.7m
$1 = escudo	154	175	185	
Population		9,873,000		
Age	*13–17*	*18–22*	*23–32*	
Men	347,000	386,000	815,000	
Women	328,000	370,000	796,000	

Total Armed Forces

ACTIVE 53,600

(11,540 conscripts; incl 4,300 Central Staff, 400 in centrally controlled formations/units)
Terms of service **Army** 4–8 months **Navy** and **Air Force** 4–12 months

RESERVES 210,930

(all services) (obligation to age 35) **Army** 210,000 **Navy** 930

Army 24,800

(10,600 conscripts)
5 Territorial Comd (1 mil governance, 2 mil zone, 2 mil region) • 1 mech inf bde (2 mech, 1 tk, 1 fd arty bn) • 3 inf bde (on mob), 1 AB bde • 1 lt intervention bde • 3 composite regt (3 inf bn, 2 coast arty, 2 AA bty) • 3 armd cav regt • 8 inf regt • 2 fd, 1 AD, 1 coast arty regt • 2 engr regt • 1 MP regt • 1 special ops centre

EQUIPMENT

MBT 180: 86 M-48A5, 94 M-60 (8 -A2, 86 -A3)
RECCE 15 V-150 *Chaimite*, 18 ULTRAV M-11
APC 251 M-113, 26 M-557, 84 V-200 *Chaimite*
TOTAL ARTY 290
  TOWED 110: **105mm**: 49 M-101, 24 M-56; **155mm**: 37 M-114A1
  SP 155mm: 6 M-109A2
  MOR 174: **107mm**: 56 M-30 (incl 14 SP); **120mm**: 118 Tampella; **81mm**: incl 22 SP
  COASTAL 20: **150mm**: 8; **152mm**: 6; **234mm**: 6
RCL 84mm: 162 *Carl Gustav*; **89mm**: 53; **90mm**: 46; **106mm**: 128 M-40
ATGW 45 TOW (incl 18 M-113, 4 M-901), 66 *Milan* (incl 6 ULTRAV-11)
AD GUNS 105, incl **20mm**: Rh202; **40mm**: L/60
SAM 15 *Stinger*, 24 *Chaparral*

DEPLOYMENT

AZORES AND MADEIRA 2,000; 3 composite regt (3 inf bn, 2 coast arty, 2 AA bty)

Navy 16,850

(incl 1,500 Marines and 940 conscripts plus 130 recalled reserves)
COMMANDS Naval Area Comd 1 **Subordinate Comds** Azores, Madeira, North Continental, Centre Continental, South Continental
BASES Lisbon (Alfeite), Portimão (HQ Continental Comd), Ponta Delgada (HQ Azores), Funchal (HQ Madeira)
SUBMARINES 3

3 *Albacora* (Fr *Daphné*) SS with 12 550mm TT
FRIGATES 10

3 *Vasco Da Gama* (MEKO 200) with 2 x 3 ASTT (US

Mk 46), plus 2 x 4 *Harpoon* SSM, 1 x 8 *Sea Sparrow* SAM, 1 100mm gun (with 2 *Super Lynx* hel in some)
3 *Commandante João Belo* (Fr *Cdt Rivière*) with 2 x 3 ASTT, 2 x 100mm gun
4 *Baptista de Andrade* with 2 x 3 ASTT; plus 1 100mm gun

PATROL AND COASTAL COMBATANTS 27
PATROL, OFFSHORE 6 *João Coutinho* PCO, hel deck
PATROL, COASTAL 10 *Cacine* PCC
PATROL, INSHORE 10
  5 *Argos*, 5< PCI
RIVERINE 1 *Rio Minho*<
AMPHIBIOUS craft only
  1 LCU, about 4 LCM
SUPPORT AND MISCELLANEOUS 13
  1 *Berrio* (UK *Green Rover*) AO, 8 AGHS, 2 trg, 1 ocean trg, 1 div spt
AIR 5 *Lynx*-Mk 95

MARINES (1,500)
3 bn (2 lt inf, 1 police), spt units
EQUIPMENT
  MOR 120mm: 36

Air Force 7,300

Flying hours F-16: 180; A-7P: 160
1 op air com (COFA)
FGA 3 sqn
  1 with A-7P, 1 with F-16A/B, 1 with *Alpha Jet*
SURVEY 1 sqn with C-212
MR 1 sqn with P-3P
TPT 4 sqn
  1 with C-130, 1 with C-212, 1 with *Falcon* 20 and *Falcon* 50, 1 with SA-330 hel
SAR 2 sqn
  1 with SA-330 hel, 1 with SA-330 hel and C-212
LIAISON 1 sqn with Reims-Cessna FTB-337G
TRG 2 sqn
  1 with *Socata* TB-30 *Epsilon*, 1 with *Alpha Jet*
EQUIPMENT
  68 cbt ac (plus 17 in store), no attack hel
  AC 33 *Alpha Jet* (FGA trg) (plus 17 in store) • 10 **A-7** (8 **-7P** (FGA), 2* **TA-7P** (trg)) • 20 **F-16A/B** (17 **-A**, 3 **-B**) • 5* **P-3P** (MR) (plus 1 in store) • 6 **C-130H** (tpt plus SAR) • 24 **C-212** (20 **-A** (12 tpt/SAR, 1 Nav trg, 2 ECM trg, 5 fisheries protection), 4 **-B** (survey)) • 12 **Cessna 337** (liaison) • 1 *Falcon* **20** (tpt, cal) • 3 *Falcon* 50 (tpt) • 16 *Epsilon* (trg)
  HEL 10 SA-330 (SAR/tpt) • 18 SA-316 (trg, utl)

Forces Abroad

UN AND PEACEKEEPING
ANGOLA (UNOMA): 80 plus 4 obs. **BOSNIA** (SFOR II): 350; 1 inf bn(-). **CROATIA** (UNMOP): 1 obs.

FYROM (UNPREDEP): 1 obs. **WESTERN SAHARA** (MINURSO): 4 obs

Paramilitary 40,900

NATIONAL REPUBLICAN GUARD 20,900
Commando Mk III APC **hel** 7 SA-315
PUBLIC SECURITY POLICE 20,000

Foreign Forces

NATO HQ IBERLANT area at Lisbon (Oeiras)
US 1,050: **Navy** 65 **Air Force** 805 (Azores)

Spain

	1996	1997	1998	1999
GDP	pts73.6tr	pts77.8tr		
	($515bn)	($531bn)		
per capita	$15,100	$16,000		
Growth	2.2%	3.6%		
Inflation	3.6%	2.0%		
Publ debt	74.8%	73.5%		
Def exp	pts1.1tr	pts1.1tr		
	($8.6bn)	($7.7bn)		
Def bdgt			pts897bn	
			($5.8bn)	
FMA (US)	$0.05m			
$1 = peseta	127	146	154	
Population		39,200,000		
Age	*13–17*	*18–22*	*23–32*	
Men	1,316,000	1,545,000	3,333,000	
Women	1,238,000	1,460,000	3,188,000	

Total Armed Forces

ACTIVE 193,950

(99,700 conscripts (to be reduced), some 200 women)
Terms of service 9 months

RESERVES 447,900
Army 436,000 **Navy** 3,900 **Air Force** 8,000

Army 127,000

(78,000 conscripts)
8 Regional Op Comd incl 2 overseas: 1 mech div (1 armd, 2 mech bde) • 2 armd cav bde (1 cadre) • 1 mtn bde • 3 lt inf bde (cadre) • 1 air-portable bde • 1 AB bde • Spanish Legion: 1 bde (3 lt inf, 1 arty, 1 engr bn, 1 ATK coy), 2 regt (each with 1 mech, 1 mot bn, 1 ATK coy) • 3 island garrison: Ceuta and Melilla, Balearic, Canary • 1 arty bde; 1 AD regt • 1 engr bde • 1 Army Avn bde (1 attack, 1 tpt hel bn, 4 utl units) • 1 AD

comd: 5 AD regt incl 1 HAWK SAM, 1 composite *Aspide*/**35mm**, 1 *Roland* bn • 1 Coastal Arty Comd (2 coast arty regt) • 3 special ops bn • Rapid Action Force (FAR) formed from 1 Spanish Legion, 1 AB and 1 air-portable bde (see above)

EQUIPMENT
MBT 725: 209 AMX-30 (150 EM2, 59 ER1), 164 M-48A5E, 244 M-60A3TTS, 108 *Leopard* 2 A4 (Ge tempy transfer)
RECCE 340 BMR-VEC (100 **90mm**, 208 **25mm**, 32 **20mm** gun)
AIFV 5 *Pizarro*
APC 1,995: 1,313 M-113 (incl variants), 682 BMR-600
TOTAL ARTY 1,260 (excluding coastal)
  TOWED 565: **105mm**: 243 M-26, 182 M-56 pack, 56 L 118; **155mm**: 84 M-114
  SP 214: **105mm**: 48 M-108; **155mm**: 102 M-109A1; **203mm**: 64 M-110A2
  COASTAL ARTY 53: **6in**: 44; **305mm**: 6; **381mm**: 3
  MRL 140mm: 14 *Teruel*
  MOR 120mm: 467 (incl 192 SP); plus **81mm**: 1,314 (incl 187 SP)
ATGW 442 *Milan*, 28 HOT, 200 TOW
RCL 106mm: 638
AD GUNS 20mm: 329 GAI-BO1; **35mm**: 92 GDF-002 twin; **40mm**: 183 L/70
SAM 24 I HAWK, 18 *Roland*, 13 *Skyguard/Aspide*, 108 *Mistral*
HELICOPTERS 175 (28 attack)
  3 AS-532UL (being delivered), 53 HU-10B, 70 HA/HR-15 (31 with **20mm** guns, 28 with HOT, 9 trg), 6 HU-18, 11 HR-12B, 18 HT-21, 17 HT-17 (incl 9-D models)
SURV 2 AN/TPQ-36 (arty, mor)

DEPLOYMENT
CEUTA AND MELILLA 11,500; 2 armd cav, 2 Spanish Legion, 2 mot inf, 2 engr, 2 arty regt; 2 lt AD bn, 1 coast arty bn
BALEARIC ISLANDS 2,400; 1 mot inf regt: 3 mot inf bn; 1 mixed arty regt: 1 fd arty, 1 AD; 1 engr bn
CANARY ISLANDS 6,000; 3 mot inf regt each 2 mot inf bn; 1 mot inf bn, 2 mixed arty regt each: 1 fd arty, 1 AD bn; 2 engr bn

Navy 36,950

(incl 860 Naval Air, 6,900 Marines and 10,700 conscripts) plus 7,900 civilians
FLEET COMMANDS 5
NAVAL ZONES Cantabrian, Strait (of Gibraltar), Mediterranean, Canary (Islands)
BASES El Ferrol (La Coruña) (Cantabrian HQ), San Fernando (Cadiz) (Strait HQ), Rota (Cadiz) (Fleet HQ), Cartagena (Murcia) (Mediterranean HQ), Las Palmas (Canary Islands HQ), Palma de Mallorca and Mahón (Menorca)

SUBMARINES 8
4 *Galerna* (Fr *Agosta*) with F-17 and L-5 HWT
4 *Delfin* (Fr *Daphné*) with F-17 and L-5 HWT

PRINCIPAL SURFACE COMBATANTS 18
CARRIERS 1 (CVV) *Príncipe de Asturias* (16,200t); air gp: typically 6 to 10 AV-8S/EAV-8B FGA, 4 to 6 SH-3D ASW hel, 2 SH-3D AEW hel, 2 utl hel

FRIGATES 17
FFG 11 (AAW/ASW)
6 *Santa Maria* (US *Perry*) with 1 x 1 SM-1 MR SAM/*Harpoon* SSM launcher, 2 SH-60B hel, 2 x 3 ASTT; plus 1 76mm gun, 1–2 S-70L hel
5 *Baleares* with 1 x 1 SM-1 MR SAM, 1 x 8 ASROC, 4 324mm and 2 484mm ASTT; plus 2 x 4 *Harpoon*, 1 127mm gun
FF 6 *Descubierta* with 2 x 3 ASTT, 1 x 2 ASW RL; plus 2 x 2 *Harpoon* SSM

PATROL AND COASTAL COMBATANTS 32
PATROL, OFFSHORE 6
4 *Serviola*, 2 *Chilreu*
PATROL, COASTAL 10 *Anaga* PCC
PATROL, INSHORE 16
6 *Barceló* PFI, 10 PCI<

MINE COUNTERMEASURES 12
3 *Guadalete* (US *Aggressive*) MSO
8 *Júcar* (US *Adjutant*) MSC
1 *Segura* MSC

AMPHIBIOUS 4
2 *Castilla* (US *Paul Revere*) amph tpt, capacity: 1,600 tps; plus some 15 amph craft
2 *Hernán Cortés* (US *Newport*) LST, capacity: 400 troops, 500t vehicles, 1 *Galicia* LPD, 3 LCVPs, 1 LCPL
Plus 13 craft: 3 LCT, 2 LCU, 8 LCM

SUPPORT AND MISCELLANEOUS 34
1 AOR, 2 AO, 5 ocean tugs, 3 diver spt, 2 tpt/spt, 3 water carriers, 6 AGHS, 1 AGOR, 1 sub salvage, 1 AK, 5 trg craft, 4 sail trg

NAVAL AIR (1,000)
(290 conscripts)
Flying hours 160
FGA 1 sqn with 9 AV-8B/9 AV-8B plus
LIAISON 1 sqn with 3 *Citation* II
HELICOPTERS 4 sqn
ASW 2 sqn
1 with SH-3D/G *Sea King* (mod to SH-3H standard)
1 with SH-60B (LAMPS-III fit)
COMD/TPT 1 sqn with AB-212
TRG 1 sqn with Hughes 500
AEW 1 flt with SH-3D (*Searchwater* radar)

EQUIPMENT
18 cbt ac, 25 armed hel
Flying hours 160
AC 9 EAV-8B, 9 EAV-8B plus (trg) • 3 *Citation* II (liaison)

HEL 10 AB-212 (ASW/SAR) • 12 SH-3D (9 -H ASW, 3 -D AEW) •10 Hughes 500 (trg) • 6 SH-60B (ASW)

MARINES (6,900)
(2,800 conscripts)
1 marine bde (3,500); 2 inf, 1 spt bn; 3 arty bty
5 marine garrison gp

EQUIPMENT
MBT 16 M-60A3
AFV 17 *Scorpion* lt tk, 19 LVTP-7 AAV, 28 BLR APC
TOWED ARTY 105mm: 12 M-56 pack
SP ARTY 155mm: 6 M-109A
ATGW 12 TOW, 18 *Dragon*
RL 90mm: C-90C
RCL 106mm: 54
SAM 12 *Mistral*

Air Force 30,000

(11,000 conscripts)
Flying hours EF-18: 180; F-5: 220; *Mirage* F-1: 180
CENTRAL AIR COMMAND (MACEN) 4 wg
FTR 2 sqn with EF-18 (F-18 *Hornet*)
RECCE 1 sqn with RF-4C
TPT 7 sqn
2 with C-212, 2 with CN-235, 1 with *Falcon* (20, 50, 900), 1 with Boeing 707 (tkr/tpt), 1 with AS-332 (tpt)
SPT 5 sqn
1 with CL-215, 1 with C-212 (EW) and *Falcon* 20, 1 with C-212, AS-332 (SAR), 1 with C-212 and Cessna *Citation*, 1 with Boeing 707
TRG 4 sqn
1 with C-212, 1 with Beech (*Baron*), 1 with C-101, 1 with Beech (*Bonanza*)

EASTERN AIR COMMAND (MALEV) 2 wg
FTR 4 sqn
2 with EF-18 (F-18 *Hornet*), 1 with EF-18 (/trg/FTR), 1 with *Mirage* F1
TPT 2 sqn
1 with C-130H, 1 tkr/tpt with KC-130H
SPT 1 sqn with **ac** C-212 (SAR) **hel** AS-330

STRAIT AIR COMMAND (MAEST) 4 wg
FTR 3 sqn
2 with *Mirage* F-1 CE/BE
1 with EF/A-18
FGA 2 sqn with F-5B
MR 1 sqn with P-3A/B
TRG 6 sqn
2 hel with *Hughes* 300C, S-76C, 1 with C-212, 1 with E-26 (*Tamiz*), 1 with C-101, 1 with C-212

CANARY ISLANDS AIR COMMAND (MACAN) 1 wg
FGA 1 sqn with *Mirage* F-1EE
TPT 1 sqn with C-212
SAR 1 sqn with **ac** F-27 **hel** AS-332 (SAR)

LOGISTIC SUPPORT COMMAND (MALOG)

1 trials sqn with C-101, C-212 and F-5A, EF/A-18

EQUIPMENT

193 cbt ac, no armed hel

AC 83 **EF/A-18 A/B** (ftr, OCU) • 23 **F-5B** (FGA) • 66 *Mirage* **F-1CF/-BE/-EE** • 14* **RF-4C** (recce) 7* **P-3** (2 **-A** (MR), 5 **-B** (MR)) • 4 **Boeing 707** (tkr/tpt) • 12 **C-130**: 7 **-H** (tpt), 5 **KC-130H** (tkr) • 78 **C-212** (34 tpt, 9 SAR, 6 recce, 26 trg, 2 EW, 1 trials) • 2 **Cessna 560** *Citation* (recce) • 76 **C-101** (trg) • 15 **CL-215** (spt) • 5 *Falcon* **20** (3 VIP tpt, 2 EW) • 1 *Falcon* **50** (VIP tpt) • 2 *Falcon* **900** (VIP tpt) • 21 **Do-27** (U-9, liaison/trg) • 3 **F-27** (SAR) • 37 **E-26** (trg) • 20 **CN-235** (18 tpt, 2 VIP tpt) • 5 **E-20** (*Baron*) trg • 25 **E-24** (*Bonanza*) trg

HEL 5 **SA-330** (SAR) • 16 **AS-332** (10 SAR, 6 tpt) • 13 **Hughes 300C** (trg) • 8 **S-76C** (trg)

MISSILES

AAM AIM-7 *Sparrow*, AIM-9 *Sidewinder*, AIM-120 AMRAAM, R-530

ASM *Maverick, Harpoon*, AGM-88A HARM

SAM *Mistral, Skyguard/Aspide*

Forces Abroad

UN AND PEACEKEEPING

ADRIATIC (*Sharp Guard* if re-implemented): 1 FFG. **BOSNIA** (SFOR II): 1,600; 1 inf bn gp, 12 Obs, 2 TACP. SFOR **Air Component** 8 F/A-18, 2 KC-130 (tkr), 1 CASA-212 (spt ac)

Paramilitary 75,760

GUARDIA CIVIL 75,000

(2,200 conscripts); 9 regions, 19 inf *tercios* (regt) with 56 rural bn, 6 traffic security gp, 6 rural special ops gp, 1 special sy bn; 22 BLR APC, 18 Bo-105, 5 BK-117 hel

GUARDIA CIVIL DEL MAR 760

32 PCI

Foreign Forces

US 2,430: **Navy** 2,200 **Air Force** 230

Turkey

	1996	1997	1998	1999
GDP	L14,345tr ($176bn)	L29,055tr ($191bn)		
per capita	$5,600	$6,000		
Growth	7.2%	6.3%		
Inflation	80.4%	85.7%		
Debt	$80bn	$85bn		
Def exp	L612tr ($7.5bn)	L1,232tr ($8.1bn)		

contd	1996	1997	1998	1999
Def bdgt			L2,179tr ($8.2bn)	
FMA (US)	$321m	$177m	$22m	$1.5m
$1 = lira	81,405	151,865	265,690	
Population	62,600,000 (Kurds ε20 23%)			
Age	*13–17*	*18–22*	*23–32*	
Men	3,268,000	3,260,000	5,809,000	
Women	3,148,000	3,075,000	5,523,000	

Total Armed Forces

ACTIVE ε639,000

(ε528,000 conscripts) *Terms of service* 18 months

RESERVES 378,700

(all to age 41) **Army** 258,700 **Navy** 55,000 **Air Force** 65,000

Army ε525,000

(ε462,000 conscripts)

4 army HQ: 9 corps HQ • 1 mech div (1 mech, 1 armd bde) • 1 mech div HQ • 1 inf div • 14 armd bde (each 2 armd, 2 mech inf, 2 arty bn) • 17 mech bde (each 2 armd, 2 mech inf, 1 arty bn) • 9 inf bde (each 4 inf, 1 arty bn) • 4 cdo bde (each 4 cdo bn) • 1 inf regt • 1 Presidential Guard regt • 5 border def regt • 26 border def bn

RESERVES

4 coastal def regt • 23 coastal def bn

EQUIPMENT

Figures in ( ) were reported to CFE on 1 Jan 1998

MBT 4,205 (2,542): 2,876 M-48 A5T1/T2, 932 M-60 (658 -A3, 274-A1), 397 *Leopard* (170-1A1, 227-1A3)

RECCE some *Akrep*

TOTAL AIFV/APC (2,529)

AIFV 280 AIFV

APC 805 AAPC, 2,813 M-113/-A1/-A2

TOTAL ARTY 4,274 (2,839)

TOWED 1,552: **105mm**: M-101A1; **150mm**: 62 Skoda (in store); **155mm**: 517 M-114A1\A2, 171 M-59 (in store); **203mm**: 162 M-115

SP 820: **105mm**: 362 M-52A1, 26 M-108T; **155mm**: 4 M-44A1, 164 M-44T1; **175mm**: 36 M-107; **203mm**: 9 M-55, 219 M-110A2

MRL 60: **107mm**: 48; **227mm**: 12 MLRS

MOR 1,842: **107mm**: 1,264 M-30 (some SP); **120mm**: 578 (some 170 SP); plus **81mm**: 3,792 incl SP

ATGW 943: 186 *Cobra*, 365 TOW SP, 392 *Milan*

RL M-72

RCL **57mm**: 923 M-18; **75mm**: 617; **106mm**: 2,329 M-40A1

AD GUNS 1,664: **20mm**: 439 GAI-DO1; **35mm**: 120

GDF-001/-003; **40mm**: 803 L60/70, 40 T-1, 262 M-42A1
SAM 108 *Stinger*, 789 *Redeye* (being withdrawn)
SURV AN/TPQ-36 (arty, mor)
AC 168: 3 Cessna 421, 34 *Citabria*, 4 B-200, 4 T-42A, 98 U-17B, 25 T-41D
ATTACK HEL 37 (26) AH-1W/P
SPT HEL 254: 8 S-70A, 19 AS-532UL, 12 AB-204B, 64 AB-205A, 23 AB-206, 2 AB-212, 28 H-300C, 3 OH-58B, 94 UH-1H
UAV CL-89 (AN/USD-501), *Gnat* 750, *Falcon* 600

Navy 51,000

(incl 3,100 Marines and 34,500 conscripts)
BASES Ankara (Navy HQ and COMEDNOREAST), Gölcük (HQ Fleet), Istanbul (HQ Northern area and Bosphorus), Izmir (HQ Southern area and Aegean), Eregli (HQ Black Sea), Iskenderun, Aksaz Bay, Mersin (HQ Mediterranean)

SUBMARINES 16

6 *Atilay* (Ge Type 209/1200) with SST-4 HWT
5 *Canakkale/Burakreis†* (plus 2 non-op) (US *Guppy*) with Mk 37 HWT
2 *Hizirreis* (US *Tang*) with Mk 37 HWT
3 *Preveze* (Ge Type 209/1400)

PRINCIPAL SURFACE COMBATANTS 21

DESTROYERS 2

2 *Kilic Ali Pasa* (US *Gearing*) with *Harpoon* SSM, 8 ASROC, 4 x 127mm gun, 6 x 324mm TT

FRIGATES 19

3 *Gaziantep* (US *Perry*)
4 *Yavuz* (Ge MEKO 200) with 1 AB-212 hel (ASW/OTHT), 2 x 3 ASTT; plus 2 x 4 *Harpoon* SSM, 1 127mm gun
2 *Berk* with 2 x 3 ASTT, 2 Mk 11 *Hedgehog*
8 *Muavenet* (US *Knox*-class) with 1 x 8 ASROC, 4 ASTT; plus *Harpoon* (from ASROC launcher), 1 127mm gun
2 *Barbaros* (MOD Ge MEKO 200) with 2 x 4 *Harpoon* SSM, 8 x *Sea Sparrow* SSM, 1 127mm gun, 6 324mm TT, 1 AB-212 hel

PATROL AND COASTAL COMBATANTS 50

MISSILE CRAFT 19

1 *Kilic* with 8 x *Harpoon* SSM, 1 x 76mm gun
8 *Dogan* (Ge Lürssen-57) PFM with 2 x 4 *Harpoon* SSM
8 *Kartal* (Ge *Jaguar*) PFM with 4 *Penguin* 2 SSM, 2 533mm TT
2 *Yildiz* with 2 x 4 *Harpoon* SSM, 1 76mm gun

PATROL CRAFT 31

COASTAL 10

1 *Girne* PFC, 6 *Sultanhisar* PCC, 3 *Trabzon* PCC (1 used as AGI)

INSHORE 21

1 *Bora* (US *Asheville*) PFI, 12 AB-25 PCI, 4 AB-21, 4 PGM-71

MINE WARFARE 29

MINELAYERS 3

1 *Nusret* (400 mines), 1 *Mersin* (US LSM) coastal (400 mines), 1 *Mehmetcik* (plus 3 ML tenders) (*Bayraktar*, *Sarucabey* and *Çakabey* LST have minelaying capability)

MINE COUNTERMEASURES 26

5 *Circe* MHC
11 *Selcuk* (US *Adjutant*) MSC
6 *Karamürsel* (Ge *Vegesack*) MSC
4 *Foça* (US *Cape*) MSI (plus 8 MCM tenders)

AMPHIBIOUS 8

1 *Osman Gazi*: capacity 980 tps, 17 tk, 4 LCVP
2 *Ertugal* (US *Terrebonne Parish*): capacity 400 tps, 18 tk
2 *Bayraktar* (US LST-512): capacity 200 tps, 16 tk
2 *Sarucabey*: capacity 600 tps, 11 tk
1 *Çakabey*: capacity 400 tps, 9 tk
Plus about 59 craft: 35 LCT, 2 LCU, 22 LCM

SUPPORT AND MISCELLANEOUS 27

1 *Akar* AO, 5 spt tkr, 2 Ge *Rhein* plus 3 other depot ships, 3 salvage/rescue, 2 survey, 3 tpt, 5 tugs, 2 repair, 1 div spt

NAVAL AVIATION

13 armed hel
ASW 3 AB-204AS, 13* AB-212 ASW
TRG 7 TB-20

MARINES (3,100)

1 regt, HQ, 3 bn, 1 arty bn (18 guns), spt units

Air Force 63,000

(31,500 conscripts) 2 tac air forces, 1 tpt comd, 1 air trg comd, 1 air log comd
Flying hours 180
FGA 11 sqn
  1 OCU with F-5A/B, 4 (1 OCU) with F-4E, 6 (1 OCU) with F-16C/D
FTR 7 sqn
  2 with F-5A/B, 2 with F-4E, 3 with F-16C/D
RECCE 2 sqn with RF-4E
TPT 5 sqn
  1 with C-130B/E, 1 with C-160D, 2 with CN-235, 1 VIP tpt unit with *Gulfstream*, *Citation* and CN 235
TKR 2 KC-135R
LIAISON 10 base flts with **ac** T-33 **hel** UH-1H
TRG 3 sqn
  1 with T-41, 1 with SF-260D, 1 with T-38 trg schools with **ac** CN-235 **hel** UH-1H
SAM 4 sqn with 92 *Nike Hercules*, 2 sqn with 86 *Rapier*
EQUIPMENT
  440 cbt ac, no attack hel
  AC 175 **F-16C/D** (149 -C, 26 -D) • 87 **F-5A/B** (FGA) • 178 **F-4E** (92 FGA, 47 ftr, 39 RF-4E (recce)) • 13 **C-130** (tpt) • 7 **KC-135R** • 19 **C-160D** (tpt) • 2 *Citation* VII (VIP) • 44 **CN-235** (tpt) • 38 **SF-**

260D (trg) • 34 **T-33** (trg) • 60 **T-37** trg • 70 **T-38** (trg) • 28 **T-41** (trg)

HEL 20 **UH-1H** (tpt, liaison, base flt, trg schools)

MISSILES

AAM AIM-7E *Sparrow*, AIM 9 S *Sidewinder*, AIM-120 AMRAAM

ASM AGM-65 *Maverick*, AGM-88 HARM, *Popeye* 1

Forces Abroad

CYPRUS 30–33,000; 1 corps; 282 M-48A5 MBT; 200 M-113, 50 AAPC APC; 126 **105mm**, 36 **155mm**, 8 **203mm** towed; 26 **155mm** SP; 30 **120mm**, 102 **107mm**, 175 **81mm** mor; 84 **40mm** AA guns; 20mm, 35mm; **ac** 3 **hel** 4

UN AND PEACEKEEPING

BOSNIA (SFOR II): 1,300; 1 inf bn gp. **IRAQ/ KUWAIT** (UNIKOM): 7 obs. **ITALY** (SFOR Air Component): 18 F-16 C

Paramilitary 182,200

GENDARMERIE/**NATIONAL GUARD** (Ministry of Interior, Ministry of Defence in war) 180,000

50,000 reserve; some *Akrep* recce, 535 BTR-60/-80, 25 *Condor* APC **ac** 2 Dornier 28D, 0-1E **hel** 19 Mi-17, 8 AB-240B, 6 AB-205A, 8 AB-206A, 1 AB-212, 14 S-70A

COAST GUARD 2,200

(1,400 conscripts); 48 PCI, 16 PCI<, plus boats, 2 tpt

Opposition

KURDISTAN WORKERS PARTY (PKK) ε5,000

plus 50,000 spt militia

Foreign Forces

NATO HQ Allied Land Forces South Eastern Europe (LANDSOUTHEAST), HQ 6 Allied Tactical Air Force (6 ATAF)

OPERATION NORTHERN WATCH

UK Air Force 230; 6 *Tornado* GR-1/1A, 1 VC-10 (tkr) **US** 1,440: **Army** 22 **Navy** 20 **Air Force** 1,4000; 1 wg (**ac** on det only), numbers vary (incl F-16, F-15C, KC-135, E-3B/C, C-12, HC-130, HH-60)

ISRAEL Periodic det of F-16 at Akinci
US Installations for seismic monitoring

United Kingdom

	1996	1997	1998	1999
GDP	£742bn	£786bn		
	($1.2tr)	($1.3tr)		
per capita	$19,600	$20,700		
Growth	2.2%	3.3%		
Inflation	2.5%	3.1%		
Publ debt	61.2%	60.3%		
Def exp	£22.1bn	£21.8bn		
	($34.5bn)	($35.7bn)		
Def bdgt			£22.3bn	
			($37.2bn)	
$1 = pound	0.64	0.61	0.60	
Population		58,644,000		

(*Northern Ireland* 1,600,000; Protestant 56%, Roman Catholic 41%)

Age	13–17	18–22	23–32
Men	1,862,000	1,839,000	4,292,000
Women	1,775,000	1,752,000	4,124,000

Total Armed Forces

ACTIVE 210,940

(incl 15,125 women, some 4,150 locally enlisted)

RESERVES

Army 246,000 (Regular 189,300) **Territorial Army** (TA) 56,700 **Navy/Marines** 27,200 (Regular 23,600, Volunteers and Auxiliary Forces 3,600) **Air Force** 46,400 (Regular 44,800, Volunteers 1,600)

Strategic Forces (1,900)

SLBM 48 msl in 3 SSBN
  SSBN 3
  3 *Vanguard* SSBN capable of carrying 16 *Trident* (D5); will not deploy with more than 48 warheads per boat (some *Trident* D5 missiles loaded with single warheads for sub-strategic role)
EARLY WARNING
Ballistic-Missile Early-Warning System (BMEWS) station at Fylingdales

Army 113,900

(incl 7,400 women and 4,150 enlisted outisde the UK, of whom 3,800 are Gurkhas)
regt normally bn size
1 Land Comd HQ • 3 Mil Districts, 3 (regenerative) div HQ (former mil districts), 1 UK Spt Comd (Germany) (UKSC(G)) • Joint Rapid Deployment Force HQ • 1 armd div with 3 armd bde, 3 arty, 4 engr, 1 avn, 1 AD regt • 1 mech div with 2 mech (*Warrior/ Saxon*), 1 AB bde, 3 arty, 2 engr, 1 avn, 1 AD regt • ARRC Corps tps: 3 armd recce, 3 MLRS, 2 AD, 1 engr

regt (EOD) • 1 air-mobile bde • 14 inf bde HQ (3 control ops in N. Ireland, remainder mixed regular and TA for trg/administrative purposes only)
Summary of combat arm units
    8 armd regt • 3 armd recce regt • 4 mech inf bn (*Saxon*) • 8 armd inf bn (*Warrior*) • 25 inf bn (incl 2 air mobile, 2 Gurkha) • 3 AB bn (2 only in para role) • 1 SF (SAS) regt • 12 arty regt (3 MLRS, 5 SP, 3 fd (1 cdo, 1 AB, 1 air-mobile), 1 trg) • 4 AD regt (2 *Rapier*, 2 *Javelin*) • 10 engr regt • 5 avn regt (2 ATK, 2 air mobile, 1 general)

HOME SERVICE FORCES

N. Ireland 4,600: 6 inf bn (2,700 full-time)
Gibraltar 360: 1 regt (160 full-time)

RESERVES

Territorial Army 1 armd recce, 4 lt recce, 1 NBC def, 1 armd delivery regt, 31 inf bn, 2 AB (not in role), 2 SF (SAS), 3 arty (2 fd, 1 obs), 3 AD, 9 engr, 1 avn regt

EQUIPMENT

Figures in ( ) were reported to CFE on 1 Jan 1998
    MBT 545 (505): 58 *Challenger* 2, 426 *Challenger*, 61 *Chieftain* (disposal in progress)
    LT TK 3 *Scorpion* (in store - for disposal)
    RECCE 315 *Scimitar*, 136 *Sabre*, 11 *Fuchs*
    AIFV 575 *Warrior* (plus 219 'look-alikes'), 11 AFV 432 *Rarden*
    APC 693 AFV 432 (plus 939 'look-alikes'), 526 FV 103 *Spartan*, 657 *Saxon* (incl 'look-alikes'), 5 *Saracen* (plus 2 in store)
    TOTAL ARTY 459
        TOWED 217: **105mm**: 162 L-118, 7 L-119; **140mm**: 1 5.5in; **155mm**: 47 FH-70
        SP 155mm: 179 AS-90
        MRL 227mm: 63 MLRS
    MOR 81mm: 543 (incl 110 SP)
    ATGW 793 *Milan*, 48 *Swingfire* (FV 102 *Striker* SP), TOW
    RL 94mm: LAW-80
    RCL 84mm: 302 *Carl Gustav* (in store)
    SAM 56 *Starstreak* (SP), some 298 *Javelin* and *Starburst*, 24 *Rapier* (some 24 SP)
    SURV 42 *Cymbeline* (mor)
    AC 7 BN-2
    ATTACK HEL 269: 154 SA-341, 115 *Lynx* AH-1/-7/-9
    TRG HEL 12 AS 350 *Ecureuil*
    UAV *Phoenix* (from 1 December 1998)
    LANDING CRAFT 2 LCL, 6 RCL, 4 LCVP, 4 workboats

Navy (RN) 44,500

(incl 6,790 Fleet Air Arm, 6,500 Royal Marines Command, 3,260 women)

ROYAL FLEET AUXILIARY (RFA)

(2,020 civilians) mans major spt vessels

ROYAL MARITIME AUXILIARY SERVICE (RMAS)

(280 civilians) provides harbour/coastal services
BASES UK Northwood (HQ Fleet, CINCEASTLANT), Devonport (HQ), Faslane, Portsmouth **Overseas** Gibraltar

SUBMARINES 15

STRATEGIC SUBMARINES 3 SSBN
TACTICAL SUBMARINES 12
    SSN 12
    5 *Swiftsure* with *Spearfish* or Mk 24 HWT and *Harpoon* USGW, one with *Tomahawk* Block III TLAM (C)
    7 *Trafalgar*

PRINCIPAL SURFACE COMBATANTS 38

CARRIERS 3 *Invincible* CVS each with **ac** 8 *Sea Harrier* V/STOL **hel** 12 *Sea King*, up to 9 ASW, 3 AEW; plus 1 x 2 *Sea Dart* SAM (includes 1 *Invincible* at extended readiness)
DDG 12 *Birmingham* with 1 x 2 *Sea Dart* SAM; plus 1 *Lynx* hel, 2 x 3 ASTT, 1 114mm gun (2 in refit)
FRIGATES 23
    4 *Cornwall* (Type 22 Batch 3) with 1 *Sea King* or 2 *Lynx* hel (*Sting Ray* LWT), 2 x 3 ASTT; plus 2 x 4 *Harpoon* SSM, 1 114mm gun
    6 *Broadsword* Type 22 Batch 2 with 2 *Lynx* hel (2 with 1 *Sea King*), 2 x 3 ASTT
    13 *Norfolk* (Type 23) with 1 *Lynx* hel, 2 x 2 ASTT, plus 2 x 4 *Harpoon* SSM, 1 114mm gun

PATROL AND COASTAL COMBATANTS 26

PATROL, OFFSHORE 10
    2 *Castle*, 6 *Island*, 2 *River* PCO
PATROL, INSHORE 16
    16 *Archer* (incl 4 trg)

MINE WARFARE 19

MINELAYER no dedicated minelayer, but all submarines have limited minelaying capability
MINE COUNTERMEASURES 19
    13 *Hunt* MCO, 6 *Sandown* MHC

AMPHIBIOUS 7

    2 *Fearless* LPD (incl 1 in extended readiness) with 4 LCU, 4 LCVP; capacity 400 tps, 15 tk, 3 hel
    5 *Sir Bedivere* LSL; capacity 340 tps, 16 tk, 1 hel (RFA manned)
    Plus 33 craft: 12 LCU, 19 LCVP
    (see Army for additional amph lift capability)

SUPPORT AND MISCELLANEOUS 21

UNDER WAY SUPPORT 9
    2 *Fort Victoria* AOR, 2 *Olwen*, 3 *Rover* AO, 2 *Fort Grange* AF
MAINTENANCE AND LOGISTIC 4 AOT
SPECIAL PURPOSE 2
    1 *Endurance*, 1 avn trg ship
SURVEY 6
    1 *Scott*, 2 *Bulldog*, 1 *Roebuck*, 1 *Herald*, 1 *Gleaner*

FLEET AIR ARM (6,790)

(320 women)

Flying hours *Harrier*: 200

A typical CVS air group consists of 8 *Harrier*, 9 *Sea King* (ASW), 3 *Sea King* (AEW)

FTR/ATK 4 ac sqn with *Sea Harrier* F/A2 plus 1 trg sqn with *Harrier* T-4/-8

ASW 5 hel sqn with *Sea King* Mk-5/6

ASW/ATK 2 sqn with *Lynx* HAS-3 HMA8 (in indep flt)

AEW 1 hel sqn with *Sea King* AEW-2

COMMANDO SPT 3 hel sqn with *Sea King* HC-4

SAR 1 hel sqn with *Sea King* MK-5

TRG 1 sqn with *Jetstream*

FLEET SPT 13 *Mystère-Falcon* (civil registration), 1 Cessna *Conquest* (civil registration), 1 Beech *Baron* (civil registration) 5 GROB 115 (op under contract)

TPT *Jetstream*

EQUIPMENT

33 cbt ac (plus 21 in store), 109 armed hel (plus 29 in store)

AC 28 *Sea Harrier* FRS-2 (plus 19 in store) • 5* **T-4/ T-8** (trg) plus 2 in store • 15 *Hawk* (spt) • 9 *Jetstream* • 7 **T-2** (trg) • 2 **T-3** (spt) (plus 4 in store)

HEL 92 *Sea King* (49 **HAS-5/6** (plus 13 in store), 33 **HC-4** (plus 4 in store), 10 **AEW-2** (plus 3 in store) • 40 *Lynx* **HAS-3** (plus 13 in store) • 20 *Lynx* **HAS-8** (plus 3 in store), 3 **EH-101** *Merlin*

MISSILES

ASM *Sea Skua, Sea Eagle*

AAM AIM-9 *Sidewinder*, AIM-120C AMRAAM

ROYAL MARINES COMMAND (6,500, incl RN and Army)

1 cdo bde: 3 cdo; 1 cdo arty regt (Army) incl 1 bty (TA); 1 cdo log regt (joint service); 1 cdo AD bty (Army), 2 cdo engr (1 Army, 1 TA), 1 aslt sqn; 3 hel sqn ((RN) 1 lt, 2 spt) • 1 bde patrol • 1 AD tp • 2 aslt sqn • 1 gp (*Commachio*) • Special Boat Service (SF) HQ. 5 sqn

EQUIPMENT

MOR 81mm

ATGW *Milan*

SAM *Javelin, Blowpipe*

HEL 9 SA-341 (*Gazelle*); plus 3 in store, 6 *Lynx* AH-7

AMPH 24 RRC, 1 LCVP, 4 LACV

Air Force (RAF) 52,540

(incl 4,465 women)

Flying hours *Tornado* 215; *Harrier*: 184; *Jaguar*: 200

FGA/BBR 6 sqn

4 with *Tornado* GR-1, 2 with *Tornado* GR-1B (maritime attack)

FGA 5 sqn

3 with *Harrier* GR-7, 2 with *Jaguar* GR-1A/B

FTR 6 sqn with *Tornado* F-3 plus 1 flt in the Falklands

RECCE 4 sqn

2 with *Tornado* GR-1A, 1 with *Canberra* PR-9, 1 with *Jaguar* GR-1A/B

MR 3 sqn with *Nimrod* MR-2

AEW 2 sqn with E-3D *Sentry*

ELINT 1 ELINT with *Nimrod* R-1

TPT/TKR 3 sqn

2 with VC-10 C1-K-2/-3/-4, 1 with *Tristar* K-1/KC-1/-2 (tkr/tpt), plus 1 flt in the Falklands

TPT 4 sqn with *Hercules* C-1/-3

LIAISON 1 comms VIP sqn with **ac** HS-125, BAe 146 **hel** AS-355 (*Twin Squirrel*)

TARGET FACILITY/CAL 1 sqn with *Hawk* T-1/T-1A

OCU 7: *Tornado* GR-1 (with 1 wpn conversion unit), *Tornado* F-3, *Jaguar* GR-1A/T2A, *Harrier* GR-7/-T10, *Hercules, Nimrod* MR-2

TRG *Hawk* T-1/-1A/-1W, *Jetstream* T-1, *Bulldog* T-1, HS-125 *Dominie* T-1, *Tucano* T-1, *Firefly*

TAC HEL 8 sqn

1 with CH-47 (*Chinook*), and SA-341 (*Gazelle* HT3), 1 with *Wessex* HC-2, 2 with SA-330 (*Puma*), 1 with CH-47 and *Sea King* HAR3, 2 with CH-47, 1 with *Wessex* HC-2 and SA-330 (*Puma*)

SAR 2 hel sqn with *Sea King* HAR-3

TRG *Sea King*, Tri-Service Defence Helicopter School with AS-350 (*Single Squirrel*) and Bell 412

EQUIPMENT

450 cbt ac, incl 25 MR (plus 105 in store), no armed hel

AC 248 *Tornado* (90 **GR-1**, 26 **GR-1A**, 26 **GR-1B**, 106 **F-3** (plus 40 *Tornado* in store)• 54 *Jaguar* (44 **GR-1A/-B**, 10 **T-2A/B** (plus 26 in store)) • 69 *Harrier* (58 **GR-7**, 11 **T-10** (plus 22 **GR-7** in store)) • 98 *Hawk* **T-1/1-A-W** (54* (T1-A) tac weapons unit *Sidewinder*-capable) (plus 22 in store) • 7 *Canberra* (2 **T-4**, 5 **PR-9**) • 28 *Nimrod* (3 **R-1** (ECM), 25* **MR-2** (MR)) • 7 *Sentry* (**E-3D**) (AEW) • 9 *Tristar* (2 **K-1** (tkr/tpt), 4 **KC-1** (tkr/cgo), 3 **C-2A** (tpt)) • 24 **VC-10** (12 **C-1/C-1K** (strategic tpt to be mod to tkr/tpt), 3 **K-2** (tkr), 4 **K-3** (tkr), 5 **K-4**) • 55 *Hercules* **C-1/C-3** • 16 **BAe-125** (10 **T-1** (trg), 6 **CC-2/-3** (liaison)) • 2 *Islander* **CC-MK2** • 3 **BAe-146** (VIP tpt) • 73 *Tucano* (trg) (plus 41 in store) • 11 *Jetstream* (trg) • 106 *Bulldog* (trg) • 43 *Firefly*

HEL 15 *Wessex* • 34 **CH-47** • 39 **SA-330** (*Puma*) • 25 *Sea King* • 38 **AS-350B** (*Single Squirrel*) • 2 **AS-355** (*Twin Squirrel*) • 9 **Bell-412EP**

MISSILES

ASM AGM-84D-1 *Harpoon, Sea Eagle*

AAM ASRAAM, AIM-9L *Sidewinder, Sky Flash*

ARM ALARM

ROYAL AIR FORCE REGIMENT

5 fd sqn, 6 SAM sqn with 40 *Rapier* fire units

RESERVES (Royal Auxiliary Air Force): 3 fd def sqn, 3 Maritime HQ Units, 1 sqn Air Movements, 1 sqn Aero-medical

4 sqn, two covering Intelligence, one each covering Photographic Interpretation and Public Relations, 7 role support sqn, 2 covering Training and Standardisation, one each covering Helicopter Support, Air

Transportable Surgical, Offensive Air Support, Air
tpt/tkr

Deployment

ARMY
LAND COMMAND
Assigned to ACE Rapid Reaction Corps **Germany** 1
armd div plus Corps cbt spt tps **UK** 1 mech inf div, 1
air mobile bde; additional TA units incl 8 inf bn, 2 SAS,
3 AD regt **Allied Command Europe Mobile Force**
(*Land*) (AMF(L)): UK contribution 1 inf BG (incl 1 inf
bn, 1 arty bty, 1 sigs sqn)

HQ NORTHERN IRELAND
(some 9,900, plus 4,600 Home Service); 3 inf bde HQ,
up to 12 major units in inf role (5 in province, 1
committed reserve, up to 6 roulement inf bn), 1 engr, 1
avn egt, 6 Home Service inf bn. Remainder of Army
regular and TA units for Home Defence and the
defence of Dependent Territories, the Cyprus
Sovereign Base Areas and Brunei

NAVY
FLEET (CinC is also CINCEASTLANT and
COMNAVNORTHWEST): almost all regular RN
forces are declared to NATO, split between SACLANT
and SACEUR
MARINES 1 cdo bde (declared to SACLANT)

AIR FORCE
STRIKE COMMAND responsible for all RAF front-
line forces. Day-to-day control delegated to 3 Groups
No. 1 (Offensive Support and Suppport Helicopters)
No. 11/18 (Air Defence/Maritime) **No. 38** (Air
Transport/AAR)
PERSONNEL AND TRAINING COMMAND
responsible for personnel management and ground/
flying trg; incl Training Group Defence Agency and
Personnel Management Agency
LOGISTIC COMMAND responsible for log spt for
RAF units world-wide; Joint Service spt for RN and
Army units for rationalised eqpt

Forces Abroad

ANTARCTICA 1 ice patrol ship (in seasonal summer)
ASCENSION ISLAND RAF 23
BRUNEI Army some 1,050; 1 Gurkha inf bn, 1 hel flt
  (3 hel)
CANADA Army trg and liaison unit **RAF** 130; routine
  training deployment of ac *Tornado, Harrier, Jaguar*
CYPRUS 3,700: **Army** 2,500; 2 inf bn, 1 engr spt sqn, 1
  hel flt **RAF** 1,237; 1 hel sqn (5 *Wessex* HC-2), plus **ac**
  on det

FALKLAND ISLANDS Army 1 inf coy gp, 1 engr sqn
  (fd, plant) **RN** 1 DD/FF, 1 OPV, 1 spt, 1 AR **RAF**, 4
  Tornado F-3, 1 *Hercules* C-1, 1 VC-10 K-2 (tkr), 2 *Sea
  King* HAR-3, 2 CH-47 hel, 1 sqn RAF regt (*Rapier*
  SAM)
GERMANY about 28,100: **Army** 23,600; 1 corps HQ
  (multinational), 1 armd div, 1 armd recce, 1 fd arty, 1
  AD regt **RAF** 4,567; 4 sqn with 52 *Tornado*, 2 sqn
  with 33 *Harrier*, RAF regt; 1 *Rapier* SAM sqn, 2 fd sqn
GIBRALTAR 440: **Army** 70; Gibraltar regt (350) **RN/
  Marines** 270; 2 PCI; Marine det, 2 twin *Exocet*
  launchers (coastal defence), base unit **RAF** some 60;
  periodic ac det
INDIAN OCEAN (*Armilla Patrol*): 2.DD/FF, 1 spt
  Diego Garcia 1 Marine/naval party
NEPAL Army ε500 (Gurkha trg org)
WEST INDIES 1 DD/FF, 1 spt
MILITARY ADVISERS 455 in 30 countries

UN AND PEACEKEEPING
BAHRAIN (*Southern Watch*): RAF 50 2 VC-10 (tkr).
BOSNIA (SFOR II): 4,900 (incl log and spt tps in
Croatia); 1 Augmented Brigade HQ (multinational)
with 2 recce sqn, 1 armd inf bn, 1 tk sqn, 2 arty bty, 1
engr regt, 1 hel sqn **hel** 2 *Sea King* MK4 (RN), 8 *Lynx*
AH-7 (Army), 3 *Gazelle* (Army) 3 CH-47 *Chinook*
(RAF). **CYPRUS** (UNFICYP): 314; 1 bn in inf role, 1 hel
flt, engr spt (incl spt for UNIFIL). **GEORGIA**
(UNOMIG): 6 obs. **IRAQ/KUWAIT** (*Southern Watch*)
RAF 400; 12 *Tornado* GRI. (UNIKOM): 11 obs. **ITALY**
(SFOR Air Component): 350; 8 *Harrier* GR-7, 2 K-1
Tristar (tkr), 2 E-3D *Sentry*. **SAUDI ARABIA** (*Southern
Watch*): RAF 400; 6 *Tornado* GR-IA, (tkr). **SIERRA
LEONE** (UNOMSIL): 2 obs. **TURKEY** (*Northern
Watch*): RAF: 160; 6 *Tornado*, GRI, 1 VC-10 tkr

Foreign Forces

US 11,646: **Army** 376 **Navy** 1,540 **Air Force** 9,000; 1 Air
Force HQ (3rd Air Force) 1 ftr wg, 66 cbt ac, 2 sqn with
48 F-15E, 1 sqn with 18 F-15C/D. 1 Special Ops Gp, 3
sqn: 1 with 5 MH-53J, 1 with 4 HC-130, 1 with 4 MC-
130H, 1 air refuelling wg with 9 KC-135, 3 RC-135, 3
C-12
GERMANY/ITALY tri-national *Tornado* trg sqn
NATO HQ Allied Forces North-west Europe
(AFNORTHWEST), HQ Allied Naval Forces North-
west Europe (NAVNORTHWEST), HQ Allied Air
Forces North-west Europe (AIR NORTH WEST), HQ
Eastern Atlantic Area (EASTLANT), HQ Maritime
Forces Northern Sub-Area (NORLANT), HQ Maritime
Forces Central Sub-Area (CENTLANT), HQ Maritime
Forces Eastern Atlantic (AIREASTLANT), HQ
Submarines Eastern Atlantic (SUBEASTLANT)

Non-NATO Europe

Albania

	1996	1997	1998	1999
GDP	leke266bn	leke386bn		
	($1.5bn)	($1.4bn)		
per capita	$3,600	$3,400		
Growth	9.1%	-7.0%		
Inflation	7.7%	12.8%		
Debt	$781m	$826m		
Def exp	εleke10.5bn	εleke14.0bn		
	($100m)	($94m)		
Def bdgt			εleke10.5bn	
			($70m)	
FMA[a] (US)	$0.4m	$0.7m	$0.6m	$0.6m
$1 = leke	105	149	151	

[a] *Operation Alba* **1997** ε$150m

Population		3,689,000		

(Muslim 70%, Albanian Orthodox 20%, Roman
Catholic 10%; Greek ε3–8%)

Age	*13–17*	*18–22*	*23–32*
Men	184,000	174,000	324,000
Women	169,000	159,000	300,000

Total Armed Forces

The Albanian armed forces have yet to be re-constituted following the civil unrest in early 1997. Personnel str and eqpt
details are those reported prior to the unrest and should be
treated with caution

EQUIPMENT

MBT 138 T-34 (in store), 721 T-59
LT TK 35 Type-62
RECCE 15 BRDM-1
APC 103 PRC Type-531
TOWED ARTY 122mm: 425 M-1931/37, M-30, 208
  PRC Type-60; **130mm**: 100 PRC Type-59-1;
  152mm: 90 PRC Type-66
MRL 107mm: 270 PRC Type-63
MOR 82mm: 259; **120mm**: 550 M-120; **160mm**: 100
  M-43
RCL 82mm: T-21
ATK GUNS 45mm: M-1942; **57mm**: M-1943; **85mm**:
  61 D-44 PRC Type-56; **100mm**: 50 Type-86
AD GUNS 23mm: 12 ZU-23-2/ZPU-1; **37mm**: 100
  M-1939; **57mm**: 82 S-60; **85mm**: 30 KS-12; **100mm**:
  56 KS-19

Navy 2,500

(incl ε250 conscripts)
BASES Durrës, Sarandë, Shëngjin Vlorë
SUBMARINES 1
1 Sov *Whiskey* with 533mm TT †
PATROL AND COASTAL COMBATANTS† 22
TORPEDO CRAFT 12 PRC *Huchuan* PHT with 2
  533mm TT
PATROL CRAFT 10
  1 Sov *Kronshlut* PCO, 2 PRC *Shanghai* II, 4 Sov Po-2
  PFI, 3 (US) PB Mk3
MINE COUNTERMEASURES† 6
  3 Sov T-43 (in reserve), 3 Sov T-301 MSI
SUPPORT 3
  1 AO, 1 AGOR, 1 tug

Air Force 6,000

(1,500 conscripts); 98 cbt act†, no armed hel
Flying hours 10–15
FGA 1 air regt with 10 J-2 (MiG-15), 14 J-6 (MiG-17), 23
  J-6 (MiG-19)
FTR 2 air regt
  1 with 20 J-6 (MiG-19), 10 J-7 (MiG-21)
  1 with 21 J-6 (MiG-19)
TPT 1 sqn with 10 C-5 (An-2), 3 Il-14M, 6 Li-2 (C-47)
HEL 1 regt with 20 Z-5 (Mi-4)
TRG 8 CJ-5, 15 MiG-15UTI, 6 Yak-11
SAM† some 4 SA-2 sites, 22 launchers

Forces Abroad

UN AND PEACEKEEPING
BOSNIA (SFOR II): 100. **GEORGIA** (UNOMIG): 1 obs

Paramilitary

INTERNAL SECURITY FORCE
PEOPLE'S MILITIA
BORDER POLICE (Ministry of Public Order)

Armenia

	1996	1997	1998	1999
GDP	d660bn	d762bn		
	($1.6bn)	($1.6bn)		
per capita	$2,500	$2,600		
Growth	5.9%	3.3%		
Inflation	18.7%	13.9%		
Debt	$614m	$798m		
Def exp	εd51bn	εd68bn		
	($122m)	($138m)		
Def bdgt			εd41.7bn	
			($83m)	
FMA (US)	$0.3m			
$1 = dram	414	491	502	

Population	3,925,000		
(Armenian Orthodox 94%, Russian 2%, Kurd 1%)			
Age	*13–17*	*18–22*	*23–32*
Men	182,000	168,000	286,000
Women	178,000	164,000	278,000

Total Armed Forces some 53,400

incl 1,400 MoD and comd staff
Terms of service conscription, 18 months

RESERVES

some mob reported, possibly 300,000 with mil service
within 15 years

Army some 52,000

(incl 3,700 Air and AD Component; conscripts)
4 Army Corps HQ
   1 with 1 mot rifle bde, 1 MRR
   1 with 3 MRR
   1 with 1 mot rifle bde, 3 MRR, 1 tk bn
   1 with 3 MRR, 1 tk bn, 2 arty regt (1 SP), 1 ATK regt
1 mot rifle trg bde
1 SAM bde, 2 SAM regt
1 mixed avn regt, 1 avn sqn
1 SF, 1 engr regt
EQUIPMENT (CFE-declared totals as at 1 Jan 1998)
   MBT 102 T-72
   AIFV 158 BMP-1/-2, 10 BMD-1
   APC 14 BTR-60, 32 BTR-70, 4 BTR-80
   TOTAL ARTY 225
   TOWED 121: **122mm**: 59 D-30; **152mm**: 2 D-1, 34
      D-20, 26 2A36
   SP 38: **122mm**: 10 2S1; **152mm**: 28 2S3
   MRL 122mm: 47 BM-21
   MOR 120mm: 19 M-120
   ATK GUNS 105: **85mm**: D-44; **100mm**: T-12
   ATGW 18 AT-3 *Sagger*, 27 AT-6 *Spiral*
   SAM 25 SA-2/-3, 27 SA-4, 20 SA-8, SA-13
   SURV GS-13 (veh), *Long Trough* ((SNAR-1) arty),
      Pork Trough ((SNAR-2/-6) arty), *Small Fred/Small*
      Yawn (arty), *Big Fred* ((SNAR-10) veh/arty)
   AIR COMPONENT (3,700 incl AD):
      FGA 6 cbt ac, 16 armd hel
         5* Su-25, 1* MiG-25 1 hel sqn with 9 Mi-2, 7
         Mi-24 (attack), 2 Mi-9, 8 Mi-8, 9* Mi-24K/P/
         R/MT
      AIR TRG CENTRE 7 Mi-2 hel, 24 ac (An-2, Yak-
         52, Yak-55, Yak-18T)

Paramilitary 1,000

MINISTRY OF INTERIOR ε1,000

4 bn: 34 BMP-1, 33 BTR-60/-70/-152

Foreign Forces

RUSSIA 4,100: **Army** 1 mil base (bde+) with 74 MBT,
17 APC, 148 ACV, 84 arty/MRL/mor **Air Defence** 1
sqn MiG-23

Austria

	1996	1997	1998	1999
GDP	OS2.4tr	OS2.5tr		
	($213bn)	($220bn)		
per capita	$20,700	$21,600		
Growth	1.6%	2.1%		
Inflation	1.8%	1.3%		
Publ Debt	69.5%	65.2%		
Def exp	OS21.7bn	OS20.9bn		
	($2.1bn)	($1.7bn)		
Def bdgt			OS22.3bn	OS22.5bn
			($1.7bn)	($1.8bn)
$1 = OS*	10.6	12.2	12.8	
* Austrian schilling				
Population	8,075,000			
Age	*13–17*	*18–22*	*23–32*	
Men	241,000	249,000	623,000	
Women	230,000	239,000	601,000	

Total Armed Forces

(Air Service forms part of the Army)

ACTIVE some 45,500

(incl 28,400 active and short term; 16,600 conscripts;
some 66,000 reservists a year undergo refresher trg, a
proportion at a time)
Terms of service 7 months recruit trg, 30 days reservist
refresher trg during 10 years (or 8 months trg, no
refresher); 60–90 days additional for officers, NCO and
specialists

RESERVES

100,700 ready (72 hrs) reserves; 990,000 with reserve
trg, but no commitment. Officers, NCO and specialists
to age 65, remainder to age 50

Army some 45,500

(16,600 conscripts)
(being re-org)
2 corps
   1 with 2 inf bde (each 3 inf bn), 1 mech inf bde (2
      mech inf, 1 tk, 1 recce, 1 SP arty bn), 1 SP arty regt,
      1 recce, 2 engr, 1 ATK bn
   1 with 1 inf bde (3 inf bn), 1 mech inf bde (1 mech
      inf, 2 tk, 1 SP arty bn), 1 SP arty regt, 1 recce, 1
      engr bn
   1 Provincial mil comd with 1 inf regt (plus 5 inf bn
      on mob)

8 Provincial mil comd (15 inf bn on mob)
EQUIPMENT
    MBT 169 M-60A3, 5 *Leopard* 2A4
    APC 465 Saurer 4K4E/F, ε68 *Pandur* (being delivered)
    TOWED ARTY 105mm: 108 IFH (M-2A1)
    SP ARTY 155mm: 178 M-109/-A2/-A5Ö
    FORTRESS ARTY 155mm: 24 SFK M-2 (deactivated)
    MRL 128mm: 18 M-51 (in store)
    MOR 81mm: 498; 120mm: 242 M-43
    ATGW 226 RBS-56 *Bill*
    RCL 2,196 incl **74mm**: *Miniman*; **84mm**: *Carl Gustav*;
      106mm: 445 M-40A1 (in store)
    ANTI-TANK GUNS
      SP 105mm: 284 *Kuerassier* JPz SK (50 in store)
      TOWED 85mm: 205 M-52/-55 (in store)
      STATIC 105mm: some 227 L7A1 (*Centurion* tk)
    AD GUNS 20mm: 426

MARINE WING
    (under School of Military Engineering)
    2 river patrol craft<; 10 unarmed boats

Air Force (4,250)

(3,400 conscripts); 53 cbt ac, no armed hel
Flying hours 130
1 air div HQ, 3 air regt, 3 AD regt, 1 air surv regt
FTR/FGA 1 wg with 24 SAAB J-35Oe
HELICOPTERS
    LIAISON 11 OH-58B, 11 AB-206A
    TPT 22 AB-212; 8 AB-204 (9 in store)
    SAR 24 SA-319 *Alouette* III
TPT 2 *Skyvan* 3M
LIAISON 14 O-1 (L-19A/E), 12 PC-6B
TRG 16 PC-7, 29* SAAB 105Oe
AD 76 *Mistral*; 132 **20mm** AA guns: 74 Twin **35mm** AA
    towed guns with *Skyguard* radars; air surv *Goldhaube*
    with *Selenia* MRS-403 3D radars

Forces Abroad

UN AND PEACEKEEPING
BOSNIA (SFOR II): 200. **CYPRUS** (UNFICYP): 257; 1
inf bn. **GEORGIA** (UNOMIG): 2 obs. **IRAQ/KUWAIT**
(UNIKOM): 34 plus 6 obs. **MIDDLE EAST** (UNTSO):
11 obs. **SYRIA** (UNDOF): 429; 1 inf bn. **TAJIKISTAN**
(UNMOT): 4 obs. **WESTERN SAHARA** (MINURSO):
5 obs

Azerbaijan

	1996	1997	1998	1999
GDP	m10.5tr	m14.3tr		
	($2.5bn)	($2.8bn)		
per capita	$1,500	$1,600		

contd	1996	1997	1998	1999
Growth	1.3%	5.8%		
Inflation	19.8%	4.0%		
Debt	$560m	$567m		
Def exp	εm560bn	εm580bn		
	($130m)	($146m)		
Def bdgt			εm750bn	
			($190m)	
$ = manat	4,301	3,985	3,950	
Population		7,625,000		

(Daghestani 3%, Russian 2%, Armenian 2–3% (mostly
in Nagorno-Karabakh))

Age	13–17	18–22	23–32	
Men	393,000	349,000	610,000	
Women	371,000	331,000	641,000	

Total Armed Forces

ACTIVE 72,150

(incl 4,000 MOD and centrally controlled units/
formations)
Terms of service 17 months, but can be extended for
ground forces

RESERVES
some mob 575,700 with mil service within 15 years

Army 55,600

3 Army Corps HQ • 1 MRD • 18 MR bde • 2 arty bde,
1 ATK regt
EQUIPMENT (CFE declared totals as at 1 Jan 1998)
    MBT 270: 147 T-72, 123 T-55
    AIFV 287: 114 BMP-1, 96 BMP-2, 3 BMP-3, 41 BMD,
      33 BRM-1
    APC 74: 25 BTR-60, 28 BTR-70, 11 BTR-80, 10 BTR-D
    TOTAL ARTY 301
      TOWED 151: **122mm**: 95 D-30; **152mm**: 32 D-20,
      24 2A36
      SP 122mm: 14 2S1
      COMBINED GUN/MOR 120mm: 28 2S9
      MRL 122mm: 56 BM-21
      MOR 120mm: 52 PM-38
    SAM 60+ SA-4/-8/-13
    SURV GS-13 (veh); *Long Trough* ((SNAR-1) arty),
      Pork Trough (SNAR-2/-6) arty), *Small Fred/Small*
      Yawn (veh, arty), *Big Fred* ((SNAR-10) veh, arty)

Navy 2,200

BASE Baku
PRINCIPAL SURFACE COMBATANTS 2
FRIGATES 2 *Petya* II with 4 76mm gun, 5 406mm TT
PATROL AND COASTAL COMBATANTS 18
MISSILE CRAFT 3 *Osa* II PFM with 4 SS-N-2B *Styx* SSM

PATROL, INSHORE 15

10 *Stenka* PFI, 1 *Zhuk* PCI, 3 SO-1 PCI, 1 *Svetlyak* PCI

MINE COUNTERMEASURES 15

5 *Sonya* MSC, 4 *Yevgenya* MSI, 2 *Yurka* MCC, 3 *Vanya* MCC, 1 T-43 MSC

AMPHIBIOUS 4

4 *Polnochny* LSM capacity 180 tps

SUPPORT AND MISCELLANEOUS 2

1 *Vadim Popov* (research), 1 *Balerian Uryvayev* (research)

Air Force and Air Defence 10,350

37 cbt ac, 15 attack hel

FGA regt with 4* Su-17, 5* Su-24, 2* Su-25, 5* MiG-21, 18 L-29, 12 L-39

FTR sqn with 16* MiG-25, 3* MiG-25UB

RECCE sqn with 2* MiG-25

TPT 5 ac (An-2, An-12, Yak-40)

HEL 1 regt with 7 Mi-2, 13 Mi-8, 15* Mi-24

IN STORE 20 **ac** incl 17 MiG-25, MiG-21, Su-24

SAM 100 SA-2/-3/-5

Paramilitary ε15,000+

MILITIA (Ministry of Internal Affairs) 10,000+

EQPT incl 3 T-55 MBT; 17 ACV incl BMP-1, BMD, BTR-60/-70/-80; 2 122mm D-30 arty; 2 120mm mor

BORDER GUARD (Ministry of Internal Affairs) ε5,000

EQPT incl 100 BMP-2 AIFV, 19 BTR-60/-70/-80 APC

Opposition

ARMENIAN ARMED GROUPS

ε20–25,000 in Nagorno-Karabakh

(incl ε8,000 personnel from Armenia)

EQPT (reported) incl 162+ T-72, 91 T-55 MBT; 298 ACV incl BTR-70/-80, BMP-1/-2; 298 arty incl D-44, 102 D-30, 53 D-20, 99 2A36, 44 BM-21, KS-19

Belarus

	1996	1997	1998	1999
GDP	r184tr	r351tr		
	($12bn)	($13bn)		
per capita	$5,500	$6,300		
Growth	2.8%	10.0%		
Inflation	53%	64%		
Debt	$1.1bn	$991m		
Def exp	εr7.6tr	εr11.7tr		
	($490m)	($381m)		
Def bdgt			r6.0tr	
			($172m)	

contd	1996	1997	1998	1999
FMA[a] (US)	$0.8m	$0.3m	$0.1m	$0.1m
$1 = rubel[b]	15,500	30,740	34,710	

[a] Excl US Cooperative Threat Reduction programme:
1992–96 $119m budget, of which $44m spent by Sept 1996. Programme continues through 1999.
[b] Market rate **July 1998** $1 = r70,500

Population		10,196,000		
(Russian 13%, Polish 4%, Ukrainian 3%)				
Age	13–17	18–22	23–32	
Men	402,000	385,000	701,000	
Women	389,000	376,000	702,000	

Total Armed Forces

ACTIVE 83,000

(incl about 14,600 in centrally controlled units and MoD staff, 3,400 women; 40,000 conscripts)
Terms of service 18 months

RESERVES some 289,500

with mil service within last 5 years

Army 43,000

MoD tps: 2 MRD (1 trg), 1 ABD, 1 indep AB bde, 1 arty div, 2 MRL regt
1 rear defence div (reserve inf units only)
2 SSM, 1 ATK, 1 *Spetsnaz*, 2 SAM bde
3 Corps
  1 with 2 tk, 1 mech, 1 SSM, 1 SAM bde, 1 arty, 1 MRL regt
  1 with 3 mech, 1 tk, 1 SSM, 1 SAM bde, 1 arty, 1 MRL regt
  1 with no manned cbt units

EQUIPMENT

MBT 1,778: T-55, T-62, T-72, some T-80

AIFV 1,590 incl BMP-1, BMP-2, BRM, BMD-1

APC 930: 188 BTR-60, 446 BTR-70, 195 BTR-80, 30 BTR-D, 71 MT-LB

TOTAL ARTY 1,529 incl

TOWED 392: **122mm**: 200 D-30; **152mm**: 6 M-1943 (D-1), 136 2A65, 50 2A36

SP 586: **122mm**: 239 2S1; **152mm**: 166 2S3, 120 2S5; **152mm**: 13 2S19; **203mm**: 48 2S7

COMBINED GUN/MOR 120mm: 54 2S9

MRL 419: **122mm**: 275 BM-21, 11 9P138; **130mm**: 1 BM-13; **220mm**: 84 9P140; **300mm**: 48 9A52

MOR 120mm: 78 2S12

ATGW 480: AT-4 *Spigot*, AT-5 *Spandrel* (some SP), AT-6 *Spiral* (some SP), AT-7 *Saxhorn*

SSM 60 *Scud*, 36 FROG/SS-21

SAM 350 SA-8/-11/-12/-13

SURV GS-13 (arty), *Long Trough* ((SNAR-1) arty), *Pork Trough* ((SNAR-2/-6) arty), *Small Fred/Small Yawn* (veh, arty), *Big Fred* ((SNAR-10) veh, arty)

Air Force 22,000

(incl 10,000 Air Defence); 1 air army, 276 cbt ac, 74 attack hel
Flying hours 40
FGA 30 Su-24, 99 Su-25
FTR 82 MiG-29, 26 Su-27, 27 MiG-23
RECCE 12* Su-24
HELICOPTERS
   ATTACK 74 Mi-24
   EW 25 Mi-8
   CBT SPT 4 Mi-24K, 6 Mi-24P, 100 Mi-8
TPT ac 29 Il-76, 6 An-12, 7 An-24, 1 An-26, 1 Tu-134
   hel 26 Mi-2, 14 Mi-26

AIR DEFENCE (10,000)
SAM 175 SA-3/-5/-10

Paramilitary 8,000

BORDER GUARDS (Ministry of Interior) 8,000

Bosnia-Herzegovina

	1996	1997	1998	1999
GDP	ε$5bn	ε$6.5bn		
per capita	ε$4,000	ε$5,300		
Growth	ε50%	ε30%		
Inflation	ε-25%	ε14%		
Debt	ε$2bn	ε$2bn		
Def exp[a]	ε$250m	ε$327m		
Def bdgt[a]			ε$188m	
FMA[bc] (US)	$0.3m	$0.5m	$0.6m	$0.6m
$ = convertible mark		150	182	

[a] Excl Bosnian Serb def exp
[b] Eqpt and trg valued at ε$450m from US, Sau, Kwt, UAE, Et and Tu in 1996–98
[c] UNMIBH **1996** ε$118m **1997** ε$190m; IFOR **1996** ε$5bn; SFOR **1997** ε$4bn

Population	ε4,000,000		
(Bosnian Muslim 44%, Serb 33%, Croat 17%)			
Age	*13–17*	*18–22*	*23–32*
Men	192,000	180,000	346,000
Women	181,000	170,000	327,000

The data outlined below represent the situation prior to the signing of a comprehensive peace agreement on 14 December 1995. BiH and HVO forces are to merge and form the armed forces of a Muslim–Croat Federation with a probable structure of 4 Corps, 15 bde (incl 1 rapid-reaction) and an arty div. It is reported that this force will be equipped with 273 MBT (45), 227 ACV (80), 1,000 arty (60), 14 attack hel. Figures in ( ) denote eqpt delivered in country, but under US control

Total Armed Forces

ACTIVE some 40,000

RESERVES some 100,000

Army (BiH) some 40,000

1 'Army' HQ • 4 'Corps' HQ • 2 div HQ • 28 inf bde • 1 SF 'bde' • 1 recce bde • 10 mot inf, 3 armd, 11 arty regt
EQUIPMENT
   MBT T-34, 10 T-55, 50 AMX-30, M-60A3
   RECCE 44 AML-90
   APC 70 incl M-113A2
   TOTAL ARTY (incl hy mor) 3,850
      ARTY incl **105mm:** 36 L-118; **122mm:** 12 D-30; **130mm:** M-59; **155mm:** 126 M-114; **203mm**
      MRL incl **262mm:** M-87 *Orkan*
      MOR 82mm; 120mm
   ATGW 100 AT-3 *Sagger*, *Red Arrow* (TF-8) reported
   AD GUNS 20mm; 23mm: 19 ZU-23; **30mm**
   SAM SA-7/-14
   HEL 10 Mi-8/-17, 15 UH-1H
   AC 3 UTVA-75

Other Forces

CROAT (Croatian Defence Council (HVO)) 16,000
4 MD • 4 guard, 1 arty bde, 1 inf regt, 1 armd, 1 MP bn, 1 Home Def regt

   RESERVES 24 Home Def, 1 inf, 1 arty regt, 7 Home Def, 2 arty, 1 AD, 1 SF bn

   EQUIPMENT
   MBT ε50, incl T-34, T-55, M-84/T-72M, M-47
   AFV ε30 M-60, M-80
   TOTAL ARTY some 1,250 incl
      TOWED incl **76mm:** M-48; **105mm:** M-56; **122mm:** D-30; **130mm:** M-46
      MRL 122mm: BM-21; **128mm:** M-63, M-77
      MOR 82mm
   ATGW AT-3 *Sagger*, AT-4 *Fagot*, AT-6 (reported)
   RL ε100 *Armbrust*, M-79, RPG-7/-22
   RCL 84mm: 30 *Carl Gustav*
   AD GUNS 20mm: M-55, Bov-3; **30mm:** M-53; **57mm:** S-60
   SAM SA-7/-9/-14/-16
   HEL Mi-8, Mi-24, MD-500

SERB (Army of the Serbian Republic of Bosnia and Herzegovina–SRB (BH)) 30,000+
3 'Corps' HQ • 40+ inf/armd/mot inf bde • 1 SF 'bde' • 11 arty/ATK/AD regt

   EQUIPMENT
   MBT 570 incl T-34, T-55, M-84, T-72
   APC 360

TOTAL ARTY some 4,000 incl
  TOWED 122mm: D-30, M-1938 (M-30); **130mm**:
    M-46; **152mm**: D-20
  SP 122mm: 2S1
  MRL 128mm: M-63; **262mm**: M-87 *Orkan*
  MOR 120mm
SSM FROG-7
AD GUNS 975: incl **20mm, 23mm** incl ZSU 23-4;
  30mm: M53/59SP; **57mm**: ZSU-57-2; **90mm**
SAM SA-2, some SA-6/-7B/-9/-13
AC some 20 *Galeb, Jastreb*, G-4 *Super Galeb* and *Orao*,
  UTVA, *Kraguj*, Cessna
HEL 12 Mi-8, 12 SA-341 *Gazela*

Foreign Forces

NATO (SFOR II): up to 33,200: Be, Ca, Da, Fr, Ge, Gr,
It, Lu, Nl, No, Por, Sp, Tu, UK, US **Non-NATO** Alb, A,
Cz, Ea, Et, HKJ, Hu, Lat, L, Mor, Pl, R, RSA, RF, Ukr

Bulgaria

	1996	1997	1998	1999
GDP	L1,749bn	L17tr		
	($11.0bn)	($10.1bn)		
per capita	$4,200	$4,000		
Growth	-10.9%	-7.4%		
Inflation	123%	1,082%		
Debt	$9.8bn	$10.0bn		
Def exp	L65bn	L570bn		
	($365m)	($339m)		
Def bdgt			L488bn	
			($270m)	
FMA (US)	$5.0m	$0.9m	$1.0m	$1.0m
$1 = leva	178	1,682	1,808	
Population		8,349,000		
(Turkish 9%, Macedonian 3%, Romany 3%)				
Age	*13–17*	*18–22*	*23–32*	
Men	295,000	311,000	585,000	
Women	279,000	295,000	562,000	

Total Armed Forces

ACTIVE ε101,500

(incl ε49,300 conscripts, about 22,300 centrally controlled,
3,400 MoD staff, but excl some 10,000 construction tps)
Terms of service 12 months

RESERVES 303,000

Army 250,500 **Navy** (to age 55, officers 60 or 65) 7,500
Air Force (to age 60) 45,000

Army 50,400

(ε33,300 conscripts)
3 Mil Districts/Corps HQ
  1 with 1 MRD, 1 tk, 2 mech bde • 1 with 1 MRD, 1
  Regional Training Centre (RTC), 1 tk bde • 1 with 2
  MRD, 2 tk, 1 mech bde
Army tps: 4 *Scud*, 1 SS-23, 1 SAM bde, 3 arty, 3 ATK, 3
  AD arty, 1 SAM regt
1 AB bde

EQUIPMENT

MBT 1,475: 1,042 T-55, 433 T-72
ASLT GUN 68 SU-100
RECCE 58 BRDM-1/-2
AIFV 100 BMP-1, 114 BMP-23, BMP-30
APC 1,894: 781 BTR-60, 1,113 MT-LB (plus 1,270
  'look-alikes')
TOTAL ARTY 1,744 (CFE total as at 1 Jan 98)
  TOWED 100mm: M-1944 (BS-3); **122mm**: M-30,
    M-1931/37 (A-19); **130mm**: M-46; **152mm**: M-1937
    (ML-20), D-20
  SP 122mm: 2S1
  MRL 122mm: BM-21
  MOR 444: **120mm**: M-38, 2B11, B-24, *Tundzha* SP
SSM launchers: 28 FROG-7, 36 *Scud*, 8 SS-23
ATGW 200 AT-3 *Sagger*
ATK GUNS 85mm: 150 D-44; **100mm**: 200 T-12
AD GUNS 400: **23mm**: ZU-23, ZSU-23-4 SP; **57mm**:
  S-60; **85mm**: KS-12; **100mm**: KS-19
SAM 20 SA-3, 27 SA-4, 20 SA-6
SURV GS-13 (veh), *Long Trough* ((SNAR-1) arty),
  Pork Trough ((SNAR-2/-6) arty), *Small Fred/Small
  Yawn* (veh, arty), *Big Fred* ((SNAR-10) veh, arty)

Navy ε6,100

(ε2,000 conscripts)
BASES Coastal Varna (HQ), Atya **Danube** Vidin
(HQ), Balchik, Sozopol. Zones of operational control at
Varna and Burgas
SUBMARINES 2 *Pobeda* (Sov Romeo)-class with
533mm TT†
FRIGATES 1 *Smeli* (Sov Koni) with 1 x 2 SA-N-4
SAM, 2 x 12 ASW RL; plus 2 x 2 76mm guns
PATROL AND COASTAL COMBATANTS 25
CORVETTES 7
  4 *Poti* ASW with 2 ASW RL, 4 ASTT
  1 *Tarantul* II ASUW with 2 x 2 SS-N-2C *Styx*, 2 x 4
    SA-N-5 *Grail* SAM; plus 1 76mm gun
  2 *Pauk* I with 1 SA-N-5 SAM, 2 x 5 ASW RL; plus 4
    406mm TT
MISSILE CRAFT 6 *Osa* I/II PFM with 4 SS-N-2A/B
  Styx SSM
PATROL, INSHORE 12
  2 *Pauk* 1 with 1 x 4 SA-N-5 SAM, 1 x 76mm gun, 4 x
    406mm TT
  10 *Zhuk* PFI

MINE WARFARE 20

MINE COUNTERMEASURES 20

4 *Sonya* MSC, 16 MSI (4 *Vanya*, 4 *Yevgenya*, 6 *Olya*, 2 PO-2)

AMPHIBIOUS 2 Sov Polnocny LSM, capacity 150 tps, 6 tk

Plus 19 LCU (incl 16 in reserve)

SUPPORT AND MISCELLANEOUS 16

3 AGS, 3 AO, 1 diving tender, 1 degaussing, 1 tug, 7 misc auxiliaries

NAVAL AVIATION

9 armed hel

HEL 1 ASW sqn with 6 Mi-14, 3 Ka-25

COASTAL ARTY 2 regt, 20 bty

GUNS 100mm: ε150; **130mm:** 4 SM-4-1

SSM SS-C-1B *Sepal*, SSC-3 *Styx*

NAVAL GUARD

3 coy

Air Force 19,300

(14,000 conscripts); 217 cbt ac, 44 attack hel, 1 Tactical Aviation corps, 1 AD corps

Flying hours 30–40

FGA 3 regt

1 with 39 Su-25

2 with 41 MiG-21, 1 regt with 32 MiG-23

FTR 4 regt with some 40 MiG-23, 23 MiG-21, 21 MiG-29

RECCE 1 regt with 21 Su-22

TPT 1 regt with 2 Tu-134, 3 An-24, 4 An-26, 5 L-410, 3 Yak-40 (VIP)

SURVEY 1 An-30

HEL 2 regt with 14 Mi-2, 7 Mi-8, 25 Mi-17, 44 Mi-24 (attack)

TRG 3 trg regt with 6 Yak-18, 73 L-29, 35 L-39

MISSILES

ASM AS-7 *Kerry*

AAM AA-2 *Atoll*, AA-7 *Apex*, AA-8 *Aphid*

SAM SA-2/-3/-5/-10 (20 sites, some 110 launchers)

Forces Abroad

UN AND PEACEKEEPING

ANGOLA (UNOMA): 3 obs. **TAJIKISTAN** (UNMOT): 8 obs.

Paramilitary 34,000

BORDER GUARDS (Ministry of Interior) 12,000

12 regt; some 50 craft incl about 12 Sov PO2 PCI<

SECURITY POLICE 4,000

RAILWAY AND CONSTRUCTION TROOPS 18,000

Croatia

	1996	1997	1998	1999
GDP	k102bn	k123bn		
	($18.8bn)	($20.1bn)		
per capita	$5,700	$6,100		
Growth	4.2%	6.5%		
Inflation	3.5%	3.6%		
Debt	$4.8bn	$6.3bn		
Def exp	k7.0bn	k7.0bn		
	($1.3bn)	($1.1bn)		
Def bdgt			k7.5bn	
			($1.1bn)	
FMA[a] (US)	$0.2m	$0.4m	$0.4m	$0.4m
$1 = kuna	5.43	6.10	6.67	

[a] UNTAES **1996** $292m **1997** $266m; UNMOP (UNMIBH) **1996** $118m **1997** $190m

Population	ε4,792,000		
(Serb 3%, Slovene 1%)			
Age	*13–17*	*18–22*	*23–32*
Men	167,000	168,000	332,000
Women	157,000	159,000	319,000

Total Armed Forces

ACTIVE 56,180

(incl ε33,500 conscripts)

Terms of service 10 months

RESERVES 220,000

Army 150,000 **Home Defence** 70,000

Army 50,000

(incl ε33,500 conscripts)

6 Mil Districts • 7 Guard bde (each 3 mech, 1 tk, 1 arty bn) • 29 inf 'bde' (each 3 inf bn, 1 tk, 1 arty unit) • 1 mech bde • 1 mixed arty/MRL bde • 1 ATK bde • 4 AD bde • 1 engr bde • 38 Home Def regt

RESERVES

25 inf 'bde' (incl 1 trg), 38 Home Def regt

EQUIPMENT

MBT 298: T-34, T-55, M-47, M-84/T-72M

LT TK 1 PT-76

RECCE 7 BRDM-2

AIFV 109 M-80

APC 18 BTR-50, 19 M-60PB plus 7 'look-alikes'

TOTAL ARTY some 979

TOWED 427: **76mm:** ZIS-3; **85mm; 105mm:** 57 M-56, 90 M-2A1; **122mm:** 45 M-1938, 32 D-30; **130mm:** 83 M-46; **152mm:** 20 D-20, 21 M-84; **155mm:** 37 M-1, 12 L-33; **203mm:** 22 incl some **SP 122mm:** 8 2S1

MRL 122mm: 40 BM-21; **128mm:** 179 M-63/-91; **262mm:** 2 M-87 *Orkan*

MOR 331 incl: **82mm; 120mm**: 325 M-75, 6
UBM-52; **240mm**: reported
ATGW AT-3 *Sagger* (9 on BRDM-2), AT-4 *Spigot*, AT-
7 *Saxhorn, Milan* reported
RL **73mm**: RPG-7/-22. **90mm**: M-79
ATK GUNS **100mm**: 133 T-12
AD GUNS 600+: **14.5mm**: ZPU-2/-4; **20mm**: BOV-1
SP, M-55; **30mm**: M-53/59, BOV-3SP

Navy 3,000

BASES Split, Pula, Sibenik, Ploce, Dubrovnik **Minor
facilities** Lastovo, Vis
SUBMARINES 1
1 Velebit (Mod Una) SSI for SF ops (4 SDV or 4 mines)
PATROL AND COASTAL COMBATANTS 13
CORVETTES 1 *Kralj Petar* with 4 or 8 Saab RBS-15
SSM
MISSILE CRAFT 2
1 *Rade Koncar* PFM with 4 RBS-15 SSM
1 *Dubrovnik* (Mod Sov *Osa* 1) no missiles, can lay
mines
PATROL, INSHORE 10
4 *Mirna*, 1 RLM-301, 5 riverine
MINE WARFARE 3
MINELAYERS 2 *Cetina* (*Silba*-class, LCT hull), 94 mines
MINECOUNTERMEASURES 1 *Dubrovnik* (Con-
verted Sov *Osa* 1) MCI
AMPHIBIOUS craft only
2 *Silba* LCT, 1 DTM LCT/ML, 1 DSM-501 LCT/ML,
7 LCU
SUPPORT AND MISCELLANEOUS 5
1 *Spasilac* salvage, 1 Sov *Moma* survey, 1 AE, 2 tugs
MARINES
2 indep inf coy
COASTAL DEFENCE
some 10 coast arty bty, 2 RBS-15 SSM bty (reported)

Air Force 3,180

(incl 1,320 conscripts)
40 cbt ac, 15 armed hel
Flying hours 80
FGA/FTR 2 sqn with 20 MiG-21
TPT 4 An-2, 2 An-26, 2 An-32, 5 UTVA, 2 Do-28
HEL 16 Mi-8/17, 15* Mi-24, 2 MD-500, 1 UH-1, 9 Bell-
206B
TRG 20* PC-9
AAM AA-2 *Atoll*, AA-8 *Aphid*
SAM SA-6, SA-7, SA-9, SA-10 (non-op), SA-13, SA-14/
-16

Paramilitary 40,000

POLICE 40,000 armed

COAST GUARD boats only

Foreign Forces

UN (UNMOP): 4 obs from 23 countries; (SFOR II): not
known

Cyprus

	1996	1997	1998	1999
GDP	C£4.1bn	C£4.4bn		
	($8.3bn)	($8.7bn)		
per capita	$11,300	$11,700		
Growth	2.4%	3.0%		
Inflation	3.0%	3.6%		
Debt	$4.6bn	$6.7bn		
Def exp	C£222m	C£259m		
	($477m)	($505m)		
Def bdgt			C£265m	
			($507m)	
$1 = pound	0.47	0.51	0.52	
UNFICYP **1996** $44m	**1997** $46m			

Population	860,000 (Turkish 23%)		
Age	*13–17*	*18–22*	*23–32*
Men	32,000	28,000	55,000
Women	30,000	26,000	52,000

Total Armed Forces

ACTIVE 10,000
(8,700 conscripts; 445 women)
Terms of service conscription, 26 months, then reserve to
age 50 (officers 65)

RESERVES
88,000 **first-line** (age 20–34), 43,000 **second-line** (age
35–50)

National Guard 10,000

(8,700 conscripts) (all units classified non-active under
Vienna Document)
1 Corps HQ • 2 lt inf div HQ • 2 lt inf bde HQ • 1
armd bde (3 bn) • 1 arty comd (regt) • 1 ATK bn (div
unit) • 1 SF comd (regt of 3 bn)
EQUIPMENT
MBT 102 AMX-30 (incl 52 -B2), 41 T-80U
RECCE 124 EE-9 *Cascavel*, 15 EE-3 *Jararaca*
AIFV 27 VAB-VCI, 43 BMP-3
APC 268 *Leonidas*, 118 VAB (incl variants), 16 AMX-
VCI
TOWED ARTY **75mm**: 4 M-116A1 pack; **88mm**: 24
25-pdr (in store); **100mm**: 10 M-1944; **105mm**: 72
M-56; **155mm**: 12 TR F1
SP ARTY **155mm**: 12 F3

MRL 128mm: 12 FRY M-63 (YMRL-32)
MOR 376+: **81mm**: 170 E-44, 70+ M1/M29 (in store); **107mm**: 20 M-30/M-2; **120mm**: 116 RT61
ATGW 45 *Milan* (15 on EE-3 *Jararaca*), 22 HOT (18 on VAB)
RL 66mm: M-72 LAW; **73mm**: ε450 RPG-7; **112mm**: ε900 *Apilas*
RCL 90mm: 40 EM-67; **106mm**: 144 M-40A1
AD GUNS 20mm: 36 M-55; **35mm**: 24 GDF-003 with *Skyguard*; **40mm**: 20 M-1 (in store)
SAM 60 *Mistral* (some SP), 12 *Aspide*

MARITIME WING

1 *Salamis* PFI (plus 11 boats)
1 coastal def SSM bty with 3 MM-40 *Exocet*

AIR WING

AC 1 BN-2 *Islander*, 2 PC-9
HEL 3 Bell 206C, 4 SA-342 *Gazelle* (with HOT), 2 Mi-2 (in store)

Paramilitary some 620

ARMED POLICE about 500

1 mech rapid-reaction unit (350), 2 VAB/VTT APC, 1 BN-2A *Maritime Defender* ac, 2 Bell 412 hel

MARITIME POLICE 120

2 *Evagoras* and 1 *Kinon* PFI, 1 *Dabur* PFI, 5 SAB-12 PCC

Foreign Forces

GREECE 1,250: 1 mech inf bde incl 950 (ELDYK) (Army); 2 mech inf, 1 armd bn, plus ε200 officers/NCO seconded to Greek-Cypriot National Guard, 41 M-48A5 MOLF MBT
UK (in Sovereign Base Areas) 3,700: **Army** 2 inf bn, 1 armd recce sqn **Air Force** 1,200; 1 hel sqn, plus ac on det
UN (UNFICYP) some 1,244: 3 inf bn (Arg, A, UK), tps from Ca, SF, Hu, Irl, Nl, Slvn, plus 35 civ pol from 4 countries

'Turkish Republic of Northern Cyprus'

Data presented here represent the *de facto* situation on the island. This in no way implies international recognition as a sovereign state

	1995	1996	1997	1998
GNP	ε$792m	ε$837m	ε$909m	
per capita	ε$4,200	ε$4,500	ε$4,800	
Def exp				
(Tu)	ε$510–540m	n.k.	n.k.	
Population		ε205,000		

Total Armed Forces

ACTIVE some 4,500

Terms of service conscription, 24 months, then reserve to age 50

RESERVES 26,000

11,000 **first-line** 10,000 **second-line** 5,000 **third-line**

Army some 4,500

7 inf bn

Turkish Navy

1 *Caner Goyneli* PCI

COAST GUARD

(operated by TRNC Security Forces)
1 *Raif Denktash* PCC • 2 ex-US Mk5 PCC • 2 SG45/SG46 PCC

Paramilitary

ARMED POLICE ε150

1 Police SF unit

POLICE COAST GUARD 5 PCC

Foreign Forces

TURKEY

ARMY 30–33,000 (mainly conscripts)
1 Corps HQ, 2 Inf div

EQUIPMENT

MBT 282 M-48A5 T1/T2, 8 M-48A2 (trg)
APC 50 AAPC, 200 M-113
TOWED ARTY 105mm: 126 M-101A1; **155mm**: 36 M-114A2; **203mm**: 8 M-115
SP ARTY 105mm: 26 M-52A1; **155mm**: 36 M-114A2
MOR 81mm: 175; **107mm**: 102 M-30; **120mm**: 30 HY-12
ATGW 48 *Milan*, 36 TOW
RL 66mm: M-72 LAW
RCL 90mm: M-67; **106mm**: 176 M-40A1
AD GUNS 20mm: Rh 202; **35mm**: GDF-003; **40mm**: M-1
SAM *Stinger*
SURV AN/TPQ-36
AC 3 U-17. Periodic det of F-16C/D, F-4E
HEL 4 UH-1H. Periodic det of S-70A, AS-532UL, AH-1P

Czech Republic

	1996	1997	1998	1999
GDP	Kc1.4tr	Kc1.5tr		
	($42bn)	($45bn)		
per capita	$10,300	$10,600		
Growth	3.9%	1.0%		

contd	1996	1997	1998	1999
Inflation	8.8%	8.5%		
Debt	$20.1bn	$22.0bn		
Def exp	Kc30.6bn	Kc31.3bn		
	($1,127m)	($987m)		
Def bdgt			Kc35.6bn	Kc42.3bn
			($1,078m)	($1,282m)
FMA (US)	$9.7m	$0.7m	$1.3m	$1.4m
$1 = koruna	27.2	31.7	33.0	
Population		10,311,000		

(Slovak 3%, Polish 0.6%, German 0.5%)

Age	13–17	18–22	23–32	
Men	374,000	419,000	764,000	
Women	357,000	402,000	736,000	

Total Armed Forces

ACTIVE 59,100

(incl 35,000 conscripts, about 18,800 MoD, centrally controlled formations and HQ units)
Terms of service 12 months

Army 25,300

(15,500 conscripts)
MoD tps: 5 civil defence regt
2 Corps HQ
1 rapid-reaction bde (2 mech, 1 AB, 1 recce, 1 arty bn)
7 mech bde (each with 4 mech/trg, 1 recce, 1 arty, 1 ATK, 1 AD bn). Manning state assessed as 2 bde above 50%, 2 bde at 50%, 3 bde at 10%
1 SF bde
Corps tps:
    2 arty bde • 2 recce bde, 1 AD regt; 2 AD bn • 2 engr bde, 2 op bn

RESERVES
14–15 territorial def bde
EQUIPMENT
  MBT 938: 397 T-54/-55, 541 T-72M (250 to be upgraded)
  RECCE some 182 BRDM, OT-65
  AIFV 945: 129 BPZV, 615 BMP-1, 186 BMP-2, 15 BRM-1K
  APC 403 OT-90, 19 OT-64 plus 576 'look-alikes'
  TOTAL ARTY 754
    TOWED 122mm: 148 D-30
    SP 370: 122mm: 91 2S1; 152mm: 273 *Dana* (M-77)
    MRL 122mm: 149 RM-70
    MOR 93: 120mm: 85 M-1982, 8 MSP-85
  SSM FROG-7, SS-21
  ATGW 721 AT-3 *Sagger* (incl 621 on BMP-1, 100 on BRDM-2), 21 AT-5 *Spandrel*
  AD GUNS 30mm: M-53/-59
  SAM SA-7, ε140 SA-9/-13
  SURV GS-13 (veh), *Small Fred/Small Yawn* (veh, arty)

Air Force 15,000

(incl AD and 8,500 conscripts); 109 cbt ac, 36 attack hel
Flying hours 50
FGA/RECCE 2 sqn with 34 Su-22, MK/UM3K
FTR 2 sqn
  1 with 19 MiG-23 (to be wfs at end of 1998)
  1 with 32 MiG-21
TPT 2 sqn with 14 L-410, 8 An-24/26/30, 1 Tu-154 **hel** 2 Mi-2, 4 Mi-8, 1 Mi-9, 10 Mi-17
HEL 2 sqn (aslt/tpt/attack) with 21 Mi-2, 4 Mi-8, 20 Mi-17, 36* Mi-24, 11 PZL W-3
TEST CENTRE 7* Mig-21, 2 L-29, 2 L-39, 1 Mi-17, 1 Mi-2
TRG 1 regt with **ac** 18 L-29, 14 L-39C, 17* L-39ZO, 3 L-39MS, 8 Z-142C **hel** 8 Mi-2
AAM AA-2 *Atoll*, AA-7 *Apex*, AA-8 *Aphid*
SAM SA-2, SA-3, SA-6

Forces Abroad

UN AND PEACEKEEPING
BOSNIA (SFOR II): up to 560; 1 mech inf bn.
CROATIA (UNMOP): 1 obs; (SFOR): 7. **FYROM** (UNPREDEP): 1 obs. **GEORGIA** (UNOMIG): 4 obs.
TAJIKISTAN (UNMOT): 3 obs

Paramilitary 5,600

BORDER GUARDS 4,000
(1,000 conscripts)
INTERNAL SECURITY FORCES 1,600
(1,500 conscripts)

Estonia

	1996	1997	1998	1999
GDP	kn52.5bn	kn65.0bn		
	($4.4bn)	($4.7bn)		
per capita	$7,100	$8,000		
Growth	4.0%	9.9%		
Inflation	14.8%	11.2%		
Debt	$405m	$1,067m		
Def exp[a]	εkn1.3bn	εkn1.7bn		
	($108m)	($119m)		
Def bdgt			kn824m	
			($57m)	
FMA (US)	$1.9m	$0.6m	$0.7m	$0.7m
$1 = kroon	12.0	13.9	14.6	

[a] Incl exp on paramilitary forces

Population		1,454,000		

(Russian 9%, Ukrainian 3%, Belarussian 2%)

Age	13–17	18–22	23–32	
Men	58,000	56,000	105,000	
Women	56,000	54,000	101,000	

Total Armed Forces

ACTIVE 4,340

(incl 2,490 conscripts)
Terms of service 12 months

RESERVES some 14,000
Militia

Army 3,980

(2,250 conscripts, 160 active reserves (Defence League))
4 Defence Regions, 5 inf bn, 1 arty gp • 1 guard, 1
recce bn • 1 peacekeeping coy

RESERVES
Militia 8,200, 16 *Kaitseliit* (Defence League) units
EQUIPMENT
RECCE 7 BRDM-2
APC 32 BTR-60/-70/-80
TOWED ARTY 105mm: 19 M 61-37
MOR 81mm: 41; 120mm: 16
ATGW 10 *Mapats*
RL 82mm: 200 B-300
RCL 84mm: *Carl Gustav*; 106mm: 30 M-40A1
AD GUNS 23mm: 100 ZU-23-2

Navy 320

(incl 240 conscripts)
Lat, Ea and L have set up a joint Naval unit BALTRON
BASES Tallinn (HQ BALTRON), Miinisadam (Navy
and BALTRON)
PATROL CRAFT 3
PATROL, INSHORE 3
2 *Grif* (RF *Zhuk*) PCI, 1 *Ahti* (*Da Maagen*) PCI
MINE COUNTERMEASURES 4
2 *Sulev* (Ge *Kondor*-1) MSO
2 *Olev* (Ge *Frauenlob*) MSI
SUPPORT AND MISCELLANEOUS 2
1 *Mardus* AK, 1 *Laine* (Ru *Mayak*) AK

Air Force 36

ac 2 An-2, 1 PZL-140 *Wilga* **hel** 2 Mi-2

Forces Abroad

UN AND PEACEKEEPING
BOSNIA (SFOR II): 44. **MIDDLE EAST** (UNTSO): 1
obs

Paramilitary 2,800

BORDER GUARD (Ministry of Interior) 2,800
(940 conscripts); 1 regt, 3 rescue coy; maritime elm of

Border Guard also fulfils task of Coast Guard
BASES Tallinn
PATROL CRAFT 8
1 *Torm* PCC, 1 *Kõu* (SF *Silma*) PCO, 3 *Koskelo* (SF
Telkkä) PCI, 1 *Tiiv* (RF *Serna*) LCU capacity 100 tps,
1 *Maru* (SF *Viima*) PCI, 1 *Pikker* (RF new build) PCI
SPT AND MISC 1 *Linda* (SF *Kemio*) PCI (trg)
AVN 2 L-410 UVP-1 *Turbolet*, 5 Mi-8

Finland

	1996	1997	1998	1999
GDP	m569bn	m609bn		
	($110bn)	($117bn)		
per capita	$18,200	$19,600		
Growth	3.7%	5.9%		
Inflation	0.6%	1.3%		
Publ debt	57.6%	55.8%		
Def exp	m10.1bn	m10.2bn		
	($2.2bn)	($2.0bn)		
Def bdgt[a]			m10.0bn	
			($1.8bn)	
$1 = markka	4.59	5.19	5.53	

[a] Excl supplementary budget of m6.1bn ($1.1bn)
approved in April 1998

Population		5,152,000		
Age	*13–17*	*18–22*	*23–32*	
Men	168,000	167,000	348,000	
Women	159,000	159,000	332,000	

Total Armed Forces

ACTIVE 31,700

(24,000 conscripts, some 500 women)
Terms of service 6–12 months (12 months for officers, NCO
and soldiers with special duties)

RESERVES some 500,000

Total str on mob some 500,000 (all services), with 300,000
in general forces (bde etc) and 200,000 in local forces.
Some 30,000 reservists a year do refresher trg: total
obligation 40 days (75 for NCO, 100 for officers) between
conscript service and age 50 (NCO and officers to age 60)

Army 24,000

(19,000 conscripts)
(all bdes reserve, some with peacetime trg role)
3 Mil Comd
1 with 6 mil provinces, 2 armd (1 trg), 3 *Jaeger* (trg), 9
inf
1 with 2 mil provinces, 3 *Jaeger* (trg) bde
1 with 4 mil provinces, 4 *Jaeger* (trg), 5 inf bde
Other units
4 AD regt, 4 engr bn

RESERVES
some 200 local bn and coy
EQUIPMENT
MBT 70 T-55M, 160 T-72
AIFV 163 BMP-1, 110 BMP-2 (incl 'look-alikes')
APC 120 BTR-60, 450 XA-180/185 *Sisu*, 220 MT-LB (incl 'look-alikes')
TOWED ARTY 105mm: 54 H 61-37; **122mm**: 486 H 63 (D-30); **130mm**: 36 K 54, **152mm**: 324 incl: H 55 (D-20), H 88-40, H 88-37 (ML-20), H 38 (M-10); **155mm**: 108 M-74 (K-83), 2 K 98
SP ARTY 122mm: 72 PsH 74 (2S1); **152mm**: 18 *Telak* 91 (2S5)
MRL 122mm: 24 Rak H 76 (BM-21), 36 Rak H 89 (RM-70)
MOR 81mm: 800; **120mm**: 789: KRH 40, KRH 92
ATGW 100: incl 24 M-82 (AT-4 *Spigot*), 12 M-83 (BGM-71D TOW 2), M-82M (AT-5 *Spandrel*)
RL 112mm: APILAS
RCL 66mm: 66 KES-75, 66 KES-88; **95mm**: 100 SM-58-61
AD GUNS 23mm: 400 ZU-23; **30mm; 35mm**: GDF-005, *Marksman* GDF-005 SP; **57mm**: 12 S-60 towed, 12 ZSU-57-2 SP
SAM SAM-78 (SA-7), SAM-79 (SA-3), SAM-86M (SA-18), SAM-86 (SA-16), 20 SAM-90 (*Crotale* NG), 18 SAM-96 (SA-11)
SURV *Cymbeline* (mor)
HEL 2 Hughes 500D, 7 Mi-8

Navy 5,000

(2,600 conscripts)
BASES Upinniemi (Helsinki), Turku
4 functional sqn (2 missile, 2 mine warfare). Approx 50% of units kept fully manned; others in short-notice storage, rotated regularly
PATROL AND COASTAL COMBATANTS 14
CORVETTES 2 *Turunmaa* with 1 120mm gun, 2 x 5 ASW RL
MISSILE CRAFT 8
4 *Helsinki* PFM with 4 x 2 MTO-85 (Swe RBS-15SF) SSM
4 *Rauma* PFM with 2 x 2 and 2 x 1 MTO-85 (Sw RBS-15SF) SSM
PATROL CRAFT, INSHORE 4
2 *Rihtniemi* with 2 ASW RL
2 *Ruissalo* with 2 ASW RL
MINE WARFARE 23
MINELAYERS 10
2 *Hämeenmaa*, 150–200 mines, plus 1 x 6 Matra *Mistral* SAM
1 *Pohjanmaa*, 100–150 mines; plus 1 120mm gun and 2 x 5 ASW RL
3 *Pansio* aux minelayer, 50 mines
4 *Tuima* (ex-PFM), 20 mines
MINE COUNTERMEASURES 13

6 *Kuha* MSI, 7 *Kiiski* MSI
AMPHIBIOUS craft only
3 *Kampela* LCU tpt, 3 *Kala* LCU
SUPPORT AND MISCELLANEOUS 37
1 *Kustaanmiekka* command ship, 5 *Valas* tpt, 6 *Hauki* tpt, 4 *Hila* tpt, 2 *Lohi* tpt, 1 *Aranda* AGOR (Ministry of Trade control), 9 *Prisma* AGS, 9 icebreakers (Board of Navigation control)
COASTAL DEFENCE
1 coastal bde (trg) with **100mm**: D-10T (tank turrets); **130mm**: 195 K-54 (static) arty
COASTAL SSM 5 RBS-15

Air Force 2,700

(1,500 conscripts); 91 cbt ac, no armed hel, 3 AD areas: 3 ftr wg
Flying hours 150
FTR 3 wg
2 with 21 F/A-18C, 7 F/A-18D, 20 *Hawk* 5/51A
1 with 21 SAAB 35 *Drakens*, 10 *Hawk* 51/51A
OCU 5* SAAB SK-35C, 7* F/A-18D
RECCE some *Hawk* Mk 51 (incl in ftr sqn)
SURVEY 3 *Learjet* 35A (survey, ECM trg, target-towing)
TPT 1 **ac** sqn with 3 F-27, 3 *Learjet*-35A
TRG 22 *Hawk* Mk 51, 28 L-70 *Vinka*
LIAISON 13 Piper (7 *Cherokee Arrow*, 6 *Chieftain*), 9 L-90 *Redigo*
AAM AA-2 *Atoll*, AA-8 *Aphid*, AIM-9 *Sidewinder*, RB-27, RB-28 (*Falcon*), AIM-20 AMRAAM

Forces Abroad

UN AND PEACEKEEPING
CROATIA (UNMOP): 1 obs. **CYPRUS** (UNFICYP): 1. **FYROM** (UNPREDEP): 218; 1 inf bn, 1 obs. **INDIA/ PAKISTAN** (UNMOGIP): 5 obs. **IRAQ/KUWAIT** (UNIKOM): 5 obs. **LEBANON** (UNIFIL): 490; 1 inf bn. **MIDDLE EAST** (UNTSO): 12 obs

Paramilitary 3,400

FRONTIER GUARD (Ministry of Interior) **3,400**
(on mob 23,000); 4 frontier, 3 Coast Guard districts, 1 air comd; 5 offshore, 2 coastal, 4 inshore patrol craft (plus boats and ACVs); air patrol sqn with **hel** 3 AS-332, 4 AB-206L, 4 AB-412 **ac** 2 Do-228 (Maritime Surv)

Georgia

	1996	1997	1998	1999
GDP	lari 4.1bn	lari 4.9bn		
	($3.3bn)	($3.7bn)		
per capita	$3,800	$4,300		
Growth	10.5%	11.0%		

contd	1996	1997	1998	1999
Inflation	40.0%	7.3%		
Debt	$1.4bn	$1.6bn		
Def exp	lari 135m	lari 143m		
	($108m)	($109m)		
Def bdgt[a]			lari 82m	
			($55m)	
FMA[b] (US)	$0.3m	$0.3m	$0.4m	$0.4m
$1 = lari	1.25	1.31	1.50	

[a] Abkhazia def bdgt 1997 ε$5m
[b] UNOMIG **1996** $16m **1997** $18m

Population		5,423,000		

(Armenian 8%, Azeri 6%, Russian 6%, Ossetian 3%, Abkhaz 2%)

Age	13–17	18–22	23–32	
Men	214,000	206,000	379,000	
Women	206,000	198,000	361,000	

Total Armed Forces 33,200

(incl 15,600 MoD and centrally controlled units)
Terms of service conscription, 2 years

RESERVES up to 250,000
with mil service in last 15 years

Army 12,600

up to 24,000 planned
Some 6 bde (incl 5 mech inf, 1 gd mech, plus trg centre)
• 1 arty bde (3 bn) • 1 peacekeeping bn
EQUIPMENT
  MBT 79: 48 T-55, 31 T-72
  AIFV/APC 111: 67 BMP-1, 11 BMP-2, 11 BRM-1K, 19 BTR-70, 3 BTR-80
  TOWED ARTY 85mm: D-44; **100mm**: KS-19 (ground role); **122mm**: 57 D-30; **152mm**: 3 2A36, 11 2A65
  SP ARTY 152mm: 1 2S5, 1 2S19
  MRL 122mm: 18 BM-21
  MOR 120mm: 16 M-120
  SAM some SA-13

Navy 2,000

BASES Tbilisi (HQ), Poti
PATROL AND COASTAL COMBATANTS 12
PATROL CRAFT 12
  2 *Zhuk* PCI, 5 ex trawlers, 4 cutters, 1 PCI
MINE COUNTERMEASURES 4 *Yevgenya* MHC
AMPHIBIOUS
  2 LCT, 4 LCM

Air Force 3,000

(incl Air Defence); some 9 Su-25 **ac**, 1 Mi-2, 4 Mi-8, 3 Mi-24 **hel**

AIR DEFENCE
SAM 75 SA-2/-3/-5

Opposition

ABKHAZIA ε5,000
50+ T-72, T-55 MBT, 80+ AIFV/APC, 80+ arty
SOUTH OSSETIA ε2,000
5–10 MBT, 30 AIFV/APC, 25 arty incl BM-21

Paramilitary

COAST GUARD
  3 *Zhuk* PCI

Foreign Forces

RUSSIA 9,200: **Army** 3 mil bases (each = bde+) 140 T-72 MBT, 500 ACV, 173 arty incl **122mm** D-30, 2S1; **152mm** 2S3; **122mm** BM-21 MRL; **120mm** mor plus 118 ACV and some arty deployed in Abkhazia **Air Force** 1 composite regt, some 35 tpt **ac** and **hel** incl An-12, An-26 and Mi-8
PEACEKEEPING: ε1,500; 3 MR, 1 inf bn (Russia)
UN (UNOMIG): 83 obs from 21 countries

Hungary

	1996	1997	1998	1999
GDP	f6.8tr	f8.6tr		
	($45bn)	($46bn)		
per capita	$6,600	$7,000		
Growth	0.8%	4.0%		
Inflation	23.5%	18.3%		
Debt	$27.6bn	$24.3bn		
Def exp	f107bn	f124bn		
	($698m)	($666m)		
Def bdgt			f142bn	f168bn
			($643m)	($701m)
FMA (US)	$4.2m	$1.0m	$1.5m	$1.5m
$1 = forint	153	187	220	

Population		10,050,000		

(Romany 4%, German 3%, Serb 2%, Romanian 1%, Slovak 1%)

Age	13–17	18–22	23–32	
Men	352,000	392,000	694,000	
Women	332,000	367,000	651,000	

Total Armed Forces

ACTIVE 43,300

(ε27,500 conscripts; 8,400 HQ staff and centrally controlled formations/units)

Terms of service 9 months

RESERVES 90,300
Army 74,900 **Air Force** 15,400 (to age 50)

Land Forces 23,400

(ε17,800 conscripts)
Land Forces HQ • 1 Mil District HQ
2 mech div
　1 with 3 mech inf, 1 engr bde, 1 arty, 1 ATK, 2 recce bn
　1 with 2 trg centres
Corps tps
　1 army maritime wing, 1 counter mine bn
MoD tps (Budapest): 1 MP regt

RESERVES
5 mech inf bde
EQUIPMENT
　MBT 835: 597 T-55 (177 in store), 238 T-72 (incl 100
　　T-72M1)
　RECCE 132 FUG D-442
　AIFV 502 BMP-1, BRM-1K, 25 BTR-80A
　APC 789: 356 BTR-80, 403 PSZH D-944 (83 in store),
　　30 MT-LB (plus some 372 'look-alike' types)
　TOTAL ARTY 840
　　TOWED 532: **122mm**: 230 M-1938 (M-30) (24 in
　　store); **152mm**: 302 D-20 (108 in store)
　　SP 122mm: 151 2S1 (18 in store)
　　MRL 122mm: 56 BM-21
　　MOR 120mm: 101 M-120 (2 in store)
　ATGW 353: 117 AT-3 *Sagger*, 30 AT-4 *Spigot* (incl
　　BRDM-2 SP), 206 AT-5 *Spandrel*
　ATK GUNS 85mm: 162 D-44 (62 in store); **100mm**:
　　106 MT-12
　AD GUNS 57mm: 190 S-60 (43 in store)
　SAM 244 SA-7, 60 SA-14, 45 *Mistral* (being delivered)
　SURV PSZNR-5B, SZNAR-10

Army Maritime Wing (290)

BASE Budapest

RIVER CRAFT ε52
6 *Nestin* MSI (riverine), some 46 An-2 mine warfare/
　patrol boats

Air Force 11,500

(5,400 conscripts)
AIR DEFENCE COMMAND
114 cbt ac, 59 attack hel
Flying hours 50
FTR 2 regt with 87 MiG-21bis/MF/UM, 27 MiG-29
ATTACK HEL 59 Mi-24
SPT HEL 33 Mi-2, 47 Mi-8/-17
TPT 4 An-26, 4 Z-43
TRG 19 L-39, 12 Yak-52

AAM AA-2 *Atoll*, AA-8 *Aphid*, AA-10 *Alamo*, AA-11
　Archer
ASM AT-2 *Swatter*, AT-6 *Spiral*
SAM 2 regt with 66 SA-2/-3/-5, 12 SA-4, 20 SA-6

Forces Abroad

UN AND PEACEKEEPING
ANGOLA (UNOMA): 3 obs. **CROATIA** (SFOR II):
300; 1 engr bn. **CYPRUS** (UNFICYP): 105. **EGYPT**
(MFO): 26 mil pol. **GEORGIA** (UNOMIG): 5 obs.
IRAQ/KUWAIT (UNIKOM): 5 obs

Paramilitary 14,100

BORDER GUARDS (Ministry of Interior) 12,000 (to
reduce)
11 districts/regts plus 1 Budapest district (incl 10
　rapid-reaction coy; 33 PSZH, 68 BTR-80 APC)
INTERNAL SECURITY FORCES (Police) 2,100
　33 PSZH, 40 BTR-80APC

Ireland

	1996	1997	1998	1999
GDP	I£42bn	I£47bn		
	($67bn)	($73bn)		
per capita	$16,600	$18,700		
Growth	7.7%	10.5%		
Inflation	1.7%	1.5%		
Publ debt	76.3%	68.3%		
Def exp	I£463m	I£491m		
	($741m)	($767m)		
Def bdgt			I£558m	I£586m
			($770m)	($814m)
$1 = pound	0.63	0.64	0.72	
Population		3,673,000		
Age	*13–17*	*18–22*	*23–32*	
Men	160,000	169,000	319,000	
Women	151,000	160,000	303,000	

Total Armed Forces

ACTIVE 11,500
(incl 200 women)

RESERVES 14,800
(obligation to age 60, officers 57–65) **Army** first-line
500, second-line 14,000 **Navy** 300

Army 9,300

4 Territorial Comds

1 inf force (2 inf bn)
4 inf bde
  2 with 2 inf bn
  1 with 3 inf bn, all with 1 fd arty regt, 1 cav recce
    sqn, 1 engr coy
  1 with 2 inf bn, 1 armd recce sqn, 1 fd arty bty
Army tps: 1 lt tk sqn, 1 AD regt, 1 Ranger coy
Total units: 11 inf bn • 1 UNIFIL bn *ad hoc* with elm
from other bn, 1 lt tk sqn, 4 recce sqn (1 armd), 3 fd
arty regt (each of 2 bty) • 1 indep bty, 1 AD regt (1
regular, 3 reserve bty), 4 fd engr coy, 1 Ranger coy

RESERVES
4 Army Gp (garrisons), 18 inf bn, 6 fd arty regt, 3 cav
sqn, 3 engr sqn, 3 AD bty

EQUIPMENT
  LT TK 14 *Scorpion*
  RECCE 15 AML-90, 32 AML-60
  APC 47 Panhard VTT/M3, 2 A-180 *Sisu*
  TOWED ARTY 88mm: 42 25-pdr; **105mm**: 18 L-118
  MOR 81mm: 400; **120mm**: 67
  ATGW 21 *Milan*
  RL 84mm: AT-4
  RCL 84mm: 444 *Carl Gustav*; **90mm**: 96 PV-1110
  AD GUNS 40mm: 24 L/60, 2 L/70
  SAM 7 RBS-70

Naval Service 1,100
BASE Cork
PATROL AND COASTAL COMBATANTS 8
  PATROL OFFSHORE 8
  1 *Eithne* with 1 *Dauphin* hel, 3 *Emer*, 1 *Deirdre*, 2 *Orla*
  (UK *Peacock*)

Air Corps 1,100
7 cbt ac, 15 armed hel; 3 wg (1 trg)
CCT 1 sqn
  1 with 7 SF-260WE,
MR 2 CN-235MP
TPT 1 *Super King Air* 200, 1 *Gulfstream* IV
LIAISON 1 sqn with 6 Cessna Reims FR-172H, 1 FR-172K
HEL 4 sqn
  1 Army spt with 8 SA-316B (*Alouette* III)
  1 Navy spt with 2 SA-365FI (*Dauphin*)
  1 SAR with 3 SA-365FI (*Dauphin*)
  1 trg with 2 SA-342L (*Gazelle*)

Forces Abroad
UN AND PEACEKEEPING
CROATIA (UNMOP): 1 obs. **CYPRUS** (UNFICYP): 30.
FYROM (UNPREDEP): 1 obs. **IRAQ/KUWAIT**
(UNIKOM): 6 obs. **LEBANON** (UNIFIL): 608; 1 bn; 4
AML-90 armd cars, 10 *Sisu* APC, 4 **120mm** mor.

MIDDLE EAST (UNTSO): 11 obs. **WESTERN
SAHARA** (MINURSO): 8 obs

Latvia

	1996	1997	1998	1999
GDP	L1.7bn	L2.0bn		
	($3.0bn)	($3.4bn)		
per capita	$4,800	$5,100		
Growth	3.4%	6.6%		
Inflation	13.1%	8.4%		
Debt	$432m	$486m		
Def exp[a]	εL75m	εL90.9m		
	($136m)	($156m)		
Def bdgt			L23.2m	L43.0m
			($39m)	($72m)
FMA (US)	$1.9m	$0.5m	$0.7m	$0.7m
(Swe)		$1.5m		
$1 = lats	0.55	0.58	0.60	

[a] Incl exp on paramilitary forces.

Population	2,458,000

(Russian 34%, Belarussian 5%, Ukrainian 3%, Polish
2%)

Age	*13–17*	*18–22*	*23–32*
Men	97,000	91,000	169,000
Women	94,000	88,000	165,000

Total Armed Forces
ACTIVE 4,960
(incl 2,150 conscripts, 1,600 National Guard) *Terms of
service* 12 months

RESERVES 14,600
National Guard

Army 2,350
(incl 1,380 conscripts)
1 inf bn • 1 recce bn • 1 engr bn • 1 peacekeeping coy
• 1 SF team

RESERVES
National Guard 5 bde each of 5–7 bn
EQUIPMENT
  RECCE 2 BRDM-2
  APC 13 *Pskbil* m/42
  TOWED ARTY 100mm: 24 K-53
  MOR 82mm: 4; **120mm**: 24
  AD GUNS 14.5mm: 12 ZPU-4

Navy 880
(incl 430 conscripts, 220 Coastal Defence)

Lat, Ea and L have set up a joint Naval unit BALTRON
BASES Liepaja, Riga, Tallinn (Ea)
PATROL CRAFT 12

    1 *Osa* PFM (unarmed), 1 *Storm* PCC (unarmed), 2
    Ribnadzor PC, 5 KBV 236 PC<, 3 PCH (plus 1 tug,
    1 diving vessel)
MINE COUNTERMEASURES 2 *Kondor* II MCO

SUPPORT AND MISCELLANEOUS 2

    1 *Nyrat* AT, 1 *Goliat* AT

COASTAL DEFENCE (220)

1 coastal def bn

Air Force 130

AC 2 An-2, 1 L-410
HEL 3 Mi-2

Forces Abroad

UN AND PEACEKEEPING
BOSNIA (SFOR II): 40

Paramilitary 3,720

BORDER GUARD (Ministry of Internal Affairs) 3,500

1 bde (7 bn)

COAST GUARD 220

5 PCI<, 2 converted fishing boats, 3 PCH

Lithuania

	1996	1997	1998	1999
GDP	L32bn	L38bn		
	($2.9bn)	($3.1bn)		
per capita	$4,900	$5,300		
Growth	4.8%	5.7%		
Inflation	13.1%	8.4%		
Debt	$1,189m	$1,787m		
Def exp[a]	εL500m	εL540m		
	($125m)	($135m)		
Def bdgt			L462m	L730m
			($116m)	($183m)
FMA (US)	$1.9m	$0.5m	$0.7m	$0.7m
$1 = litas	4.0	4.0	4.0	
[a] Incl exp on paramilitary forces				
Population		3,700,000		
(Russian 9%, Polish 8%, Belarussian 2%)				
Age	*13–17*	*18–22*	*23–32*	
Men	142,000	135,000	263,000	
Women	137,000	131,000	256,000	

Total Armed Forces

ACTIVE 11,130
(incl 3,548 conscripts; 2,090 Voluntary National
Defence Force) *Terms of service* 12 months

RESERVES 355,650
27,700 **first line** (ready 72 hrs, incl 11,100 Voluntary
National Defence Service), 327,950 **second line** (age up
to 59)

Army 6,750

(incl 2,799 conscripts)
1 motor rifle bde (6 bn) • 1 Jaeger, 1 Guard, 1 engr bn •
1 peacekeeping coy
EQUIPMENT
    RECCE 11 BRDM-2
    APC 14 BTR-60, 13 *Pskbil* m/42
    MOR 120mm: 36 M-43
    RCL 84mm: 119 *Carl Gustav*

RESERVES
Voluntary National Defence Service: 10 Territorial
Defence regt, 38 territorial def bn, 134 territorial def
coy 2 air sqn

Navy 1,320 (incl 670 conscripts)

Lat, Ea and L have set up a joint Naval unit BALTRON
BASES Klaipeda, HQ BALTRON Tallinn (Ea)
FRIGATES 2
    2 Sov Grisha III, with 2 x 12 ASW RL, 4 533mm TT
PATROL AND COASTAL COMBATANTS 4
    1 *Storm* PCI, 1 SK-21 PCI, 1 SK-23 PCI, 1 SK-24 PCI
SUPPORT AND MISCELLANEOUS 1
    1 *Valerian Uryvayev* AGOR

Air Force 970

no cbt ac
Flying hours 60
Air Force HQ, 3 Air Bases, 1 Air Control Centre, 3 Air
Surveillance coy
AC 4 L-39, 2 L-410, 3 AN-26, 1 AN-24
HEL 3 Mi-8, 5 Mi-2

Forces Abroad

UN AND PEACEKEEPING
BOSNIA (SFOR II): 41

Paramilitary 3,900

BORDER POLICE 3,500

COAST GUARD 400

Macedonia, Former Yugoslav Republic of

	1996	1997	1998	1999
GDP	ε$1.3bn	ε$1.3bn		
per capita	$3,500	$3,600		
Growth	0.9%	1.5%		
Inflation	2.5%	1.3%		
Debt	$1.2bn	$1.1bn		
Def exp	d4.8bn	ε6.6bn		
	($120m)	($132m)		
Def bdgt			εd3.7bn	
			($66m)	
FMA[a] (US)	$0.3m	$0.5m	$3.4m	$0.5m
$1 = dinar	40.0	50.0	56.2	

[a] UNPREDEP **1996** $50m **1997** $45m

Population		2,284,000		
(Albanian 22%, Turkish 4%, Romany 3%, Serb 2%)				
Age	*13–17*	*18–22*	*23–32*	
Men	95,000	91,000	178,000	
Women	86,000	83,000	161,000	

Total Armed Forces

ACTIVE 20,000

(8,000 conscripts) *Terms of service* 9 months

RESERVES 102,000 planned

Army 20,000

3 Corps HQ (cadre), 3 bde
1 border gd bde

EQUIPMENT

MBT 4 T-34
RECCE 10 BRDM-2
APC M-80, 50 BTR-70, 10 BTR-80
TOWED ARTY 400 incl **76mm**: M-48, M-1942;
  105mm: 14 (ex US)
MRL 128mm: M-71 (single barrel), M-63
MOR 1,200 incl **60mm**, **82mm** and 130 **120mm**
ATGW AT-3 *Sagger*
RCL 57mm: 2,400; **82mm**

MARINE WING (400)

9 river patrol craft

Air Force

ac 4 *Zlin*-242 (trg), 10 UTVA-75 **hel** 4 Mi-17
AD GUNS 50: **20mm**; **40mm**
SAM 30 SA-7

Paramilitary 7,500

POLICE 7,500
(some 4,500 armed)

Foreign Forces

UN (UNPREDEP): some 796; 2 inf bn (US, SF), incl 34
obs and 26 civ pol from 27 countries

Malta

	1996	1997	1998	1999
GDP	ML1.1bn	ML1.3bn		
	($3.3bn)	($3.3bn)		
per capita	$7,900	$8,300		
Growth	3.6%	2.9%		
Inflation	2.6%	3.2%		
Debt	$953m	$978m		
Def exp	ML12.0m	ML11.8m		
	($33m)	($31m)		
Def bdgt			ML11.5m	
			($29m)	
FMA (US)	$0.03m	$0.1m	$0.1m	$0.1m
$1 = lira	0.36	0.39	0.40	

Population		375,000		
Age	*13–17*	*18–22*	*23–32*	
Men	14,000	14,000	26,000	
Women	14,000	14,000	25,000	

Total Armed Forces

ACTIVE 1,900

Armed Forces of Malta 1,900

Comd HQ, spt tps
No. 1 Regt (inf bn): 3 rifle, 1 spt coy
No. 2 Regt (composite regt)
  1 air wg (76) with **ac** 4 0-1 *Bird Dog*, 2 BN-2 *Islander* **hel**
    2 SA-316A, 3 SA-316B, 2 NH-369M Hughes, 1 AB-
    206A, 4 AB-47G2
  1 maritime sqn (210) with 3 ex-GDR *Kondor* 1 PCC,
    4 PCI, 3 harbour craft, 1 LCVP
  1 AD bty; **14.5mm**: 50 ZPU-4; **40mm**: 40 Bofors
No. 3 Regt (Depot Regt): 1 engr sqn, 1 workshop, 1
  ordnance, 1 airport coy

Foreign Forces

ITALY 16 **Air Force** 2 AB-212 **hel**

Moldova

	1996	1997	1998	1999
GDP	L8.6bn	L9.5bn		
	($1.1bn)	($1.2bn)		
per capita	$3,500	$3,600		
Growth	-7.8%	1.3%		
Inflation	23.5%	11.8%		
Debt	$795m	$969m		
Def exp[a]	L215m	L245m		
	($47m)	($53m)		
Def bdgt			L96m	
			($20m)	
FMA (US)	$0.6m	$0.3m	$0.4m	$0.5m
$1 = leu	4.60	4.62	4.73	

[a] Incl exp on paramilitary forces

Population	4,315,000		
(Moldovan/Romanian 65%, Ukrainian 14%, Russian 13%, Gagauz 4%, Bulgarian 2%, Jewish <1.5%)			
Age	*13–17*	*18–22*	*23–32*
Men	199,000	181,000	295,000
Women	187,000	177,000	299,000

Total Armed Forces

ACTIVE 11,050

(incl ε5,200 conscripts) *Terms of service* up to 18 months

RESERVES some 66,000

with mil service within last 5 years

Army some 10,000

(ε5,200 conscripts)
3 MR bde • 1 arty bde • 1 recce/assault, 1 gd, 1 SF, 1 engr bn

EQUIPMENT

AIFV 54 BMD
APC 11 BTR-80, 11 BTR-D, 2 BTR-60PB, 131 TAB-71, plus 126 'look-alikes'
TOTAL ARTY 154
TOWED ARTY 122mm: 17 M-30; **152mm**: 32 D-20, 21 2A36
COMBINED GUN/MOR 120mm: 9 2S9
MRL 220mm: 15 9P140 *Uragan*
MOR 82mm: 54; **120mm**: 60 M-120
ATGW 70 AT-4 *Spigot*, 19 AT-5 *Spandrel*, 27 AT-6 *Spiral*
RCL 73mm: SPG-9
ATK GUNS 100mm: 26 MT-12
AD GUNS 23mm: 30 ZU-23; **57mm**: 12 S-60
SURV GS-13 (arty), 1 L219/200 PARK-1 (arty), *Long Trough* ((SNAR-1) arty), *Pork Trough* ((SNAR-2/-6) veh, arty), *Small Fred/Small Yawn* (veh, arty), *Big Fred* ((SNAR-10) veh, arty)

Air Force 1,050

(incl AD)
TPT 1 mixed sqn **ac** An-24, 2 An-72, 1 Tu-134, 1 IL-18 **hel** 8 Mi-8
SAM 1 bde with 25 SA-3/-5

Paramilitary 3,400

INTERNAL TROOPS (Ministry of Interior) 2,500
OPON (Ministry of Interior) 900 (riot police)

Opposition

DNIESTR 5,000

incl Republican Guard (Dniestr bn), Delta bn, ε1,000 Cossacks

Foreign Forces

RUSSIA 2,500: 1 op gp
PEACEKEEPING: 2 inf bn (-) **Russia** (500) 3 inf bn **Moldova** (300) 3 bn **Dniestr** (400)

Poland

	1996	1997	1998	1999
GDP	z363bn	z444bn		
	($109bn)	($135bn)		
per capita	$6,400	$7,000		
Growth	6.0%	6.7%		
Inflation	20.1%	15.9%		
Debt	$41bn	$39bn		
Def exp	z9.8bn	z10.7bn		
	($3.7bn)	($3.1bn)		
Def bdgt			z11.6bn	z12.1bn
			($3.4bn)	($3.4bn)
FMA (US)	$17.5m	$1.0m	$1.6m	$1.6m
$1 = zloty	2.70	3.28	3.44	

Population	38,659,000		
(German 1.3%, Ukrainian 0.6%, Belarussian 0.5%)			
Age	*13–17*	*18–22*	*23–32*
Men	1,659,000	1,598,000	2,708,000
Women	1,576,000	1,521,000	2,592,000

Total Armed Forces

ACTIVE 240,650

(141,600 conscripts; incl 25,750 centrally controlled staffs, units/formations)
Terms of service all services 18 months (to be 12 months from 1 Jan 1999)

RESERVES

Army 343,000 **Navy** 14,000 (to age 50) **Air Force** 49,000 (to age 60)

Army 142,500

(incl 101,670 conscripts)
4 Mil Districts/Army HQ
Pomerania 2 mech div (incl 1 coast def), 1 arty, 1 engr, 1 territorial def bde, 1 SSM, 1 cbt hel, 2 AA arty, 1 SA-6 regt
Silesia 3 mech, 1 armd cav div, 1 mtn, 2 arty, 2 engr, 1 AD arty bde, 2 SSM regt
Warsaw 3 mech div, 1 arty, 1 engr, 1 territorial def bde, 1 cbt hel regt
Krakow 1 air cavalry div HQ, 1 armd, 1 mech, 1 air aslt, 1 mtn, 1 territorial def bde, 1 mech, 2 engr, 1 recce regt
Div tps: 10 SA-6/-8 regt
General Staff tps: 1 special ops, 1 gd regt

EQUIPMENT

MBT 1,727: 839 T-55, 772 T-72, 116 PT-91
RECCE 510 BRDM-2
AIFV 1,405: 1,367 BMP-1, 38 BRM-1
APC 35 OT-64 plus some 693 'look-alike' types
TOTAL ARTY 1,580
  TOWED 440: **122mm**: 280 M-1938 (M-30); **152mm**: 160 M-1938 (ML-20)
  SP 652: **122mm**: 533 2S1; **152mm**: 111 *Dana* (M-77); **203mm**: 8 2S7
  MRL 258: **122mm**: 228 BM-21, 30 RM-70
  MOR 230: **120mm**: 214 M-120, 16 2B11/2S12
SSM launchers: 35 FROG, SS-C-2B
ATGW 403: 263 AT-3 *Sagger*, 115 AT-4 *Spigot*, 18 AT-5 *Spandrel*, 7 AT-6 *Spiral*
ATK GUNS 85mm: 711 D-44
AD GUNS 1,116: **23mm**: ZU-23-2, ZSU-23-4 SP; **57mm**: S-60
SAM 1,290: SA-6/-7/-8/-9/-13
HELICOPTERS
  ATTACK 22 PZL-W3, 38 Mi-24, 34 Mi-2URP
  SPT 18 Mi-2URN
  TPT 36 Mi-8/Mi-17, 31 Mi-2
  SURV GS-13 (arty), 1 L219/200 PARK-1 (arty), *Long Trough* ((SNAR-1) arty), *Pork Trough* ((SNAR-2/-6) veh, arty), *Small Fred/Small Yawn* (veh, arty), *Big Fred* ((SNAR-10) veh, arty)

Navy 17,100

(incl 2,460 Naval Aviation, 9,500 conscripts)
BASES Gdynia, Hel, Swinoujscie; Kolobrzeg, Gdansk (Coast Guard)

SUBMARINES 3

1 *Orzel* SS (RF *Kilo*) with 533mm TT
2 *Wilk* (RF *Foxtrot*) with 533mm TT

PRINCIPAL SURFACE COMBATANTS 2

DESTROYERS 1 *Warszawa* DDG (Sov mod *Kashin*) with 2 x 2 SA-N-1 *Goa* SAM, 4 SS-N-2C *Styx* SSM, 5 533mm TT, 2 ASW RL
FRIGATES 1 *Kaszub* with 2 ASW RL, 4 533mm TT, 76mm gun

PATROL AND COASTAL COMBATANTS 33

CORVETTES 4 *Gornik* (Sov *Tarantul* I) with 2 x 2 SS-N-2C *Styx* SSM, 76mm gun
MISSILE CRAFT 7 Sov *Osa* I PFM with 4 SS-N-2A SSM
PATROL CRAFT 22
  COASTAL 3 *Sassnitz* with 1 x SA-N-5 SAM, 1 x 76mm gun
  INSHORE 19
  8 *Obluze* PCI, 11 *Pilica* PCI<

MINE WARFARE 24

MINELAYERS none, but SS, *Krogulec* MSC and *Lublin* LSM have minelaying capability
MINE COUNTERMEASURES 24
  5 *Krogulec* MSC, 13 *Goplo* (*Notec*) MSI, 4 *Mamry* (*Notec*) MHI, 2 *Leniwka* MSI

AMPHIBIOUS 5

5 *Lublin* LSM, capacity 135 tps, 9 tk
Plus craft: 3 *Deba* LCU (none employed in amph role), 2 LCU

SUPPORT AND MISCELLANEOUS 12

1 comd ship, 2 AGI, 3 AGHS, 2 ARS, 4 spt tkr

NAVAL AVIATION (2,460)

28 cbt ac, 11 armed hel
Flying hours (MiG-21) 60
7 sqn
  2 with 28 MiG-21 BIS/UM
  1 with **5 PZL-3RM** (SAR), 2 PZL-W3T (tpt), 3 An-28 (tpt), 25 Mi-2 (tpt)
  1 ASW with 11 Mi-14PL
  1 SAR with 3 Mi-14 PS, 3 Mi-2RM
  1 SAR with 3 PZL An-28RM, 6 PZL An-2
  1 Recce with 17 PZL TS-11 *Iskra*

Air Force 55,300

(incl AD tps, 30,430 conscripts); 297 cbt ac, 32 attack hel
Flying hours 60
FTR 3 AD Corps
  7 regt with 133 MiG-21/U, 27 MiG-23, 22 MiG-29/U
FGA 4 regt with 99 Su-22
RECCE 16* MiG-21R/U
TPT 2 regt with 32 An-2, 10 An-26, 5 An-28, 13 Yak-40, 2 Tu-154
HEL 32* PZL-W3W, 35 Mi-2, 5 Mi-8
TRG 183 TS-11 *Iskra*, 11 PZL I-22 *Iryda*, 25 PZL-130 *Orlik*
IN STORE 13 MiG-17, 1 MiG-21
AAM AA-2 *Atoll*, AA-8 *Aphid*
ASM AS-7 *Kerry*
SAM 5 bde; 1 indep regt with about 200 SA-2/-3/-4/-5

Forces Abroad

UN AND PEACEKEEPING

ANGOLA (UNOMA): 4 obs. **BOSNIA** (SFOR II): 450;
1 AB bn. **CROATIA** (UNMOP): 1 obs. **GEORGIA**
(UNOMIG): 3 obs. **IRAQ/KUWAIT** (UNIKOM): 5 obs.
LEBANON (UNIFIL): 629; 1 inf bn, mil hospital.
FYROM (UNPREDEP): 2 obs. **ROK** (Neutral Nations
Supervisory Commission – NNSC): staff. **SYRIA**
(UNDOF): 354; 1 inf bn. **TAJIKISTAN** (UNMOT): 4
obs. **WESTERN SAHARA** (MINURSO): 3 obs

Paramilitary 23,400

BORDER GUARDS (Ministry of Interior and
Administration) 13,500

12 district units, 2 trg centres

MARITIME BORDER GUARD

about 28 patrol craft: 2 PCC, 9 PCI and 17 PC1<

PREVENTION UNITS OF POLICE (OPP-Ministry of
Interior) 7,000

(1,000 conscripts)

Romania

	1996	1997	1998	1999
GDP	lei 102tr	lei 250tr		
	($33bn)	($35bn)		
per capita	$4,800	$4,600		
Growth	3.9%	-6.6%		
Inflation	38.8%	154.8%		
Debt	$8.5bn	$10.4bn		
Def exp	lei 2.3tr	lei 5.7tr		
	($745m)	($793m)		
Def bdgt			lei 6.8tr	
			($782m)	
FMA (US)	$10.0m	$0.9m	$1.0m	$1.3m
$1 = lei	3,084	7,168	8,690	
Population	22,520,000 (Hungarian 9%)			
Age	*13–17*	*18–22*	*23–32*	
Men	887,000	930,000	1,810,000	
Women	855,000	895,000	1,749,000	

Total Armed Forces

ACTIVE 219,650

(incl 133,300 conscripts, 1,800 MoD staff and 38,150 in
centrally controlled units)
Terms of service **Army, Air Force** 12 months, **Navy** 18
months

RESERVES 470,000

Army 400,000 **Navy** 30,000 **Air Force** 40,000

Army 111,300

(77,950 conscripts)
3 Army HQ, 7 Corps HQ each with 2–3 mech 1 tk, 1
mtn, 1 arty, 1 ATK, 1 mixed AAA bde
Army tps: 1 tk, 1 mech, 1 mtn, 1 arty, 1 ATK, 3 AAA
bde, 1 mech, 1 arty, 4 AAA, 4 SAM, 3 engr regt
MoD tps: 3 AB (Air Force), 1 gd bde, 2 recce bn
Land Force tps: 2 *Scud*, 1 arty, 1 engr bde; 2 engr regt
Determining the manning state of units is difficult. The following is based on the latest available information: one-third
at 100%, one-third at 50–70%, one-third at 10–20%

EQUIPMENT

MBT 1,253: 821 T-55, 30 T-72, 314 TR-85, 88 TR-580
ASLT GUN 84 SU-100
RECCE 121 BRDM-2, 44 ABC-M
AIFV 177 MLI-84
APC 1,614: 167 TAB-77, 394 TABC-79, 965 TAB-71,
88 MLVM, plus 1,015 'look-alikes'
TOTAL ARTY 1,291
TOWED 751: **122mm**: 204 M-1938 (M-
30) (A-19); **130mm**: 82 Gun 82; **150mm**: 12 Skoda
(Model 1934); **152mm**: 111 Gun-how 85, 288
Model 81, 54 M-1937 (ML-20)
SP 48: **122mm**: 6 2S1, 42 Model 89
MRL 122mm: 160 APR-40
MOR 120mm: 332 M-1982
SSM launchers: 9 FROG
ATGW 174 AT-3 *Sagger* (incl BRDM-2), 54 AT-5
Spandrel
ATK GUNS 57mm: M-1943; **85mm**: D-44; **100mm**:
880 Gun 77, 75 Gun 75
AD GUNS 1,093: **30mm; 37mm; 57mm; 85mm;
100mm**
SAM 69 SA-6/-7/-8
SURV GS-13 (arty), 1 L219/200 PARK-1 (arty), *Long
Trough* ((SNAR-1) arty), *Pork Trough* ((SNAR-2/-6)
veh, arty), *Small Fred/Small Yawn* ((veh, arty), *Big
Fred* ((SNAR-10) veh, arty)
UAV 6 *Shadow*-600 (being delivered)

Navy 22,100

(13,200 conscripts; incl 10,250 Naval Inf and Coastal
Defence)
Navy HQ with 1 Naval fleet, 1 Danube flotilla, 1 Naval
inf corps
Naval fleet with 1 missile, torpedo, minelayer,
minesweeper bde
Danube flotilla with 1 riverine naval and 1 river bde
BASES Coastal Mangalia, Constanta **Danube** Braila,
Giurgiu, Tulcea, Galati
SUBMARINES 1
1 Sov Kilo SS with 533mm TT
PRINCIPAL SURFACE COMBATANTS 7
DESTROYERS 1 *Muntena* DDG with 4 x 2 SS-N-2C
Styx SSM, plus SA-N-5 *Grail* SAM, 2 IAR-316 hel, 2 x
3 533mm TT, RBU 6000

FRIGATES 6
4 *Tetal* 1 with 2 ASW RL, 4 ASTT
2 *Tetal* II with 2 ASW RL, 4 ASTT, plus 1 SA-316 hel

PATROL AND COASTAL COMBATANTS 47

CORVETTES 3 *Zborul* (Sov *Tarantul* I) with 2 x 2 SS-N-2C *Styx*, 1 76mm gun

MISSILE CRAFT 3 Sov *Osa* I PFM with 4 SS-N-2A *Styx*

TORPEDO CRAFT 31
12 *Epitrop* PFT with 4 533mm TT
19 PRC *Huchuan* PHT with 2 533mm TT

PATROL CRAFT 10
OFFSHORE 4 *Democratia* (GDR M-40) PCO
RIVERINE 6
some 3 *Brutar* with 1 100mm gun, 1 122mm RL, 3 *Kogalniceanu* with 2 x 100mm gun

MINE WARFARE 37

MINELAYERS 2 *Cosar*, capacity 100 mines

MINE COUNTERMEASURES 35
4 *Musca* MSC, 6 T-301 MSI (plus some 9 non-op), 25 VD141 MSI<

SUPPORT AND MISCELLANEOUS 11
2 *Constanta* log spt with 1 *Alouette* hel, 3 spt tkr, 2 AGOR, 1 trg, 2 tugs, 1 tkr

HELICOPTERS 7
3 1AR-316, 4 Mi-14 PL

NAVAL INFANTRY (10,250)
1 Corps HQ
2 mech, 1 mot inf, 1 arty bde, 1 AD arty regt, 1 ATK, 1 marine bn

EQUIPMENT
MBT 120 TR-580
APC 208: 172 TAB-71, 36 TABC-79 plus 101 'look-alikes'
TOTAL ARTY 144
TOWED 90: **122mm**: 54 M-1938 (M-30); **152mm**: 36 Model 81
MRL 122mm: 18 APR-40
MOR 120mm: 36 Model 1982
ATK GUNS 100mm: 57 Gun 77

COASTAL DEFENCE
4 coastal arty bty with 32 **130mm**

Air Force 46,300

(incl 5,500 AB, 26,900 conscripts); 362 cbt ac, 16 attack hel

Flying hours 40

Air Force comd: 2 Corps, 1 avn base and Group, 1 hel base and Group, 1 trg base and Group, 1 Eng Regt, 1 SAM regt, 1 AAA regt, 1 AD arty, 3 para bde

FGA 2 regt with 74 IAR-93

FTR 6 regt with 209 MiG-21, 40 MiG-23, 18 MiG-29

RECCE 2 sqn
1 with 12* Il-28 (recce/ECM)
1 with 9* MiG-21

TPT ac 6 An-24, 11 An-26, 2 Boeing 707, 4 C-130B **hel** 5 IAR-330, 9 Mi-8, 4 SA-365

SURVEY 3 An-30

HELICOPTERS
ATTACK 16 IAR 316A
CBT SPT 74 IAR-330, 88 IAR-316, 15 Mi-8, 2 Mi-17

TRG ac 45 L-29, 32 L-39, 14 IAR-99, 36 IAR-823, 23 Yak-52

AAM AA-2 *Atoll*, AA-3 *Anab*, AA-7 *Apex*, AA-11 *Archer*

ASM AS-7 *Kerry*

AD 2 div bde
20 SAM sites with 120 SA-2, SA-3 *Strella*

Forces Abroad

UN AND PEACEKEEPING

ANGOLA (UNOMA): 142. **BOSNIA** (SFOR II): 150; 1 engr bn. **KUWAIT** (UNIKOM): 6 obs

Paramilitary 75,900

BORDER GUARDS (Ministry of Interior) 22,900
(incl conscripts) 6 bde, 7 naval gp
33 TAB-71 APC, 18 SU-100 aslt gun, 12 M-1931/37 (A19) **122mm** how, 18 M-38 **120mm** mor, 7 PRC *Shanghai* II PFI

GENDARMERIE (Ministry of Interior) 53,000

Slovakia

	1996	1997	1998	1999
GDP	Ks576bn	Ks654bn		
	($18.8bn)	($19.5bn)		
per capita	$6,600	$7,100		
Growth	7.0%	5.7%		
Inflation	5.8%	6.1%		
Debt	$7.8bn	$10.7bn		
Def exp	Ks13.8bn	Ks13.9bn		
	($450m)	($414m)		
Def bdgt			Ks14.6bn	
			($416m)	
FMA (US)	$4.2m	$0.6m	$0.6m	$0.6m
$ = koruna	30.7	33.6	35.2	
Population		5,391,000		
(Hungarian 11%, Romany ε5%, Czech 1%)				
Age	*13–17*	*18–22*	*23–32*	
Men	228,000	232,000	410,000	
Women	220,000	225,000	400,000	

Total Armed Forces

ACTIVE 45,450

(incl 13,600 conscripts, 2,100 centrally controlled staffs, 7,550 log and spt)

Terms of service 12 months

RESERVES ε20,000 on mob
National Guard Force

Army 23,800

(incl 13,600 conscripts)
2 Corps HQ
3 tk bde (each 3 tk, 1 mech, 1 recce, 1 arty bn)
3 mech inf bde (each 3 mech inf, 1 tk, 1 recce, 1 arty bn)

RESERVES

National Guard Force 6 bde plus 32 indep coy

EQUIPMENT

MBT 478 (103 in store): 272 T-72M, 206 T-55
RECCE 129 BRDM, 90 OT-65, 72 BPVZ
AIFV 383 BMP-1, 93 BMP-2
APC 207 OT-90
TOTAL ARTY 382 (68 in store)
  TOWED 122mm: 76 D-30
  SP 191: 122mm: 49 2S1; 152mm: 134 *Dana* (M-77);
  155mm: 8 *Zuzana* 2000
  MRL 122mm: 87 RM-70
  MOR 120mm: 36 M-1982
SSM 9 FROG-7, SS-21, SS-23, *Scud*
ATGW 538 (incl BMP-1/-2 and BRDM mounted):
  AT-3 *Sagger*, AT-5 *Spandrel*
AD GUNS ε200: 30mm: M-53/-59, *Strop* SP; 57mm:
  S-60
SAM SA-7, ε48 SA-9/-13
SURV GS-13 (veh), *Long Trough* (SNAR-1), *Pork
Trough* ((SNAR-2/-6) arty), *Small Fred/Small Yawn*
(veh, arty), *Big Fred* (SNAR-10) veh, arty)

Air Force 12,000

121 cbt ac, 19 attack hel
Flying hours 45
FGA 20 Su-22, 12 Su-25
FTR 57 MiG-21, 24 MiG-29
RECCE 8* MiG-21 RF
TPT 1 An-12, 2 An-24, 2 An-26, 4 L410M
TRG 14 L-29, 20 L-39
ATTACK HEL 19 Mi-24
ASLT TPT 13 Mi-2, 7 Mi-8, 17 Mi-17
AAM AA-2 *Atoll*, AA-7 *Apex*, AA-8 *Aphid*, AA-10
  Alamo, AA-11 *Archer*
AD SA-2, SA-3, SA-6, SA-10B

Forces Abroad

UN AND PEACEKEEPING

ANGOLA (UNOMA): 3 obs. SYRIA (UNDOF): 35

Paramilitary 2,600

INTERNAL SECURITY FORCES 1,400

CIVIL DEFENCE TROOPS 1,200

Slovenia

	1996	1997	1998	1999
GDP	t2.6tr	t2.9tr		
	($16bn)	($18bn)		
per capita	$7,000	$7,400		
Growth	3.1%	3.3%		
Inflation	9.7%	9.1%		
Debt	$4.0bn	$4.3bn		
Def exp	t31bn	t50bn		
	($226m)	($310m)		
Def bdgt			t41.4bn	
			($241m)	
FMA (US)	$0.7m	$0.4m	$0.6m	$0.7m
$1 = tolar	135	160	172	
Population		2,015,000		
(Croat 3%, Serb 2%, Muslim 1%)				
Age	13–17	18–22	23–32	
Men	72,000	75,000	148,000	
Women	67,000	71,000	146,000	

Total Armed Forces

ACTIVE 9,550

(5,500 conscripts) *Terms of service* 7 months

RESERVES 53,000

Army (incl 300 maritime)

Army 9,550

(5,500 conscripts)
7 Mil Regions, 27 Mil Districts • 7 inf bde (each 1
active, 3 reserve inf bn) • 1 SF 'bde' • 1 SAM 'bde' (bn)
• 2 indep mech bn • 1 avn 'bde' • 1 arty bn

RESERVES

2 indep mech, 1 arty, 1 coast def, 1 ATK bn

EQUIPMENT

MBT 44 M-84, 46 T-55, 6 T-34
RECCE 16 BRDM-2
AIFV 52 M-80
APC Voluk (*Pandur* – being delivered)
TOWED ARTY 105mm: 18 M-2; 155mm: 10
SP ARTY 122mm: 8 2S1
MRL 128mm: 56 M-71 (single tube), 4 M-63
MOR 120mm: 120 M-52
ATGW AT-3 *Sagger* (incl 12 BOV-1SP)

MARITIME ELEMENT (100)

(effectively police) (plus 300 reserve)
BASE Koper
2 PCI<

AIR ELEMENT (120)
8 armed hel
AC 3 PC-9, 3 *Zlin-242*, 1 LET L-410, 3 UTVA-75
HEL 1 AB-109, 3 B-206, 8* B-412
SAM 9 SA-9
AD GUNS 20mm: 9 SP; **30mm**: 9 SP; **57mm**: 21 SP

Forces Abroad

UN AND PEACEKEEPING
CYPRUS (UNFICYP): 10

Paramilitary 4,500

POLICE 4,500
armed (plus 5,000 reserve) **hel** 2 AB-206 *Jet Ranger*, 1
AB-109A, 1 AB-212, 1 AB-412

Sweden

	1996	1997	1998	1999
GDP	Skr1.6tr	Skr1.7tr		
	($213bn)	($225bn)		
per capita	$20,000	$20,700		
Growth	1.3%	1.8%		
Inflation	0.0%	0.8%		
Publ Debt	77.5%	77.1%		
Def exp	Skr42.7bn	Skr41.8bn		
	($6.4bn)	($5.5bn)		
Def bdgt			Skr36.8bn	Skr38.1bn
			($4.6bn)	($4.8bn)
$1 = kronor	6.71	7.63	8.07	
Population		8,882,000		
Age	*13–17*	*18–22*	*23–32*	
Men	264,000	270,000	613,000	
Women	248,000	255,000	582,000	

Total Armed Forces

ACTIVE 53,100
(34,900 conscripts and active reservists)
Terms of service **Army, Navy** 7–15 months **Air Force** 8–12 months

RESERVES[a] 570,000
(obligation to age 47) **Army** (incl Local Defence and
Home Guard) 450,000 **Navy** 50,000 **Air Force** 70,000

[a] About 48,000 reservists carry out refresher trg each year;
length of trg depends on rank (officers up to 31 days, NCO
and specialists, 24 days, others 17 days). Commitment is five
exercises during reserve service period, plus mob call-outs

Army 35,100

(24,200 conscripts and active reservists)
3 joint (tri-service) comd each with: Army div and def
districts, Naval Comd (2 in Central Joint Comd)
Air Comd, logistics regt
No active units (as defined by Vienna Document)
3 div with total of 2 armd, 4 mech, 4 inf, 3 arctic bde, 3
arty regt HQ, 12 arty bn
15 def districts
EQUIPMENT
  MBT 60 *Centurion*, 239 Strv-103B (in store), 160 Strv-
    121 (*Leopard* 2), 78 Strv-122 (*Leopard* 2 (S))
  LT TK 211 Ikv-91
  AIFV 514 Pbv-302, 202 Strf-9040
  APC 401 Pbv 401A (MT-LB), 126 *Pskbil* M/42 (plus
    323 ACV 'look-a-likes')
  TOWED ARTY 105mm: 483 m/40; **155mm**: 276 FH-
    77A, 114 Type F
  SP ARTY 155mm: 24 BK-1C
  MOR 81mm: 200; **120mm**: 474
  ATGW 55 TOW (Pvrbv 551 SP), RB-55, RB-56 *Bill*
  RL 84mm: AT-4
  RCL 84mm: *Carl Gustav*; **90mm**: PV-1110
  AD GUNS 40mm: 600
  SAM RBS-70 (incl Lvrbv SP), RB-77 (I HAWK), RBS-
    90
  SURV *Green Archer* (mor)
  AC 1 C-212
  HEL 20 Hkp-9A ATK, 25 Hkp-3 tpt, 12 Hkp-4, 25
    Hkp-5B trg, 32 Hkp-6A utl, 5 Hkp-11

Navy 9,200

(incl 1,100 Coastal Defence, 320 Naval Air, 3,500
conscripts and 2,500 reserve officers)
BASES Muskö, Karlskrona, Härnösand, Göteborg (spt
only)
SUBMARINES 10
  3 *Gotland* with 4 533mm TT, TP-613 and TP-431/451
    (AIP powered)
  4 *Västergötland* with 6 533mm TT, TP-613 and TP-
    431/451
  2 *Näcken* with 6 533mm TT, TP-613 and TP-421
  1 *Spiggen* II (ASW target)
PATROL AND COASTAL COMBATANTS 27
MISSILE CRAFT 24 PFM
  4 *Göteborg* with 4 x 2 RBS-15 SSM; plus 4 400mm TT,
    4 ASW mor
  2 *Stockholm* with 4 x 2 RBS-15 SSM (or up to 4
    additional 533 TT); plus 2 533mm, 4 400mm TT, 4
    ASW mor
  4 *Hugin* with 6 RB-12 *Penguin* SSM
  8 *Kaparen* with 6 RB-12 *Penguin* SSM
  6 *Norrköping* with 4 x 2 RBS-15 SSM or up to 6
    533mm TT
PATROL CRAFT 3 PCI

MINE WARFARE 27

MINELAYERS 2

1 *Carlskrona* (200 mines) trg, 1 *Visborg* (200 mines) (Mines can be laid by all submarine classes)

MINE COUNTERMEASURES 25

4 *Styrsö* MSO, 1 *Utö* MCMV spt, 1 *Skredsvic* MCM/ diver support, 7 *Landsort* MHC, 12 MSI

SUPPORT AND MISCELLANEOUS 28

1 AGI, 1 sub rescue/salvage ship, 2 survey, 7 icebreakers, 16 tugs, 1 SES PCI (trials)

COASTAL DEFENCE (1,100)

2 mobile coastal arty bde: 5 naval bde, 6 amph, 3 mobile arty (**120mm**), 12 specialist protection (incl inf, static arty (**75mm, 105mm, 120mm**), SSM and mor units)

EQUIPMENT

APC 5 *Piranha*
GUNS 40mm, incl L/70 AA; **75mm, 105mm, 120mm** 24 CD-80 *Karin* (mobile); **120mm** *Ersta* (static)
MOR 81mm, 120mm: 70
SSM 90 RBS-17 *Hellfire*, 6 RBS-15KA
SAM RBS-70
MINELAYERS 5 inshore
PATROL CRAFT 12 PCI
AMPH 10 LCM, 65 LCU, 77 LCA

NAVAL AIR (320)

1 cbt ac, no armed hel
ASW 1 C-212 ac
HEL 14 Hkp4C (CH-46)(3 MCM, 11 SAR), 10 Hkp6 (Bell-206) (utl)

Air Force 8,800

(incl 3,000 conscripts and 1,700 active reservists); 362 cbt ac, no armed hel
Flying hours 110–140
3 Air Comd
FGA/RECCE 3 sqn with 36 SAAB AJS-37; plus 42* SAAB ASSH/AJSF-37 (recce), 1 (OCU) with 14 SAAB SK-37
MULTI-ROLE (FTR/FGA/RECCE) 1 sqn with 53 SAAB JAS-39 (second sqn forms late 1998)
FTR 9 sqn
   1 with 17 SAAB J-35
   8 with 134 SAAB JA-37
SIGINT 2 S-102B *Korpen* (*Gulfstream* IV)
AEW 4 S-100B *Argus* (SAAB-340B)
TPT 1 sqn with 8 C-130, 3 *King Air* 200, 1 *Metro* III, 13 SK-60D/E, 1 Tp-100A (SAAB 340B) (VIP), 1 Tp-102A (*Gulfstream* IV) (VIP)
TRG 122 Sk-60 (includes 66* Sk-60B/C with lt attack/ recce role) 38 SK-61 (*Bulldog*)
SAR 12 Hkp10 (*Super Puma*), 3 Hkp3 (Bell 204)
AAM RB-24 (AIM-9B/3 *Sidewinder*), RB-27 (*Improved*

Falcon), RB-28 (*Falcon*), RB-71 (*Skyflash*), RB-74 AIM 9L (*Sidewinder*), AIM 120 (AMRAAM)
ASM RB-04E, RB-05A, RB-15F, RB-75 (*Maverick*), BK-39
AD semi-automatic control and surv system, *Stric*, coordinates all AD components. *Stric* will replace from 1997 and will be fully operational by 2000

Forces Abroad

UN AND PEACEKEEPING

ANGOLA (UNOMA): 3 obs. **CROATIA** (UNMOP): 1 obs; (SFOR): 1. **FYROM** (UNPREDEP): 39 plus 1 obs. **GEORGIA** (UNOMIG): 4 obs. **INDIA/PAKISTAN** (UNMOGIP): 9 obs. **IRAQ/KUWAIT** (UNIKOM): 5 obs. **MIDDLE EAST** (UNTSO): 11 obs. **ROK** (NNSC): 6 staff. **WESTERN SAHARA** (MINURSO): 75

Paramilitary 600

COAST GUARD 600

1 *Gotland* PCO and 1 KBV-171 PCC (fishery protection), some 65 PCI
AIR ARM 2 C-212 MR
CIVIL DEFENCE shelters for 6,300,000
All between ages 16–25 liable for civil defence duty
VOLUNTARY AUXILIARY ORGANISATIONS some 35,000

Switzerland

	1996	1997	1998	1999
GDP	fr364bn	fr367bn		
	($250bn)	($253bn)		
per capita	$26,400	$27,200		
Growth	-0.2%	0.7%		
Inflation	0.9%	0.4%		
Publ Debt	48.7%	48.0%		
Def exp	fr5.7bn	fr5.6bn		
	($4.6bn)	($3.8bn)		
Def bdgt			fr5.3bn	
			($3.4bn)	
$1 = franc	1.24	1.45	1.54	
Population		7,070,000		
Age	*13–17*	*18–22*	*23–32*	
Men	207,000	210,000	554,000	
Women	195,000	204,000	560,000	

Total Armed Forces

ACTIVE about 3,300
plus recruits (2 intakes in 1996 (1 of 8,160, 1 of 14,800) each for 15 weeks only)

Terms of service 15 weeks compulsory recruit trg at age 19–20, followed by 10 refresher trg courses of 3 weeks over a 22-year period between ages 20–42. Some 240,900 attended trg in 1996

RESERVES 390,000

Army 357,460 (to be mobilised)

Armed Forces Comd (All units non-active/Reserve status)

Comd tps: 2 armd bde, 2 inf, 1 arty, 1 airport, 2 engr regt

3 fd Army Corps, each 2 fd div (3 inf, 1 arty regt), 1 armd bde, 1 arty, 1 engr, 1 cyclist, 1 fortress regt, 1 territorial div (5/6 regt)

1 mtn Army corps with 3 mtn div (2 mtn inf, 1 arty regt), 3 fortress bde (each 1 mtn inf regt), 2 mtn inf, 2 fortress, 1 engr regt, 1 territorial div (6 regt), 2 territorial bde (1 regt)

EQUIPMENT

MBT 769 (incl 27 in store): 186 Pz-68, 186 Pz-68/88, 370 Pz-87 (*Leopard* 2)

RECCE 154 *Eagle*

AIFV 513 (incl 6 in store): 192 M-63/73, 315 M-63/89 (all M-113 with **20mm**)

APC 836 M-63/73 (M-113) incl variants, 122 *Piranha* (incl 36 with *Dragon* ATGW)

TOTAL ARTY 796 (incl 22 in store)

TOWED 105mm: 216 Model-46

SP 155mm: 558 PzHb 66/74/-74/-79/-88 (M-109U)

MOR 81mm: 1,200 M-33, M-72; **120mm**: 577 (incl 44 in store): 402 M-87, 132 M-64 (M-113)

ATGW 2,850 *Dragon*, 303 TOW-2 SP (MOWAG) *Piranha*

RL 13,540 incl: **60mm**: *Panzerfaust*; **83mm**: M-80

AD GUNS 20mm: 630

SAM 56 B/L-84 (*Rapier*), some *Stinger*

UAV *Scout, Ranger*/ADS 95

HEL 60 *Alouette* III

MARINES

10 *Aquarius* patrol boats

Air Force 32,600 (to be mobilised)

(incl AD units, mil airfield guard units); 171 cbt ac, no armed hel

1 Air Force bde, 1 AAA bde, 1 Air-Base bde and 1 Comd-and-Control bde

Flying hours: 150–200; reserves 50–70

FTR 11 sqn

7 with 89 *Tiger* II/F-5E, 12 *Tiger* II/F-5F

2 with 29 *Mirage* IIIS, 4 -III DS

2 with 21 F/A-18 C/D

RECCE 3 sqn with 16* *Mirage* IIIRS 2 (being withdrawn from service)

TPT 1 sqn with 16 PC-6, 1 *Learjet* 36, 2 Do-27, 1 *Falcon*-50

HEL 3 sqn with 15 AS-332 M-1 (*Super Puma*), 12 SA-316 (*Alouette* III)

TRG 19 *Hawk* Mk 66, 38 PC-7, 12 PC-9 (tgt towing)

AAM AIM-9 *Sidewinder*, AIM-26 *Falcon*, AIM-120 AMRAAM

AIR DEFENCE

1 SAM regt with 1 bn with 3 bty, *Bloodhound*

1 AD bde: 1 SAM regt (3 bn, each with 2 or 3 bty: *Rapier*)

Forces Abroad

UN AND PEACEKEEPING

CROATIA (UNMOP): 1 obs. **FYROM** (UNPREDEP): 1 obs plus 4 civ pol. **GEORGIA** (UNOMIG): 3 obs. **KOREA** (NNSC): 6 Staff. **MIDDLE EAST** (UNTSO): 7 obs. **TAJIKISTAN** (UNMOT): 6 obs

Paramilitary

CIVIL DEFENCE 350,000 (not part of Armed Forces) 300,000 trained

Ukraine

	1996	1997	1998	1999
GDP	h82bn	h92bn		
	($45bn)	($50bn)		
per capita	$4,400	$4,400		
Growth	-10.0%	-3.2%		
Inflation	80.3%	15.9%		
Debt	$9.3bn	$10.4bn		
Def exp[a]	h2.4bn	h2.5bn		
	($1.3bn)	($1.3bn)		
Def bdgt			h1.7bn	
			($813m)	
FMA[b] (US)	$3.5m	$1.0m	$1.3m	$1.3m
$1 = hryvnia	1.82	1.86	2.11	

[a] Incl exp on paramilitary forces

[b] Excl US Cooperative Threat Reduction programme: **1992–96** $395m, of which $171m spent by Sept 1996. Programme continues through 1999

Population	50,480,000			
(Russian 22%, Polish ε4%, Jewish 1%)				
Age	*13–17*	*18–22*	*23–32*	
Men	1,891,000	1,852,000	3,538,000	
Women	1,826,000	1,810,000	3,514,000	

Total Armed Forces

ACTIVE 346,400

(excl Strategic Nuclear Forces and Black Sea Fleet; incl 38,200 in central staffs and units not covered below)

Terms of service **Army**, **Air Force** 18 months **Navy** 2 years

RESERVES some 1,000,000
mil service within 5 years

Strategic Nuclear Forces

(to be eliminated under START)
ICBM 115 (none with warheads)
  69 SS-19 *Stiletto* (RS-18) (without warheads); at two
  sites
  40 SS-24 *Scalpel* (RS-22); silo-based (without warheads), one site co-located with SS-19
BBR 44
  20 Tu-95H16
  5 Tu-95H6 (with AS-15 ALCM)
  19 Tu-160 (with AS-15 ALCM)
  plus 2 Tu-95A/B in store (under Ukr comd)

Ground Forces 171,300

3 Op Comd (North, South, West)
MoD tps: 1 air mobile, 2 SSM, 1 arty (trg) bde, 2 engr
WESTERN OP COMD
Comd tps 1 arty div (2 arty, 1 MRL bde), 1 air mobile,
  1 SSM, 1 *Spetsnaz* bde, 1 avn gp
2 Corps 1 with 2 mech div, 2 mech, 1 SSM, 1 arty bde, 1
  MRL, 1 ATK regt, 1 avn gp
  1 with 2 mech div, 1 mech, 1 SSM, 1 arty bde, 1 MRL,
  1 ATK regt, 1 avn gp
SOUTHERN OP COMD
Comd tps 1 mech, 1 air mobile, 1 arty div (1 arty, 1
  MRL, 1 ATK bde), 1 air mobile, 1 SSM bde, 2 avn gp
2 Corps 1 with 1 tank, 2 mech div, 2 arty bde, 1 MRL
  regt
  1 with 2 mech, 1 arty, 1 *Spetsnaz* bde, 1 MRL, 1 ATK
  regt
NORTHERN OP COMD
Comd tps 2 mech, 1 trg div (include 1 active tank regt),
  1 tank, 1 SSM bde, 1 MRL, 1 ATK regt
1 Corps with 1 tank, 1 trg div, 1 arty bde, 2 avn gp
EQUIPMENT
  MBT 4,014 (917 in store): 154 T-55, 1 T-62, 2,281 T-
    64, 1,305 T-72, 273 T-80
  RECCE some 1,500
  AIFV 3,079 (399 in store): 1,010 BMP-1, 458 BRM-
    1K, 1,468 BMP-2, 4 BMP-3, 61 BMD-1, 78 BMD-2
  APC 1,823 (238 in store): 203 BTR-60, 1,105 BTR-70,
    473 BTR-80, 42 BTR-D; plus 2,000 MT-LB, 4,700
    'look-alikes'
  TOTAL ARTY 3,749 (582 in store)
    TOWED 1,139: **122mm**: 435 D-30, 3 M-30; **152mm**:
      219 D-20, 8 ML-20, 185 2A65, 289 2A36
    SP 1,307: **122mm**: 642 2S1; **152mm**: 501 2S3, 24
      2S5, 40 2S19; **203mm**: 100 2S7
    COMBINED GUN/MOR 120mm: 62 2S9, 2 2B16
    MRL 634: **122mm**: 373 BM-21, 24 9P138; **132mm**: 4
      BM-13; **220mm**: 139 9P140; **300mm**: 94 9A52

  MOR 605: **120mm**: 347 2S12, 257 PM-38; **160mm**:
    1 M-160
  SSM 132 *Scud*, 140 FROG/SS-21
  ATGW AT-4 *Spigot*, AT-5 *Spandrel*, AT-6 *Spiral*
  SAM SA-4/-6/-8/-11/-12A/-15
  ATTACK HEL 236 Mi-24
  SPT HEL 4 Mi-2, 31 Mi-6, 162 Mi-8, 17 Mi-26
  SURV SNAR-10 (*Big Fred*), *Small Fred* (arty)

Navy† ε12,500

(incl nearly 2,500 Naval Aviation, ε1,250 Naval
Infantry)
On 31 May 1997, Russian President Yeltsin and Ukrainian
President Kuchma signed an inter-governmental agreement
on the status and terms of the Black Sea Fleet's deployment
on the territory of Ukraine and parametres for the Fleet's di-
vision. The Russian Fleet will lease bases in Sevastopol for
the next 20 years. It is based at Sevastopol and Karantinnaya
Bays and jointly with Ukrainian warships at Streletskaya Bay.
The overall serviceability of the Fleet is very low

BASES Sevastopol, Donuzlav, Odessa, Kerch,
Ochakov, Chernomorskaye (Balaklava, Nikolaev
construction and repair yards)
SUBMARINES 4
  3 *Foxtrot*, 1 *Tango*
PRINCIPAL SURFACE COMBATANTS 9
  2 *Krivak* 1 with 4 SS-N-14 SSM/ASW, 2 SA-N-4
    SAM, 4 76mm gun, 8 533mm TT
  1 *Krivak* 2 with 4 SS-N-14 SSM, 2 100mm gun, 8
    533mm TT
  1 *Krivak* 3 with 2 SA-N-4 SAM, 1 100mm gun, 8
    533mm TT, 1 KA-27 hel
  5 *Grisha* I/II/V with 2 SA-N-4 SAM, 1 76mm gun, 4
    533mm TT
PATROL AND COASTAL COMBATANTS 11
  2 *Pauk* 1 PFT with 4 SA-N-5 SAM, 1 76mm gun, 4
    406mm TT
  5 *Matka* PHM with 2 SS-N-2C SSM, 1 76mm gun
  1 *Mukha* PHT with 8 406mm TT, 1 76mm gun
  2 *Tarantul* 1 with 4 SS-N-2D SSM, 4 SA-N-5 SAM, 1
    76mm gun
  1 *Zhuk* PCI
MINE COUNTERMEASURES 5
  1 *Yevgenya* MHC, 2 *Sonya* MSC, 2 *Natya* MSC
AMPHIBIOUS 7
  4 *Pomornik* ACV with 2 SA-N-5 capacity 30 tps and
    crew
  1 *Ropucha* LST with 4 SA-N-5 SAM, 2 x 2 57mm gun,
    92 mines; capacity 190 tps or 24 veh
  1 *Alligator* LST with 2/3 SA-N-5 SAM capacity 300
    tps and 20 tk
  1 *Polnocny* LSM capacity 180 tps and 6 tk
SUPPORT AND MISCELLANEOUS 9
  1 Mod *Kamkatka* research, 2 *Vytegrales* AK, 1 *Lama*

msl spt, 1 Mod *Moma* AGI, 1 *Primore* AGI, 1 *Kashtan* buoytender, 1 *Passat* AGOS, 1 *Elbrus* ASR

NAVAL AVIATION (7,000)
32 MiG-29, 69 Su-17, 44 Su-25, 39 Tu-22M

NAVAL INFANTRY (1,250)
2 inf bn

Air Force 124,400

some 786 cbt ac (plus 380 in store MiG-21, MiG-23, MiG-25, MiG-27, MiG-29, Su-24, Yak-28), 24 attack hel
3 air corps
BBR 1 div HQ, 2 regt with 28 Tu-22M
FGA/BBR 2 div HQ, 5 regt (1 trg) with 166 Su-24
FGA 1 regt with 34 Su-25
FTR 2 div, 6 regt with 140 MiG-23, 73 MiG-25, 144 MiG-29, 66 Su-27
RECCE 4 regt (1 trg) with 17* Tu-22, 41* Su-17, 41* Su-24, 13* MiG-25
ECM 1 sqn with 29 Mi-8
TPT 172 Il-76, 16 Il-78 (tkr/tpt), 100 others incl An-12
TRG 7 regt with 23* Tu-22M, 429 L-39
ATTACK HEL 24 Mi-24
SPT HEL 16 Mi-6, 144 Mi-8, 8 Mi-26
SAM 825: SA-2/-3/-5/-10/-12A

Forces Abroad

UN AND PEACEKEEPING
ANGOLA (UNOMA): 4 incl 3 obs. **BOSNIA** (SFOR II): 300. **CROATIA** (UNMOP): 1 obs. **FYROM** (UNPREDEP): 1 obs. **TAJIKISTAN** (UNMOT): 6 obs

Paramilitary

MVS (Ministry of Internal Affairs) 32,000
internal security tps
NATIONAL GUARD 23,000
3 regions, 1 armd, 1 hel unit
BORDER GUARD 34,000
HQ and 3 regions
MARITIME BORDER GUARD
The Maritime Border Guard is an independent subdivision of the State Commission for Border Guards, is not part of the Navy and is org with:
4 cutter, 2 river bde • 1 gunship, 1 MCM sqn • 1 aux ship gp • 1 trg div • 3 air sqn
PATROL AND COASTAL COMBATANTS 36
3 *Pauk* 1 with 4 SA-N-5 SAM, 1 76mm gun, 4 406mm TT
3 *Muravey* PHT with 1 76mm gun, 2 406mm TT
10 *Stenka* PFC with 4 30mm gun, 4 406mm TT
20 *Zhuk* PCI

AIRCRAFT
An-24, An-26, An-72, An-8, Ka-27
COAST GUARD 14,000
3 patrol boats, 1 water jet boat, 1 ACV, 1 landing ship, 1 OPV, 1 craft

Yugoslavia, Federal Republic of (Serbia–Montenegro)

	1996	1997	1998	1999
GDP	sd58bn	sd106bn		
	($17bn)	($19bn)		
per capita	$4,500	$5,000		
Growth	5.5%	7.4%		
Inflation	58.7%	9.0%		
Debt	$13.4bn	$14bn		
Def exp	εsd7.5bn	εsd8.5bn		
	($1.5bn)	($1.5bn)		
Def bdgt			sd6.6bn	
			($599m)	
$1 = super dinar	5.10	5.71	10.9	
Population	ε10,600,000			

Serbia ε9,900,000 (Serb 66%, Albanian 17%, Hungarian 4%)
Montenegro ε700,000 (Montenegrin 62%, Serb 9%, Albanian 7%)
(ε2,032,000 Serbs were living in the other Yugoslav republics before the civil war)

Age	13–17	18–22	23–32
Men	420,000	426,000	836,000
Women	396,000	402,000	794,000

Total Armed Forces

ACTIVE some 114,200
(43,000 conscripts) *Terms of service* 12–15 months

RESERVES some 400,000

Army (JA) some 90,000

(37,000 conscripts)
3 Army, 7 Corps (incl 1 capital def) • 3 div HQ • 6 tk bde • 1 gd bde (-), 1 SF bde • 4 mech bde • 1 AB bde • 8 mot inf bde (incl 1 protection) • 5 mixed arty bde • 7 AD bde • 1 SAM bde

RESERVES
27 mot inf, 42 inf, 6 mixed arty bde
EQUIPMENT
MBT 785 T-55, 239 M-84 (T-74; mod T-72), 181 T-34, 65 T-72
LT TK PT-76
RECCE 88 BRDM-2

AIFV 568 M-80
APC 169 M-60P, 68 BOV VP M-86
TOWED 105mm: 265 M-56, 15 M-18, 54 M2A1;
  122mm: 90 M-38, 310 D-30; **130mm**: 276 M-46;
  152mm: 25 D-20, 52 M-84; **155mm**: 139 M-1, 6 M-65
SP 122mm: 83 2S1
MRL 107mm; **122mm**: BM-21; **128mm**: 103 M-63, 64
  M-77, **262mm**: M-87 *Orkan*
MOR 82mm: 1,665; **120mm**: 6 M-38/-39, 123 M-52,
  320 M-74, 854 M-75
SSM 4 FROG
ATGW 135 AT-3 *Sagger* incl SP (BOV-1, BRDM-1/2),
  AT-4 *Fagot*
RCL 57mm: 1,550; **82mm**: 1,000 M-60PB SP; **105mm**:
  650 M-65
ATK GUNS 750: **76mm**: 24 M-42, 94 M-48; **90mm**:
  M-36B2 (incl SP), M-3; **100mm**: 138 T-12, MT-12
AD GUNS 1,850: **20mm**: M-55/-75, BOV-3 SP triple;
  30mm: M-53, M-53/-59, BOV-30 SP; **57mm**: ZSU-57-2 SP
SAM 60 SA-6, SA-7/-9/-13/-14/-16

Navy ε7,500

(incl 3,000 conscripts and 900 Marines)
BASES Kumbor, Tivat, Bar, Novi Sad (River Comd)
(Most former Yugoslav bases are now in Croatian
hands)
SUBMARINES 4
  2 *Sava* SS with 533mm TT (1 in refit)
  2 *Heroj* SS with 533mm TT (1 in refit)
  (Plus 3 *Una* SSI for SF ops, 3 non-op)
FRIGATES 4
  2 *Kotor* with 4 SS-N-2C *Styx* SSM, 1 x 2 SA-N-4
    SAM, 2 x 12 ASW RL, 2 x 3 ASTT
  2 *Split* (Sov *Koni*) with 4 SS-N-2C, 1 x 2 SA-N-4 SAM,
    Styx SSM, 2 x 12 ASW RL
PATROL AND COASTAL COMBATANTS 34
MISSILE CRAFT 10
  5 *Rade Koncar* PFM with 2 SS-N-2B *Styx* (some †)
  5 *Mitar Acev* (Sov *Osa* I) PFM with 4 SS-N-2A
PATROL CRAFT 24
  PATROL, INSHORE 6 *Mirna*
  PATROL, RIVERINE about 18 < (some in reserve)
MINE COUNTERMEASURES 10
  2 *Vukov Klanac* MHC, 1 UK *Ham* MSI, 7 *Nestin* MSI

AMPHIBIOUS 20
  1 *Silba* LCT/ML: capacity 6 tk or 300 tps, 1 x 4 SA-
    N-5 SAM, can lay 94 mines
  1 DSM 501 LCT/ML capacity 3 mbt or 200 tps, can
    lay 100 mines
  8 Type 22 LCU
  6 Type 21 LCU
  4 Type 11 LCVP
SUPPORT AND MISCELLANEOUS 9
  1 PO-91 *Lubin* tpt, 1 water carrier, 4 tugs, 2 AK, 1
    degassing

MARINES (900)
2 mot inf 'bde' (2 regt each of 2 bn) • 1 lt inf bde
(reserve) • 1 coast arty bde • 1 MP bn

Air Force 16,700

(3,000 conscripts); 238 cbt ac, 52 armed hel
2 Corps (1 AD)
FGA 4 sqn with 30 *Orao* 2, 50 *Galeb*, 9 *Super Galeb* G-4
FTR 5 sqn with 47 MiG-21F/PF/M/bis, 17 MiG-21U,
  15 MiG-29
RECCE 2 sqn with some 20* *Orao*, 18* MiG-21R
ARMED HEL 44 Gazelle
ASW 1 hel sqn with 3* Mi-14, 3* Ka-25, 2* Ka-28
TPT 15 An-26, 4 CL-215 (SAR, fire-fighting), 2 *Falcon*
  50 (VIP), 6 Yak-40
LIAISON ac 32 UTVA-66 **hel** 14 *Partizan*
TRG ac 16* *Super Galeb*, 16* *Orao*, 25 UTVA **hel** 16
  Gazelle
AAM AA-2 *Atoll*, AA-8 *Aphid*, AA-10 *Alamo*, AA-11
  Archer
ASM AGM-65 *Maverick*, AS-7 *Kerry*
AD 8 SAM bn, 8 sites with 24 SA-2, 16 SA-3
  15 regt AD arty

Paramilitary

MINISTRY OF INTERIOR TROOPS str n.k.
internal security; eqpt incl 150 AFV, 170 mor

Opposition

Kosovo Liberation Army (KLA) str n.k.

MILITARY DEVELOPMENTS

Restructuring and reform remain the most serious challenges facing the Russian armed forces, but the process continued to lack clear strategic direction in 1998. The military doctrine which was supposed to spell out the forces' new missions is still being worked out, despite Defence Ministry promises to complete it by May 1998. It is now expected to be ready in 'autumn 1998'. Some guidance on the direction of the reforms can be gleaned from Russia's 'national security concept', approved by President Boris Yeltsin on 17 December 1997 and developed further in a presidential policy document, known as the 'Fundamentals of Russian Federation State Policy for Military Development up to the Year 2005', published on 4 August 1998. However, both documents define Russia's national security interests, and the threats to them, very broadly. Their essential elements are:

- Large-scale external aggression will not be the main threat to Russia's national security for at least the next 10–15 years, although the possibility cannot be ruled out in the longer term (30–35 years).
- The principal security threat currently derives from the acute economic, social and ethnic problems that threaten the country's integrity.
- Resources should be switched from the over-heavy defence industry to rebuilding the country's economy.
- Russia must strengthen its ability to defend its global interests through an 'aggressive' foreign policy aimed at increasing its influence in international organisations.
- In the 'leaner' military structure, nuclear deterrence will have an even more important role than before.

In the absence of clear strategic direction, the reform programme has been primarily driven by economic expediency. The Russian government faces many competing claims for funds as social tensions increase in Russia. At the same time, it is under pressure to cut spending from the International Monetary Fund (IMF). In July 1998, the Fund added to its earlier loans a new $22bn, 18-month lending package, with $11.2bn paid out initially and the remainder only to come if the government worked towards balancing the budget.

Shortage of funds is therefore the most serious obstacle to progress in military reform, and the resources that are available are not being properly allocated to cover the cost of closing down units and bases and discharging personnel. The funds shortage also hinders the redeployment of the military assets and personnel that are to remain. The government's ambitious plan to end conscription and develop an all-professional restructured force by 2005 seems difficult to achieve.

The scale of the personnel reductions is illustrated by the impact of the merger between the Air Defence and Air forces. This will result in the discharge of 45% of their combined strength, or 122,000 personnel. In 1998 alone, the Navy will dismiss 210,000 personnel, representing 19% of its current strength. Another problem facing the armed forces is that, while they are trying to reduce the number of troops, they have difficulty retaining well-qualified officers, particularly younger ones, which they badly need. The majority of officers' contracts expire in late 1998 and early 1999, and indications are that 40–50% are not planning to renew. Already, 32% of warrant officer posts are vacant, as are 22% of commissioned officer posts. In 1999, the Army will be short of 19,000 officers, with 70% of the vacancies for commanders of motor-rifle, tank, artillery and mortar platoons. The difficulties are compounded by the piecemeal approach to dealing with the funds shortage. For example, in 1998 the Ministry of Defence decided to discharge 15,000 1998 graduates from the military colleges.

A step that has been taken to try to improve management of the reform process was the merger, in January 1998, of the two government commissions, one headed by the Prime Minister and the other by the First Deputy Prime Minister, which were set up to deal with reform issues. The merged commission, headed by Kiriyenko, is primarily concerned with economic and social factors. A particular concern is providing housing for retiring military personnel, as required under the 'Law on the Status of Servicemen' which was signed by the President on 27 May 1998 after the Duma had, in March 1998, overcome an earlier presidential veto with the required two-thirds majority vote. More than 100,000 apartments are needed to meet the requirement. One of the main results of the commission's work in 1998 was the announcement of a programme of housing certificates to cover 80% of the cost of dwellings bought by retiring officers. The programme's success is vital to maintaining the momentum of the reform process and implementing the planned reductions.

The top priority for available funds is the strategic nuclear force, which is being improved by the introduction of the SS-27 (*Topol*-M2) missile for the ground-based element (the first of which entered service in December 1997), and new air-launched cruise missiles for the Tu-95 and Tu-160 strategic bombers. Plans were also approved in July 1998 to develop the *Bark* submarine-launched ballistic missile (SLBM) to be fitted to the new *Borey*-class ballistic missile submarine (SSBN), which is expected to enter service in 2003. By that time, all SSBNs are expected to have been withdrawn from the Pacific Fleet and remain only in the Northern Fleet. At present levels of expenditure, maintenance and production capabilities, it will be difficult for Russia to maintain its overall strategic nuclear forces at Strategic Arms Reduction Treaty (START) 1 levels for much longer. Even if START II is ratified by the Duma, it will be difficult for the new permitted level of 2,300 warheads to be maintained in operational condition. There are already difficulties with SSBNs. For nearly three months from early May 1998, Russia had no operational SSBN at sea. Apart from a brief stretch of around a week in 1996, this is the only prolonged period in which there has been no Russian SSBN at sea since the SSBN force became operational in 1960.

The major outside contributor to Russia's efforts to restructure its nuclear programmes and dismantle its other weapons of mass destruction (WMD) programmes has been the US, through its Co-operative Threat Reduction (CTR) programme. Congressional constraints have prevented the full sum appropriated being spent since the programme's inception in 1993, but by 1998, $438m had been contributed for nuclear materials protection control and accounting (MPC&A) alone. US expenditure on MPC&A is expected to total $800m by 2002. The Russian chemical weapons destruction programme has also benefited from this funding, as have the International Science and Technology Centres (to which the European Union and Japan also contribute) that run projects to employ former weapons scientists and engineers. The US has also provided more specifically targeted funds, such as the $3.1m committed in July 1998 for the conversion to civil purposes of the Russian nuclear weapons research facilities in 'closed' military towns.

The restructuring of the armed forces also involves the territorial military districts. They will be reduced from eight to six 'military zones', whose boundaries will eventually be common to all defence and law enforcement agencies. The military zones will be the Northwest (formerly Leningrad), Moscow, Southwest (formerly North Caucasus), Siberia (formerly the separate Siberian and Transbaykal Districts), Central Asia (formerly the separate Volga and Urals Districts) and Far East. An essential aspect of the new structure is that the senior military zone commanders will be given operational control over all military assets in their district. Interior Ministry military commanders will take the lead for operations within Russia, while the 'Ministry of Defence and the General Staff' will take charge within the Commonwealth of Independent States (CIS) of what are described as 'local wars', involving troop deployment outside Russia. An example of the effect of these reforms on combat units can be seen in Kaliningrad, where an operational strategic group has been created through the merger of the 11th Guards Army and the Baltic Fleet. Elements of this group, including air defence troops, marines and parachute forces, took part in joint exercises in the Baltic Fleet's April 1998 annual manoeuvres.

A plan is underway to reduce the Interior Troops by a third from their present 237,000 and reorganise them to fit in with the new military zone structure. Their focus in peacetime is to be less on guarding key points like communications facilities and convoys, and more on dealing with 'internal conflicts'. In a second phase of reorganisation, beginning in 2001, they will become known as the Federal Internal Security Police. They will not use conscripts, but only employ on contract. The Border Troops will also be reorganised. According to a statement by Andrei Kokoshin, the Secretary of the Russian Security Council, the Border Troops will 'transition to mainly non-military forms of service' as 'border protection personnel' and their military component will be 'appropriately reduced'.

The main threats faced by Russia's armed forces remain internal. In the south, violence and instability reign in the Transcaucasus region, where the Army is needed to support the civil authorities and Interior Troops. One of the largest Russian ground force exercises in 1998 was held in July and August in the north Caucasus region, where the Interior Ministry has set up a new operational headquarters in Stavropol to control the operations of all military forces in the region. Beyond Russia's borders, there are still 23,000 troops in Tajikistan, where the situation remains unstable; 15,000 of these are made up of Border Troops, mainly recruited locally. About 10,000 peacekeeping and garrison troops remain in the Abkhazia region of Georgia, and some 2,500 Russian troops remain in Moldova from the former complement of about 5,000. Among the other small groups of forces stationed abroad, the largest is the Stabilisation Force (SFOR) II contingent, numbering some 1,400 in two airborne battalions and headquarters staff.

While some units manage to maintain a good level of operational readiness, for example the SFOR contingent, the general standard continues to decline. This is principally due to shortage of money for operations and maintenance and failure to replace unserviceable or obsolete equipment. In particular, the operational capability of aircrew remains very low because lack of fuel and shortage of serviceable aircraft have meant insufficient flying hours.

DEFENCE SPENDING

The Russian economy, contracting since 1992, improved slightly in 1997, when Gross Domestic Product (GDP) rose by about 1% compared with a 3% decline in 1996. Retail price inflation dropped from 48% to 15%, while the rouble exchange rate remained stable at around six (redenominated) roubles to the dollar. This did not lead to a boost in military spending, despite efforts by the Duma and by the military, which put in a request for a budget of R240bn. They had to make do with a revised figure of R83bn after the May 1997 fiscal crisis forced a reduction from R104bn. The persistent tax collection difficulties, which, since 1993, have forced the government to resort to sequestration, resulted, as usual, in much lower revenues than expected throughout the calendar year. Official defence outlays in 1997 were some (redenominated) R62bn. Further disbursements followed in early 1998 to give a final outlay of some R79.7bn. This outturn represented 95% of the budgeted funding under defence for 1997, but was the closest the Russian government has come to meeting its defence spending commitments since the Soviet Union broke up.

Table 12 Official Russian defence budgets and outlays, 1992–1998

(Redenominated roubles m)	Defence budget	% Federal budget	Defence outlay
1992	901	16.0	855
1993	3,116	16.6	n.a.
1993 Revised	8,327	n.a.	7,210
1994	40,626	20.9	28,028
1995	48,577	19.6	n.a.
1995 Revised	59,379	21.3	47,800
1996	80,185	18.4	63,900
1997	104,300	19.7	n.a.
1997 Revised	83,200	19.7	79,700
1998	81,765	16.4	n.a.

The 1998 defence budget of nearly R82bn was passed under the Russian Federation Law 'On the 1998 Federal Budget', which was approved by the Duma on 4 March 1998, and by the Federation Council on 12 March, and was signed by Yeltsin on 26 March. A change from previous years was that the budget no longer covers funding for military pensions. These now come under the social security budget in line with the August 1996 law on budget classifications. An earlier draft defence budget of R102bn contained nearly R12bn for military pensions.

Table 13 Official Russian defence budgets by function, 1991–1998

(Redenominated roubles m)	1991 (USSR)	%	1992	%	1993	%	1994	%	1995	%
Personnel, O&M	30.3	31.4	499	55.4	1,556	50	22,105	54.4	21,982	45.3
Procurement	38.8	40.2	185	20.5	570	18.3	8,442	20.8	10,275	21.2
R&D	12.7	13.2	75	8.3	225	7.2	2,433	6.0	4,936	10.2
Infrastructure	5.9	6.1	122	13.5	514	16.5	4,778	11.8	6,138	12.6
Pensions	3.9	4.0	n.a.	n.a.	171	5.5	1,994	4.9	4,015	8.3
Nuclear, other	4.9	5.1	21	2.3	80	2.6	874	2.2	1,231	2.5
Military reform	n.a.	n.a.	n.a.	n.a.	n.a.	n.a.	n.a.	n.a.	n.a.	n.a.
Total	97	100	901	100	3,116	100	40,626	100	48,577	100

	1995 revised	%	1996	%	1997[1]	%	1998 draft	%	1998 actual	%
Personnel, O&M	31,880	53.7	41,120	51.3	48,364	46.4	49,800	48.7	44,527	54.5
Procurement	10,275	17.3	13,213	16.5	20,963	20.1	15,100	14.8	17,048	20.8
R&D	4,936	8.3	6,475	8.1	11,574	11.1	10,100	9.9	10,800	13.2
Infrastructure	6,138	10.3	7,637	9.5	5,017	4.8	5,400	5.3	3,300	4.0
Pensions	4,867	8.2	9,899	12.3	13,858	13.3	11,600	11.4		
Nuclear, other	1,283	2.2	1,842	2.3	2,095	2	2,200	2.2	2,095	2.6
Military reform	n.a.	n.a.	n.a.	n.a.	2,429	2.3	8,000	7.8	3,995	4.9
Total	59,379	100	80,185	100	104,300	100	102,200	100	81,765	100

Note [1]The 1997 budget was reduced to R83bn in May 1997.

Although pensions are now outside the defence budget, the 1998 budget is only some R1.4bn less than the revised 1997 allocation, or about 7% lower in real terms, given inflation projected at 6% for the year, and 3% below the 1997 outturn. Personnel and Operations and Maintenance together account for nearly 55% of the total allocation. Some R4bn has been funded for military reform, to be spent chiefly on financial provision for retiring military personnel and their housing. The government is relying heavily on revenue from the sale of state land, property and industrial assets to fund the military reform and defence conversion programmes. At the same time, it is expecting the Defence Ministry to tighten up its accounting procedures following criticism by senior government figures. In 1998, the armed forces will introduce the cost-accounting practices used by government ministries, including the Finance Ministry.

As in previous years, the defence budget does not include all military spending. For example, funding for paramilitary organisations – Federal Security, Internal and Border Troops in particular – is covered elsewhere. Some allocations for research and development are also excluded. This mainly applies to the Russian Space Agency (RSA) and the defence industry, which use their retained profits for R&D. While some provision is made for military housing within the defence budget, the government has approved a five-year R25bn house building programme for retired and soon-to-be-retired personnel. This is to be funded from sales of government property and by donor or creditor countries like Germany, which has made a grant over $5bn to date, and Japan, which made a $1.5bn loan in 1998. While the official defence budget accounts for around 16% of projected government spending in 1998, actual allocations to fund military-related activities continue to account for up to a third of government spending.

According to industry sources, the Defence Ministry's accumulated debts to the defence industry (for which the government does not hold itself accountable) amount to nearly R20bn. The total owed by the Defence Ministry in unpaid wages and unpaid bills to suppliers in the defence, electricity and food industries may amount to around R100bn. One example cited by Kiriyenko on 12 May 1998 makes the point. The Defence Ministry consumed heat, light and electricity worth R9bn in 1997, whereas the budget provided for R2bn and the Ministry actually paid out only R1.2bn for all communal services, including R600m for heat, light and electricity. A similar situation is likely to arise in 1998, as the defence budget allocates R1.5bn against projected supply worth R10bn. When calculating real military spending in standardised (US dollar) terms, the mismatch between outlay and the real costs of supply can be addressed either by using the actual cost of supply (if known), or by applying a purchasing-power-parity value to the budgeted figure instead of a market exchange rate.

	IMF	SIPRI	SIPRI	NATO	IISS	IISS	ACDA	ACDA
	% GDP	1997 $bn	% GDP	% GDP	1997 $bn	% GDP	1997 $bn	% GDP
1992	4.7	50	5.5	>10	146	12	178	20
1993	4.4	44	5.3	>10	114	9	137	17
1994	4.6	42	5.8	>10	101	9	99	14
1995	2.9	25	3.7	>7	86	8	79	11
1996	3.6	24	3.7	7	73	7	n.a.	n.a.
1997	3.3	25	3.8	>6	64	6	n.a.	n.a.

Table 14 **Independent estimates of Russian military expenditure, 1992–1997**

The lack of transparency in Russian military accounting continues to make estimates of Russia's real military spending difficult and vulnerable to manipulation for political purposes. Given the size and capability of Russia's armed forces, it is more useful to have some estimate of real military expenditure rather than none, or, worse, a figure based on market exchange rates applied to the defence budget only. The second approach yields a figure for Russian defence spending on a par with countries like South Korea and Taiwan and somewhat less than Italy – which is clearly not realistic. Similarly, to adhere to the notion, as does the Russian government (and the IMF), that defence spending accounts for 3–4% of GDP is also misleading. While few would dispute that Russia's military expenditure has contracted greatly since the end of the Cold War, the evidence suggests that real military spending still accounts for about 6% of GDP, or about $64bn in 1997. This means Russia continues to be a clear, if distant, second to the US in terms of military spending and well ahead of Japan, France and the UK.

WEAPONS PROGRAMMES, ARMS EXPORTS AND THE DEFENCE INDUSTRY

Funding for equipment programmes has improved in recent years and accounts for 34% of the 1998 defence budget, compared to 28% in the early 1997 budget. The Defence Ministry has set a target for procurement to take at least 40% of the budget by 2005. No details of funding for individual weapons programmes are released, although between 40 and 50 major programmes received government funding in 1997. Near-term plans indicate continuing priority for strategic forces, which currently take 15–16% of the overall budget, and research and development, which receives additional funding from allocations to the science budget and the RSA, as well as the RSA's foreign currency earnings. Priority is also given to the arms export organisation *Rosvooruzheniye* and individual defence firms. The bulk of domestically produced weapons are exported, with production for the armed forces remaining at a low level, apart from strategic systems. Medium-term plans call for production to be increased from 2001 to meet the needs of armed forces' modernisation. There are currently a number of long-running development programmes which have reached pre-production status and await long-deferred orders from the forces.

Table 15 Estimated production of major weapon systems, 1990–1997

(Units)	1990 (USSR)	1991 (USSR)	1992	1993	1994	1995	1996	1997
Main battle Tanks	1,600	850	500	200	40	30	5	5
Inf fighting vehicles	3,400	3,000	700	300	380	400	250	350
SP artillery	500	300	200	100	85	15	20	10
Bombers	40	30	20	10	2	2	1	0
Fighters/FGA	430	250	150	100	50	20	25	35
Transport aircraft	120	60	5	5	5	4	3	0
Helicopters[1]	450	350	175	150	100	95	75	70
Submarines	12	6	6	4	4	3	2	2
Major surface ships	2	3	1	1	0	1	1	0
ICBMs/SLBMs	115	100	55	35	25	10	10	2
SRBMs[2]	0	0	80	105	55	45	35	30

Notes [1] Includes civilian production

[2] Production relocated from Kazakstan to Russia in 1992

Source UK Ministry of Defence

Russia's once-massive defence industry continues to contract in a disorganised way because of the failure to implement plans for much-needed restructuring. Employment in the industry has fallen from some 7m in 1987, with 4m directly engaged in defence work, to about 2.5m, with 925,000 directly engaged in defence work, in 1997. The government's main strategy continues to be defence conversion and dual-use technological diversification. Countervailing concerns about the security implications of defence industry rationalisation, allied to fears of the social consequences of large-scale unemployment, have made the government unwilling to use preferential contract allocations to force defence firms to merge or leave the industry. As a result, there is massive over-capacity, since Russia has many more design bureaux and defence firms than it needs to meet current military requirements. The 1993 privatisation programme has been only partially implemented. By late 1997, the state still controlled 42% of the defence industry and partially controlled a further 29%, leaving 29% under nominal private-sector control. The government's immediate objective, announced in November 1997, is to reduce the number of defence firms, design bureaux and research institutes from around 1,750 to fewer than 700, while promoting an increase in private financial-industrial groups (FIGs) from about 30 to 80. The plan is supposed to be completed by 2005.

Russian arms exports in 1997, as reported by *Rosvooruzheniye*, amounted to $2.5bn, down from $3.5bn in the previous year. The 1997 figures included about $2bn in hard currency transactions, with the balance involving barter and government debt repayment to, for example, Hungary, South Korea and Finland. In practice, Russian arms exports were almost certainly higher than the *Rosvooruzheniy* figures, since the organisation no longer monopolises export transactions and it does not take account of other authorised exporters' earnings.

Russia

	1996	1997	1998	1999
GDP[a]	r2,256bn	r2,602bn		
	($1.1tr)	($1.1tr)		
per capita	$6,600	$6,800		
Growth	-2.8%	0.8%		
Inflation	47.5%	14.6%		
Debt	$125bn	$131bn		
Def exp[a]	$71bn	$64bn		
Def bdgt[a]			r81.8bn	
			($34bn)	
FMA[b] (US)	$2.3m	$0.9m	$1.0m	$0.9m
(Ge) **1991–97** $5.0bn				
$1 = rouble*	5.12	5.75	6.43	

* (redenominated)

[a] PPP est

[b] Under the US Cooperative Threat Reduction programme, $754m was authorised for FY1992–96 to support START implementation and demilitarisation in Russia. By September 1996, $328m had been spent. The 1999 budget request is $442m (1997 $328m, 1998 $382m) of which Russia's share is 50–60%.

Population	146,600,000		

(Tatar 4%, Ukrainian 3%, Chuvash 1%, Bashkir 1%, Belarussian 1%, Moldovan 1%, other 8%)

Age	*13–17*	*18–22*	*23–32*
Men	5,818,000	5,484,000	10,239,000
Women	5,601,000	5,328,000	9,973,000

Total Armed Forces

ACTIVE ε1,159,000

(perhaps 381,000 conscripts, 153,000 women; incl about 200,000 MoD staff, centrally controlled units for EW, trg, rear services, not incl elsewhere)
Terms of service 18–24 months. Women with medical and other special skills may volunteer

RESERVES some 20,000,000

some 2,400,000 with service within last 5 years; Reserve obligation to age 50

Strategic Nuclear Forces ε149,000

(incl 49,000 assigned from Air Force, Air Defence and Navy)

NAVY (ε13,000)

412 msl in 26 operational SSBN†
SSBN 26 (all based in Russian ports)
  4 *Typhoon* with 20 SS-N-20 *Sturgeon* (80 msl)
  7 *Delta* IV with 16 SS-N-23 *Skiff* (112 msl)
  10 *Delta* III with 16 SS-N-18 *Stingray* (160 msl)
  5 *Delta* I with 12 SS-N-8 *Sawfly* (60 msl)
(The following non-op SSBNs remain START-accountable, with a total of 228 msl

  2 *Typhoon* with 40 SS-N-20
  1 *Yankee* 1 with 16 SS-N-6
  4 *Delta* II with a total of 64 SS-N-8
  9 *Delta* I with a total of 108 SS-N-8
In the 1 January START I declaration, Russia stated a total of 648 'deployed' SLBMs. The above figures represent holdings as of 1 August 1998.)

STRATEGIC MISSILE DEFENCE TROOPS (ε100,000 incl 50,000 conscripts)

5 rocket armies, org in div, regt, bn and bty, launcher gp normally with 10 silos (6 for SS-18) and one control centre; 12 SS-24 rail each 3 launchers
ICBM 756
  180 SS-18 *Satan* (RS-20) at 4 fields; mostly mod 4/5, 10 MIRV; in **Russia**
  188 SS-19 *Stiletto* (RS-18) at 4 fields; mostly mod 3, 6 MIRV; 168 in **Russia**, 20 in **Ukraine** (without warheads)
  92 SS-24 *Scalpel* (RS-22) 10 MIRV; 10 silo, 36 rail in **Russia**, 46 silo in **Ukraine** (without warheads)
  360 SS-25 *Sickle* (RS-12M) mobile, single-warhead; 2 SS-25 *Sickle* (RS-12M) variant for silo launcher; 10 bases with some 40 units in **Russia**
ABM 100: 36 SH-11 (mod *Galosh*), 64 SH-08 *Gazelle*

WARNING SYSTEMS

ICBM/SLBM launch-detection capability, others include photo recce and ELINT
RADARS
OVER-THE-HORIZON-BACKSCATTER (OTH-B)
2 near Kiev and Komsomolsk (Ukraine), covering US and polar areas
1 near Nikolayevsk-na-Amure, covering China (these sites are non-op)
LONG-RANGE EARLY-WARNING ABM-ASSOCIATED
6 long-range phased-array systems **Operational** Olenegorsk (Kola), Lyaki (Azerbaijan), Pechora (Urals) **Under test** Sary-Shagan (Kazakstan) **Under construction** Baranovichi (Belarus), Mishelevka (Irkutsk)
11 *Hen House*-series; range 6,000km, 6 locations covering approaches from the west and south-west, north-east and south-east and (partially) south. Engagement, guidance, battle management: 1 *Pill Box* phased-array at Pushkino (Moscow)

STRATEGIC AVIATION (ε3,000)

Long-Range Forces (Moscow)
BBR 66, plus 5 trg, 14 test ac (plus 44 in Ukraine)
  28 Tu-95H6 (with AS-15 ALCM) (plus 5 in Ukraine)
  32 Tu-95H16 (with AS-15 ALCM) (plus 20 in Ukraine)
  6 Tu-160 (with AS-15 ALCM) (plus 19 in Ukraine)
TEST AC 8 Tu-95, 6 Tu-160
TRG AC 5 Tu-95G

Army ε420,000

(ε144,000 conscripts, ε170,000 on contract)
7 Mil Districts (MD)
5 Army HQ, 6 Corps HQ
6 TD (3 tk, 1 motor rifle, 1 arty, 1 SAM regt; 1 armd recce bn; spt units)
19 MRD (incl trg) (3 motor rifle, 1 arty, 1 SAM regt; 1 indep tk, 1 ATK, 1 armd recce bn; spt units)
5 ABD (each 2 para, 1 arty regt) (plus 1 trg div)
4 MG/arty div
3 arty div; no standard org: perhaps 4 bde (12 bn): 152mm SP, 152mm towed and MRL: plus ATK bde
Some 32 arty bde/regt; no standard org, perhaps 4 bn: 2 each of 24 152mm towed guns, 2 each of 24 152mm SP guns, some only MRL
4 hy arty bde (each with 4 bn of 12 203mm 2S7 SP guns)
3 AB bde (each 3 inf bn; arty, SAM, ATK; spt tps)
1 indep tk bde
11 indep MR bde
8 SF (Spetsnaz) bde (5 op incl 1 trg, 3 cadre)
13 SSM bde
9 ATK bde/regt
21 SAM bde/regt
12 attack hel regt
7 aslt tpt hel regt
7 hel trg regt
Other Front and Army tps
  engr, pontoon-bridge, pipe-line, signals, EW, CW def, tpt, supply bde/regt/bn

EQUIPMENT
Figures in () were reported to CFE on 1 Jan 1998 and include those held by Naval Infantry and Coastal Defence units
  MBT about 15,500 (5,559), incl: T-54/-55 (37), T-62 (97), T-64A/-B (189), T-72L/-M (2,028) and T-80/-U/UD/UM (3,178), T-90 (2), plus some 11,000 in store east of Urals (incl Kazakstan, Uzbekistan)
  LT TK 200 PT-76 (2)
  RECCE some 2,000 BRDM-2
  TOTAL AIFV/APC ε26,300 (9,839)
  AIFV (6,594): BMP-1 (1,513), BMP-2 (3,232), BMP-3 (97), some 1,600 BMD-1/-2/-3 (AB) (1,187), BRM (565)
  APC (3,245): BTR-60P/-70/-80 (2,018), BTR-D (483); MT-LB (744), plus 'look-alikes'
  TOTAL ARTY ε15,700 (5,999), plus some 13,000, mainly obsolete types, in store east of the Urals
    TOWED (1,956) incl: **122mm**: M-30 (16); D-30 (871); **130mm**: M-46 (1); **152mm**: ML-20 (1); D-20 (213), Giatsint-B 2A36 (524), MSTA-B 2A65 (330); **203mm**: B-4M
    SP (2,573) incl: **122mm**: Gvozdika 2S1 (592); **152mm**: Acatsia 2S3 (1,061), Giatsint-S 2S5 (471), MSTA-S 2S19 (416); **203mm**: Pion 2S7 (33)
    COMBINED GUN/MOR (333): **120mm**: Nona-S 2S9 SP (328), Nona-K 2B16 (2), 3 S23 (3)
  MRL (869) incl: **122mm**: BM-21 (336), BM-13 (6), 9P138 (13); **220mm**: 800 (409) 9P140 Uragan; **300mm**: 105 (105) Smerch 9A52
  MOR (268) incl: **120mm**: 2S12 (170), PM-38 (79); **160mm**: M-160; **240mm**: Tulpan 2S4 SP (19)
  SSM (nuclear-capable) ε200 SS-21 Scarab (Tochka), ε116 Scud-B/-C mod (R-17) (FROG (Luna) units mostly disbanded)
  ATGW AT-2 Swatter, AT-3 Sagger, AT-4 Spigot, AT-5 Spandrel, AT-6 Spiral, AT-7 Saxhorn, AT-9, AT-10
  RL 64mm: RPG-18; **73mm**: RPG-7/-16/-22/-26; **105mm**: RPG-27/-29
  RCL 73mm: SPG-9; **82mm**: B-10
  ATK GUNS 57mm: ASU-57 SP; **76mm**; **85mm**: D-44/SD-44, ASU-85 SP; **100mm**: T-12/-12A/M-55 towed
  AD GUNS 23mm: ZU-23, ZSU-23-4 SP; **37mm**; **57mm**: S-60, ZSU-57-2 SP; **85mm**: M-1939; **100mm**: KS-19; **130mm**: KS-30
  SAM
    500 SA-4 A/B Ganef (twin) (Army/Front weapon)
    400 SA-6 Gainful (triple) (div weapon)
    400 SA-8 Gecko (2 triple) (div weapon)
    200 SA-9 Gaskin (2 twin) (regt weapon)
    250 SA-11 Gadfly (quad) (replacing SA-4/-6)
    100 SA-12A/B (Gladiator/Giant)
    350 SA-13 Gopher (2 twin) (replacing SA-9)
    100 SA-15 (replacing SA-6/SA-8)
    SA-19 (2S6 SP) (8 SAM, plus twin **30mm** gun)
    SA-7, SA-14 being replaced by SA-16, SA-18 (man-portable)
  HELICOPTERS some 2,300
    ATTACK 1,000 Mi-24 (801), 4 Ka-50 Hokum
    TPT some 1,300 Mi-6, Mi-8 (some armed), Mi-26 (hy)

Navy ε180,000

(ε17,000 conscripts, ε13,000 Strategic Forces, ε35,000 Naval Aviation, ε12,500 Coastal Defence Forces/Naval Infantry)
SUBMARINES 98
STRATEGIC 26 (see p. 108)
TACTICAL 72
  SSGN 15
  11 Oscar with 24 SS-N-19 Shipwreck USGW (VLS); plus T-65 HWT
  3 Yankee 'Notch' with 20+ SS-N-21 Sampson SLCM
  1 Yankee (trials) with ε12 SS-NX-24 SLCM
  SSN 25
  10 Akula with T-65 HWT; plus SS-N-21
  3 Sierra with T-65 HWT; plus SS-N-21
  12 Victor III with T-65 HWT; plus SS-N-15
  SS 23
  17 Kilo, 5 Tango, 1 Foxtrot (all with T-53 HWT)
OTHER ROLES 9
  SSN 6
  3 Uniform, 1 Echo II experimental/trials, 2 Yankee

SS 3

1 *X-Ray* trials, 2 *Losos* SF

IN STORE probably some *Foxtrot*, *Tango* and *Kilo*

PRINCIPAL SURFACE COMBATANTS 44

CARRIERS 1 *Kuznetsov* CVV (67,500t) capacity 20 fixed wing ac (Su-33) and 15–17 ASW hel with 12 SS-N-19 *Shipwreck* SSM, 4 x 6 SA-N-9 SAM, 8 CADS-1, 2 RBU-12 (not fully op)

CRUISERS 17

CGN 2 *Kirov* (AAW/ASUW) with 12 x 8 SA-N-6 *Grumble*, 20 SS-N-19 *Shipwreck* SSM, 3 Ka-25/-27 hel for OTHT/AEW/ASW; plus 1 with 1 x 2 130mm guns, 1 with 1 x 2 SS-N-14 *Silex* SUGW (LWT or nuc payload), 10 533mm TT

CG 15

3 *Slava* (AAW/ASUW) with 8 x 8 SA-N-6 *Grumble*, 8 x 2 SS-N-12 *Sandbox* SSM, 1 Ka-25/-27 hel (AEW/ASW); plus 8 533mm TT, 1 x 2 130mm guns

8 *Udaloy* (ASW) with 2 x 4 SS-N-14 *Silex* SUGW, 2 x 12 ASW RL, 8 533mm TT, 2 Ka-27 hel; plus 2 100mm guns

1 *Udaloy* II with 8 x 4 SS-N-22 *Sunburn*, 8 SA-N-9, 2 Cads-N-1, 8 SA-N-11, 10 533mm TT, 2 Ka-27 hel plus 2 100mm guns

2 *Kara* (ASW) with 2 x 4 SS-N-14 *Silex* SUGW, 10 533mm TT, 1 Ka-25 hel; plus 2 x 2 SA-N-3 *Goblet* (1 (*Azov*) with 3 x 8 SA-N-6, only 1 SA-N-3 and other differences)

1 *Kynda* (ASUW) with 8 SS-N-3B plus 2 SA-N-1 *Goa* SAM, 6 533mm TT

DDG 13

11 *Sovremennyy* with 2 x 4 SS-N-22 *Sunburn* SSM, 2 x 1 SA-N-7 *Gadfly* SAM, 2 x 2 130mm guns, 1 Ka-25 (B) hel (OTHT); plus 4 533mm TT

1 mod *Kashin* with 4 SS-N-2C *Styx* SSM, 2 x 2 SA-N-1 SAM; plus 5 533mm TT (non-op)

1 *Kashin* with 2 x 12 ASW RL, 5 533mm TT; plus 2 x 2 SA-N-1 SAM

FRIGATES 13

3 *Krivak* II with 1 x 4 SS-N-14 *Silex* SUGW, 8 533mm TT, 2 x 12 ASW RL; plus 2 100mm guns

9 *Krivak* I (weapons as *Krivak* II, but with 2 twin 76mm guns)

1 *Neustrashimyy* with 2 x 12 ASW RL

PATROL AND COASTAL COMBATANTS 124

CORVETTES 42

30 *Grisha* I, -III, -IV, -V, with 2 x 12 ASW RL, 4 533mmTT

12 *Parchim* II (ASW) with 2 x 12 ASW RL, 4 406mm ASTT

MISSILE CRAFT 55

25 *Tarantul* (ASUW), 3 -I, 17 -II, both with 2 x 2 SS-N-2C *Styx*; 29 -III with 2 x 2 SS-N-22 *Sunburn*

21 *Nanuchka* (ASUW) -I, -III and -IV with 2 x 3 SS-N-9 *Siren*

2 *Dergash* ACV with 8 x SS-N-22 SSM, 1 SAN-4 SAM, 1 76mm gun

3 *Osa* PFM with 4 SS-N-2C (non-op)

4 *Matka* PHM with 2 x 1 SS-N-2C

TORPEDO CRAFT 15 *Turya* PHT with 4 533mm TT

PATROL CRAFT 12

COASTAL 12

1 *Vtka* PCI

8 *Pauk* PFC (ASW) with 2 ASW RL, 4 ASTT

1 *Babochka* PHT (ASW) with 8 ASTT

2 *Mukha* PHT (ASW) with 8 ASTT

MINE WARFARE about 106

MINE COUNTERMEASURES about 106

OFFSHORE 22

2 *Gorya* MCO

20 *Natya* I and -II MSO

COASTAL 44

9 *Yurka* MSC

35 *Sonya* MSC

INSHORE 40

40 MSI<

AMPHIBIOUS about 27

LPD 1 *Ivan Rogov* with 4–5 Ka-27 hel, capacity 520 tps, 20 tk

LST 24

19 *Ropucha*, capacity 225 tps, 9 tk

5 *Alligator*, capacity 300 tps, 20 tk

LSM about 2 *Polnocny*, capacity 180 tps, 6 tk

Plus about 40 craft: about 6 *Ondatra* LCM; about 34 LCAC and SES (incl 6 *Pomornik*, 6 *Aist*, 6 *Tsaplya*, 12 *Lebed*, 1 *Utenok*, 2 *Orlan* WIG and 1 *Utka* WIG (wing-in-ground-experimental))

Plus about 80 smaller craft

SUPPORT AND MISCELLANEOUS about 480

UNDER WAY SUPPORT 18

1 *Berezina*, 5 *Chilikin*, 12 other AO

MAINTENANCE AND LOGISTIC about 219

some 15 AS, 38 AR, 20 AOT, 15 msl spt/resupply, 90 tugs, 12 special liquid carriers, 12 water carriers, 17 AK

SPECIAL PURPOSES about 55

some 18 AGI (some armed), 2 msl range instrumentation, 7 trg, about 24 icebreakers (civil-manned), 4 AH

SURVEY/RESEARCH about 188

some 28 naval, 39 civil AGOR; 80 naval, 35 civil AGHS; 6 space-associated ships (civil-manned)

MERCHANT FLEET (aux/augmentation)

about 2,800 ocean-going vessels (17 in Arctic service) incl 125 ramp-fitted and ro-ro, some with rails for rolling stock, 3 roll-on/float-off, 14 barge carriers, 48 passenger liners, 500 coastal and river ships, plus miscellaneous craft

NAVAL AVIATION (ε35,000)

some 329 cbt ac; 387 armed hel

Flying hours 40

HQ Naval Air Force

FLEET AIR FORCES 4

each org in air div, each with 2–3 regt of HQ elm and
2 sqn of 9–10 ac each; recce, ASW, tpt/utl org in
indep regt or sqn
BBR some 71
5 regt with some 71 Tu-22M (AS-4 ASM)
FGA 75 Su-24, 9 Su-25, 30 Su-27
ASW ac 9 Tu-142, 35 Il-38, 54 Be-12 **hel** 70 Mi-14, 53
Ka-25, 119 Ka-27
MR/EW ac incl 14 Tu-95, 8 Tu-22, 24 Su-24, 7 An-12, 2
Il-20 **hel** 20 Ka-25
MCM 25 Mi-14 hel
CBT ASLT 25 Ka-29 hel
TPT ac 120 An-12, An-24, An-26 **hel** 70 Mi-6/-8
ASM AS-4 *Kitchen*, AS-7 *Kerry*, AS-10 *Karen*, AS-11
Kilter, AS-12 *Kegler*, AS-13 *Kingbolt*, AS-14 *Kedge*

COASTAL DEFENCE (ε12,500)

(incl Naval Infantry, Coastal Defence Troops)

NAVAL INFANTRY (Marines) (ε7,500)
1 inf div (2,500: 3 inf, 1 tk, 1 arty bn) (Pacific Fleet)
2 indep bde (4 inf, 1 tk, 1 arty, 1 MRL, 1 ATK bn), 1
indep regt
3 fleet SF bde (1 op, 2 cadre): 2–3 underwater, 1 para
bn, spt elm
EQUIPMENT
MBT 160: T-55, T-64, T-72, T-80
RECCE 60 BRDM-2/*Sagger* ATGW
APC some 1,500: BTR-60/-70/-80, 250 MT-LB
TOTAL ARTY 389
SP **122mm**: 96 2S1; **152mm**: 18 2S3
MRL **122mm**: 96 9P138
COMBINED GUN/MOR **120mm**: 168 2S9 SP,
11 2S23 SP
ATGW 72 AT-3/-5
AD GUNS **23mm**: 60 ZSU-23-4 SP
SAM 250 SA-7, 20 SA-8, 50 SA-9/-13

COASTAL DEFENCE TROOPS (5,000)
(all units reserve status)
1 coastal defence div
1 coastal defence bde
1 arty regt
2 SAM regt
EQUIPMENT
MBT 350 T-64
AIFV 450 BMP
APC 280 BTR-60/-70/-80, 400 MT-LB
TOTAL ARTY 364 (152)
TOWED 280: **122mm**: 140 D-30; **152mm**: 40
D-20, 50 2A65, 50 2A36
SP **152mm**: 48 2S5
MRL **122mm**: 36 BM-21

NAVAL DEPLOYMENT

NORTHERN FLEET (Arctic and Atlantic)
(HQ Severomorsk)
BASES Kola Inlet, Motovskiy Gulf, Gremikha,
Polyarnyy, Litsa Gulf, Ura Guba, Severodovinsk

SUBMARINES 57
strategic 18 SSBN **tactical** 39 (10 SSGN, 20 SSN, 9 SS
(incl 6 SSN/SS other roles))
PRINCIPAL SURFACE COMBATANTS 18
1 CV, 8 cruisers, 5 destroyers, 4 frigates
OTHER SURFACE SHIPS about 30 patrol and coastal
combatants, 25 MCM, 8 amph, some 130 spt and
misc
NAVAL AVIATION
108 cbt ac; 85 armed hel
BBR 37 Tu-22M
FTR/FGA 30 Su-24/-25, 30 Su-27
ASW ac 11 Il-38, 5 Be-12 **hel** (afloat) 5 Ka-25, 55 Ka-
27
MR/EW ac 2 An-12, 30 Tu-95 **hel** 5 Ka-25
MCM 8* Mi-14 hel
CBT ASLT HEL 12 Ka-29
COMMS 5 Tu-142

BALTIC FLEET (HQ Kaliningrad)
BASES Kronshtadt, Baltiysk
SUBMARINES 2
2 SS
PRINCIPAL SURFACE COMBATANTS 6
2 destroyers, 4 frigates
OTHER SURFACE SHIPS about 30 patrol and coastal
combatants, 19 MCM, 5 amph, some 130 spt and
misc
NAVAL AVIATION
93 cbt ac, 25 armed hel
FGA 5 regt: 55 Su-24, 28 Su-27
ASW ac 10 Be-12 **hel** 3* Ka-25, 22* Ka-27
MR/EW ac 2 An-12, 5 Su-24 **hel** 5 Ka-25
MCM 6 Mi-14 BT hel
CBT ASLT HEL 4 Ka-29

BLACK SEA FLEET (HQ Sevastopol)
The Russian Fleet are leasing bases in Sevastopol for the
next 20 years, and be based at Sevastopol and Karantinnaya Bays, and jointly with Ukrainian warships at Strelet-
skaya Bay. The Fleet's overall serviceability is low.
BASES Sevastopol, Temryuk, Novorossiysk
SUBMARINES 10
tactical 9 **other roles** 1
PRINCIPAL SURFACE COMBATANTS 8
4 cruisers, 2 destroyers, 2 frigates
OTHER SURFACE SHIPS about 19 patrol and coastal
combatants, 20 MCM, 5 amph, some 90 spt and misc
NAVAL AVIATION
17 cbt ac; 30 armed hel
BBR some 7 Tu-22M
ASW ac 10* Be-12 **hel** 35 Mi-14, 25* Ka-25, 5* Ka-27
MR/EW ac 4 An-12 **hel** 3 Ka-25
MCM 5 Mi-14 BT hel

CASPIAN SEA FLOTILLA
BASE Astrakhan (Russia)
The Caspian Sea Flotilla has been divided among Azer-

baijan (about 25%), and Russia, Kazakstan and Turkmenistan, which are operating a joint flotilla under Russian command currently based at Astrakhan.

SURFACE COMBATANTS

15 patrol and coastal combatants, 9 MCM, some 6 amph, about 20 spt

PACIFIC FLEET (HQ Vladivostok)

BASES Vladivostok, Petropavlovsk, Kamchatskiy, Magadan, Sovetskaya Gavan

SUBMARINES 28

strategic 7 SSBN **tactical** 21 (5 SSGN, 11 SSN, 5 SS incl 2 SS other roles)

PRINCIPAL SURFACE COMBATANTS 12

5 cruisers, 4 destroyers, 3 frigates

OTHER SURFACE SHIPS about 30 patrol and coastal combatants, 33 MCM, 4 amph, some 110 spt and misc

NAVAL AVIATION (Pacific Fleet Air Force)

(HQ Vladivostok) 96 cbt ac, 80 cbt hel

BBR 1 regt with 9 Tu-22M

FGA 1 regt with 15 Su-24

ASW ac 27 Tu-142, 20 Il-38, 25 Be-12 **hel** afloat 25 Ka-25, 30 Ka-27; ashore 25 Mi-14

MR/EW ac some 8 An-12, Tu-95

MCM hel 6 Mi-14 BT

CBT ASLT HEL 10 Ka-29

COMMS 7 Tu-142

Air Force (Integrated Air Force and Air Defence Forces) (VVS) ε210,000

On the 1 March 1998 the Air Defence Troops (VPVO) amalgamated with the Air Force under one Air Force Command. The reorganisation is still in progress. The units and formations are those existing on 1 March 1998.
Some 1,855 cbt ac, 2 comd, 5 tac air armies, trg org. Force strengths vary, mostly org with div of 3 regt of 3 sqn (total 90–120 ac), indep regt (30–40 ac). Regt roles incl AD, interdiction, recce, tac air spt

Flying hours For aircrew that do fly the average annual flying time for Long Range Aviation is about 27 hours and in Tactical Aviation about 14 hours.

LONG-RANGE AVIATION COMMAND (DA)

3 div

BBR about 125 Tu-22M-3, plus 30 decommissioned Tu-22M-2 in store and 92 Tu-22 (incl 30 recce) awaiting destruction

TKR 20 Il-78

TRG 10 Tu-22M-2/3, 60 Tu-134

TACTICAL AVIATION

5 tac air armies

Flying hours 40

BBR/FGA some 725: incl 475 Su-24, 250 Su-25

FTR some 415: incl 315 MiG-29, 100 Su-27

RECCE some 200: incl 40 MiG-25, 160 Su-24

ECM 60 Mi-8

TRG 1 centre for op conversion: 180 **ac** incl 80 MiG-29, 80 Su-24, 20 Su-25

1 centre for instructor trg: 65 **ac** incl 10 MiG-25, 20 MiG-29, 15 Su-24, 10 Su-25, 10 Su-27

AAM AA-8 *Aphid*, AA-10 *Alamo*, AA-11 *Archer*

ASM AS-7 *Kerry*, AS-10 *Karen*, AS-11 *Kilter*, AS-12 *Kegler*, AS-13 *Kingbolt*, AS-14 *Kedge*, AS-16 *Kickback*, AS-17 *Krypton*, AS-18 *Kazoo*

AIR DEFENCE

3 AD armies: 4 indep AD corps: air regt and indep sqn; SAM bde/regt, 965 cbt ac

AIRCRAFT

FTR some 800, incl, 100 MiG-23, 425 MiG-31, 275 Su-27 (plus some 20 cbt capable MiG-23 trg variants in regts)

AEW AND CONTROL 20 Il-76

TRG 1 trg school, 4 regt: 165 MiG-23, 200 L-39

DECOMMISSIONED AIRCRAFT IN STORE 300 **ac** inc MiG-23, MiG-25

MISSILES

AAM AA-8 *Aphid*, AA-9 *Amos*, AA-10 *Alamo*, AA-11 *Archer*

SAM some 2,150 launchers in some 225 sites
50 SA-2 *Guideline* (being replaced by SA-10)
200 SA-5 *Gammon* (being replaced by SA-10)
some 1,900 SA-10

MILITARY TRANSPORT AVIATION COMMAND (VTA)

3 div, each 3 regt, each 30 ac; some indep regt

EQUIPMENT

some 340 **ac**, incl Il-76M/MD *Candid* B, An-12, An-21, An-124

Additional long- and medium-range tpt **ac** in comd other than VTA some 250: Tu-134, Tu-154, An-12, An-72, Il-18, Il-62

CIVILIAN FLEET 1,500 medium- and long-range passenger ac, incl some 350 An-12 and Il-76

AIR FORCE AVIATION TRAINING SCHOOLS

TRG 5 schools (incl 1 for foreign students) subordinate to Air Force HQ: 1,225 **ac** incl 900 L-39, 250 L-410/Tu-134, 75 MiG-29/Su-22/Su-25/Su-27

DECOMMISSIONED AIRCRAFT IN STORE some 1,000 **ac** incl MiG-23, MiG-27, Su-17, Su-22

COMBAT AIRCRAFT (CFE totals as at 1 Jan 1998 for all air forces less maritime)

ac 2,868 : 192 **Su-17** • 56 **Su-22** • 425 **Su-24** • 195 **Su-25** • 299 **Su-27** • 545 **MiG-23** • 139 **MiG-25** • 169 **MiG-27** • 461 **MiG-29** • 237 **MiG-31** • 92 **Tu-22** • 58 **Tu-22M**

hel 805: 720 **Mi-24** • 38 **Mi-24(K)** • 43 **Mi-24(R)** • 4 **Ka-50**

Deployment

The manning state of Russian units is difficult to determine. The following assessment of units within the Atlantic to the Urals (ATTU) region is based on the latest available information. Above 75% – none reported; above 50% – possibly 2 TD, 6 MRD, 4 ABD, 1 arty and 1 AB bde. The remainder are assessed as 20–50%. Units outside the ATTU are likely to be at a lower level. All bde are maintained at or above 50%. TLE in each MD includes active and trg units and in store

KALININGRAD

These forces are now commanded by The Ground and Coastal Defence Forces of the Baltic Fleet.

GROUND 14,500: 2 MRD, 2 tk, 1 SSM, 1 SAM bde/regt, 1 attack hel regt, 790 MBT, 1,000 ACV, 305 arty/MRL/mor, 18 Scud/Scarab, 42 attack hel

NAVAL INFANTRY (1,800)

1 bde (25 MBT, 34 arty/MRL) (Kaliningrad)

COASTAL DEFENCE

2 arty regt (133 arty)
1 SSM regt: some 8 SS-C-1b *Sepal*
AD 1 regt: 28 Su-27 (Baltic Fleet)
SAM 50

RUSSIAN MILITARY DISTRICTS

With effect from 1 August 1998 President Yeltsin authorised the establishment of a unified system for the military-administrative regions of the Russian Federation. Details of the reorganisation of Military Districts are at p. 102.

LENINGRAD MD (HQ St Petersburg)(to be re-named Northwest Zone)

GROUND 49,000: 1 ABD; plus 2 indep MR bde, 2 arty bde/regt, 1 SSM, 1 *Spetsnaz*, 4 SAM bde, 1 ATK, 1 aslt tpt hel regt, 980 MBT, 800 ACV, 1,130 arty/MRL/mor, 18 Scud/Scarab, 18 attack hel

NAVAL INFANTRY (1,700)

1 bde (77 MBT, 100 ACV, 41 arty)

COASTAL DEFENCE

1 Coastal Defence (360 MT-LB, 134 arty), 1 SAM regt
AIR 1 hy bbr regt (20 Tu-22M), 1 tac air army: 1 bbr div (80 Su-24), 1 recce regt (25 MiG-25, 10 Su-24), 1 ftr div (35 Su-27, 60 MiG-29), 1 hel ECM sqn (20 Mi-8)
AD 7 regt: 100 MiG-31, 90 Su-27
SAM 525

MOSCOW MD (HQ Moscow)

GROUND 105,000: 2 Army HQ, 2 TD, 2 MRD, 2 ABD, plus 1 arty div HQ, 6 arty bde/regt, 1 ATK, 3 SSM, 2 indep MR, 1 *Spetsnaz*, 4 SAM bde, 5 attack hel, 1 aslt tpt hel regt, 1,900 MBT, 3,500 ACV, 2,650 arty/MRL/mor, 48 Scud/Scarab, 180 attack hel
AIR 1 hy bbr regt (20 Tu-22M), 1 tac air army: 1 bbr div (90 Su-24), 1 ftr div (120 MiG-29), 1 FGA regt (50 Su-25), 1 recce regt (30 Su-24/MiG-25), 2 hel ECM sqn with 40 Mi-8
TRG 1 Long Range Aviation trg centre, 2 Tactical Aviation trg centre, trg regts of Air Force Aviation Schools; storage bases
AD 6 regt: 30 MiG-23, 75 MiG-31, 65 Su-27, 1 trg centre
SAM 850

VOLGA MD (HQ Kuybyshev (Samarra))(to be merged

with Ural as Central Asian Zone)

GROUND 33,300: 1 MRD, 1 ABD plus 1 AB, 1 arty bde/regt, 1 SSM, 1 SAM bde, 1 aslt tpt hel, 5 hel trg regt, 900 MBT, 1,500 ACV, 1,000 arty/MRL/mor, 18 *Scarab*, 130 attack hel
AIR trg regts of tac aviation; trg centres and Air Force aviation schools, storage bases
AD 1 PVO Corps, 2 regt: 30 MiG-23, 25 MiG-31

NORTH CAUCASUS MD (HQ Rostov)

GROUND 54,500: 1 Army HQ, 2 Corps HQ, 2 MRD, 1 ABD, 3 MR bde, 1 *Spetsnaz*, 2 arty bde, 1 SSM, 4 SAM bde, 1 ATK, 2 attack hel, 1 aslt tpt hel regt, 500 MBT, 2,270 ACV, 500 arty/MRL/mor, 18 Scud/Scarab, 60 attack hel

NAVAL INFANTRY (ε1,500)

1 regt (36 MBT, 130 APC, 24 arty (2S1, 2S9))
AIR 1 tac Air Army: 1 bbr div (90 Su-24), 1 FGA div (100 Su-25), 1 ftr div (100 MiG-29), 1 recce regt (35 Su-24), 1 hel ECM sqn with 20 Mi-8, trg regt of tac aviation and Air Force aviation schools
AD 3 regt: 25 MiG-31, 60 Su-27; 1 aviation school, 4 regt: 165 MiG-23, 200 L-39
SAM 125

URAL MD (HQ Yekaterinburg)(to be merged with Volga MD as Central Asian Zone)

GROUND 1 TD, 1 MRD, 1 *Spetsnaz*, 2 arty bde/regt, 1 ATK bde/regt, 1 SSM bde, 1,300 MBT, 1,600 ACV, 900 arty/MRL/mor, 18 *Scarab*
AIR Air Force aviation schools
AD Covering Ural, Siberian, Transbaykal and Far Eastern MDs: 40 MiG-23, 200 MiG-31, 65 Su-27
SAM 600

SIBERIAN MD (HQ Novosibirsk)

GROUND 1 MRD, 1 arty div, 3 MR bde, 5 arty bde/regt, 1 SAM, 1 *Spetsnaz* bde, 1 ATK, 1 attack hel regt, 1,468 MBT, 3,000 ACV, 2,300 arty/MRL/mor, 30 attack hel
AIR Air Force aviation schools
AD See Ural MD

TRANSBAYKAL MD (HQ Chita)(to be merged with Siberian MD as Siberian Zone)

GROUND 2 Corps HQ, 3 TD (1 trg), 1 MRD, plus 2 MG/arty div, 5 arty bde/regt, 2 SSM, 1 AB, 1 *Spetsnaz*, 3 ATK, 1 SAM bde, 1 attack hel, 1 aslt tpt hel regt, 3,000 MBT, 3,000 ACV, 2,000 arty/MRL/mor, 36 Scud/Scarab, 18-SS-21, 80 attack hel
AIR Covering Transbaykal and Far Eastern MDs: 2 LRA DIV, 2 tac air armies
BBR 85 Tu-22M
FGA 315 Su-24/25
FTR 100 Su-27/MiG-29
RECCE 100 Su-24
AD See Ural MD

FAR EASTERN MD (HQ Khabarovsk)

GROUND 2 Army, 2 Corps HQ, 10 MRD (2 trg), plus 2 MG/arty div, 1 arty div, 9 arty bde/regt, 1 MR, 1 AB, 3 SSM, 5 SAM, 1 *Spetsnaz*, 1 ATK bde, 2 attack

hel, 2 aslt tpt hel regt, 3,900 MBT, 6,400 ACV, 3,000
arty/MRL/mor, 54 *Scud/Scarab*, 120 attack hel

NAVAL INFANTRY (2,500)
1 div HQ, 3 inf, 1 tk and 1 arty bn

COASTAL DEFENCE
1 Coastal Defence div

AIR See Transbaykal MD
  AD See Ural MD

Forces Abroad

Declared str of forces deployed in Armenia and Georgia as
at 1 Jan 1998 was 13,300. These forces are now subordinate
to the North Caucasus MD. Total probably excludes locally
enlisted personnel.

ARMENIA
GROUND (4,100): 1 mil base (bde), 74 MBT, 17
  APC, 148 ACV, 84 arty/MRL/mors
AD 1 sqn MiG-23

GEORGIA
GROUND (9,200): 3 mil bases (each = bde+), 140 T-
  72 MBT, 500 ACV, 173 arty incl **122mm** D-30, 2S1
  SP; **152mm** 2S3; **122mm** BM-21 MRL; **120mm**
  mor, 5 attack hel. Plus 118 ACV and some arty
  deployed in Abkhazia
AD 60 SA-6
AIR 1 composite regt with some 35 **ac** An-12, An-26
  hel Mi-8

MOLDOVA (Dniestr)
GROUND 2,500: 120 MBT, 130 ACV, 130 arty/
  MRL/mor. These forces are now subordinate to
  the Moscow MD

TAJIKISTAN
GROUND (ε8,200): 1 MRD, 190 MBT, 303 ACV, 180
  arty/MRL/mor; plus 14,500 Frontier Forces
  (Russian officers, Tajik conscripts)
AFRICA 100. **CUBA** some 800 SIGINT and ε10 mil
advisers. **SYRIA** 50
VIETNAM 700; naval facility and SIGINT station.
Used by RF aircraft and surface ships on reduced basis

Peacekeeping

BOSNIA (SFOR II): 1,500; 2 AB bn
GEORGIA/ABKHAZIA ε1,500; 1 AB regt, 2 MR bn
GEORGIA/SOUTH OSSETIA ε500; 1 MR bn
MOLDOVA/TRANSDNIESTR 500; 1 MR bn
UNITED NATIONS
ANGOLA (UNOMA): 136 incl 3 obs. **BOSNIA**
(UNMIBH): 1 plus 36 civ pol. **CROATIA** (UNPSG): 31
plus 1 civ pol; (UNMOP): 1 obs. **FYROM**
(UNPREDEP): 2 obs plus 2 civ pol. **GEORGIA**:

(UNOMIG) 3 obs. **IRAQ/KUWAIT** (UNIKOM): 11
obs. **MIDDLE EAST** (UNTSO): 4 obs. **WESTERN
SAHARA** (MINURSO): 25 obs

Paramilitary ε543,000 active

FRONTIER FORCES 200,000
directly subordinate to the President; 7 frontier
districts, Arctic, Kaliningrad, Moscow units (to re-org
into 8 regional directorates, 6 frontier districts, 3
frontier gps)

EQUIPMENT
1,700 ACV (incl BMP, BTR), 90 arty (incl 2S1, 2S9,
  2S12)
ac some 70 Il-76, Tu-134, An-72, An-24, An-26, Yak-
  40, 16 SM-92 **hel** some 200+ Mi-8, Mi-24, Mi-26,
  Ku-27
PATROL AND COASTAL COMBATANTS about
  237
PATROL, OFFSHORE 23
7 *Krivak*-III with 1 Ka-27 hel, 1 100mm gun, 12
  Grisha-II, 4 *Grisha*-III
PATROL, COASTAL 35
20 *Pauk*, 15 *Svetlyak*
PATROL, INSHORE 95
65 *Stenka*, 10 *Muravey*, 20 *Zhuk*
RIVERINE MONITORS about 84
10 *Yaz*, 7 *Piyavka*, 7 *Vosh*, 60 *Shmel*
SUPPORT AND MISCELLANEOUS about 26
8 *Ivan Susanin* armed icebreakers, 18 *Sorum* armed
  ocean tugs

MINISTERSTVO VNUTRENNIKH DEL (MVD)
ε237,000
internal security tps; 7 regions (to be 6), some 20 'div'
incl 4 indep special purpose div (ODON – 2 to 5 op
regt), 29 indep bde incl 10 indep special designation
bde (OBRON – 3 mech, 1 mor bn); 65 regt/bn incl
special motorised units, avn, guards and escorts

EQUIPMENT
incl 1,700 ACV (incl BMP-1/-2, BTR-80), 20 D-30

**FORCES FOR THE PROTECTION OF THE
RUSSIAN FEDERATION** 25,000
org incl elm of Ground Forces (1 mech inf bde, 1 AB
regt, 1 Presidential Guard regt)

FEDERAL SECURITY SERVICE ε9,000 armed incl
Alfa, Beta and Zenit cdo units

**FEDERAL COMMUNICATIONS AND
INFORMATION AGENCY** ε54,000

MILITARY DEVELOPMENTS

The military situation in the region has changed little since 1997. The Middle East peace process remains stalled and **Iraq** continues to test the resolve of the US and the rest of the UN Security Council. Despite positive internal political developments, **Iran** continues to raise security concerns with its missile and nuclear weapon programmes. These, along with other security threats such as the conflict in **Algeria**, contribute to maintaining the region's position as the world's leading arms importer.

Middle East

In August 1998, the US proposal for 13% of the West Bank to be handed over by **Israel** to the Palestinian Authority (PA) remained the basis of discussion between the two sides. The lack of progress in negotiations means that the security situation remains unstable. Terrorist attacks in Israel by *Hamas* and *Hizbollah* persist, and Israel continues to maintain the 15-kilometre 'security zone' in **Lebanese** territory along their mutual border. The level of Israeli Defence Force (IDF) activity in south Lebanon – particularly air operations – remains high. By mid-August 1998, Israel had carried out nearly 70 air attacks on suspected guerrilla (mostly *Hizbollah*) positions in south Lebanon. In general, land-force operations in 1998 have been less frequent and smaller-scale than in the previous year. The 1996 agreement between Israel and *Hizbollah* to avoid attacks on or near civilian areas has generally held. The agreement was negotiated following an incident in May 1996 in which over 200 civilians were killed by Israeli artillery aimed at a *Hizbollah* group positioned next to a large number of refugees sheltering in a UN post. Both sides have alleged breaches of the agreement. Nonetheless it appears to have contributed to the lower level of civilian casualties in 1997 and 1998.

The Gulf

Iraq continues to obstruct the work of the UN Special Commission (UNSCOM) and the International Atomic Energy Agency (IAEA). The regime forced US members of the UN inspection teams to leave Iraq in October 1997; UNSCOM and the IAEA were compelled to stop all inspections in January 1998. The UN Security Council was divided over its response, although there was no disagreement that Iraq had not met its obligations under the terms of the 1991 UN cease-fire resolution (SCR687). The US, supported by the UK and some other countries, strengthened its forces in the Gulf region and threatened to use force unless Iraq complied. The reinforcement was complicated by allies in the region declining permission for facilities to be used for launching attacks on Iraq. **Saudi Arabia**, **Bahrain** and the **United Arab Emirates** (UAE) were among those that refused permission for planes to fly from their airfields directly for missions over Iraq. The Turkish government has also refused to allow combat aircraft to use its bases to fly sorties directly to Iraq. This reinforced the importance of carrier-based forces to reduce dependence on host-nation support in such situations. By mid-February 1998, the US had two carrier groups in the Gulf with 94 Naval combat aircraft (F-14, F/A-18) and about 140 US Air Force combat aircraft in the region (F-15, F-16, B-1B, F-117, A-10 and 14 B-52s based in Diego Garcia). In addition, the US deployed some 110 combat-support aircraft and helicopters. The UK provided a carrier with 15 combat aircraft aboard (*Sea Harriers* and *Harrier* GR-7s) and 14 *Tornado* GR-1s. The US also deployed 6,500 marines ashore in Kuwait from its Marine Amphibious Group in the region. In addition to the numbers in the Gulf, forces in the Mediterranean and elsewhere were earmarked as reinforcements or replacements. This level of deployment was sustained until mid-

June 1998 (nearly six months), but its significant economic costs and drain on personnel resources showed the limits to what even the US could deploy for protracted periods. The cost of the deployment to the US is indicated by the administration's request for a supplementary appropriation of $1.4 billion.

Under the shadow of an unambiguous threat of force, the Iraqi regime negotiated with UN Secretary-General Kofi Annan who, on 23 February 1998, announced an agreement which allowed the inspection process to resume. Until August 1998, a more politicised inspection process was conducted which nevertheless resulted in further evidence of Iraq's failure to declare in full its weapons of mass destruction (WMD) and missile programmes. On 2 August, Iraq further limited its cooperation with UNSCOM and the IAEA, effectively ending searches for evidence of WMD and missile programmes. Iraq was only prepared to countenance inspections for the purpose of long-term monitoring and compliance – and even placed restrictions on these inspections that the heads of UNSCOM and the IAEA declared unacceptable. It is unclear whether military force will again need to be threatened or used to compel Iraqi compliance with its obligations.

In July 1998, Iran flight-tested its *Shihab*-3 medium-range ballistic missile (MRBM). The *Shihab*-3, which is reportedly based on North Korean *Nodong*-1 technology, is designed to have a maximum range of just over 1,000km. It is not known whether the test was successful; reports indicate that the missile exploded just two minutes into its flight, although this could have been deliberate since this is the point at which the missile's fuel would be exhausted. The warhead would then separate and continue to the target. While the missile is not yet operational, its range means that it is capable of reaching targets anywhere in Iraq, and could reach Israel. Iran is also reported to be developing a longer-range *Shihab*-4 MRBM.

North Africa

Conflict continues in Algeria; since the current round of violence began in 1992, an estimated 70,000 people have died. A high-level UN fact-finding mission visited the country in July and August 1998 to talk to massacre survivors, prisoners, opposition parties and government and military officers. Annan was due to report the mission's findings to the UN General Assembly in September 1998. Although this political development is encouraging, the killings continue. The security forces are able to protect key elements of the national infrastructure, including the flow of oil for export, but are unable to prevent attacks by militant Islamic armed groups on people in villages and rural areas. There have been allegations that government forces have been responsible for some massacres but no substantive evidence has emerged. The *Groupe Islamique Armée* (GIA) is now the only effective fighting opposition force since the disbanding of the *Armée Islamique du Salut* (AIS) by August 1998 following a decision by the AIS' political wing, the *Front Islamique du Salut* (FIS), to cooperate with the government.

DEFENCE SPENDING

In 1997, regional military expenditure increased from $54bn in 1996 to $56bn, or some 5% in real terms, according to *The Military Balance* estimates. At 7–8% of gross domestic product (GDP), the region continues to spend significantly more than any other as a proportion of GDP. Defence budgets in 1998 indicate a further real increase of about 1%, despite the prospect of declining oil revenues for many regional governments. Countries increasing their military spending in 1997 included Algeria, where the costs of civil war continued to escalate; Iran, which has a growing number of expensive indigenous weapons programmes, including MRBMs; and Saudi Arabia, the UAE and **Qatar**, where arms imports accounted for the increase. The region remains the largest market in the world, in value terms, for direct sales of advanced weaponry. Regional arms deliveries in 1997 were estimated at $17bn, compared to $15bn in 1996.

Israel's defence budget remains at between 10% and 12% of GDP, depending on how it is calculated. As noted in *The Military Balance 1997/98*, significant military-related expenditure is excluded from the defence budget. Excluding US Foreign Military Assistance (FMA) of $1.8bn for procurement and $1.2bn in military-related economic assistance, the 1998 budget published in September 1997 was NIS24.5bn, plus $170 million in reserve, giving a total of $7bn – about 3% down on the 1997 budget in real terms. The direct cost of the Iraq crisis of November 1997–March 1998 was NIS285m ($80m), shared by the Defence and Health ministries. Due to lower than expected tax revenues caused by Israel's slow economic-growth rate in 1997 (1.9%), the Ministry of Finance opposes increases in defence spending in a year when population growth reached 2.5% (40% from immigration). From 1998, biannual grants of NIS5,000 ($1,400), funded outside the defence budget, are to be given to military personnel eligible for family allowances to encourage service in field units. Pending final agreement between Israel and the US, the arrangements for US FMA are to change over the next 10–12 years starting in 2000. Under the proposed new arrangements, Foreign Military Financing (FMF), the direct military component of US grant aid, is to increase by $600m a year to $2.4bn, while economic aid is to be phased out. Under Israeli proposals, the extra $600m would be spent on R&D and equipment from Israeli rather than US suppliers (at present, about a quarter of US FMF ($475m) is spent on equipment from Israeli suppliers). In July 1998, the US Congress cut $100m from the US government's 1999 FMA request for both Israel and **Egypt** (and diverted $50m of this to military assistance to **Jordan**). The Israeli Air Force took delivery of the first of 25 F-15I aircraft (equipped with the US advanced medium-range air-to-air missile (AMRAAM) and the new Israeli *Python*-4 air-to-air missile (AAM)) in January 1998 under the terms of a 1993 contract valued at $2.2bn over ten years. In May 1998, production of the joint US–Israeli *Homa* (formerly *Arrow*) for ballistic-missile defence (BMD) was approved. The first delivery is planned for late 1999, followed by deployment of the first two batteries in 2000. An Israeli funding request for a third *Homa* battery was part-approved under the US budget authorisation for Fiscal Year (FY) 1999. The value of Israeli arms exports in 1997 exceeded $1.5bn, up from $1.4bn in 1996, and Israel remains one of the top five exporters in the international arms trade.

It remains difficult to assess real military spending in both Iran and **Syria**. Iran's defence budget for 1998 is r101tr ($5.8bn), up from r82tr ($4.7bn) in 1997 – a nominal increase of some 23%. Official figures show that Iran's defence spending has almost tripled since 1993. Iran's civil nuclear programme, the subject of international concern given the country's ample oil and gas reserves, involves Russia building a 1,000MW reactor at Bushehr under a contract worth $800m. Iran has so far invested about $6bn, including the Russian contract, in nuclear power. In October 1997, the Iranian government announced its plans to produce 20% of its energy from nuclear-power plants. The plan involves increasing the present 16,000MW power output to 27,000MW by March 2000. Iran's indigenous conventional-weapons programmes include 122mm and 155mm self-propelled artillery built under Russian licence. Iran also produces Russian-designed T-72 main battle tanks (MBTs) and BMP-derivative *Boragh* armoured personnel carriers (APCs) under Russian licence based on a 1988–89 agreement. In Lebanon, the defence budget for 1998 is LP901bn ($592m), up from LP805bn ($523m) in 1997. In Jordan, where deliveries of 16 F-16A/B aircraft from the US were completed in April 1998, the defence and security budget rose to D390m ($548m) in 1998 from D352m ($496m) in 1997.

Details of defence expenditure in Egypt are difficult to obtain in advance. Official figures for 1996–97 show outlays of E£8bn ($2.4bn), excluding US foreign military assistance for equipment purchases ($1.3bn) and economic aid ($815m). Follow-on orders for 21 F-16C/D aircraft from the US (assembled in Turkey) are planned for delivery from 1999 after completion of the first batch of 46. There is also a follow-on order for 80 M1A1 MBTs (assembled in Egypt) for delivery from 1999, after delivery of 555 units mostly assembled in Egypt is completed by the same year.

Defence spending in the Gulf States, boosted by imports of advanced weaponry, remains high. There were no direct commitments by the Gulf States to contribute towards the costs of US and UK reinforcements in the region during the 1997–98 confrontation with Iraq. Saudi Arabia's defence spending in 1997 was R68bn ($18bn). The Kingdom pays for a third ($300m) of the cost of the *Southern Watch* no-fly zone in southern Iraq operated by the US and UK. The value of arms imports increased from $9bn to $11bn, mainly as a result of combat-aircraft acquisitions. Deliveries of 72 F-15S fighters ordered from the US in 1992 are at the half-way stage and will continue until 2000, while deliveries of 48 *Tornado* bombers ordered in 1993 from the UK should be completed in 1998. Six *Tornados* were delivered in 1996 and 36 in 1997. Qatar took delivery of the last two of four *Barzan* fast-attack Naval vessels from the UK in April 1998, and deliveries of 12 *Mirage* 2000-5 fighters from France should be completed in 1998 following delivery of the first three in 1997. After a prolonged international competition to meet its fighter requirements, the UAE ordered:

- 30 new *Mirage* 2000-9 (plus 33 upgrades to 2000-9-standard for its existing *Mirage* fighters) from France in December 1997;
- 18 *Hawk* 200 single-seat combat aircraft from the UK in April 1998, and;
- 80 F-16 Block 60 fighters from the US in May 1998 for delivery from 2002.

The F-16 purchase was the largest single export order in the international arms trade since the Saudi F-15 purchase in 1992 and that of the *Tornados* in 1993. The combined value of the UAE's fighter acquisitions exceeds $11bn.

Kuwait's defence budget in 1997 was D460m ($1.5bn), with a further D76m ($250m) for the National Guard. These figures exclude procurement spending. Kuwait pays two-thirds of the annual cost of the UN Iraq–Kuwait Observer Force (UNIKOM), which cost the country $50m in 1997. The initial phase of Kuwait's rearmament programme following the war with Iraq in 1990–91 is almost complete, apart from the *Patriot* surface-to-air missile (SAM) system ordered from the US in 1992 and eight *Almaradin* (*Combattante*) fast-patrol craft from France, armed with British *Sea-Skua* missiles, for delivery from 1998. After prolonged delay, Kuwait ordered 16 AH-64D attack helicopters from the US in October 1997 and, in December, 27 PLZ45 155mm self-propelled howitzers from China. Bahrain ordered 8 F-16C/D aircraft from the US in January 1998 for delivery from 2001. **Oman** ordered a second batch of 20 *Challenger* II MBTs from the UK in November 1997. **Yemen**'s 1998 defence and security budget is R54bn ($414m), up from R52bn ($400m) in 1997.

Algeria's defence budget increased to D112bn ($1.8bn) from D101bn ($1.7bn) in 1997. Because of the civil war, the defence budget has almost doubled since 1992; indications are that actual outlays are likely to be higher than budgeted. Algeria took delivery of the *Seeker* unmanned aerial vehicle (UAV) system from South Africa in 1997. In July 1995, there were reports that the Air Force had ordered 36 used MiG-29 aircraft from Belarus. In **Morocco**, the 1997 defence budget was D13.2bn ($1.4bn); the **Tunisian** defence budget in 1998 is D397m ($340m), up from D369m ($333m) in 1997.

Table 16 Arms orders and deliveries, Middle East and North Africa, 1996–1998

Supplier	Classification	Designation	Units	Order Date	Delivery Date	Comment
Algeria						
Slvk	APC	BVP-2	48	1994	1995	Deliveries complete 1996
RSA	UAV	*Seeker*		1997	1997	
Bel	FGA	MiG-29	36	1998	1999	
Bel	FGA	Su-24	2	1996	1997	
Bahrain						
US	ftr	F-16C/D	8	1998	2001	Option for further 2
US	hel	AH-1	12	1994	1997	10 delivered 1997
US	FFG	OH *Perry*	1	1995	1997	
US	MBT	M-60A3	60	1995	1996	Ex-ROK, on lease
US	SAM	*Hawk*	8	1996	1997	Improved *Hawk*. Ex-US, 8 batteries
US	arty	M-110	49	1995	1997	
Egypt						
US	FGA	F-16C/D	46	1991	1994	Last delivery 1996, assembled in Tu
US	FGA	F-16C/D	21	1996	1999	Follow-on order
US	AH	AH-64A	36	1990	1994	Deliveries to 1999. 6 delivered 1997
US	hel	UH-60L	2	1995	1998	VIP configuration
US	hel	CH-47D	4	1997	1999	Possibly delivered 2000
US	FFG	OH *Perry*	3	1997	1997	ex-US. Deliveries 1997–98
US	hel	SH-2G	10	1994	1997	
US	SSM	*Harpoon*	42	1998		Part of OH *Perry* FFG transaction
US	FF	*Knox*	4	1997		2 to be used for spare parts
US	MBT	M1A1	555	1988	1993	Deliveries to 1999
US	MBT	M1A1	80	1996	1999	Follow-on order
Nl	AIFV	YPR-765	611	1995	1996	
Domestic	APC	*Al-Akhbar*		1998		Development completed
US	arty	SP 122	24		1998	Follow-on order
US	SAM	*Avenger*	50	1998		
US	APC	M-113	378	1995	1997	
Iran						
Domestic	SSM	*Shihab-2*		1994	1998	Domestically produced *Scud*
Domestic	SSM	*Shihab-3*		1994	1999	Reportedly based on *Nodong*-1
Domestic	MRBM	*Shihab-4*		1994		Development. Reportedly based on SS-4
Domestic	FGA	*Azarakhsh*		1986		Development. Also known as *Owj*
Fr	trg	TB-21	12	1996		6 TB-21, 6 *Socata* TB-200
PRC	tpt	Y-7	14	1996	1998	Deliveries 1998–2006
RF	SS	*Kilo*-class	3	1989	1996	Deliveries completed 1997
Domestic	SS	Submarine		1997		Small submarine development
Domestic	corvette		3	1998	2002	In development
PRC	PFM	*Hudong*-class	10	1992	1994	Deliveries completed 1996
RF	MBT	T-72	200	1989	1994	Some licensed production; 200+ delivered
Domestic	MBT	Type-72Z			1996	Upgrade package for T-54/55
Domestic	MBT	*Zulfiqar*		1994	1997	In production
Domestic	lt tk	*Towsan*				Reportedly to enter production
Domestic	APC	*Boragh*	40			In production. 40 in service with IRGC
Domestic	arty	*Thunder*-1			1996	122mm. In production
Domestic	arty	*Thunder*-2			1996	155mm. In production
Domestic	RL	*Zelzal* 2				610mm. In production
Domestic	MRL	*Fadjr* 3				240mm. In production

Supplier	Classification	Designation	Units	Order Date	Delivery Date	Comment
Domestic	MRL	*Hadid*				122mm. In production
Domestic	UAV	*Stealth*			1997	Development
Israel						
Domestic	BMD	*Homa*	2	1986	1999	Deployment 1999; joint venture with US
Domestic	SAM	*Nautilus*				In development. Joint venture with US
Domestic	BMD	MOAB				In development. Air-launched ABM
Domestic	Sat	*Ofeq* 3			1995	Reconnaissance satellite
Domestic	Sat	*Ofeq* 4			1999	In development. Jan 1998 malfunction
Domestic	Sat	*Amos*-1	1		1996	Communications satellite
US	FGA	F-15I	25	1993	1998	
US	AAM	AMRAAM	64	1993	1998	
Domestic	AAM	*Python*-4		1993	1998	
Domestic	PGM	MSOV			1998	Long-range glide bomb
US	tpt	KC-135	1		1997	Multirole passenger/ tanker
US	AH	AH-64D		1998		Upgrade to *Longbow*-standard
US	hel	AH-1	14	1995	1996	
US	tpt hel	S-70A	15	1996	1998	
Fr	hel	AS-565	8	1994	1997	5 delivered 1997
Ge	SSK	*Dolphin*	3	1991	1998	First delivered 1998. Funded by Ge
US	corvette	*Saar* 5	3	1989	1995	Fitted out in Il
Domestic	PFC	*Super Dvora*	2	1997	1999	
US	LST	*Newport*	1	1997		
Domestic	MBT	*Merkava* IV		1991		In development
US	MRL	MLRS	42	1994	1995	Completed 1998.16 delivered 1997
US	SAM	*Chaparral*	36	1995	1996	
Domestic	UAV	*Silver Arrow*		1997		In development. Prototype Apr 1998
Kuwait						
US	SAM	*Patriot*	5	1992		5 batteries, 210 missiles
Fr	PFM	*Almaradim*	8	1995	1998	Commissioning to begin late 1998
UK	SSM	*Sea-Skua*	60	1997	1998	
US	cbt hel	AH-64D	16	1997		*Longbow* radar will not initially be fitted
US	MBT	M1A2	218	1992	1994	Deliveries continuing 1996–97
UK	AIFV	*Warrior*	254	1993	1995	Deliveries to 1998, 72 delivered 1997
RF	AIFV	BMP-3	126	1994	1995	Deliveries continue
RF	AIFV	BMP-2	46	1993	1996	Deliveries complete 1996
A	APC	*Pandur*	70	1996		Option for further 130
Aus	APC	S-600	22	1997	1998	
PRC	arty	PLZ45	27	1997		Option for further 27
US	arty	M-109A6	48	1998		Option for further 24. Order delayed
Fr	APC	VBL	20	1995	1997	
Lebanon						
US	hel	UH-1H			1998	Follow-on order
US	APC	M-113	88	1995	1997	
Libya						
Domestic	MRBM	*Al-Fatah*				Development
Mauritania						
Fr	PCI	VSA 14	1		1996	
PRC	tpt	Y-7	1		1997	
Morocco						
Fr	AK	408	1	1995	1997	
Fr	OPV	OPV-64	5		1995	Deliveries completed 1997
US	arty	M-110	60	1995	1997	

Supplier	Classification	Designation	Units	Order Date	Delivery Date	Comment
US	arty	M-198	26	1996	1997	ex-US
Fr	APC	AMX-13	10	1996	1997	
Jordan						
US	FGA	F-16A/B	16	1995	1997	Deliveries complete Apr 1998
US	tpt	C-130-H	1		1997	Ex-US
US	hel	UH-60L	4	1995	1998	
US	tac hel	UH-1H	18		1996	Ex-US
US	MBT	M-60A3	50		1996	Ex-US
US	MBT	M-60A3	38		1998	Ex-US
US	arty	203mm	18		1998	Ex-US
Oman						
UK	ftr	*Jaguar*	15	1997		Upgrade
UK	Corvette	VT-83	2	1992	1996	Second delivered 1997
UK	MBT	*Challenger* II	20	1997		
US	MBT	M60A3	50	1995	1996	Ex-US
CH	APC	*Piranha*	80	1993	1994	Final deliveries 1997
RSA	arty	G-6	25	1995	1996	
CH	AAA	35mm			1996	4 batteries
Fr	APC	VBL	41	1995	1997	
Qatar						
Sp	FGA	F-1	5	1995	1997	
Fr	FGA	*Mirage* 2000-5	12	1994	1997	*Mirage* 2000-5. 3 delivered 1997
UK	trg	*Hawk* 100	15	1996	1999	Possibly 18
UK	PFC	*Barzan*	4	1992	1997	
UK	SAM	*Starburst*		1996		
Fr	MBT	AMX-30	10	1997		
CH	LAV	*Piranha* II	38	1996	1997	2 delivered 1997 via UK
Saudi Arabia						
US	FGA	F-15S	72	1992	1995	Deliveries to 2000. 16 delivered 1997
UK	FGA	*Tornado* IDS	48	1993	1996	6 1996, 36 1997
US	AWACS	E-3	5	1997		Upgrade
UK	trg	*Hawk* 65	20	1993	1997	Deliveries complete 1997
CH	trg	PC-9	20	1993	1996	Deliveries complete in 1996
Fr	hel	AS-532	12	1996	1998	
It	sar hel	AB-412TP	40	1997		
Fr	FF	*La Fayette*	3	1994	2003	Deliveries to 2004. Known as *Sawari* 2
UK	MHC	*Sandown*	3	1988	1997	Second delivered 1997
RSA	arty	G6	30	1997		
UK	mor	LAV-AMS	73	1996	1998	120mm mortar on LAV chassis
Syria						
PRC	SSM	M-9			1997	Unknown whether missiles are operational
Ukr	MBT	T-55MV	200	1995	1997	
United Arab Emirates						
US	ftr	F-16	80	1998	2002	Block 60 variant
Fr	ftr	*Mirage* 2000-9	30	1997	2001	
Fr	ftr	*Mirage* 2000	33	1997	2000	Upgrade to 2000-9-standard
Fr	ASM	*Apache*		1998		
UK	trg	*Hawk*	26	1989	1992	Final deliveries 1996
UK	FGA	*Hawk* 200	18	1998	2001	

Supplier	Classification	Designation	Units	Order Date	Delivery Date	Comment
Ge	trg	G-115 TA	12	1996	1997	UAE has option for further 12
RF	tpt	Il-76	4			
Indo	tpt	CN-235	7	1997		
Indo	MPA	CN-235-200	4	1998		
US	cbt hel	AH-64A	10	1996		Follow-on order to 20 previously delivered
Fr	hel	AS-565	7	1995	1997	Option for further 2
Fr	hel	SA 342	5	1997		Option for further 5
It	hel	A-109	3	1994	1995	Deliveries completed 1996
It	hel	AB-412	5	1994	1996	At least 5 ordered
Nl	FFG	*Kortenaer*	2	1996	1997	Deliveries completed 1998
US	SSM	*Harpoon*	24	1997		To equip 2 ex-Nl *Kortenaer*-class frigates
Fr	MBT	*Leclerc*	430	1993	1994	396 MBTs, 34 CRVs. 68 delivered 1997
RF	AIFV	BMP-3	330	1992	1996	
Tu	APC	AAPC	136	1997	1999	M-113
Nl	arty	M-109	87	1995	1997	
Yemen						
Fr	FAC	*Vigilante*	6	1996	1997	Commissioning delayed

Algeria

	1996	1997	1998	1999
GDP	D2.5tr	D2.7tr		
	($45bn)	($46bn)		
per capita	$6,300	$6,400		
Growth	4.0%	1.2%		
Inflation	21.7%	5.7%		
Debt	$33bn	$31bn		
Def exp	D99bn	D122bn		
	($1.8bn)	($2.1bn)		
Def bdgt			D112bn	
			($1.9bn)	
FMA (US)	$0.1m	$0.1m	$0.1m	$0.1m
$1 = dinar	54.7	57.7	60.2	
Population		29,200,000		
Age	*13–17*	*18–22*	*23–32*	
Men	1,891,000	1,693,000	2,689,000	
Women	1,761,000	1,584,000	2,524,000	

Total Armed Forces

ACTIVE ε122,000

(ε75,000 conscripts)
Terms of service **Army** 18 months (6 months basic, 12 months civil projects)

RESERVES

Army some 150,000, to age 50

Army 105,000

(ε75,000 conscripts)
6 Mil Regions; re-org into div structure on hold
2 armd div (each 3 tk, 1 mech regt) • 2 mech div (each 3 mech, 1 tk regt) • 1 AB div • 1 indep armd bde • 4–5 indep mot/mech inf bde • 6 arty, 1 ATK, 5 AD bn

EQUIPMENT

MBT 951: 324 T-54/-55, 332 T-62, 295 T-72
RECCE 75 BRDM-2
AIFV 700 BMP-1, 225 BMP-2
APC 530 BTR-50/-60, 150 OT-64, some BTR-80 (reported)
TOWED ARTY 122mm: 28 D-74, 100 M-1931/37, 60 M-30 (M-1938), 198 D-30; **130mm**: 10 M-46; **152mm**: 20 ML-20 (M-1937)
SP ARTY 185: **122mm**: 150 2S1; **152mm**: 35 2S3
MRL 122mm: 48 BM-21; **140mm**: 48 BM-14-16; **240mm**: 30 BM-24
MOR 82mm: 150 M-37; **120mm**: 120 M-1943; **160mm**: 60 M-1943
ATGW AT-2 *Swatter*, AT-3 *Sagger*
RCL 82mm: 120 B-10; **107mm**: 58 B-11
ATK GUNS 57mm: 156 ZIS-2; **85mm**: 80 D-44; **100mm**: 12 T-12, 50 SU-100 SP
AD GUNS 14.5mm: 80 ZPU-2/-4; **20mm**: 100;

23mm: 100 ZU-23 towed, 210 ZSU-23-4 SP; **37mm**: 150 M-1939; **57mm**: 75 S-60; **85mm**: 20 KS-12; **100mm**: 150 KS-19; **130mm**: 10 KS-30
SAM SA-7/-8/-9

Navy ε7,000

(incl ε500 Coast Guard)
BASES Mers el Kebir, Algiers, Annaba, Jijel
SUBMARINES 2
2 Sov *Kilo* with 533mm TT
FRIGATES 3
3 *Mourad Rais* (Sov *Koni*) with 4 x 76mm gun, 2 x 12 ASW RL
PATROL AND COASTAL COMBATANTS 19
CORVETTES 3 *Rais Hamidou* (Sov *Nanuchka* II) with 4 SS-N-2C *Styx* SSM, 2 C-58
MISSILE CRAFT 11 *Osa* with 4 SS-N-2 SSM
PATROL CRAFT 5
  COASTAL 2 *Djebel Chinoise*
  INSHORE 3 *El Yadekh* PCI
MINE COUNTERMEASURES 11
11 Sov T-43 MSC
AMPHIBIOUS 3
2 *Kalaat beni Hammad* LST: capacity 240 tps, 10 tk, hel deck
1 *Polnocny* LSM: capacity 180 tps, 6 tk
SUPPORT AND MISCELLANEOUS 3
1 *El Idrissi* AGHS, 1 div spt, 1 *Poluchat* torpedo recovery vessel

COAST GUARD (ε500)
Some 7 PRC *Chui-E* PCC, about 6 *El Yadekh* PCI, 16 PCI<, 1 spt, plus boats

Air Force 10,000

181 cbt ac, 65 armed hel
Flying hours ε160
FGA 3 sqn
  1 with 10 Su-24 • 2 with 40 MiG-23BN
FTR 5 sqn
  1 with 10 MiG-25 • 1 with 30 MiG-23B/E • 3 with 70 MiG-21MF/bis
RECCE 1 sqn with 4* MiG-25R, 1 sqn with 6* MiG-21
MR 2 sqn with 15 *Super King Air* B-200T
TPT 2 sqn with 10 C-130H, 6 C-130H-30, 5 Il-76
VIP 2 *Falcon* 900, 3 *Gulfstream* III, 2 F-27
HELICOPTERS
  ATTACK 35 Mi-24, 1 with 30 Mi-8/-17
  TPT 2 Mi-4, 5 Mi-6, 46 Mi-8/17, 10 AS 355
TRG 3* MiG-21U, 5* MiG-23U, 3* MiG-25U, 6 T-34C, 30 L-39, plus 30 ZLIN-142
UAV *Seeker*
AAM AA-2, AA-6
AD GUNS 3 bde+: **85mm, 100mm, 130mm**
SAM 3 regt with SA-3, SA-6, SA-8

Paramilitary ε146,200

GENDARMERIE (Ministry of Defence) 25,000

6 regions; 44 Panhard AML-60/M-3, 200 *Fahd* APC, BRDM-2 recce **hel** Mi-2

NATIONAL SECURITY FORCES (Directorate of National Security) 20,000

small arms

REPUBLICAN GUARD 1,200

AML-60, M-3 recce

LEGITIMATE DEFENCE GROUPS ε100,000

self-defence militia, communal guards

Opposition

GROUPE ISLAMIQUE ARMÉE (GIA) small groups each ε50–100

perhaps 2–3,000

ARMED FRONT FOR ISLAMIC *JIHAD* (FIDA)
ISLAMIC LEAGUE FOR THE CALL AND *JIHAD* (LIDD)

Bahrain

	1996	1997	1998	1999
GDP	D2.0bn	D2.1bn		
	($5.4bn)	($5.6bn)		
per capita	$8,000	$8,900		
Growth	3.1%	3.1%		
Inflation	-0.2%	1.0%		
Debt	$2.1bn	$2.8bn		
Def exp	D109m	D137m		
	($289m)	($364m)		
Def bdgt			D151m	
			($402m)	
FMA (US)	$0.1m	$0.1m	$0.3m	$0.2m
$1 = dinar	0.38	0.38	0.38	
Population		612,200		

(Nationals 63%, Asian 13%, other Arab 10%, Iranian 8%, European 1%)

Age	13–17	18–22	23–32
Men	30,000	24,000	40,000
Women	29,000	23,000	40,000

Total Armed Forces

ACTIVE 11,000

Army 8,500

1 armd bde (-) (2 tk, 1 recce bn) • 1 inf bde (2 mech, 1 mot inf bn) • 1 arty 'bde' (1 hy, 2 med, 1 lt, 1 MRL bty) • 1 SF, 1 *Amiri* gd bn • 1 AD bn (2 SAM, 1 AD gun bty)

EQUIPMENT

MBT 106 M-60A3
RECCE 22 AML-90, 8 *Saladin*, 8 *Ferret*, 8 Shorland
AIFV 25 YPR-765 (with **25mm**)
APC some 10 AT-105 *Saxon*, 110 Panhard M-3, 220 M-113A2
TOWED ARTY **105mm**: 8 lt; **155mm**: 28 M-198
SP ARTY **203mm**: 13 M-110
MRL **227mm**: 9 MLRS
MOR **81mm**: 9; **120mm**: 9
ATGW 15 TOW
RCL **106mm**: 30 M-40A1; **120mm**: 6 MOBAT
AD GUNS **35mm**: 12 Oerlikon; **40mm**: 12 L/70
SAM 40+ RBS-70, 15 *Stinger*, 7 *Crotale*, 8 I HAWK (being delivered)

Navy 1,000

BASE Mina Sulman

PRINCIPAL SURFACE COMBATANTS 1

FRIGATES 1 *Sabah* (US OH *Perry*) with 4 *Harpoon* SSM, 1 *Standard* SAM, 1 76mm gun (hel deck)

PATROL AND COASTAL COMBATANTS 12

CORVETTES 2 *Al Manama* (Ge Lürssen 62m) with 2 x 2 MM-40 *Exocet* SSM, 1 x 76mm gun, hel deck
MISSILE CRAFT 4 *Ahmad el Fateh* (Ge Lürssen 45m) with 2 x 2 MM-40 *Exocet*
PATROL CRAFT 6
INSHORE 6
2 *Al Riffa* (Ge Lürssen 38m) PFI
2 PFI<
2 *Swift* FPB-20

SUPPORT AND MISCELLANEOUS 5

4 *Ajeera* LCU-type spt
1 *Tiger* ACV, **hel** 2 B-105

Air Force 1,500

24 cbt ac, 26 armed hel

FGA 1 sqn with 8 F-5E, 4 F-5F
FTR 1 sqn with 8 F-16C, 4 F-16D
TPT 2 *Gulfstream* (1 -II, 1 -III; VIP), 1 Boeing 727
HEL 1 sqn with 12 AB-212 (10 armed), 14 AH-1E (atk), 5 Bo-105, 1 UH-60L (VIP), 1 S-70A (VIP)

MISSILES

ASM AS-12, AGM-65 *Maverick*
AAM AIM-9P *Sidewinder*, AIM-7F *Sparrow*

Paramilitary ε9,850

POLICE (Ministry of Interior) 9,000

2 Hughes 500, 2 Bell 412, 1 BO-105 hel

NATIONAL GUARD str ε600

3 bn to form; 1 PCI, some 20 PCI<, 2 spt/landing craft, 1 hovercraft

COAST GUARD (Ministry of Interior) ε250
1 PCI, some 20 PCI<, 2 spt/landing craft, 1 hovercraft

Foreign Forces

US Air Force periodic detachments of ttr and support
ac **Navy** (HQ CENTCOM and 5th Fleet) 230
UK RAF 40 (Southern Watch), 2 VC-10 tkr

Egypt

	1996	1997	1998	1999
GDP	E£228bn	E£256bn		
	($60bn)	($65bn)		
per capita	$4,100	$4,400		
Growth	4.9%	5.6%		
Inflation	7.2%	4.6%		
Debt	$31bn	$27bn		
Def exp	εE£9.1bn	εE£9.3bn		
	($2.7bn)	($2.7bn)		
Def bdgt			εE£9.5bn	
			($2.8bn)	
FMA[a] (US)	$2.1bn	$2.1bn	$2.1bn	$2.1bn
$1 = pound	3.39	3.39	3.39	

[a] UNTSO **1996** $27m **1997** $27m

Population		61,300,000	
Age	13–17	18–22	23–32
Men	3,486,000	3,026,000	4,900,000
Women	3,291,000	2,850,000	4,599,000

Total Armed Forces

ACTIVE 450,000
(some 320,000 conscripts)
Terms of service 3 years (selective)

RESERVES 254,000
Army 150,000 **Navy** 14,000 **Air Force** 20,000 **AD** 70,000

Army 320,000

(perhaps 250,000+ conscripts)
4 Mil Districts, 2 Army HQ • 4 armd div (each with 2
armd, 1 mech, 1 arty bde) • 8 mech inf div (each with 2
mech, 1 armd, 1 arty bde) • 1 Republican Guard armd
bde • 4 indep armd bde • 1 air-mobile bde • 2 indep
inf bde • 1 para bde • 4 indep mech bde • 6 cdo gp •
15 indep arty bde • 2 SSM bde (1 with FROG-7, 1 with
Scud-B)

EQUIPMENT[a]
  MBT 840 T-54/-55, 260 *Ramses* II (mod T-54/55), 500
   T-62, 1,700 M-60 (400 M-60A1, 1,300 M-60A3), 400
   M1A1 *Abrams*
  RECCE 300 BRDM-2, 112 *Commando Scout*
  AIFV 220 BMP-1 (in store), 260 BMR-600P, 310 YPR-
   765 (with **25mm**)
  APC 650 *Walid*, 165 *Fahd*/-30, 1,075 BTR-50/OT-62
   (most in store), 1,944 M-113A2 (incl variants), 70
   YPR-765
  TOWED ARTY 122mm: 36 M-31/37, 359 M-1938,
   156 D-30M; **130mm**: 420 M-46
  SP ARTY 122mm: 76 SP 122 (delivery reported),
   155mm: 200 M-109A2
  MRL 122mm: 96 BM-11, 200 BM-21/as-Saqr-10/-18/
   -36
  MOR 82mm: 500 (some 50 SP); **107mm**: 100+ M-30
   SP; **120mm**: 1,800 M-38; **160mm**: 60 M-160
  SSM 12 FROG-7, *Saqr*-80 (trials), 9 *Scud*-B
  ATGW 1,400 AT-3 *Sagger* (incl BRDM-2); 220 *Milan*;
   200 *Swingfire*; 840 TOW (incl I-TOW, TOW-2A
   (with 52 on M-901, 210 on YPR-765 SP))
  RCL 107mm: B-11
  AD GUNS 14.5mm: 475 ZPU-2/-4; **23mm**: 550 ZU-
   23-2, 117 ZSU-23-4 SP, 45 *Sinai*; **37mm**: 150 M-
   1939; **57mm**: 300 S-60, 40 ZSU-57-2 SP
  SAM 2,000 SA-7/'*Ayn as-Saqr*, 20 SA-9, 26 M-54 SP
   Chaparral
  SURV AN/TPQ-37 (arty/mor), RASIT (veh, arty),
   Cymbeline (mor)
  UAV R4E-50 *Skyeye*

[a] Most Sov eqpt now in store, incl MBT and some cbt ac

Navy ε20,000

(incl ε2,000 Coast Guards and ε10,000 conscripts)
BASES Mediterranean Alexandria (HQ), Port Said,
Mersa Matruh, Safaqa, Port Tewfig **Red Sea**
Hurghada (HQ)
SUBMARINES 4
  4 PRC Romeo with sub-*Harpoon* and 533mm TT
PRINCIPAL SURFACE COMBATANTS 9
DESTROYERS 1 *El Fateh* (UK 'Z') (trg) with 4 114mm
  guns, 5 533mm TT
FRIGATES 8
  2 *Mubarak* (ex-US *Perry*) with 4 *Harpoon* SSM, 36
   Standard SAM, 1 76mm gun, 2 hel
  2 *El Suez* (Sp *Descubierta*) with 2 x 3 ASTT, 1 x 2 ASW
   RL; plus 2 x 4 *Harpoon* SSM
  2 *Al Zaffir* (PRC *Jianghu* I) with 2 ASW RL; plus 2
   CSS-N-2 (*HY* 2) SSM
  2 *Damyat* (US *Knox*) with 8 *Harpoon*, 127mm gun, 4
   324mm TT
  1 *Tariq* (UK *Black Swan*) with 6 102mm gun
PATROL AND COASTAL COMBATANTS 42
MISSILE CRAFT 24
  6 *Ramadan* with 4 *Otomat* SSM
  4 Sov *Osa* I with 4 SS-N-2A *Styx* SSM (plus 1 non-op)
  6 *6th October* with 2 *Otomat* SSM
  2 Sov *Komar* with 2 SSN-2A *Styx* (plus 2 non-op)
  6 PRC *Hegu* (*Komar*-type) with 2 SSN-2A *Styx* SSM
PATROL CRAFT 18
  8 PRC *Hainan* PFC with 6 324mm TT, 4 ASW RL

6 Sov *Shershen* PFI; 2 with 4 533mm TT and BM-21 (8-tube) 122mm MRL; 4 with SA-N-5 and 1 BM-24 (12-tube) 240mm MRL

4 PRC *Shanghai* II PFI

MINE COUNTERMEASURES 13

4 *Aswan* (Sov *Yurka*) MSC (plus 1 non-op)

6 *Assiout* (Sov T-43 class) MSC (1 in reserve)

3 *Swiftship* MHI

AMPHIBIOUS 12

3 Sov *Polnocny* LSM, capacity 100 tps, 5 tk

9 *Vydra* LCU, capacity 200 tps

SUPPORT AND MISCELLANEOUS 20

7 AOT (small), 5 trg, 6 tugs, 1 diving spt, 1 *Tariq* (ex-UK FF) trg

NAVAL AVIATION

24 armed Air Force **hel** 5 *Sea King* Mk 47 (ASW, anti-ship), 9 SA-342 (anti-ship), 10 SH-2G

COASTAL DEFENCE (Army tps, Navy control)

GUNS 130mm: SM-4-1

SSM *Otomat*

Air Force 30,000

(10,000 conscripts); 585 cbt ac, 125 armed hel

FGA 7 sqn

2 with 42 *Alpha Jet*, 2 with 44 PRC J-6, 2 with 29 F-4E, 1 with 20 *Mirage* 5E2

FTR 21 sqn

2 with 25 F-16A, 6 with 74 MiG-21, 6 with 114 F-16C, 3 with 53 *Mirage* 5D/E, 3 with 53 PRC J-7, 1 with 18 *Mirage* 2000C

RECCE 2 sqn with 6* *Mirage* 5SDR, 14* MiG-21

EW ac 2 C-130H (ELINT), 4 Beech 1900 (ELINT) **hel** 4 *Commando* 2E (ECM)

AEW 5 E-2C

MR 2 Beech 1900C surv **ac**

TPT 19 C-130H, 5 DHC-5D, 1 *Super King Air*, 3 *Gulfstream* III, 1 *Gulfstream* IV, 3 *Falcon* 20

HELICOPTERS

ASW 9* SA-342L, 5* *Sea King* 47, 10* SH-2G (with Navy)

ATTACK 4 sqn with 65 SA-342K (44 with HOT, 25 with 20mm gun), 36 AH-64A

TAC TPT hy 14 CH-47C, 14 CH-47D **med** 40 Mi-8, 25 *Commando* (3 VIP), 2 S-70 (VIP) **lt** 12 Mi-4, 17 UH-12E (trg), 2 UH-60A, 2 UH-60L (VIP), 3 AS-61

TRG incl 4 DHC-5, 54 EMB-312, 10* F-16B, 29* F-16D, 36 *Gumhuria*, 16* JJ-6, 40 L-29, 48 L-39, 30* L-59E, MiG-21U, 5* *Mirage* 5SDD, 3* *Mirage* 2000B

UAV 29 Teledyne-Ryan 324 *Scarab*

MISSILES

ASM AGM-65 *Maverick*, Exocet AM-39, AS-12, AS-30, AS-30L HOT

ARM *Armat*

AAM AA-2 *Atoll*, AIM-7E/F/M *Sparrow*, AIM-9F/L/P *Sidewinder*, MATRA R-530, MATRA R-550 *Magic*

Air Defence Command 80,000

(50,000 conscripts)

4 div: regional bde, 100 AD arty bn, 40 SA-2, 53 SA-3, 14 SA-6 bn, 12 bty I HAWK, 12 bty *Chaparral*, 14 bty *Crotale*

EQUIPMENT

AD GUNS some 2,000: **20mm, 23mm, 37mm, 57mm, 85mm, 100mm**

SAM some 282 SA-2, 212 SA-3, 56 SA-6, 78 I HAWK, 36 *Crotale*

AD SYSTEMS some 18 *Amoun* (*Skyguard*/RIM-7F *Sparrow*, some 36 twin **35mm** guns, some 36 quad SAM); *Sinai*-23 short-range AD (Dassault 6SD-20S radar, **23mm** guns, '*Ayn as-Saqr* SAM)

Forces Abroad

Advisers in Oman, Saudi Arabia, Zaire

UN AND PEACEKEEPING

ANGOLA (UNOMA): 3 obs. **BOSNIA** (SFOR II): 300. **CAR** (MINURCA): 125. **CROATIA** (UNMOP): 1 obs. **FYROM** (UNPREDEP): 1 obs. **GEORGIA** (UNOMIG): 1 obs. **WESTERN SAHARA** (MINURSO): 19 obs

Paramilitary 230,000 active

CENTRAL SECURITY FORCES (Ministry of Interior) 150,000

110 *Hotspur Hussar*, *Walid* APC

NATIONAL GUARD 60,000

8 bde (each of 3 bn; cadre status); lt wpns only

BORDER GUARD FORCES 20,000

19 Border Guard Regt; lt wpns only

COAST GUARD ε2,000 (incl in Naval entry)

PATROL, INSHORE 40

20 *Timsah* PCI, 9 *Swiftships*, 5 *Nisr†*, 6 *Crestitalia* PFI<, plus some 60 boats

Foreign Forces

PEACEKEEPING

MFO Sinai: some 1,896 from **Aus, Ca, Co, Fji, Fr, Hu, It, NZ, No, Ury, US**

Iran

	1996	1997	1998	1999
GDP[a]	r233tr	r277tr		
	($67bn)	($71bn)		
per capita	$5,100	$5,200		
Growth	5.1%	3.2%		
Inflation	28.9%	17.2%		
Debt	$21.2bn	$18.8bn		

contd	1996	1997	1998	1999
Def exp[a]	r5.9tr	r8.2tr		
	($3.4bn)	($4.7bn)		
Def bdgt			r10.1tr	
			($5.8bn)	
$1 = rial[b]	1,751	1,753	1,753	

[a] Excl defence industry funding
[b] Market rate **1998** $1 = r5,500–6,300

Population	70,699,000

(Persian 51%, Azeri 24%, Gilaki/Mazandarani 8%, Kurdish 7%, Arab 3%, Lur 2%, Baloch 2%, Turkman 2%)

Age	13–17	18–22	23–32
Men	4,290,000	3,560,000	5,394,000
Women	4,123,000	3,415,000	5,107,000

Total Armed Forces

ACTIVE 540,000–545,600

(perhaps 250,000 plus conscripts)
Terms of service 24 months

RESERVES

Army 350,000, ex-service volunteers

Army ε350,000

(perhaps 220,000 conscripts)
4 Corps HQ • 4 armd div (each 3 armd, 1 mech bde, 4–5 arty bn) • 6 inf div (each 4 inf bde, 4-5 arty bn) • 1 AB bde • 1 cdo div, 1 SF div • some indep armd, inf, cdo bde • 5 arty gps

EQUIPMENT†

MBT some 1,400+, incl: 110 T-54/-55, some 75 T-62, 230 T-72, 250 *Chieftain* Mk 3/5, 150 M-47/-48, 160 M-60A1, 220 PRC Type-59, 200 PRC Type-69

LT TK 80 *Scorpion*

RECCE 35 EE-9 *Cascavel*

AIFV 300 BMP-1, 140 BMP-2

APC 550: BTR-50/-60, M-113

TOWED 2,170: **105mm**: 130 M-101A1; **122mm**: 600 D-30, 100 PRC Type-54; **130mm**: 1,100 M-46/Type-59; **152mm**: 30 D-20; **155mm**: 20 WAC-21, 70 M-114; 100 GHN-45; **203mm**: 20 M-115

SP 290: **122mm**: 60 2S1; **155mm**: 160 M-109; **170mm**: 10 M-1978; **175mm**: 30 M-107; **203mm**: 30 M-110

MRL 764+: **107mm**: 600 PRC Type-63; **122mm**: 50 *Hadid/Arash/Noor*, 100 BM-21, 5 BM-11; **240mm**: 9 M-1985; **320mm**: *Oghab*; **333mm**: *Shahin* 1/-2; **355mm**: *Nazeat*

MOR 6,500 incl: **60mm**; **81mm**; **82mm**; **107mm**: 4.2in M-30; **120mm**

SSM ε10 *Scud*-B/-C (210 msl), ε25 CSS-8 (200 msl), *Fajr*

ATGW TOW, AT-3 *Sagger* (some SP)

RL 73mm: RPG-7

RCL 75mm: M-20; **82mm**: B-10; **106mm**: M-40; **107mm**: B-11

AD GUNS 1,700: **14.5mm**: ZPU-2/-4; **23mm**: ZU-23 towed, ZSU-23-4 SP; **35mm; 37mm**: M-1939, PRC Type-55; **57mm**: ZSU-57-2 SP

SAM SA-7

AC incl 50 Cessna (150, 180, 185, 310), 19 F-27, 8 *Falcon* 20

HEL 100 AH-1J **attack**; 40 CH-47C **hy tpt**; 130 Bell 214A, 35 AB-214C; 40 AB-205A; 90 AB-206; 12 AB-212; 30 Bell 204; 5 Hughes 300C; 9 RH-53D; 10 SH-53D, 10 SA-319; 45 UH-1H

Revolutionary Guard Corps (*Pasdaran Inqilab*) some 125,000

GROUND FORCES some 100,000

grouped into perhaps 16–20 div incl 2 armd, 5 mech, 10 inf, 1 SF and 15–20 indep bde, incl inf, armd, para, SF, arty (incl SSM), engr, AD and border defence units, serve indep or with Army; limited numbers of tk, APC and arty; controls *Basij* (see *Paramilitary*) when mob

NAVAL FORCES some 20,000

BASES Al Farsiyah, Halul (oil platform), Sirri, Abu Musa, Larak

some 40 Swe Boghammar Marin boats armed with ATGW, RCL, machine guns; 5 *Hudong* with C-802 SSM; controls coast-defence elm incl arty and CSSC-3 (*HY* 2) *Seersucker* SSM bty. Under joint command with Navy

MARINES some 5,000 1 bde

Navy 20,600

(incl 2,600 Naval Air and Marines)

BASES Bandar Abbas (HQ), Bushehr, Kharg, Bandar-e-Anzelli, Bandar-e-Khomeini, Chah Bahar

SUBMARINES 3

3 Sov *Kilo* SS with 6 533mm TT (possibly wake homing) (plus some 2 SS1s)

PRINCIPAL SURFACE COMBATANTS 3

FRIGATES 3 *Alvand* (UK Vosper Mk 5) with 1 x 4 *Sea Killer* II, with 4 x C-802 SSM, 1 x 3 AS mor, 1 114mm gun

PATROL AND COASTAL COMBATANTS 65

CORVETTES 2 *Bayandor* (US PF-103) with 2 76mm gun

MISSILE CRAFT 21

10 *Kaman* (Fr *Combattante* II) PFM with 2 or 4 C-802 SSM

10 *Houdong* PFM with 4 C-802 SSM

1 *Osa* II with 4 x SS-N-2B SSM

PATROL, INSHORE 42

3 *Kaivan*, 3 *Parvin* PCI, 1 ex-Irq *Bogomol* PFI, some 35 other PFI<, plus some 9 hovercraft< (not all op), 60 small craft

MINE WARFARE 7

MINE LAYERS

2 *Hejaz* LST

MINE COUNTERMEASURES 5

3 *Shahrokh* MSC (in Caspian Sea as trg ship)

2 *Riazi* (US *Cape*) MSI

AMPHIBIOUS 9

4 *Hengam* LST, capacity 225 tps, 9 tk, 1 hel

3 *Iran Hormuz 24* (ROK) LST, capacity 140 tps, 8 tk

2 *Foque* LSL

Plus craft: 3 LCT, 6 ACV

SUPPORT AND MISCELLANEOUS 25

1 *Kharg* AOE with 2 hel, 2 *Bandar Abbas* AOR with 1
hel, 1 repair, 4 water tkr, 2 *Delvar* and 13 *Hendijan*
spt vessels, 1 AT, 1 *Shahrokh* msc trg

NAVAL AIR (2,000)

8 cbt ac, 9 armed hel

MR 3 P-3F, 5 Do-228

ASW 1 hel sqn with ε3 SH-3D, 6 AB-212 ASW

MCM 1 hel sqn with 2 RH-53D

TPT 1 sqn with 4 *Commander*, 4 F-27, 1 *Falcon* 20 **ac** AB-
205, AB-206 **hel**

MARINES 2 bde

Air Force 45–50,000

(incl 15–20,000 Air Defence); some 307 cbt ac (serviceability probably about 60% for US ac types and about
80% for Chinese/Russian ac); no armed hel

FGA 9 sqn

4 with some 60 F-4D/E, 4 with some 60 F-5E/F, 1
with 30 Su-24 (including former Irq ac)

FTR 7 sqn

4 with 60 F-14, 1 with 24 F-7, 2 with 30 MiG-29 (incl
former Irq ac)

MR 5* C-130H-MP

RECCE 1 sqn (det) with some 8* RF-4E

TKR/TPT 1 sqn with 4 Boeing 707, 1 Boeing 747

TPT 5 sqn with 9 Boeing 747F, 11 Boeing 707, 1 Boeing
727, 18 C-130E/H, 3 *Commander* 690, 15 F-27, 4
Falcon 20 1 *Jetstar*, 10 PC-6B, 2 Y-7

HEL 2 AB-206A, 39 Bell 214C, 5 CH-47

TRG incl 26 Beech F-33A/C, 10 EMB-312, 45 PC-7, 7 T-
33, 5* MiG-29B, 5* FT-7, 20* F-5B, 8 TB-21, 4 TB-200

MISSILES

ASM AGM-65A *Maverick*, AS-10, AS-11, AS-14, C-
801

AAM AIM-7 *Sparrow*, AIM-9 *Sidewinder*, AIM-54
Phoenix, probably AA-8, AA-10, AA-11 for MiG-
29, PL-7

SAM 12 bn with 150 I HAWK, 5 sqn with 30 *Rapier*,
15 *Tigercat*, 45 HQ-2J (PRC version of SA-2), SA-5,
FM-80 (PRC version of *Crotale*)

Forces Abroad

LEBANON: ε150 Revolutionary Guard
SUDAN: mil advisers

Paramilitary 40,000 active

BASIJ ('Popular Mobilisation Army') (R) ε200,000
peacetime volunteers, mostly youths; str up to
1,000,000 during periods of offensive ops. Small arms
only; not currently embodied for mil ops

LAW-ENFORCEMENT FORCES ε40,000

incl border-guard elm **ac** Cessna 185/310 lt **hel** AB-205/
-206; about 90 patrol inshore, 40 harbour craft

Opposition

KURDISH COMMUNIST PARTY OF IRAN
(KOMALA) str n.k.

KURDISH DEMOCRATIC PARTY OF IRAN (KDP–
Iran) ε8,000

NATIONAL LIBERATION ARMY (NLA) some 15,000

Iraq-based; org in bde, armed with captured eqpt.
Perhaps 160+ T-54/-55 tanks, BMP-1 AIFV, D-30
122mm arty, BM-21 **122mm** MRL, Mi-8 **hel**

Iraq

	1996	1997	1998	1999
GDP	ε$15bn	ε$17bn		
Growth	ε2%	ε10%		
Inflation	ε30%	ε45%		
Debt	ε$23bn	ε$23bn		
Def exp	ε$1.3bn	ε$1.3bn	ε$1.3bn	
$1 = dinar[a]	0.31	0.31	0.31	

[a] Market rate **1998** $1 = d1,200

Population		23,144,000		

(Arab 75–80% (of which Shi'a Muslim 55%, Sunni
Muslim 45%), Kurdish 20–25%)

Age	13–17	18–22	23–32
Men	1,416,000	1,194,000	1,762,000
Women	1,353,000	1,145,000	1,702,000

Total Armed Forces

ACTIVE ε429,000

Terms of service 18–24 months

RESERVES ε650,000

Army ε375,000

(incl ε100,000 recalled Reserves)
7 corps HQ • 3 armd div, 3 mech div[a] • 12 inf div[a] • 6

Republican Guard Force div (2 armd, 3 mech, 1 inf) • 4
Special Republican Guard bde • 10 cdo bde • 2 SF bde

EQUIPMENT[b]

MBT perhaps 2,700, incl 1,000 T-54/-55/M-77, PRC
Type-59/ 69, 200 T-62, 700 T-72 (total incl *Chieftain*
Mk 3/5, M-60 and M-47, mostly inop)

RECCE BRDM-2, AML-60/-90, EE-9 *Cascavel*, EE-3
Jararaca

AIFV perhaps 900 BMP-1/-2

APC perhaps 2,000, incl BTR-50/-60/-152, OT-62/-
64, MTLB, YW-531, M-113A1/A2, Panhard M-3,
EE-11 *Urutu*

TOWED ARTY perhaps 1,800, incl **105mm**: incl M-
56 pack; **122mm**: D-74, D-30, M-1938; **130mm**: incl
M-46, Type 59-1; **155mm**: some G-5, GHN-45, M-
114

SP ARTY 150, incl **122mm**: 2S1; **152mm**: 2S3;
155mm: M-109A1/A2, AUF-1 (GCT)

MRL perhaps 150, incl **107mm**; **122mm**: BM-21;
127mm: ASTROS II; **132mm**: BM-13/-16, **262mm**:
Ababeel

MOR 81mm; **120mm**; **160mm**: M-1943; **240mm**

SSM up to 6 *Scud* launchers (ε27 msl) reported

ATGW AT-3 *Sagger* (incl BRDM-2), AT-4 *Spigot*
reported, SS-11, *Milan*, HOT (incl 100 VC-TH)

RCL 73mm: SPG-9; **82mm**: B-10; **107mm**

ATK GUNS 85mm; **100mm** towed

HELICOPTERS ε500 (120 armed)

    ATTACK ε120 Bo-105 with AS-11/HOT, Mi-24,
SA-316 with AS-12, SA-321 (some with *Exocet*),
SA-342

    TPT ε350 **hy** Mi-6 **med** AS-61, Bell 214 ST, Mi-4,
Mi-8/-17, SA-330 **lt** AB-212, BK-117 (SAR),
Hughes 300C, Hughes 500D, Hughes 530F

SURV RASIT (veh, arty), *Cymbeline* (mor)

[a] All divisions less Republican Guard at a reported 50% cbt
effectiveness

[b] 50% of all eqpt lacks spares

Navy ε2,000

BASES Basra (limited facilities), Az Zubayr, Umm
Qasr (currently closed for navy, commercials only)

FRIGATES 2

    2 *Mussa Ben Nussair* (It *Assad*) with 2 *Otomat* SSM, 1
Aspide SAM, 1 76mm gun, 1 AB 212 hel (1
currently in Italy)

PATROL AND COASTAL COMBATANTS 6

MISSILE CRAFT 1 Sov *Osa* I with 4 SS-N-2A *Styx*

PATROL, INSHORE 5

    1 Sov *Bogomol* PFI<, 3 PFI<, 1 PCI< plus 80 boats†

MINE COUNTERMEASURES 4

    2 Sov *Yevgenya*, 2 *Nestin* MSI<

SUPPORT AND MISCELLANEOUS 3

    1 *Damen* AGS, 1 *Aka* (Yug *Spasiluc*-class) AR, 1 yacht
with hel deck

(Plus 1 *Agnadeen* (It *Stromboli*) AOR laid-up in
Alexandria, 3 *Al Zahraa* ro-ro AK with hel deck,
capacity 16 tk, 250 tps, inactive in foreign ports)

Air Force ε35,000

Serviceability of fixed-wg **ac** about 55%, serviceability
of **hel** poor

Flying hours senior pilots 90–120, junior pilots as low
as 20

BBR ε6, incl H-6D, Tu-22

FGA ε130, incl MiG-23BN, *Mirage* F1EQ5, Su-7, Su-20,
Su-25

FTR ε180 incl F-7, MiG-21, MiG-23, MiG-25, *Mirage* F-
1EQ, MiG-29

RECCE incl MiG-25

TKR incl 2 Il-76

TPT incl An-2, An-12, An-24, An-26, Il-76

TRG incl AS-202, EMB-312, some 50 L-39, *Mirage* F-
1BQ, 25 PC-7, 30 PC-9

MISSILES

    ASM AM-39, AS-4, AS-5, AS-11, AS-9, AS-12, AS-
30L, C-601

    AAM AA-2/-6/-7/-8/-10, R-530, R-550

Air Defence Command ε17,000

AD GUNS ε6,000: **23mm**: ZSU-23-4 SP; **37mm**: M-
1939 and twin; **57mm**: incl ZSU-57-2 SP; **85mm**;
100mm; **130mm**

SAM SA-2/-3/-6/-7/-8/-9/-13/-14/-16, *Roland*

Paramilitary 45–50,000

SECURITY TROOPS ε15,000

BORDER GUARDS ε20,000

lt wpns and mor only

SADDAM'S FEDAYEEN ε10–15,000

Opposition

KURDISH DEMOCRATIC PARTY (KDP) ε15,000
(plus 25,000 tribesmen); small arms, some Iranian lt
arty, MRL, mor, SAM-7

PATRIOTIC UNION OF KURDISTAN (PUK) ε10,000
(plus 22,000 tribesmen); 450 mor (**60mm, 82mm,
120mm**); **106mm** RCL; some 200 **14.5mm** AA guns;
SA-7 SAM

SOCIALIST PARTY OF KURDISTAN ε500

**SUPREME ASSEMBLY OF THE ISLAMIC
REVOLUTION** (SAIRI)
ε4,000; ε1 'bde'; Iran-based; Iraqi dissidents, ex-
prisoners of war

Foreign Forces

UN (UNIKOM): some 904 tps and 194 mil obs from 33 countries

Israel

	1996	1997	1998	1999
GDP	NS304bn	NS338bn		
	($93bn)	($97bn)		
per capita	$17,300	$17,800		
Growth	4.4%	1.9%		
Inflation	11.3%	9.0%		
Debt	$47bn	$56bn		
Def exp	εNS35bn	εNS39bn		
	($11.0bn)	($11.1bn)		
Def bdgt			NS25.1bn	
			($7.0bn)	
FMA*a* (US)	$3bn	$3bn	$3bn	$3bn
$1 = new sheqalim				
	3.19	3.50	3.58	

a UNDOF **1996** $32m **1997** $38m

Population*b*		5,910,000		

(Jewish 82%, Arab 14%, Christian 3%, Druze 2%, Circassian ε3,000)

Age	*13–17*	*18–22*	*23–32*
Men	275,000	267,000	506,000
Women	260,000	258,000	498,000

b Incl ε170,000 Jewish settlers in Gaza and the West Bank, ε215,000 in East Jerusalem and ε15,000 in Golan

Total Armed Forces

ACTIVE ε175,000

(ε138,500 conscripts)
Terms of service **officers** 48 months **men** 36 months **women** 21 months (Jews and Druze only; Christians, Circassians and Muslims may volunteer). Annual trg as cbt reservists to age 42 (some specialists to age 54) for men, 24 (or marriage) for women

RESERVES 430,000

Army 365,000 **Navy** 10,000 **Air Force** 55,000. Reserve service can be followed by voluntary service in Civil Guard or Civil Defence

Strategic Forces

Israel is widely believed to have a nuclear capability with up to 100 warheads. Delivery means could include **ac** *Jericho* 1 SSM (range up to 500km), *Jericho* 2 (tested 1987–89, range ε1,500km)

Army 134,000

(114,700 conscripts, male and female); some 598,000 on mob
3 territorial, 1 home front comd • 3 corps HQ • 3 armd div (2 armd, 1 arty bde, plus 1 armd, 1 mech inf bde on mob) • 2 div HQ (op control of anti-*intifada* units) • 3 regional inf div HQ (border def) • 4 mech inf bde (incl 1 para trained) • 3 arty bn with 203mm M-110 SP

RESERVES

9 armd div (2 or 3 armd, 1 affiliated mech inf, 1 arty bde) • 1 air-mobile/mech inf div (3 bde manned by para trained reservists) • 10 regional inf bde (each with own border sector) • 4 arty bde

EQUIPMENT

MBT 4,300: 1,080 *Centurion*, 500 M-48A5, 400 M-60, 600 M-60A1, 200 M-60A3, 150 *Magach* 7, 300 Ti-67 (T-54/-55), 70 T-62, 1,000 *Merkava* I/II/III
RECCE about 400, incl RAMTA RBY, BRDM-2, ε8 *Fuchs*
APC 5,900 M-113A1/A2, ε80 *Nagmashot* (*Centurion*), ε300 *Achzarit*, *Puma*, BTR-50P, 3,500 M-2/-3 half-track
TOWED ARTY 400: **105mm**: 60 M-101; **122mm**: 100 D-30; **130mm**: 100 M-46; **155mm**: 40 Soltam M-68/-71, 50 M-839P/-845P, 50 M-114A1
SP ARTY 1,150: **105mm**: 34 M-7; **155mm**: 200 L-33, 120 M-50, 530 M-109A1/A2; **175mm**: 230 M-107; **203mm**: 36 M-110
MRL 100+: **122mm**: 40 BM-21; **160mm**: LAR-160; **227mm**: 12 MLRS; **240mm**: 30 BM-24; **290mm**: MAR-290.
MOR 60mm: ε5,000; **81mm**: 1,600; **120mm**: 900; **160mm**: 240 (some SP)
SSM 20 *Lance* (in store), some *Jericho* 1/2
ATGW 200 TOW (incl *Ramta* (M-113) SP), 780 *Dragon*, AT-3 *Sagger*, 25 *Mapats*
RL 82mm: B-300
RCL 84mm: *Carl Gustav*; **106mm**: 250 M-40A1
AD GUNS 20mm: 850: incl TCM-20, M-167 *Vulcan*, 35 M-163 *Vulcan*/M-48 *Chaparral* gun/msl systems; **23mm**: 100 ZU-23 and 60 ZSU-23-4 SP; **37mm**: M-39; **40mm**: L-70
SAM *Stinger*, 900 *Redeye*, 45 *Chaparral*
SURV EL/M-2140 (veh), AN/TPQ-37 (arty), AN/PPS-15 (arty)

Navy ε9,000

(2,000–3,000 conscripts), 10,000–12,000 on mob
BASES Haifa, Ashdod, Eilat
SUBMARINES 3

1 *Dolphin* (Ge prob Type 212 variant)
2 *Gal* (UK Vickers) SSC with Mk 37 HWT, *Harpoon* USGW (plus 1 in maintenance)

PATROL AND COASTAL COMBATANTS 51

CORVETTES 3 *Eilat* (*Sa'ar* 5) with 8 *Harpoon*, 8 *Gabriel* II SSM, 2 *Barak* VLS SAM (2 32 mls), 6 324mm ASTT plus 1 SA-366G hel

MISSILE CRAFT 18 PFM
- 2 *Aliya* with 4 *Harpoon*, 4 *Gabriel* SSM, 1 SA-366G *Dauphin* hel (OTHT)
- 3 *Romat* with 8 *Harpoon*, 8 *Gabriel*
- 4 *Hetz* (*Sa'ar* 4.5) with 4 *Harpoon*, 6 *Gabriel* and *Barak* VLS (plus 1 trials)
- 7 *Reshef* (*Sa'ar* 4) with 2–4 *Harpoon*, 4–6 *Gabriel*
- 2 *Mivtach* with 2–4 *Harpoon*, 3–5 *Gabriel*

PATROL, INSHORE 30
- 14 *Super Dvora/Dabur* PFI<, some with 2 324mm TT, 3 *Nashal* PCI, 13 *Dabur* PFI with 2 324mm TT

AMPHIBIOUS 1
- 1 *Bat Sheva* LST type tpt
- Plus craft: 3 *Ashdod* LCT, 1 US type LCM

NAVAL COMMAND 300 mainly underwater trained

Air Force 32,000

(21,800 conscripts, mainly in AD), 37,000 on mob; 474 cbt ac (plus perhaps 250 stored), 137 armed hel
Flying hours regulars: 188; reserves: 75
FGA/FTR 17 sqn
- 5 with 50 F-4E-2000, 25 F-4E
- 3 with 61 F-15 (36 -A, 2 -B, 18 -C, 5 -D)
- 1 with 18 F-15I (further 7 to be delivered)
- 7 with 203 F-16 (67 -A, 7 -B, 75 -C, 54 -D)
- 1 with 20 *Kfir* C7 (plus 120 C2/C7 in store)

FGA 4 sqn with 50 A-4N, plus 130 in store
RECCE 14* RF-4E, 6* *Kfir* RC-2, 2* F-15D
AEW 2 Boeing 707 with *Phalcon* system
EW 6 Boeing 707 (ELINT/ECM), 6 RC-12D, 3 IAI-200, 15 Do-28, 6 *King Air* 2000
MR 3 IAI-1124 *Seascan*
TKR 5 KC-130H
TPT 1 wg incl 8 Boeing 707 (3 tpt/tkr), 12 C-47, 24 C-130H, 7 IAI-201
LIAISON 2 *Islander*, 20 Cessna U-206, 8 *Queen Air* 80
TRG 80 CM-170 *Tzukit*, 10 *Kfir* TC2/7, 30 *Super Cub*, 9* TA-4H, 4* TA-4J, 4 *Queen Air* 80
HELICOPTERS
  ATTACK 14 AH-1E, 38 AH-1F, 35 Hughes 500MD, 42 AH-64A
  ASW/SAR 1 HH-65A, 8* AS-565
  TPT 40 CH-53D, 10 UH-60; 15 S-70A *Blackhawk*, 54 Bell 212, 39 Bell 206
UAV *Scout, Pioneer, Searcher, Firebee, Samson, Delilah, Hunter Silver Arrow*
MISSILES
  ASM AGM-45 *Shrike*, AGM-62A *Walleye*, AGM-65 *Maverick*, AGM-78D *Standard*, *Gabriel* III (mod), *Hellfire*, TOW, *Popeye*
  AAM AIM-7 *Sparrow*, AIM-9 *Sidewinder*, AIM-120B, R-530, *Shafrir*, *Python* III, *Python* IV, *Shafrir*
  SAM 17 bty with MIM-23 I HAWK, 3 bty *Patriot*, 50 *Chapparal*, *Stinger*

Forces Abroad

TURKEY: periodic det of Air Force F-16 ac to Akinci air base

Paramilitary ε6,050

BORDER POLICE 6,000
  some *Walid* 1, 600 BTR-152 APC
COAST GUARD ε50
  1 US PBR, 3 other patrol craft

Foreign Forces

UN (UNTSO): 153 mil obs from 20 countries

Jordan

	1996	1997	1998	1999
GDP	D5.1bn	D5.5bn		
	($7.0bn)	($7.7bn)		
per capita	$4,500	$4,700		
Growth	5.0%	5.0%		
Inflation	6.5%	3.1%		
Debt	$7.5bn	$6.8bn		
Def exp	D320m	D352m		
	($451m)	($496m)		
Def bdgt			D390m	
			($548m)	
FMA[a] (US)	$271m	$32m	$52m	$47m
$1 = dinar	0.71	0.71	0.71	
[a] Excl US military debt waiver 1997 $15m 1998 $12m				
Population	4,867,000 (Palestinian ε50–60%)			
Age	*13–17*	*18–22*	*23–32*	
Men	263,000	240,000	432,000	
Women	256,000	233,000	414,000	

Total Armed Forces

ACTIVE ε104,050

RESERVES 35,000 (all services)
Army 30,000 (obligation to age 40)

Army 90,000

2 armd div (each 2 tk, 1 mech inf, 1 arty, 1 AD bde)
2 mech inf div (each 2 mech inf, 1 tk, 1 arty, 1 AD bde)
1 indep Royal Guard bde
1 SF bde (2 SF, 2 AB, 1 arty bn)
1 fd arty bde (4 bn)
Southern Mil Area (3 inf bn)
EQUIPMENT
  MBT some 1,217: 300 M-47/-48A5 (in store), 354 M-60A1/A3, 270 *Khalid/Chieftain*, 293 *Tariq*

(*Centurion*)
LT TKS 19 *Scorpion*
RECCE 170 *Ferret*
AIFV some 35 BMP-2
APC 1,100 M-113
TOWED ARTY 115: **105mm**: 50 M-102; **155mm**: 30 M-114 towed, 10 M-59/M-1; **203mm**: 25 M-115 towed (in store)
SP ARTY 406: **105mm**: 30 M-52; **155mm**: 20 M-44, 220 M-109A1/A2; **203mm**: 136 M-110
MOR 81mm: 450 (incl 130 SP); **107mm**: 50 M-30; **120mm**: 300 Brandt
ATGW 330 TOW (incl 70 SP), 310 *Dragon*
RL 94mm: 2,500 LAW-80; **112mm**: 2,300 APILAS
RCL 106mm: 330 M-40A1
AD GUNS 360: **20mm**: 100 M-163 *Vulcan* SP; **23mm**: 44 ZSU-23-4 SP; **40mm**: 216 M-42 SP
SAM SA-7B2, 50 SA-8, 50 SA-13, 300 SA-14, 240 SA-16, 250 *Redeye*
SURV AN-TPQ-36/-37 (arty, mor)

Navy ε480

BASE Aqaba
PATROL AND COASTAL COMBATANTS 3
PATROL CRAFT, INSHORE 3
3 *Al Hussein* (Vosper 30m) PFI
Plus 3 *Al Hashim* (Rotork) PCI< and 4 other armed boats

Air Force 13,500

(incl 3,400 AD); 93 cbt ac, 16 armed hel
Flying hours 180
FGA 3 sqn with 50 F-5E/F
FTR 3 sqn
2 with 25 *Mirage* F-1 CJ/EJ/BJ
1 with 16 F-16A/B (12 -A, 4 -B)
TPT 1 sqn with 8 C-130 (3 -B, 5 -H), 4 C-212A
VIP 1 sqn with **ac** 2 *Gulfstream* III, IL-1011 **hel** 3 S-70, SA-319
HELICOPTERS 3 sqn
ATTACK 2 with 16 AH-1S (with TOW ASM)
TPT 1 with 9 AS-332M, 3 Bo-105, 8 Hughes 500D, 18 UH-1H, 8 UH-60 *Blackhawk*
TRG 4 sqn with 16 *Bulldog*, 15 C-101, 12 PA-28-161, 6 PA-34-200, 2* *Mirage* F-1B
AD 2 bde: 14 bty with 80 I HAWK
MISSILES
ASM TOW, AGM-65D *Maverick*
AAM AIM-9 *Sidewinder*, MATRA R-530, MATRA R-550 *Magic*

Forces Abroad

UN AND PEACEKEEPING
ANGOLA (UNOMA): 3 obs. **BOSNIA** (SFOR II): 100.

CROATIA (UNMOP): 1 obs. **FYROM** (UNPREDEP): 2 obs. **GEORGIA** (UNOMIG): 2 obs. **TAJIKISTAN** (UNMOT): 8 obs

Paramilitary ε10,000 active

PUBLIC SECURITY DIRECTORATE (Ministry of Interior) ε10,000
(incl Police Public Sy bde); some *Scorpion* lt tk, 25 EE-11 *Urutu*, 30 *Saracen* APC
CIVIL MILITIA 'PEOPLE'S ARMY' (R) ε20,000
(to be 5,000) **men** 16–65 **women** 16–45

Kuwait

	1996	1997	1998	1999
GDP	D9.3bn	D9.6bn		
	($31bn)	($32bn)		
per capita	$16,200	$16,400		
Growth	1.6%	1.5%		
Inflation	3.4%	1.7%		
Debt	$9.1bn	$8.3bn		
Def exp[a]	D1.2bn	D1.2bn		
	($3.9bn)	($4.0bn)		
Def bdgt			εD1.2bn	
			($4.0bn)	
$1 = dinar	0.30	0.30	0.31	

[a] UNIKOM **1996** $62m **1997** $50m

Population		2,200,000		

(Nationals 35%, other Arab 35%, South Asian 9%, Iranian 4%, other 17%)

Age	*13–17*	*18–22*	*23–32*
Men	113,000	93,000	145,000
Women	84,000	70,000	106,000

Total Armed Forces

ACTIVE 15,300
(some conscripts)
Terms of service voluntary, conscripts 2 years

RESERVES 23,700
obligation to age 40; 1 month annual trg

Land Force 11,000

(incl 1,600 foreign personnel)
2 armd bde • 1 force arty bde • 1 mech inf bde • 1 force engr bde • 1 recce (mech) bde

ARMY
1 reserve bde • 1 Amiri gd bde • 1 cdo bn
EQUIPMENT
MBT 150 M-84 (ε50% in store), 174 M-1A2 (being delivered), 17 *Chieftain* (in store)

AIFV 46 BMP-2, 55 BMP-3, 254 *Desert Warrior*
APC 60 M-113, 40 M-577, 40 *Fahd* (in store)
SP ARTY 155mm: 23 M-109A2, 18 GCT (in store), 18 F-3
MRL 300mm: 27 *Smerch* 9A52
MOR 81mm: 44; **107mm**: 6 M-30
ATGW 118 TOW/TOW II (incl 8 M-901 ITV; 66 HMMWV)

Navy ε1,800

(incl 400 Coast Guard)
BASE Ras al Qalaya
PATROL AND COASTAL COMBATANTS 11
MISSILE CRAFT 6
  4 *Um Almaradim* PFM (Fr P-37 BRL) with 4 *Sea Skua* SSM, 1 x 6 Sadral SAM, 1 x 40mm gun
  1 *Istiqlal* (Ge Lürssen FPB-57) PFM with 2 x 2 MM-40 *Exocet* SSM
  1 *Al Sanbouk* (Ge Lürssen TNC-45) with 2 x 2 MM-40 *Exocet*
PATROL INSHORE 5
  1 *Al Shaheed* PCI
  4 *Inttisar* OPV
  plus about 30 boats<
SUPPORT AND MISCELLANEOUS 6
  2 LCM, 4 spt

Air Force ε2,500

76 cbt ac, 20 armed hel
Flying hours 210
FTR/FGA 40 F/A-18 (-C 32, -D 8)
FTR 8 *Mirage* F1-CK/BK
CCT 1 sqn with 12 *Hawk* 64, 16 Shorts *Tucano*
TPT ac 3 L-100-30, 1 DC-9 **hel** 4 AS-332 (tpt/SAR/attack), 8 SA-330
TRG/ATK hel 16 SA-342 (with HOT)

AIR DEFENCE
4 *Hawk* Phase III bty with 24 launchers
6 bty *Amoun* (each bty, 1 *Skyguard* radar, 2 *Aspide* launchers, 2 twin **35mm** Oerlikon), 48 *Starburst*

Paramilitary 5,000 active

NATIONAL GUARD 5,000
3 gd, 1 armd car, 1 SF, 1 mil police bn
COAST GUARD
4 *Inttisar* (Aust 31.5m) PFI, 3 LCU
Plus some 30 armed boats

Foreign Forces

UN (UNIKOM): some 904 tps and 194 obs from 33 countries
UK: **Air Force** (Southern Watch) 12 Tornado-GR1/1A.

US: **Army** 1,200; prepositioned eqpt for 1 armd bde (2 tk, 1 mech, 1 arty bn **Air Force** (Southern Watch) Force structure varies with aircraft detachments **Navy** 1,000

Lebanon

	1996	1997	1998	1999
GDP	LP21tr	LP23tr		
	($13bn)	($15bn)		
per capita	$4,500	$4,800		
Growth	4.0%	4.0 %		
Inflation	9.5%	7.8%		
Debt	$4.0bn	$4.2bn		
Def exp	LP760bn	LP1,041bn		
	($484m)	($676m)		
Def bdgt			LP901bn	
			($592m)	
FMA[a] (US)	$4.8m	$0.5m	$0.6m	$0.7m
$1 = pound	1,571	1,540	1,521	

[a] UNIFIL **1996** $135m **1997** $121m

Population	4,209,000

(Christian 30%, Druze 6%, Armenian 4% excl ε300,000 Syrian nationals and ε500,000 Palestinian refugees)

Age	*13–17*	*18–22*	*23–32*
Men	207,000	196,000	379,000
Women	211,000	202,000	394,000

Total Armed Forces

ACTIVE some 55,100
Terms of Service 1 year

Army 53,300

11 inf bde (-) • 1 Presidential Guard bde • 1 cdo/Ranger, 3 SF regt • 2 arty regt • 1 air aslt regt
EQUIPMENT
  MBT some 110 M-48A1/A5, 205 T-54/-55
  LT TK 35 AMX-13
  RECCE 40 *Saladin*, 5 *Ferret*, 80 AML-90, 30 *Staghound*
  APC 725 M-113A1/A2, 20 *Saracen*, 30 VAB-VCI, 30 VAB-VTT, 75 AMX-VCI, 15 Panhard M3/VTT
  TOWED ARTY 105mm: 15 M-101A1, 10 M-102; **122mm**: 33 M-1938, 10 D-30; **130mm**: 25 M-46; **155mm**: 60, incl some Model 50, 15 M-114A1, 35 M-198
  MRL 122mm: 5 BM-11, 25 BM-21
  MOR 81mm: 150; **120mm**: 130
  ATGW ENTAC, *Milan*, 20 BGM-71A TOW
  RL 85mm: RPG-7; **89mm**: M-65
  RCL 106mm: M-40A1
  AD GUNS 20mm; 23mm: ZU-23; **40mm**: 10 M-42A1

Navy 1,000 (incl ε100 Marines)

BASES Juniye, Beirut, Tripoli
PATROL AND COASTAL COMBATANTS 14
PATROL CRAFT, INSHORE 14
    7 PCI<, 5 UK *Attacker* PCI<, 2 UK *Tracker* PCI<, plus
    27 armed boats
AMPHIBIOUS craft only
    2 *Sour* (Fr *Edic*) LCT (33 tps)

Air Force some 800

3† cbt ac; 4† armed hel
EQUIPMENT
FTR 3 *Hunter*† (F-70/FGA-70A)
HELICOPTERS
    ATTACK 4† SA-342 with AS-11/-12 ASM
    TPT 16 UH-1H, 5† AB-212, 3† SA-330; 4† SA-319
TRG 3† *Bulldog*, 3† CM-170

Paramilitary ε13,000 active

INTERNAL SECURITY FORCE (Ministry of Interior)
ε13,000
(incl Regional and Beirut *Gendarmerie* coy plus Judicial
Police); 30 *Chaimite* APC
CUSTOMS
    2 *Tracker* PCI<, 5 *Aztec* PCI<

Opposition

MILITIAS
most militias, except *Hizbollah* and the South Lebanon
Army, have been substantially disbanded and hy wpn
handed over to the National Army
HIZBOLLAH ('Party of God'; Shi'a, fundamentalist,
    pro-Iranian): ε3–500 (-) active; about 3,000 in spt
    EQUIPMENT arty, MRL, RL, RCL, ATGW (AT-3
    Sagger, AT-4 *Spigot*), AA guns, SAM
SOUTH LEBANESE ARMY (SLA) 2–3,000 active
    (was mainly Christian but increasingly Shi'a, some
    Druze, trained, equipped and supported by Israel,
    occupies the 'Security Zone' between Israeli border
    and area controlled by UNIFIL)
    EQUIPMENT
        MBT 30 T-54/-55
        APC M-113, BTR-50
        TOWED ARTY 122mm: D-30; **130mm**: M-46;
        155mm: M-1950
        MOR some **160mm**

Foreign Forces

UN (UNIFIL): some 4,473; 6 inf bn 1 each from **Fji, SF,
Gha, Irl, N, No**, plus spt units from **Fr, It, No, Pl**
IRAN ε150 Revolutionary Guard

SYRIA 30,000 **Beirut** elm 1 mech inf bde, 5 SF regt
Metn elm 1 mech inf bde **Bekaa** 1 mech inf div HQ,
elm 2 mech inf, elm 1 armd bde **Tripoli** 1 SF regt
Batrum 1 SF Regt **Kpar Fallus** elm 3 SF regt

Libya

	1996	1997	1998	1999
GDP	ε$26bn	ε$27bn		
per capita	$5,600	$5,700		
Growth	ε2.0%	ε2.6%		
Inflation	ε7.0%	ε6.0%		
Debt	ε$3.7bn	ε$4.1bn		
Def exp	εD474m	εD480m		
	($1.3bn)	($1.3bn)		
Def bdgt			εD495m	
			($1.3bn)	
$1 = dinar[a]	0.37	0.38	0.38	
[a] Market rate **1998** $1 = D3.5–4.5				
Population		6,005,000		
Age	*13–17*	*18–22*	*23–32*	
Men	350,000	291,000	441,000	
Women	337,000	281,000	420,000	

Total Armed Forces

ACTIVE ε65,000
Terms of service selective conscription, 1–2 years

RESERVES some 40,000
People's Militia

Army ε35,000

(ε25,000 conscripts)
7 Mil Districts • 5 elite bde (regime sy force) • 10 tk bn
• 22 arty bn • 21 inf bn • 8 AD arty bn • 8 mech inf bn
• 15 para/cdo bn • 5 SSM bde
EQUIPMENT
    MBT 560 T-54/-55, 280 T-62, 145 T-72 (plus some
        1,040 T-54/-55, 70 T-62, 115 T-72 in store†)
    RECCE 250 BRDM-2, 380 EE-9 *Cascavel*
    AIFV 1,000 BMP-1
    APC 750 BTR-50/-60, 100 OT-62/-64, 40 M-113, 100
        EE-11 *Urutu*
    TOWED ARTY some 720: **105mm**: some 60 M-101;
        122mm: 270 D-30, 60 D-74; **130mm**: 330 M-46.
    SP ARTY: 450: **122mm**: 130 2S1; **152mm**: 60 2S3, 80
        DANA; **155mm**: 160 *Palmaria*, 20 M-109
    MRL 107mm: Type 63; **122mm**: 350 BM-21/RM-70,
        300 BM-11
    MOR 82mm; 120mm: M-43; **160mm**: M-160
    SSM launchers: 40 FROG-7, 80 *Scud*-B
    ATGW 3,000: *Milan*, AT-3 *Sagger* (incl BRDM SP),
        AT-4 *Spigot*

RCL **106mm**: 220 M-40A1
AD GUNS 600: **23mm**: ZU-23, ZSU-23-4 SP; **30mm**: M-53/59 SP
SAM SA-7/-9/-13, 24 quad *Crotale*
SURV RASIT (veh, arty)

Navy 8,000

(incl Coast Guard)
BASES Tripoli, Benghazi, Derna, Tobruk, Sidi Bilal, Al Khums

SUBMARINES 2 *Al Badr* † (Sov *Foxtrot*) with 533mm and 406mm TT (plus 2 non-op)

FRIGATES 3
2 *Al Hani* (Sov *Koni*) with 4 ASTT, 2 ASW RL; plus 4 SS-N-2C SSM (1 non-op)
1 *Dat Assawari*† (UK Vosper Mk 7) with 2 x 3 ASTT; plus 4 *Otomat* SSM, 1 114mm gun

PATROL AND COASTAL COMBATANTS 33
CORVETTES 4
1 *Assad al Bihar*† (It *Assad*) with 4 *Otomat* SSM; plus 2 x 3 ASTT (A244S LWT) (plus 3 more non-op)
3 *Ean al Gazala* (Sov *Nanuchka* II) with 2 x 2 SS-N-2C *Styx* SSM
MISSILE CRAFT 21
9 *Sharaba* (Fr *Combattante* II) with 4 *Otomat* SSM, 1 x 76mm gun (5 non-op)
12 *Al Katum* (Sov *Osa* II) with 4 SS-N-2C SSM (6 non-op)
PATROL, INSHORE 8
4 *Garian*, 3 *Benina*, 1 Sov *Poluchat*

MINE COUNTERMEASURES 8
8 *Ras al Gelais* (Sov *Natya* MSO)
(*El Temsah* and about 5 other ro-ro tpt have mine-laying capability)

AMPHIBIOUS 5
2 *Ibn Ouf* LST, capacity 240 tps, 11 tk, 1 SA-316B hel
3 Sov *Polnocny* LSM, capacity 180 tps, 6 tk (1 non-op)
Plus craft: 3 LCT

SUPPORT AND MISCELLANEOUS 10
1 *Zeltin* log spt/dock, 1 *Tobruk* trg, 1 salvage, 1 diving spt, 1 *El Temsah* and about 5 other ro-ro tpt

COASTAL DEFENCE
1 SSC-3 *Styx* bty

NAVAL AVIATION
32 armed hel
HEL 2 sqn
1 with 25 Mi-14 PL (ASW), 1 with 7 SA-321 (Air Force assets)

Air Force 22,000

(incl Air Defence Command); 420 cbt ac, 52 armed hel (many ac in store, number n.k.) **Flying hours** 85

BBR 1 sqn with 6 Tu-22
FGA 13 sqn
12 with 40 MiG-23BN, 15 MiG-23U, 30 *Mirage* 5D/DE, 14 *Mirage* 5DD, 14 *Mirage* F-1AD, 6 Su-24, 45 Su-20/-22
1 with 30 J-1 *Jastreb*
FTR 9 sqn with 50 MiG-21, 75 MiG-23, 60 MiG-25, 3 -25U, 15 *Mirage* F-1ED, 6 -BD
RECCE 2 sqn with 4 *Mirage* 5DR, 7 MiG-25R
TPT 9 sqn with 15 An-26, 12 Lockheed (7 C-130H, 2 L-100-20, 3 L-100-30), 16 G-222, 20 Il-76, 15 L-410
ATTACK HEL 40 Mi-25, 12 Mi-35
TPT HEL hy 18 CH-47C **med** 34 Mi-8/17 **lt** 30 Mi-2, 11 SA-316, 5 AB-206
TRG ac 80 *Galeb* G-2 **hel** 20 Mi-2 **other ac** incl 1 Tu-22, 150 L-39ZO, 20 SF-260WL
MISSILES
ASM AT-2 *Swatter* ATGW (hel-borne), AS-7, AS-9, AS-11
AAM AA-2 *Atoll*, AA-6 *Acrid*, AA-7 *Apex*, AA-8 *Aphid*, R-530, R-550 *Magic*

AIR DEFENCE COMMAND
Senezh AD comd and control system
4 bde with SA-5A: each 2 bn of 6 launchers, some 4 AD arty gun bn; radar coy
5 Regions: 5–6 bde each 18 SA-2; 2–3 bde each 12 twin SA-3; ε3 bde each 20–24 SA-6/-8

Paramilitary

CUSTOMS/COAST GUARD (Naval control)
a few patrol craft incl in naval totals, plus armed boats

Mauritania

	1996	1997	1998	1999
GDP	OM150bn	OM165bn		
	($1.1bn)	($1.1bn)		
per capita	$1,700	$1,800		
Growth	3.2%	4.7%		
Inflation	4.7%	3.0%		
Debt	$2.4bn	$2.4bn		
Def exp	OM3.7bn	OM3.7bn		
	($27m)	($24m)		
Def bdgt			εOM4.7bn	
			($27m)	
FMA (Fr)	$1.0m	$1.1m	$1.0m	
$1 = OM*	137	152	176	
* Mauritanian ouguiya				
Population		2,467,000		
Age	*13–17*	*18–22*	*23–32*	
Men	136,000	115,000	178,000	
Women	132,000	110,000	175,000	

Total Armed Forces

ACTIVE ε15,650

Terms of service conscription 24 months authorised

Army 15,000

6 Mil Regions • 7 mot inf bn • 3 arty bn • 8 inf bn • 4 AD arty bty • 1 para/cdo bn • 1 Presidential sy bn • 2 Camel Corps bn • 1 engr coy • 1 armd recce sqn

EQUIPMENT
MBT 35 T-54/-55
RECCE 60 AML (20 -60, 40 -90), 40 *Saladin*, 5 *Saracen*
TOWED ARTY 105mm: 35 M-101A1/HM-2; 122mm: 20 D-30, 20 D-74
MOR 81mm: 70; 120mm: 30
ATGW *Milan*
RCL 75mm: M-20; 106mm: M-40A1
AD GUNS 23mm: 20 ZU-23-2; 37mm: 15 M-1939; 57mm: S-60; 100mm: 12 KS-19
SAM SA-7

Navy ε500

BASES Nouadhibou, Nouakchott
PATROL CRAFT 11
OFFSHORE 4
1 *Aboubekr Ben Amer* (Fr OPV 54) OPV
1 *N'Madi* (UK *Jura*) PCO (fishery protection)
1 *Z'Bar* (Ge *Neustadt*) PFO
1 *El Nasr* (Fr *Patra*) PCO
INSHORE 7
3 *El Vaiz* (Sp *Barcelo*) PFI†
4 *Mandovi* PCI

Air Force 150

7 cbt ac, no armed hel
CCT 5 BN-2 *Defender*, 2 FTB-337 *Milirole*
MR 2 *Cheyenne* II
TPT 2 Cessna F-337, 1 DHC-5D, 1 *Gulfstream* II

Paramilitary ε5,000 active

GENDARMERIE (Ministry of Interior) ε3,000
6 regional coy
NATIONAL GUARD (Ministry of Interior) 2,000
plus 1,000 auxiliaries
CUSTOMS
1 *Dah Ould Bah* (Fr *Amgram* 14)

Morocco

	1996	1997	1998	1999
GDP	D321bn	D320bn		
	($37bn)	($34bn)		
per capita	$3,600	$3,600		
Growth	12.0%	-2.1%		
Inflation	3.0%	1.0%		
Debt	$21.8bn	$22.1bn		
Def exp	D12.2bn	D13.2bn		
	($1.4bn)	($1.4bn)		
Def bdgt			D14.2bn	
			($1.4bn)	
FMAᵃ (US)	$0.8m	$0.8m	$0.9m	$0.9m
$1 = dirham	8.72	9.53	9.87	

ᵃ MINURSO **1996** $59m **1997** $29m

Population	29,303,000			
Age	*13–17*	*18–22*	*23–32*	
Men	1,690,000	1,526,000	2,521,000	
Women	1,633,000	1,473,000	2,455,000	

Total Armed Forces

ACTIVE 196,300

(ε100,000 conscripts)
Terms of service conscription 18 months authorised; most enlisted personnel are volunteers

RESERVES
Army 150,000; obligation to age 50

Army 175,000

(ε100,000 conscripts)
2 Comd (Northern Zone, Southern Zone) • 3 mech inf bde • 1 lt sy bde • 2 para bde • 8 mech inf regt •
Indep units
12 arty bn • 3 mot (camel corps) bn • 1 AD gp • 2 cav bn • 10 armd bn • 1 mtn bn • 37 inf bn • 7 engr bn • 4 cdo units • 2 AB bn

ROYAL GUARD 1,500

1 bn, 1 cav sqn
EQUIPMENT
MBT 224 M-48A5, 300 M-60 (60 -A1, 240 -A3)
LT TK 100 SK-105 *Kuerassier*
RECCE 16 EBR-75, 80 AMX-10RC, 190 AML-90, 38 AML-60-7, 20 M-113
AIFV 60 *Ratel* (30 -20, 30 -90), 45 VAB-VCI, 10 AMX-10P
APC 420 M-113, 320 VAB-VTT, some 45 OT-62/-64 may be op
TOWED ARTY 105mm: 35 lt (L-118), 20 M-101, 36 M-1950; 130mm: 18 M-46; 155mm: 20 M-114, 35 FH-70, 26 M-198
SP ARTY 105mm: 5 Mk 61; 155mm: 98 F-3, 44 M-109, 20 M-44

MRL 122mm: 39 BM-21
MOR 81mm: 1,100; **120mm**: 600 (incl 20 VAB SP)
ATGW 440 *Dragon*, 80 *Milan*, 150 TOW (incl 42 SP), 50 AT-3 *Sagger*
RL 89mm: 150 3.5in M-20
RCL 106mm: 350 M-40A1
ATK GUNS 90mm: 28 M-56; **100mm**: 8 SU-100 SP
AD GUNS 14.5mm: 200 ZPU-2, 20 ZPU-4; **20mm**: 40 M-167, 60 M-163 *Vulcan* SP; **23mm**: 90 ZU-23-2; **100mm**: 15 KS-19 towed
SAM 37 M-54 SP *Chaparral*, 70 SA-7
SURV RASIT (veh, arty)
UAV R4E-50 *Skyeye*

Navy 7,800

(incl 1,500 Marines)
BASES Casablanca, Agadir, Al Hoceima, Dakhla, Tangier
FRIGATES 1 *Lt Col. Errhamani* (Sp *Descubierta*) with 2 x 3 ASTT (Mk 46 LWT), 1 x 2 375mm AS mor (fitted for 4 MM-38 *Exocet* SSM)

PATROL AND COASTAL COMBATANTS 27
MISSILE CRAFT 4 *Cdt El Khattabi* (Sp *Lazaga* 58m) PFM with 4 MM-38 *Exocet* SSM
PATROL CRAFT 23
    COASTAL 17
    2 *Okba* (Fr PR-72) PFC
    6 *LV Rabhi* (Sp 58m B-200D) PCC
    4 *El Hahiq* (Dk *Osprey* 55) PCC (incl 2 with customs)
    5 *Rais Bargach* (navy marine for fisheries dept)
    INSHORE 6 *El Wacil* (Fr P-32) PFI< (incl 4 with customs)

AMPHIBIOUS 4
    3 *Ben Aicha* (Fr *Champlain* BATRAL) LSM, capacity 140 tps, 7 tk
    1 *Sidi Mohammed Ben Abdallah* (US Newport) LST, capacity 400 troops
    Plus craft: 1 *Edic*-type LCT

SUPPORT AND MISCELLANEOUS 4
    2 log spt, 1 tpt, 1 AGOR (US lease)

MARINES (1,500)
1 naval inf bn

Air Force 13,500

89 cbt ac, 24 armed hel
Flying hours F-5 and *Mirage*: over 100
FGA 10 F-5A, 3 F-5B, 16 F-5E, 4 F-5F, 14 *Mirage* F-1EH
FTR 1 sqn with 15 *Mirage* F-1CH
RECCE 2 C-130H (with side-looking radar), 4* OV-10
EW 2 C-130 (ELINT), 1 *Falcon* 20 (ELINT)
TKR 1 Boeing 707, 2 KC-130H (tpt/tkr)
TPT 11 C-130H, 7 CN-235, 3 Do-28, 3 *Falcon* 20, 1 *Falcon* 50 (VIP), 2 *Gulfstream* II (VIP), 5 *King Air* 100, 3 *King Air* 200

HELICOPTERS
    ATTACK 24 SA-342 (12 with HOT, 12 with cannon)
    TPT hy 7 CH-47 **med** 27 SA-330, 27 AB-205A **lt** 20 AB-206, 3 AB-212, 4 SA-319
TRG 10 AS-202, 2 CAP-10, 4 CAP-230, 12 T-34C, 23* *Alpha Jet*
LIAISON 2 *King Air 200*, 2 UH-60 *Blackhawk*
AAM AIM-9B/D/J *Sidewinder*, R-530, R-550 *Magic*
ASM AGM-65B *Maverick* (for F-5E), HOT

Forces Abroad

UN AND PEACEKEEPING
BOSNIA (SFOR II): ε800; 1 mot inf bn

Paramilitary 42,000 active

GENDARMERIE ROYALE 12,000
1 bde, 4 mobile gp, 1 para sqn, air sqn, coast guard unit
    EQPT 18 boats **ac** 2 *Rallye* **hel** 3 SA-315, 3 SA-316, 2 SA-318, 6 *Gazelle*, 6 SA-330, 2 SA-360
FORCE AUXILIAIRE 30,000
incl 5,000 Mobile Intervention Corps
CUSTOMS/COAST GUARD
4 *Erraid* PCI, 32 boats, 3 SAR craft

Opposition

POLISARIO ε3–6,000
Mil wing of Sahrawi People's Liberation Army, org in bn
    EQPT 100 T-55, T-62 tk; 50+ BMP-1, 20–30 EE-9 *Cascavel* MICV; 25 D-30/M-30 **122mm** how; 15 BM-21 **122mm** MRL; 20 **120mm**, mor; AT-3 *Sagger* ATGW; 50 ZSU-23-2, ZSU-23-4 **23mm** SP AA guns; SA-6/-7/-8/-9 SAM (Captured Moroccan eqpt incl AML-90, *Eland* armd recce, *Ratel* 20, Panhard APC, Steyr SK-105 *Kuerassier* lt tks)

Foreign Forces

UN (MINURSO): some 161 tps, 202 mil obs in Western Sahara from 27 countries

Oman

	1996	1997	1998	1999
GDP	R5.7bn	R6.2bn		
	($14.7bn)	($16.2bn)		
per capita	$9,000	$9,100		
Growth	3.5%	3.6%		
Inflation	0.3%	-0.2%		
Debt	$3.1bn	$3.4bn		
Def exp	R737m	R698m		
	($1.9bn)	($1.8bn)		

contd	1996	1997	1998	1999
Def bdg[a]			R695m	
			($1.8bn)	
FMA[b] (US)	$0.1m	$0.2m	$0.2m	$0.2m
$1 = rial	0.38	0.38	0.38	

[a] Five-year plan 1996–2000 allocates R3.3bn ($8.6bn) for defence
[b] Excl ε$100m over 1990–99 from US Access Agreement renewed in 1990

Population		2,130,000 (expatriates 27%)	
Age	*13–17*	*18–22*	*23–32*
Men	121,000	97,000	143,000
Women	117,000	94,000	132,000

Total Armed Forces

ACTIVE 43,500

(incl Royal Household tps, and some 3,700 foreign personnel)

Army 25,000

(regt are bn size)
1 armd, 2 inf bde HQ • 2 armd regt (3 tk sqn) • 1 armd recce regt (3 sqn) • 4 arty (2 fd, 1 med (2 bty), 1 AD (2 bty)) regt • 8 inf regt (incl 2 Baluch) • 1 inf recce regt (3 recce coy), 2 indep recce coy • 1 fd engr regt (3 sqn) • 1 AB regt • Musandam Security Force (indep rifle coy)

EQUIPMENT
MBT 6 M-60A1, 73 M-60A3 (20 to be delivered), 24 *Qayid al-Ardh* (*Chieftain* Mk 7/-15) (in store), 18 *Challenger* 2
LT TK 37 *Scorpion*
APC 6 *Spartan*, 13 *Sultan*, 4 *Stormer*, 50 *Piranha* (being delivered)
TOWED ARTY 91: **105mm**: 42 ROF lt; **122mm**: 25 D-30; **130mm**: 12 M-46, 12 Type 59-1
SP ARTY 155mm: 18 G-6
MOR 81mm: 69; **107mm**: 20 4.2in M-30
ATGW 18 TOW, 50 *Milan* (incl 2 VCAC)
AD GUNS 23mm: 4 ZU-23-2; **40mm**: 12 Bofors L/60
SAM *Blowpipe*, 28 *Javelin*, 34 SA-7

Navy 4,200

BASES Seeb (HQ), Wudam (main base), Raysut, Ghanam Island, Alwi
PATROL AND COASTAL COMBATANTS 11
MISSILE CRAFT 4 *Dhofar*, 1 with 2 x 3 MM-40, 3 with 2 x 4 MM-40 *Exocet* SSM
PATROL CRAFT 7
3 *Al Bushra* (Fr P-400) with 1 76m gun, 4 406mm TT
4 *Seeb* (Vosper 25m) PCI<
CORVETTES 2 *Qahir Al Amwaj* with 8 MM-40 *Exocet* SSM, 8 *Crotale* SAM, 1 76mm gun, 6 x 324mm TT, hel deck

AMPHIBIOUS 2
1 *Nasr el Bahr* LST†, capacity 240 tps, 7 tk, hel deck
1 *Al Munassir* LST, capacity 200 tps, 8 tk, hel deck (non-op, harbour trg)
Plus craft: 3 LCM, 1 LCU
SUPPORT AND MISCELLANEOUS 5
1 *Al Sultana*, 1 *Al Mabrukah* trg with hel deck (also used in offshore patrol role), 1 supply, 1 survey, 1 Royal Yacht + craft

Air Force 4,100

40 cbt ac, no armed hel
FGA 2 sqn with 8 *Jaguar* S(O) Mk 1, 4 T-2
FGA/RECCE 12 *Hawk* 203
CCT 1 sqn with 12* BAC-167 Mk 82, 4* *Hawk* 103
TPT 3 sqn
1 with 3 BAC-111
2 with 15 *Skyvan* 3M (7 radar-equipped, for MR), 3 C-130H
HEL 2 med tpt sqn with 20 AB-205, 3 AB-206, 3 AB-212, 5 AB-214
TRG 4 AS-202-18, 7 MFI-17B *Mushshak*
AD 2 sqn with 28 *Rapier* SAM, *Martello* radar
AAM AIM-9P *Sidewinder*

Royal Household 6,500

(incl HQ staff) 2 SF regt (1,000)
Royal Guard bde (5,000) 9 VBC-90 lt tk, 14 VAB-VCI APC, 9 VAB-VDAA, *Javelin* SAM
Royal Yacht Squadron (based Muscat) (150) 1 Royal Yacht, 3,800t with hel deck, 1 *Fulk Al Salamah* tps and veh tpt with up to 2 AS-332C *Puma* hel, 1 *Zinat Al Bihaar Dhow*
Royal Flight (250) **ac** 2 Boeing-747 SP, 1 DC-8-73CF, 2 *Gulfstream* IV **hel** 3 AS-330, 2 AS-332C, 1 AS-332L

Paramilitary 4,400 active

TRIBAL HOME GUARD (*Firqat*) 4,000
org in teams of ε100
POLICE COAST GUARD 400
3 CG 29 PCI, plus 14 craft
POLICE AIR WING
ac 1 Do-228, 2 CN 235M, 1 BN-2T Islander **hel** 3 Bell 205A, 6 Bell 214ST

Palestinian Autonomous Areas Of Gaza And Jericho

	1996	1997	1998	1999
GDP	ε$3.3bn	ε$3.4bn		
per capita	$1,700	$1,600		
Growth	ε0.7%	ε1.0%		

contd	1996	1997	1998	1999
Inflation	ε11.0%	ε9.0%		
Debt	ε$800m	ε$290m		
Sy bdgt	ε$248m	ε$250m	ε$300m	
FMA(US)	$75m	$75m	$85m	$100m
Population				

West Bank and Gaza ε2,890,000 (Israeli 6% excl East Jerusalem) *Gaza* ε1,190,000 (Israeli ε5,500) *West Bank excl East Jerusalem* ε1,700,000 (Israeli ε6%) *East Jerusalem* Israeli ε215,000

Gaza	13–17	18–22	23–32	
Men	50,000	41,000	64,000	
Women	49,000	40,000	63,000	
West Bank				
Men	70,000	63,000	109,000	
Women	67,000	60,000	101,000	

Total Armed Forces

ACTIVE Nil

Paramilitary ε35,000

PUBLIC SECURITY 6,000 Gaza, 8,000 West Bank

CIVIL POLICE 4,000 Gaza, 6,000 West Bank

PREVENTIVE SECURITY 1,200 Gaza, 1,800 West Bank

GENERAL INTELLIGENCE 3,000

MILITARY INTELLIGENCE 500

PRESIDENTIAL SECURITY 3,000

Others include **Coastal Police, Civil Defence, Air Force, Customs and Excise Police Force, University Security Service**
> **EQPT** incl small arms, 45 APC **ac** 1 Lockheed *Jet Star* **hel** 2 Mi-8, 2 Mi-17

PALESTINIAN GROUPS

All significant Palestinian factions are listed irrespective of where they are based. Est number of active 'fighters' are given; these could perhaps be doubled to give an all-told figure. In 1991, the Lebanon Armed Forces (LAF), backed by Syria, entered refugee camps in southern Lebanon to disarm many Palestinian groups of their heavier weapons, such as tk, arty and APCs. The LAF conducted further disarming operations against *Fatah* Revolutionary Council (FRC) refugee camps in spring 1994

PLO (Palestine Liberation Organisation) **Leader** Yasser Arafat
> *FATAH* Political wing of the PLO
> **PNLA** (Palestine National Liberation Army) ε8,000 Effectively mil wing of the PLO **Based** Ag, Et, RL, LAR, HKJ, Irq, Sdn, Ye. Units closely monitored by host nations' armed forces.

PLF (Palestine Liberation Front) **Leader** Al Abas; ε300–400 **Based** Irq **Tal al Yaqub faction** ε100–150 **Based** Syr

DFLP (Democratic Front for the Liberation of Palestine) **Leader** Hawatmah; ε500–600 **Based** Syr, RL, elsewhere **Abd Rabbu faction** ε150–20 **Based** HKJ

PFLP (Popular Front for the Liberation of Palestine) **Leader** Habash; ε800 **Based** Syr, RL, Occupied Territories

PSF (Popular Struggle Front) **Leader** Samir Ghansha; ε600–700 **Based** Syr

ARAB LIBERATION FRONT ε500 **Based** RL, Irq

GROUPS OPPOSED TO THE PLO

FATAH **DISSIDENTS** (Abu Musa gp) ε1,000 **Based** Syr, RL

FRC (*Fatah* Revolutionary Council, Abu Nidal Group) ε300 **Based** RL, Syr, Irq, elsewhere

PFLP (GC) (Popular Front for the Liberation of Palestine (General Command)) **Leader** Jibril; ε600

PFLP (SC) (Popular Front for the Liberation of Palestine – Special Command) ε50–100 **Based** RL, Irq, Syr

SAIQA Leader al-Khadi; ε1,000 **Based** Syr

HAMAS ε300 **Based** Occupied Territories

PIJ (Palestine Islamic *Jihad*) ε350 all factions **Based** Occupied Territories

PALESTINE LIBERATION FRONT Abd al-Fatah Ghanim faction **Based** Syr

PLA (Palestine Liberation Army) ε4,500 Based Syr

Qatar

	1996	1997	1998	1999
GDP	R31bn	R36bn		
	($8.5bn)	($9.8bn)		
per capita	$17,700	$20,500		
Growth	9.9%	15.5%		
Inflation	2.5%	2.6%		
Debt	$7bn	$10bn		
Def exp	εR2.8bn	εR4.9bn		
	($755m)	($1,346m)		
Def bdgt			εR4.5bn	
			($1.2bn)	
$1 = rial	3.64	3.64	3.64	
Population		576,000		

(*nationals* 25%, *expatriates* 75%, of which Indian 18%, Iranian 10%, Pakistani 18%)

Age	13–17	18–22	23–32
Men	24,000	20,000	36,000
Women	25,000	21,000	31,000

Total Armed Forces

ACTIVE ε11,800

Army 8,500

1 Royal Guard regt • 1 SF 'bn' (coy) • 1 tk bn • 1 fd

arty regt • 4 mech inf bn • 1 mor bn

EQUIPMENT
MBT 34 AMX-30
RECCE 16 VBL, 12 AMX-10RC, 8 V-150
AIFV 40 AMX-10P
LAV some *Piranha* II
APC 160 VAB, 12 AMX-VCI
TOWED ARTY 155mm: 12 G5
SP ARTY 155mm: 28 F-3
MRL 4 ASTROS II
MOR 81mm: 24 L16 (some SP); 120mm: 15 Brandt
ATGW 100 *Milan*, HOT (incl 24 VAB SP)
RCL 84mm: *Carl Gustav*

Navy ε1,800

(incl Marine Police)
BASE Doha
PATROL AND COASTAL COMBATANTS 7
MISSILE CRAFT 3 *Damsah* (Fr *Combattante* III) with 2
x 4 MM-40 *Exocet* SSM
PATROL, INSHORE 4 *Barzan* (UK *Vita*) PCI with 8
Exocet SSM, 6 *Mistral* SAM, 1 76mm gun
Plus some 40 small craft operated by Marine Police
AMPHIBIOUS craft only
1 LCU

COASTAL DEFENCE
4 x 3 *quad* MM-40 *Exocet* bty

Air Force 1,500

18 cbt ac, 18 armed hel
FGA/FTR 2 sqn
1 with 6 *Alpha* jets
1 with 9 *Mirage* - 2000-5 EDA, 3 *Mirage* - 2000-5 DDA
TPT 1 sqn with 2 Boeing 707, 1 Boeing 727, 2 *Falcon*
900, 1 *Airbus* A340
ATTACK HEL 10 SA-342L (with HOT), 8 *Commando*
Mk 3 (*Exocet*)
TPT 4 *Commando* (3 Mk 2A tpt, 1 Mk 2C VIP)
LIAISON 2 SA-341G
MISSILES
ASM *Exocet* AM-39, *HOT, Apache*
AAM MATRA R550 *Magic*, MATRA *Mica*
SAM 9 *Roland* 2, *Mistral, Stinger*, SA-7 *Grail*

Foreign Forces

US Army: 13; prepositioned eqpt for 1 armd bde
(forming)

Saudi Arabia

	1996	1997	1998	1999
GDP	R511bn	R547bn		
	($136bn)	($146bn)		
per capita	$9,800	$10,000		
Growth	4.5%	2.7%		
Inflation	1.2%	1.0%		
Debt	$15.6bn	$21.1bn		
Def exp	R65bn	R68bn		
	($17.4bn)	($18.2bn)		
Def bdgt			εR69bn	
			($18.4bn)	
$1 = rial	3.75	3.75	3.75	
Population		17,450,000		

(*nationals* 73%, of which Bedouin up to 10%, Shi'a
6%, *expatriates* 27%, of which Asians 20%, Arabs
6%, Africans 1% and Europeans <1%)

Age	13–17	18–22	23–32
Men	1,260,000	1,043,000	1,561,000
Women	1,128,000	927,000	1,317,000

Total Armed Forces

ACTIVE ε105,500
(plus 57,000 active National Guard)

Army 70,000

3 armd bde (each 3 tk, 1 mech, 1 fd arty, 1 recce, 1 AD,
1 ATK bn) • 5 mech bde (each 3 mech, 1 tk, 1 fd arty, 1
AD, 1 spt bn) • 1 AB bde (2 AB bn, 3 SF coy) • 1 Royal
Guard regt (3 bn) • 8 arty bn • 1 army avn comd
EQUIPMENT
MBT 315 M-1A2 *Abrams* (ε200 in store), 290 AMX-
30 (50% in store), 450 M60A3
RECCE 235 AML-60/-90
AIFV 570+ AMX-10P, 400 M-2 *Bradley*
APC 1,700 M-113 (incl variants), 150 Panhard M-3
TOWED ARTY 105mm: 100 M-101/-102; 155mm:
50 FH-70 (in store), 90 M-198, M-114; 203mm: 8
M-115 (in store)
SP ARTY 155mm: 110 M-109A1B/A2, 90 GCT
MRL 60 ASTROS II
MOR 400, incl: 107mm: 4.2in M-30; 120mm: 110
Brandt
SSM some 10 PRC CSS-2 (40 msl)
ATGW TOW-2 (incl 200 VCC-1 SP), M-47 *Dragon*,
HOT (incl 90 AMX-10P SP)
RCL 84mm: 300 *Carl Gustav*; 90mm: M-67; 106mm:
M-40A1
HEL 12 AH-64, 12 S-70A-1, 10 UH-60 (tpt, 4
medevac), 6 SA-365N (medevac), 15 Bell 406CS
SAM *Crotale, Stinger*, 500 *Redeye* SURV AN/TPQ-
36/-37 (arty, mor)

Navy ε13,500

(incl 3,000 Marines)

BASES Riyadh (HQ Naval Forces) **Western Fleet** Jiddah (HQ), Yanbu **Eastern Fleet** Al-Jubayl (HQ), Ad-Dammam, Ras al Mishab, Ras al Ghar, Jubail

FRIGATES 8

4 *Madina* (Fr F-2000) with 4 533mm, 1 SA 365F hel, 8 *Otomat* 2 SSM, 8 *Crotale* SAM, 1 100mm gun (1 in refit)

4 *Badr* (US Tacoma) (ASUW) with 2 x 4 *Harpoon* SSM, 2 x 3 ASTT (Mk 46 LWT), 1 76mm gun

PATROL AND COASTAL COMBATANTS 29

MISSILE CRAFT 9 *Al Siddiq* (US 58m) PFM with 2 x 2 *Harpoon*, 1 76mm gun

TORPEDO CRAFT 3 *Dammam* (Ge *Jaguar*) with 4 533mm TT

PATROL CRAFT 17 US Halter Marine PCI< (some with Coast Guard) plus 40 craft

MINE COUNTERMEASURES 6

2 *Al Jawf* (UK *Sandown* MCC)

4 *Addriyah* (US MSC-322) MCC

AMPHIBIOUS craft only

4 LCU, 4 LCM

SUPPORT AND MISCELLANEOUS 7

2 *Boraida* (mod Fr/*Durance*) AO with 1 or 2 hel, 3 ocean tugs, 1 salvage tug, 1 Royal Yacht with hel deck

NAVAL AVIATION

21 armed hel

HEL 19 AS-565 (4 SAR, 15 with AS-15TT ASM), 12 AS 332B/F (6 tpt, 6 with AM-39 *Exocet*)

MARINES (3,000)

1 inf regt (2 bn) with 140 BMR-600P

Air Force 18,000

432 cbt ac

FGA 7 sqn

3 with 56 F-5E, 14 F-5F

4 with 90 *Tornado* IDS

FTR 24 *Tornado* ADV, 70 F-15C, 25 F-15D, 72 F-15S (being delivered)

RECCE 1 sqn with 10* RF-5E (plus 10 *Tornado* in FGA sqn)

AEW 1 sqn with 5 E-3A

TKR 8 KE-3A (tkr/tpt), 7 KC-130H

OCU 2 sqn with 14* F-5B, 7* F-5F

TPT 3 sqn with 41 C-130 (7 -E, 34 -H), 8 L-100-30HS (hospital ac)

HEL 2 sqn with 22 AB-205, 25 AB-206B, 27 AB-212, 12 AS-332 B/F, 12 AS-532A2

TRG 30* *Hawk* Mk 65, 20* *Hawk* Mk 65A, 50 PC-9, 1 *Jetstream* 31, 4 Cessna 172

ROYAL FLT ac 1 Boeing-747SP, 1 Boeing-737-200, 4 BAe 125-800, 2 C-140, 4 CN-235, 2 *Gulfstream* III, 2 *Learjet* 35, 6 VC-130H, 1 Cessna 310 **hel** 3 AS-61, AB-212, 1 -S70

MISSILES

ASM AGM-65 *Maverick*, AS-15, AS-30, *Sea Eagle*, *Shrike* AGM-45, ALARM

AAM AIM-9J/L/P *Sidewinder*, AIM-7F *Sparrow*, *Skyflash*

Air Defence Forces 4,000

33 SAM bty

16 with 128 I HAWK

17 with 68 *Shahine* fire units and AMX-30SA 30mm SP AA guns

73 *Shahine/Crotale* fire units as static defence

EQUIPMENT

AD GUNS 20mm: 92 M-163 *Vulcan*; **30mm**: 50 AMX-30SA; **35mm**: 128; **40mm**: 150 L/70 (in store)

SAM 141 *Shahine*, 128 MIM-23B I HAWK, 40 *Crotale*

National Guard 77,000

(57,000 active, 20,000 tribal levies)

3 mech inf bde, each 4 all arms bn

5 inf bde

1 ceremonial cav sqn

EQUIPMENT

LAV 450 LAV-25

APC 290 V-150 *Commando* (plus 810 in store), 440 *Piranha*

TOWED ARTY 105mm: 40 M-102; **155mm**: 30 M-198

MOR 81mm

RCL 106mm: M-40A1

ATGW TOW

Paramilitary 15,500+ active

FRONTIER FORCE 10,500

COAST GUARD 4,500

EQPT 4 *Al Jouf* PFI, about 30 PCI<, 16 hovercraft, 1 trg, 1 Royal Yacht (5,000t) with 1 Bell 206B hel, about 350 armed boats

GENERAL CIVIL DEFENCE ADMINISTRATION UNITS

10 KV-107 **hel**

SPECIAL SECURITY FORCE 500

UR-416 APC

Foreign Forces

PENINSULAR SHIELD FORCE ε7,000

1 inf bde (elm from all GCC states)

FRANCE: 130; (Southern Watch) 6 *Mirage* 2000C, 3 C 135FR

UK: ε200; (Southern Watch) 6 *Tornado* GR-1A

US: ε5,000 **Army** 1,400 incl 1 *Patriot* SAM, 1 sigs unit plus those on short-term duty (6 months) **Air Force** (Southern Watch) 1,820; units on rotational det, numbers vary (incl: F-15, F-16, F-117, C-130, KC-135, U-2, E-3)

Syria

	1996	1997	1998	1999
GDP	S£673bn	S£727bn		
	($33bn)	($35bn)		
per capita	$6,400	$6,700		
Growth	7.1%	5.0%		
Inflation	8.3%	2.5%		
Debt	$21.4bn	$21.0bn		
Def exp[a]	S£48bn	S£51bn		
	($2.0bn)	($2.2bn)		
Def bdgt			S£39.5bn	
			($1.7bn)	
$1 = pound[a]	11.2	11.2	11.2	
[a] Market rate **1998** $1 = S£45				
Population		15,874,000		
Age	*13–17*	*18–22*	*23–32*	
Men	973,000	793,000	1,175,000	
Women	937,000	768,000	1,136,000	

Total Armed Forces

ACTIVE ε320,000

Terms of service conscription, 30 months

RESERVES (to age 45) 500,000
Army 400,000 active **Navy** 8,000 **Air Force** 92,000

Army ε215,000

(incl conscripts)
3 corps HQ • 6 armd div (each 3 armd, 1 mech bde, 1 arty regt) • 3 mech div (-) (each 2 armd, 2 mech bde, 1 arty regt) • 1 Republican Guard div (3 armd, 1 mech bde, 1 arty regt) • 1 SF div (3 SF regt) • 3 indep inf bde • 1 Border Guard bde • 2 indep arty bde • 2 indep ATK bde • 8 indep SF regt • 1 indep tk regt • 3 SSM bde (each of 3 bn): 1 with FROG, 1 with *Scud*, 1 with SS-21 • 1 coastal def SSM bde with SS-C-1B *Sepal* and SS-C-3 *Styx*
RESERVES
1 armd div HQ (cadre), 30 inf, arty regt
EQUIPMENT
   MBT 4,600: 2,100 T-54/-55, 1,000 T-62M/K, 1,500 T-72/-72M (incl some 1,200 in static positions and in store)
   RECCE 700 BRDM-2
   AIFV 2,250 BMP-1, 60 BMP-2, some BMP-3
   APC 1,500 BTR-40/-50/-60/-152
   TOWED ARTY some 1,630, incl: **122mm**: 100 M-

1931/-37 (in store), 150 M-1938, 500 D-30; **130mm**: 800 M-46; **152mm**: 20 D-20, 50 M-1937; **180mm**: 10 S23
   SP ARTY 122mm: 400 2S1; **152mm**: 50 2S3
   MRL 107mm: 200 Type-63; **122mm**: 280 BM-21
   MOR 82mm: 200; **120mm**: 350 M-1943; **160mm**: 100 M-160; **240mm**: ε8 M-240
   SSM launchers: 18 FROG-7, some 18 SS-21, 26 Scud-B/-C; SS-C-1B *Sepal*, SS-C-3 coastal
   ATGW 3,000 AT-3 *Sagger* (incl 2,500 SP), 150 AT-4 *Spigot*, 40 AT-5 *Spandrel*, AT-14 Komet (reported) and 200 *Milan*
   AD GUNS 2,060: **23mm**: 650 ZU-23-2 towed, 400 ZSU-23-4 SP; **37mm**: 300 M-1939; **57mm**: 675 S-60, 10 ZSU-57-2 SP; **100mm**: 25 KS-19
   SAM 4,000 SA-7, 20 SA-9, 35 SA-13

Navy ε5,000

(plus 4,000 reserves)
BASES Latakia, Tartus, Minet el-Baida
SUBMARINES 3
   3 Sov *Romeo* with 533mm TT (all non-op)
FRIGATES 2
   2 Sov *Petya* II with 4 ASW RL, 5 533mm TT
PATROL AND COASTAL COMBATANTS 21
MISSILE CRAFT 10
   10 Sov *Osa* I and II PFM with 4 SS-N-2 *Styx* SSM
PATROL CRAFT 11
   8 Sov *Zhuk* PFI< • 1 Sov *Natya* (ex-MSO) • About 2 *Hamelin* PFI< (ex-PLF)
MINE COUNTERMEASURES 5
   1 Sov T-43, 1 *Sonya* MSC, 3 *Yevgenya* MSI
AMPHIBIOUS 3
   3 *Polnocny* LSM, capacity 100 tps, 5 tk
SUPPORT AND MISCELLANEOUS 4
   1 spt, 1 trg, 1 div spt, 1 AGOR

NAVAL AVIATION
24 armed hel
ASW 20 Mi-14, 4 Ka-28 (Air Force manpower)

Air Force 40,000

589 cbt ac; 72 armed hel (some may be in store)
Flying hours 30
FGA 9 sqn
   5 with 90 Su-22 • 2 with 44 MiG-23 BN • 2 with 20 Su-24
FTR 17 sqn
   8 with 170 MiG-21 • 5 with 90 MiG-23 • 2 with 30 MiG-25 • 2 with 20 MiG-29
RECCE 6 MiG-25R, 8 MiG-21H/J
EW 10 Mi-8 *Hip* J/K
TPT 4 An-24, civil-registered **ac** incl 5 An-26, 2 *Falcon* 20, 4 Il-76, 7 Yak-40, 1 *Falcon* 900, 6 Tu-134 **hel** 10 Mi-2, 100 Mi-8/-17

ATTACK HEL 49 Mi-25, 23 SA-342L
TRG incl 80* L-39, 20 MBB-223, 20* MiG-21U, 6* MiG-23UM, 5* MiG-25U, 6 *Mashshak*
MISSILES
  ASM AT-2 *Swatter*, AS-7 *Kerry*, AS-12, HOT
  AAM AA-2 *Atoll*, AA-6 *Acrid*, AA-7 *Apex*, AA-8 *Aphid*, AA-10 *Alamo*

Air Defence Command ε60,000

25 AD bde (some 130 SAM bty)
Some 450 SA-2/-3, 200 SA-6 and AD arty
2 SAM regt (each 2 bn of 2 bty) with some 48 SA-5, 60 SA-8

Forces Abroad

LEBANON 30,000; 1 mech div HQ, elm 1 armd, 4 mech inf bde, elm 10 SF, 2 arty regt

Paramilitary 8,000+

GENDARMERIE (Ministry of Interior) 8,000

WORKERS' MILITIA (PEOPLE'S ARMY) (*Ba'ath* Party)

Foreign Forces

UN (UNDOF): 1,045; contingents from **A** 429 **Ca** 182 **J** 45 **Pl** 354
RUSSIA: ε50 advisers, mainly AD

Tunisia

	1996	1997	1998	1999
GDP	D19bn ($19bn)	D21bn ($19bn)		
per capita	$5,500	$5,800		
Growth	6.9%	5.6%		
Inflation	3.7%	3.7%		
Debt	$9.9bn	$10.1bn		
Def exp	D387m ($397m)	D369m ($334m)		
Def bdgt			D398m ($340m)	
FMA (US)	$0.7m	$0.8m	$0.9m	$0.9m
$1 = dinar	0.97	1.11	1.17	
Population		9,616,000		
Age	*13–17*	*18–22*	*23–32*	
Men	514,000	478,000	828,000	
Women	493,000	460,000	804,000	

Total Armed Forces

ACTIVE ε35,000
(ε23,400 conscripts)

Terms of service 12 months selective

Army 27,000

(22,000 conscripts)
3 mech bde (each with 1 armd, 2 mech inf, 1 arty, 1 AD regt) • 1 Sahara bde • 1 SF bde • 1 engr regt
EQUIPMENT
  MBT 54 M-60A3, 30 M-60A1
  LT TK 55 SK-105 *Kuerassier*
  RECCE 24 *Saladin*, 35 AML-90
  APC 140 M-113A1/-A2, 18 EE-11 *Urutu*, 110 Fiat F-6614
  TOWED ARTY 105mm: 48 M-101A1/A2; **155mm**: 12 M-114A1, 57 M-198
  MOR 81mm: 95; **107mm**: 66 4.2in
  ATGW 65 TOW (incl some SP), 500 *Milan*
  RL 89mm: 300 LRAC-89, 300 3.5in M-20
  RCL 57mm: 140 M-18; **106mm**: 70 M-40A1
  AD GUNS 20mm: 100 M-55; **37mm**: 15 Type-55/-65
  SAM 48 RBS-70, 25 M-48 *Chaparral*
  SURV RASIT (veh, arty)

Navy ε4,500

(incl ε700 conscripts)
BASES Bizerte, Sfax, Kelibia
PATROL AND COASTAL COMBATANTS 20
MISSILE CRAFT 6
  3 *La Galite* (Fr *Combattante* III) PFM with 8 MM-40 *Exocet* SSM
  3 *Bizerte* (Fr P-48) with 8 SS-12 SSM
PATROL, INSHORE 14
  2 *Gafsah* (PRC *Shanghai*) PFI (plus 3 non-op), 2 *Tazarka* (UK Vosper 31m) PCI, some 10 PCI<
SUPPORT AND MISCELLANEOUS 3
  1 *Salambo* (US *Conrad*) survey/trg, 2 AGS

Air Force 3,500

(700 conscripts); 44 cbt ac, 7 armed hel
FGA 15 F-5E/F
CCT 3 MB-326K, 2 MB-326L
TPT 5 C-130B, 2 C-130H, 1 *Falcon* 20, 3 LET-410
LIAISON 2 S-208M
TRG 18 SF-260 (6 -C, 12* -W), 5 MB-326B, 12* L-59
ARMED HEL 5 SA-341 (attack) 2 HH-3 (ASW)
TPT HEL 1 wg with 15 AB-205, 6 AS-350B, 1 AS-365, 6 SA-313, 3 SA-316, 2 UH-1H, 2 UH-1N
AAM AIM-9J *Sidewinder*

Paramilitary 12,000

NATIONAL GUARD (Ministry of Interior) 12,000
incl Coastal Patrol with 5 (ex-GDR) *Kondor* I-class PCC, 5 (ex-GDR) *Bremse*-class PCI<, 4 *Gabes* PCI<, plus some 10 other PCI< **ac** 5 P-6B **hel** 8 SA-318/SA-319

United Arab Emirates

	1996	1997	1998	1999
GDP	Dh158bn	Dh160bn		
	($40.0bn)	($43.7bn)		
per capita	$16,800	$16,900		
Growth	2.0%	2.6%		
Inflation	7.0%	4.0%		
Debt	$10.9bn	$12.2bn		
Def exp	εDh7.6bn	εDh8.9bn		
	($2.1bn)	($2.1bn)		
Def bdgt[a]			εDh13.7bn	
			($3.7bn)	
$1 = dirham	3.67	3.67	3.67	

[a] Including extra-budgetary funding for procurement

Population	2,580,000		

(*nationals* 24%, *expatriates* 76%, of which Indian 30%, Pakistani 20%, other Arab 12%, other Asian 10%, UK 2%, other European 1%)

Age	*13–17*	*18–22*	*23–32*
Men	85,000	79,000	142,000
Women	83,000	74,000	98,000

Total Armed Forces

The Union Defence Force and the armed forces of the UAE (Abu Dhabi, Dubai, Ras Al Khaimah and Sharjah) were formally merged in 1976 and centred on Abu Dhabi. Dubai still maintains its independence, and other emirates to a smaller degree

ACTIVE ε64,500 (perhaps 30% expatriates)

Army 59,000

(incl **Dubai** 15,000) **MoD** Dubai **GHQ** Abu Dhabi
INTEGRATED
1 Royal Guard 'bde' • 1 armd bde • 2 mech inf bde • 2 inf bde • 1 arty bde
NOT INTEGRATED
2 inf bde (Dubai)
EQUIPMENT
   MBT 45 AMX-30, 36 OF-40 Mk 2 (*Lion*), 150 *Leclerc*
   LT TK 76 *Scorpion*
   RECCE 49 AML-90, 20 *Saladin* (in store)
   AIFV 18 AMX-10P, 415 BMP-3
   APC 80 VCR (incl variants), 370 Panhard M-3, 120 EE-11 *Urutu*
   TOWED ARTY 105mm: 26 ROF lt; 130mm: 20 PRC Type-59-1
   SP ARTY 155mm: 18 Mk F-3, 72 G-6, 85 M-109A3 (being upgraded before delivery in ε1999)
   MRL 70mm: 18 LAU-97; 122mm: 48 FIROS-25 (ε24 op)
   MOR 81mm: 114 L16; 120mm: 21 Brandt
   SSM 6 *Scud*-B (Dubai only)
   ATGW 230 *Milan*, *Vigilant*, 25 TOW, HOT (20 SP)

   RCL 84mm: *Carl Gustav*; 106mm: 12 M-40
   AD GUNS 20mm: 42 M-3VDA SP; 30mm: 20 GCF-BM2
   SAM 20+ *Blowpipe*, *Mistral*

Navy ε1,500

BASE Abu Dhabi
NAVAL FACILITIES Dalma, Mina Zayed, Ajman **Dubai** Mina Rashid, Mina Jabal, Al Fujairah **Ras al Khaimah** Mina Sakr **Sharjah** Mina Khalid, Khor Fakkan
FRIGATES 2 *Abu Dhabi* (NL *Kortenaer*) FFG with 8 *Harpoon* SSM, 8 x *Sea Sparrow* SAM, 1 x 76mm gun, 4 x 324mm TT, 2 x AS565 hel

PATROL AND COASTAL COMBATANTS 19
CORVETTES 2 *Muray Jip* (Ge Lürssen 62m) with 2 x 2 MM-40 *Exocet* SSM, plus 1 SA-316 hel
MISSILE CRAFT 8
   6 *Ban Yas* (Ge Lürssen TNC-45) with 2 x 2 MM-40 *Exocet* SSM
   2 *Mubarraz* (Ge Lürssen 45m) with 2 x 2 MM-40 *Exocet* SSM, plus 1 6 *Sadral* SAM
PATROL, INSHORE 9
   6 *Ardhana* (UK Vosper 33m) PFI
   3 *Kawkab* PCI< plus boats
AMPHIBIOUS craft only
   3 *Al Feyi* LCT, 1 LCM, 1 LCU
SUPPORT AND MISCELLANEOUS 3
   1 div spt, 1 log spt, 1 tug

Air Force 4,000

(incl Police Air Wing) 99 cbt ac, 49 armed hel
Flying hours 110
FGA 3 sqn
   1 with 9 *Mirage* 2000E
   1 with 17 *Hawk* 102
   1 with 17 *Hawk* Mk 63/63A/63C (FGA/trg)
FTR 1 sqn with 22 *Mirage* 2000 EAD
CCT 1 sqn with 8 MB-326 (2 -KD, 6 -LD), 5 MB-339A
OCU *5 *Hawk* Mk 61, *2 MB-339A, *6 *Mirage* 2000 DAD
RECCE 8* *Mirage* 2000 RAD
TPT incl 1 BN-2, 4 C-130H, 2 L-100-30, 4 C-212, 7 CN-235M-100, 4 Il-76 (on lease)
HELICOPTERS
   ATTACK 5 AS-332F (anti-ship, 3 with *Exocet* AM-39), 10 SA-342K (with HOT), 7 SA-316/-319 (with AS-11/-12), 20 AH-64A, 7 AS-565 *Panther*
   TPT 2 AS-332 (VIP), 1 AS-350, 26 Bell (8 -205, 9 -206, 5 -206L, 4 -214), 10 SA-330, 2 *King Air* 350 (VIP)
   SAR 3 Bo-105, 3 *Agusta* -109 K2
TRG 30 PC-7, 5 SF-260 (4 -TP, 1 -W), 12 Grob G-115TA
MISSILES
   ASM HOT, AS-11/-12, AS-15 *Exocet* AM-39, *Hellfire*, Hydra-70, PGM1, PGM2
   AAM R-550 *Magic*, AIM 9L

AIR DEFENCE
1 AD bde (3 bn)
5 bty I HAWK
12 *Rapier*, 9 *Crotale*, 13 RBS-70, 100 *Mistral* SAM

Paramilitary

COAST GUARD (Ministry of Interior)
some 40 PCI<, plus boats

Yemen, Republic of

	1996	1997	1998	1999
GDP	R655bn	R741bn		
	($5.0bn)	($5.7bn)		
per capita	$1,300	$1,300		
Growth	3.2%	5.5%		
Inflation	47.9%	5.0%		
Debt	$6.4bn	$6.4bn		
Def exp	εR47bn	εR52bn		
	($362m)	($403m)		
Def bdgt			R53.8bn	
			($414m)	
FMA (US)		$0.05m	$0.1m	$0.1m
$1 = rial	94.2	129.2	130.1	
Population		15,890,000		
(North 79% South 21%)				
Age	*13–17*	*18–22*	*23–32*	
Men	904,000	756,000	1,224,000	
Women	878,000	719,000	1,113,000	

Total Armed Forces

ACTIVE 66,3000
(incl conscripts)
Terms of service conscription, 3 years

RESERVES perhaps 40,000
Army

Army 61,000

(incl conscripts)
9 armd bde • 1 SF bde • 18 inf bde • 5 arty bde • 7 mech bde • 3 SSM bde • 2 AB/cdo bde • 1 central guard force • 3 AD arty bn • 2 AD bn (1 with SA-2 SAM)
EQUIPMENT
  MBT 1,320: 290 T-34, 720 T-54/-55, 250 T-62, 60 M-60A1
  RECCE 60 AML-245, 130 AML-90, 160 BRDM-2
  AIFV 300 BMP-1/-2
  APC 60 M-113, 580 BTR-40/-60/-152
  TOWED ARTY some 452: **100mm**: 50 M-1944, 45

M-1955; **105mm**: 35 M-101A1; **122mm**: 30 M-1931/37, 50 M-1938, 130 D-30; **130mm**: 90 M-46; **152mm**: 10 D-20; **155mm**: 12 M-114
  ASLT GUNS 100mm: 30 SU-100
  COASTAL ARTY 130mm: 36 SM-4-1
  MRL 122mm: 185 BM-21; **140mm**: BM-14
  MOR 600 incl **81mm**; **82mm**; **120mm**; **160mm**
  SSM 12 FROG-7, 12 SS-21, 6 *Scud*-B
  ATGW 12 TOW, 24 *Dragon*, 35 AT-3 *Sagger*
  RL 66mm: M72 LAW
  RCL 75mm: M-20; **82mm**: B-10; **107mm**: B-11
  ATK GUNS 85mm: D-44; **100mm**
  AD GUNS 20mm: 52 M-167, 20 M-163 *Vulcan* SP; **23mm**: 100 ZSU-23-4; **37mm**: 150 M-1939; **57mm**: 120 S-60; **85mm**: KS-12
  SAM SA-7/-9/-13/-14

Navy 1,800

BASES Aden, Hodeida
FACILITIES Al Mukalla, Perim Island, Socotra (these have naval support equipment)
PATROL AND COASTAL COMBATANTS 15
  MISSILE CRAFT 7
  3 *Huangfen* with C-801 SSM (only 4 C-801 between the 4 craft)
  2 *Tarantul* 1 PFM with 4 SS-N-2C *Styx* SSM
  2 Sov *Osa* II with 4 SSN-2B *Styx* SSM, plus 6 boats
  PATROL, INSHORE 8
  3 *Sana'a* (US *Broadsword* 32m) PFI, 5 Sov *Zhuk* PFI<
MINE COUNTERMEASURES 6
  1 Sov *Natya* MSO
  5 Sov *Yevgenya* MSI
AMPHIBIOUS 3
  2 Sov *Ondatra* LCM
  1 *Ropucha* LST, capacity 190tps

Air Force 3,500

49 cbt ac (plus some 40 in store), 8 attack hel
FGA 10 F-5E, 17 Su-20/-22
FTR 11 MiG-21, 5 MiG-29
TPT 2 An-12, 4 An-26, 3 C-130H, 4 IL-14, 3 IL-76
HEL 2 AB-212, 14 Mi-8, 1 AB-47, 8 Mi-35 (attack)
TRG 2* F-5B,4* MiG-21U, 14 YAK-11

AIR DEFENCE
SAM some SA-2, SA-3, SA-6
AAM AA-2 *Atoll*, AIM-9 *Sidewinder*

Paramilitary 70,000

MINISTRY OF THE INTERIOR FORCES 50,000
TRIBAL LEVIES at least 20,000
COAST GUARD
(slowly being established)
5 Fr *Interceptor* PCI<

MILITARY DEVELOPMENTS

Nuclear tests by **India** and **Pakistan** in May 1998 finally brought their nuclear programmes into the open. While the situation is little changed in military and technical terms, the political land-scape has altered significantly. The tests have given both countries confidence that their weapons work and removed any lingering doubts elsewhere. They revealed little about how advanced the weapons are or the quantities held, but one military fact is clear: each side is capable of striking a devastating blow against the other. There is now a risk that, should relations between them deteriorate badly, one might be tempted to make a pre-emptive strike against the other's nuclear capability – either the warheads, the means of delivery or both. It is unlikely that there is sufficient redundancy on either side to guarantee that their nuclear capability would survive such action. Pakistan's inferiority in conventional forces introduces further uncertainty. Both sides have said that they have no plans for further testing and have indicated willingness to join the Compre-hensive Test Ban Treaty (CTBT) under certain conditions.

Pakistan would appear to have some advantage over India in land-based missile delivery. In particular, its *Ghauri* missile, with a range of up to 1,500 kilometres, is based on proven tech-nology – *Nodong*-1 components originating in North Korea. (It is not clear what types of warhead have been supplied or designed.) India's intermediate-range *Agni* missile is mainly indigenously developed and has been subject to difficulties and delay. The simplest and most likely means of delivery by either state remains combat aircraft. India could have a submarine-launched missile capability by 2004 if development programmes continue and are successful.

Indian and Pakistani forces continue to exchange fire across the demarcation line in Jammu & Kashmir. The insurgency on the Indian side has remained well contained since 1997 although Islamic militant armed groups, such as the *Harkat-ul-Mujahideen*, still pose a challenge with attacks on Hindu civilians and Indian security forces.

In **Sri Lanka**, the deadly combat between government forces and the Liberation Tigers of Tamil Eelam (LTTE) rages on. The mounting death toll is now estimated to be over 50,000 since fighting began 15 years ago. Despite major offensives, government forces have yet to achieve decisive military success. Mediation attempts have not proved successful.

In **Bangladesh**, longstanding insurgency finally ended with a peace accord between *Chakma* (Buddhist) guerrillas and the government in May 1998. There were violent demonstrations by Bangladeshis, who felt that the government had made too many concessions on territory and autonomy to the *Chakma*. Nevertheless, more than 1,500 fighters had handed in their weapons by the end of June 1998 and so far the settlement appeared secure.

In **Nepal**, more than 50 Maoist rebels have been killed since the security forces stepped-up their campaign against them in May 1998. Something of an anachronism, the Maoists oppose Nepal's constitutional monarchy and are fighting to establish a communist republic.

Central Asia

The least stable of the Central Asian republics, **Tajikistan** is in a state of uneasy peace. Central government control is limited and tensions persist between the various armed groups and the centre. The law passed by the Tajik parliament on 23 May 1998 banning religious political parties could be a serious obstacle to the fragile peace process. It means that the country's main oppo-sition party, the Islamic Revival Party, will not be able to take part in elections. The governments of both Tajikistan and **Uzbekistan** are taking a strong line, with Russian encouragement, against Islamic groups. In Uzbekistan, a number of mosques are being closed as part of the campaign to root out armed opposition. This is likely to incite terrorist action rather than damp it down. Instability in neighbouring **Afghanistan** fuels the trade in weapons of all kinds, much of it funded from the region's rapidly expanding narcotics trade. In Afghanistan, the *Taleban* has still not completely overcome the Northern Group of forces and are unable to extend their control to the far northern areas of the country. The uneasy military stalemate is punctuated by fierce clashes when one side or the other sees an opportunity to gain military advantage. Mediation attempts by the UN, Pakistan and Iran have failed so far.

DEFENCE SPENDING

Regional defence spending showed real growth of some 3% in 1997 to $19.2bn from $18.7bn in 1996 (in 1997 US dollars), according to *The Military Balance* estimates. In most cases, nominal increases in defence budgets were much larger because of inflation (still over 50% on average in the Central Asian republics and around 8% in South Asia) and depreciation of local currencies. In South Asia, real growth in gross domestic product (GDP) averaged around 5% in 1997 (the same as in 1996), and the East Asian financial crisis did not appear to have affected regional economies significantly by mid-1998. In the Central Asian republics, economic performance in 1997 continued to improve modestly in Kazakstan and Uzbekistan, the largest sub-regional economies, and more emphatically in **Kyrgyzstan**, while Tajikistan registered economic growth for the first time since the break-up of the Soviet Union. **Turkmenistan**'s economy continued to decline (by 26%); the country is the only former Soviet republic whose economy has not grown since independence.

India and Pakistan between them account for over 80% of regional defence spending, but other countries in the region also spend heavily. Military expenditure as a proportion of GDP across the region is, at 5%, higher than anywhere except the Middle East. The opacity of defence accounting in the Central Asian republics, most notably Uzbekistan, probably means that military outlays are under-stated in official figures and underestimated by independent sources. While budgetary data for 1998 suggest that regional defence spending is at similar levels to 1997 in real terms, it is more likely that actual military outlays will grow in 1998.

South Asia

India's 1998 defence budget, released on 1 June 1998, amounts to Rs412bn ($9.9bn) – an increase of 16% on the previous year's budget (Rs356bn) and 14% up on 1997 outlays (Rs360bn). This represents a real increase of around 7% measured against 1998 price inflation expectations. In US dollar terms, 1998 defence spending is marginally down on 1997, because of rupee depreciation. The Indian Navy's allocation increases by some 22% in real terms, which raises its share of the budget to 14.5%, while funding for the Army and Air Force declines from 1997 levels. Defence

Table 17 India's defence budget by service/department, 1994–1998										
(1998 US$m)	1994	%	1995	%	1996	%	1997	%	1998	%
Army	4,273	52.9	4,673	53.0	4,630	53.4	5,663	56.6	5,150	52.2
Air Force	2,236	27.7	2,274	25.8	2,221	25.6	2,468	24.7	2,242	22.7
Navy	1,043	12.9	1,246	14.1	1,175	13.5	1,168	11.7	1,430	14.5
R&D	432	5.3	454	5.1	429	4.9	471	4.7	425	4.3
DP&S[1], other	99	1.2	165	1.9	221	2.6	237	2.4	610	6.2
Total	8,083	100	8,812	100	8,676	100	10,007	100	9,856	100

Note [1]Department of Defence Production and Supplies

Research and Development Organisation (DRDO) funding also declines in real terms, as does spending on tri-service R&D, but non-specified spending in 'other' categories increases by $373m.

The Indian government does not identify defence-specific nuclear spending and it is not clear under which budget the nuclear weapons programme is funded. Funding is probably broken up under several departmental headings to maintain secrecy. While the sunk costs of India's nuclear programme are sure to be substantial (perhaps $15bn since 1971), the annual running costs of a mature programme probably account for between 5% and 10% of the cost of indigenous development or foreign purchase of delivery systems, or perhaps $200–300m a year. India has increased funding for both atomic energy and space to a combined $705m in 1998, and activities in this department, while mainly in the civilian sphere, may contribute to the nuclear weapons programme.

India has a range of indigenous weapons programmes where production has started or is close to doing so. The Integrated Guided Missile Development Programme (IGMDP), which began in 1983, now incorporates five systems whose development is advanced or complete. Development of the *Agni* medium-range ballistic missile (MRBM) continues, while development of the 2,500km-range *Agni* 2 variant might have been accelerated following the testing of Pakistan's *Ghauri* MRBM in April 1998. There have also been reports that India is developing a strategic missile, the *Surya* intercontinental ballistic missile (ICBM). Development work on the *Sagarika* 300km-range submarine-launched missile (probably ballistic) continues as part of a nuclear-powered submarine project. The first submarine in this series, the Advanced Technology Vessel (ATV), is due to enter service in 2004. At least two of the three *Prithvi* surface-to-surface missile (SSM) variants are reported to be in production following the Army order for 75 of the 150km variant and the Air Force order for 25 of the 250km variant. Tactical missiles currently undergoing user trials include the *Akash* medium-range surface-to-air missile (SAM), the *Trishul* short-range SAM, and the *Nag* anti-tank guided weapon (ATGW).

The Indian Navy commissioned the first of six *Delhi*-class destroyers with SAMs (DDGs) in November 1997. Two more are to be commissioned in 1998 and 1999. Development of India's other large, conventional weapon platforms continues to face technical difficulties. In user trials, the *Arjun* main battle tank (MBT) programme has failed to demonstrate acceptable reliability, which has delayed full-scale production. While the tank may enter production in 1998-99, no production order has yet been issued and there might be no more than 124 vehicles in service by 2001. Difficulties with the *Arjun* programme have reportedly led India to consider licensed production of T-80 or T-90 MBTs as an alternative. Production of the first batch of advanced light helicopters (ALH) is underway and first deliveries are due by the end of 1998. Deliveries to the Indian Navy are likely to be delayed, as these variants use a US engine now embargoed under US sanctions imposed after the May 1998 nuclear tests. Army variants use a French engine which is also subject to embargo following the tests. US sanctions are additionally expected to delay the first flight of the Light Combat Aircraft (LCA) to mid-1999, rather than December 1998 as scheduled. India began small-scale production of its *Nishant* unmanned aerial vehicle (UAV) and continued development of the *Lakshya* UAV, but technical difficulties are reported to have led India to consider technical cooperation with Israeli UAV producers and licensed production of Israeli UAVs.

India maintains several paramilitary organisations, with a combined manpower in excess of one million, whose funding comes under the Ministry of Home Affairs. Combined allocations for these organisations, which include the Border Security Force, Indo-Tibetan Border Police, and the Assam Rifles, amount to $773m in 1998.

Pakistan only provides an aggregate figure for defence spending. The 1998 defence budget, released on 13 June 1998, amounts to Rs145bn ($3.3bn) which is 8% up on 1997 (Rs134bn) in

Table 18 India's defence and other budgets, 1997–1998

(US$m)	1997 budget	1997 outturn	1998 budget
Personnel, Operations & Maintenance			
MoD	80	89	62
Defence Pensions	1,023	1,362	1,417
Army	5,289	5,056	5,150
Navy	622	671	700
Air Force	1,326	1,427	1,369
Defence ordnance factories	120	227	159
Sub-total (excluding recoveries and receipts)	8,459	8,832	8,857
Recoveries and receipts	1,103	1,452	1,479
Sub-total	7,356	7,381	7,378
R&D, Procurement & Construction			
Tri-Service Defence R&D	192	192	167
Army	588	588	661
Navy	522	643	730
Air Force	1,088	1,088	872
Other	63	49	48
Sub-total	2,453	2,560	2,478
Total Defence Budget	9,809	9,941	9,856
Total Defence Budget (1998 US$)	10,007	10,142	9,856
Other Military-relevant Funding			
Paramilitary forces	611	815	773
Department of Atomic Energy	354	272	375
Department of Space	273	234	330
Intelligence Bureau	43	59	55
Total	1,281	1,380	1,533

nominal terms, and about the same in real terms. No details are provided on funding for Pakistan's nuclear programme which is likely to be outside, and in addition to, the defence allocation. Pakistan claims its *Hatf* and *Ghauri* series of ballistic missiles, in support of its nuclear weapons, are based on indigenous resources, but its outlays on missile programmes are likely to be significantly less than those of India on the *Prithvi*, *Agni* and similar programmes because of reported direct imports of North Korean *Nodong* and Chinese M-11 missile components. Pakistan tested the *Ghauri* in April 1998, and is developing the *Shaheen* 1 SSM (also known as the *Hatf-3* and based on the Chinese M-9) and the 2,500km-range *Shaheen* 2 MRBM (which may be based on the North Korean *Taepo-Dong*). Pakistan's *Al-Khalid* MBT, designed with Chinese assistance, has yet to overcome technical difficulties and enter production. The K-8 aircraft trainer programme, undertaken jointly with China, has stalled after delivery of six prototypes for user trials, pending an agreement with China on joint orders.

Like India, Pakistan has substantial paramilitary forces (numbering nearly a quarter of a million) whose federal funding in 1997 amounted to nearly $200m.

In Sri Lanka, the government has stated that military expenditures will be increased in 1998 if the war against the LTTE continues at present levels. The 1998 defence budget is Rs44.8bn

($691m) compared to Rs44bn in 1997, and accounts for 14% of government spending. In Bangladesh, the defence budget is increased to T29bn ($627m) from a budget of T24.6bn ($560m) and outlay of T26bn in 1997. In Nepal, the 1998 defence budget is NR2.5bn ($39m), against a budget of NR2.4bn and outturn of NR2.3bn in 1997.

Central Asia

Central Asian defence budgets continue to be hidden from public scrutiny and include considerable military spending under Internal Security allocations. Kazakstan's 1998 budget has increased to T19.9bn ($259m) from T16.3bn in 1996, while Internal Security funding goes up from T21.6bn to T34.1bn, nearly half of which is directly related to military activity. The Uzbekistan government claims that defence expenditure accounts for just 4% of government spending and 1.4% of GDP. Given the growth in the state's armed forces since 1996, official figures may understate real outlays. These could account for up to 20% of government spending and up to 6–7% of GDP. The most recent International Monetary Fund (IMF) audit of Uzbekistan's government finances, published in October 1997, commented that military expenditures are not reported by the government under a defence budget heading, but are included under the category of 'other expenditures' which accounted for 6% of GDP in 1996.

Table 19 **Kazakstan's defence budget, 1997–1998**		
(US$m) **Defence**	**1997**	**1998**
MoD	193	235
Republican Guard	8	8
Emergency funds	15	16
Sub-total	**216**	**259**
Internal Security		
Ministry of the Interior	9	9
Internal Troops	34	39
Border Guard	52	63
Intelligence	54	91
Sub-total	**150**	**201**
Total Military-related Budget	**366**	**460**

REGIONAL ARMS SALES

Russia continues to be India's major foreign arms supplier. In June 1998, India ordered Russian S-300V SAM systems comprising some 24–36 launchers. The Indian Navy ordered three improved *Krivak* 3 frigates from Russia in May 1998 and took delivery of the ninth Russian *Kilo* 877-class submarine in January 1998. Two *Kilo* 636-class submarines are on order for 2000–2001 delivery. Two more German-licensed Type-209s are on order for production in India and delivery in 2003–2005. The first *Delhi*-class destroyer has been fitted with 16 Russian SS-N-25 *Zveda* SSMs. The Air Force should be receiving eight more Su-30 ground-attack fighter aircraft (FGAs) from Russia in 1998, following delivery of the first eight in 1997. The balance of 24 of the 40 ordered is due for delivery in 1999/or 2000. The Su-30s are to be equipped with Kh-31P-2 (AS-17 *Kryton*) anti-radiation missiles (ARMs) on order from Russia.

Deliveries of around 100 T-80UD MBTs to Pakistan, out of 320 on order from Ukraine, had taken place by March 1998. Work on the first of the Pakistan Navy's new *Agosta*-class submarines is nearing completion. The second submarine has been laid down in France, but will be fitted out in Pakistan, while the third in the series will be produced entirely in Pakistan. Deliveries are expected between 1999 and 2002. The Pakistan Air Force started to take delivery of 40 upgraded *Mirage* III fighters in 1998.

Sri Lanka's procurement has included an order for a British M-10 hovercraft and two Ukrainian Mi-24 helicopters. The Bangladesh Air Force took delivery of eight F-7 fighters from China in late 1997 and ordered 8–10 MiG-29s from Russia in early 1998.

Table 20 **Arms orders and deliveries, Central and South Asia, 1996–1998**						
Supplier	**Classification**	**Designation**	**Units**	**Order Date**	**Delivery Date**	**Comment**
Bangladesh						
US	trg	T-37	12	1995	1996	Ex-US, EDA
Ukr	tpt	AN-32	1	1995	1996	
RF	ftr	MiG-29B	8	1998		
PRC	ftr	F-7	8	1996	1997	
PRC	MSO	T-43	4	1995	1997	
ROK	OPV	*Madhumati*	1	1995	1998	
India						
RF	SAM	S-300	24	1998	1998	24–36 launchers
Domestic	SAM	*Akash*		1983	1997	
Domestic	SSM	*Prithvi*	125	1983	1998	SS350 in development
Domestic	SSM	*Agni* 1		1983	1999	*Agni* 2 in development
Domestic	ICBM	*Surya*		1983		
Domestic	satellite	IRS-1C	1	1995	1996	
Domestic	SLCM	*Sagarika*		1983	2005	May be SLBM
Domestic	UAV	*Nishant*	14	1991	1998	In development
Domestic	hel	ALH	300	1984	1998	Delays may occur
Domestic	SAM	*Trishul*		1983	1996	In development
RF	tkr ac	IL-78	6	1996	1998	First 2 delivered in early 1998
UK	FGA	*Jaguar* GR1	16	1994	1997	Licensed production in Ind
RF	FGA	Su-30MK	40	1996	1997	8 in 1997 and 1998, 12 in 1999 and 2000
Domestic	FGA	LCA	7	1983	1997	In-service date 2008–2010
RF	FGA	MiG-21	125	1996	1997	Fr and Il avionics upgrade
RF	hel	KA-31	3	1997	2000	
RF	AO	A-58	1	1995	1996	Possibly *Boris Chilikin*-class
UK	ftr	*Harrier* TMk4	2	1997	1999	Two ex-UK RN aircraft
RF	FFG	P1135.6	3	1998	2000	Modified *Krivak* 3
Domestic	FFG	*Brahmaputra*	3	1989	1998	2nd in 1999, 3rd in 2003
Domestic	corvette	*Kuhkri*-class	1	1990	1999	Sixth of class of eight
Domestic	DDG	*Delhi*	1	1987	1997	First of 6
RF	ASSM	SS-N-25	16	1996	1997	More for delivery 1998
Ge	SS	Type-209	2	1997	2003	Second for delivery in 2005
Il	FAC	*Super Dvora*	6	1997	1997	2 bought. 4 local build 2000–2002
RF	SS	*Kilo*	2	1997	2001	Type-636
RF	SS	*Kilo*	1	1997	1997	Type-877
Domestic	SSN	ATV	1	1982	2004	Possibly SLBM compatible
Domestic	LST	*Magyar*	1	1991	1997	Second of class
RF	PFM	*Tarantul* 1	1	1995	1997	11th of class
Domestic	SAM	*Trishul*		1983	1998	Trials for Naval use
Domestic	OPV	*Samar*	4	1993	1996	1 delivered, 3 building
RF	arty	2S6M	12	1995	1996	
Domestic	ATGW	*Nag*		1983		User trials scheduled for mid-1998

Supplier	Classification	Designation	Units	Order Date	Delivery Date	Comment
Domestic	MBT	*Arjun*	124	1998	2001	Development began in 1972
Il	UAV	*Searcher*	12	1997		12 systems, 32 vehicles
Il	arty	130mm	500	1997	1998	To be upgraded by *Soltam*
RF	arty	152mm	120	1997	1998	
Domestic	UAV	*Lakshya*		1991	1998	Entering serial production
Kazakstan						
RF	ftr	Su-27	10	1997	1997	
RF	PFC	*Zhuk*	3	1996	1996	Designated coastal defence cutters
Ge	PCI	KW 15	4	1995	1996	
US	PCI	*Dauntless*	1	1996	1997	
Pakistan						
PRC	SSM	M-11	34	1994	1996	In kit form
Domestic	SSM	*Hatf* 2		1984	1996	M-11 parts also called *Shaheen* 1
Domestic	IRBM	*Ghauri*		1984	1998	*Nodong*. Also known as *Hatf* 5
Domestic	SSM	*Hatf* 3		1994		Based on PRC M-9
Domestic	SSM	*Shaheen* 2		1998		
Fr	FGA	*Mirage* III	40	1996	1998	
PRC	FGA	FC-1	150	1993	2005	In co-development with PRC
US	AAM	AIM-L	360	1995	1997	
PRC	tpt	Y-12(11)	1	1997	1998	
Fr	MSC	M-163	3	1992	1997	
Fr	SS	*Agosta*-class	3	1994	1998	Deliveries 1999–2002
US	MPA	PC-3C	3	1995	1996	With 28 *Harpoon* missiles, deliveries to 1997
Domestic	PFM	Mod. *Larkana*	1	1996	1997	Commissioned August 1997
Domestic	MBT	*Al-Khalid*		1991	1998	In acceptance trials
RF	hel	Mi-17	12	1995	1996	
Ukr	MBT	T-80UD	320	1996	1996	105 delivered in 1997
US	APC	M113	775	1989	1990	Licensed production; deliveries to 1999
Sri Lanka						
US	MPA	*Beech* 200	4	1995	1997	
Ukr	tpt	AN-32	4	1995	1996	
Ukr	hel	Mi-17	3	1995	1996	
Ukr	hel	Mi-24	2	1995	1996	For electronic warfare
US	tpt	C-130	3	1997	1999	
Il	FAC	*Colombo*	4	1994	1996	Similar to *Super Dvora* in design
Il	FAC	*Super Dvora*	6	1995	1997	Built in Ska
Il	PFC	*Dvora*-class	6	1996	1997	
US	PCI	*Trinity*	6	1997	1997	
PRC	PCO	*Haiqing*	3	1994	1996	1 in service in 1996; 2 delivered in 1997
Il	UAV	*Super Hawk*	5	1994	1996	
Ukr	hel	Mi-24	2	1998	1999	

Afghanistan

	1996	1997	1998	1999
GDP	ε$1.5bn	ε$1.6bn		
per capita	ε$600	ε$700		
Growth	ε6%	ε6%		
Inflation	ε14%	ε14%		
Debt	ε$5.7bn	ε$6.0bn		
Def exp	ε$200m	ε$200m		
$1 = afgani[a]	2,333	3,000	3,000	

[a] Market rate **1998** ε$1 = Afs4,750

Population[b]		ε23,400,000		

(Pashtun 38%, Tajik 25%, Hazara 19%, Uzbek 12%, Aimaq 4%, Baluchi 0.5%)

Age	*13–17*	*18–22*	*23–32*
Men	1,354,000	1,146,000	1,934,000
Women	1,299,000	1,088,000	1,822,000

[b] Includes ε1,500,000 refugees in Pakistan, ε1,000,000 in Iran, ε150,000 in Russia and ε50,000 in Kyrgyzstan

Total Armed Forces

ACTIVE Nil

Taleban now controls two-thirds of Afghanistan, and continues to mount mil ops against an alliance of former President Burhanuddin Rabbani's government troops, led by former Defence Minister Ahmad Shah Masoud and the National Islamic Alliance (NIA) of General Abdul Rashid Dostam. The alliance appears to receive little support from Shi'a opposition groups.

EQUIPMENT

It is impossible to show the division of ground force equipment among the different factions. The list below represents weapons known to be in the country in April 1992. Individual weapons quantities are unknown.

MBT T-54/-55, T-62
LT TK PT-76
RECCE BRDM-1/-2
AIFV BMP-1/-2
APC BTR-40/-60/-70/-80/-152
TOWED ARTY 76mm: M-1938, M-1942; **85mm**: D-48; **100mm**: M-1944; **122mm**: M-30, D-30; **130mm**: M-46; **152mm**: D-1, D-20, M-1937 (ML-20)
MRL 122mm: BM-21; **140mm**: BM-14; **220mm**: 9P140 *Uragan*
MOR 82mm: M-37; **107mm**; **120mm**: M-43
SSM *Scud*, FROG-7
ATGW AT-1 *Snapper*, AT-3 *Sagger*
RCL 73mm: SPG-9; **82mm**: B-10
AD GUNS: 14.5mm; **23mm**: ZU-23, ZSU-23-4 SP; **37mm**: M-1939; **57mm**: S-60; **85mm**: KS-12; **100mm**: KS-19
SAM SA-7/-13

Air Force

Only the former government–NIM alliance and *Taleban* have aircraft. These groups have a quantity of SU-17/22 and MiG-21s and both have some Mi-8/17. The inventory shows ac in service in April 1992. Since then, an unknown number of fixed-wing ac and hel have either been shot down or destroyed on the ground, however, it is believed that the *Taleban* have about 4 Su-17/22 and 30 MiG-21 and the NIM have about 30 Su-17/22, 30 MiG-21 and 10 L-39. The number of helicopters each side have is unknown.
FGA 30 MiG-23, 80 Su-7/-17/-22
FTR 80 MiG-21F
ARMED HEL 25 Mi-8, 35 Mi-17, 20 Mi-25
TPT ac 2 Il-18D; 50 An-2, An-12, An-26, An-32 **hel** 12 Mi-4
TRG 25 L-39*, 18 MiG-21*

AIR DEFENCE

SAM 115 SA-2, 110 SA-3, *Stinger*, SAM-7, SAM-14, **37mm**, **85mm** and **100mm** guns

Opposition Groups

Afghan insurgency was a broad national movement, united only against the Najibullah government.

GROUPS ORIGINALLY BASED IN PESHAWAR
Islamic Fundamentalist
TALEBAN ε25,000 **Leaders** Maulewi Mohamed Omar, Maulewi Mohamed Rabbi **Area** southern Afghanistan **Ethnic group** Pashtun. Formed originally from religious students in Madrassahs (both Pashtun and non-Pashtun)

Traditionalist Moderate
ISLAMIC REVOLUTIONARY MOVEMENT (*Haraka't-Inqila'b-Isla'mi*) ε25,000 **Leader** Mohammed Nabi Mohammed **Area** Farah, Zabol, Paktika, southern Ghazni, eastern Lowgar, western Paktia, northern Nimruz, northern Helmand, northern Kandahar **Ethnic group** Pashtun. Has backed *Taleban*
NATIONAL ISLAMIC FRONT (*Mahaz-Millin Isla'mi*) ε15,000 **Leader** Sayyed Amhad Gailani **Area** eastern Paktia (Vardak–Lowgar border) **Ethnic group** Pashtun
NATIONAL LIBERATION FRONT[a] (*Jabha't-Nija't-Milli'*) ε15,000 **Leader** Sibghatullah Modjaddi **Area** enclaves in Kandahar, Zabol provinces, eastern Konar **Ethnic group** Pashtun
ISLAMIC SOCIETY (*Jamia't Isla'mi*) ε60,000 **Leader** Burhanuddin Rabbani **Area** eastern and northern Farah, Herat, Ghowr, Badghis, Faryab, northern Jowzjan, northern Balkh, northern Kondoz, Takhar, Baghlan, Kapisa, northern Laghman, Badakhshan **Ethnic groups** Turkoman, Uzbek, Tajik
ISLAMIC PARTY (*Hizbi-Isla'mi-Gulbuddin*)[a] ε50,000 **Leader** Gulbuddin Hekmatyar **Area** northern and southern Kabul, Parvan, eastern Laghman, northern

Nangarhar, south-eastern Konar; large enclave at Badghis–Ghowr–Jowzjan junction, western Baghlan; enclaves in Farah, Nimruz, Kandahar, Oruzgan and Zabol **Ethnic groups** Pashtun, Turkoman, Tajik

ISLAMIC PARTY (*Hizbi-Isla'mi-Kha'lis*) ε40,000 **Leader** Yu'nis Kha'lis **Area** central Paktia, Nangarhar, south-east Kabul **Ethnic group** Pashtun

ISLAMIC UNION (*Ittiha'd-Isla'mi Barai Azadi*) ε18,000 **Leader** Abdul Rasul Sayyaf **Area** east of Kabul **Ethnic group** Pashtun

GROUPS ORIGINALLY BASED IN IRAN

HEZBI-WAHDAT (Unity Party)[a] umbrella party of Shi'a groups

Sazman-e-Nasr some 50,000 **Area** Bamian, northern Oruzgan, eastern Ghowr, southern Balkh, southern Samangan, south-western Baghlan, south-eastern Parvan, northern Vardak **Ethnic group** Hazara

Shura-Itifaq-Islami some 30,000+ **Area** Vardak, eastern Bamian **Ethnic group** Hazara

Harakat-e-Islami 20,000 **Area** west of Kabul; enclaves in Kandahar, Ghazni, Vardak, Samangan, Balkh **Ethnic groups** Pashtun, Tajik, Uzbek

Pasdaran-e-Jehad 8,000

Hizbollah 4,000

Nehzat 4,000

NATIONAL ISLAMIC MOVEMENT (NIM)[a] Formed in March 1992, mainly from troops of former Afghan Army Northern Comd. Predominantly Uzbek, Tajik, Turkoman, Ismaeli and Hazara Shi'a. Str ε65,000 (120–150,000 in crisis). 2 Corps HQ, 5–7 inf div, some indep bde

[a] Form the Supreme Coordination Council

Bangladesh

	1996	1997	1998	1999
GDP	Tk1.3tr	Tk1.4tr		
	($31bn)	($32bn)		
per capita	$1,500	$1,600		
Growth	5.4%	5.7%		
Inflation	2.7%	5.7%		
Debt	$16.1bn	$18.7bn		
Def exp	Tk22.7bn	Tk26.0bn		
	($542m)	($593m)		
Def bdgt			Tk27.9bn	
			($602m)	
FMA (US)	$0.3m	$0.3m	$0.4m	$0.4m
$1 = taka	41.8	43.9	46.3	
Population	127,894,000 (Hindu 12%)			
Age	*13–17*	*18–22*	*23–32*	
Men	7,900,000	7,216,000	11,283,000	
Women	7,513,000	6,796,000	10,684,000	

Total Armed Forces

ACTIVE 121,000

Army 101,000

7 inf div HQ • 17 inf bde (some 26 bn) • 1 armd bde (2 armd regt) • 2 armd regt • 1 arty div (6 arty regt) • 1 engr bde • 1 AD bde

EQUIPMENT†

MBT some 80 PRC Type-59/-69, 60 T-54/-55

LT TK some 40 PRC Type-62

APC 20 BTR-80, some MT-LB

TOWED ARTY 105mm: 30 Model 56 pack, 50 M-101; **122mm**: 20 PRC Type-54; **130mm**: 40+ PRC Type-59

MRL 122mm: reported

MOR 81mm; 82mm: PRC Type-53; **120mm**: 50 PRC Type-53

RCL 106mm: 30 M-40A1

ATK GUNS 57mm: 18 6-pdr; **76mm**: 50 PRC Type-54

AD GUNS 37mm: 16 PRC Type-55; **57mm**: PRC Type-59

SAM some HN-5A

Navy† 10,500

BASES Chittagong (HQ), Dhaka, Khulna, Kaptai

FRIGATES 4

1 *Osman* (PRC *Jianghu* I) with 2 x 5 ASW mor, plus 2 x 2 CSS-N-2 *Hai Ying* 2 (*HY* 2) SSM, 2 x 2 100mm guns

1 *Umar Farooq* (UK *Salisbury*) with 1 x 3 *Squid* ASW mor, 1 x 2 115mm guns

2 *Abu Bakr* (UK *Leopard*) with 2 x 2 115mm guns

PATROL AND COASTAL COMBATANTS 41

MISSILE CRAFT 10

5 *Durdarsha* (PRC *Huangfeng*) with 4 *HY* 2 SSM

5 *Durbar* (PRC *Hegu*) PFM< with 2 *SY*-1 SSM

TORPEDO CRAFT 4 PRC *Huchuan* PFT< with 2 533mm TT

PATROL, OFFSHORE 1 *Madhumati* (J *Sea Dragon*) with 1 x 76mm gun

PATROL, COASTAL 3

1 *Durjoy* (PRC *Hainan*) with 4 x 5 ASW RL

2 *Meghna* fishery protection

PATROL, INSHORE 18

8 *Shahead Daulat* (PRC *Shanghai* II) PFI, 2 *Karnaphuli*, 1 *Bishkali* PCI, 1 *Bakarat* PCI, 4 Type 123K PFT, 2 *Akshay* PCI

PATROL, RIVERINE 5 *Pabna*<

MINE COUNTERMEASURES 4

3 *Shapla* (UK *River*) MSI, 1 *Sagar* MSO

AMPHIBIOUS 14

7 LCU, 4 LCM, 3 LCVP

SUPPORT AND MISCELLANEOUS 8

1 coastal tkr, 1 repair, 1 ocean tug, 1 coastal tug, 2 *Yuch'in* AGHS, 1 *Shaibal* AGOR (UK *River*) (MCM capable), 1 *Shaheed Ruhul Amin* (trg)

Air Force† 9,500

49 cbt ac, no armed hel **Flying hours** 100–120
   FGA/FTR 4 sqn with 12 A-5, 11 F-6, 14 F-7M, 4 FT-7B
   TPT 3 An-32
   HEL 3 sqn with 11 Bell 212, 7 Mi-8, 11 Mi-17
   TRG 46 PT-6, 12 T-37B, 8 CM-170, 8* L-39ZA, 2 Bell 206L
   AAM AA-2 *Atoll*

Forces Abroad

UN AND PEACEKEEPING

ANGOLA (UNOMA): 4 incl 3 obs. **CROATIA** (UNMOP): 1 obs. **FYROM** (UNPREDEP): 2 obs. **GEORGIA** (UNOMIG): 9 obs. **IRAQ/KUWAIT** (UNIKOM): 807 incl 5 obs. **TAJIKISTAN** (UNMOT): 3 obs. **WESTERN SAHARA** (MINURSO): 6 obs

Paramilitary 49,700

BANGLADESH RIFLES 30,000

border guard; 41 bn

ARMED POLICE 5,000

rapid action force (forming)

ANSARS (Security Guards) 14,500 in bn
A further 180,000 unembodied

COAST GUARD 200

(HQ Chittagong and Khulma)
1 *Bishkhali* PCI
(force in its infancy and expected to expand)

India

	1996	1997	1998	1999
GDP	Rs12.8tr	Rs14.0tr		
	($360bn)	($385bn)		
per capita	$1,500	$1,600		
Growth	6.8%	5.0%		
Inflation	8.9%	7.2%		
Debt	$90bn	$114bn		
Def exp[a]	Rs419bn	Rs443bn		
	($11.8bn)	($12.2bn)		
Def bdgt			Rs412bn	
			($9.9bn)	
FMA[b] (US)	$0.4m	$0.4m	$0.5m	$0.5m
(Aus)	$0.3m	$0.2m	$0.2m	$0.2m
$1 = rupee	35.4	36.3	41.8	

[a] Incl exp on paramil org

[b] UNMOGIP **1996** $7m **1997** $7m

Population	983,436,000		
(Hindu 80%, Muslim 14%, Christian 2%, Sikh 2%)			
Age	13–17	18–22	23–32
Men	52,158,000	47,927,000	84,141,000
Women	48,713,000	44,310,000	76,812,000

Total Armed Forces

ACTIVE 1,175,000 (incl 200 women)

RESERVES 528,400

Army 300,000 (first-line reserves within 5 years' full-time service, a further 500,000 have commitment until age 50) **Territorial Army** (volunteers) 33,400 **Air Force** 140,000 **Navy** 55,000

Army 980,000

HQ: 5 Regional Comd, 4 Fd Army, 11 Corps
3 armd div (each 2–3 armed, 1 SP arty (2 SP fd, 1 med regt) bde) • 4 RAPID div (each 2 inf, 1 mech bde) • 18 inf div (each 2–5 inf, 1 arty bde; some have armd regt) • 9 mtn div (each 3–4 bde, 1 or more arty regt) • 1 arty div (3 bde) • 15 indep bde: 7 armd, 5 inf, 2 mtn, 1 AB/cdo • 1 SSM regt (*Privthi*) • 4 AD bde (plus 14 cadre) • 3 engr bde
These formations comprise
   59 tk regt (bn) • 355 inf bn (incl 25 mech, 8 AB, 3 cdo) • 190 arty regt (bn) reported: incl 1 SSM, 2 MRL, 50 med (11 SP), 69 fd (3 SP), 39 mtn, 29 AD arty regt; perhaps 2 SAM gp (3–5 bty each) plus 15 SAM regt • 14 hel sqn: 6 atk, 8 air obs

EQUIPMENT

   MBT ε3,414 (ε1,100 in store): some 700 T-55, ε1,500 T-72/-M1, 1,200 *Vijayanta*, ε14 *Arjun*
   LT TK ε90 PT-76
   RECCE ε100 BRDM-2
   AIFV 350 BMP-1, 1,000 BMP-2 (*Sarath*)
   APC 157 OT-62/-64 (in store)
   TOWED ARTY 4,175 (perhaps 600 in store) incl:
   75mm: 900 75/24 mtn, 215 FRY M-48; **105mm**: some 1,300 IFG Mk I/II, 50 M-56; **122mm**: some 550 D-30; **130mm**: 750 M-46; **155mm**: 410 FH-77B
   SP ARTY 105mm: 80 *Abbot* (ε30 in store); **130mm**: 100 mod M-46 (ε70 in store)
   MRL 122mm: 150 incl BM-21, LRAR; **214mm**: *Pinacha* (being deployed)
   MOR 81mm: L16A1, E1; **120mm**: 500 Brandt AM-50, E1; **160mm**: 500 M-1943, 200 Tampella M-58 (150 in store)
   SSM *Prithvi* (3–5 launchers)
   ATGW *Milan*, AT-3 *Sagger*, AT-4 *Spigot* (some SP), AT-5 *Spandrel* (some SP)
   RCL 57mm: 500 M-18; **84mm**: *Carl Gustav*; **106mm**: 1,000+ M-40A1

AD GUNS some 2,400: **20mm:** Oerlikon (reported); **23mm:** 300 ZU 23-2, 100 ZSU-23-4 SP; **30mm:** 8 2S6 SP (reported); **40mm:** 1,200 L40/60, 800 L40/70

SAM 180 SA-6, 620 SA-7, 50 SA-8B, 400 SA-9, 45 SA-3, SA-13, 500 SA-16

SURV MUFAR, *Green Archer* (mor)

HEL 199 *Chetak, Cheetah*

LC 2 LCVP

RESERVES

Territorial Army 25 inf bn, plus 29 'departmental' units

DEPLOYMENT

North 2 Corps with 8 inf, 2 mtn div **West** 3 Corps with 1 armd, 5 inf div, 3 RAPID **Central** 1 Corps with 1 armd, 1 inf, 1 RAPID **East** 3 Corps with 1 inf, 7 mtn div **South** 2 Corps with 1 armd, 3 inf div

Navy 55,000

(incl 7,000 Naval Aviation and ε1,200 Marines, ε2,000 women)

PRINCIPAL COMMAND Western, Eastern, Southern, Far Eastern

SUB-COMMAND Submarine, Naval Air

BASES Mumbai (Bombay) (HQ Western Comd), Goa (HQ Naval Air), Karwar (under construction), Kochi (Cochin) (HQ Southern Comd), Visakhapatnam (HQ Eastern and submarines), Calcutta, Madras, Port Blair (Andaman Is) (HQ Far Eastern Comd), Arakonam (Naval Air)

FLEETS Western base Bombay **Eastern base** Visakhapatnam

SUBMARINES 19

8 *Sindhughosh* (Sov *Kilo*) with 533mm TT

4 *Shishumar* (Ge T-209/1500) with 533mm TT

7 *Kursura* (Sov *Foxtrot*)† with 533mm TT (inc 2 in refit)

PRINCIPAL SURFACE COMBATANTS 25

CARRIERS 1 *Viraat* (UK *Hermes*) (29,000t) CVV Air group typically **ac** 12 *Sea Harrier* ftr/attack **hel** 7 *Sea King* ASW/ASUW (*Sea Eagle* ASM)

DESTROYERS 6

5 *Rajput* (Sov *Kashin*) with 2 x 2 SA-N-1 *Goa* SAM; plus 4 SS-N-2C *Styx* SSM, 5 533mm TT, 2 ASW RL, 1 Ka-25 or 28 hel (ASW)

1 *Delhi* with 16 SS-N-25 SSM, 2 x SA-N-7 SAM, 1 100mm gun, 5 533mm TT, 2 hel

FRIGATES 18

3 *Godavari* FFH with 1 *Sea King* hel, 2 x 3 324mm ASTT; plus 4 SS-N-2C *Styx* SSM and 1 x 2 SA-N-4 SAM

5 *Nilgiri* (UK *Leander*) with 2 x 3 ASTT, 4 with 1 x 3 *Limbo* ASW mor, 1 *Chetak* hel, 2 with 1 *Sea King*, 1 x 2 ASW RL; plus 2 114mm guns (plus 1 in reserve)

1 *Krishna* (UK *Leander*) (trg role)

5 *Arnala* (Sov *Petya*) with 4 ASW RL, 3 533mm TT

4 *Khukri* (ASUW) with 2 or 4 SS-N-2C *Styx* SSM, hel deck

PATROL AND COASTAL COMBATANTS 49

CORVETTES 19

3 *Vijay Durg* (Sov *Nanuchka* II) with 4 SS-N-2B *Styx* SSM

6 *Veer* (Sov *Tarantul*) with 4 *Styx* SSM

6 *Vibhuti* (similar to *Tarantul*) with 4 *Styx* SSM

4 *Abhay* (Sov *Pauk* II) (ASW) with 4 ASTT, 2 ASW mor

MISSILE CRAFT 8 *Vidyut* (Sov *Osa* II) with 4 *Styx* (plus 6 *Osa* 1 reserve and 2 *Osa* 1 for special forces penetration)

PATROL, OFFSHORE 9 *Sukanya* PCO

PATROL, INSHORE 13

11 SDB Mk 2/3

2 *Super Dvora*

MINE WARFARE 20

MINELAYERS 0

none, but *Kamorta* FF and *Pondicherry* MSO have minelaying capability

MINE COUNTERMEASURES 20

12 *Pondicherry* (Sov *Natya*) MSO, 2 *Bulsar* (UK *Ham*) MSI, 6 *Mahé* (Sov *Yevgenya*) MSI<

AMPHIBIOUS 10

2 *Magar* LST, capacity 500 tps, 18 tk, 1 hel (plus 1 fitting out)

8 *Ghorpad* (Sov *Polnocny* C) LSM, capacity 140 tps, 6 tk

Plus craft: 7 *Vasco da Gama* LCU

SUPPORT AND MISCELLANEOUS 28

1 *Jyoti* AO, 5 small AO, 1 *Amba* (Sov *Ugra*) sub spt, 1 div spt , 2 ocean tugs, 6 *Sandhayak* and 4 *Makar* AGHS, 1 *Tir* trg, 1 *Sagardhwani* AGOR, 3 torpedo recovery vessels, 1 AH, 2 *Osa* 1 (special forces insertion)

NAVAL AVIATION (5,000)

67 cbt ac, 83 armed hel **Flying hours** some 180

ATTACK 2 sqn with 17 *Sea Harrier* FRS Mk-51, 2 T-60 trg

ASW 6 hel sqn with 26 *Chetak*, 7 Ka-25, 18 Ka-28, 32 *Sea King* Mk 42A/B

AEW 3 Ka-31

MR 3 sqn with 5 Il-38, 8 Tu-142M *Bear* F, 20 Do-228, 15 BN-2 *Defender*

COMMS 1 sqn with **ac** 5 BN-2 *Islander*, 10 Do-228 **hel** 3 *Chetak*

SAR 1 **hel** sqn with 6 *Sea King* Mk 42C

TRG 2 sqn with **ac** 6 HJT-16, 8 HPT-32 **hel** 2 *Chetak*, 4 Hughes 300

MISSILES

AAM R-550 *Magic* I and II

ASM Sea Eagle, Sea Skua

MARINES (1,200)

1 regt (3 gp)

Air Force 140,000

772 cbt ac, 32 armed hel. 5 Air Comd **Flying hours** 150
FGA 17 sqn
    3 with 53 MiG-23 BN/UM, 4 with 88 *Jaguar* S(I), 6
      with 147 MiG-27, 4 with 79 MiG-21 MF/PFMA
FTR 20 sqn
    4 with 66 MiG-21 FL/U, 10 with 169 MiG-21 bis/U,
      1 with 26 MiG-23 MF/UM, 3 with 64 MiG-29, 2
      with 35 *Mirage* 2000H/TH, 8 SU-30MK
ECM 4 *Canberra* B(I) 58 (ECM/target towing, plus 2
    Canberra TT-18 target towing)
ELINT 2 Boeing 707, 2 Boeing 737
AEW 4 HS-748
TANKER 6 IL-78
MARITIME ATTACK 6 *Jaguar* S(I) with *Sea Eagle*
ATTACK HEL 3 sqn with 32 Mi-25
RECCE 2 sqn
    1 with 8 *Canberra* (6 PR-57, 2 PR-67)
    1 with 6* MiG-25R, 2* MiG-25U
MR/SURVEY 2 *Gulfstream* IV SRA, 2 *Learjet* 29
TRANSPORT
    ac 12 sqn
      6 with 105 An-32 *Sutlej*, 2 with 45 Do-228, 2 with
      28 BAe-748, 2 with 25 Il-76 *Gajraj*
    hel 11 sqn with 73 Mi-8, 36 Mi-17, 10 Mi-26 (hy tpt)
VIP 1 HQ sqn with 2 Boeing 737-200, 7 BAe-748, 6 Mi-8
TRG ac 28 BAe-748 (trg/tpt), 120 *Kiran* I, 56 *Kiran* II,
    88 HPT-32, 38 *Hunter* (20 F-56, 18 T-66), 14* *Jaguar*
    B(1), 9* MiG-29UB, 44 TS-11 *Iskara* **hel** 20 *Chetak*, 2
    Mi-24, 2* Mi-35
MISSILES
    ASM AS-7 *Kerry*, AS-11B (ATGW), AS-12, AS-30, *Sea*
    Eagle, AM 39 *Exocet*, AS-17 *Krypton*
    AAM AA-7 *Apex*, AA-8 *Aphid*, AA-10 *Alamo*, AA-11
    Archer, R-550 *Magic*, *Super* 530D
    SAM 38 sqn with 280 *Divina* V75SM/VK (SA-2),
    Pechora (SA-3), SA-5, SA-10

Forces Abroad

UN AND PEACEKEEPING
ANGOLA (UNOMA): 151 incl 5 obs. **IRAQ/KUWAIT**
(UNIKOM): 5 obs. **SIERRA LEONE** (UNOMSIL): 6
obs. **WESTERN SAHARA** (MINURSO): 10 obs

Paramilitary 1,090,000 active

NATIONAL SECURITY GUARDS (Cabinet
Secretariat) 7,400
Anti-terrorism contingency deployment force,
comprising elements of the armed forces, CRPF and
Border Security Force

SPECIAL PROTECTION GROUP 3,000
Protection of VVIP
SPECIAL FRONTIER FORCE (Cabinet Secretariat)
9,000
mainly ethnic Tibetans
RASHTRIYA RIFLES (Ministry of Defence) 40,000
36 bn in 12 Sector HQ
DEFENCE SECURITY CORPS 31,000
provides security at Defence Ministry sites
INDO-TIBETAN BORDER POLICE (Ministry of Home
Affairs) 32,200
28 bn, Tibetan border security
ASSAM RIFLES (Ministry of Home Affairs) 52,500
7 HQ, 31 bn, security within north-eastern states,
mainly Army-officered; better trained than BSF
RAILWAY PROTECTION FORCES 70,000
CENTRAL INDUSTRIAL SECURITY FORCE
(Ministry of Home Affairs)[a] 88,600
guards public-sector locations
CENTRAL RESERVE POLICE FORCE (CRPF)
(Ministry of Home Affairs) 165,300
130–135 bn incl 10 rapid action, 2 *Mahila* (women);
internal security duties, only lightly armed,
deployable throughout the country
BORDER SECURITY FORCE (BSF) (Ministry of Home
Affairs) 185,000
some 150 bn, small arms, some lt arty, tpt/liaison air
spt
HOME GUARD (R) 472,000
authorised, actual str 416,000 in all states except
Arunachal Pradesh and Kerala; men on lists, no trg
STATE ARMED POLICE 400,000
For duty primarily in home state only, but can be
moved to other states, incl 24 bn India Reserve Police
(commando-trained)
CIVIL DEFENCE 394,000 (R)
in 135 towns in 32 states
COAST GUARD over 6,000
    PATROL CRAFT 35
    3 *Samar* OPV, 9 *Vikram* OPV, 21 *Jija Bai*, 2 SDB-2 plus
      17 boats
    AVIATION
    3 sqn with **ac** 17 Do-228, **hel** 15 *Chetak*

[a] Lightly armed security guards only

Foreign Forces

UN (UNMOGIP): 45 mil obs from 8 countries

Kazakstan

	1996	1997	1998	1999
GDP	t1.3tr	t1.7tr		
	($19bn)	($22bn)		
per capita	$3,300	$3,600		
Growth	1.1%	2.5%		
Inflation	39%	17%		
Debt	$3.9bn	$4.3bn		
Def exp[a]	t36bn	t38bn		
	($541m)	($503m)		
Def bdgt			t19.9bn	
			($259m)	
FMA[b] (US)	$0.4m	$0.4m	$0.6m	$0.6m
$1 = tenge	67.3	75.4	77.0	

[a] Incl exp on paramilitary forces
[b] Excl US Cooperative Threat Reduction Programme funds for nuclear dismantlement and demilitarisation. In 1992–96, $35m of $173m budget was spent. Programme continues through 1999

Population	15,900,000		

(Kazak 51%, Russian 32%, Ukrainian 5%, German 2%, Tatar 2%, Uzbek 2%)

Age	*13–17*	*18–22*	*23–32*
Men	875,000	786,000	1,316,000
Women	856,000	773,000	1,285,000

Total Armed Forces

ACTIVE ε55,100
Terms of service 31 months

Army ε40,000

2 Army Corps HQ • 1 TD • 2 MRD (1 trg) • 1 MR, 1 AB • 2 arty bde • 1 indep MRR • 2 arty regt
EQUIPMENT
  MBT 630 T-72 (plus some 300+ in store)
  RECCE 140 BRDM
  ACV 1,000 incl BMP-1/-2, BRM AIFV, BTR-70/-80, MT-LB APC (plus some 1,000 in store)
  TOWED ARTY 550: **122mm**: D-30; **152mm**: D-20, 2A65, 2A36
  SP ARTY 150: **122mm**: 2S1; **152mm**: 2S3
  MRL 170: **122mm**: BM-21; **220mm**: 9P140 *Uragan*
  MOR 130: **120mm**: 2B11, M-120
  SSM 10 SS-21
  ATK GUNS 100mm: 125 T-12
(In 1991, the former Soviet Union transferred some 2,680 T-64/-72s, 2,428 ACVs and 6,900 arty to storage bases in Kazakstan. This eqpt is under Kazak control, but has deteriorated considerably).

Navy ε100

BASES Aktau

PATROL AND COASTAL COMBATANTS 10
  5 *Guardian* PCI, 1 *Dauntless* PCI, 4 *Almaty* PCI, plus 2 boats

Air Force ε15,000

(incl Air Defence)
1 Air Force div, 123 cbt ac (plus some 75 in store)
Flying hours 25
FTR 1 regt with 12 MiG-29, 4 MiG-29UB, 12 MiG-23, 4 MiG-23UB
FGA 3 regt
  1 with 34 MiG-27, 9 MiG-23UB
  1 with 26 Su-24
  1 with 10 Su-27
RECCE 1 regt with 12 Su-24*
HEL 1 regt (tpt), 44 Mi-8
STORAGE some 75 MiG-27/MiG-23/MiG-23UB/ MiG-25/MiG-29/SU-27
AIR DEFENCE
1 regt, 32 cbt ac (plus 15 MiG-25 in store)
  FTR 1 regt with 32 MiG-31
  SAM 100 SA-2, SA-3, SA-5
MISSILES
  ASM AS-7 *Kerry*, AS-9 *Kyle*, S-10 *Karen*, AS-11 *Killer*
  AAM AA-6 Acrid, AA-7 *Apex*, AA Aphid

Forces Abroad

TAJIKISTAN ε350 1 border gd bn

Paramilitary 34,500

INTERNAL SECURITY TROOPS (Ministry of Interior) ε20,000

BORDER GUARDS (National Security Committee) ε12,000

PRESIDENTIAL GUARD 2,000

GOVERNMENT GUARD 500

Kyrgyzstan

	1996	1997	1998	1999
GDP	s22bn	s30bn		
	($1.6bn)	($1.8bn)		
per capita	$1,800	$2,000		
Growth	5.6%	12.0%		
Inflation	37.0%	25.6%		
Debt	$789m	$934m		
Def exp[a]	s625m	s775m		
	($49m)	($45m)		
Def bdgt			s573m	
			($31m)	
FMA (US)	$0.2m	$0.3m	$0.3m	$0.3m
$1 = som	12.8	17.4	18.3	

a Incl exp on paramilitary forces

Population	4,550,000		
(Kyrgyz 56%, Russian 17%, Uzbek 13%, Ukrainian 3%)			
Age	13–17	18–22	23–32
Men	270,000	228,000	351,000
Women	266,000	225,000	346,000

Total Armed Forces

ACTIVE 12,200 (incl 11,000 conscripts)

Terms of service 18 months

RESERVES 57,000

Army 9,800

1 MRD (3 MR, 1 tk, 1 arty, 1 AA regt)
1 indep MR bde (mtn)
EQUIPMENT
  MBT 210 T-72
  RECCE 34 BRDM-2
  AIFV 98 BMP-1, 101 BMP-2, 20 BRM-1K
  APC 45 BTR-70
  TOWED ARTY 161: **100mm**: 18 M-1944 (BS-3);
    122mm: 72 D-30, 37 M-30; **152mm**: 34 D-1
  COMBINED GUN/MOR 120mm: 12 2S9
  MOR 120mm: 6 2S12, 48 M-120
  ATGW 26 AT-3 *Sagger*
  AD GUNS 57mm: 24 S-60
  SAM SA-7

Air Force 2,400

ac and hel assets inherited from Sov Air Force trg school;
Kgz failed to maintain pilot trg for foreign students
AC 67 L-39, plus 53 decommissioned MiG-21/MiG-
  21UB
HEL 15 Mi-24, 28 Mi-8, 2 Mi-17, 2 Mi-25/35
AIR DEFENCE
  SAM SA-2, SA-3, SA-7

Forces Abroad

TAJIKISTAN ε300 incl Army and Border Guards

Paramilitary ε5,000

BORDER GUARDS ε5,000

Nepal

	1996	1997	1998	1999
GDP	NR250bn	NR273bn		
	($4.4bn)	($4.7bn)		
per capita	$1,300	$1,400		
Growth	6.1%	4.5%		
Inflation	9.4%	7.5%		
Debt	$2.4bn	$2.5bn		
Def exp	NR2.2bn	NR2.4bn		
	($38m)	($42m)		
Def bdgt			εNR2.6bn	
			($41.0m)	
FMA (US)	$0.1m	$0.2m	$0.2m	$0.2m
$1 = rupee	56.7	58.0	63.4	
Population	23,053,000			
(Hindu 90%, Buddhist 5%, Muslim 3%)				
Age	13–17	18–22	23–32	
Men	1,387,000	1,144,000	1,734,000	
Women	1,307,000	1,063,000	1,590,000	

Total Armed Forces

ACTIVE 46,000 (to be 50,000)

Army 46,000

1 Royal Guard bde (incl 1 MP bn) • 7 inf bde (16 inf
bn) • 44 indep inf coy • 1 SF bde (incl 1 AB bn, 2 indep
SF coy, 1 cav sqn (*Ferret*)) • 1 arty bde (1 arty, 1 AD
regt) • 1 engr bde (4 bn)
EQUIPMENT
  RECCE 40 *Ferret*
  TOWED ARTY† **75mm**: 6 pack; **94mm**: 5 3.7in mtn
    (trg); **105mm**: 14 pack (ε6 op)
  MOR 81mm; 120mm: 70 M-43 (ε12 op)
  AD GUNS 14.5mm: 30 PRC Type 56; **37mm**: PRC
    40mm: 2 L/60

AIR WING (215)
no cbt ac, or armed hel
TPT ac 1 BAe-748, 2 *Skyvan* **hel** 2 SA-316B *Chetak*, 1
  SA-316B, 1 AS-332L (*Puma*), 2 AS-332L-1 (*Super
  Puma*), 1 Bell 206, 2 Bell 206L, 1 AS-350 (*Ecureuil*)

Forces Abroad

UN AND PEACEKEEPING
CROATIA (UNMOP): 1 obs. **FYROM** (UNPREDEP): 1
Obs. **LEBANON** (UNIFIL) 601: 1 inf bn. **TAJIKISTAN**
(UNMOT): 5 obs.

Paramilitary 40,000

POLICE FORCE 40,000

Pakistan

	1996	1997	1998	1999
GDP	Rs2.2tr	Rs2.5tr		
	($60bn)	($61bn)		
per capita	$2,300	$2,400		
Growth	4.1%	3.4%		
Inflation	10.4%	11.4%		
Debt	$29.9bn	$28.6bn		
Def exp	Rs129bn	Rs139bn		
	($3.6bn)	($3.4bn)		
Def bdgt			Rs143bn	
			($3.2bn)	
FMA[a] (US)	$2.5m	$2.5m	$1.5m	$2.9m
(Aus)	$0.02m	$0.02m	$0.02m	$0.02m
$1 = rupee	36.1	41.1	44.5	

[a] UNMOGIP **1996** $7m **1997** $7m

Population	140,689,000 (less than 3% Hindu)		
Age	*13–17*	*18–22*	*23–32*
Men	8,286,000	7,133,000	11,516,000
Women	7,765,000	6,429,000	10,234,000

Total Armed Forces

ACTIVE 587,000

RESERVES 513,000

Army ε500,000; obligation to age 45 (men) or 50 (officers), active liability for 8 years after service **Navy** 5,000 **Air Force** 8,000

Army 520,000

9 Corps HQ • 2 armd div • 9 Corps arty bde • 19 inf div • 7 engr bde • 1 area comd (div) • 3 armd recce regt • 7 indep armd bde • 1 SF gp (3 bn) • 9 indep inf bde • 1 AD comd (3 AD gp: 8 bde)
AVN 17 sqn
  7 ac, 8 hel, 1 VIP, 1 obs flt
EQUIPMENT
  MBT 2,120+: 15 M-47, 345 M-48A5, 50 T-54/-55, 1,200 PRC Type-59, 250 PRC Type-69, 200+ PRC Type-85, ε100 T-80UD
  APC 850 M-113
  TOWED ARTY 1,590: **85mm**: 200 PRC Type-56; **105mm**: 300 M-101, 50 M-56 pack; **122mm**: 200 PRC Type-60, 400 PRC Type-54; **130mm**: 200 PRC Type-59-1; **155mm**: 30 M-59, 60 M-114, 124 M-198; **203mm**: 26 M-115
  SP ARTY 240: **105mm**: 50 M-7; **155mm**: 150 M-109A2; **203mm**: 40 M-110A2
  MRL 122mm: 45 *Azar* (PRC Type-83)
  MOR 81mm: 500; **120mm**: 225 AM-50, M-61
  SSM 18 *Hatf* 1, *Hatf* 2 (under development)
  ATGW 800 incl: *Cobra*, 200 TOW (incl 24 on M-901 SP), *Green Arrow* (PRC *Red Arrow*)

RL 89mm: M-20 3.5in
RCL 75mm: Type-52; **106mm**: M-40A1
AD GUNS 2,000+ incl: **14.5mm; 35mm**: 200 GDF-002; **37mm**: PRC Type-55/-65; **40mm**: M1, 100 L/60; **57mm**: PRC Type-59
SAM 350 *Stinger, Redeye,* RBS-70, 500 *Anza* Mk-1/-2
SURV RASIT (veh, arty), AN/TPQ-36 (arty, mor)
AIRCRAFT
  SURVEY 1 *Commander* 840
  LIAISON 1 Cessna 421, 2 *Commander* 690, 80 *Mashshaq*, 1 F-27
  OBS 40 O-1E, 50 *Mashshaq*
HELICOPTERS
  ATTACK 20 AH-1F (TOW)
  TPT 12 Bell 47G, 7 -205, 10 -206B, 16 Mi-8, 6 IAR/SA-315B, 23 IAR/SA-316, 35 SA-330, 5 UH-1H

Navy 22,000

(incl Naval Air, ε1,200 Marines and ε2,000 Maritime Security Agency (see *Paramilitary*))
BASE Karachi (Fleet HQ)
SUBMARINES 9
  2 *Hashmat* (Fr *Agosta*) with 533mm TT (F-17 HWT), *Harpoon* USGW
  4 *Hangor* (Fr *Daphné*) with 533mm TT (L-5 HWT), *Harpoon* USGW
  3 MG110 SSI SF *Midget* submarines
PRINCIPAL SURFACE COMBATANTS 10
DESTROYERS 2 *Alamgir* (US *Gearing*) (ASW) with 1 x 8 ASROC; plus 2 x 3 ASTT, 2 x 2 127mm guns, 3 x 2 *Harpoon* SSM and hel deck (1 trg)
FRIGATES 8
  6 *Tariq* (UK *Amazon*) with 4 x *Harpoon* SSM (in 3 of class), 1 x LY-60N SAM (in 3 of class), 2 x 3 324mm ASTT (in 2 of class); 1 114mm gun (2 *Lynx* hel delivered)
  2 *Shamsher* (UK *Leander*) with SA-319B hel, 1 x 3 ASW mor, plus 2 114mm guns
PATROL AND COASTAL COMBATANTS 10
MISSILE CRAFT 5
  4 PRC *Huangfeng* with 4 HY 2 SSM
  1 x *Jalat* II with 4 C-802 SSM
PATROL, COASTAL 1 *Larkana* PCO
PATROL, INSHORE 4
  2 *Quetta* (PRC *Shanghai*) PFI
  1 *Rajshahi* PCI
  1 *Larkana* PCI
MINE COUNTERMEASURES 2
  2 *Munsif* (Fr *Eridan*) MHC
SUPPORT AND MISCELLANEOUS 9
  1 *Behr Paima* (survey), 2 *Gwadar* AOT, 1 *Attack* AOT, 1 *Nasr* AO, 1 *Moawin* AOR, 3 tugs

NAVAL AIR
7 cbt ac, 12 armed hel

ASW/MR 1 sqn with 4 *Atlantic* plus 3 in store, 3 P-3C (operated by Air Force)
ASW/SAR 2 hel sqn with 4 SA-319B (ASW), 6 *Sea King* Mk 45 (ASW), 2 *Lynx* HAS Mk-3 (ASW)
COMMS 3 Fokker F-27 **ac** (Air Force)
ASM *Exocet* AM 39

MARINES (ε1,200)

1 cdo/SF gp

Air Force 45,000

410 cbt ac, no armed hel **Flying hours** some 210
FGA 7 sqn
  1 with 18 *Mirage* (15 IIIEP (some with AM-39 ASM), 3 IIIDP (trg))
  3 (1 OCU) with 56 *Mirage* 5 (54 -5PA/PA2, 2-5DPA/DPA2)
  3 with 49 Q-5 (A-5 *Fantan*)
FTR 10 sqn
  4 with 88 J-6/JJ-6, (F-6/FT-6), 3 (1 OCU) with 32 F-16A/B, 2 (1 OCU) with 78 J-7 (F-7P), 1 with 30 *Mirage* 1110
RECCE 1 sqn with 12* *Mirage* IIIRP
ASW/MR 1 sqn with 4* *Atlantic*, 3* P-3C
SAR 1 hel sqn with 6 SA-319
TPT ac 12 C-130 (5 -B, 7 -E), 1 L-100, 2 Boeing 707, 3 Boeing 737, 3 *Falcon* 20, 2 F-27-200 (1 with Navy), 2 Beech (1 *Travel Air*, 1 *Baron*), 1-Y12 **hel** 1 sqn with 12 SA-316, 4 SA-321, 12 SA-315B *Lama*
TRG 12 CJ-6A (PT-6A), 30 JJ-5 (FT-5), 40* MFI-17B *Mashshaq*, 6 MiG-15UTI, 10 T-33A, 44 T-37B/C, 18 K-8
AD 7 SAM bty
  6 each with 24 *Crotale*, 1 with 6 CSA-1 (SA-2)
MISSILES
  ASM AM-39 *Exocet*, AGM-65 *Maverick*
  AAM AIM-7 *Sparrow*, AIM-9 *Sidewinder*, R-530, R-550 *Magic*

Forces Abroad

UN AND PEACEKEEPING

ANGOLA (UNOMA): 6 incl 5 obs. **CROATIA** (UNMOP): 1 obs. **FYROM** (UNPREDEP): 2 obs. **GEORGIA** (UNOMIG): 6 obs. **IRAQ/KUWAIT** (UNIKOM): 6 obs. **WESTERN SAHARA** (MINURSO): 64 incl 5 obs

Paramilitary ε247,000 active

NATIONAL GUARD 185,000

incl *Janbaz* Force, *Mujahid* Force, National Cadet Corps, Women Guards

FRONTIER CORPS (Ministry of Interior) 35,000

11 regt (40 bn), 1 indep armd car sqn; 45 UR-416 APC

PAKISTAN RANGERS (Ministry of Interior) ε25,000

MARITIME SECURITY AGENCY ε2,000

1 *Alamgir* (US *Gearing* DD) (no ASROC or TT), 4 *Barakat* PCC, 4 (PRC *Shanghai*) PFI

COAST GUARD

some 23 PFI, plus boats

Foreign Forces

UN (UNMOGIP): 43 mil obs from 8 countries

Sri Lanka

	1996	1997	1998	1999
GDP	Rs769bn	Rs891bn		
	($13.7bn)	($14.8bn)		
per capita	$3,500	$3,800		
Growth	3.8%	6.0%		
Inflation	15.9%	9.6%		
Debt	$8.0bn	$9.2bn		
Def exp	Rs48bn	Rs53bn		
	($868m)	($898m)		
Def bdgt			Rs47bn	
			($725m)	
FMA (US)	$0.2m	$0.2m	$0.2m	$0.2m
$1 = rupee	55.3	59.0	64.8	
Population	18,653,000			

(Sinhalese 74%, Tamil 18%, Moor 7%, Buddhist 69%, Hindu 15%, Christian 8%, Muslim 8%)

	13–17	18–22	23–32
Age			
Men	928,000	886,000	1,566,000
Women	891,000	853,000	1,540,000

Total Armed Forces

ACTIVE some 110–115,000
(incl recalled reservists)

RESERVES 4,200
Army 1,100 **Navy** 1,100 **Air Force** 2,000
Obligation 7 years, post regular service

Army ε90–95,000

(incl 42,000 recalled reservists; ε1,000 women)
8 div HQ • 1 mech inf bde • 1 air mobile bde • 23 inf bde • 1 indep SF bde (1 cdo, 1 SF regt) • 1 armd regt • 3 armd recce regt (bn) • 4 fd arty (1 reserve) • 4 fd engr regt (1 reserve)
EQUIPMENT
  MBT ε25 T-55 (perhaps 18 op)
  RECCE 26 *Saladin*, 15 *Ferret*, 12 Daimler *Dingo*
  AIFV 16 BMP (12 -1, 4 -2) (trg)
  APC 35 PRC Type-85, 10 BTR-152, 31 *Buffel*, 30 *Unicorn*, 8 *Shorland*, 9 *Hotspur*, 30 *Saracen*

TOWED ARTY 76mm: 14 FRY M-48; 85mm: 12
PRC Type-56; 88mm: 12 25-pdr; 130mm: 12 PRC
Type-59-1
MRL 107mm: 1
MOR 81mm: 276; 82mm: 19; 107mm: 12; 120mm: 36
M-43
RCL 105mm: 15 M-65; 106mm: 34 M-40
AD GUNS 40mm: 7 L-40; 94mm: 3 3.7in
SURV AN/TPQ-36 (arty)
UAV 1 *Seeker*

Navy 10,000

(incl 1,100 recalled reservists)
BASES Colombo (HQ), Trincomalee (main base),
Karainagar, Tangalle, Kalpitiya, Galle, Welisara
PATROL AND COASTAL COMBATANTS 54
PATROL, COASTAL 1 *Jayesagara* PCC
PATROL, INSHORE 53
3 *Sooraya*, 2 *Rana* (PRC MOD *Shanghai* II) PFI
1 *Parakrambahu* (PRC *Houxin*) PFC
3 Il *Dvora* PFI<
8 Il *Super Dvora* PFI<
3 ROK *Killer* PFI<
6 *Trinity Marine* PCF
2 *Shaldag* PCF
4 *Colombo* PCF
1 *Ranarisi* PFI
22 PCI<
some 36 boats
AMPHIBIOUS 8
1 *Wuhu* LSM, 2 LCM, 2 fast personnel carrier, 2
LCU, 1 ACV

Air Force 10,000

22 cbt ac, 15 armed hel **Flying hours** 420
FGA 4 F-7M, 1 FT-7, 2 FT-5, 4 *Kfir*-C2, 1 *Kfir*-TC2
ARM AC 8 SF-260TP, 2 FMA IA58A *Pucara*
ATTACK HEL 11 Bell 212, 2 Mi-24V, 2 Mi-35
TPT 1 sqn with ac 3 BAe 748, 1 Cessna 421C, 1 *Super
King Air*, 1 Y-8, 7 Y-12, 4 An-24, 4 An-32B, 1 Cessna
150 hel 3 Bell 412 (VIP)
HEL 9 Bell 206, 5 Mi-17 (plus 6 in store)
TRG incl 4 DHC-1, 4 SF-260 W, 3 Bell 206
RESERVES Air Force Regt, 3 sqn; Airfield
Construction, 1 sqn
UAV 1 *Superhawk*

Paramilitary ε110,200

POLICE FORCE (Ministry of Defence) 80,000
incl reserves, 1,000 women and Special Task Force:
3,000-strong anti-guerrilla unit
NATIONAL GUARD ε15,000
HOME GUARD 15,200

Opposition

LIBERATION TIGERS OF TAMIL EELAM (LTTE)
ε6,000
Leader Velupillai Prabhakaran

Tajikistan

	1996	1997	1998	1999
GDP*a*	Tr309bn	Tr443bn		
	($1.1bn)	($1.1bn)		
per capita	$800	$900		
Growth	-4.4%	1.7%		
Inflation	418%	164%		
Debt	$868m	$893m		
Def exp*a*	ε$115m	ε$132m		
Def bdgt*a*			ε$109m	
$1 = rouble	295	600	700	

a UNMOT **1996** $7m **1997** $8m

Population	6,150,000		
(Tajik 67%, Uzbek 25%, Russian 2%, Tatar 2%)			
Age	*13–17*	*18–22*	*23–32*
Men	389,000	309,000	459,000
Women	378,000	301,000	452,000

Total Armed Forces

ACTIVE some 7–9,000
Terms of service 24 months
A number of potential officers are being trained at the
Higher Army Officers and Engineers College, Dushanbe.
It is planned to form an Air Force sqn and to acquire Su-25
from Belarus, 5 Mi-24 and 10 Mi-8 have been procured.

Army some 7,000

2 MR bde (incl 1 trg), 1 mtn bde
1 SF bde, 1 SF det (εbn+)
1 SAM regt

EQUIPMENT
MBT 40 T-72
AIFV 85 BMP-1/-2
APC 40 BTR-60/-70/-80
TOWED ARTY 122mm: 12 D-30
MOR 122mm: 12
SAM 20 SA-2/-3

Paramilitary ε1,200

BORDER GUARDS (Ministry of Interior) ε1,200

Opposition

ISLAMIC MOVEMENT OF TAJIKISTAN some 5,000
Signed peace accord with government on 27 June
1997. Integration with govt forces slowly proceeding.

Foreign Forces

UN (UNMOT): 71 mil obs from 14 countries
RUSSIA Frontier Forces ε14,500 (Tajik conscripts,
Russian officers) **Army** 8,200; 1 MRD
  EQUIPMENT
    MBT 190 T-72
    AIFV/APC 313 BMP-2, BRM-1K, BTR-80
    SP ARTY 122mm: 66 2S1; **152mm**: 54 2S3
    MRL 122mm: 12 BM-21; **220mm**: 12 9P140
    MOR 120mm: 36 PM-38
  AIR DEFENCE
    SAM 20 SA-8
KAZAKSTAN ε350: 1 border gd bn
KYRGYZSTAN ε300 incl Army and Border Guard
UZBEKISTAN 1 MR bn plus border gd

Turkmenistan

	1996	1997	1998	1999
GDP	ε$4.9bn	ε$3.9bn		
per capita	$2,400	$1,800		
Growth	ε7.7%	ε-25.9%		
Inflation	ε992%	ε84%		
Debt	$825m	$1,248m		
Def exp	ε$138m	ε$107m		
Def bdgt			$139m	
FMA (US)	$0.2m	$0.3m	$0.3m	$0.3m
$1 = manat	3,978	5,400	5,400	
Population		4,600,000		

(Turkmen 77%, Uzbek 9%, Russian 7%, Kazak 2%)

Age	*13–17*	*18–22*	*23–32*	
Men	250,000	210,000	339,000	
Women	245,000	207,000	334,000	

Total Armed Forces

ACTIVE 17–19,000
Terms of service 24 months

Army 14–16,000

4 MRD (1 trg) • 1 arty bde • 1 MRL regt • 1 ATK regt
• 1 SSM bde • 1 engr bde • 2 SAM bde • 1 indep air
aslt bn
EQUIPMENT
  MBT 570 T-72
  RECCE 14 BRDM-2

AIFV 156 BMP-1, 405 BMP-2, 51 BRM
APC 728 BTR (-60/-70/-80)
TOWED ARTY 122mm: 197 D-30; **152mm**: 76 D-1,
  72 2A65
SP ARTY 152mm: 16 2S3
COMBINED GUN/MOR 120mm: 12 2S9
MRL 122mm: 60 BM-21; **220mm**: 54 9P140
MOR 82mm: 31; **120mm**: 42 PM-38
SSM 12 *Scud*
ATGW AT-2 *Swatter*, AT-3 *Sagger*, AT-4 *Spigot*, AT-5
  Spandrel
ATK GUNS 85mm: 6 D-44; **100mm**: 48 MT-12
AD GUNS 23mm: 28 ZSU-23-4 SP; **57mm**: 22 S-60
SAM 27 SA-4

Navy none

Has announced intention to form a Navy/Coast Guard.
Caspian Sea Flotilla (see **Russia**) is operating as a joint RF,
Kaz and Tkm flotilla under RF comd based at Astrakhan.

Air Force 3,000

(incl Air Defence)
171 cbt ac (plus 218 in store)
FGA/FTR 1 composite regt with 22 MiG-29, 2 MiG-
  29U, 65 Su-17
TRG 1 unit with 3 Su-7B, 3 MiG-21, 2 L-39, 8 Yak-28, 3
  An-12
TPT/GENERAL PURPOSE 1 composite sqn with 1
  An-24, 10 Mi-24, 10 Mi-8
AIR DEFENCE
  FTR 2 regt with 48 MiG-23, 10 MiG-23U 24 MiG-25
  SAM 50 SA-2/-3/-5
  IN STORE 172 MiG-23, 46 Su-25

Uzbekistan

	1996	1997	1998	1999
GDP	s560bn	s850bn		
	($11.0bn)	($11.5bn)		
per capita	$2,400	$2,500		
Growth	1.6%	2.4%		
Inflation	64%	45%		
Debt	$2.3bn	$2.6bn		
Def exp[a]	ε$432m	ε$447m		
Def bdgt			ε$109m	
FMA (US)	$0.3m	$0.3m	$0.4m	$0.5m
$1 = som	44.0	73.8	82.9	

[a] Incl exp on paramilitary forces

Population		23,300,000		

(Uzbek 73%, Russian 6%, Tajik 5%, Kazak 4%, Kara-
kalpak 2%, Tatar 2%, Korean <1%, Ukrainian <1%)

Age	*13–17*	*18–22*	*23–32*	
Men	1,415,000	1,179,000	1,837,000	
Women	1,388,000	1,164,000	1,839,000	

Total Armed Forces

ACTIVE ε80,000 (to be 100,000)
(incl MoD staff and centrally controlled units)
Terms of service conscription, 18 months

Army 50,000

3 Corps HQ • 2 tk, 4 MR, 1 lt mtn, 1 mot bde • 2 air
aslt, 1 air-mobile, 1 *Spetsnaz* bde • 4 arty, 1 MRL bde •
1 National Guard bde
EQUIPMENT
  MBT 370 incl T-54, T-62, T-64 plus some T-72
  RECCE 35 BRDM-2
  AIFV 273 BMP-2, 130 BMD-1
  APC 36 BTR-70, 290 BTR-80, 145 BTR-D
  TOWED ARTY 122mm: 90 D-30; **152mm:** 28 D-1, 49
    D-20, 32 2A36
  SP ARTY 122mm: 18 2S1; **152mm:** 17 2S3, 2S5
    (reported); **203mm:** 48 2S7
  COMBINED GUN/MOR 120mm: 69 2S9
  MRL 122mm: 33 BM-21; **220mm:** 48 9P140
  MOR 120mm: 18 PM-120, 19 2S12, 5 2B11
  ATK GUNS 100mm: 39 MT-12
(In 1991 the former Soviet Union transferred some 2,000 tanks
(T-64), 1,200 ACV and 750 arty to storage bases in Uzbekistan.
This eqpt is under Uzbek control, but has deteriorated
considerably.)

Air Force some 4,000

108 cbt ac, 43 attack hel
FGA 30 Su-17/Su-17UB, 4 Su-24
FTR 32 MiG-29/MiG-29UB, 32 Su-27/Su-27UB
RECCE 10* Su-24
TPT 30 An-2, plus 20 light tpt ac
TRG 15 L-39
HELICOPTERS
  ATTACK 43 Mi-24
  ASLT 43 Mi-8T
  TPT 23 Mi-6, 1 Mi-26
  RECCE 6 Mi-24K, 2 Mi-24 R
SAM 45 SA-2/-3/-5

Forces Abroad

TAJIKISTAN 1 MR bn plus border gd

Paramilitary ε18-20,000

INTERNAL SECURITY TROOPS (Ministry of Interior)
ε17–19,000

NATIONAL GUARD (Ministry of Defence) 1,000
1 bde

MILITARY DEVELOPMENTS

Regional Trends

Armed conflict in the region is at a relatively low level, but other kinds of upheavals pose challenges for the military. There has been cathartic political change with the fall of President Suharto in **Indonesia**. Natural disasters costing thousands of lives – floods in **China** and **South Korea** and the tidal wave in **Papua New Guinea** – placed more demands on armed forces and caused far more casualties than any armed conflict in the region. The economic crisis sweeping across East Asia forced some countries to cancel or postpone major weapons programmes, particularly in South-east Asia.

China

China continues to improve its military capabilities, but it will be some years before a significant advance is seen. The focus remains on enhancing the operational standards of field formations in all branches of the services as well as on technological advance. The People's Liberation Army (PLA) continues to be restructured, with a stated goal of cutting active military personnel by some 500,000 to around 2.3m. There has been renewed government effort to induce the PLA to divest its non-military businesses, not only to prevent revenue escaping government control and crack down on corruption, but also to ensure that military resources are concentrated on military tasks so that professional standards improve. However, business activities probably detract less from military efficiency than the widespread use of the PLA by regional governments on public works. The importance of the military to the maintenance and development of the national infrastructure is demonstrated in the government's own statements, which record that over the past decade the armed forces have, for example, built 200,000kms of irrigation channels, dams and dikes; laid 20,000kms of optical cable and developed 40 civil and military airfields. Civil emergency tasks arising from the widespread flooding have placed additional demands on the PLA in 1998. The diversion of the military to supporting the infrastructure and maintaining internal security has led to there being few military resources fully trained and capable for modern military operations. China's ability to project significant conventional forces beyond its borders remains limited. However, the government's July 1998 paper on National Defence, when referring to **Taiwan**, does not rule out the use of force to 'achieve the reunification of the country'. China does not have the resources to carry out an opposed landing, on Taiwan or anywhere else, but it could cause serious disruption to shipping and economic activity and possibly capture one or more of the smaller islands near the mainland. Its capabilities could advance significantly over the next ten years, however, as a result of its vigorous acquisition of technology from abroad.

Taiwan has continued to strengthen its military capabilities in 1998 with, in particular, the acquisition of F-16 and *Mirage* 2000-5 combat aircraft, frigates and destroyers and *Patriot* air defence systems.

North Asia

Japan's military capabilities are essentially unchanged from 1997. The planned reform of its equipment procurement system to contain costs has become even more important with the falling value of the yen. The redeployment of US forces from bases in Okinawa continues, although this call on public funds is unwelcome in the current economic climate. The military situation in **North Korea** is also little changed. While economic difficulties must detract from military efficiency, there appears little sign of a reduction in the forces deployed near the border with

South Korea. Some estimates suggest that 65% of North Korea's armed forces, including up to 80% of its artillery and missile capability, are within 60 miles of the southern border. Seoul is within range of medium artillery. Pyongyang appears determined to press ahead with its ballistic missile programmes which are an important means of earning badly-needed hard currency. Its missile technology exports contribute to rising tension in South Asia and the Gulf region, particularly the export of *Nodong* missile technology to Pakistan and Iran. North Korea has even threatened to restart its nuclear weapons programme if no solution is found to the funding problems holding up the supply of oil and construction of nuclear power stations under the Korean Peninsula Energy Development Organisation (KEDO). As the North Korean regime struggles to survive, the missile and nuclear programmes are its only means of exerting influence on the major powers

South-east Asia

In Indonesia, the resignation of President Suharto in May 1998, the assumption of the presidency by Bacharuddin Jusuf Habibie, and the dismantling of the Suharto family's interests are reducing the military's influence on key economic and political decisions. However, their role as a bulwark against the prevailing civil unrest and deep entrenchment in the national infrastructure mean the forces remain a key influence on the development of the country's political structures. There are divisions among their ranks, with younger officers wanting to distance themselves from corruption and direct military involvement in political affairs. An increasing number feel that these activities detract from the armed forces' ability to ensure internal stability (an estimated 1,200 people died in the nationwide turmoil surrounding Suharto's fall) and deal with the challenges to the central government in East Timor, Sumatra, Irian Jaya and Kalimantan. The government has offered East Timor more political autonomy and reduced the garrison there to around 5,000 troops. In August 1998, the Ministry of Defence announced that it was 'ceasing all military operations' in the province of Aceh in northern Sumatra, where armed forces have been deployed since 1991 against separatist insurgency being waged by the Islamic Aceh *Merdeka* group. The security situation is further complicated by ethnic tensions which led to civilian attacks on the Indonesian Chinese community in May and August 1998.

In the **Philippines,** conflict persists on the island of Mindanao. Despite the 1996 peace accord signed by the main insurgent group, the Moro National Liberation Front (MNLF), confrontation continues between the Moro Islamic Liberation Front (MILF) and government forces. In July 1998, for example, a battle in Pigcawayan forced hundreds of people to flee their homes, although casualties were low. In August 1998, the US Secretary for Defense William Cohen visited the Philippines for talks on ratifying an agreement on US military visits and joint military exercises. While the new Philippine President Joseph Estrada led the campaign for the withdrawal of US forces from the Subic Bay base, he supports this more modest, visiting, US military presence in the region, despite opposition from left-wing and nationalist groups.

Papua New Guinea, now struggling to recover from the devastating tidal wave, which caused up to 6,000 deaths in July 1998, is still trying to end insurgency on the island of Bougainville. The nine year conflict, in which an estimated 10,000 people died, was officially ended on 30 May 1998, after secessionist rebels and the government signed a cease-fire accord, now being supervised by the Australian-led Peace Monitoring Group, Operation *Belisi*, of 300 troops with UN observers.

Military activity in **Cambodia** fell sharply in 1998 with the decline of the Khmer Rouge and the engagement of Prime Minister Hun Sen and his political opponents, in particular Prince Norodom Ranarridh, in an election campaign. While some degree of political violence will continue, a return to armed conflict convulsing the whole country seems unlikely. The military still retain a grip on power in **Myanmar**, with substantial reliance on economic support and military supplies from China. The armed forces are still conducting operations against Karen rebel groups near the Thai border, which on occasions, as in March 1998, have led to cross-border raids on Karen refugee camps in **Thailand**.

DEFENCE SPENDING

Defence expenditure in East Asia and Australasia is estimated to have fallen by around 5% in real terms in 1997, to $142bn from $149bn in 1996, measured in 1997 dollars. The economic crisis that developed in the region from mid-1997 had only a limited effect on nominal defence expenditures for that year, but the depreciation of Asian currencies against the dollar increased the cost of foreign equipment and operations and forced some countries to cancel orders for expensive weapons systems. The real impact is seen on the dollar value of 1998 budgets, which are set to fall by around 18% across the region with Japan, South Korea and the Association of South-East Asian Nations (ASEAN) region accounting for most of the decline. It remains to be seen whether supplementary allocations will be raised, but over the short-term there is certain to be a moratorium on new procurement of major equipment in the worst affected countries.

Japan

Japan's 1998 defence budget is down by 16% measured in constant dollars, from $40.9bn in 1997 to $34.5bn. The yen value has only fallen by a marginal 0.3% to ¥4,929bn from ¥4,940bn in 1997, but this still marks the first nominal decrease in the defence budget since the Japanese Defence Agency (JDA) was established in 1954. The budget excludes ¥10.7bn ($76m) for the Special Action Committee on Okinawa (SACO), whose funds contribute to the cost of redeploying US forces from their Okinawa bases. The JDA contribution to the overall costs of US forces in Japan is ¥254bn ($1.8bn) in 1998.

Table 21 Japan's defence budget by function and selected other budgets, 1993–1998

(1997 US$bn)		1993	1994	1995	1996	1997	1998
Personnel		19.1	20.9	23.0	19.5	17.6	15.2
Supplies		26.5	28.1	29.4	26.0	23.3	19.3
of which	Procurement	10.6	10.5	9.6	8.6	7.7	6.6
	R&D	1.2	1.3	1.6	1.4	1.3	0.9
	Maintenance	7.4	8.3	9.2	8.2	7.4	6.3
	Infrastructure and others	7.3	8.0	9.0	7.8	6.8	5.6
Total defence budget		**45.6**	**49.0**	**52.4**	**45.5**	**40.9**	**34.5**
SACO						0.050	0.076
Maritime Safety Agency		1.5	1.6	1.7	1.5	1.4	1.2
Veterans (Imperial Japanese Army)		15.2	16.1	16.7	13.7	11.6	9.5
Space		1.6	1.9	2.0	2.3	2.6	2.6

The government reduced the 1996–2000 Five-Year Mid-Term Defence Programme (MTDP) in June 1997 from ¥25,150bn to ¥24,230bn, with the front-line equipment allocation falling from ¥4,280bn to ¥3,970bn. The Research and Development budget for 1998 is down from ¥160bn in 1997 to ¥128bn as the programmes of indigenous F-2 fighters (45, reduced from 47, on order for 1996–2000 and a final requirement for 130) and OH-1 observation helicopters (193 required) move towards peak production. The JDA continues to conduct its feasibility study on theatre missile defence which has cost about ¥557m since it began in 1995.

Table 22 **Japan's defence budget by armed service, 1993–1997**					
(1997 US$bn)	**1993**	**1994**	**1995**	**1996**	**1997**
Japanese Defense Agency	40.5	43.3	46.1	40.1	36.1
of which Ground Self-Defense Force	16.4	17.8	19.8	16.8	15.0
Maritime Self-defense Force	10.7	11.6	11.7	10.7	9.4
Air Self-Defense Force	11.6	11.9	12.3	10.5	9.7
Other	1.9	2.0	2.3	2.1	2.1
Defense Facility Administration Agency	5.1	5.7	6.3	5.4	4.8
Total defence budget	**45.6**	**49.0**	**52.4**	**45.5**	**40.9**

Confronted by escalating equipment costs, the JDA is introducing more competition into weapons procurement which is expected to cut over $1.5bn from expenditure on major programmes by 2003. Much of the JDA's procurement has not been subject to competitive tender. The small-scale of Japanese indigenous programmes also increases unit costs and the JDA's preferred suppliers tend to be large Japanese conglomerates with high overheads for low production runs. The JDA has mainly chosen to procure US equipment under licence.

Australasia

Australia plans to keep defence expenditure between 1998–2002 at the same level in real terms as the 1997 budget, reflecting the savings proposed in the July 1997 Defence Reform Programme (DRP). Most of the savings are expected to come from a 3,800 reduction in armed forces personnel and contracting out support functions which will cut another 11,200 jobs. Cumulative savings are expected to be A$1.1bn by 2001. The cost of the Peace Monitoring Group in Papua New Guinea, known as Operation *Belisi,* to the 1998 Australian defence budget rose to A$24m ($16m) compared with A$8m in 1997 for the preceding truce monitoring operations. New equipment commitments in the 1998 budget include upgrades for F-18 fighters and M113 armoured personnel carriers (APCs) and the acquisition of *Penguin* anti-ship missiles (ASMs) for the SH-2 helicopters carried by the *Anzac*-class frigates. Two more CH-47D *Chinooks* were ordered from the US in June 1998 and the Navy takes delivery during 1998 of a third *Collins*-class submarine, the first of its order of *Huon*-class coastal minesweepers, and two hydrographic survey ships. The first C-130J *Hercules* is also due for delivery from the US in the 1998–1999 fiscal year.

New Zealand is due to take delivery of a second *Anzac*-class frigate in February 1999, following delivery of the first in May 1997. The programme cost has risen to NZ$1.2bn. The first of four SH-2G helicopters for the new frigates is scheduled for delivery in mid-to-late 2000. Meanwhile, four used SH-2Fs have been leased from the US Navy to replace *Wasp* helicopters. The Army is to replace its M-113 APCs with 81 armoured vehicles. An order is expected in 1999. Six Air Force PC-3K *Orion* maritime patrol aircraft are undergoing airframe refurbishment, with the programme scheduled for completion in 2001.

China and Taiwan

Military expenditure continues to rise in China and Taiwan. China's 1998 defence budget increased from Y80.6bn ($9.7bn) in 1997 to Y91bn ($11bn) in 1998. Real expenditure in 1997 is estimated at over $36bn according to IISS definitions of defence spending and purchasing-power-parity calculations. Chinese indigenous weapons programmes now cover a widening range of strategic, conventional and tactical systems, and the PLA continues to make large scale purchases of weapons and technology from Russia, directly and under licence. While the US government embargo on military sales to the PLA, imposed after the events in Tianamen Square in 1989, is still effective, Western European sales of military sub-systems and licensed technology are growing.

China has three strategic missiles in development. The 8,000km range *Dong Feng*-31 (DF-31) intercontinental ballistic missile (ICBM) may enter service in 1999. Between ten and 20 missiles of this three-stage solid propellant type may be deployed. The 12,000km DF-41 ICBM may enter service between 2002 and 2005. Development of the second generation JL-2 submarine-launched ballistic missile (SLBM) may be completed by 2002 and 16 will be carried by the first Project 094 nuclear-fuelled ballistic submarine (SSBN) when it enters service in 2009 or 2010. The Navy continues construction of its Type 093 nuclear submarine with dedicated non-ballistic missile launchers (SSGN) whose launch is expected in 2000. The first *Song*-class submarine is conducting sea trials. Two more are under construction. The second *Kilo* 636 submarine is due for delivery from Russia in October 1998. The first of the new *Luhai*-class destroyers is under construction. Its launch is scheduled for June 1999 and it will probably be commissioned at approximately the same time as the two *Sovremennyy*-class destroyers bought from Russia in December 1996. In April 1998, China ordered SS-N-22 anti-ship missiles (ASSMs) to equip its *Sovremennyys* and possibly its *Luhai* destroyer. The PLA Air Force's major acquisition programme now appears to be the Russian Su-27 ground-attack fighter (FGA). Production under licence has started, with orders for up to 150 reported. Development of the F-10 FGA continues with Israeli technical assistance. The first flight by one of four prototypes took place in March 1998. The in-service date has slipped and production deliveries are unlikely to start before 2001, with an operational capability from 2005. Low-volume production of the Z-9A and Z-11 helicopters continues under French licence. China's *Red Arrow* 8E anti-tank missile (ATGW) is set to enter production. The PLA has also acquired air-portable armoured vehicles from Russia and is to produce under licence the Russian RPO-A *Shmel* rocket launcher which can fitted with a fuel-air explosive or a hollow-charge warhead.

Taiwan's 1998 defence budget is NT$275bn ($8bn), compared to NT$269bn ($9.8bn) in 1997, while the plan for 1999 is NT$286bn ($8.3bn). These figures exclude the special budget covering the purchase of 150 F-16s and 60 *Mirage* 2000s which amounts to NT$301bn ($11–12bn) between 1993 and 2001. Of this, NT$289bn had been spent by 1998 with over 30 F-16s and over 30 *Mirages* delivered by August 1998. The indigenous *Ching-Kuo* IDF fighter programme is scheduled for completion at the end of 1998 after deliveries of 130 to the Air Force. Final deliveries of the Navy's seven *Perry*-class *Cheng-Kung* frigates, produced domestically under licence, and six *LaFayette*-class frigates from France take place in 1998. Six *Patriot* surface-to-air missile (SAM) launchers will have been delivered by the end of 1998.

South Korea's initial defence allocation for 1998 was won 14.2tr ($10.2bn), compared to won 14tr ($14.7bn) in 1997. Two supplementary allocations in March and July 1998 have increased the budget by some 12% over the initial allocation, but still leave it below 1997 US dollar levels because of currency depreciation. Direct support for US forces in South Korea required re-negotiation to keep the cost at the budgeted level of $400m for 1998. It is estimated that indirect support to the US presence – provision of land, utilities and other facilities – is worth some $1.4bn. South Korean orders in the pipeline for US equipment were worth over $8bn in 1998. These include the outstanding 32 F-16C/Ds, domestically-built under licence, of the original order for 120 for delivery by the end of 1999. The Air Force requirement for 4 B-767 airborne warning and control system (AWACS) aircraft, announced in September 1997, may slip, as may the schedule for the KTX-2 advanced training aircraft, whose full development was approved in late 1997 after prolonged uncertainty. Licensed production continues of German Type-209 submarines. Six of the nine have been delivered by 1998.

Military expenditure has been reduced substantially in the ASEAN region, apart from **Singapore** and Myanmar, with extensive cuts by Thailand and Indonesia and smaller reductions by **Malaysia** and the Philippines. Singapore's 1998 budget of S$7.3bn ($4.3bn) is little changed in real terms from 1997's S$6.1bn ($4.1bn). The equipment budget is S$775m. The Air Force took delivery of the first F16C of 42 F-16C/Ds on order in April 1998.

Malaysia's five-year capital budget under the Seventh Malaysia Plan 1996–2000 amounted to RM9.2bn ($3.7bn) over five years at 1996 values, but the dollar purchasing power has fallen by up to a third in 1998. Several planned procurements have been put on hold, including the purchase of up to 27 Offshore Patrol Vessels (OPVs) and naval and combat helicopters. The 1998 defence budget has been trimmed by 2% to RM6.1bn but its dollar value is down from $2.2bn to $1.5bn, while the capital allocation for equipment is RM2.4bn ($610m). The Navy has delayed acceptance of 2 *Lekiu*-class frigates from the UK for technical reasons.

The Philippines has also scaled back the initial phase of its P50bn ($2.9bn) modernisation programme for 1996–2000 because its dollar purchasing power had fallen by nearly a half by 1998. The purchase of 12 combat aircraft and 3 OPVs is still planned over the five-year period. Tendering for these contracts began in April 1998. Thailand's 1997 outlay was b102bn ($3.2bn), cut from b104bn (worth over $4bn when approved), while the 1998 budget is B81bn ($2bn) and the plan for 1999 is B77bn ($1.8bn). The first-quarter outlay in 1998 was b22bn, suggesting that the budget was on course at that time. The Navy's 1996 order for 8 F-18C/Ds from the US was cancelled in January 1998.

There has been a large nominal increase in Myanmar's 1998 defence budget to K24.5bn from K19.3bn in 1997. Chinese deliveries to Myanmar resumed during 1997–1998 when the Navy received deliveries of two *Jianghu* frigates and the Air Force four K-8 training aircraft. These acquisitions were reportedly funded by long-term soft-loans similar to earlier deals concluded between 1990 and 1994.

Indonesia's August 1997 orders for 12 Su-30 FGAs and 8 Mi-17 helicopters from Russia were postponed indefinitely in January 1998. The five Type-206 submarines ordered from Germany in March 1997 have been cancelled.

Table 23 Arms orders and deliveries, East Asia and Australasia, 1996–1998

Supplier	Classification	Units Designation	Units	Order Date	Delivery Date	Comment
Australia						
Domestic	FGA	F-111	71	1990	1999	Upgrade of F/RF-111C
UK	AAM	ASRAAM	100	1998	1999	
US	tpt	C-130J	12	1996	1997	Deliveries slipped to 1999
UK	trg	*Hawk*-100	33	1997	1999	Deliveries 1999-2006
Domestic	MPA	P-3C	19	1996	1999	Upgrade
Swe	SS	*Collins*	6	1987	1996	One delivered 1996, two in 1997
Domestic	FF	*Anzac*	6	1989	1996	3 delivered by end 1998
US	hel	SH-2G	11	1997	2001	
No	ASM	*Penguin*		1998	2002	
Domestic	MHC	*Huon/Gaeta*	6	1994	1998	Deliveries to 2002
Domestic	AGS	*Pacific*	2	1995	1998	Second to commission in 1999
US	LPH	*Newport*	2	1996	1998	Conversion
Ca	LAV	ASLAV	111	1992	1996	Customisation in Aus
Ca	LAV	ASLAV	150	1998	1999	Follow on order
US	hel	CH-47D	4	1997	1999	Deliveries to 2000
Brunei						
Indo	tpt	CN-235	1	1995	1996	
HG	trg	PC-7 *Pilatus*	4	1996	1997	

Supplier	Classification	Designation	Units	Order Date	Delivery Date	Comment
UK	trg	*Hawk* 100/200				
			10	1996	1999	
US	hel	UH-60L	4	1996	1997	
Indo	MPA	CN-235	3	1996	1999	Requirement for up to 12
UK	Corvette	12-1500t	3	1995	2000	First delivery in 2000
UK	FAC	*Waspada*	3	1997	1998	Upgrade
Fr	SAM	*Mistral*		1998	1999	
Cambodia						
Il	trg	L-39	8	1994	1996	Second-hand
Il	FGA	MiG-21	19	1995	1997	Upgrade
RF	FAC	*Stenka*-class	2	1994	1996	Upgrade
Ger	PCR	*Kaoh Chlam*	2	1996	1997	
China						
Domestic	ICBM	DF-31	10	1985	1999	Might build 20
Domestic	ICBM	DF-41	12	1985	2005	Development programme
Domestic	SLBM	JL-2		1985	2002	Development programme
Domestic	SRBM	DF-15	50	1988	1996	CSS-6/M-9. Of a total of 300
Domestic	SRBM	DF-11	20	1988	1996	CSS-7/M-11. Of a total of 100
Domestic	bbr	H-6			1998	Still in production
RF	FGA	Su-27	50	1992	1993	Deliveries to 1996
RF	FGA	Su-27	150	1997	1999	Licensed production. PRC desig J-11
Il	AWACS	IL-76	4	1997		
Domestic	FGA	F-10		1993	2005	Development continues
Domestic	FGA	F-8IIM		1993	1996	Modernisation completed
Domestic	FGA	FC-1		1991	2005	Joint venture with Pak
Domestic	ASM	KR-1		1997		In development with RF
RF	SAM	Tor-MI	15	1995	1997	SA-15
Domestic	SSBN	Type 094	1	1985	2010	Development continues
Domestic	SSGN	Type 093	1	1985	2005	Launch expected 2000
Domestic	SS	*Ming*	6	1994	1997	4 more under construction
RF	SS	*Kilo* 636	2	1993	1997	First delivered, 2 in late 1998
Domestic	SS	*Song*	3	1994	2002	2 others building to 2002
Domestic	DDG	*Luhai*	1	1996	1999	
RF	DDG	*Sovremennyy*	2	1996	2000	
RF	hel	Ka-28	8	1998	1999	Original deal in 1996
RF	ASSM	SS-N-22		1998	2000	
Domestic	FF	*Luhu*	3	1991	1996	Second commissioned in 1996
RF	AO	*Nanchang*	1	1988	1996	
Domestic	SLCM	C-801(mod)		1997		Development (also known as YJ-82)
RF	AIFV	BMD-3		1997		Could be BMD-1s
Domestic	ATGW	*Red Arrow* 8E		1996	1998	
RF	hel	Mi-17	35	1995	1997	30 delivered by 1997
RF	RL	*Shmel*		1997		Licensed production
Fr	hel	AS-350	12	1988	1996	Locally assembled. Known as Z-11
Fr	hel	AS-365		1992		Locally assembled. Known as Z-9A
Taiwan						
US	SAM	*Patriot*	6	1993	1997	Deployment 1998
Domestic	SSM	*Sky Halberd*		1984	1997	
Domestic	FGA	IDF	130		1994	Deliveries complete end 1998
Fr	FGA	*Mirage* 2000-5	60	1992	1997	20 delivered
US	FGA	F-16A/B	150	1992	1997	20 delivered
Domestic	trg	AT-3	40	1997		Order resheduled
US	sar hel	S-70C	4	1994	1998	

Supplier	Classification	Designation	Units	Order Date	Delivery Date	Comment
Fr	FF	*LaFayette*	6	1992	1996	Deliveries to 1998
US	FF	*Perry*	7	1979	1998	7th to commission Nov 98
US	FF	*Knox*	5	1997	1998	First 2 in 1998
US	LST	*Newport*	2	1994	1997	Leased from US
Domestic	PFM	*Kuang Hua* IV				
			50	1998	2001	
US	MBT	M-60A3	340	1995	1997	Ex-US. 30 in 1997
US	arty	M-109A5	28	1995	1998	
US	hel	AH-1W	21	1997	2000	9 in 1997
US	hel	OH-58D	13	1998	2001	
US	hel	TH-67	30	1996	1998	
US	SAM	*Stinger*	465	1996	1998	
Fr	SAM	*Mistral*	550	1995	1997	
US	SAM	*Avenger*	74	1996	1998	
Indonesia						
RF	FGA	Su-30K	12	1997	1998	Postponed indefinitely
UK	trg	*Hawk* 109/209				
			24	1993	1996	Deliveries 1996-97
UK	FGA	*Hawk* 209	16	1996	1998	Deliveries 1998-99
Domestic	MPA	CN-235MP	3	1996	1998	
Aus	tpt	*Nomad*	20		1997	
Ge	hel	BO-105	3	1996	1998	
Ge	Corvette	*Parchim*	16	1992	1996	
RF	AK		1		1997	Military transport ship
Ge	SS	Type 206	5	1997	1998	Order cancelled
US	hel	B-412	2	1994	1996	Licence
US	hel	UH-1H	20	1995	1996	Surplus
US	hel	NB-412	1	1996	1998	Licence
Fr	SAM	*Mistral*		1996	1998	
UK	lt tk	*Scorpion*	50	1993	1994	Deliveries to 1996
RF	hel	Mi-17	8	1997	1998	Postponed
Nl	tpt	F-28	8	1996	1998	
Fr	APC	VAB/VBL	36	1995	1997	
UK	APC	*Stormer*	10	1995	1997	
UK	APC	*Tactica*	12	1995	1997	
UK	APC		7	1995	1996	
Japan						
US	SAM	*Patriot*		1994		
US	FGA	F-15	13	1994	1996	Licensed production
Domestic	FGA	F-2	47	1996	2000	Final requirement 120
US	tpt	C-130H	1	1995	1997	
US	AEW	E-767	4	1991	1998	2 for delivery in 1999
US	hel	CH-47J	6	1994	1996	Licensed production
US	hel	UH-JA	10	1994	1996	Licensed production
Domestic	trg	T-4	59	1996	1996	Deliveries to 2000
Domestic	DD	*Kongo*-class	4	1987	1993	Deliveries 1993-98
Domestic	DD	*Murasame*	11	1991	1996	Deliveries 1996-02
Domestic	SS	*Oyashio*	5	1993	1998	Deliveries 1998-02
Domestic	MCMV	*Sugashima*	5	1996	1996	Deliveries to 2001
US	hel	SH-60J	37	1996	1996	Licensed production
US	MPA	EP-3 & UP-3	4	1994	1997	Licensed production
Domestic	MBT	Type-90	96	1996	1996	Deliveries to 2000
Domestic	AIFV	Type-89	21	1994	1996	Deliveries to 2000

Supplier	Classification	Designation	Units	Order Date	Delivery Date	Comment
Domestic	AOC	Type-73/96	98	1994	1996	Deliveries to 2000
Collab.	arty	FH-70	77	1994	1996	Licensed production
US	MRL	MLRS	45	1996	1996	Deliveries to 2000
US	hel	AH-1S	7	1994	1996	Licensed production
Domestic	hel	OH-1	5	1997	2000	Final requirement 193
US	hel	UH-60JA	15	1994	1996	Licensed production
US	hel	UH-1J	40	1994	1996	Licensed production
US	hel	CH-47J	9	1994	1996	Licensed production
North Korea						
Domestic	MRBM	*Taepo-dong* 1				Development programme
Domestic	MRBM	*Nodong*		1988	1997	Deployment reported
South Korea						
US	AEW	B-767	4	1998		
US	FGA	F-16C/Ds	120	1992	1995	Delivery to 1999. 12 in 1997
US	AAM	AMRAAM	190	1992	1997	190 delivered in 1997
Il	UAV	*Hawk* 800	10	1996	1999	
US	trg	T-38	30	1996	1997	Ex-US, lease
US	hel	CH-47	6	1993	1997	
Domestic	trg	KTX-2	94	1997	2009	Full development approved late 1997
Indo	tpt	CN-235	8	1997	1999	
Domestic	FF	KDX-2000	3	1995	1998	Deliveries continue in 1999-2000
UK	hel	*Lynx*	13	1997	1999	
Ger	SS	Type-209	9	1991	1996	Licensed production, delivery to 2002
Domestic	ARS	*Chonghaejin*	1	1995	1997	
RF	MBT	T-80U	33	1995	1997	Deliveries to 1998. 27 in 1997
Domestic	MBT	K1A1		1996	1998	120mm gun upgrade for K1
US	MRL	MLRS	29	1997	1999	
Ger	hel	BO-105	12	1998	1999	
Fr	SAM	*Mistral*	1294	1997	1998	
RF	APC	BTR-80		1995	1996	Deliveries to 1998
RF	AIFV	BMP-3	33	1995	1996	Deliveries to 1998. 13 in 1997
Il	UAV	*Searcher*	100	1997	1999	
Domestic	SAM	*Pegasus*		1990	1999	In limited production
Laos						
RF	hel	Mi-17V	12	1997	1997	Deliveries 1997-98
Malaysia						
US	FGA	F/A-18	8	1993	1997	All delivered in 1997
UK	tkr	C-130H	2	1995	1996	Upgrade
US	hel	S-70A	2	1995	1998	
It	trg	MB-339	2	1997	1999	
Indo	tpt	CN-235	6	1995	1998	
US	LST	*Newport*-class	1	1997	1998	
UK	FF	*Lekiu*-class	2	1992	1998	Delivery delayed
It	Corvette	*Assad*-class	2	1995	1997	Ex-Iraqi new build
Ge	OPV	MEKO 100	6	1998		
Myanmar						
RF	hel	M-17	6	1995	1996	
PRC	FGA	F-7	4	1996	1998	
PRC	trg	K-8	4	1997	1998	
Pl	hel	W-3	35	1996	1996	Deliveries in 1996 and 1997
PRC	FF	Mod *Jianghu*	2	1994	1998	1 delivered 1 building
Domestic	PFC	*Houxin*	2	1991	1996	
PRC	APC	Type-85	150	1991	1996	

Supplier	Classification	Designation	Units	Order Date	Delivery Date	Comment
PRC	MBT	Type-69	50	1993	1996	
DPRK	arty	130mm	20	1997	1998	
New Zealand						
US	tpt	C-130J	8	1996	1999	Joint procurement with Aus
Domestic	trg	CT-4E	13	1996	1998	
Aus	FFG	*Anzac*	2	1990	1997	Second in 1998
US	hel	SH-2F	4	1997	1997	Leased until arrival of SH-2G
US	hel	SH-2G	4	1997	2000	
US	TAGOS	*Stalwart*	1	1996	1997	Towed array ship
Fr	SAM	*Mistral*	12	1996	1997	Delivery of 2 launchers in late 1997
Papua New Guinea						
Indo	tpt	CN-235	2	1998	2001	
Aus	PCC	*Pacific Forum*	4	1995	1997	
Philippines						
ROK	ftr	F-5A	5	1997	1998	Ex ROK
US	tpt	C-130B	2	1995	1998	
US	trg	T-41	5	1997	1998	Ex-US
US	hel	B-412	4	1995	1997	
UK	OPV	*Peacock*-class	3	1996	1997	Ex-RN
Singapore						
US	FGA	F-16C/D	42	1995	1998	First deliveries in 1998
US	tkr	KC-135	4	1996	1997	Ex-US
US	tk	KC-130B/H	5	1994	1996	
US	hel	CH-47D	12	1997	2000	Delivery of first 6 1994-97
Swe	SS	A12	4	1995	1997	Deliveries 1997-2001
Domestic	OPV	*Fearless*	1	1993	1998	Last of class of 12
Domestic	LST	*Endurance*	4	1994	1999	
Domestic	PCO	PG-94	2	1993	1998	Total of 12 likely
Domestic	AIFV	M113	500	1991	1998	Upgrade
Il	UAV	*Searcher*	40	1997	1997	
Thailand						
US	FGA	A-7	23	1995	1996	
US	FGA	F/A-18C/D	8	1996	1999	Cancelled
Sp	FGA	AV-8S	9	1995	1997	All delivered in 1997
Cz	trg	L-39	2	1991	1997	Last 2 of 42 delivered from 1993
Indo	tpt	CN-235	2	1996	1999	
US	hel	SH-60	6	1993	1996	
US	hel	S-76N	6	1993	1996	
Sp	CV	CV - 911	1	1992	1997	
Domestic	Corvette		3	1996	1998	Cancelled
Domestic	LCU	*Man Nok*	3	1997	2000	
It	MCMV	*Gaeta*	2	1996	1998	
US	MBT	M-60	125	1995	1996	24 in 1996, 101 in 1997
US	APC	M113	65	1995	1997	Ex-US
Fr	arty	105mm	24	1995	1996	All delivered in 1996
It	MHC	*Lat Ya*	2	1996	1998	Deliveries to December 1999
Fr	hel	AS-532	3	1995	1996	2 delivered in 1996, 3rd in 1997
US	ACV	Various	63	1995	1997	21 M-125, 12 M-1064, 12 M-577, 18 M-901
Vietnam						
RF	ftr	Su-27	6	1995	1997	Follow-on order. Delivered 1997/98
Ukr	FGA	MIG-21UM	6	1995	1996	For training
Il	FGA	MiG-21		1996		Il upgrade
RF	PGG	BPS 500	2	1996	1998	Assembled in Vn
RF	ASM	X-35	16	1998	1999	

Australia

	1996	1997	1998	1999
GDP	A$502bn	A$525bn		
	($371bn)	($391bn)		
per capita	$20,000	$21,000		
Growth	3.4%	3.1%		
Inflation	2.6%	0.3%		
Publ Debt	41.8%	38.7%		
Def exp	A$11.0bn	A$11.4bn		
	($8.6bn)	($8.5bn)		
Def bdgt			A$10.9bn	A$11.5bn
			($6.6bn)	($6.9bn)
US$1 = A$	1.28	1.34	1.65	
Population		18,871,000		

(Asian 4%, Aborigines <1%)

Age	*13–17*	*18–22*	*23–32*	
Men	681,000	688,000	1,514,000	
Women	642,000	655,000	1,463,000	

Total Armed Forces

ACTIVE 57,400

(incl 7,500 women)

RESERVES 33,650
GENERAL RESERVE
Army 25,100 **Navy** 4,700 **Air Force** 3,850

Army 25,400

(incl 2,600 women)
1 Land HQ, 1 northern comd • 1 inf div, 1 bde HQ, 1
Task Force HQ • 1 armd regt HQ (1 active, 2 reserve
sqn) • 1 recce regt (2 sqn) • 1 APC sqn • 5 inf bn (incl 1
AB, 1 mech) • 2 arty regt (1 fd, 1 med (each 2 bty)) • 1
AD regt (2 bty) • 2 cbt engr regt • 1 SAS regt (3 sqn) •
2 avn regt

RESERVES

GENERAL RESERVE 25,100
1 div HQ, 6 bde HQ, 1 armd sqn, 1 APC regt, 2 APC
sqn, 2 recce regt, 1 recce sqn, 1 APC/recce regt, 14 inf
bn, 1 cdo (2 coy), 4 arty regt (3 fd, 1 med), 4 indep arty
bty, 5 engr regt (3 cbt, 2 construction), 4 indep engr
sqn, 3 regional surv units

EQUIPMENT

MBT 71 *Leopard* 1A3 (excl variants)
AIFV 46 M-113 with **76mm** gun
LAV 111 ASLAV-25
APC 463 M-113 (excl variants, 364 to be upgraded,
119 in store)
TOWED ARTY 105mm: 246 M2A2/L5, 104 *Hamel*;
155mm: 35 M-198
MOR 81mm: 296
RCL 84mm: 577 *Carl Gustav*; **106mm**: 74 M-40A1

SAM 19 *Rapier*, 17 RBS-70
AC 4 *King Air* 200, 2 DHC-6 (all on lease)
HEL 36 S-70 A-9, 43 Bell 206 B-1 *Kiowa* (to be
upgraded), 25 UH-1H (armed), 17 AS-350B, 4 CH-
47D
MARINES 15 LCM, 53 LARC 5 amph craft
SURV 14 RASIT (veh, arty), AN-TPQ-36 (arty, mor)

Navy 14,300

(incl 990 Fleet Air Arm, 2,200 women)
Maritime Comd, Support Comd, Training Comd
BASES Sydney, NSW (Maritime Comd HQ) 3 DDG, 3
FFG, 2 PFI, 1 LSH, 1 AO, 2 LCH, 2 MSI, 5 MSA
Garden Island, WA 3 SS, 3 FFG, 1 DD, 1 FFH, 1 AO, 2
PFC, 1 AGS, 1 ASR **Cairns, Qld** 5 PFC, 5 AGS, 2 LCH
Darwin, NT 6 PFC, 1 LCH

SUBMARINES 4

2 *Oxley* (mod UK *Oberon*) (incl 1 in refit) with Mk 48
HWT and *Harpoon* SSM (plus 1 alongside trg)
2 *Collins* with sub-*Harpoon* and MK48 HW7

PRINCIPAL SURFACE COMBATANTS 11

DESTROYERS 3 *Perth* (US *Adams*) DDG with 1 SM-1
MR SAM/*Harpoon* SSM launcher; plus 2 x 3 ASTT
(Mk 46 LWT), 2 127mm guns
FRIGATES 8

6 *Adelaide* (US *Perry*), with S-70B-2 *Sea Hawk*, 2 x 3
ASTT; plus 1 SM-1 MR SAM/*Harpoon* SSM
launcher
2 *Anzac* with *Sea Sparrow* VLS, 1 127mm gun, 6
324mm TT, plus hel

PATROL AND COASTAL COMBATANTS 15
PATROL, INSHORE 15 *Fremantle* PFI
MINE COUNTERMEASURES 7

2 *Rushcutter* MHI, 2 *Bandicoot*, 2 *Kooraaga* MSA, 1
Brolga MSI
AMPHIBIOUS 7

5 *Balikpapan* LCH, capacity 3 tk (plus 3 in store)
1 *Tobruk* LST (decommission mid-to-late 1998)
1 *Kanimbla* (US *Newport*) LST. Capacity 450 tps, 2
LCM **hel** 4 Army *Blackhawk* or 3 *Sea King*. No
beach landing capability
SUPPORT AND MISCELLANEOUS 8

1 *Success* (mod Fr *Durance*), 1 *Westralia* AO, 1*Protec-
tor* sub trials and safety, 1 AGS, 4 small AGHS
FLEET AIR ARM (990)
no cbt ac, 16 armed hel
ASW 1 hel sqn with 16 S-70B-2 *Sea Hawk*
UTL/SAR 1 sqn with 6 AS-350B, 3 Bell 206B and 2
BAe-748 (EW trg), 1 hel sqn with 7 *Sea King* Mk 50/
50A

Air Force 17,700

(incl 2,700 women); 126 cbt ac incl MR, no armed hel

Flying hours F-111, 200; F/A-18, 175
FGA/RECCE 2 sqn with 17 F-111C, 15 F-111G, 4 RF-111C
FTR/FGA 3 sqn with 52 F/A-18 (50 -A, 2 -B)
OCU 1 with 17* F/A-18B
TAC TRG 1 sqn with 16 MB-326H, 3 PC-9A
AIRCRAFT R&D 2* F/A-18, 4 C-47
MR 2 sqn with 19* P-3C, 3 TAP-3B
FAC 1 flt with 3 PC-9
TKR 4 Boeing 707
TPT 7 sqn
　2 with 24 C-130 (12 -E, 12 -H)
　1 with 5 Boeing 707 (4 fitted for AAR)
　2 with 14 DHC-4 (*Caribou*)
　1 VIP with 5 *Falcon* 900
　1 with 10 HS-748 (8 for navigation trg, 2 for VIP tpt)
TRG 59 PC-9, 14 MB-326, 2 Beech-200 *Super King Air*
AD *Jindalee* OTH radar: 1 experimental, 3 planned, 3 control and reporting units (1 mobile)
MISSILES
　ASM AGM-84A, AGM-142
　AAM AIM-7 *Sparrow*, AIM-9M *Sidewinder*

Forces Abroad

Advisers in **Fji**, **Indo**, **Solomon Islands**, **Th**, **Vanuatu**, **Tonga**, **Western Samoa**, **Kiribati**
MALAYSIA Army ε115; 1 inf coy (on 3-month rotational tours) **Air Force** 33; det with 2 P-3C **ac**
PAPUA NEW GUINEA 38; trg unit

UN AND PEACEKEEPING

EGYPT (MFO): 26 obs. **MIDDLE EAST** (UNTSO): 12 obs. **PAPUA NEW GUINEA**: ε100 (Bougainville Truce Monitoring Group)

Paramilitary

AUSTRALIAN CUSTOMS SERVICE

　ac 3 DHC-8, 3 *Reims* F406, 6 BN-2B-20, 1 *Strike Aerocommander* 500 **hel** 1 Bell 206L-4; about 6 boats

Foreign Forces

US Navy 35; joint facilities at NW Cape, Pine Gap and Nurrungar
NEW ZEALAND Air Force 47; 6 A-4K/TA-4K, (trg for Australian Navy); 10 navigation trg
SINGAPORE 230; Flying Training School with 27 S-211 ac

Brunei

	1996	1997	1998	1999
GDP	B$7.3bn	B$7.5bn		
	($5.0bn)	($5.3bn)		
per capita	$7,000	$7,200		

contd	1996	1997	1998	1999
Growth	2.8%	3.5%		
Inflation	6.0%	2.0%		
Debt	$268m	$1,166m		
Def exp	εB$475m	εB$530m		
	($337m)	($353m)		
Def bdgt			εB$550m	
			($345m)	
US$1 = B$	1.41	1.43	1.6	
Population		317,000		

(Muslim 71%; also Malay 67%, Chinese 16%, non-Malay indigenous 6%)

Age	13–17	18–22	23–32
Men	15,000	14,000	28,000
Women	15,000	14,000	25,000

Total Armed Forces

ACTIVE 5,000
(incl 600 women)

RESERVES 700
Army 700

Army 3,900

(incl 250 women)
3 inf bn • 1 armd recce sqn • 1 SAM bty: 2 tps with *Rapier* • 1 engr sqn

EQUIPMENT

　LT TK 16 *Scorpion*
　APC 26 VAB, 2 *Sultan*, 24 AT-104 (in store)
　MOR 81mm: 24
　RL *Armbrust* (reported)
　SAM 12 *Rapier* (with *Blindfire*)

RESERVES

1 bn

Navy 700

BASE Muara
PATROL AND COASTAL COMBATANTS 9†
MISSILE CRAFT 3 *Waspada* PFM with 2 MM-38 *Exocet* SSM
PATROL, INSHORE 3 *Perwira* PFI<
PATROL, RIVERINE 3 *Rotork* Marine FPB plus boats
AMPHIBIOUS craft only
　4 LCU<; 1 SF sqn plus boats

Air Force 400

no cbt ac, 6 armed hel
HEL 2 sqn
　1 with 10 Bell 212, 1 Bell 214 (SAR), 4 UH-60L, 4 S-70
　1 with 6 Bo-105 armed hel (**81mm** rockets)

VIP TPT 2 S-70 hel, 2 Bell 412ST
TRG ac 2 SF-260W, 4 PC-7, 1 CN235 **hel** 2 Bell 206B

Paramilitary 4,050

GURKHA RESERVE UNIT 2,300+
2 bn
ROYAL BRUNEI POLICE 1,750
7 PCI<

Foreign Forces

UK Army some 1,050; 1 Gurkha inf bn, 1 hel flt
SINGAPORE 500; trg school incl hel det (5 UH-1)

Cambodia

	1996	1997	1998	1999
GDP	r8.5tr	r10.2tr		
	($3.2bn)	($3.5bn)		
per capita	$700	$700		
Growth	7.6%	6.5%		
Inflation	7.2%	7.9%		
Debt	$2.1bn	$2.2bn		
Def exp	εr475bn	εr748bn		
	($181m)	($254m)		
Def bdgt			εr560bn	
			($142m)	
FMA (US)	$1.4m	$1.5m		
(Aus)	$2.0m	$0.1m	$0.3m	
(PRC)	$3.0m			
$1 = riel	2,624	2,946	3,955	
Population		10,430,000		
(Khmer 90%, Vietnamese 5%, Chinese 1%)				
Age	*13–17*	*18–22*	*23–32*	
Men	572,000	467,000	870,000	
Women	561,000	459,000	869,000	

Total Armed Forces

ACTIVE 139,000
(incl Provincial Forces, perhaps only 19,000 cbt capable)
Terms of service conscription authorised but not
implemented since 1993

Army 90,000

6 Mil Regions (incl 1 special zone for capital) • 12 inf
div[a] • 3 indep inf bde • 1 protection bde (4 bn) • 9
indep inf regt • 3 armd bn • 1 AB/SF regt • 4 engr
regt (3 fd, 1 construction) • some indep recce, arty, AD
bn
EQUIPMENT
MBT 100+ T-54/-55, plus PRC Type-59

LT TK 10 PT-76
APC 210 BTR-60/-152, M-113, 30 OT-64 (SKOT)
TOWED ARTY some 400: **76mm**: M-1942; **122mm**:
M-1938, D-30; **130mm**: Type 59
MRL **107mm**: Type-63; **122mm**: 8 BM-21; **132mm**:
BM 13-16; **140mm**: 20 BM-14-16
MOR **82mm**: M-37; **120mm**: M-43; **160mm**: M-160
RCL **82mm**: B-10; **107mm**: B-11
AD GUNS **14.5mm**: ZPU 1/-2/-4; **37mm**: M-1939;
57mm: S-60
SAM SA-7

[a] Inf div established str 3,500, actual str some 1,500

Navy 2,000
(proposed to increase to 5,000)

(incl 1,500 Naval Infantry)
PATROL AND COASTAL COMBATANTS 33
PATROL, INSHORE 6
2 Sov *Turya* PFI (no TT)
4 Sov *Stenka* PFI (no TT), 1 x 2 23mm gun
RIVERINE 27
4 Sov *Shmel* PCI< †, 2 Sov *Zhuk* PCI<, 8 LCVP, 2 Koh
Chhlam, 2 PCF, 9 *Kano*

NAVAL INFANTRY (1,500)
7 inf, 1 arty bn

Air Force 2,000

20 cbt ac†; no armed hel
FTR 24† MiG-21 (only 8 serviceable)
TPT 2 An-24, 1 An-26, Tu-134, 2 Y-12, 1 BN-2
HEL 1 Mi-8, 7 Mi-17, 2 Mi-26
TRG 5* L-39, 5 *Tecnam* P-92

Provincial Forces some 45,000

Reports of at least 1 inf regt per province, with varying
numbers of inf bn with lt wpn

Paramilitary

MILITIA
org at village level for local defence: ε10–20 per village;
not all armed

Opposition

KHMER ROUGE (National Army of Democratic
Kampuchea) perhaps 600–1,000
***FUNCINPEC/KHMER PEOPLE'S LIBERATION
FRONT*** (KPNLF) ε1–2,000
alliance between Prince Ranariddh's party and the
KPNLF

China, Peoples' Republic of

	1996	1997	1998	1999
GDP	Y6.8tr	Y7.5tr		
	($616bn)	($639bn)		
per capita	$3,100	$3,400		
Growth	9.7%	8.8%		
Inflation	8.3%	2.8%		
Debt	$129bn	$133bn		
Def exp[a]	ε$35.4bn	ε$36.6bn		
Def bdgt[b]			Y90.9bn	
			($11.0bn)	
$1 = yuan	8.33	8.29	8.28	

[a] PPP est incl extra-budgetary mil exp
[b] Def bdgt shows official figures at market rates

Population	1,232,765,000		

(Tibetan, Uighur and other non-Han 8%; *Xinjiang* Muslim ε60% of which Uighur ε44%; *Tibet* Chinese ε60%, Tibetan ε40%)

Age	*13–17*	*18–22*	*23–32*
Men	50,570,000	51,806,000	121,342,000
Women	47,624,000	48,487,000	113,596,000

Total Armed Forces

ACTIVE some 2,820,000

(perhaps 1,275,000 conscripts, some 136,000 women), being reduced
Terms of service selective conscription
Army, Marines 3 years **Navy, Air Force** 4 years

RESERVES 1,200,000+

militia reserves being formed on a province-wide basis

Strategic Missile Forces

OFFENSIVE (125,000)

org in 6 bases (army level) with bde/regt incl 1 msl testing and trg regt; org varies by msl type
ICBM 17+
  7 CSS-4 (DF-5); mod tested with MIRV
  10+ CSS-3 (DF-4)
IRBM ε46+
  38+ CSS-2 (DF-3), some updated
  ε8 CSS-5 (DF-21)
SLBM 1 *Xia* SSBN with 12 CSS-N-3 (J-1)
SRBM 4 DF-15 (CSS-6/M-9) (range 600km), DF-11 (CSS-7/M-11) (range 120–300+km)

DEFENSIVE

Tracking stations Xinjiang (covers Central Asia) and Shanxi (northern border)
Phased-array radar complex ballistic-missile early-warning

Army 2,090,000

(perhaps 1,075,000 conscripts) (reductions continue)
7 Mil Regions, 27 Mil Districts, 3 Garrison Comd
24 Integrated Group Armies (GA: about 60,000, equivalent to Western corps), org varies, normally with 3 inf div, 1 tk, 1 arty, 1 AAA bde or 3 inf, 1 tk div, 1 arty, 1 AAA bde, cbt readiness category varies
Summary of cbt units
Group Army 59 inf div (ε 3 mech inf) incl 3 with national level rapid-reaction role and at least 9 with regional rapid-reaction role ready to mobilise in 24-48 hours; 11 tk div, 13 tk bde, 5 arty div, 20 arty bde, 7 hel regt
Independent 5 inf div, 1 tk, 2 inf bde, 1 arty div, 3 arty bde, 4 AAA bde
Local Forces (Garrison, Border, Coastal) 12 inf div, 1 mtn bde, 4 inf bde, 87 inf regt/bn
AB (manned by Air Force) 1 corps of 3 div
Support Troops incl 50 engr, 50 sigs regt
EQUIPMENT
  MBT some 8,800: incl 700 T-34/85 (trg), 6,000 Type-59-I/-II, 200 Type-69-I/-II (mod Type-59), 800 Type-69III/-79, 500 Type-80, 600 Type-85-IIM
  LT TK 1,200 Type-63 amph, 800 Type-62
  AIFV/APC 5,500 incl Type-63, some Type-77 (BTR-50PK), Type-90, WZ-523, WZ-551, WZ-501
  TOWED ARTY 14,500: **100mm**: Type-59 (fd/ATK); **122mm**: Type-54-1, Type-60, Type-83, D-30; **130mm**: Type-59/-59-1; **152mm**: Type-54, Type-66, Type-83; **155mm**: WAC-21
  SP ARTY 122mm: Type-70 (Type-63 APC chassis), Type-85; **152mm** : Type-83
  MRL 122mm: Type-81, Type-89 SP; **130mm**: Type-70 SP, Type-82, Type-85 SP; **273mm**: Type-83
  MOR 82mm: Type-53/-67/-W87/-82 (incl SP); **100mm**: Type-71 reported; **120mm** : Type-55 (incl SP); **160mm**: Type-56
  ATGW HJ-73 (*Sagger*-type), HJ-8 (TOW/*Milan*-type)
  RCL 75mm: Type-52, Type-56; **82mm**: Type-65; **105mm**: Type-75
  RL 90mm: Type-51
  ATK GUNS 57mm: Type-55; **76mm**: Type-54; **100mm**: Type-73, Type-86; **120mm** : Type-89 SP
  AD GUNS 23mm: Type-80; **37mm**: Type-55/-65/-74; **57mm**: Type-59, -80 SP; **85mm**: Type-56; **100mm**: Type-59
  SAM HN-5A/-C (SA-7 type), QW-1, HQ-61A, HQ-7
  SURV *Cheetah* (arty), Type-378 (veh), RASIT (veh, arty)
  HEL 28+ Mi-17, 25 Mi-8, Mi-6, 30 Z-9/-WZ-9, 8 SA-342 (with HOT), 20 S-70
  UAV ASN-104/-105

RESERVES

(undergoing major re-org on provincial basis): perhaps 1,000,000; 50 inf, arty and AD div, 100 indep inf, arty regt

DEPLOYMENT

(GA units only)

North-east Shenyang MR (Heilongjiang, Jilin, Liaoning MD): 5 GA, 3 tk, 13 inf, 1 arty div

North Beijing MR (Beijing, Tianjin Garrison, Nei Mong-gol, Hebei, Shanxi MD): 6 GA, 3 tk, 13 inf, 1 arty div

West Lanzhou MR (incl Ningxia, Shaanxi, Gansu, Qing-hai, Xinjiang MD): 2 GA, 1 tk, 4 inf div

South-west Chengdu MR (incl Sichuan, Guizhou, Yunnan, Xizang MD): 2 GA, 5 inf, 1 arty div

South Guangzhou MR (Hubei, Hunan, Guangdong, Guangxi, Hainan MD): 2 GA, 5 inf, 2 AB (Air Force) div. Hong Kong: ε4,500: 1 inf bde (3 inf, 1 mot inf, 1 arty, 1 engr regt), 1 hel unit

Centre Jinan MR (Shandong, Henan MD): 4 GA, 2 tk, 11 inf, 1 AB (Air Force), 1 arty div

East Nanjing MR (Shanghai Garrison, Jiangsu, Zhejiang, Fujian, Jiangxi, Anhui MD): 3 GA, 2 tk, 8 inf, 1 arty div

Navy ε260,000

(incl 26,000 Coastal Regional Defence Forces, 26,000 Naval Air Force, some 5,000 Marines and some 40,000 conscripts)

SUBMARINES 63

(some may be armed with Russian wake-homing torpedoes)

STRATEGIC 1 SSBN

TACTICAL 62

SSN 5 *Han* with 533mm TT. Can carry YJ 8-2 (C-801 derivative) SLCM (submerged launch)

SSG 1 mod *Romeo* (Type S5G), with 6 C-801 (YJ-6, *Exocet* derivative) SSM; plus 533mm TT (test platform)

SS 56

1 *Song* with YJ 8-2 SLCM (C802 derivative) SLCM (submerged launch), 6 533mm TT (not fully op)

2 *Kilo*-class (Type EKM 877) with 533mm TT, prob wake-homing torpedo

1 *Kilo*-class (Type EKM 636) with 533mm TT, prob wake-homing torpedo

16 imp *Ming* (Type ES5E) with 533mm TT

36 *Romeo* (Type ES3B)† with 533mm TT (some 32 additional *Romeo*-class mothballed)

OTHER ROLES 1 *Golf* (SLBM trials)

PRINCIPAL SURFACE COMBATANTS 53

DESTROYERS 18

2 *Luhu* with 4 x 2 YJ-8/CSS-N-4 SSM, 1 x 2 100mm gun, 2 Z-9A (Fr *Dauphin*) hel, plus 2 x 3 ASTT, 1 x 8 *Crotale* SAM

1 *Luda* III with 4 x 2 YJ-8/CSS-N-4 SSM, 4 130mm gun, 6 324mm TT

1 mod *Luda*, 2 with 1 x 2 130mm guns, 2 Z-9A (Fr *Dauphin*) hel (OTHT), 2 x 3 ASTT, 1 x 8 *Crotale* SAM

14 *Luda* (Type-051) (ASUW) with 2 x 3 CSS-N-2/C-

201/HY 2, 2 x 2 130mm guns; plus 2 x 12 ASW RL

FRIGATES about 35

4 *Jiangwei* with 2 x 3 C-801 SSM, 6 XHQ-61/CSA-N-1 SAM, 2 x 5 ASW RL, 1 x 2 100mm gun, 1 Z-9A (Fr *Dauphin*) hel

About 31 *Jianghu*; 3 variants:

About 26 Type I, with 4 x 5 ASW RL, plus 2 x 2 HY, 2/C-201/CSS-N-2 SSM, 2 100mm guns

About 1 Type II, with 2 x 5 ASW RL, plus 2 x 2 HY 2, 2 x 2 100mm guns

About 4 Type III, with 8 C-801 SSM, 2 x 2 100mm guns; plus 4 x 5 ASW RL

PATROL AND COASTAL COMBATANTS about 747

MISSILE CRAFT about 163

1 *Huang* with 6 C-801 SSM

12 *Houxin* with 4 C-801 SSM

Some 100 *Huangfeng/Hola* (Sov *Osa* I-Type) with 4 HY-2 SSM

About 50 *Houku* (*Komar*-Type) with 2 SY-1 SSM

TORPEDO CRAFT about 125

100 *Huchuan* PHT

some 25 P-6, all < with 2 533mm TT

PATROL CRAFT about 459

COASTAL about 103

2 *Haijui* with 3 x 5 ASW RL

About 96 *Hainan* with 4 ASW RL

5 *Haiqing* with 2 x 6 ASW mor

INSHORE about 311

300 *Shanghai*, 11 *Haizhui*

RIVERINE about 45<

(Some minor combatants have reportedly been assigned to paramilitary forces (People's Armed Police, border guards, the militia) to the Customs Service, broken up or into store. Totals, therefore, may be high.)

MINE WARFARE about 119

MINELAYERS 1

1 *Wolei*

In addition, *Luda* and *Jiangnan*-class DD/FF, *Hainan*, *Shanghai* PC and T-43 MSO have minelaying capability

MINE COUNTERMEASURES about 118

27 Sov T-43 MSO

7 *Wosao* MSC

About 80 *Lienyun* aux MSC

3 *Wochang* and 1 *Shanghai* II MSI; plus about 4 drone MSI and 42 reserve

AMPHIBIOUS 73

8 *Yukan* LST, capacity about 200 tps, 10 tk

3 *Shan* (US LST-1) LST, capacity about 150 tps, 16 tk

6 *Yuting* LST, capacity 4 *Jingsah* ACV, 2 hel plus tps

31 *Yuliang*, 1 *Yuling*, 1 *Yudeng* LSM, capacity about 100 tps, 3 tk

9 *Wuhu-A* LSM capacity 250 tps, 2 tk

9 *Yuhai* LSM capacity 250 tps 2tk

1 *Yudao* LSM

6 *Quonsha* shock tpt capacity 400 tps, 350 tons cargo

Plus about 140 craft: 90 LCU, 40 LCP, 10 LCT

SUPPORT AND MISCELLANEOUS about 167

1 *Nanchang* AOR
2 *Fuqing* AO, 33 AOT, 14 AF, 10 submarine spt, 1 submarine rescue, 2 repair, 9 *Qiongsha* tps tpt, 30 tpt, 33 survey/research/experimental, 4 ice-breakers, 1 DMS, 25 ocean tugs, 1 hel trg, 1 trg

COASTAL REGIONAL DEFENCE FORCES (25,000)

ε35 indep arty and SSM regt deployed in 25 coastal defence regions to protect naval bases, offshore islands and other vulnerable points

GUNS 85mm, 100mm, 130mm
SSM *HY* 2/CSS-C-3, *HY* 4/CSS-C-7

MARINES (some 5,000)

1 bde (3 marine, 1 mech inf, 1 lt tk, 1 arty bn); special recce units
RESERVES on mob to total 8 div (24 inf, 8 tk, 8 arty regt), 2 indep tk regt. 3 Army div also have amph role

EQUIPMENT

MBT Type-59
LT TK Type-63 amph
APC Type-77-II
ARTY 122mm: Type-54, Type-70 SP
MRL 107mm: Type-63
ATGW HJ-8
SAM HN-5

NAVAL AIR FORCE (25,000)

541 shore-based cbt ac, 25 armed hel
BBR 7 H-6, 15 H-6D reported with 2 YJ-6 anti-ship ALCM; about 60 H-5 torpedo-carrying lt bbr
FGA some 40 Q-5
FTR some 295 J-6, 66 J-7, 30 J-8
RECCE 7 HZ-5
MR/ASW 4* ex-Sov Be-6 *Madge*, 4* PS-5 (SH-5)
HEL
   ASW 9 SA-321, 4 Z-8, 12 Z-9
   TPT 50 Y-5, 4 Y-7, 6 Y-8, 2 YAK-42, 6 An-26, 10 Mi-8
TRG 53 PT-6, 16* JJ-6, 4* JJ-7
MISSILES
   ALCM YJ-6/C-601, YJ-BK/C-801K, YJ-8IIK/C-802K
(Naval ftr integrated into national AD system)

DEPLOYMENT AND BASES

NORTH SEA FLEET

coastal defence from Korean border (Yalu River) to south of Lianyungang (approx 35°10'N); equates to Shenyang, Beijing and Jinan MR, and to seaward
BASES Qingdao (HQ), Dalian (Luda), Huludao, Weihai, Chengshan, Yuchi; 9 coastal defence districts
FORCES 2 submarine, 3 escort, 1 mine warfare, 1 amph sqn; plus Bohai Gulf trg flotillas; about 300 patrol and coastal combatants

EAST SEA FLEET

coastal defence from south of Lianyungang to Dongshan (approx 35°10'N to 23°30'N); equates to Nanjing Military Region, and to seaward
BASES HQ Dongqian Lake (Ninbo), Shanghai Naval base, Dinghai, Hangzhou, Xiangshan; 7 coastal defence districts
FORCES 2 submarine, 2 escort, 1 mine warfare, 1 amph sqn; about 250 patrol and coastal combatants
   Naval Infantry 1 cadre div
   Coastal Regional Defence Forces Nanjing Coastal District

SOUTH SEA FLEET

coastal defence from Dongshan (approx 23°30'N) to Vietnamese border; equates to Guangzhou MR, and to seaward (including Paracel and Spratly Islands)
BASE Hong Kong
   PATROL AND COASTAL COMBATANTS 8
      4 *Houjian* PGG with 6 C-801 SSM, 4 PCI
   SUPPORT AND MISCELLANEOUS 5
      2 *Wuhu* LSM capacity 250 tps 2 tk; 3 *Catamaran*
OTHER BASES Zhanjiang (HQ), Shantou, Guangzhou, Haikou, Dongguan City, Yulin, Beihai, Huangpu; plus outposts on Paracel and Spratly Islands; 9 coastal defence districts
FORCES 2 submarine, 2 escort, 1 mine warfare, 1 amph sqn; about 300 patrol and coastal combatants
   Naval Infantry 1 bde

Air Force 470,000

(incl strategic forces, 220,000 AD personnel and 160,000 conscripts); some 3,566 cbt ac, few armed hel
Flying hours H-6: 80; J-7 and J-8: 110; Su-27: 110+
7 Mil Air Regions, HQ Beijing
Combat elm org in 7 armies of varying numbers of air div (each with 3 regt of 3 sqn of 3 flt of 3–4 ac, 1 maint unit, some tpt and trg ac); tpt ac in regt only
BBR med 3 regt with 120 H-6 (some may be nuclear-capable), some carry YJ-6/C-601 ASM **lt** some 200+ H-5 (some with YJ-8 ASM)
FGA 400+ Q-5
FTR 2,556, some 60 regt with about 1,800 J-6/B/D/E, 500 J-7, 150 J-8, 46 Su-27SK/UBK
RECCE ε290: ε40 HZ-5, 150 JZ-5, 100 JZ-6 ac
TPT incl 18 BAe *Trident* 1E/2E, 10 Il-18, 10 Il-76, 300 Y-5, 25 Y-7, 45 Y-8 (some tkr), 15 Y-11, 2 Y-12
HEL some 210: incl 6 AS-332, 4 Bell 214, 30 Mi-8, 100 Z-5, 70 Z-9
TRG incl HJ-5, JJ-6
MISSILES
   AAM PL-2/-2A, PL-5B, PL-7, PL-8, PL-9, 50+ AA-8, 250+ AA-10, 250+ AA-11
   ASM YJ-1/2, C-801/802, YJ-6/C-601, C-601 sub-sonic ALCM (anti-ship, perhaps *HY* 2 SSM derivative); YJ-8 K/C-801K, YJ-8IIK/C-802K
AD ARTY 16 div: 16,000 **35mm**, **57mm**, **85mm** and **100mm** guns; 28 indep AD regts (100+ SAM units with HQ-2/2A/2B, -2J (CSA-1), SA-10, SA-12)

Forces Abroad

UN AND PEACEKEEPING
MIDDLE EAST (UNTSO): 5 obs. **IRAQ/KUWAIT** (UNIKOM): 11 obs. **WESTERN SAHARA** (MINURSO): 16 obs

Paramilitary ε1,000,000 active

PEOPLE'S ARMED POLICE (Ministry of Defence)
ε1,000,000 (to increase)

45 div incl **Internal security** ε730,000 **Border defence** 200,000 **Guards, Comms** ε69,000

Fiji

	1996	1997	1998	1999
GDP	F$3.0bn	F$3.1bn		
	($1.9bn)	($1.9bn)		
per capita	$5,500	$5,800		
Growth	3.3%	3.6%		
Inflation	3.1%	3.4%		
Debt	$217m	$210m		
Def exp	F$68m	F$70m		
	($48m)	($48m)		
Def bdgt			εF$61m	
			($30m)	
FMA (Aus)	$3m	$2m	$2m	
US$1 = F$	1.41	1.44	2.03	
Population		798,000		

(Indian 49%, Fijian 46%, European/other 5%)

Age	*13–17*	*18–22*	*23–32*
Men	46,000	43,000	64,000
Women	44,000	40,000	62,000

Total Armed Forces

ACTIVE some 3,500
(incl recalled reserves)
RESERVES some 6,000
(to age 45)

Army 3,200

(incl 300 recalled reserves)
7 inf bn (incl 4 cadre) • 1 engr bn • 1 arty bty • 1 special ops coy
EQUIPMENT
    TOWED ARTY 88mm: 4 25-pdr (ceremonial)
    MOR 81mm: 12

Navy 300

BASES Walu Bay, Viti (trg)

PATROL AND COASTAL COMBATANTS 9
PATROL, INSHORE 9
    3 *Kulu* (*Pacific Forum*) PCI, 4 *Vai* (Il *Dabur*) PCI<, 2 *Levuka* PCI<
SUPPORT AND MISCELLANEOUS 1
    1 *Cagi Donu* presidential yacht (trg)

Forces Abroad

UN AND PEACEKEEPING
EGYPT (MFO): 339; 1 inf bn(-). **IRAQ/KUWAIT** (UNIKOM): 5 obs. **LEBANON** (UNIFIL): 582; 1 inf bn. **PAPUA NEW GUINEA**: Bougainville Truce Monitoring Group

Indonesia

	1996	1997	1998	1999
GDP	Rp533tr	Rp624tr		
	($227bn)	($215bn)		
per capita	$4,200	$4,500		
Growth	7.8%	5.0%		
Inflation	8.0%	7.6%		
Debt	$129bn	$136bn		
Def exp[a]	εRp11tr	εRp14tr		
	($4.7bn)	($4.8bn)		
Def bdgt[b]			εRp20tr	
			($1.7bn)	
FMA (US)	$0.6m	$0.1m	$0.4m	$0.4m
(Aus)	$4.0m	$4.5m	$3.5m	
$1 = rupiah	2,342	2,909	11,650	

[a] Incl mil exp on procurement and def industry
[b] Revised from Rp9.4tr in July 1998

Population		200,745,000	

(Muslim 87%; also Javanese 45%, Sundanese 14%, Madurese 8%, Malay 8%, Chinese 3%, other 22%)

Age	*13–17*	*18–22*	*23–32*
Men	11,084,000	10,567,000	16,890,000
Women	10,601,000	10,177,000	17,521,000

Total Armed Forces

ACTIVE 476,000
(incl some 177,000 Police (*POLRI*), see *Paramilitary*)
Terms of service 2 years selective conscription authorised

RESERVES 400,000
Army cadre units; numbers, str n.k., obligation to age 45 for officers

Army 235,000

Strategic Reserve (KOSTRAD) (35,000)
    2 inf div HQ • 3 inf bde (9 bn) • 3 AB bde (9 bn) • 2

fd arty regt (6 bn) • 1 AD arty regt (2 bn) • 2 armd bn • 2 engr bn

10 Mil Area Comd (KODAM) (160–170,000) (Provincial (KOREM) and District (KODIM) comd) 2 inf bde (6 bn) • 67 inf bn (incl 4 AB) • 9 cav bn • 11 fd arty, 10 AD bn • 9 engr bn • 1 composite avn sqn, 1 hel sqn

Special Forces (KOPASSUS) (6–7,000 incl 4,800 cbt) subject to re-org; to be 5 SF gp (incl 2 cbt, 1 counter-terrorist, 1 int, 1 trg)

EQUIPMENT

LT TK some 275 AMX-13 (to be upgraded), 30 PT-76, 50 *Scorpion* (incl 30 with **90mm**)

RECCE 69 *Saladin* (16 upgraded), 55 *Ferret* (13 upgraded), 18 VBL

APC 200 AMX-VCI, 55 *Saracen* (14 upgraded), 60 V-150 *Commando*, 22 *Commando Ranger*, 80 BTR-40, 9 BTR-50, 20 *Stormer* (incl variants)

TOWED ARTY 76mm: M-48; **105mm**: 170 M-101, 10 M-56

MOR 81mm: 800; **120mm**: 75 Brandt

RCL 90mm: 90 M-67; **106mm**: 45 M-40A1

RL 89mm: 700 LRAC

AD GUNS 20mm: 125; **40mm**: 90 L/70; **57mm**: 200 S-60

SAM 51 *Rapier*, 42 RBS-70

AC 1 BN-2 *Islander*, 2 C-47, 4 NC-212, 2 Cessna 310, 2 *Commander* 680, 18 *Gelatik* (trg), 3 DHC-5

HEL 8 Bell 205, 14 Bo-105, 20 NB-412, 10 Hughes 300C (trg)

Navy ε43,000 (increasing to 47,000)

(incl ε1,000 Naval Air and 12,000 Marines)

PRINCIPAL COMMAND

WESTERN FLEET HQ Teluk Ratai (Jakarta)
  BASES Primary Teluk Ratai, Belawan **Other** 10 plus minor facilities
EASTERN FLEET HQ Surabaya
  BASES Primary Surabaya, Ujung Pandang, Jayapura **Other** 13 plus minor facilities

MILITARY SEALIFT COMMAND (KOLINLAMIL)

controls some amph and tpt ships used for inter-island comms and log spt for Navy and Army (assets incl in Navy and Army listings)

SUBMARINES 2

2 *Cakra* (Ge T-209/1300) with 533mm TT (Ge HWT) (1 in long-term refit) (plus 2 Ge 206 late 1997)

FRIGATES 17

6 *Ahmad Yani* (Nl *Van Speijk*) with 1 *Wasp* hel (ASW) (Mk 44 LWT), 2 x 3 ASTT; plus 2 x 4 *Harpoon* SSM, 1 76mm gun

3 *Fatahillah* with 2 x 3 ASTT (not *Nala*), 1 x 2 ASW mor, 1 *Wasp* hel (*Nala* only); plus 2 x 2 MM-38 *Exocet*, 1 120mm gun

3 *M. K. Tiyahahu* (UK *Tribal*) with 1 *Wasp* hel, 1 x 3

Limbo ASW mor; plus 2 114mm guns

1 *Hajar Dewantara* (FRY) (trg) with 2 533mm TT, 1 ASW mor; plus 2 x 2 MM-38 *Exocet*, 1 57mm gun

4 *Samadikun* (US *Claud Jones*) with 2 x 3 ASTT

PATROL AND COASTAL COMBATANTS 57

CORVETTES 16 *Kapitan Patimura* (GDR *Parchim*)

MISSILE CRAFT 4 *Mandau* (Ko *Dagger*) PFM with 4 MM-38 *Exocet* SSM, 1 57mm gun

TORPEDO CRAFT 2 *Singa* (Ge Lürssen 57m (NAV I)) with 2 533mm TT and 1 57mm gun

PATROL CRAFT 35

COASTAL 6

2 *Pandrong* (Ge Lürssen 57m (NAV II)) PFC, with 1 57mm gun

3 *Kakap* (Ge Lürssen 57m (NAV III)) PFC, with 40mm gun and hel deck

1 *Barakuda* PCI

INSHORE 29

8 *Sibarau* (Aust *Attack*) PCI

2 *Bima Samudera* PHT

1 *Barabzuda* PCI

18<

MINE COUNTERMEASURES 13

2 *Pulau Rengat* (mod Nl *Tripartite*) MCC (sometimes used for coastal patrol)

2 *Pulau Rani* (Sov T-43) MCC (mainly used for coastal patrol)

9 *Palau Rote* (Ge *Kondor* II)† MSC (mainly used for coastal patrol, 7 non-op)

AMPHIBIOUS 26

6 *Teluk Semangka* LST, capacity about 200 tps, 17 tk, 2 with 3 hel (1 fitted as hospital ship)

1 *Teluk Amboina* LST, capacity about 200 tps, 16 tk

7 *Teluk Langsa* (US LST-512) and 2 *Teluk Banten* (mod US LST-512) LST, capacity 200 tps, 16 tks

12 *Teluk Gilimanuk* (Ge *Frosch* I/II) LST)

Plus about 65 LCM and LCVP

SUPPORT AND MISCELLANEOUS 15

1 *Sorong* AO, 1 *Arun* AOR (UK *Rover*), 2 Sov *Khobi* AOT, 1 cmd/spt/replenish, 1 repair, 2 ocean tug, 6 survey/research, 1 *Barakuda* (Ge *Lürsson Nav* IV) presidental yacht

NAVAL AIR (ε1,000)

49 cbt ac, 21 armed hel

ASW 6 *Wasp* HAS-1

MR 9 N-22 *Searchmaster* B, 6 *Searchmaster* L, 11 NC-212 (MR/ELINT), 14 N-22B, 6 N-24, 3 CN-235 MP

TPT 4 *Commander*, 10 NC-212, 2 DHC-5, 20 *Nomad* (6 VIP)

TRG 2 *Bonanza* F33, 6 PA-38

HEL 4* NAS-332F, 7* NBo-105, 4* Bell-412

MARINES (12,000)

2 inf bde (6 bn) • 1 SF bn(-) • 1 cbt spt regt (arty, AD)

EQUIPMENT

LT TK 100 PT-76†

RECCE 14 BRDM
AIFV 10 AMX-10 PAC 90
APC 24 AMX-10P, 60 BTR-50P
TOWED ARTY 48: **105mm**: 20 LG-1 Mk II; **122mm**: 28 M-38
MOR 81mm
MRL 140mm: 15 BM-14
AD GUNS 40mm, 57mm

Air Force 21,000

91 cbt ac, no armed hel; 2 Air Operations Areas
FGA 5 sqn
    1 with 20 A-4 (18 -E, 2 TA-4H)
    1 with 10 F-16 (6 -A, 4 -B)
    2 with 8 *Hawk* Mk 109 and 16 *Hawk* Mk 209 (FGA/ftr)
    1 with 13 *Hawk* Mk 53 (FGA/trg)
FTR 1 sqn with 12 F-5 (8 -E, 4 -F)
RECCE 1 sqn with 12* OV-10F
MR 1 sqn with 3 Boeing 737-200
TKR 2 KC-130B
TPT 19 C-130 (9 -B, 3 -H, 7 -H-30), 3 L100-30, 1 Boeing 707, 4 Cessna 207, 5 Cessna 401, 2 C-402, 6 F-27-400M, 1 F-28-1000, 2 F-28-3000, 10 NC-212, 1 *Skyvan* (survey), 6 CN-235-110
HEL 10 S-58T, 10 Hughes 500, 11 NAS-330, 2 NAS-332L (VIP), 4 NBO-105CD
TRG 3 sqn with 31 AS-202, 2 Cessna 172, 18 T-34C, 2 T-41D

Deployment

ARMY
EAST TIMOR ε5,000

Forces Abroad

UN AND PEACEKEEPING
CROATIA (UNMOP): 1 obs. **FYROM** (UNPREDEP): 53 incl 2 obs. **GEORGIA** (UNOMIG): 4 obs. **IRAQ/KUWAIT** (UNIKOM): 5 obs. **TAJIKISTAN** (UNMOT): 4 obs

Paramilitary

POLICE (*POLRI*) some 177,000
incl 6,000 police 'mobile bde' (BRIMOB) org in 49 coy (to be 56), incl counter-terrorism unit (*Gegana*)
    EQPT APC 34 *Tactica*; **ac** 1 *Commander*, 2 Beech 18, 1 PA-31T, 1 Cessna-U206, 2 NC- 212 **hel** 19 NBO-105, 3 Bell 206
MARINE POLICE (12,000)
    about 10 PCC, 9 PCI and 6 PCI< (all armed)
KAMRA (People's Security) (R) 1,500,000
some 300,000 undergo 3 weeks' basic trg each year;

part-time police auxiliary
WANRA (People's Resistance) (R)
part-time local military auxiliary force under Regional Military Comd (KOREM)
CUSTOMS
    about 72 PFI<, armed
SEA COMMUNICATIONS AGENCY (responsible to Department of Communications)
    5 Kujang PCI, 4 Golok PCI (SAR), plus boats

Opposition

FRETILIN (Revolutionary Front for an Independent East Timor) some 70 incl spt
FALINTIL mil wing; small arms
FREE PAPUA ORGANISATION (OPM) perhaps 2–300 (100 armed)
FREE ACEH MOVEMENT (*Gerakan Aceh Merdeka*) 50 armed reported

Japan

	1996	1997	1998	1999
GDP	¥500tr	¥507tr		
	($4.4tr)	($4.2tr)		
per capita	$23,200	$23,500		
Growth	3.6%	-0.7%		
Inflation	0.2%	1.7%		
Publ Debt	82.7%	87.1%		
Def exp	¥4.8tr	¥4.9tr		
	($44.5bn)	($40.9bn)		
Def bdgt			¥4.9tr	
			($35.2bn)	
$1 = yen	109	121	140	
Population	126,189,000 (Korean <1%)			
Age	*13–17*	*18–22*	*23–32*	
Men	3,862,000	4,402,000	9,363,000	
Women	3,676,000	4,189,000	8,953,000	

Total Armed Forces

ACTIVE some 242,600
(incl 1,400 Central Staffs; 9,900 women)

RESERVES 48,600

READY RESERVE Army (GSDF) 700
GENERAL RESERVE Army (GSDF) 46,000 **Navy** (MSDF) 1,100 **Air Force** (ASDF) 800

Army (Ground Self-Defense Force) some 151,800

5 Army HQ (Regional Comds) • 1 armd div • 12 inf div (7 at 7,000, 5 at 9,000 each) • 2 composite bde • 1 AB bde • 1 arty bde; 2 arty gp • 2 AD bde; 4 AD gp • 4 trg bde (incl 1 spt); 2 trg regt • 5 engr bde •1 hel bde • 5 ATK hel sqn

EQUIPMENT

MBT some 70 Type-61 (retiring), some 870 Type-74, some 150 Type-90

RECCE some 90 Type-87

AIFV some 60 Type-89

APC some 300 Type-60, some 340 Type-73, some 230 Type-82

TOWED ARTY 105mm: some 30 M2A1; **155mm**: some 450 FH-70

SP ARTY 105mm: some 20 Type-74; **155mm**: some 200 Type-75; **203mm**: some 90 M-110A2

MRL 130mm: some 70 Type-75 SP; **227mm**: some 40 MLRS

MOR incl **81mm**: some 740 (some SP); **107mm**: some 360 (some SP); **120mm**: some 250 (some SP)

SSM some 80 Type-88 coastal

ATGW some 200 Type-64, some 240 Type-79, some 240 Type-87

RL 89mm: some 1,470

RCL 84mm: some 2,720 *Carl Gustav*; **106mm**: some 330 (incl Type 60 SP)

AD GUNS 35mm: some 40 twin, some 40 Type-87 SP

SAM 320 *Stinger*, some 60 Type 81, some 100 Type 91, some 30 Type 93, some 200 I HAWK

AC some 20 LR-1

ATTACK HEL some 90 AH-1S

TPT HEL 3 AS-332L (VIP), some 40 CH-47J/JA, some V-107, some 190 OH-6D/J, some 140 UH-1H/J, some UH-60JA

SURV Type-92 (mor), J/MPQ-P7 (arty)

Navy (Maritime Self-Defense Force) 43,800

(incl ε12,000 Air Arm and 1,900 women)
BASES Yokosuka, Kure, Sasebo, Maizuru, Ominato
FLEET Surface units org into 4 escort flotillas of 8 DD/FF each **Bases** Yokosuka, Kure, Sasebo, Maizuru
SS org into 2 flotillas **Bases** Kure, Yokosuka
Remainder assigned to 5 regional districts

SUBMARINES 16

7 *Harushio* with 6 x 533mm TT (J Type-89 HWT) with *Harpoon* USGW

8 *Yuushio* with 533mm TT (J Type-89 HWT), 7 with *Harpoon* USGW

1 *Oyashio* with 6 x 533mm TT, Sub *Harpoon* USGW

PRINCIPAL SURFACE COMBATANTS 57

DESTROYERS 9

4 *Kongo* DDG with 2 VLS for *Standard* SAM and ASROC SUGW (29 cells forward, 61 cells aft); plus 2 x 4 *Harpoon* SSM, 1 127mm gun, 2 x 3 ASTT and

hel deck

2 *Hatakaze* with 1 SM-1-MR Mk 13 SAM; plus 2 x 4 *Harpoon* SSM, 1 x 8 ASROC SUGW (Mk 46 LWT) 2 x 3 ASTT, 2 127mm guns

3 *Tachikaze* with 1 SM-1-MR; plus 1 x 8 ASROC, 2 x 3 ASTT, 2 127mm guns

FRIGATES 48

FFH 26

2 *Shirane* with 3 SH-60J ASW hel, 1 x 8 ASROC, 2 x 3 ASTT; plus 2 127mm guns

2 *Haruna* with 3 SH-60J hel, 1 x 8 ASROC, 2 x 3 ASTT; plus 2 127mm guns

8 *Asagiri* with 1 SH-60J hel, 1 x 8 ASROC, 2 x 3 ASTT; plus 2 x 4 *Harpoon* SSM

12 *Hatsuyuki* with 1 SH-60J, 1 x 8 ASROC, 2 x 3 ASTT; plus 2 x 4 *Harpoon* SSM

2 *Murasame* with 1 SH-60J hel, 1 VLS *Sea Sparrow* SAM, 1 VLS ASROC ASW, 2 x 3 ASTT, 8 SSM-1B

FF 22

6 *Abukuma* with 1 x 8 ASROC, 2 x 3 ASTT; plus 2 x 4 *Harpoon* SSM

2 *Takatsuki* with 1 x 8 ASROC, 2 x 3 ASTT, 1 x 4 ASW RL; plus 2 127mm gun

3 *Yamagumo* with 1 x 8 ASROC, 2 x 3 ASTT, 1 x 4 ASW RL

2 *Yubari* with 2 x 3 ASTT, 1 x 4 ASW RL; plus 2 x 4 *Harpoon* SSM

1 *Ishikari* with 2 x 3 ASTT, 1 x 4 ASW RL; plus 2 x 4 *Harpoon* SSM

8 *Chikugo* with 1 x 8 ASROC, 2 x 3 ASTT

PATROL AND COASTAL COMBATANTS 6

MISSILE CRAFT 3 *Ichi-Go* Type PHM with 4 SSM-1B
PATROL CRAFT, INSHORE 3 *Jukyu-Go* PCI<

MINE COUNTERMEASURES 32

2 *Uraga* MCM spt with hel deck; can lay mines
16 *Hatsushima* MCC
9 *Uwajima* MCC
3 *Yaeyama* MSO
1 *Fukue* coastal MCM spt
1 *Nijima* coastal MCM spt

AMPHIBIOUS 6

1 *Osumi* LST, capacity 330 tps, 10 tk, 2 LCAC (large flight deck)
3 *Miura* LST, capacity 200 tps, 10 tk
2 *Atsumi* LST, capacity 130 tps, 5 tk
Plus craft: 2 *Yura* and 2 *Ichi-Go* LCM, 2 LCAC, 11 LCM

SUPPORT AND MISCELLANEOUS 23

3 *Towada* AOE, 1 *Sagami* AOE (all with hel deck), 2 sub depot/rescue, 3 *Minegumo* trg, 2 *Uraga* minesweeping lenders, 1 *Kashima* (trg), 2 trg spt, 8 survey/experimental, 1 icebreaker

AIR ARM (ε12,000)

100 cbt ac, 106 armed hel
Flying hours P-3: 500
7 Air Groups

MR 10 sqn (1 trg) with 100 P-3C
ASW 6 land-based hel sqn (1 trg) with 45 HSS-2B, 4 shipboard sqn with 61 SH-60J
MCM 1 hel sqn with 10 MH-53E
EW 1 sqn with 4 EP-3
TPT 1 sqn with 4 YS-11M
SAR 10 US-1A, 10 S-61 hel, 12 UH-60J
TRG 4 sqn with **ac** 30 T-5, 26 TC-90/UC-90, 7 YS-11T/M **hel** 9 OH-6D/J

Air Force (Air Self-Defense Force) 45,600

329 cbt ac, no armed hel, 7 cbt air wings
Flying hours 150
FGA 2 sqn with 50 F-I, 1 sqn with 20 F-4EJ
FTR 10 sqn
    8 with 180 F-15J/DJ
    2 with 49 F-4EJ
RECCE 1 sqn with 20* RF-4E/EJ
AEW 1 sqn with 13 E-2C, 2 Boeing E-767 (AWACS)
EW 2 sqn with 1 EC-1, 10 YS-11 E
AGGRESSOR TRG 1 sqn with 10 F-15DJ
TPT 4 sqn, 4 flt
    3 with 20 C-1, 10 C-130H, 10 YS-11
    1 with 2 747-400 (VIP)
    4 flt heavy-lift hel with 16 CH-47J
SAR 1 wg (10 det) with **ac** 20 MU-2, 10 U-125 **hel** 20 KV-107, 20 UH-60J
CAL 1 sqn with 1 YS-11, 10 U-125-800
TRG 5 wg, 12 sqn with 40 T-1A/B, 40* T-2, 40 T-3, 40 T-4, 10 T-400
LIAISON 1 B-65, 10 T-33, 90 T-4, 2 U-4
TEST 1 wg with F-15J, 10 T-4

AIR DEFENCE

ac control and warning: 4 wg, 28 radar sites
6 SAM gp (24 sqn) with 120 *Patriot*
Air Base Defence Gp with **20mm** *Vulcan* AA guns, Type 81, Type 91, *Stinger* SAM
ASM ASM-1, ASM-2
AAM AAM-1, AAM-3, AIM-7 *Sparrow*, AIM-9 *Sidewinder*

Forces Abroad

UN AND PEACEKEEPING
SYRIA/ISRAEL (UNDOF): 45

Paramilitary 12,000

MARITIME SAFETY AGENCY (Coast Guard) (Ministry of Transport, no cbt role) 12,000
    PATROL VESSELS some 328
    Offshore (over 1,000 tons) 42, incl 1 *Shikishima* with 2 *Super Puma* hel, 2 *Mizuho* with 2 Bell 212, 8 *Soya* with 1 Bell 212 hel, 2 *Izu*, 28 *Shiretok* and 1 *Kojima* (trg) **Coastal** (under 1,000 tons) 36 **Inshore** some 250 patrol craft most<

MISC about 90 service, 80 tender/trg vessels
AC 5 NAMC YS-11A, 2 Short *Skyvan*, 16 *King Air*, 1 Cessna U-206G
HEL 32 Bell 212, 4 Bell 206, 2 Hughes 369

Foreign Forces

US 39,100: **Army** 1,800; 1 Corps HQ **Navy** 6,700; bases at Yokosuka (HQ 7th Fleet) and Sasebo **Marines** 16,600; 1 MEF in Okinawa **Air Force** 14,000; 1 Air Force HQ (5th Air Force), 90 cbt ac, 1 ftr wg, 2 sqn with 36 F-16, 1 wg, 3 sqn with 54 F-15C/D, 1 sqn with 15 KC-135, 1 SAR sqn with 8 HH-60, 1 sqn with 2 E-3 AWACS; 1 airlift wg with 16 C-130E/H, 4 C-21, 3 C-9; 1 special ops gp with 4 MC-130P, 4 MC-130E

Korea, Democratic People's Republic Of (North)

	1996	1997	1998	1999
GNP[a]	ε$20bn	ε$18bn		
per capita	$1,000	$900		
Growth	ε-3.6%	ε6.8%		
Inflation	ε5%	ε5%		
Debt	ε$12bn	ε$12bn		
Def exp	ε$5.4bn	ε$5.4bn		
Def bdgt			ε$2.4bn	
$1 = won[b]	2.2	2.2	2.2	

[a] PPP est. GNP is larger than GDP because of remitted earnings of DPRK expatriates in Japan and ROK
[b] Market rate **1997** $1 = 70–100 won

Population		25,057,000		
Age	*13–17*	*18–22*	*23–32*	
Men	1,016,000	1,037,000	2,520,000	
Women	1,040,000	1,091,000	2,308,000	

Total Armed Forces

ACTIVE ε1,055,000
Terms of service **Army** 5–8 years **Navy** 5–10 years **Air Force** 3–4 years, followed by compulsory part-time service to age 40. Thereafter service in the Worker/Peasant Red Guard to age 60

RESERVES 4,700,000
Army 600,000 **Navy** 65,000 are assigned to units (see *Paramilitary*)

Army ε923,000

20 Corps (1 armd, 4 mech, 12 inf, 2 arty, 1 capital defence) • 26 inf div • 15 armd bde • 24 truck mobile inf bde • 3 indep inf bde
Special Purpose Forces Comd (88,000): 10 *Sniper* bde

(incl 2 amph, 2 AB), 14 lt inf bde (incl 3 AB), 17 recce, 1 AB bn, 'Bureau of Reconnaissance SF' (8 bn)
Army tps: 6 hy arty bde (incl MRL), 1 *Scud* SSM bde, 1 FROG SSM regt
Corps tps: 14 arty bde incl 122mm, 152mm SP, MRL

RESERVES

26 inf div, 18 inf bde

EQUIPMENT

MBT some 3,000: T-34, T-54/-55, T-62, Type-59
LT TK 500 PT-76, M-1985
APC 2,500 BTR-40/-50/-60/-152, PRC Type-531, VTT-323 (M-1973)
TOTAL ARTY (excl mor) 10,600
TOWED ARTY 3,500: **122mm**: M-1931/-37, D-74, D-30; **130mm**: M-46; **152mm**: M-1937, M-1938, M-1943
SP ARTY 4,500: **122mm**: M-1977, M-1981, M-1985, M-1991; **130mm**: M-1975, M-1981, M-1991; **152mm**: M-1974, M-1977; **170mm**: M-1978, M-1989
COMBINED GUN/MOR: 120mm: (reported)
MRL 2,600: **107mm**: Type-63; **122mm**: BM-21, BM-11, M-1977/-1985/-1992/-1993; **240mm**: M-1985/-1989/-1991
MOR 8,100: **82mm**: M-37; **120mm**: M-43 (some SP); **160mm**: M-43
SSM 24 FROG-3/-5/-7; some 30 *Scud*-C
ATGW AT-1 *Snapper*, AT-3 *Sagger* (some SP), AT-4 *Spigot*, AT-5 *Spandrel*
RCL 82mm: 1,700 B-10
AD GUNS 4,800 plus 3,000 in static positions: **14.5mm**: ZPU-1/-2/-4 SP, M-1984 SP; **23mm**: ZU-23, M-1992 SP; **37mm**: M-1939, M-1992; **57mm**: S-60, M-1985 SP; **85mm**: KS-12; **100mm**: KS-19
SAM ε10,000+ SA-7/-16

Navy ε46,000

BASES East Coast Toejo (HQ), Changjon, Munchon, Songjon-pardo, Mugye-po, Mayang-do, Chaho Nodongjagu, Puam-Dong, Najin **West Coast** Nampo (HQ), Pipa Got, Sagon-ni, Chodo-ri, Koampo, Tasa-ri 2 Fleet HQ

SUBMARINES 26

22 PRC Type-031/Sov *Romeo* with 533mm TT
4 Sov *Whiskey*† with 533mm and 406mm TT
(Plus some 45 midget and 13 coastal submarines (incl 21 *Sang-O*) mainly used for SF ops, but some with 2 TT)

FRIGATES 3

1 *Soho* with 4 ASW RL, plus 4 SS-N-2 *Styx* SSM, 1 100mm gun and hel deck
2 *Najin* with 2 x 5 ASW RL, plus 2 SS-N-2 *Styx* SSM, 2 100mm guns

PATROL AND COASTAL COMBATANTS some 424

CORVETTES 5

3 *Sariwon* with 1 85mm gun
2 *Tral* with 1 85mm gun
MISSILE CRAFT 43
15 *Soju*, 8 Sov *Osa*, 4 PRC *Huangfeng* PFM with 4 SS-N-2 *Styx*, 6 *Sohung*, 10 Sov *Komar* PFM with 2 SS-N-2
TORPEDO CRAFT some 198
3 Sov *Shershen* with 4 533mm TT
Some 155 with 2 533mm TT
40 *Sin Hung* PHT
PATROL CRAFT 178
COASTAL 25
6 *Hainan* PFC with 4 ASW RL, 13 *Taechong* PFC with 2 ASW RL, 6 *Chong-Ju* with 1 85mm gun, 2 ASW mor
INSHORE some 153
18 SO-1, 12 *Shanghai* II, 3 *Chodo*, some 120<

MINE COUNTERMEASURES about 25 MSI<

AMPHIBIOUS 10

10 *Hantal* LSM, capacity 350 tps, 3 tk
plus craft 15 LCM, 15 LCU, about 100 Nampo LCVP, plus about 130 hovercraft

SUPPORT AND MISCELLANEOUS 7

2 ocean tugs, 1 AS, 1 ocean and 3 inshore survey

COASTAL DEFENCE

2 SSM regt: *Silkworm* in 6 sites, and probably some mobile launchers
GUNS 122mm: M-1931/-37; **130mm**: SM-4-1, M-1992; **152mm**: M-1937

Air Force 85,000

607 cbt ac, armed hel
Flying hours some 30
BBR 3 lt regt with 82 H-5 (Il-28)
FGA/FTR 15 regt
3 with 107 J-5 (MiG-17), 4 with 159 J-6 (MiG-19), 4 with 130 J-7 (MiG-21), 1 with 46 MiG-23, 1 with 30 MiG-29, 1 with 18 Su-7, 1 with 35 Su-25
TPT ac 282 An-2/Y-5, 6 An-24, 2 Il-18, 4 Il-62M, 2 Tu-134, 4 Tu-154 **hel** 80 Hughes 500D, 139 Mi-2, 15 Mi-8/-17, 48 Z-5
TRG incl 10 CJ-5, 7 CJ-6, 6 MiG-21, 170 Yak-18, 35 FT-2 (MiG-15UTI)
MISSILES
AAM AA-2 *Atoll*, AA-7 *Apex*
SAM 300+ SA-2, 36 SA-3, 24 SA-5

Forces Abroad

advisers in some 12 African countries

Paramilitary 189,000 active

SECURITY TROOPS (Ministry of Public Security)
189,000
incl border guards, public safety personnel

WORKER/PEASANT RED GUARD some 3,500,000

Org on a provincial/town/village basis; comd structure is bde – bn – coy – pl; small arms with some mor and AD guns (but many units unarmed)

Korea, Republic Of (South)

	1996	1997	1998	1999
GDP	won390tr	won421tr		
	($433bn)	($443bn)		
per capita	$12,300	$13,100		
Growth	7.1%	5.5%		
Inflation	4.9%	4.5%		
Debt	$161bn	$154bn		
Def exp	won12.7tr	won14.0tr		
	($15.8bn)	($14.7bn)		
Def bdgt			won14.2tr	
			($10.2bn)	
$1 = won	804	951	1,395	
Population		46,500,000		
Age	*13–17*	*18–22*	*23–32*	
Men	1,883,000	2,057,000	4,377,000	
Women	1,759,000	1,918,000	4,096,000	

Total Armed Forces

ACTIVE 672,000

(ε159,000 conscripts)
Terms of service conscription **Army** 26 months **Navy** and **Air Force** 30 months; First Combat Forces (Mobilisation Reserve Forces) or Regional Combat Forces (Homeland Defence Forces) to age 33

RESERVES 4,500,000

being re-org

Army 560,000

(140,000 conscripts)
HQ: 3 Army, 11 Corps
3 mech inf div (each 3 bde: 3 mech inf, 3 tk, 1 recce, 1 engr bn; 1 fd arty bde) • 19 inf div (each 3 inf regt, 1 recce, 1 tk, 1 engr bn; 1 arty regt (4 bn)) • 2 indep inf bde • 7 SF bde • 3 counter-infiltration bde • 3 SSM bn with NHK-I/-II (*Honest John*) • 3 AD arty bde • 3 I HAWK bn (24 sites), 2 *Nike Hercules* bn (10 sites) • 1 avn comd

RESERVES
1 Army HQ, 23 inf div
EQUIPMENT
MBT 800 Type 88, 80 T-80U, 400 M-47, 850 M-48
AIFV 40 BMP-3
APC incl 1,700 KIFV, 420 M-113, 140 M-577, 200 Fiat 6614/KM-900/-901, 40 BMP-3

TOWED ARTY some 3,500: **105mm:** 1,700 M-101, KH-178; **155mm:** M-53, M-114, KH-179; **203mm:** M-115
SP ARTY 155mm: 1,040 M-109A2; **175mm:** M-107; **203mm:** M-110
MRL 130mm: 156 *Kooryong* (36-tube)
MOR 6,000: **81mm:** KM-29; **107mm:** M-30
SSM 12 NHK-I/-II
ATGW TOW-2A, *Panzerfaust*, AT-7
RCL 57mm, 75mm, 90mm: M67; **106mm:** M40A2
ATK GUNS 58: **76mm:** 8 M-18; **90mm:** 50 M-36 SP
AD GUNS 600: **20mm:** incl KIFV (AD variant), 60 M-167 *Vulcan*; **30mm:** 20 B1 HO SP; **35mm:** 20 GDF-003; **40mm:** 80 L60/70, M-1
SAM 350 *Javelin*, 60 *Redeye*, 130 *Stinger*, 170 *Mistral*, SA-16, 110 I HAWK, 200 *Nike Hercules*
SURV RASIT (veh, arty), AN/TPQ-36 (arty, mor), AN/TPQ-37 (arty)
AC 5 O-1A
HELICOPTERS
  ATTACK 75 AH-1F/-J, 68 Hughes 500 MD.
  TPT 15 CH-47D
  UTL 170 Hughes 500, 130 UH-1H, 98 UH-60P

Navy 60,000

(incl 25,000 Marines and ε19,000 conscripts)
BASES Chinhae (HQ), Cheju, Inchon, Mokpo, Mukho, Pukpyong, Pohang, Pusan
FLEET COMMAND 3
SUBMARINES 14
  6 *Chang Bogo* (Ge T-209/1200) with 8 533 TT; plus 3 KSS-1 *Dolgorae* SSI (175t) with 2 406mm TT, 8 *Dolphin* SSI (175t) with 2 406mm TT
PRINCIPAL SURFACE COMBATANTS 38
DESTROYERS 1 *King Kwanggaeto* with 8 *Harpoon* SSM, 1 *Sea Sparrow* SAM, 1 127mm gun, 1 *Super Lynx* hel, 4 *Chung Buk* (US *Gearing*) with 2 or 3 x 2 127mm guns; plus 2 x 3 ASTT; 5 with 2 x 4 *Harpoon* SSM, 2 with 1 x 8 ASROC, 1 *Alouette* III hel (OTHT)
FRIGATES 33
  9 *Ulsan* with 2 x 3 ASTT (Mk 46 LWT); plus 2 x 4 *Harpoon* SSM
  24 *Po Hang* with 2 x 3 ASTT; some with 2 x 1 MM-38 *Exocet*
PATROL AND COASTAL COMBATANTS 105
CORVETTES 4 *Dong Hae* (ASW) with 2 x 3 ASTT
MISSILE CRAFT 11
  8 *Pae Ku-52* (US *Asheville*), 3 with 4 *Standard* (boxed) SSM, 5 with 2 x 2 *Harpoon* SSM
  1 *Pae Ku-51* (US *Asheville*), with 2 *Standard* SSM
  2 *Kilurki-71* (*Wildcat*) with 2 MM-38 *Exocet* SSM
PATROL, INSHORE 90
  75 *Kilurki-11* (*Sea Dolphin*) 37m PFI
  15 *Chebi-51* (*Sea Hawk*) 26m PFI< (some with 2 MM-38 *Exocet* SSM)
MINE COUNTERMEASURES 14

6 *Kan Keong* (mod It *Lerici*) MHC
8 *Kum San* (US MSC-268/289) MSC

AMPHIBIOUS 16

2 *Alligator* (RF) LST, capacity 700 tons vehicles
7 *Un Bong* (US LST-511) LST, capacity 200 tps, 16 tk
7 *Ko Mun* (US LSM-1) LSM, capacity 50 tps, 4 tk
Plus about 36 craft; 6 LCT, 10 LCM, about 20 LCVP

SUPPORT AND MISCELLANEOUS 13

2 AOE, 2 spt tankers, 2 ocean tugs, 2 salv/div spt, 1
ASR, about 4 survey (civil-manned, Ministry of
Transport-funded)

NAVAL AIR

23 cbt ac; 47 armed hel
ASW 3 sqn
2 **ac** 1 with 15 S-2E, 1 with 8 P-3C
1 **hel** with 25 Hughes 500MD
1 flt with 8 SA-316 hel, 12 *Lynx* (ASW)

MARINES (25,000)

2 div, 1 bde • spt units
EQUIPMENT
MBT 60 M-47
AAV 60 LVTP-7
TOWED ARTY 105mm, 155mm
SSM *Harpoon* (truck-mounted)

Air Force 52,000

488 cbt ac, no armed hel. 8 cbt, 2 tpt wg
FGA 10 sqn
4 with 88 F-16C/D (a further 72 for delivery)
6 with 195 F-5E/F
FTR 4 sqn with 130 F-4D/E
CCT 1 sqn with 22* A-37B
FAC 10 O-2A
RECCE 1 sqn with 18* RF-4C, 10* RF-5A
SAR 1 hel sqn, 15 UH-60
TPT ac 2 BAe 748 (VIP), 1 Boeing 737-300 (VIP), 1 C-
118, 10 C-130H, 15 CN-235M **hel** 16 UH-1H/N, 6
CH-47, 3 Bell-412, 3 AS-332, 3 VH-60
TRG 25* F-5B, 50 T-37, 30 T-38, 25 T-41B, 18 *Hawk* Mk-
67
UAV 3 *Searcher*
MISSILES
ASM AGM-65A *Maverick*, AGM-88 HARM, AGM-
130, AGM-142
AAM AIM-7 *Sparrow*, AIM-9 *Sidewinder*, AIM-120B
AMRAAM
SAM *Nike-Hercules*, I HAWK, *Javelin*, *Mistral*

Forces Abroad

UN AND PEACEKEEPING

GEORGIA (UNOMIG) 3 obs: **INDIA/PAKISTAN**
(UNMOGIP): 9 obs. **WESTERN SAHARA**
(MINURSO): 20

Paramilitary ε4,500 active

CIVILIAN DEFENCE CORPS (to age 50) 3,500,000
MARITIME POLICE ε4,500
PATROL CRAFT 81
OFFSHORE 10
3 *Mazinger* (HDP-1000) (1 CG flagship), 1 *Han
Kang* (HDC-1150), 6 *Sea Dragon/Whale* (HDP-600)
COASTAL 33
22 *Sea Wolf/Shark*, 2 *Bukhansan*, 7 *Hyundai*-type, 2
Bukhansan
INSHORE 38
18 *Seagull*, about 20<, plus numerous boats
SUPPORT AND MISCELLANEOUS 3 salvage
HEL 9 Hughes 500

Foreign Forces

US 36,120: **Army** 27,460; 1 Army HQ, 1 inf div **Air
Force** 8,660; 1 HQ (7th Air Force): 90 cbt ac, 2 ftr wg; 3
sqn with 72 F-16, 1 sqn with 6 A-10, 12 OA-10, 1
special ops sqn with 5MH -53J

Laos

	1996	1997	1998	1999
GDP	kip1.7tr	kip2.0tr		
	($1.6bn)	($1.6bn)		
per capita	$2,500	$2,700		
Growth	7.5%	7.2%		
Inflation	13.1%	14.2%		
Debt	$2.3bn	$2.3bn		
Def exp	kip71bn	εkip79bn		
	($77m)	($63m)		
Def bdgt			εkip110bn	
			($55m)	
FMA (US)	$2.0m	$2.5m	$3.5m	$4.0m
$1 = kip	921	1,257	2,009	
Population		5,200,000		

(*lowland* Lao Loum 68% *upland* Lao Theung 22%
highland Lao Soung incl Hmong and Yao 9%,
Chinese and Vietnamese 1%)

Age	*13–17*	*18–22*	*23–32*
Men	289,000	233,000	363,000
Women	284,000	230,000	362,000

Total Armed Forces

ACTIVE ε29,100
Terms of service conscription, 18 months minimum

Army 25,000

4 Mil Regions • 5 inf div • 7 indep inf regt • 5 arty, 9

AD arty bn • 3 engr (2 construction) regt • 65 indep inf coy • 1 lt ac liaison flt

EQUIPMENT
MBT 30 T-54/-55, T-34/85
LT TK 25 PT-76
APC 70 BTR-40/-60/-152
TOWED ARTY 75mm: M-116 pack; **105mm**: 25 M-101; **122mm**: 40 M-1938 and D-30; **130mm**: 10 M-46; **155mm**: M-114
MOR 81mm; 82mm; 107mm: M-2A1, M-1938; **120mm**: M-43
RCL 57mm: M-18/A1; **75mm**: M-20; **106mm**: M-40; **107mm**: B-11
AD GUNS 14.5mm: ZPU-1/-4; **23mm**: ZU-23, ZSU-23-4 SP; **37mm**: M-1939; **57mm**: S-60
SAM SA-3, SA-7

Navy (Army Marine Section) ε600

PATROL AND COASTAL COMBATANTS some 16
PATROL, RIVERINE some 16
some 12 PCI<, 4 LCM, plus about 40 boats

Air Force 3,500

26 cbt ac; no armed hel
FGA 2 sqn with some 20 MiG-21
TPT 1 sqn with 4 An-2, 5 An-24, 4 An-26, 4 Yak-12, 2 Yak-40
HEL 1 sqn with 2 Mi-6, 10 Mi-8, 12 Mi-17, 3 SA-360
TRG *6 MiG-21UB, 8 Yak-18
AAM AA-2 *Atoll*

Paramilitary

MILITIA SELF-DEFENCE FORCES 100,000+
village 'home-guard' org for local defence

Opposition

Numerous factions/groups; total armed str: ε2,000
United Lao National Liberation Front (ULNLF) largest group

Malaysia

	1996	1997	1998	1999
GDP	RM250bn	RM255bn		
	($86bn)	($91bn)		
per capita	$10,100	$10,800		
Growth	8.2%	7.0%		
Inflation	3.6%	3.7%		
Debt	$40bn	$41bn		
Def expᵃ	RM9.1bn	RM9.5bn		
	($3.6bn)	($3.4bn)		

contd	1996	1997	1998	1999
Def bdgᵇ			RM8.5bn	
			($2.1bn)	
FMA (US)	$0.5m	$0.6m	$0.6m	$0.7m
(Aus)	$4.0m	$4.3m	$3.5m	
$1 = ringgit	2.52	2.81	3.99	

ᵃIncl procurement and def industry exp
ᵇExcl est procurement allocation

Population	22,000,000

(Muslim 39%; also Malay and other indigenous 64%, Chinese 27%, Indian 9%; in *Sabah* and *Sarawak* non-Muslim Bumiputras form the majority of the population; 1,000,000+ Indonesian and Filipino illegal immigrants in 1997)

Age	13–17	18–22	23–32
Men	1,167,000	988,000	1,719,000
Women	1,111,000	945,000	1,675,000

Total Armed Forces

ACTIVE 110,000

RESERVES 40,600
Army 37,800 **Navy** 2,200 **Air Force** 600

Army 85,000

(reducing to 80,000)
2 Mil Regions • 1 HQ fd comd, 4 area comd (div) • 1 mech inf, 10 inf bde • 1 AB bde (3 AB bn, 1 lt arty regt, 1 lt tk sqn – forms Rapid Deployment Force)
Summary of combat units
5 armd regt • 31 inf bn • 3 AB bn • 5 fd arty, 1 AD arty, 5 engr regt
1 SF regt (3 bn)
AVN 1 hel sqn

RESERVES
Territorial Army 1 bde HQ; 12 inf regt, 4 highway sy bn

EQUIPMENT
LT TK 26 *Scorpion* (**90mm**)
RECCE 162 SIBMAS, 140 AML-60/-90, 92 *Ferret* (60 mod)
APC 111 KIFV (incl variants), 184 V-100/-150 *Commando*, 25 *Stormer*, 459 *Condor* (150 to be upgraded), 37 M-3 Panhard
TOWED ARTY 105mm: 75 Model 56 pack, 40 M-102A1 († in store); **155mm**: 12 FH-70
MOR 81mm: 300
ATGW SS-11, *Eryx*
RL 89mm: M-20; **92mm**: FT5
RCL 84mm: *Carl Gustav*; **106mm**: 150 M-40
AD GUNS 35mm: 24 GDF-005; **40mm**: 36 L40/70
SAM 48 *Javelin, Starburst*, 12 *Rapier*
HEL 10 SA-316B
ASLT CRAFT 165 *Damen*

Navy 12,500

(incl 160 Naval Air)
Fleet Operations Comd (HQ Lumut)
Naval Area 1 Kuantan **Naval Area 2** Labuan
BASES Naval Area 1 Kuantan **Naval Area 2** Labuan,
Sandakan (Sabah) **Naval Area 3** Lumut **Naval Area 4**
Sungei Antu (Sarawak) plus trg base at Penerang

SUBMARINES 0
but personnel training in India, Italy and Turkey

PRINCIPAL SURFACE COMBATANTS 6

FFG 2
  2 *Leiku* with 8 x MM-40 *Exocet* SSM, 1 x VLS *Seawolf*
  SAM, 6 x 324mm TT

FF 4
  2 *Kasturi* (FS-1500) with 2 x 2 ASW mor, deck for
  Wasp hel; plus 2 x 2 MM-38 *Exocet* SSM, 1 100mm
  gun
  1 *Hang Tuah* (UK *Mermaid*) with 1 x 3 *Limbo* ASW
  mor, hel deck for *Wasp*; plus 1 x 2 102mm gun (trg)
  1 *Rahmat* with 1 x 3 ASW mor, 1 114mm gun hel
  deck (trg)

PATROL AND COASTAL COMBATANTS 39

CORVETTES 2 *Hang Nadim* (It *Assad*) with 6 OTO
  Melara SSM, 1 *Selenia* SAM 1 76mm gun 6 324mm TT
MISSILE CRAFT 8
  4 *Handalan* (Swe *Spica*) with 4 MM-38 *Exocet* SSM
  4 *Perdana* (Fr *Combattante* II) with 2 *Exocet* SSM
PATROL CRAFT 29
  OFFSHORE 2 *Musytari* with 1 100mm gun, hel deck
  INSHORE 27
  6 *Jerong* PFI, 3 *Kedah*, 4 *Sabah*, 14 *Kris* PCI

MINE COUNTERMEASURES 5
  4 *Mahamiru* (mod It *Lerici*) MCO
  1 diving tender (inshore)

AMPHIBIOUS 3
  2 *Sri Banggi* (US LST-511) LST, capacity 200 tps, 16 tk
  (but usually employed as tenders to patrol craft)
  1 *Sri Inderapura* (US *Newport*) LST, capacity 400 tps,
  10 tk
  Plus 178 craft: 115 (LCM/LCP/LCU)

SUPPORT AND MISCELLANEOUS 3
  2 log/fuel spt, 1 survey

NAVAL AIR (160)
no cbt ac, 12 armed hel
  HEL 12 *Wasp* HAS-1

Air Force 12,500

89 cbt ac, no armed hel; 4 Air Div
Flying hours 60
FGA 4 sqn
  3 with 8 *Hawk* 108, 17 *Hawk* 208, 11 MB-339
  1 with 8 F/A-18D
FTR 3 sqn

  1 with 11 F-5E, 2 F-5F, 2 RF-5E
  2 with 16 MiG-29, 2 MiG-29U
MR 1 sqn with 4 Beech-200T
TKR 6 A-4, 2 KC-130H
TRANSPORT 4 sqn
  1 with 12 DHC-4
  1 with 5 C-130H
  1 with 6 C-130H-30, 1 C-130H-MP, 2 KC-130, 10
    Cessna 402B
  1 with ac 1 *Falcon*-900 (VIP), 2 BAC-125, 1 F-28 **hel** 2
    AS-61N, 1 Agusta-109, 2 S-70A
  HEL 3 sqn with 30 S-61A, 20 SA-316A/B
TRAINING
  AC 37 PC-7 (12* wpn trg), 20 MD3-160
  HEL 13 SA-316
AAM AIM-9 *Sidewinder*, AA-10 *Alamo*, AA-11 *Archer*,
AA-12 *Adder*
ASM AGM-65 *Maverick*, *Harpoon*

AIRFIELD DEFENCE
1 field sqn
SAM 1 sqn with *Starburst*

Forces Abroad

UN AND PEACEKEEPING
ANGOLA (UNOMA): 4 obs. **BOSNIA** (SFOR II): up
to 50. **IRAQ/KUWAIT** (UNIKOM): 6 obs. **WESTERN
SAHARA** (MINURSO): 13 obs

Paramilitary ε20,100

GENERAL OPS FORCE 18,000
5 bde HQ: 21 bn (incl 2 Aboriginal, 1 Special Ops
  Force), 4 indep coy
  EQPT ε100 Shorland armd cars, 140 AT-105 *Saxon*,
  ε30 SB-301 APC
MARINE POLICE about 2,100
  BASES Kuala, Kemaman, Penang, Tampoi,
  Kuching, Sandalean
  PATROL CRAFT, INSHORE 30
  15 *Lang Hitam* (38m) PFI, 6 *Sangitan* (29m), 9
    improved PX PFI, plus 6 tpt, 2 tugs, 120 boats
POLICE AIR UNIT
  ac 6 Cessna *Caravan* I, 4 Cessna 206, 7 PC-6 **hel** 1 Bell
  206L, 2 AS-355F
AREA SECURITY UNITS (aux Police Field Force) 3,500
89 units
BORDER SCOUTS (in Sabah, Sarawak) 1,200
PEOPLE'S VOLUNTEER CORPS (RELA) 240,000
some 17,500 armed
CUSTOMS SERVICE
  PATROL CRAFT, INSHORE 56
  6 *Perak* (Vosper 32m) armed PFI, about 50 craft<

Foreign Forces

AUSTRALIA 148 **Army** 115; 1 inf coy **Air Force** 33; det with 2 P-3C **ac**

Mongolia

	1996	1997	1998	1999
GDP	t532bn	t701bn		
	($841m)	($887m)		
per capita	$2,000	$2,100		
Growth	2.3%	3.5%		
Inflation	53.2%	40.0%		
Debt	$524m	$634m		
Def exp	t7.9bn	t18.2bn		
	($14m)	($23m)		
Def bdgt			t18.7bn	
			($24m)	
FMA (US)	$0.1m	$0.4m	$0.4m	$0.4m
$1 = tugrik	548	790	785	
Population		2,404,000		

(Kazak 4%, Russian 2%, Chinese 2%)

Age	*13–17*	*18–22*	*23–32*
Men	151,000	134,000	219,000
Women	145,000	128,000	212,000

Total Armed Forces

ACTIVE 9,800

(incl 6,100 conscripts, 500 construction tps and 500 Civil Defence – see *Paramilitary*)
Terms of service conscription: males 18–28 years, 1 year

RESERVES 137,000

Army 137,000

Army 8,000 (5,300 conscripts)

7 MR bde (all under str) • 1 arty bde • 1 lt inf bn (rapid-deployment) • 1 AB bn
EQUIPMENT
  MBT 600 T-54/-55/-62
  RECCE 120 BRDM-2
  AIFV 400 BMP-1
  APC 250 BTR-60
  TOWED ARTY 300: **122mm**: M-1938/D-30; **130mm**: M-46; **152mm**: ML-20
  MRL 122mm: 130+ BM-21
  MOR 140: **82mm, 120mm, 160mm**
  ATK GUNS 200 incl: **85mm**: D-44/D-48; **100mm**: BS-3, MT-12

Air Defence 800

9 cbt ac; 12 armed hel

Flying hours 22
2 AD regt
FTR 1 sqn with 8 MiG-21, 1 Mig-21U
ATTACK HEL 12 Mi-24
TPT (Civil Registration) 15 An-2, 12 An-24, 3 An-26, 1 An-30, 2 Boeing 727, 3 Y-12, 1 Airbus A310-300
AD GUNS: 150: **14.5mm**: ZPU-4, **23mm**: ZU-23, ZSU-23-4, **57mm**: S-60
SAM 250 SA-7

Paramilitary 7,200 active

BORDER GUARD 6,000 (incl 4,700 conscripts)
INTERNAL SECURITY TROOPS 1,200 (incl 800 conscripts) 4 gd units
CIVIL DEFENCE TROOPS (500)
CONSTRUCTION TROOPS (500)

Myanmar

	1996	1997	1998	1999
GDP[a]	K715bn	εK820bn		
	($26bn)	($28bn)		
per capita	$1,000	$1,100		
Growth	7.0%	7.0%		
Inflation	20.0%	10.0%		
Debt	$5.2bn	$5.0bn		
Def exp[a]	K25bn	K28bn		
	($2.0bn)	($2.2bn)		
Def bdgt[a]			K24.5bn	
			($1.9bn)	
$1 = kyat[b]	5.90	6.24	6.25	

[a] PPP est
[b] Market rate **1998** $1 = K250–300

Population		49,500,000		

(Burmese 68%, Shan 9%, Karen 7%, Rakhine 4%, Chinese 3+% *Other* Chin, Kachin, Kayan, Lahu, Mon, Palaung, Pao, Wa, 9%)

Age	*13–17*	*18–22*	*23–32*
Men	2,602,000	2,376,000	4,136,000
Women	2,538,000	2,322,000	4,137,000

Total Armed Forces

ACTIVE some 434,800 reported (incl People's Police Force and People's Militia – see *Paramilitary*)

Army 325,000

10 lt inf div (each 3 tac op comd (TOC))
12 Regional Comd (each with 10 regt)
32 TOC with 145 garrison inf bn
Summary of cbt units
  245 inf bn • 7 arty bn • 4 armd bn • 2 AA arty bn

EQUIPMENT†

MBT 26 *Comet*, 80 PRC Type-69II, 20 PRC Type-80 (reported)

LT TK 105 Type-63 (ε 60 serviceable)

RECCE 45 *Ferret*, 40 *Humber*, 30 *Mazda* (local manufacture)

APC 20 *Hino* (local manufacture), 250 Type-85

TOWED ARTY 76mm: 100 M-1948; **88mm**: 50 25-pdr; **105mm**: 96 M-101; **140mm**: 5.5in

MRL 107mm: 30 Type-63

MOR 81mm; 82mm: Type-53; **120mm**: Type-53, 80 Soltam

RCL 84mm: 500 *Carl Gustav*; **106mm**: M40A1

ATK GUNS 60: **57mm**: 6-pdr; **76.2mm**: 17-pdr

AD GUNS 37mm: 24 Type-74; **40mm**: 10 M-1; **57mm**: 12 Type-80

SAM HN-5A (reported)

Navy† 15,800

(incl 800 Naval Infantry)

BASES Bassein, Mergui, Moulmein, Seikyi, Yangon (Monkey Point), Sittwe

PATROL AND COASTAL COMBATANTS 65

CORVETTES 2

1 *Yan Taing Aung* (US PCE-827)†

1 *Yan Gyi Aung* (US *Admirable* MSF)†

MISSILE CRAFT 6 *Houxin* with 4 C-801 SSM

PATROL, COASTAL 10 *Yan Sit Aung* (PRC *Hainan*)

PATROL, INSHORE 18

12 US PGM-401/412, 3 FRY PB-90 PFI<, 3 *Swift* PGM 421

PATROL, RIVERINE about 29

2 *Nawarat*, 2 imp FRY Y-301 and 10 FRY Y-301, about 15<, plus some 25 boats

AMPHIBIOUS 15

5 LCU, 10 LCM

SUPPORT 15

6 coastal tpt, 1 AOT, 1 diving spt, 1 buoy tender, 6 boats

NAVAL INFANTRY (800) 1 bn

Air Force 9,000

121 cbt ac, 22 armed hel

FTR 3 sqn with 30 F-7, 6 FT-7

FGA 2 sqn with 36 A-5M

CCT 2 sqn with 24 PC-7, 5 PC-9, 20 *Super Galeb* G4

TPT 1 F-27, 4 FH-227, 5 PC-6A/-B, 2 Y-8D

LIAISON/TRG 6 Cessna 180, 1 Cessna *Citation* II, 4 K-8

HEL 4 sqn with 12 Bell 205, 6 Bell 206, 9 SA-316, 10* Mi-2, 12* Mi-17, 25 PZL W-3 *Sokol*

Paramilitary ε85,250

PEOPLE'S POLICE FORCE 50,000

PEOPLE'S MILITIA 35,000

PEOPLE'S PEARL AND FISHERY MINISTRY ε250

11 patrol boats (3 *Indaw* (Dk *Osprey*) PCC, 3 US *Swift* PGM PCI, 5 Aus *Carpentaria* PCI<)

Opposition and Former Opposition

GROUPS WITH CEASE-FIRE AGREEMENTS

UNITED WA STATE ARMY (UWSA) ε12,000 **Area** Wa hills between Salween river and Chinese border; formerly part of CPB

KACHIN INDEPENDENCE ARMY (KIA) some 8,000 **Area** northern Myanmar, incl Kuman range, the Triangle. Reached cease-fire agreement with government in October 1993

MONG TAI ARMY (MTA) (formerly Shan United Army) ε3,000+ **Area** along Thai border and between Lashio and Chinese border

SHAN STATE ARMY (SSA) ε3,000 **Area** Shan state

MYANMAR NATIONAL DEMOCRATIC ALLIANCE ARMY (MNDAA) 2,000 **Area** northeast Shan state

MON NATIONAL LIBERATION ARMY (MNLA) ε1,000 **Area** on Thai border in Mon state

NATIONAL DEMOCRATIC ALLIANCE ARMY (NDAA) ε1,000 **Area** eastern corner of Shan state on China–Laos border; formerly part of CPB

PALAUNG STATE LIBERATION ARMY (PSLA) ε700 **Area** hill tribesmen north of Hsipaw

NEW DEMOCRATIC ARMY (NDA) ε500 **Area** along Chinese border in Kachin state; former Communist Party of Burma (CPB)

DEMOCRATIC KAREN BUDDHIST ORGANISATION (DKBO) ε100–500 armed

GROUPS STILL IN OPPOSITION

MONG TAI ε8,000

KAREN NATIONAL LIBERATION ARMY (KNLA) ε4,000 **Area** based in Thai border area; political wg is Karen National Union (KNU)

ALL BURMA STUDENTS DEMOCRATIC FRONT ε2,000

KARENNI ARMY (KA) >1,000 **Area** Kayah state, Thai border

New Zealand

	1996	1997	1998	1999
GDP	NZ$96bn ($56bn)	NZ$99bn ($58bn)		
per capita	$17,100	$17,600		
Growth	2.1%	1.5%		
Inflation	2.3%	1.3%		
Publ debt	47.0%	37.3%		
Def exp	NZ$1.5bn ($1,000m)	NZ$1.4bn ($901m)		

contd	1996	1997	1998	1999
Def bdgt			NZ$1.4bn	
			($764m)	
US$1 = NZ$	1.45	1.56	1.95	
Population		3,620,000		
(Maori 9%, Pacific Islander 3%)				
Age	*13–17*	*18–22*	*23–32*	
Men	130,000	134,000	294,000	
Women	123,000	127,000	280,000	

Total Armed Forces

ACTIVE 9,550
(incl some 1,340 women)

RESERVES some 6,960
Regular some 2,310 **Army** 1,500 **Navy** 800 **Air Force** 10
Territorial 4,650 **Army** 3,900 **Navy** 400 **Air Force** 350

Army 4,400

(incl 500 women)
1 Land Force Comd HQ • 2 Land Force Gp HQ • 1
APC/Recce regt (-) • 2 inf bn • 1 arty regt (2 fd bty) •
1 engr regt (-) • 1 AD tp (forming) • 2 SF sqn (incl 1
reserve)

RESERVES
Territorial Army 6 inf bn, 4 fd arty bty, 2 armd sqn
(incl 1 lt recce)

EQUIPMENT
  LT TK 20 *Scorpion*
  APC 78 M-113 (incl variants)
  TOWED ARTY 105mm: 19 M-101A1, 24 *Hamel*
  MOR 81mm: 50
  RL 94mm: LAW
  RCL 84mm: 63 *Carl Gustav*
  SAM 12 *Mistral*
  SURV *Cymbeline* (mor)

Navy 2,100

(incl 340 women)
BASE Auckland (Fleet HQ)
FRIGATES 3
  2 *Waikato* (UK *Leander*) with 1 SH-2F hel, 2 x 3 ASTT
  and 3 with 2 114mm guns (1 in long refit)
  1 *Anzac* with 8 *Sea Sparrow* VLS SAM, 1 127mm gun,
  6 324mm TT, *Seasprite* hel
PATROL AND COASTAL COMBATANTS 4
  4 *Moa* PCI (reserve trg)
SUPPORT AND MISCELLANEOUS 2
  1 *Resolution* AGS (US *Stalwart*), 1 *Endeavour* AO

NAVAL AIR
no cbt ac, 4 armed hel

HEL 4 SH-2F *Sea Sprite* (see Air Force)

Air Force 3,050

(incl 500 women); 42 cbt ac, no armed hel
Flying hours A-4: 180

AIR COMMAND
FGA 2 sqn with 14 A-4K, 5 TA-4K
MR 1 sqn with 6* P-3K *Orion*
LIGHT ATTACK/TRG 1 sqn for *ab initio* and ftr lead-
  in trg with 17* MB-339C
ASW 4 SH-2F (Navy-assigned)
TPT 2 sqn
  ac 1 with 5 C-130H, 2 Boeing 727
  hel 1 with 13 UH-1H, 5 Bell 47G (trg)
TRG 1 sqn with 13 CT-4E
MISSILES
  ASM AGM-65B/G *Maverick*
  AAM AIM-9L *Sidewinder*

Forces Abroad

AUSTRALIA 47; 3 A-4K, 3 TA-4K, 9 navigation trg
SINGAPORE 11; spt unit
UN AND PEACEKEEPING
ANGOLA (UNOMA): 3 obs. **BOSNIA** (SFOR): 22.
CROATIA (UNMOP): 1 obs. **EGYPT** (MFO): 25.
FYROM (UNPREDEP): 1 obs. **MIDDLE EAST**
(UNTSO): 7 obs. **PAPUA NEW GUINEA**: 130
(Bougainville Truce Monitoring Group)

Papua New Guinea

	1996	1997	1998	1999
GDP	K7.2bn	K7.4bn		
	($5.4bn)	($5.2bn)		
per capita	$2,700	$2,500		
Growth	2.3%	-6.2%		
Inflation	11.6%	3.9%		
Debt	$2.4bn	$2.6bn		
Def exp	K104m	K90m		
	($79m)	($63m)		
Def bdgt			εK115m	
			($56m)	
FMA (US)	$0.2m	$0.1m	$0.2m	$0.2m
(Aus)	$9.0m	$13.8m	$9.6m	
$1 = kina	1.32	1.43	2.07	
Population		4,655,000		
Age	*13–17*	*18–22*	*23–32*	
Men	264,000	238,000	402,000	
Women	250,000	221,000	363,000	

Total Armed Forces

ACTIVE ε4,300

Army ε3,800

2 inf bn • 1 engr bn
EQUIPMENT
  MOR 81mm; 120mm: 3

Maritime Element 400

BASES Port Moresby (HQ), Lombrum (Manus Island)
(patrol boat sqn); forward bases at Kieta and Alotau
PATROL AND COASTAL COMBATANTS 4
PATROL, INSHORE 4 *Tarangau* (Aust *Pacific Forum*
  32-m) PCI
AMPHIBIOUS craft only
  2 *Salamaua* (Aust *Balikpapan*) LCH, plus 4 other
    landing craft, manned and operated by the civil
    administration

Air Force 100

no cbt ac, no armed hel
TPT 2 CN-235, 3 IAI-201 *Arava*
HEL †4 UH-1H

Foreign Forces

AUSTRALIA 38; trg unit
BOUGAINVILLE TRUCE MONITORING GROUP
some 260 tps from Aus (ε100), NZ (130), Fiji, Tonga,
Vanuatu

Philippines

	1996	1997	1998	1999
GDP	P2.2tr	P2.5tr		
	($74bn)	($83bn)		
per capita	$2,900	$3,000		
Growth	5.7%	5.1%		
Inflation	8.4%	5.1%		
Debt	$41.2bn	$41.9bn		
Def exp[a]	P39bn	P42bn		
	($1.5bn)	($1.4bn)		
Def bdgt[b]			P47bn	
			($1.2bn)	
FMA (US)	$1.2m	$1.3m	$1.4m	$1.4m
(Aus)	$3.0m	$2.9m	$3.0m	
$1 = peso	26.2	27.5	39.2	

[a] Incl paramil exp
[b] A five-year supplementary procurement budget of P50bn
($1.9bn) for 1996–2000 was approved in Dec 1996

Population	74,044,000

(Muslim 5–8%; *Mindanao provinces* Muslim 40–
90%; Chinese 2%)

Age	13–17	18–22	23–32
Men	4,103,000	3,640,000	6,051,000
Women	3,962,000	3,508,000	5,865,000

Total Armed Forces

ACTIVE 117,800

RESERVES 131,000
Army 100,000 (some 75,000 more have commitments)
Navy 15,000 **Air Force** 16,000 (to age 49)

Army 74,500

5 Area Unified Comd (joint service) • 8 inf div (each
with 3 inf bde) • 1 special ops comd with 1 lt armd
bde ('regt'), 1 scout ranger, 1 SF regt • 3 engr bde; 1
construction bn • 8 arty bn • 1 Presidential Security
Group

EQUIPMENT
  LT TK 41 *Scorpion*
  AIFV 85 YPR-765 PRI
  APC 100 M-113, 20 *Chaimite*, 165 V-150, some 90
    Simba
  TOWED ARTY 105mm: 230 M-101, M-102, M-26
    and M-56; 155mm: 12 M-114 and M-68
  MOR 81mm: M-29; 107mm: 40 M-30
  RCL 75mm: M-20; 90mm: M-67; 106mm: M-40 A1

Navy† ε25,900

(incl 9,000 Marines)
6 Naval Districts
BASES Sangley Point/Cavite, Zamboanga, Cebu
FRIGATES 1 *Rajah Humabon* (US *Cannon*) with ASW
mor, 76mm gun
PATROL AND COASTAL COMBATANTS 67
PATROL, OFFSHORE 14
  3 *Emilio Jacinto* (ex-UK *Peacock*) with 1 76mm gun
  2 *Rizal* (US *Auk*) with hel deck
  8 *Miguel Malvar* (US PCE-827)
  1 *Magat Salamat* (US-MSF)
PATROL, INSHORE 53
  2 *Aguinaldo*, 3 *Kagitingan*, 22 *José Andrada* PCI<, 5
    Thomas Batilo (ROK *Sea Dolphin*), and about 21
    other PCI<
AMPHIBIOUS some 9
  2 US *F. S. Beeson*-class LST, capacity 32 tk plus 150
    tps, hel deck
  Some 7 *Zamboanga del Sur* (US LST-1/511/542) LST,
    capacity either 16tk or 10tk plus 200 tps
  Plus about 39 craft: 30 LCM, 3 LCU, some 6 LCVP

SUPPORT AND MISCELLANEOUS 11

2 AOT (small), 1 repair ship, 3 survey/research, 3 spt, 2 water tkr

NAVAL AVIATION

8 cbt ac, no armed hel

MR/SAR ac 8 BN-2A *Defender*, 1 *Islander* **hel** 11 Bo-105 (SAR)

MARINES (9,000)

3 bde (10 bn) – to be 2 bde (6 bn)

EQUIPMENT

APC 30 LVTP-5, 55 LVTP-7, 24 LAV-300 (reported)

TOWED ARTY 105mm: 150 M-101

MOR 4.2in (**107mm**): M-30

Air Force 17,400

39 cbt ac, some 99 armed hel

FTR 1 sqn with 6 F-5A/B

ARMED HEL 3 sqn with 62 Bell UH-1H/M, 16 AUH-76 (S-76 gunship conversion), 21 Hughes 500/520MD

MR 2 F-27M

RECCE 6 RT-33A, 21* OV-10 *Broncos*

SAR ac 4 HU-16 **hel** 10 Bo-105C

PRESIDENTIAL AC WG ac 1 F-27, 1 F-28 **hel** 2 Bell 212, 4 Bell-412, 2 S-70A, 2 SA-330

TPT 3 sqn

1 with 2 C-130B, 3 C-130H, 3 L-100-20, 5 C-47, 7 F-27

2 with 22 BN-2 *Islander*, 14 N-22B *Nomad Missionmaster*

HEL 2 sqn with 55 Bell 205, 16 UH-1H

LIAISON 10 Cessna (7 -180, 2 -210, 1 -310), 5 DHC-2, 12 U-17A/B

TRG 4 sqn

1 with 6 T-33A, 1 with 15 T-41D, 1 with 15 SF-260TP, 1 with 12* S-211

AAM AIM-9B *Sidewinder*

Paramilitary 42,500 active

PHILIPPINE NATIONAL POLICE (Department of Interior and Local Government) 40,500

62,000 active aux; 15 Regional, 73 Provincial Comd

COAST GUARD 3,500

Command devolving initially to the President before settling under the Department of Transport and Communications

EQPT 1 *Kalinga* PCO, 4 *Basilan* (US PGM-39/42 PCI, 2 *Tirad Pass* PCI (SAR), 4 ex-US Army spt ships, plus some 50 patrol boats; 2 lt **ac**

CITIZEN ARMED FORCE GEOGRAPHICAL UNITS (CAFGU) 60,000

Militia, 56 bn; part-time units which can be called up for extended periods

Opposition and Former Opposition

Groups with Cease-fire Agreements

BANGSA MORO ARMY (armed wing of Moro National Liberation Front (MNLF); Muslim) ε5,000

Groups Still in Opposition

NEW PEOPLE'S ARMY (NPA; communist) ε8,000

MORO ISLAMIC LIBERATION FRONT (breakaway from MNLF; Muslim) ε6–10,000

MORO ISLAMIC REFORMIST GROUP (breakaway from MNLF; Muslim) 900

ABU SAYAF GROUP ε500

Singapore

	1996	1997	1998	1999
GDP	S$133bn ($88bn)	S$143bn ($96bn)		
per capita	$23,400	$25,400		
Growth	7.0%	7.8%		
Inflation	1.3%	2.0%		
Debt	$9.0bn	$9.9bn		
Def exp	S$5.7bn ($4.0bn)	S$6.1bn ($4.1bn)		
Def bdgt			S$7.3bn ($4.3bn)	
FMA (US)	$0.02m			
(Aus)	$1.0m	$0.7m	$0.5m	
US$1 = S$	1.41	1.48	1.7	
Population		3,076,000		
(Chinese 76%, Malay 15%, Indian 6%)				
Age	*13–17*	*18–22*	*23–32*	
Men	113,000	109,000	251,000	
Women	107,000	104,000	245,000	

Total Armed Forces

ACTIVE ε72,500

(39,800 conscripts)

Terms of service conscription 24–30 months

RESERVES ε250,000

Army 240,000; annual trg to age 40 for men, 50 for officers **Navy** ε6,300 **Air Force** ε7,500

Army 50,000

(35,000 conscripts/op ready reserve)

3 combined arms div each with 2 inf bde (each 3 inf bn), 1 mech bde, 1 recce, 2 arty, 1 AD, 1 engr bn (mixed active/reserve formations)

1 Rapid Deployment div with 3 inf bde (incl 1 air mob, 1 amph, mixed active/reserve formations)

1 mech bde
Summary of active units
9 inf bn • 4 lt armd/recce bn • 4 arty bn • 1 cdo (SF)
bn • 4 engr bn

RESERVES

1 op reserve div, some inf bde HQ; ε40 inf, ε8 lt armd
recce, ε8 arty, ε1 cdo (SF), ε8 engr bn
People's Defence Force: some 30,000; org in 2 comd, 7+
bde gp, ε20+ bn

EQUIPMENT

MBT some 60 *Centurion* (reported)
LT TK ε350 AMX-13SM1
RECCE 22 AMX-10 PAC 90
AIFV 22 AMX-10P, some IFV-25
APC 750+ M-113A1/A2 (some with 40mm AGL,
  some with 25mm gun), 30 V-100, 250 V-150/-200
  Commando
TOWED ARTY 105mm: 37 LG1; **155mm**: 38 Soltam
  M-71S, 16 M-114A1 (may be in store), M-68 (may
  be in store), 52 FH88, 17 FH2000
MOR 81mm (some SP); **120mm**: 50 (some SP in M-
  113); **160mm**: 12 Tampella
ATGW 30+ *Milan*
RL *Armbrust*; **89mm**: 3.5in M-20
RCL 84mm: ε200 *Carl Gustav*; **106mm**: 90 M-40A1
  (in store)
AD GUNS 20mm: 30 GAI-CO1 (some SP)
SAM RBS-70 (some SP in V-200) (Air Force), *Mistral*
  (Air Force)
SURV AN/TPQ-36/-37 (arty, mor)

Navy ε9,000

incl 4,500 full time (2,700 regular and 1,800 national
service) plus 4,500 op ready reserve
COMMANDS Fleet (1st and 3rd Flotillas) **Coastal**
and **Naval Logistic**, **Training Command**
BASES Pulau Brani, Tuas (Jurong)

SUBMARINES 1

1 *Challenger* (Swe A 12) with 4 533mm TT (tng in Swe)

PATROL AND COASTAL COMBATANTS 24

CORVETTES 6 *Victory* (Ge Lürssen 62m) with 8
Harpoon SSM, 2 x 3 ASTT (1 x 2 *Barak* SAM being
fitted)
MISSILE CRAFT 18
  6 *Sea Wolf* (Ge Lürssen 45m) PFM with 2 x 2 *Harpoon*, 4 x 2 *Gabriel* SSM, 1 x 2 *Sinbad/Mistral* SAM
  12 *Fearless* OPV with 2 *Mistral Sadral* SAM, 1 76mm
  gun, 6 with 6 324mm TT

MINE COUNTERMEASURES 4

4 *Bedok* (SW *Landsort*) MHC (*Jupiter* diving spt has
  mine-hunting capability)

AMPHIBIOUS 3

1 *Perseverance* (UK *Sir Lancelot*) LSL with 1 x 2 *Simbad*
  (navalised *Mistral*) SAM capacity: 340 tps, 16 tk,
  hel deck

2 *Excellence* (US LST-511) LST, capacity 200 tps, 16 tk,
  hel deck, 1 x 2 *Sinbad/Mistral* SAM (plus 3 in store)
Plus craft: 6 LCM, 30 LCU, 1 hovercraft and boats

SUPPORT AND MISCELLANEOUS 2

1 *Jupiter* diving spt and salvage, 1 trg

Air Force 13,500

(incl 3,000 conscripts; 7,500 op ready reserve); 157 cbt
ac, 20 armed hel
FGA 4 sqn
  3 with 51 A-SU, 24 TA-SU
  1 with 7 F-16 (3 -A, 4 -B) (with a further 12 F-16C/D
  in US)
  8 F-16C and 10 F-16D being delivered
FTR 2 sqn with 28 F-5E, 9 F-5F
RECCE 1 sqn with 8* RF-5S
AEW 1 sqn with 4 E-2C
MPA 1 sqn with 5 F-50 *Enforcer*
ARMED HEL 2 sqn with 20 AS 550A2/C2
TRANSPORT 5 sqn
  AC 3 sqn
    1 with 4 KC-130B (tkr/tpt), 5 C-130H (1 ELINT),
    1 KC-130H (tkr)
    1 with 4 *Fokker* 50 (tpt/MR)
  HEL 3 sqn
    1 with 19 UH-1H, 1 with 21 AS-332M (incl 5 SAR),
    1 with 20 AS-550, 6 CH-47D (in USA)
TRG 2 sqn
  1 with 27 SIAI S-211
  1 with 26 SF-260
UAV 1 sqn with *Searcher*

AIR DEFENCE SYSTEMS DIVISION

4 field def sqn
Air Defence Bde 1 sqn with **35mm** Oerlikon, 1 sqn
  with I HAWK, 1 sqn with blind fire *Rapier*
Air Force Systems Bde 1 sqn mobile RADAR, 1 sqn
  LORADS
Divisional Air Def Arty Bde (attached to Army
  Division) 1 bn with *Mistral* (SAM), 3 sqn RBS 70
  (SAM), SA-18 *Igla* (being delivered)

MISSILES

AAM AIM-7P *Sparrow*, AIM-9 N/P *Sidewinder*
ASM AGM-65B *Maverick*, AGM-65G *Maverick*

Forces Abroad

AUSTRALIA 230; flying trg school with 27 S-211, 12
AS-332M
BRUNEI 500; trg school, incl hel det (with 5 UH-1H)
FRANCE 100: trg 10 A-4 (Cazaux AFB)
TAIWAN 3 trg camps (incl inf and arty)
THAILAND 1 trg camp (arty)
US 6 CH-47D (ANG facility Grand Prairie, TX); 12 F-
16C/D (leased from USAF at Luke AFB, AZ), 12 F-
16C/D (at Cannon AFB, NM)

UN AND PEACEKEEPING
IRAQ/KUWAIT (UNIKOM): 6 obs

Paramilitary ε108,000+ active

SINGAPORE POLICE FORCE
incl Police Coast Guard
12 *Swift* PCI< and about 60 boats
Singapore Gurkha Contingent (750)
CIVIL DEFENCE FORCE 108,000
(incl 1,500 regulars, 3,600 conscripts, 62,100 former
Army reservists, 40,500+ volunteers); 1 construction
bde (2,500 conscripts)

Foreign Forces

NEW ZEALAND 11; spt unit
US 140 **Navy** 100 **Air Force** 40

Taiwan (Republic Of China)

	1996	1997	1998	1999
GNP	NT$7.5tr	NT$8.0tr		
	($285bn)	($293bn)		
per capita	$12,800	$13,800		
Growth	5.6%	6.0%		
Inflation	3.5%	3.1%		
Debt	$24.4bn	$24.6bn		
Def expᵃNT$357bn	NT$375bn			
	($13.6bn)	($13.6bn)		
Def bdgt			NT$275bn	NT$286bn
			($8.3bn)	($8.3bn)
US$1 = NT$	26.3	27.5	34.3	

NT$ = New Taiwan dollar
ᵃ Incl special appropriations for procurement and infrastructure amounting to NT$301bn ($11bn) 1993–2001.
Between 1993–98 NT$208bn ($8bn) was spent out of
NT$289bn ($11bn) appropriated for these years.

Population	21,631,000		
(Taiwanese 84%, mainland Chinese 14%)			
Age	*13–17*	*18–22*	*23–32*
Men	991,000	976,000	1,845,000
Women	944,000	922,000	1,747,000

Total Armed Forces

ACTIVE ε376,000
Terms of service 2 years

RESERVES 1,657,500
Army 1,500,000 with some obligation to age 30 **Navy**
32,500 **Marines** 35,000 **Air Force** 90,000

Army ε240,000

(incl mil police)
3 Army, 1 AB Special Ops HQ • 10 inf div • 2 mech inf
div • 2 AB bde • 6 indep armd bde • 1 tk gp • 2 AD
SAM gp with 6 SAM bn: 2 with *Nike Hercules*, 4 with I
HAWK • 2 avn gp, 6 avn sqn

RESERVES
7 lt inf div
EQUIPMENT
MBT 100 M-48A5, 450+ M-48H, 169 M-60A3
LT TK 230 M-24 (**90mm gun**), 675 M-41/Type 64
AIFV 225 M-113 with **20–30mm** cannon
APC 650 M-113, 300 V-150 *Commando*
TOWED ARTY **105mm**: 650 M-101 (T-64); **155mm**:
    M-44, 90 M-59, 250 M-114 (T-65); **203mm** : 70 M-
    115
SP ARTY **105mm**: 100 M-108; **155mm**: 45 T-69, 110
    M-109A2/A5; **203mm**: 60 M-110
COASTAL ARTY **127mm**: US Mk 32 (reported)
MRL **117mm**: KF VI; **126mm**: KF III/IV towed
    and SP
MOR **81mm**: M-29 (some SP); **107mm**
ATGW 1,000 TOW (some SP)
RCL **90mm**: M-67; **106mm**: 500 M-40A1, Type 51
AD GUNS **40mm**: 400 (incl M-42 SP, Bofors)
SAM 40 Nike *Hercules* (to be retired), 100 HAWK,
    Tien Kung (*Sky Bow*) -1/-2, 2 *Chaparral*, ε6 *Patriot*
AC 20 O-1
HEL 110 UH-1H, 42 AH-1W, 13 TH-55, 8 TH-67, 24
    OH-58D, 12 KH-4, 7 CH-47, 5 Hughes 500
UAV *Mastiff* III

DEPLOYMENT
Quemoy 35–40,000; 4 inf div **Matsu** 8–10,000; 1 inf div

Navy 68,000

(incl 30,000 Marines)
3 Naval Districts
BASES Tsoying (HQ), Makung (Pescadores), Keelung
(New East Coast fleet set up and based at Suo; 6 *Chin
Yang*-class FF)
SUBMARINES 4
2 *Hai Lung* (Nl mod *Zwaardvis*) with 533mm TT
2 *Hai Shih* (US *Guppy* II) with 533mm TT (trg only)
PRINCIPAL SURFACE COMBATANTS 36
DESTROYERS 18
DDG 7 *Chien Yang* (US *Gearing*) (*Wu Chin* III
    conversion) with 10 SM-1 MR SAM (boxed), plus
    1 x 8 ASROC, 2 x 3 ASTT, plus 1 *Hughes* MD-500
    hel
DD 11
6 *Fu Yang* (US *Gearing*) (ASW); 5 with 1 *Hughes* MD
    500 hel, 1 with 1 x 8 ASROC, all with 2 x 3 ASTT;
    plus 1 or 2 x 2 127mm guns, 3 or 5 *Hsiung Feng* I
    (*HF* 1) (Il *Gabriel*) SSM
2 *Po Yang* (US *Sumner*)† with 1 or 2 x 2 127mm guns;
    plus 2 x 3 ASTT; 5 or 6 *HF* 1 SSM, 1 with 1 *Hughes*

MD-500 hel

3 *Kun Yang* (US *Fletcher*) with 2 or 3 127mm guns; 1 76mm gun; plus 2 x 3 ASTT with 5 *HF* 1 SSM†

FRIGATES 18

FFG 6 *Cheng Kung* with 8 HF2 SSM, 1 SM-1 MR SAM, 2 x 3 ASTT, 2 S-70C hel

FF 12

6 *Kang Ding* (Fr *La Fayette*) with 8 HF2 SSM, 4 *Sea Chaparral* SAM, 1 76mm gun, 6 324mm TT, 1 S-70C hel

6 *Chin Yang* (US *Knox*) with 1 x 8 ASROC, 1 SH-2F hel, 4 ASTT; plus *Harpoon* (from ASROC launchers), 1 127mm gun

PATROL AND COASTAL COMBATANTS 101

CORVETTES 3 *Ping Ching* (US *Auk*) with 4 40mm gun

MISSILE CRAFT 53

2 *Lung Chiang* PFM with 2 *HF* 1 SSM

1 *Jinn Chiang* PFM with 4 *HF* 1 SSM

50 *Hai Ou* (mod Il *Dvora*)< with 2 *HF* 1 SSM

PATROL, INSHORE 45 (op by Maritime Police)

22 Vosper-type 32m PFI, 7 PCI, about 16 PCI<

MINE COUNTERMEASURES 12

4 *Yung Chou* (US *Adjutant*) MSC

4 (ex-US) *Aggressive* ocean-going minesweepers

4 *Yung Feng* MSC converted from oil-rig spt ships

AMPHIBIOUS 19

2 *Chung Ho* (US *Newport*) LST capacity 400 troops, 500 tons vehicles, 4 LCVP

1 *Kao Hsiung* (US LST 511) amph comd

10 *Chung Hai* (US LST 511) LST, capacity 16 tk, 200 tps

4 *Mei Lo* (US LSM-1) LSM, capacity about 4 tk

2 *Chung Cheng* (US *Cabildo*) LSD, capacity 3 LCU or 18 LCM

Plus about 325 craft; some 20 LCU, 205 LCM, 100 LCVP and assault LCVP

SUPPORT AND MISCELLANEOUS 20

3 spt tkr, 2 repair/salvage, 1 *Wu Yi* combat spt with hel deck, 2 *Yuen Feng* and 2 *Wu Kang* attack tpt with hel deck, 2 tpt, 7 ocean tugs, 1 *Te Kuan* (research)

COASTAL DEFENCE 1

1 SSM coastal def bn with *Hsiung Feng* (*Gabriel*-type)

NAVAL AIR

31 cbt ac; 21 armed hel

MR 1 sqn with 31 S-2 (24 -E, 7 -G) (Air Force-operated)

HEL 12* Hughes 500MD, 9* S-70C ASW *Defender*, 9 S-70C(M)-1

MARINES (30,000)

2 div, spt elm

EQUIPMENT

AAV LVTP-4/-5

TOWED ARTY 105mm, 155mm

RCL 106mm

Air Force 68,000

529 cbt ac, no armed hel

Flying hours 180

FGA/FTR 20 sqn

10 with 272 F-5 (7 -B, 213 -E, 52 -F)

4 with 100 *Ching-Kuo* (plus 10 test)

3 with 30 *Mirage* 2000-5 (on-going delivery of 30 more)

3 with 60 F-16A/B (on-going delivery of 120 more)

AEW 4 E-2T

SAR 1 sqn with 17 S-70C

TPT 4 ac sqn

2 with 8 C-47, 1 C-118B, 1 DC-6B

1 with 19 C-130H (1 EW)

1 VIP with 4 -727-100, 12 Beech 1900

HEL 5 CH-34, 1 S-62A (VIP), 14 S-70

TRG ac incl 58* AT-3A/B, 40 T-38A, 42 T-34C

MISSILES

ASM AGM-65A *Maverick*

AAM AIM-4D *Falcon*, AIM-9J/P *Sidewinder*, *Shafrir*, *Sky Sword* I and II, MATRA *Mica*, MATRA R550 *Magic* 2

Paramilitary ε26,650

SECURITY GROUPS 25,000

National Police Administration (Ministry of Interior); **Bureau of Investigation** (Ministry of Justice); **Military Police** (Ministry of Defence)

MARITIME POLICE ε1,000

about 38 armed patrol boats; also man many of the patrol craft listed under Navy

CUSTOMS SERVICE (Ministry of Finance) 650

5 PCO, 2 PCC, 1 PCI, 5 PCI<; most armed

Foreign Forces

SINGAPORE 4 trg camps

Thailand

	1996	1997	1998	1999
GDP	b4.6tr	b4.8tr		
	($166bn)	($154bn)		
per capita	$8,200	$8,400		
Growth	6.7%	0.6%		
Inflation	5.9%	5.0%		
Debt	$91bn	$98bn		
Def exp	b109bn	b102bn		
	($4.3bn)	($3.2bn)		
Def bdgt			b81.0bn	b77.4bn
			($2.0bn)	($1.8bn)
FMA (US)	$2.9m	$4.8m	$3.9m	$4.6m
(Aus)	$3.0m	$2.5m	$2.5m	
$1 = baht	25.3	31.4	43.3	

Population	62,910,000		
(Thai 75%, Chinese 14%, Muslim 4%)			
Age	*13–17*	*18–22*	*23–32*
Men	3,170,000	3,165,000	6,024,000
Women	3,064,000	3,070,000	5,865,000

Total Armed Forces

ACTIVE 306,000

RESERVES 200,000

Army 190,000

4 Regional Army HQ, 2 Corps HQ • 2 cav div • 3 armd inf div • 3 mech inf div • 1 lt inf div • 2 SF div • 1 arty div, 1 AD arty div (6 AD arty bn) • 1 engr div • 4 economic development div • 1 indep cav regt • 8 indep inf bn • 4 recce coy • armd air cav regt with 3 air-mobile coy • Some hel flt • Rapid Reaction Force (1 bn per region forming)

RESERVES
4 inf div HQ

EQUIPMENT
MBT 50+ PRC Type-69 (trg/in store), 150+ M-48A5, 77 M-60A1/-A3
LT TK 154 *Scorpion*, 250 M-41, 106 *Stingray*
RECCE 32 Shorland Mk 3
APC 340 M-113A1 (plus 82 A3 being delivered), 162 V-150 *Commando*, 18 *Condor*, 450 PRC Type-85 (YW-531H)
TOWED ARTY 105mm: 24 LG1 Mk 2, 285 M-101/-101 mod, 12 M-102, 32 M-618A2 (local manufacture); **130mm**: 15 PRC Type-59; **155mm**: 56 M-114, 62 M-198, 32 M-71, 36 GHN-45/A1
SP ARTY 155mm: 20 M-109A2
MOR 81mm, 107mm
ATGW TOW, 300 *Dragon*
RL M-72 LAW
RCL 75mm: M-20; **106mm**: 150 M-40
AD GUNS 20mm: 24 M-163 *Vulcan*, 24 M-167 *Vulcan*; **37mm**: 122 Type-74; **40mm**: 80 M-1/M-42 SP, 28 L/70; **57mm**: 24+ PRC Type-59
SAM *Redeye*, some *Aspide*, HN-5A
AIRCRAFT
TPT 2 C-212, 2 Beech 1900C-1, 4 C-47, 10 Cessna 208, 2 Short 330UTT, 1 Beech King Air, 2 Jetstream 41
LIAISON 60 O-1A, 17 -E, 5 T-41A, 13 U-17A
TRG 16 T-41D, 20+ MX-7-235
HELICOPTERS
ATTACK 4 AH-1F
TPT 8 CH-47, 8 Bell 206, 9 B-212, 6 B-214, 69 UH-1H
TRG 36 Hughes 300C, 3 OH-13, 7 TH-55
SURV RASIT (veh, arty), AN-TPQ-36 (arty, mor)

Navy 73,000

(incl 1,700 Naval Air, 20,000 Marines, 7,000 Coastal Defence)
FLEETS 1st North Thai Gulf **2nd** South Thai Gulf 1 Naval Air Division
BASES Bangkok, Sattahip (Fleet HQ), Songkhla, Phang Nga, Nakhon Phanom (HQ Mekong River Operating Unit)

PRINCIPAL SURFACE COMBATANTS 15
AIRCRAFT CARRIER 1 *Chakri Naruebet* with 8 AV-8S *Matador* (*Harrier*), 6 S-70B *Seahawk* hel, 3 x 6 *Sadral* SAM, 8 VLS *Sea Sparrow*
FRIGATES 14
FFG 8
2 *Naresuan* with 2 x 4 *Harpoon* SSM, 8 cell *Sea Sparrow* SAM, 1 127mm gun, 6 324mm TT, 1 SH-2F hel
2 *Chao Phraya* (PRC *Jianghu* III) with 8 C-801 SSM, 2 x 2 100mm guns; plus 2 x 5 ASW RL (plus 1 undergoing weapons fit)
2 *Kraburil* (PRC *Jianghu* IV type) with 8 C-801 SSM, 1 x 2 100mm guns; plus 2 x 5 ASW RL and *Bell* 212 hel
2 *Phutthayotfa Chulalok* (US *Knox*) (to be leased) with 8 *Harpoon* SSM, 8 ASROC ASTT, 1 127mm gun, 1 Bell 212 hel
FF 6
1 *Makut Rajakumarn* with 2 x 3 ASTT (*Sting Ray* LWT); plus 2 114mm guns
2 *Tapi* (US PF-103) with 2 x 3 ASTT (Mk 46 LWT)
2 *Tachin* (US *Tacoma*) with 2 x 3 ASTT (trg)
1 *Pin Klao* (US *Cannon*) with 1 76mm gun, 6 324mm TT

PATROL AND COASTAL COMBATANTS 87
CORVETTES 5
2 *Rattanakosin* with 2 x 3 ASTT (*Sting Ray* LWT); plus 2 x 4 *Harpoon* SSM, 8 *Aspide* SAM
3 *Khamronsin* with 2 x 3 ASTT; plus 1 76mm gun
MISSILE CRAFT 6
3 *Ratcharit* (It Breda 50m) with 4 MM-38 *Exocet* SSM
3 *Prabparapak* (Ge Lürssen 45m) with 5 *Gabriel* SSM
PATROL CRAFT 76
COASTAL 12
3 *Chon Buri* PFC, 6 *Sattahip*, 3 PCD
INSHORE 64
7 T-11 (US PGM-71), 9 T-91, about 33 PCF and 15 PCR plus boats
MINE COUNTERMEASURES 5
2 *Bang Rachan* (Ge Lürssen T-48) MCC
2 *Ladya* (US *Bluebird*) MSC
1 *Thalang* MCM spt with minesweeping capability (Plus some 12 MSB)
AMPHIBIOUS 9
2 *Sichang* (Fr PS-700) LST, capacity 14 tk, 300 tps with hel deck (trg)
5 *Angthong* (US LST-511) LST, capacity 16 tk, 200 tps

2 *Kut* (US LSM-1) LSM, capacity about 4 tk
Plus about 51 craft: 9 LCU, about 24 LCM, 1 LCG, 2 LSIL, 3 hovercraft, 12 LCVP

SUPPORT AND MISCELLANEOUS 16

1 *Similan* AO (1 hel) , 1 *Chula* AO, 5 small tkr, 3 survey, 6 trg

NAVAL AIR (1,700)

(300 conscripts); 54 cbt ac; 5 armed hel
FTR 9 *Harrier* (7 AV-8, 2 TAV-8)
MR/ATTACK 11 Cessna T-337 *Skymasters*, 14 A-7E, 4 TA-7C, 5 O-1G, 4 U-17B
MR/ASW 3 P-3T *Orion* (plus 2 P-3A in store), 1 UP-3T, 6 Do-228, 2 F-27 MPA, 4 S-2F, 5 N-24A *Nomad*
ASW HEL 5 S-70B
SAR/UTILITY 2 CL-215, 7 Bell 212, 5 Bell 412, 4 UH-1H, 6 S-76N
ASM AGM-84 *Harpoon* (for F-27MPA, P-3T)

MARINES (20,000)

1 div HQ, 2 inf regt, 1 arty regt (3 fd, 1 AA bn); 1 amph aslt bn; recce bn

EQUIPMENT

AAV 33 LVTP-7
TOWED ARTY 155mm: 12 GC-45
ATGW TOW, *Dragon*

Air Force 43,000

206 cbt ac, no armed hel
Flying hours 100
FGA 3 sqn
1 with 8 F-5A/B • 2 with 36 F-16 (26 -A, 10 -B)
FTR 2 sqn with 35 F-5E, 6 -F
ARMED AC 5 sqn
1 with 7 AC-47 • 3 with 24 AU-23A • 1 with 20* N-22B *Missionmaster* (tpt/armed)
ELINT 1 sqn with 3 IAI-201
RECCE 2 sqn with 30* OV-10C, 4* RF-5A, 3*RT-33A
SURVEY 2 *Learjet* 35A, 3 *Merlin* IVA, 3 GAF N-22B *Nomads*
TPT 3 sqn
1 with 6 C-130H, 6 C-130H-30, 3 DC-8-62F
1 with 3 C-123-K, 4 BAe-748
1 with 6 G-222
VIP Royal flight **ac** 1 Airbus A-310-324, 1 Boeing 737-200, 1 *King Air* 200, 2 BAe-748, 3 *Merlin* IV **hel** 2 Bell 412, 3 AS-532A2
TRG 24 CT-4, 30 Fantrainer-400, 16 Fantrainer-600, 16 SF-260, 10 T-33A, 20 PC-9, 6 -C, 11 T-41, 34 L-39ZA/MP
LIAISON 3 *Commander*, 2 *King Air* E90, 30 O-1 *Bird Dog*, 2 *Queen Air*, 3 *Basler Turbo*-67
HEL 2 sqn
1 with 18 S-58T • 1 with 21 UH-1H
AAM AIM-9B/J *Sidewinder*, AIM-120 AMRAAM, *Python* 3
AIR DEFENCE
1 AA arty bty: 4 *Skyguard*, 1 *Flycatcher* radars, each

with 4 fire units of 2 30mm Mauser/Kuka guns
SAM *Blowpipe*, *Aspide*, RBS NS-70, *Starburst*

Forces Abroad

UN AND PEACEKEEPING
IRAQ/KUWAIT (UNIKOM): 5 obs

Paramilitary ε71,000 active

THAHAN PHRAN (Hunter Soldiers) 18,500
volunteer irregular force; 27 regt of some 200 coy
NATIONAL SECURITY VOLUNTEER CORPS 50,000
MARINE POLICE 2,500
3 PCO, 3 PCC, 8 PFI, some 110 PCI<
POLICE AVIATION 500
ac 1 *Airtourer*, 6 AU-23, 2 Cessna 310, 1 Fokker 50, 1 CT-4, 2 CN 235, 8 PC-6, 2 Short 330 **hel** 27 Bell 205A, 14 Bell 206, 3 Bell 212, 6 UH-12, 5 KH-4
BORDER PATROL POLICE 18,000
PROVINCIAL POLICE ε50,000
incl ε500 Special Action Force

Foreign Forces

SINGAPORE 2 trg camps (arty)

Vietnam

	1996	1997	1998	1999
GDP	d259tr	d284tr		
	($23.5bn)	($24.3bn)		
per capita	$1,000	$1,100		
Growth	9.5%	7.5%		
Inflation	6.0%	3.6%		
Debt	$27bn	$29bn		
Def exp	ε$950m	ε$990m		
Def bdgt			ε$950m	
$1 = dong	11,000	11,659	12,980	
Population	78,852,000 (Chinese 3%)			
Age	*13–17*	*18–22*	*23–32*	
Men	4,324,000	3,916,000	6,784,000	
Women	4,174,000	3,795,000	6,669,000	

Total Armed Forces

ACTIVE ε484,000
(referred to as 'Main Force')
Terms of service 2 years, specialists 3 years, some ethnic minorities 2 years

RESERVES some 3–4,000,000
'Strategic Rear Force' (see also *Paramilitary*)

Army ε412,000

8 Mil Regions, 2 special areas • 14 Corps HQ • 58 inf div[a] • 4 mech inf div • 10 armd bde • 15 indep inf regt • SF incl AB bde, demolition engr regt • Some 10 fd arty bde • 8 engr div • 10–16 economic construction div • 20 indep engr bde

EQUIPMENT

MBT 45 T-34, 850 T-54/-55, 70 T-62, 350 PRC Type-59
LT TK 300 PT-76, 320 PRC Type-62/63
RECCE 100 BRDM-1/-2
AIFV 300 BMP
APC 1,100 BTR-40/-50/-60/-152, YW-531, M-113
TOWED ARTY 2,300: **76mm; 85mm; 100mm**: M-1944, T-12; **105mm**: M-101/-102; **122mm**: Type-54, Type-60, M-1938, D-30, D-74; **130mm**: M-46; **152mm**: D-20; **155mm**: M-114
SP ARTY 152mm: 30 2S3; **175mm**: M-107
COMBINED GUN/MOR 120mm: 2S9 reported
ASLT GUNS 100mm: SU-100; **122mm**: ISU-122
MRL 107mm: 360 Type 63; **122mm**: 350 BM-21; **140mm**: BM-14-16
MOR 82mm, 120mm: M-43; **160mm**: M-43
ATGW AT-3 Sagger
RCL 75mm: PRC Type-56; **82mm**: PRC Type-65, B-10; **87mm**: PRC Type-51
AD GUNS 12,000: **14.5mm; 23mm**: incl ZSU-23-4 SP; **30mm; 37mm; 57mm; 85mm; 100mm**
SAM SA-7/-16

[a] Inf div str varies from 5,000 to 12,500

Navy ε42,000

(incl 27,000 Naval Infantry)
Four Naval Regions
BASES Hanoi (HQ), Cam Ranh Bay, Da Nang, Haiphong, Ha Tou, Ho Chi Minh City, Can Tho, plus several smaller bases

SUBMARINES

2 DPRK Yugo (midget subs)

FRIGATES 7

1 Barnegat (US Cutter) with 2 SS-N-2A Styx SSM, 1 127mm gun
3 Sov Petya II with 2 ASW RL, 10 406mm TT, 4 76mm gun
2 Sov Petya III with 2 ASW RL, 3 533mm TT, 4 76mm gun
1 Dai Ky (US Savage) with 2 x 3 ASTT (trg hulk)

PATROL AND COASTAL COMBATANTS 44

MISSILE CRAFT 10
8 Sov Osa II with 4 SS-N-2 SSM
2 Sov Tarantul with 4 SS-N-2D Styx SSM
TORPEDO CRAFT 15
7 Sov Turya PHT with 4 533mm TT
8 Sov Shershen PFT with 4 533mm TT
PATROL, INSHORE 19
4 Sov SO-1, 3 US PGM-59/71, 10 Zhuk<, 2 Sov

Poluchat PCI; plus large numbers of river patrol boats

MINE COUNTERMEASURES 11

2 Yurka MSC, 4 Sonya MSC, 2 PRC Lienyun MSC, 1 Vanya MSI, 2 Yevgenya MSI, plus 5 K-8 boats

AMPHIBIOUS 6

3 US LST-510-511 LST, capacity 200 tps, 16 tk
3 Sov Polnocny LSM, capacity 180 tps, 6 tk
Plus about 30 craft: 12 LCM, 18 LCU

SUPPORT AND MISCELLANEOUS 30+

incl 1 trg, 1 survey, 4 small tkr, about 12 small tpt, 2 ex-Sov floating docks and 3 div spt. Significant numbers of small merchant ships and trawlers are taken into naval service for patrol and resupply duties. Some of these may be lightly armed

NAVAL INFANTRY (27,000)

(amph, cdo)

Air Force 15,000

201 cbt ac, 43 armed hel (plus many in store). 4 Air Div
FGA 2 regt with 65 Su-22, 12 Su-27
FTR 5 regt with 124 MiG-21bis/PF
ATTACK HEL 24 Mi-24
MR 4 Be-12
ASW HEL 8 Ka-25, 5 Ka-28, 6 Ka-32
SURVEY 2 An-30
TPT 3 regt incl 12 An-2, 4 An-24, 30 An-26, 8 Tu-134, 13 Yak-40
HEL some 70 incl Mi-6, Mi-8/-17
TRG 3 regt with 52 ac, incl L-39, MiG-21U, Yak-18
AAM AA-2 Atoll, AA-8 Aphid, AA-10 Allamo
ASM AS-9 Kyle

Air Defence Force 15,000

14 AD div
SAM some 66 sites with SA-2/-3/-6
AD 4 arty bde: **37mm, 57mm, 85mm, 100mm, 130mm**
People's Regional Force: ε1,000 units, 6 radar bde: 100 sites

Paramilitary 40,000 active

LOCAL FORCES some 4–5,000,000

incl **People's Self-Defence Force** (urban units), **People's Militia** (rural units); these comprise static and mobile cbt units, log spt and village protection pl; some arty, mor and AD guns; acts as reserve

BORDER DEFENCE CORPS ε40,000

COAST GUARD

being established; to come into effect on 1 Sept 1998

Foreign Forces

RUSSIA 700: naval facilities; ELINT station

MILITARY DEVELOPMENTS

The region's armed forces were mainly occupied during 1997 and 1998 with internal security and wide-scale civil emergencies caused by El Ninõ-related weather disturbance. The consolidation of civilian control over the military continues in most of the region, although haltingly in some countries, particularly where military officers retire and take up key positions in government or business. In **Chile,** while General Augusto Pinochet formally retired on 10 March 1998, he and some of his old guard exercise influence through the senate and their informal networks. Nevertheless, Chile continues to lead the region in greater openness on defence budget matters. In June 1998, the Chilean government announced it had suspended plans to re-equip its Air Force with new combat aircraft. In **Paraguay,** General Lino César Silva Orvieto briefly attempted to restore his authority, while still awaiting trial for his failed coup attempt in April 1996, when the *Associación Nacional Republicana* (ANR) party put him forward as its candidate for the presidency in September 1997. This effort to re-establish military control with a quasi-civilian president failed when Orvieto was tried and jailed prior to the May 1998 presidential election.

In contrast to this positive trend, a disturbing development is the growth in armed vigilante groups flourishing in a number of countries, some with government encouragement, which includes supplying weapons. This is happening in areas where central government is failing to contain armed opposition groups and large-scale organised crime. The trend is particularly marked in **Colombia** and in some provinces of **Mexico**. In Colombia, Bogotá has not regained control over significant territory still held by the two main armed opposition groups, the Revolutionary Armed Forces of Colombia (FARC) and the National Liberation Army (ELN). FARC, the bigger of the two groups, reported to be some 12,000–15,000 strong in May 1998, has inflicted heavy casualties on the Colombian Army's élite Mobile Brigade. During the first week of March 1998 alone, for example, 84 regular troops were killed, 30 injured and 27 taken hostage. The government tries to exert some control through the irregular armed groups, essentially right wing, that cooperate with the police and armed forces to try to erode support for the left-wing guerrilla movements. These have gained stature, but they are not under firm control and cause unnecessary suffering to civilians through their indiscriminate operations. The most prominent, the United Self-Defence Forces of Colombia (AUC), has been responsible for numerous killings, including the murder of 21 people in Puerto Alvira in May 1998. Hopes for peace were raised in July 1998 when then President-elect Andrés Pastrana met the leaders of the various armed factions to prepare the way for talks. Vigilante groups have also been operating in the Chiapas region of Mexico where there was an upsurge of violence in May and June 1998. A cease-fire has yet to be agreed, despite central government efforts to achieve a peace settlement with the *Ejército Zapatista de Liberación Nacional* (EZLN) guerilla movement. Attempts to bring in outside mediators to resolve differences have also failed. Supporters of the Institutional Revolutionary Party (PRI) in the region have exploited the vacuum left by lack of progress to attack ELZN supporters. Their victims have been mainly unarmed civilians. One of the most gruesome incidents was the murder, in December 1997, of 45 people, mainly women and children, in Chenalho, a stronghold of the EZLN. While conflict has been at a relatively low level during much of the past year, the upward spiral of violence resumed in mid-1998.

The one international dispute in the region, between **Ecuador** and **Peru,** looked nearer resolution in 1998. However, despite ministerial meetings in June 1998, a settlement has proved elusive. The disputed border region is still being overseen by international military observers from Brazil,

Argentina, Venezuela and the US. All military forces were withdrawn from the UN Transition Mission in **Haiti** (UNTMIH) in November 1997, leaving only a civilian police element to train and advise the Haitian National Police.

ORGANISED CRIME

Organised crime, typically narcotics-related and transnational, places increasing demands on the armed forces in operations to support the civil authorities. According to the Inter-American Development Bank, criminal violence costs Latin America some $168bn a year, or about 14% of regional GDP. The countries worst affected are Colombia, **Brazil**, Mexico and **Venezuela**. International drug cartels (and related arms-smuggling and money-laundering) pose a security threat in their own right; this is compounded when the cartels sponsor armed opposition groups (most notably in Colombia) or corrupt politicians and military leaders. The relative poverty of indigenous ethnic groups (as in the Chiapas region of Mexico) aggravates the problem, as do the unresolved grievances of former civil war belligerents elsewhere in Central America.

DEFENCE SPENDING

Regional defence spending continued to rise in real terms during 1997, as it has done each year since 1992. Outlays in 1997 are estimated at some $33bn (in 1997 dollars), compared to just over $32bn in 1996. The real increase of about 6% outpaced economic growth of 4.5% across the region. Since 1992, military outlays have risen in real terms by about 35% compared to economic growth of some 22%. Brazil has been the largest single contributor, both in absolute and relative terms, with outlays more than doubling since 1992. Large spending increases have also occurred in Mexico, Colombia and Peru. There have been smaller rises in Chile and Ecuador, while military spending has declined in **Argentina** and Venezuela, together with the Central American republics **El Salvador, Honduras, Nicaragua** and most recently **Guatemala**. While much of the increased funding has gone towards raising military salaries, there has also been more weapons procurement. Defence budgets in 1998 indicate spending at or slightly above 1997 levels in real terms.

Despite some improvement in the political and security environments, there is not yet a parallel improvement in the transparency of military accounting and it is very difficult to make accurate estimates of defence expenditures. Official figures cite defence budgets funded from general taxation, but may exclude: war taxes and specific levies for military application on, for example, exported commodities like oil and copper; subsidies for military enterprises; extra-budgetary funding from state-run firms; commercial enterprises operated by the military; and the draw-down from military pension funds. According to the latest International Monetary Fund (IMF) figures (1997), regional defence spending accounts for just 1.3% of GDP on average, whereas *The Military Balance* shows an average figure of 2%. The use of varying definitions of defence expenditure accounts for the difference. In *The Military Balance*, spending on military equipment (however funded), on paramilitary forces and on pensions for retired military personnel, funded out of current government revenue (as opposed to past contributions), are all counted as defence expenditure. Of the 28 countries covered in the Caribbean and Latin America region, four provided information for 1996 to the annual UN military expenditure exercise. Only Argentina included spending on paramilitary forces and pensions to retired military personnel, although this is an explicit UN response requirement. Brazil excluded military pensions to retired personnel and funding for the Military Police. The Mexican response excluded pensions and funding for paramilitary forces, while that of Ecuador excluded the 15% share of oil export revenues taken by the military. In Chile, the official budget covers about 40% of actual spending.

Procurement is funded outside the fiscal budget (the armed forces take 10% of the export revenues of the state copper company Codelco); military pensions (17% of real spending in 1998) are listed as social security; the paramilitary *Caribineros* come under the Interior Ministry; and no fiscal account is taken of other sources of revenue for the armed forces, such as sales of military (state) property and military industries. Such accounting practices are not confined to Chile, but widespread throughout Central and South America. The picture would be clearer if the region's governments were more open about all their accounting. The IMF is no more successful than the UN in eliciting information on defence spending from member and client states. Only **Bolivia**, Chile, El Salvador and **Uruguay** reported 1996 outlays to the Fund for late 1997 publication. While the response rate has improved, a reporting lag of three years and more for the majority of countries shows how far from transparent regional accounting practice remains.

Table 24 Countries reporting defence expenditures to the UN, 1996

(US$m)	Argentina	Brazil	Ecuador	Mexico
Personnel	3,964	7,579	245	717
Operations & Maintenance	472	1,050	45	500
Procurement	81	379	1	137
Research & Development	12	79	0	0
Infrastructure	16	184	1	29
Total	**4,546**	**9,271**	**291**	**1,383**

Table 25 Argentina and Chile: defence funding, 1998

(US$m)	Argentina	%	Chile	%
Army	925	22.6	553	16.5
Navy	580	14.2	496	14.8
Air Force	529	13.0	266	7.9
Military Pensions	1,205	29.5	560	16.7
Other	155	3.8	337	10.1
Sub-Total	**3,394**	**83.1**	**2,212**	**66.1**
Paramilitary	690	16.9	800	23.9
Armed Forces Commercial Revenue	n.a.	n.a.	335	10.0
Total	**4,084**	**100.0**	**3,347**	**100.0**

The impact of demands for greater parliamentary oversight of military spending is limited. In Mexico, where it was reported in October 1997 that the Congress is to audit defence spending for the first time, the 1998 defence and public order and safety (internal security) budgets each account for 0.8% of GDP. A total security outlay of 1.6% of GDP is a very low figure in absolute and relative terms, given the country's continuing problems in the Chiapas and other regions. However, this figure excludes both military pensions and state-level funding for paramilitary police forces. Adding these expenditures to the federal security budget would raise the real spend to over 2% of GDP. In Guatemala, where the 1996 peace agreement was conditional on a 33% reduction in military spending, the parliamentary opposition has criticised the 1998 defence budget of Q798m ($127m) both because of the increase on the 1997 figure of Q729m, and because it excludes funding for the paramilitary force under the presidential budget allocation (Q75m). In Honduras, the military handed over control of the Public Security Force in October 1997 to a civilian ministry, but the 1998 defence allocation increased from L330m in 1997 to L479m ($36m), after the Honduran Congress added to the administration's 1998 request for L364m. Outside parliament, there is increasing criticism of the resources controlled by the Honduran military pension fund (Military Welfare Institute). In Nicaragua, the 1998 security allocation is C546m ($54m) split between the military (C314m) and the Police (C232m) after a 20% salary increase for all enlisted personnel. In May 1998, the Nicaraguan Comptroller-General announced an official inquiry into the military pension fund (Military Social Welfare Institute). In **Costa Rica,** the security budget has risen from C13.6bn: ($69m) to C17.6bn ($79m) in 1998. In 1997, according to official figures, the security forces spent $594,000 on equipment, while the 1998 equipment budget is $518, 000.

Another reason for the lack of openness in military accounting is that it enables both governments and military establishments to mask their real priorities and avoid accountability for failures to address contemporary security challenges. The real dilemma for governments is whether to continue rewarding senior and retired military personnel for their political loyalty with large salaries and pensions and uncritical approval of expensive procurement programmes, or to use the funds to address real immediate and future security needs. In general, the current distribution of military funds favours those identified with the military regimes of the past. Immediate security needs have taken second place, which may, in part, explain the relative inability of the military to deal with the current security challenges effectively. Professionalisation of the armed forces remains too expensive or, in some countries in the region, would arouse strong political opposition. The exception among countries with larger armed forces is Argentina, which made a commitment to develop a professional military in 1995. Until professionalisation takes hold across the region, junior enlisted personnel will not get appropriate financial rewards and incentives. This means that there will be continued reliance on conscripted personnel, with low motivation and poor skills. At the same time operations and maintenance (O&M) budgets are under-financed to the detriment of training and operational effectiveness. Where procurement is concerned, reactionary central military establishments, out of touch with field operations, remain prone to waste limited resources on traditional, but expensive, weapons and equipment that do not meet the real needs of the armed forces. Chile, by suspending plans to acquire new and more advanced combat aircraft, may be signalling an end to this tendency.

There has been little evidence, beyond declarations, of substantive regional security cooperation. Following the US decision to relax restrictions on advanced weapon exports to the region, the Organisation of American States announced, in July 1997, that it was drafting a proposal calling for pre-notification of arms transfers. Agreement on such a measure (which would be an advance on the reporting requirements of the UN Register of Conventional Arms) has not yet been achieved.

There are revised figures for Brazil's defence spending over the past few years in this edition of *The Military Balance,* due partly to new information becoming available from the Brazilian Ministry of Planning.

Table 26 Brazil's defence expenditure, 1995–1998

(US$m)	1995 Budget	1995 Outlay	1996 Budget	1996 Outlay	1997 Budget	1997 Revised	1997 Outlay	1998 Budget
Army	7,920	6,444	7,060	6,595	6,906	7,001	6,606	6,648
Navy	5,420	3,914	4,273	3,749	4,032	4,088	3,769	3,844
Air Force	4,609	3,759	4,212	3,604	3,697	3,774	3,439	3,433
MoD	95	252	101	101	132	132	132	256
Total	18,045	14,369	15,646	14,050	14,767	14,995	13,945	14,181

Brazil's 1998 defence budget authorisation is R16.1bn ($14.2bn) compared to last year's initial authorisation of R15.9bn, increased to R16.2bn, and outlay of R15bn. Salaries and pensions accounted for 73% of the 1997 budget. R&D and Procurement spending (some $481m in 1996) is on the increase, particularly in the Navy and Air Force. The federal defence budget excludes funding for the Military Police (with an estimated establishment of nearly 400,000). Although these forces are considered an army reserve and come ultimately under army control, they are funded under the individual budgets of the 27 Brazilian states. Following the series of strikes by the Military Police in 13 states, which began in May 1997, the government has awarded them (along with the armed forces) a 25% pay increase in 1998.

Table 27 Brazil's defence budget by function, 1997

(US$m)	Army	%	Navy	%	Air Force	%	MoD	%	Total	%
Personnel										
and Pensions	5,663	82.0	2,765	68.6	2,298	62.1	74	56.3	10,801	73.1
O&M, Procurement										
& Construction	1,243	18.0	1,267	31.4	1,399	37.9	58	43.7	3,966	26.9
Total	**6,906**	100.0	**4,032**	100.0	**3,697**	100.0	**132**	100.0	**14,767**	100.0

Venezuela's 1998 defence budget shows a large nominal increase to B685bn ($1,315m) from B470bn at mid-1998 exchange rates. This is also the case in Bolivia, where the military are requesting B1,016m ($187m), up from B786m.

In Mexico, the 1998 defence budget rises to P20.1bn from P19bn in 1997, which represents a decline in dollar terms from $2.4bn in 1997 to $2.3bn. Paraguay's defence budget for 1998 is Pg280bn ($109m) compared to Pg260bn in 1997, and Colombia's is pC3.6tr ($2.7bn), compared to pC2.2tr.

Table 28 Colombia's defence and security budget, 1998

	pC (bn)	US$ (m)
Ministry of National Defence	454	326
Army	976	700
Navy	273	196
Air Force	247	177
Other services	157	113
Sub-total MND	**2,107**	**1,513**
National Police	1,554	1,116
State funding for security	1,353	971
Total Security Budget	**5,015**	**3,600**

WEAPONS PROGRAMMES

Arms transfers in the region were an estimated $1.6bn in 1995 and $1.7bn in 1996, double the very low levels recorded in 1993–94. Modernisation programmes are beginning to take effect in several countries, notably Brazil and Chile, while both Peru and Ecuador are re-equipping their armed forces following the border conflict in January–February 1995.

The major orders and deliveries during 1997 and 1998 were from and to Brazil, Chile, Peru and Ecuador. Brazil's AMX light combat aircraft programme, in collaboration with Italy, is drawing to a close after deliveries of 56 aircraft to the Air Force. In 1998, the Air Force ordered 99 EMB-312H

Super Tucanos for delivery from 1999. These will be used for training and internal security operations in conjunction with the *Sistema de Viligencia de Amazonia* (SIVAM) area radar surveillance system, initiated in 1997 at an estimated programme cost of some $1.5bn. The Navy has taken delivery of nine new *Lynx* helicopters for the four ex-UK Type 22 frigates accepted between 1995 and 1997. Following the commissioning in 1994 and 1996 of two *Tupi* Type 209 submarines, built under licence from a German company, two more locally-built *Tupi* submarines are due to be launched in 1998 for delivery in 1999 and 2000. In 1998, the Navy also received 22 A-4 aircraft (ex-Kuwait) of which they plan to use 12 operationally with the remainder for spares. Brazilian law had to be changed to allow the Navy to fly fixed-wing aircraft, much to the chagrin of the Air Force. Chile's 1997 order for two submarines (at a reported cost of around $400m) from a Franco-Spanish consortium was confirmed in December 1997 and deliveries are expected in 2003 and 2005. The Navy has also announced a new requirement for four frigates, on which work is due to start in 2000, marking the first indigenous Chilean programme for a principal surface combatant. In early 1998, the Chilean Air Force ordered 12 UH-60 *Blackhawk* helicopters, one of which is to be delivered in 1998. Peru's acquisition of 18 used MiG-29s from Belarus has been confirmed. Eight aircraft were delivered in 1996 and the balance in 1997. The Peruvian Air Force has also taken delivery of 18 Su-25s during the same period. Ecuador's purchase of used Israeli *Kfir* combat aircraft has been delayed because they are powered by American engines and the US refuses to allow the technology transfer. In the meantime, there are unconfirmed reports that Ecuador ordered 18 MiG-29s from Russia in early 1998. In 1997, Ecuador ordered seven Mi-17 helicopters from Russia for 1998 delivery, while 1997 deliveries of large numbers of SA-18 surface-to-air missiles (SAMs) of Russian design via Bulgaria have also been reported but not confirmed. Throughout the region, procurement activity appears to be increasing at a modest rate after several years at a virtual standstill.

Table 29 **Arms orders and deliveries, Caribbean and Latin America, 1996–1998**

Supplier	Classification	Designation	Units	Order Date	Delivery Date	Comment
Argentina						
US	FGA	A-4AR	36	1995	1997	Upgrade. All delivered in 1997
US	FGA	A-4M	8	1997		Further 11 on order for parts
A	APC	*Pandur*	6	1996	1997	
Domestic	arty	155mm		1995	1996	In low-volume production
US	hel	UH-1H	26	1995		Unconfirmed
US	tpt	C-130B	2	1996	1997	
US	TKR AC	KC-135	1	1998		
Fr	hel	AS-555	4	1991	1997	
US	MPA	P-3B	8	1996	1998	6 delivered in 1997
UK	APC	*Tactica*	9	1996	1997	
Bahamas						
US	OPV	*Bahamas*	2	1997	1999	Contract options for 4 more
Belize						
UK	OPV	*Daphne*	1	1996	1996	Ex-Da; refurbished in UK 1996
Bolivia						
US	ftr	TA-4J	18	1997	1998	12 for operations and 6 for spare parts
Brazil						
UK	hel	*Lynx*	9	1993	1996	Deliveries continued in 1997
Fr	SAM	*Mistral*		1995	1997	
Fr	ATGW	*Eryx*		1995	1997	

Supplier	Classification	Designation	Units	Order Date	Delivery Date	Comment
RF	hel	Mil-34	10	1995	1996	For police use
Kwt	ftr	A-4	22	1998	1998	For use on a carrier
Collab.	FGA	AMX	56	1980	1989	With It; deliveries 1989–98
Ge	SSK	Type 209	5	1985	1999	4th and 5th launched in 1998
Domestic	AEW	EMB-145	8	1997	2001	
US	MBT	M-60A3	91	1995	1997	
Be	MBT	Leopard	87	1995	1997	
US	hel	UH-1H	20	1995	1997	All delivered in 1997
Ge	PCI	Grauna	2		1997	Last 2 of total order of 10
Domestic	MRL	SS-80		1995	1998	Development completed
Domestic	MRL	ASTROS II	4	1998	1999	
Domestic	trg	EMB-312H	99	1998	1999	AL-X. First 33 to be delivered 1999
US	hel	S-70A	4	1996	1997	29 delivered in 1997
Ge	hel	BO-105	1	1994	1996	
It	PCI	Grajau	16	1998	2000	Based on Meatini (G-11) class
UK	arty	105mm	18	1994	1996	
It	arty	105mm	10	1996	1997	

Chile

Supplier	Classification	Designation	Units	Order Date	Delivery Date	Comment
Il	tkr	B-707	1	1995	1996	
Il	PFC	Saar-class	2	1995	1997	
Be	MBT	Leopard	67	1997		Delivery delayed
It	APC	M-113	128	1995	1997	Deliveries to 1998
Fr	SS	Scorpene	2	1997	2003	1st to commission 2003 and 2nd 2005
US	hel	UH-60	12	1998	1998	
Ge	FAC	Type 148	4	1995	1997	Ex-Ge Navy; built in Fr
US	tpt	C-130B	4	1996	1997	
Fr	trg	C-101	3	1995	1997	Upgrade
US	tpt	B-737	1	1997	1997	
Domestic	MRL	Rayo		1997		In trials until mid-1998
Sp	tpt	C-212	5	1995	1996	
US	hel	AS-332	4	1995	1996	
US	hel	MD-530-F	6	1995	1996	
Fr	msl	Mistral	12	1996	1997	
Fr	MBT	AMX-30	10	1997	1998	
Sp	tpt	CN-235	4	1995	1997	

Colombia

Supplier	Classification	Designation	Units	Order Date	Delivery Date	Comment
US	hel	F-28F	12	1994	1996	Training
RF	hel	Mi-17	10	1997	1997	
Domestic	utl	Gavilan	12	1997		
US	tpt	C-130B	7	1995	1997	
US	hel	UH-1H	20	1994	1996	
US	hel	UH-60L	3	1998	1999	
Sp	PCI	Lazaga	2	1997	1999	
Sp	tpt	CN-235	3	1997	2000	
US	PCI	Tenerife	9	1993	1996	Acquired through US FMA
RSA	APC	RG-31	4	1995	1996	
Fr	hel	AS-555	2	1995	1997	

Dominican Republic

Supplier	Classification	Designation	Units	Order Date	Delivery Date	Comment
US	cutter	cutter	1	1995	1996	

Ecuador

Supplier	Classification	Designation	Units	Order Date	Delivery Date	Comment
Fr	FGA	Mirage F-1	12	1998	1999	
Il	FGA	Kfir	4	1995	1996	To date US refused export of engines

Supplier	Classification	Designation	Units	Order Date	Delivery Date	Comment
US	tpt	C-130B	4	1993	1996	
Nic	AAA	ZU-23	34	1996	1997	
Nic	MBT	T-55	3	1996	1997	
Il	AAM	*Python 3*	100	1995	1996	
RF	ftr	MiG-29	18	1998		Unconfirmed
RF	hel	Mi-17	7	1997	1998	
El Salvador						
Chl	trg	T-35	5	1997	1998	
US	hel	MD-520N	2	1997	1998	
Guatemala						
Chl	trg	T-35	5	1997	1998	
Domestic	APC	*Danto*		1994	1998	Designed for internal security duties
Haiti						
Ge	hel	BO-105	1	1994	1996	
Honduras						
Domestic	ftr	*Super Mystère*	11	1997	1998	Upgrade
Mexico						
US	hel	UH-1H	24	1996	1996	
RF	hel	Mi-17	12	1995	1997	
US	hel	B-206	18	1994	1996	
US	FF	*Knox*-class	2	1996	1998	3rd approved by US Congress
Domestic	PCO		1	1993	1997	First domestically-built warship
US	hel	Bell 208	18	1995	1996	
Nicaragua						
Il	PFC	*Dabur*-class	3	1994	1996	
Panama						
ROC	hel	UH-1H	5	1997	1997	
Paraguay						
Sp	PCI	*Rodman* 101/557		1995	1997	2 *Rodman* 101, 1 *Rodman* 55
ROC	ftr	F-5E/F	12	1997	1998	
US	hel	UH-1H	2	1996	1997	Ex-ROC
Peru						
US	tpt	B-737	2	1995	1996	Ex-Fr
Bel	ftr	MiG-29	18	1995	1996	8 delivered 1996; 10 in 1997
Bel	FGA	Su-25	18	1995	1997	All delivered in 1997
Suriname						
Sp	MPA	C-212	2	1997	1998	1 delivered, 2nd due in 1999
Uruguay						
UK	hel	*Wessex* HC2	11	1997	1998	
Il	MBT	T-55	15	1996	1997	
Venezuela						
RF	hel	Mi-17	18	1995	1996	Refurbished in Pl
Fr	hel	AS-532	6	1997	2000	
US	hel	Bell 412	2	1997	1999	
Pl	tpt	An-28	6	1996	1997	All delivered with option for 12 more
It	trg	SF-260E	12	1998	2000	Option to purchase 18 more
US	hel	UH-1H	5	1997	1999	
US	ftr	F-16B	2	1997	1999	
Sp	tpt	C-212	3	1997	1998	
US	PCI		10	1998	1999	Aluminium 50-foot craft
US	PCI		12	1998	1999	Aluminium 80-foot craft
US	FF	*Lupo*	2	1998	2000	Upgrade and modernisation

Dollar GDP figures for several countries in Latin America are based on Inter-American Development Bank estimates. In some cases, the dollar conversion rates are different from the average exchange rate values shown under the country entry. Dollar GDP figures may vary from those cited in *The Military Balance* in previous years. Defence budgets and expenditures have been converted at the dollar exchange rate used to calculate GDP.

Antigua and Barbuda

	1996	1997	1998	1999
GDP	EC$1.5bn	EC$1.5bn		
	($540m)	($570m)		
per capita	$5,100	$5,300		
Growth	5.4%	3.0%		
Inflation	1.7%	n.k.		
Ext Debt	$274m	n.k.		
Def exp	εEC$9m	EC$7m		
	($3m)	($3m)		
Def bdgt			εEC$11m	
			($4m)	
US$1 = EC$*	2.7	2.7	2.7	

*East Caribbean dollar

Population		70,000		
Age	*13–17*	*18–22*	*23–32*	
Men	5,000	5,000	5,000	
Women	5,000	5,000	7,000	

Total Armed Forces

ACTIVE (all services form combined Antigua and Barbuda Defence Force) 150

RESERVES 75

Army 125

Navy 25

BASE St Johns
PATROL CRAFT 2
PATROL, INSHORE 3
1 *Swift* PCI with 1 12.7mm, 2 7.62mm gun
1 *Dauntless* PCI with 1 7.62mm gun
1 *Point* PCI

Argentina

	1996	1997	1998	1999
GDP	P297bn	P327bn		
	($248bn)	($273bn)		
per capita	$8,900	$9,700		

	1996	1997	1998	1999
Growth	4.3%	7.8%		
Inflation	0.2%	0.5%		
Debt	$94bn	$109bn		
Def exp	P4.5bn	P4.7bn		
	($4.5bn)	($4.7bn)		
Def bdgt			P3.4bn	P3.6bn
			($3.4bn)	($3.6bn)
FMA (US)	$0.6m	$0.6m	$0.6m	$0.6m
$1 = peso	1.0	1.0	1.0	
Population		35,164,000		
Age	*13–17*	*18–22*	*23–32*	
Men	1,632,000	1,571,000	2,652,000	
Women	1,578,000	1,525,000	2,589,000	

Total Armed Forces

ACTIVE 73,000

RESERVES 375,000

Army 250,000 (National Guard 200,000 **Territorial Guard** 50,000 **Navy** 75,000 **Air Force** 50,000

Army 41,000

3 Corps
1 with 1 armd, 1 mech bde, 1 trg bde
1 with 1 inf, 1 mtn bde
1 with 1 armd, 2 mech, 1 mtn bde
Corps tps: 1 lt armd cav regt (recce), 1 arty, 1 AD arty, 1 engr bn in each Corps

STRATEGIC RESERVE

1 AB bde
1 mech bde (4 mech, 1 armd cav, 2 SP arty bn)
Army tps
1 mot inf bn (Army HQ Escort Regt) • 1 mot cav regt (Presidential Escort) • 1 SF coy, 3 avn bn • 1 AD arty bn, 2 engr bn

EQUIPMENT

MBT 96 M-4 *Sherman* (in store), 230 TAM
LT TK 56 AMX-13, 106 SK-105 *Kuerassier*
RECCE 48 AML-90
AIFV 30 AMX-VCI, 88 VCTP
APC 129 M-3 half-track, 319 M-113, 70 MOWAG *Grenadier* (mod *Roland*)
TOWED ARTY 105mm: 84 M-56; **155mm**: 109 CITEFA Models 77/-81
SP ARTY 155mm: 24 Mk F3
MRL 105mm: 30 SLAM *Pampero*; **127mm**: 20 SLAM SAPBA-1
MOR 81mm: 1,000; **120mm**: 309 Brandt (37 SP in VCTM AIFV)
ATGW 600 SS-11/-12, *Cobra (Mamba)*, 2,100 *Mathogo*
RCL 75mm: 75 M-20; **90mm**: 100 M-67; **105mm**: 930 M-1968
AD GUNS 20mm: 30; **30mm**: 30; **35mm**: 100 GDF-

001; **40mm**: 95 L/60/-70 (in store); **90mm**: 20
SAM *Tigercat, Blowpipe*, 6 *Roland*
SURV RASIT (veh, arty), *Green Archer* (mor)
AC 1 C212-200, 5 *Cessna 207*, 5 *Commander 690*, 2
    DHC-6, 3 G-222, 1 *Merlin IIIA*, 5 *Merlin IV*, 3
    Queen Air, 1 *Sabreliner*, 5 T-41, 23 OV-1D
HEL 6 A-109, 3 AS-332B, 5 Bell 205, 4 FH-1100, 4 SA-
    315B, 1 SA-330, 9 UH-1H, 8 UH-12

Navy 20,000

(incl 2,500 Naval Aviation and 3,500 Marines)
NAVAL AREAS Centre from River Plate to 42° 45' S
South from 42° 45' S to Cape Horn **Antarctica**
BASES Buenos Aires, Ezeiza (Naval Air), La Plata, Rio
Santiago (submarine base), Puerto Belgrano (HQ
Centre), Punta Indio (Naval Air), Mar del Plata
(submarine base), Ushuaia (HQ South)
SERVICEABILITY very poor throughout Navy

SUBMARINES 3

2 *Santa Cruz* (Ge TR-1700) with 533mm TT (SST-4
    HWT)
1 *Salta* (Ge T-209/1200) with 533mm TT (SST-4
    HWT) (plus 1 in major refit/mod)

PRINCIPAL SURFACE COMBATANTS 13
DESTROYERS 6

2 *Hercules* (UK Type 42) with 1 x 2 *Sea Dart* SAM; plus
    1 SA-319 hel (ASW), 2 x 3 ASTT, 4 MM-38 *Exocet*
    SSM, 1 114mm gun (incl 1 in reserve)
4 *Almirante Brown* (Ge MEKO 360) ASW with 2 SA-
    316 hel, 2 x 3 ASTT; plus 8 MM-40 *Exocet* SSM, 1
    127mm gun

FRIGATES 7

4 *Espora* (Ge MEKO 140) with 2 x 3 ASTT, hel deck;
    plus 4 MM-38 *Exocet* SSM
3 *Drummond* (Fr A-69) with 2 x 3 ASTT; plus 4 MM-
    38 *Exocet*, 1 100mm gun

PATROL AND COASTAL COMBATANTS 14

TORPEDO CRAFT 2 *Intrepida* (Ge Lürssen 45m) PFT
    with 2 533mm TT (SST-4 HWT) (one poss with 2
    MM-38 SSM)
PATROL, OFFSHORE 8
    1 *Teniente Olivieri* (ex-US oilfield tug)
    3 *Irigoyen* (US *Cherokee* AT)
    2 *King* (trg) with 3 105mm guns
    2 *Sorbral* (US *Sotoyomo* AT)
PATROL, INSHORE 4 *Baradero* (Il *Dabur*) PCI<

AMPHIBIOUS 20 (craft only)

4 LCM, 16 LCVP

SUPPORT AND MISCELLANEOUS 9

1 AGOR, 3 tpt, 1 ocean tug, 1 icebreaker, 2 trg, 1
    research

NAVAL AVIATION (2,500)

52 cbt ac, 11† armed hel

Carrier air crew training on Brazilian CV *Minas Gerais*
ATTACK 1 sqn with 2 *Super Etendard*
MR/ASW 1 sqn with 2 L-188, 5 S-2E/T, 8 P-3B, 4 *Super
King Air* 200, 10 Cessna-337
EW 2 L-188E
HEL 2 sqn
    1 ASW/tpt with 7 ASH-3H (ASW) and 4 AS-61D
        (tpt), 4 AS-555
    1 spt with 6 SA-316
TPT 1 sqn with 3 F-28-3000, 3 L-188, 4 *Queen Air* 80, 9
    Super King Air
SURVEY 3 PC-6B (Antarctic flt)
TRG 2 sqn with 7* EMB-326, 9* MB-326 *Xavante*, 5*
    MB-339A, 10 T-34C

MISSILES

ASM AM-39 *Exocet*, AS-12, *Martín Pescador*
AAM R-550 *Magic*

MARINES (3,500)

FLEET FORCES 2, each with 2 bn, 1 amph recce coy, 1
    fd arty bn, 1 atk, 1 engr coy
AMPH SPT FORCE 1 marine inf bn
1 AD arty regt (bn)
2 SF bn

EQUIPMENT

RECCE 12 ERC-90 *Lynx*
AAV 21 LVTP-7
APC 6 MOWAG *Grenadier*, 35 Panhard VCR
TOWED ARTY 105mm: 15 M-101/M-56; **155mm**: 6
    M-114
MOR 81mm: 70
ATGW 50 *Bantam, Cobra (Mamba)*
RL 89mm: 60 M-20
RCL 105mm: 30 1974 FMK1
AD GUNS 30mm: 10 HS-816; **35mm**: GDF-001
SAM *Blowpipe, Tigercat*
HEL 8 UH-1H (reported)

Air Force 12,000

200 cbt ac, 14 armed hel, 9 air bde, 10 AD arty bty, 1 SF
(AB) coy

AIR OPERATIONS COMMAND (9 bde)

FGA/FTR 7 sqn
    1 with 7 *Mirage 5P*, 21 *Dagger Nesher* (18 -A, 3 -B)
    4 with 15 A-4B/C, 32 A-4M, 4 OA-4M
    2 with 45 IA-58A, 30 MS-760
MR 1 Boeing 707
SURVEY 3 *Learjet 35A*, 4 1A-50
TKR 2 Boeing 707, 2 KC-130H, 1 KC-135
SAR 4 SA-315 hel
TPT 5 sqn
    ac 4 Boeing 707, 2 C-130E, 5 C-130B, 5 -H, 1 L-100-
    30, 6 DHC-6, 9 F-27, 4 F-28, 15 IA-50, 2 *Merlin IVA*, 1
    S-70A (VIP); Antarctic spt unit with 1 DHC-6
    hel 5 Bell 212, 2 CH-47C, 1 S-61R (*Sea King*), 11 MD-
    500 (armed), 3 UH-1H (armed)

CAL 1 sqn with 2 Boeing 707, 3 IA-50, 2 *Learjet* 35, 1 PA-31
LIAISON 1 sqn with 20 Cessna 182, 1 C-320, 7 *Commander*, 1 *Sabreliner*

AIR TRAINING COMMAND

AC 28 EMB-312, 16* IA-63, 30* MS-760, 28 T-34B, 8 Su-29
HEL 3 Hughes 500D

MISSILES

ASM ASM-2 *Martín Pescador*
AAM AIM-9B *Sidewinder*, R-530, R-550, *Shafrir*

Forces Abroad

UN AND PEACEKEEPING

CROATIA (UNMOP): 1 obs. **CYPRUS** (UNFICYP) 421: 1 inf bn. **ECUADOR/PERU** (MOMEP): some obs. **FYROM** (UNPREDEP): 1 obs. **IRAQ/KUWAIT** (UNIKOM): 50 engr plus 4 obs. **MIDDLE EAST** (UNTSO): 3 obs. **WESTERN SAHARA** (MINURSO): 1 obs

Paramilitary 31,240

GENDARMERIE (Ministry of Interior) 18,000

5 Regional Comd, 16 bn
EQPT Shorland recce, 40 UR-416; **81mm** mor; **ac** 3 Piper, 5 PC-6 **hel** 5 SA-315

PREFECTURA NAVAL (Coast Guard) 13,240

7 comd
SERVICEABILITY much better than Navy
EQPT 5 *Mantilla*, 1 *Delfin* PCO, 1 *Mandubi* PCO; 4 PCI, 21 PCI< plus boats; **ac** 5 C-212 **hel** 2 AS-330L, 1 AS-365, 3 AS-565MA, 2 Bell-47, 2 Schweizer-300C

Bahamas

	1996	1997	1998	1999
GDP	B$3.2bn	B$3.4bn		
	($3.2bn)	($3.4bn)		
per capita	$12,900	$13,600		
Growth	4.2%	3.5%		
Inflation	1.4%	0.5%		
Debt	$361m	$398m		
Def exp	B$21m	B$29m		
	($21m)	($29m)		
Def bdgt			εB$35m	
			($35m)	
FMA (US)	$0.8m	$1.1m	$1.1m	$1.1m
US$1 = B$	1.0	1.0	1.0	
Population		288,000		
Age	*13–17*	*18–22*	*23–32*	
Men	14,000	16,000	31,000	
Women	13,000	14,000	29,000	

Total Armed Forces

ACTIVE 860

Navy (Royal Bahamian Defence Force) 860

(incl 70 women)
BASE Coral Harbour, New Providence Island
MILITARY OPERATIONS PLATOON 1
ε120; Marines with internal and base sy duties
PATROL AND COASTAL COMBATANTS 7
PATROL, INSHORE 7
3 *Yellow Elder* PFI, 1 *Marlin*, 2 *Cape* PFI, 1 *Kieth Nelson* PFI
SUPPORT AND MISCELLANEOUS 8
1 *Fort Montague* (aux), 2 *Dauntless* (aux), 2 converted fishing vessels, 1 diving boat, 1 LCM, 1 small auxiliary
HARBOUR PATROL UNITS 6
4 *Boston* whaler, 2 *Wahoo*
AIRCRAFT 4
1 Cessna 404, 1 Cessna 421C, 2 C-26

Barbados

	1996	1997	1998	1999
GDP	B$4.1bn	B$4.4bn		
	($2.1bn)	($2.2bn)		
per capita	$6,100	$6,200		
Growth	8.9%	0.9%		
Inflation	2.4%	7.7%		
Debt	$597m	$696m		
Def exp	εB$27m	εB$28m		
	($13m)	($14m)		
Def bdgt			εB$30m	
			($15m)	
US$1 = B$	2.0	2.0	2.0	
Population		264,000		
Age	*13–17*	*18–22*	*23–32*	
Men	11,000	12,000	24,000	
Women	11,000	11,000	22,000	

Total Armed Forces

ACTIVE 610

RESERVES 430

Army 500

Navy 110

BASES St Ann's Fort Garrison (HQ), Bridgetown
PATROL AND COASTAL COMBATANTS 3
PATROL, OFFSHORE 2
  1 *Kebir* PCO with 2 12.7mm gun
  1 *Dauntless* PCI
PATROL, INSHORE 1 *Guardian* II PCI< plus boats

Belize

	1996	1997	1998	1999
GDP	BZ$1.2bn	BZ$1.2bn		
	($580m)	($610m)		
per capita	$2,600	$2,700		
Growth	1.5%	4.4%		
Inflation	6.4%	1.0%		
Debt	$283m	$233m		
Def exp	εBZ$29m	εBZ$31m		
	($14m)	($16m)		
Def bdgt			εBZ$17m	
			($8m)	
FMA (US)	$0.2m	$0.2m	$0.25m	$0.25m
US$1 = BZ$	2.0	2.0	2.0	
Population		231,000		
Age	*13–17*	*18–22*	*23–32*	
Men	14,000	12,000	18,000	
Women	14,000	12,000	18,000	

Total Armed Forces

ACTIVE ε1,050

RESERVES 700

Army ε1,000

3 inf bn (each 3 inf coy), 1 spt gp, 3 Reserve coy
EQUIPMENT
  MOR 81mm: 6
  RCL 84mm: 8 *Carl Gustav*

MARITIME WING 50
  PATROL CRAFT 2 *Wasp* PCI, plus some 9 armed
    boats and 3 LCU

AIR WING
2 cbt ac, no armed hel
  MR/TPT 2 BN-2B *Defender*
  TRG 1 T 67-200 *Firefly*

Bolivia

	1996	1997	1998	1999
GDP	B36.5bn	B41.1bn		
	($7.2bn)	($7.8bn)		
per capita	$2,600	$2,700		
Growth	3.9%	4.3%		
Inflation	12.4%	4.7%		
Debt	$5.1bn	$4.5bn		
Def exp	B745m	B786m		
	($155m)	($155m)		
Def bdgt			B1,016m	B1,200m
			($187m)	($218m)
FMA (US)	$16m	$46m	$46m	$46m
$1 = boliviano	5.1	5.2	5.4	
Population		8,690,000		
Age	*13–17*	*18–22*	*23–32*	
Men	486,000	431,000	663,000	
Women	480,000	432,000	683,000	

Total Armed Forces

ACTIVE 33,500 (to be 35,000)
(some 21,800 conscripts)
Terms of service 12 months, selective

Army 25,000

(some 18,000 conscripts)
HQ: 6 Mil Regions
Army HQ direct control
  2 armd bn • 1 mech cav regt • 1 Presidential Guard
  inf regt
10 'div'; org, composition varies; comprise
  8 cav gp (5 horsed, 2 mot, 1 aslt) • 1 mot inf 'regt'
  with 2 bn • 22 inf bn (incl 5 inf aslt bn) • 10 arty
  'regt' (bn) • 1 AB 'regt' (bn) • 6 engr bn
EQUIPMENT
  LT TK 36 SK-105 *Kuerassier*
  RECCE 24 EE-9 *Cascavel*
  APC 50 M-113, 10 V-100 *Commando*, 24 MOWAG
    Roland, 24 EE-11 *Urutu*
  TOWED ARTY 75mm: 70 incl M-116 pack, ε10
    Bofors M-1935; **105mm**: 30 incl M-101, FH-18;
    122mm: 36 PRC Type-54
  MOR 81mm: 50; **107mm**: M-30
  AC 2 C-212, 1 *King Air* B90, 1 *Cheyenne* II, 1 *Seneca*
    III, 5 Cessna (4 -206, 1 -421B)

Navy 4,500

(incl Naval Aviation, 2,000 Marines and 1,800
conscripts)
NAVAL DISTRICTS 6, covering Lake Titicaca and the
rivers; each 1 flotilla
BASES Riberalta (HQ), Tiquina (HQ), Puerto Busch,

Puerto Guayaramerín (HQ), Puerto Villaroel, Trinidad (HQ), Puerto Suárez (HQ), Cobija (HQ)

PATROL CRAFT, RIVERINE some 43

some 43 riverine craft/boats, plus 11 US *Boston* whalers

SUPPORT AND MISCELLANEOUS 18

some 18 logistic support and patrol craft

NAVAL AVIATION

AC 1 Cessna U206G, 1 Cessna 402C

MARINES (2,000)

6 bn (1 in each District)

Air Force 4,000

(perhaps 2,000 conscripts); 50 cbt ac, 10 armed hel
FTR 1 sqn with 6 AT-33N
FGA 12 TA-4J (6 in store)
ARMED HEL 1 sqn with 10 Hughes 500M hel
SAR 1 hel sqn with 4 HB-315B, 2 SA-315B, 1 UH-1
SURVEY 1 sqn with 5 Cessna 206, 1 C-210, 1 C-402, 3 *Learjet* 25/35
TPT 3 sqn
1 VIP tpt with 1 L-188, 1 *Sabreliner*, 2 *Super King Air*
2 tpt with 14 C-130A/B/H, 4 F-27-400, 1 IAI-201, 2 *King Air*, 2 C-47, 4 *Convair* 580
LIAISON ac 9 Cessna 152, 1 C-185, 13 C-206, 1 C-208, 2 C-402, 2 Beech *Bonanza*, 2 Beech *Barons*, PA-31, 4 PA-34 **hel** 2 Bell 212, 22 UH-1H
TRG 1 Cessna 152, 2 C-172, 20* PC-7, 4 SF-260CB, 15 T-23, 12* T-33A, 1 *Lancair* 320
AD 1 air-base def regt (Oerlikon twin **20mm**, 18 PRC Type-65 **37mm**, some truck-mounted guns)

Paramilitary 37,100

NATIONAL POLICE some 31,100
9 bde, 2 rapid action regt, 27 frontier units

NARCOTICS POLICE some 6,000

Brazil

	1996	1997	1998	1999
GDP	R766bn	R821bn		
	($580bn)	($596bn)		
per capita	$5,900	$6,100		
Growth	3.0%	3.0%		
Inflation	18.2%	7.5%		
Debt	$178bn	$188bn		
Def exp	R14.0bn	R15.0bn		
	($13.9bn)	($13.9bn)		
Def bdgt			R16.1bn	
			($14.2bn)	
FMA (US)	$0.5m	$0.9m	$0.7m	$1.4m
$1 = real	1.0	1.1	1.1	

Population		167,886,000		
Age	13–17	18–22	23–32	
Men	8,646,000	8,076,000	14,229,000	
Women	8,575,000	8,077,000	14,331,000	

Total Armed Forces

ACTIVE 313,250

(132,000 conscripts)
Terms of service 12 months (can be extended to 18)

RESERVES

Trained first-line 1,115,000; 400,000 subject to immediate recall **Second-line** 225,000

Army 195,000

(incl 125,000 conscripts)
HQ: 7 Mil Comd, 11 Mil Regions; 8 div (3 with Regional HQ)
1 armd cav bde (2 mech, 1 armd, 1 arty bn), 3 armd inf bde (each 2 inf, 1 armd, 1 arty bn), 4 mech cav bde (each 3 inf, 1 arty bn) • 13 motor inf bde (26 bn) • 1 mtn bde • 4 jungle bde • 1 frontier bde (6 bn) • 1 AB bde (3 AB, 1 arty, 1 SF bn) • 2 coast and AD arty bde • 3 cav guard regt • 28 arty gp (4 SP, 6 med, 18 fd) • 2 engr gp each 4 bn • 10 bn (incl 2 railway) (to be increased to 34 bn)
AVN 1 hel bde (1 bn of 4 sqn)

EQUIPMENT

MBT 60 *Leopard* 1 (27 to be delivered)
LT TK 287 M-41B/C
RECCE 409 EE-9 *Cascavel*
APC 219 EE-11 *Urutu*, 584 M-113
TOWED ARTY 105mm: 320 incl M-101/-102, 56 Model 56 pack, 22 L118; **155mm**: 92 M-114
SP ARTY 105mm: 72 M-7/-108
COASTAL ARTY 152mm: 31
MRL 108mm: SS-06; 4 ASTROS II
MOR 81mm; **107mm**: 209 M-30; **120mm**: 77 K6A3
ATGW 12 *Milan*
RL 84mm: 540 AT-4
RCL 57mm: 240 M-18A1; **75mm**: 20 M-20; **84mm**: 126 *Carl Gustav*; **105mm**; **106mm**: M-40A1
AD GUNS 200 incl **20mm**; **35mm**: GDF-001; **40mm**: L-60/-70 (some with BOFI)
SAM 2 *Roland* II
HEL 4 S-70A, 36 SA-365, 20 AS-550 *Fennec*, 16 AS-350 (armed)

Navy 68,250

(incl 1,200 Naval Aviation, 15,100 Marines and 12,400 conscripts)
OCEANIC NAVAL DISTRICTS 5 plus 1 Riverine; 1 Comd

BASES Ocean Rio de Janeiro (*HQ I Naval District*), Salvador (*HQ II District*), Recife (*HQ III District*), Belém (*HQ IV District*), Floriancholis (*HQ V District*) **River** Ladario (*HQ VI District*), Manaus

SUBMARINES 6

3 *Tupi* (Ge T-209/1400) with 533mm TT (UK *Tigerfish* HWT)

3 *Humaitá* (UK *Oberon*) with 533mm TT (UK *Tigerfish* HWT) (1 in refit)

PRINCIPAL SURFACE COMBATANTS 19

CARRIERS 1 *Minas Gerais* (UK *Colossus*) CV (ASW), typically ASW **hel** 4–6 ASH-3H, 3 AS-332 and 2 AS-355; has been used by Argentina for embarked aircraft training

FRIGATES 18

4 *Greenhaigh* (ex-UK *Broadsword*) with 4 MM-38 *Exocet* SSM, *Seawolf* MOD 4 SAM

4 *Para* (US *Garcia*) with 1 x 8 ASROC, 2 x 3 ASTT, 1 *Lynx* hel; plus 2 127mm guns

2 *Constitução* ASW with 1 *Lynx* hel, 2 x 3 ASTT, *Ikara* SUGW, 1 x 2 ASW mor; plus 2 MM-40 *Exocet* SSM, 1 114mm gun

4 *Niteroi*; weapons as ASW, except 4 MM-40 *Exocet*, 2 114mm guns, no *Ikara*

4 *Inhauma*, with 1 *Lynx* hel, 2 x 3 ASTT, plus 4 MM-40 *Exocet*, 1 114mm gun

PATROL AND COASTAL COMBATANTS 36

PATROL, OFFSHORE 16

7 *Imperial Marinheiro* PCO, 9 *Grajaü* PCC

PATROL, INSHORE 15

6 *Piratini* (US PGM) PCI, 3 *Aspirante Nascimento* PCI (trg), 6 *Tracker* PCI<

PATROL, RIVERINE 5

3 *Roraima* and 2 *Pedro Teixeira*

MINE COUNTERMEASURES 6

6 *Aratü* (Ge *Schütze*) MSI

AMPHIBIOUS 4

2 *Ceara* (US *Thomaston*) LSD capacity 350 tps, 38 tk

1 *Duque de Caxais* (US *de Soto County* LST), capacity 600 tps, 18 tk

1 *Mattoso Maia* (US *Newport* LST) capacity 400 tps, 500 tons veh, 3 LCVP, 1 LCPL

Plus some 48 craft: 3 LCU, 10 LCM, 35 LCVP

SUPPORT AND MISCELLANEOUS 25

2 *Polar research*, 1 AGOR, 5 AGS, 16 buoy tenders, 1 Mod *Niteroi* (tng)

NAVAL AVIATION (1,300)

22 cbt ac, 54 armed hel

FGA 22 A-4/TA-4 (being delivered)

ASW 6 SH-3B, 7 SH-3D, 6 SH-3G/H

ATTACK 14 Lynx MK-21A

UTL 2 sqn with 5 AS-332, 12 AS-350 (armed), 9 AS-355 (armed)

TRG 1 hel sqn with 13 TH-57

ASM AS-11, AS-12, *Sea Skua*

MARINES (15,100)

FLEET FORCE 1 amph div (1 comd, 3 inf bn, 1 arty gp)

REINFORCEMENT COMD 5 bn incl 1 engr, 1 SF

INTERNAL SECURITY FORCE 8+ regional gp

EQUIPMENT

RECCE 6 EE-9 Mk IV *Cascavel*

AAV 11 LVTP-7A1, 12 AAV-7A1

APC 28 M-113, 5 EE-11 *Urutu*

TOWED ARTY 105mm: 15 M-101, 18 L118; **155mm**: 6 M-114

MOR 81mm; 120mm: 8 K 6A3

RL 89mm: 3.5in M-20

RCL 106mm: 8 M-40A1

AD GUNS 40mm: 6 L/70 with BOFI

Air Force 50,000

(5,000 conscripts); 278 cbt ac, 29 armed hel

AIR DEFENCE COMMAND 1 gp

FTR 2 sqn with 16 F-103E/D (*Mirage* IIIE/DBR)

TACTICAL COMMAND 10 gp

FGA 3 sqn with 46 F-5E/-B/-F, 45 AMX

CCT 2 sqn with 58 AT-26 (EMB-326)

RECCE 2 sqn with 4 RC-95, 10 RT-26, 12 *Learjet* 35 recce/VIP, 3 RC-130E

LIAISON/OBS 7 sqn

1 with **ac** 8 T-27

5 with **ac** 31 U-7

1 with **hel** 29 UH-1H (armed)

MARITIME COMMAND 4 gp

MR/SAR 3 sqn with 10 EMB-110B, 20 EMB-111

TRANSPORT COMMAND

6 gp (6 sqn)

1 with 9 C-130H, 2 KC-130H • 1 with 4 KC-137 (tpt/tkr) • 1 with 12 C-91 • 1 with 17 C-95A/B/C • 1 with 17 C-115 • 1 (VIP) with **ac** 1 VC-91, 12 VC/VU-93, 2 VC-96, 5 VC-97, 5 VU-9, 2 Boeing 737-200 **hel** 3 VH-4

7 regional sqn with 7 C-115, 86 C-95A/B/C, 6 EC-9 (VU-9)

HEL 6 AS-332, 8 AS-355, 4 Bell 206, 27 HB-350B

LIAISON 50 C-42, 3 Cessna 208, 30 U-42

TRAINING COMMAND

AC 38* AT-26, 97 C-95 A/B/C, 25 T-23, 98 T-25, 61* T-27 (*Tucano*), 14* AMX-T

HEL 4 OH-6A, 25 OH-13

CAL 1 unit with 2 C-95, 1 EC-93, 4 EC-95, 1 U-93

MISSILES

AAM AIM-9B *Sidewinder*, R-530, *Magic* 2, MAA-1 *Piranha*

Forces Abroad

UN AND PEACEKEEPING

ANGOLA (UNOMA): 6 incl 4 obs. **CROATIA**

(UNMOP): 1 Obs. **ECUADOR/PERU** (MOMEP): Obs plus log spt. **FYROM** (UNPREDEP): 2 Obs

Paramilitary

PUBLIC SECURITY FORCES (R) some 385,600

in state mil pol org (state militias) under Army control and considered Army Reserve

Chile

	1996	1997	1998	1999
GDP	pCh29.6tr	pCh32.3tr		
	($71.9bn)	($77.0bn)		
per capita	$10,600	$11,300		
Growth	7.2%	5.5%		
Inflation	7.3%	6.3%		
Debt	$27.4bn	$28.6bn		
Def exp	pCh823bn	pCh901bn		
	($2.0bn)	($2.1bn)		
Def bdgt			pCh969bn	
			($2.1bn)	
FMA (US)	$0.3m	$0.4m	$0.5m	$0.5m
$1 = pCh*	412	419	453	
Chilean peso				
Population		14,749,000		
Age	*13–17*	*18–22*	*23–32*	
Men	683,000	628,000	1,226,000	
Women	658,000	607,000	1,198,000	

Total Armed Forces

ACTIVE 94,500

(32,300 conscripts)
Terms of service **Army** 1 year **Navy** and **Air Force** 22 months

RESERVES 50,000
Army

Army 51,000

(27,000 conscripts)
7 Mil Regions, 2 Corps HQ
8 div; org, composition varies; comprise
  14 mot inf, 9 mtn inf, 10 armd cav, 8 arty, 7 engr regt
1 bde with 1 armd cav, 1 mtn regt
1 bde with 1 mot inf, 1 cdo regt
Army tps: 1 avn bde, 1 engr, 1 AB regt (1 AB, 1 SF bn)

EQUIPMENT

MBT 100 M-4A3, 30 AMX-30
LT TK 21 M-24, 60 M-41
RECCE 50 EE-9 *Cascavel*
AIFV 20 MOWAG *Piranha* with **90mm** gun

APC 228 M-113 (plus 127 to be delivered), 180 Cardoen/MOWAG *Piranha*, 30 EE-11 *Urutu*
TOWED ARTY 105mm: 66 M-101, 36 Model 56; **155mm**: 12 M-71, 28 G5 (being delivered)
SP ARTY 155mm: 12 Mk F3
MOR 81mm: 300 M-29; **107mm**: 15 M-30; **120mm**: 125 FAMAE (incl 50 SP)
ATGW *Milan/Mamba, Mapats*
RL 89mm: 3.5in M-20
RCL 150 incl: **57mm**: M-18; **106mm**: M-40A1
AD GUNS 20mm: 60 incl some SP (*Cardoen/MOWAG*)
SAM 50 *Blowpipe, Javelin, Mistral*

AIRCRAFT

TPT 9 C-212, 1 *Citation* (VIP), 5 CN-235, 4 DHC-6, 3 PA-31, 8 PA-28 Piper *Dakota*, 3 Cessna-208 *Caravan*
TRG 16 Cessna R-172, some Cessna R-182 (being delivered)
HEL 2 AB-206, 3 AS-332, 15 Enstrom 280 FX, 21 Hughes MD-530F (armed trg), 10 SA-315, 9 SA-330

Navy 30,000

(incl 800 Naval Aviation, 3,200 Marines, 1,800 Coast Guard and 3,800 conscripts)

DEPLOYMENT AND BASES

MAIN COMMAND Fleet (includes DD and FF), submarine flotilla, tpt. Remaining forces allocated to 4 Naval Zones **1st** 26°S–36°S approx: Valparaiso (HQ), Vina Del Mar **2nd** 36°S–43°S approx: Talcahuano (HQ), Puerto Montt **3rd** 43°S to Cape Horn: Punta Arenas (HQ), Puerto Williams **4th** north of 26°S approx: Iquique (HQ)

SUBMARINES 4

2 *O'Brien* (UK *Oberon*) with 8 533mm TT (Ge HWT)
2 *Thompson* (Ge T-209/1300) with 8 533mm TT (HWT)

PRINCIPAL SURFACE COMBATANTS 8

DESTROYERS 4

2 *Prat* (UK *Norfolk*) DDG with 1 x 2 *Seaslug* 2 SAM, 4 MM-38 *Exocet* SSM, 1 x 2 114mm guns, 1 AB-206B hel plus 2 x 3 ASTT (Mk 44) 1 to decom end 1998 (1 unit retains *Seaslug*, both have *Barak* SAM)
2 *Blanco Encalada* (UK *Norfolk*) DDH with 4 MM-38, *Exocet* SSM, 1 x 2 114 mm guns, 2 AS-332F hel; plus 2 x 3 ASTT (Mk 44), 2 x 8 *Barak* 1 SAM, 1 with 1 x 2 *Seaslug* SAM in addition
FRIGATES 4 *Condell* (mod UK *Leander*), 2 with 2 x 3 ASTT (Mk 44), 1 hel; plus 1 with 2 x 2 MM-40 *Exocet* SSM, 1 with 2 MM-38 *Exocet* SSM, 1 x 2 114mm guns 1 to decom end 1998

PATROL AND COASTAL COMBATANTS 28

MISSILE CRAFT 7

3 *Casma* (Il *Sa'ar* 4) PFM with 4 *Gabriel* SSM, 2 76mm gun
2 *Iquique* (Il *Sa'ar* 3) with 6 *Gabriel* SSM, 1 76mm gun
2 *Tiger* (Ge Type 148) PFM with 4 *Exocet* SSM, 1 76mm gun

TORPEDO CRAFT 4 *Guacolda* (Ge Lürssen 36-M) with 4 533mm TT
PATROL, OFFSHORE 4
1 PCO (ex-US tug), 2 *Taito* OPV, 1 *Viel* (ex-Ca) icebreaker
PATROL, INSHORE 13
3 *Micalvi* PCC, 10 *Grumete Diaz* (Il *Dabur*) PCI<
AMPHIBIOUS 4
3 *Maipo* (Fr *Batral*) LSM, capacity 140 tps, 7 tk
1 *Valdivia†* (US *Newport*) LST, capacity 400 tps, 500t vehicles (non-op)
Plus craft: 2 *Elicura* LCT, 1 *Pisagua* LCU
SUPPORT AND MISCELLANEOUS 12
1 *Almirante Jorge Montt* (UK *Tide*) AO, 1 *Araucano* AO, 1 tpt, 1 survey, 1 *Uribe* trg, 1 Antarctic patrol, 1 *Almirante Merino* (Swe *Alvsborg*) submarine depot ship with minelaying capability, 5 tugs/spt

NAVAL AVIATION (800)
14 cbt ac, 12 armed hel
MR 1 sqn with 6* EMB-111N, 2* P-3A *Orion*, 6* UP-3B, 8 Cessna *Skymaster* (plus 2 in store)
ASW HEL 1 sqn with 6 AS-532 (4 with AM-39 *Exocet*, 2 with torpedoes), 6 AS-332 (with AM-39 *Exocet*)
LIAISON 1 sqn with 3 C-212A, 3 EMB-110CN, 1 Falcon-200
HEL 1 sqn with 6 AB-206-B, 8 BO-105, 1 AS-332
TRG 1 sqn with 7 PC-7, *Skymaster* (SAR)
ASM AM-39 *Exocet*

MARINES (3,200)
4 gp: 2 inf, 2 trg bn, 1 cdo coy, 1 fd arty, 1 AD arty bty • 1 amph bn
EQUIPMENT
LT TK 30 *Scorpion*
AAV 20 LVTP-5 (in store)
APC 40 MOWAG *Roland*
TOWED ARTY 105mm: 16 KH-178, **155mm:** 36 M-114, 28 G-5 (being delivered)
COASTAL GUNS 155mm: 16 GPFM-3
MOR 81mm: 50
SSM *Excalibur*
RCL 106mm: ε30 M-40A1
SAM *Blowpipe*

COAST GUARD (1,800)
(integral part of the Navy)
PATROL CRAFT 24
2 PCC (buoy tenders), 1 *Castor* PCI, 2 *Alacalufe*, 4 *Guacola* PCI, 15 *Rodman* PCI, plus about 12 boats

Air Force 13,500

(1,500 conscripts); 92 cbt ac, no armed hel
Flying hours: 100
5 Air Bde, 5 wg
FGA 2 sqn
1 with 15 *Mirage* 5BA (MRIS), 6 *Mirage* BD (MRIS)

1 with 16 F-5 (13 -E, 3 -F)
CCT 2 sqn with 24 A-37B, 12 A-36
FTR/RECCE 1 sqn with 15 *Mirage* 50 (8 -FCH, 6 -CH, 1 -DCH), 4 *Mirage* 5-BR
RECCE 2 photo units with 1 *King Air* A-100, 2 *Learjet* 35A
AEW 1 IAI-707 *Phalcon*
TPT ac 3 Boeing 707(tkr), 1 Boeing 737-500 (VIP), 2 C-130H, 4 C-130B, 4 C-212, 9 Beech 99 (ELINT, tpt, trg), 14 DHC-6 (5 -100, 9 -300), 1 *Gulfstream* III (VIP), 1 *Beechcraft* 200 (VIP), 1 Cessna 206 (amph) **hel** 5 SA-315B, 1 S-70A
TRG 1 wg, 3 flying schools **ac** 16 PA-28, 19 T-35A/-B, 20 T-36, 15 T-37B/C, 6 *Extra* 300 **hel** 9 UH-1H
MISSILES
ASM AS-11/-12
AAM AIM-9B *Sidewinder, Shafrir, Python* III
AD 1 regt (5 gp) with **20mm:** S-639/-665, GAI-CO1 twin; **35mm:** Oerlikon GDF-005, MATRA *Mistral, Mygalle*

Forces Abroad

UN AND PEACEKEEPING
ECUADOR/CHILE (MOMEP): some obs. **INDIA/PAKISTAN** (UNMOGIP): 4 obs. **MIDDLE EAST** (UNTSO): 3 obs

Paramilitary 29,500

CARABINEROS (Ministry of Defence) 29,500
8 zones, 38 districts
APC 20 MOWAG *Roland*
MOR 60mm, 81mm
AC 22 Cessna (6 C-150, 10 C-182, 6 C-206), 1 *Metro*
HEL 2 Bell 206, 12 Bo-105

Opposition

FRENTE PATRIOTICO MANUEL RODRIGUEZ – AUTONOMOUS FACTION (FPMR-A) ε800
leftist

Colombia

	1996	1997	1998	1999
GDP	pC89tr ($72bn)	pC104tr ($76bn)		
per capita	$5,900	$6,100		
Growth	2.0%	3.2%		
Inflation	20.2%	18.5%		
Debt	$29bn	$29bn		
Def exp	pC2.6tr ($2.5bn)	pC3.5tr ($3.1bn)		

contd	1996	1997	1998	1999
Def bdgt			pC3.5tr ($2.7bn)	
FMA (US)	$16m	$33m	$67m	$46m
$1 = pC*	1,037	1,141	1,357	
*Colombian peso				
Population		36,524,000		
Age	*13–17*	*18–22*	*23–32*	
Men	1,937,000	1,813,000	3,289,000	
Women	1,849,000	1,746,000	3,245,000	

Total Armed Forces

ACTIVE 146,300

(some 67,300 conscripts)
Terms of service 12–18 months, varies (all services)

RESERVES 60,700

(incl 2,000 first-line) **Army** 54,700 **Navy** 4,800 **Air Force** 1,200

Army 121,000

(63,800 conscripts)
5 div HQ
17 regional bde
  6 mech each with 3 inf, 1 mech cav, 1 arty, 1 engr bn
  2 air-portable each with 2 inf bn
  9 inf (8 with 2 inf bn, 1 with 4 inf bn)
2 arty bn
Army tps
  3 Mobile Counter Guerrilla Force (bde) (each with 1 cdo unit, 4 bn)
  2 trg bde with 1 Presidential Guard, 1 SF, 1 AB, 1 mech, 1 arty, 1 engr bn
  1 AD arty bn
  army avn (forming)

EQUIPMENT
LT TK 12 M-3A1 (in store)
RECCE 12 M-8, 120 EE-9 *Cascavel*
APC 80 M-113, 76 EE-11 *Urutu*, 4 RG-31 *Nyala*
TOWED ARTY 105mm: 130 M-101
MOR 81mm: 125 M-1; **120mm**: 120 Brandt
ATGW TOW
RCL 106mm: M-40A1
AD GUNS 40mm: 30 Bofors
HEL 10 Mi-17 (being delivered), OH-6A (reported)

Navy (incl Coast Guard) 18,000

(incl 9,000 Marines and 100 Naval Aviation)
BASES Ocean Cartagena (main), Buenaventura, Málaga (Pacific) **River** Puerto Leguízamo, Barranca-bermeja, Puerto Carreño (tri-Service Unified Eastern Command HQ), Leticia, Puerto Orocue, Puerto Inirida
SUBMARINES 2

2 *Pijao* (Ge T-209/1200) with 8 533mm TT (Ge HWT)
(Plus 2 *Intrepido* (It SX-506) SSI (SF delivery))
FRIGATES 4
4 *Almirante Padilla* with 1 Bo-105 hel (ASW), 2 x 3 ASTT; plus 8 MM-40 *Exocet* SSM
PATROL AND COASTAL COMBATANTS 104
PATROL, OFFSHORE 6
3 *Pedro de Heredia* (ex-US tugs), 1 *Esperanta* (Sp *Cormoran*) PCO, 2 *Lazaga* PCF
PATROL, INSHORE 9
1 *Quito Sueno* (US *Asheville*) PFI, 2 *Castillo Y Rada* (*Swiftship* 32m) PCI, 2 *José Palas* PCI<, 2 *José Garcia* PCI<, 2 *Jaime Gomez* PCI
PATROL, RIVERINE 89
3 *Arauca*, 10 *Diligente*, 9 *Tenerife*, 5 *Rio Magdalena*, 20 *Delfin*, 42 *Pirana*
SUPPORT AND MISCELLANEOUS 42
3 AGOS, 21 AG, 17 Tugs, 1 trg

MARINES (9,000)
2 bde (each of 2 bn), 1 amph aslt, 1 river ops (15 amph patrol units), 1 SF, 1 sy bn
No hy eqpt (to get EE-9 *Cascavel* recce, EE-11 *Urutu* APC)

NAVAL AVIATION (100)
AC 2 *Commander*, 2 PA-28, 2 PA-31
HEL 2 Bo-105

Air Force 7,300

(some 3,500 conscripts); 72 cbt ac, 72 armed hel
AIR COMBAT COMMAND
FGA 2 sqn
  1 with 12 *Mirage* 5, 1 with 13 *Kfir* (11 -C2, 2 -TC2)
TACTICAL AIR SUPPORT COMMAND
CBT ac 1 AC-47, 2 AC-47T, 3 IA-58A, 22 A-37B, 6 AT-27
ARMED HEL 12 Bell 205, 5 Bell 212, 2 Bell 412, 2 UH-1B, 25 UH-60, 11 MD-500ME, 2 MD-500D, 3 MD-530F, 10 Mi-17
RECCE 8 *Schweizer* SA 2-37A, 13* OV-10, 3 C-26
MILITARY AIR TRANSPORT COMMAND
AC 1 Boeing 707, 2 Boeing 727, 14 C-130B, 2 C-130H, 1 C-117, 2 C-47, 2 CASA 212, 2 *Bandeirante*, 1 F-28, 3 CN-235
HEL 17 UH-1H
AIR TRAINING COMMAND
AC 14 T-27 (*Tucano*), 6 T-34M, 13 T-37, 8 T-41
HEL 2 UH-1B, 4 UH-1H, 12 F-28F
MISSILES
AAM AIM-9 *Sidewinder*, R-530

Forces Abroad

UN AND PEACEKEEPING
EGYPT (MFO): 358; 1 inf bn

Paramilitary 87,000

NATIONAL POLICE FORCE 87,000

ac 2 C-47, 2 DHC-6, 9 Cessna (2 C-152, 6 C-206G, 1 C-208), 1 Beech C-99, 5 *Turbo Thrush* **hel** 7 Bell-206L, 5 Bell-212, 3 Hughes 500D, 11 UH-1H, 3 UH-60L

COAST GUARD

integral part of Navy

Opposition

COORDINADORA NACIONAL GUERRILLERA SIMON BOLIVAR (CNGSB) loose coalition of guerrilla gp incl **Revolutionary Armed Forces of Colombia (FARC)** ε12–15,000 active; **National Liberation Army (ELN)** ε5,000, pro-Cuban; **People's Liberation Army (EPL)** ε500

Costa Rica

	1996	1997	1998	1999
GDP	C1.9tr	C2.2tr		
	($8.3bn)	($8.8bn)		
per capita	$6,400	$6,600		
Growth	-0.6%	3.2%		
Inflation	17.5%	13.2%		
Debt	$3.4bn	$3.4bn		
Sy exp[a]	C10.2bn	C13.6bn		
	($52m)	($59m)		
Sy bdgt			C17.6bn	
			($79m)	
FMA (US)	$0.2m	$0.2m	$0.2m	$0.2m
$1 = colon	208	233	249	

[a] No defence forces. Budgetary data are for border and maritime policing and internal security.

Population		3,595,000		
Age	*13–17*	*18–22*	*23–32*	
Men	188,000	168,000	297,000	
Women	180,000	161,000	288,000	

Total Armed Forces

ACTIVE Nil

Paramilitary 8,400

CIVIL GUARD 4,400

7 urban *comisaria*[a] • 1 tac police *comisaria* • 1 special ops unit • 6 provincial *comisaria*

BORDER SECURITY POLICE 2,000

2 Border Sy Comd (8 *comisaria*)
MARITIME SURVEILLANCE UNIT (300)

BASES Pacific Golfito, Punta Arenas, Cuajiniquil, Quepos **Atlantic** Limon, Moin, Barra del Colorado
PATROL CRAFT, INSHORE 8†
1 *Isla del Coco* (US *Swift* 32m) PFI
1 *Astronauta Franklin Chang* (US *Cape Higgon*) PCI
6 PCI<; plus about 10 boats
AIR SURVEILLANCE UNIT (300)
ac 4 Cessna 206, 1 DHC-4, 2 PA-31, 1 PA-34 **hel** 2 *Hughes* 500E, 1 Mi-17

RURAL GUARD (Ministry of Government and Police) 2,000

8 comd; small arms only

[a] *comisaria* = reinforced coy

Cuba

	1996	1997	1998	1999
GDP	ε$13bn	ε$14bn		
per capita	$2,100	$2,200		
Growth	7.8%	3.0%		
Inflation	10.0%	3.0%		
Debt	$12bn	$12bn		
Def exp	ε$700m	ε$720m		
Def bdgt		ε$390m		
$1 = peso	22	22	23	
Population		11,189,000		
Age	*13–17*	*18–22*	*23–32*	
Men	403,000	424,000	1,082,000	
Women	378,000	398,000	1,023,000	

Total Armed Forces

ACTIVE ε50–60,000

(incl Ready Reserves, conscripts)
Terms of service 2 years

RESERVES

Army 39,000 **Ready Reserves** (serve 45 days per year) to fill out Active and Reserve units; see also *Paramilitary*

Army ε38,000

(incl conscripts and Ready Reservists)
HQ: 3 Regional Comd, 3 Army
4–5 armd bde • 9 mech inf bde (3 mech inf, 1 armd, 1 arty, 1 AD arty regt) • 1 AB bde • 14 reserve bde • 1 frontier bde
AD AD arty regt and SAM bde
EQUIPMENT † (some 75% in store)
MBT ε1,500 incl: T-34, T-54/-55, T-62
LT TK some PT-76
RECCE some BRDM-1/-2

AIFV 400 BMP-1
APC ε700 BTR-40/-50/-60/-152
TOWED ARTY 700: **76mm**: ZIS-3; **122mm**: M-1938,
  D-30; **130mm**: M-46; **152mm**: M-1937, D-1
SP ARTY 40: **122mm**: 2S1; **152mm**: 2S3
MRL 300: **122mm**: BM-21; **140mm**: BM-14
MOR 1,000: **82mm**: M-41/-43; **120mm**: M-38/-43
STATIC DEF ARTY JS-2 (**122mm**) hy tk, T-34
  (**85mm**)
ATGW AT-1 *Snapper*, AT-3 *Sagger*
ATK GUNS 85mm: D-44; **100mm**: SU-100 SP, T-12
AD GUNS 255 incl: **23mm**: ZU-23, ZSU-23-4 SP;
  30mm: M-53 (twin)/BTR-60P SP; **37mm**: M-1939;
  57mm: S-60 towed, ZSU-57-2 SP; **85mm**: KS-12;
  100mm: KS-19
SAM SA-6/-7/-8/-9/-13/-14/-16

Navy ε5,000

(incl 550+ Naval Infantry, ε3,000 conscripts), 4 op
flotillas
NAVAL DISTRICTS Western HQ Cabanas **Eastern**
HQ Holquin
BASES Cienfuegos, Cabanas, Havana, Mariel, Punta
Movida, Nicaro
SUBMARINES 1
  1 Sov *Foxtrot* with 533mm and 406mm TT (non-op)
FRIGATES 2
  2 Sov *Koni* with 2 ASW RL (non-op)
PATROL AND COASTAL COMBATANTS 5
MISSILE CRAFT 4 Sov *Osa* I/II with 4 SS-N-2 *Styx*
  SSM†
PATROL, COASTAL 1 Sov *Pauk* II PFC with 2 ASW
  RL, 4 ASTT
MINE COUNTERMEASURES 6
  2 Sov *Sonya* MSC, 4 Sov *Yevgenya* MSI
SUPPORT AND MISCELLANEOUS 2
  1 AGI, 1 survey
NAVAL INFANTRY (550+)
2 amph aslt bn
COASTAL DEFENCE
  ARTY 122mm: M-1931/37; **130mm**: M-46; **152mm**:
  M-1937
  SSM 2 SS-C-3 systems, some mobile *Bandera* IV
  (reported)

Air Force ε10,000

(incl AD and conscripts); 130† cbt ac, 45 armed hel
Flying hours less than 50
FGA 2 sqn with 10 MiG-23BN
FTR 4 sqn
  2 with 30 MiG-21F, 1 with 50 MiG-21bis, 1 with 20
  MiG-23MF, 6 MiG-29
  (Probably only some 3 MiG-29, 10 MiG-23, 5 MiG-
  21bis in operation)

ATTACK HEL 45 Mi-8/-17, Mi-25/35
ASW 5 Mi-14 hel
TPT 4 sqn with 8 An-2, 1 An-24, 15 An-26, 1 An-30, 2
  An-32, 4 Yak-40, 2 Il-76 (Air Force ac in civilian
  markings)
HEL 40 Mi-8/-17
TRG 25 L-39, 8* MiG-21U, 4* MiG-23U, 2* MiG-29UB,
  20 Z-326
MISSILES
  ASM AS-7
  AAM AA-2, AA-7, AA-8, AA-10, AA-11
  SAM 13 active SA-2, SA-3 sites
CIVIL AIRLINE
  10 Il-62, 7 Tu-154, 12 Yak-42, 1 An-30 used as troop tpt

Paramilitary 19,000 active

YOUTH LABOUR ARMY 65,000

CIVIL DEFENCE FORCE 50,000

TERRITORIAL MILITIA (R) ε1,000,000

STATE SECURITY (Ministry of Interior) 15,000

BORDER GUARDS (Ministry of Interior) 4,000
  about 20 Sov *Zhuk* and 3 Sov *Stenka* PFI<, plus boats

Foreign Forces

US 1,420: **Navy** 1,000 **Marines** 420
RUSSIA 810: 800 SIGINT, ε10 mil advisers

Dominican Republic

	1996	1997	1998	1999
GDP	pRD182bn	pRD213bn		
	($9bn)	($10bn)		
per capita	$4,300	$4,700		
Growth	7.3%	8.2%		
Inflation	5.4%	6.7%		
Debt	$4.1bn	$3.9bn		
Def exp	pRD2.2bn	pRD2.4bn		
	($114m)	($120m)		
Def bdgt			εpRD1.1bn	
			($72m)	
FMA (US)	$0.5m	$0.6m	$0.5m	$0.5m
$1 = pRD*	13.8	14.3	14.7	
*peso República Dominicana				
Population		8,042,000		
Age	*13–17*	*18–22*	*23–32*	
Men	444,000	402,000	707,000	
Women	433,000	393,000	695,000	

Total Armed Forces

ACTIVE 24,500

Army 15,000

3 Defence Zones • 4 inf bde (with 8 inf, 1 arty bn, 2 recce sqn) • 1 armd, 1 Presidential Guard, 1 SF, 1 arty, 1 engr bn

EQUIPMENT
LT TK 12 AMX-13 (**75mm**), 12 M-41A1 (**76mm**)
RECCE 8 V-150 *Commando*
APC 20 M-2/M-3 half-track
TOWED ARTY 105mm: 22 M-101
MOR 81mm: M-1; **120mm**: 24 ECIA

Navy 4,000

(incl marine security unit and 1 SEAL unit)
BASES Santo Domingo (HQ), Las Calderas

PATROL AND COASTAL COMBATANTS 17
PATROL, OFFSHORE 6
1 *Mella* (Ca *River*) (comd/trg), 2 *Cambiaso* (US *Cohoes*), 2 *Canopus* PCO, 1 *Prestol* (US *Admirable*)
PATROL, INSHORE 9
1 *Betelgeuse* (US PGM-71), 1 *Capitan Alsina* (trg), 1 *Balsam* PCI, some 6 PCI<

AMPHIBIOUS craft only
2 LCU
SUPPORT AND MISCELLANEOUS 4
1 AOT (small harbour), 3 ocean tugs

Air Force 5,500

10 cbt ac, no armed hel
Flying hours probably less than 60
CCT 1 sqn with 8 A-37B
TPT 1 sqn with 3 C-47, 1 *Commander* 680
LIAISON 1 Cessna 210, 2 PA-31, 3 *Queen Air* 80, 1 *King Air*
HEL 8 Bell 205, 2 SA-318C, 1 SA-365 (VIP)
TRG 2* AT-6, 6 T-34B, 3 T-41D
AB 1 SF (AB) bn
AD 1 bn with 4 **20mm** guns

Paramilitary 15,000

NATIONAL POLICE 15,000

Ecuador

	1996	1997	1998	1999
GDP	ES61tr	ES79tr		
	($17bn)	($20bn)		
per capita	$4,400	$4,600		
Growth	2.0%	3.3%		
Inflation	24.4%	30.7%		
Debt	$14bn	$15bn		
Def exp[a]	εES1.7tr	εES2.4tr		
	($612m)	($692m)		
Def bdgt[a]			εES2.0tr	
			($571m)	
FMA[b] (US)	$1m	$1m	$1m	$2m
$1 = ES*	3,190	3,998	4,660	

*Ecuadorean sucre
[a] incl extra-budgetary funding
[b] MOMEP **1996**ε $15m **1997**ε $15m

Population	12,419,000		
Age	*13–17*	*18–22*	*23–32*
Men	692,000	634,000	1,072,000
Women	672,000	618,000	1,051,000

Total Armed Forces

ACTIVE 57,100
Terms of service conscription 1 year, selective

RESERVES 100,000
Ages 18–55

Army 50,000

4 Defence Zones
1 div with 2 inf bde (each 3 inf, 1 armd, 1 arty bn) • 1 armd bde (3 armd, 1 mech inf, 1 SP arty bn) • 2 inf bde (5 inf, 3 mech inf, 2 arty bn) • 3 jungle bde (2 with 3, 1 with 4 jungle bn)
Army tps: 1 SF (AB) bde (4 bn), 1 AD arty gp, 1 avn gp (4 bn), 3 engr bn
EQUIPMENT
MBT 3 T-55 (reported)
LT TK 45 M-3, 108 AMX-13
RECCE 27 AML-60/-90, 22 EE-9 *Cascavel*, 10 EE-3 *Jararaca*
APC 20 M-113, 60 AMX-VCI, 20 EE-11 *Urutu*
TOWED ARTY 105mm: 50 M2A2, 30 M-101, 24 Model 56; **155mm**: 12 M-198, 12 M-114
SP ARTY 155mm: 10 Mk F3
MRL 122mm: 6 RM-70
MOR 81mm: M-29; **107mm**: 4.2in M-30; **160mm**: 12 Soltam
RCL 90mm: 380 M-67; **106mm**: 24 M-40A1
AD GUNS 14.5mm: 128 ZPU-1/-2; **20mm**: 20 M-1935; **23mm**: 34 ZU-23; **35mm**: 30 GDF-002 twin; **37mm**: 18 Ch; **40mm**: 30 L/70

SAM 75 *Blowpipe*, 90 SA-18 (reported), SA-8 (being delivered)

AIRCRAFT

SURVEY 1 Cessna 206, 1 *Learjet* 24D

TPT 1 CN-235, 1 DHC-5, 3 IAI-201, 1 *King Air* 200, 2 PC-6

LIAISON/TRG/OBS 1 Cessna 172, 1 -182

HELICOPTERS

SURVEY 3 SA-315B

TPT/LIAISON 10 AS-332, 4 AS-350B, 1 Bell 214B, 3 SA-315B, 3 SA-330, 30 SA-342

Navy 4,100

(incl 250 Naval Aviation and 1,500 Marines)
BASES Guayaquil (main base), Jaramijo, Galápagos Islands

SUBMARINES 2

2 *Shyri* (Ge T-209/1300) with 533mm TT (Ge SUT HWT)

FRIGATES 2

2 *Presidente Eloy Alfaro* (ex-UK *Leander Batch* II) with 1 206B hel; plus 4 MM-38 *Exocet* SSM

PATROL AND COASTAL COMBATANTS 12

CORVETTES 6 *Esmeraldas* with 2 x 3 ASTT, hel deck; plus 2 x 3 MM-40 *Exocet* SSM

MISSILE CRAFT 6

3 *Quito* (Ge Lürssen 45m) with 4 MM-38 *Exocet*
3 *Manta* (Ge Lürssen 36m) with 4 *Gabriel* II SSM

AMPHIBIOUS 1

1 *Hualcopo* (US LST-511) LST, capacity 200 tps, 16 tk

SUPPORT AND MISCELLANEOUS 8

1 survey, 1 ex-GDR depot ship, 1 AOT (small), 1 *Calicuchima* (ex-UK *Throsk*) armament carrier, 1 water carrier, 2 armed ocean tugs, 1 trg

NAVAL AVIATION (250)

LIAISON 1 *Super King Air* 200, 1 *Super King Air* 300, 1 CN-235

TRG 3 T-34C

HEL 2 Bell 230, 4 Bell 206, 4 TH-57

MARINES (1,500)

3 bn: 2 on garrison duties, 1 cdo (no hy weapons/veh)

Air Force 3,000

45 cbt ac, no armed hel

OPERATIONAL COMMAND

2 wg, 5 sqn

FGA 3 sqn

1 with 8 *Jaguar* S (6 -S(E), 2 -B(E))
1 with 9 *Kfir* C-2, 2 TC-2
1 with 8 A-37B

FTR 1 sqn with 13 *Mirage* F-1JE, 1 F-1JB

CCT 4 *Strikemaster* Mk 89A

MILITARY AIR TRANSPORT GROUP

2 civil/military airlines:

TAME 6 Boeing 727, 2 BAe-748, 4 C-130B, 2 C-130H, 3 DHC-6, 1 F-28, 1 L-100-30

ECUATORIANA 3 Boeing 707-320, 1 DC-10-30, 2 Airbus A-310

LIAISON 1 *King Air* E90, 1 *Sabreliner*

LIAISON/SAR hel 2 AS-332, 1 Bell 212, 6 Bell-206B, 5 SA-316B, 1 SA-330, 2 UH-1B, 24 UH-1H

TRG incl 20 Cessna 150, 5 C-172, 17 T-34C, 1 T-41

MISSILES

AAM R-550 *Magic*, *Super 530*, *Shafrir*, *Python* 3 (possibly)

AB 1 AB sqn

Paramilitary 270

COAST GUARD 270

PATROL, INSHORE 8

2 25 *De Julio* PCI, 2 5 *De Agosto* PCI, 2 10 *De Agosto* PCI<, 1 *Point* PCI, 1 PGM-71 PCI, plus some 8 boats

El Salvador

	1996	1997	1998	1999
GDP	C91bn ($8.5bn)	C100bn ($9.0bn)		
per capita	$2,600	$2,800		
Growth	2.1%	4.0%		
Inflation	9.8%	4.5%		
Debt	$2.9bn	$2.7bn		
Def exp	εC1.3bn ($146m)	εC1.5bn ($176m)		
Def bdgt			C986m ($92m)	
FMA (US)	$0.5m	$0.5m	$0.5m	$0.5m
$1 = colon	8.8	8.8	8.8	
Population		5,975,000		
Age	*13–17*	*18–22*	*23–32*	
Men	368,000	341,000	488,000	
Women	355,000	333,000	513,000	

Total Armed Forces

ACTIVE 24,600

Terms of service selective conscription, 1 year

RESERVES

Ex-soldiers registered

Army ε22,300

(4,000 conscripts)

6 Mil Zones • 6 inf bde (each of 2 inf bn, 1 inf det) • 1
special sy bde (2 MP, 2 border gd bn) • 8 inf det (bn) •
1 engr comd (3 engr bn) • 1 arty bde (3 fd, 1 AD bn) •
1 mech cav regt (2 bn) • 2 indep bn (1 Presidential
Guard, 1 sy) • 1 special ops gp (1 para bn, 1 naval inf,
1 SF coy)
EQUIPMENT
  RECCE 10 AML-90
  APC 40 M-37B1 (mod), 8 UR-416
  TOWED ARTY 105mm: 24 M-101, 36 M-102, 18 M-
  56 (in store)
  MOR 81mm: incl 300 M-29; **120mm:** 60 UB-M52, M-
  74 (all in store)
  RL 94mm: LAW; **82mm:** B-300
  RCL 90mm: 400 M-67; **106mm:** 20+ M-40A1 (in store)
  AD GUNS 20mm: 36 FRY M-55, 4 TCM-20
  SAM some captured SA-7 may be in service

Navy 700

(incl some 90 Naval Infantry and spt forces)
BASES La Unión, La Libertad, Acajutla, El Triunfo,
Guija Lake
PATROL AND COASTAL COMBATANTS 5
PATROL, INSHORE 5
  3 *Camcraft* 30m, 2 PCI<, plus 11 boats
AMPHIBIOUS craft only
  2 LCM

NAVAL INFANTRY (Marines) (some 90)
1 sy coy

Air Force 1,600

(incl AD and c200 conscripts); 29 cbt ac, 17 armed hel
Flying hours A-37: 90
CBT AC 1 sqn with 10 A-37B, 2 AC-47, 6 CM-170
ARMED HEL 1 sqn with 8 Hughes 500D/E, 9 UH-1M
RECCE 8* O-2A
TPT 1 sqn with ac 1 C-47, 5 Basler Turbo-67, 1 C-123K,
  1 *Commander*, 1 DC-6B, 1 *Merlin* IIIB, 9 *Rallye* **hel** 1
  sqn with 12 UH-1H tpt hel (incl 4 SAR)
LIAISON 2 Cessna-210
TRG 3 T-41C/D, 6 TH-300, 3* O-2A, 10 T-35

Forces Abroad

UN AND PEACEKEEPING
WESTERN SAHARA (MINURSO): 2 Obs

Paramilitary 12,000

NATIONAL CIVILIAN POLICE (Ministry of Public
Security) some 12,000 (to be 16,000)
  small arms; **ac** 1 Cessna O-2A **hel** 1 UH-1H, 2 MD-
  500N, 1 MD-500D

Guatemala

	1996	1997	1998	1999
GDP	q96bn	q108bn		
	($11.6bn)	($12.3bn)		
per capita	$3,700	$3,800		
Growth	3.0%	4.1%		
Inflation	11.1%	9.2%		
Debt	$3.7bn	$3.7bn		
Def exp	εq1.6bn	εq1.1bn		
	($207m)	($182m)		
Def bdgt			q874m	
			($139m)	
FMAᵃ (US)	$2m	$2m	$3m	$4m
$1 = quetzal	6.1	6.0		
ᵃMINUGUA **1997** $15m				
Population		11,575,000		
Age	*13–17*	*18–22*	*23–32*	
Men	694,000	589,000	879,000	
Women	674,000	576,000	868,000	

Total Armed Forces

(National Armed Forces are combined; the Army
provides log spt for Navy and Air Force)

ACTIVE ε31,400
(ε23,000 conscripts)
Terms of service conscription; selective, 30 months

RESERVES
Army ε35,000 (trained) **Navy** (some) **Air Force** 200

Army 29,200

(ε23,000 conscripts)
15 Mil Zones (22 inf, 1 trg bn, 6 armd sqn) • 2 strategic
bde (4 inf, 1 lt armd bn, 1 recce sqn, 2 arty bty) • 1 SF
gp (3 coy incl 1 trg) • 2 AB bn • 5 inf bn gp (each 1 inf
bn, 1 recce sqn, 1 arty bty) • 1 Presidential Guard bn •
1 engr bn
RESERVES ε19 inf bn
EQUIPMENT
  LT TK 10 M-41A3
  RECCE 7 M-8, 9 RBY-1
  APC 10 M-113, 7 V-100 *Commando*, 30 *Armadillo*
  TOWED ARTY 75mm: 8 M-116; **105mm:** 12 M-101,
  8 M-102, 56 M-56
  MOR 81mm: 55 M-1; **107mm:** 12 M-30; **120mm:** 18
  ECIA
  RL 89mm: 3.5in M-20
  RCL 57mm: M-20; **105mm:** 64 Arg M-1974 FMK-1;
  106mm: 20 M-40A1
  AD GUNS 20mm: 16 M-55, 16 GAI-DO1

Navy ε1,500

(incl some 650 Marines)
BASES Atlantic Santo Tomás de Castilla **Pacific**
Puerto Quetzal
PATROL CRAFT, INSHORE 15

1 *Kukulkan* (US *Broadsword* 32m) PFI, 2 *Stewart* PCI, 6
Cutlas PCI, 6 *Vigilante* PCI (plus 20 river patrol
craft and 2 LCP)

MARINES (some 650)
2 under-str bn

Air Force 700

14† cbt ac, 7 armed hel. Serviceability of ac is less than
50%
CBT AC 1 sqn with 4 Cessna A-37B, 6 PC-7, 4 IAI-201
ARMED HEL 6 Bell 212, 1 Bell 412
TPT 1 sqn with 1 C-47, 3 T-67 (mod C-47 *Turbo*), 2 F-27,
1 *Super King Air* (VIP), 1 DC-6B
LIAISON 1 sqn with 3 Cessna 206, 1 Cessna 310
HEL 1 sqn with 9 Bell 206, 5 UH-1D/-H, 3 S-76
TRG 6 T-41, 10 T-35B
TACTICAL SECURITY GROUP

3 CCT coy, 1 armd sqn, 1 AD bty (Army units for
air-base sy)

Paramilitary 9,800 active

NATIONAL POLICE 9,800
21 departments, 1 SF bn, 1 integrated task force (incl
mil and treasury police)
TREASURY POLICE (2,500)

Guyana

	1996	1997	1998	1999
GDP	G$104bn	G$115bn		
	($690m)	($748m)		
per capita	$3,000	$3,200		
Growth	7.4%	6.2%		
Inflation	4.5%	4.2%		
Debt	$1.6bn	$1.6bn		
Def exp	G$1.0bn	G$1.1bn		
	($7m)	($7m)		
Def bdgt			G$850m	G$900m
			($6m)	($6m)
FMA (US)	$0.2m	$0.2m	$0.2m	$0.2m
US$1 = G$	140	142	145	
Population		837,000		
Age	*13–17*	*18–22*	*23–32*	
Men	42,000	41,000	79,000	
Women	40,000	38,000	76,000	

Total Armed Forces

ACTIVE (combined Guyana Defence Force) some 1,600

RESERVES some 1,500
People's Militia (see *Paramilitary*)

Army 1,400

(incl 500 Reserves)
1 inf bn, 1 SF, 1 spt wpn, 1 engr coy
EQUIPMENT
RECCE 3 Shorland
TOWED ARTY 130mm: 6 M-46
MOR 81mm: 12 L16A1; **82mm:** 18 M-43; **120mm:** 18
M-43

Navy

Authorised 30 plus 300 reserves **Actual** 17 plus 170
reserves
BASES Georgetown, New Amsterdam
2 boats

Air Force 100

no cbt ac, no armed hel
TPT ac 1 BN-2A, 1 *Skyvan* 3M **hel** 1 Bell 206, 1 Bell 412

Paramilitary

GUYANA PEOPLE'S MILITIA (GPM) some 1,500

Haiti

	1996	1997	1998	1999
GDP	G44bn	G52bn		
	($1.8bn)	($1.9bn)		
per capita	$1,000	$1,000		
Growth	2.7%	1.1%		
Inflation	20.6%	20.6%		
Debt	$896m	$1,028m		
Sy exp	εG1.5bn	εG1.6bn		
	($99m)	($99m)		
Sy bdgt			G1.7bn	
			($98m)	
FMAᵃ (US)	$0.3m	$0.3m	$0.3m	$0.3m
$1 = gourde	15.1	16.7	17.4	
ᵃ UN **1996** $243m **1997** $57m				
Population		7,445,000		
Age	*13–17*	*18–22*	*23–32*	
Men	410,000	365,000	592,000	
Women	402,000	360,000	594,000	

Total Armed Forces

ACTIVE Nil

Paramilitary

In 1994, the military government of Haiti was replaced by a civilian administration. The former armed forces and police were disbanded and an Interim Public Security Force (IPSF) of 3,000 formed. A National Police Force of ε5,300 personnel has now formed. All Army equipment has been destroyed.

The United Nations Civilian Police Mission in Haiti (MIPONUH) maintains some 285 civ pol to assist the government of Haiti by supporting and contributing to the professionalisation of the National Police Force.

NAVY (Coast Guard) 30 (being developed)
BASE Port-au-Prince
   PATROL CRAFT boats only

AIR FORCE (disbanded in 1995)

Foreign Forces

US Army 189

Honduras

	1996	1997	1998	1999
GDP	L48bn	L61bn		
	($4.4bn)	($4.7bn)		
per capita	$2,100	$2,200		
Growth	3.7%	4.9%		
Inflation	23.8%	20.2%		
Debt	$3.2bn	$3.2bn		
Def exp	εL1,150m	εL1,310m		
	($98m)	($101m)		
Def bdgt			L479m	
			($36m)	
FMA (US)	$0.5m	$0.4m	$0.5m	
$1 = lempira	11.7	13.0	13.2	
Population		6,447,000		
Age	*13–17*	*18–22*	*23–32*	
Men	380,000	329,000	520,000	
Women	368,000	320,000	511,000	

Total Armed Forces

ACTIVE 8,300

RESERVES 60,000
Ex-servicemen registered

Army 5,500

6 Mil Zones

4 inf bde
   3 with 3 inf, 1 arty bn • 1 with 3 inf bn
1 special tac gp with 1 inf (AB), 1 SF bn
1 armd cav regt (2 mech bn, 1 lt tk, 1 recce sqn, 1 arty, 1 AD arty bty)
1 engr bn
1 Presidential Guard coy
RESERVES
1 inf bde
EQUIPMENT
   LT TK 12 *Scorpion*
   RECCE 3 *Scimitar*, 1 *Sultan*, 50 *Saladin*, 13 RBY-1
   TOWED ARTY 105mm: 24 M-102; **155mm**: 4 M-198
   MOR 60mm; **81mm**; **120mm**: 60 Brandt; **160mm**: 30 *Soltam*
   RL 84mm: 120 *Carl Gustav*
   RCL 106mm: 80 M-40A1
   AD Guns 20mm: 24 M-55A2, 24 TCM-20

Navy 1,000

(incl 400 Marines)
BASES Atlantic Puerto Cortés, Puerto Castilla **Pacific** Amapala
PATROL CRAFT, INSHORE 10
   3 *Guaymuras* (US *Swiftship* 31m) PFI
   2 *Copan* (US *Lantana* 32m) PFI<
   5 PCI<, plus 33 riverine boats
AMPHIBIOUS craft only
   1 *Punta Caxinas* LCT; plus some 3 ex-US LCM

MARINES (400)
3 indep coy (-)

Air Force some 1,800

49 cbt ac, no armed hel
FGA 2 sqn
   1 with 13 A-37B, 4 A-36 *Halcon*
   1 with 5 F-5E, 1 -F
FTR 11 *Super Mystère* B2
TPT 5 C-47, 3 C-130A, 1 IAI-201, 2 IAI-1123
LIAISON 1 sqn with 3 Cessna 172, 2 C-180, 2 C-185, 3 *Commander*, 1 PA-31, 1 PA-34
HEL 9 Bell 412, 4 Hughes 500, 6 UH-1B/H, 1 S-76
TRG 4* C-101CC, 6 U-17A, 11* EMB-312, 5 T-41A
AAM *Shafrir*

Forces Abroad

UN AND PEACEKEEPING
WESTERN SAHARA (MINURSO): 12 Obs

Paramilitary 6,000

PUBLIC SECURITY FORCES (Ministry of Public

Security and Defence) 6,000

11 regional comd

Foreign Forces

US 719 **Army** 619 **Air Force** 100

Jamaica

	1996	1997	1998	1999
GDP	J$219bn	J$225bn		
	($5bn)	($5bn)		
per capita	$3,400	$3,500		
Growth	-1.7%	-1.4%		
Inflation	15.8%	9.2%		
Debt	$3.9bn	$4.0bn		
Def exp	J$990m	J$1.1bn		
	($29m)	($29m)		
Def bdgt			εJ$1.1bn	
			($30m)	
FMA (US)	$1.2m	$1.2m	$1.1m	$1.3m
US$1 = J$	37.1	35.4	36.4	
Population		2,489,000		
Age	*13–17*	*18–22*	*23–32*	
Men	124,000	122,000	227,000	
Women	122,000	119,000	229,000	

Total Armed Forces

ACTIVE (combined Jamaican Defence Force) some 3,320

RESERVES some 950

Army 877 **Coast Guard** 60 **Air Wing** 16

Army 3,000

2 inf bn, 1 spt bn

EQUIPMENT

APC 13 V-150 *Commando*

MOR 81mm: 12 L16A1

RESERVES 877

1 inf bn

Coast Guard ε150

BASE Port Royal

PATROL CRAFT, INSHORE 8

1 *Fort Charles* PFI (US 34m), 1 *Paul Bogle* (US-31m), 2 *Bay* PCI, 4 *Dauntless* PCI, plus 5 boats

Air Wing 170

no cbt ac, no armed hel

AC 2 BN-2A, 1 Cessna 210, 1 *King Air*

HEL 4 Bell 206, 3 Bell 212, 3 UH-1H

Mexico

	1996	1997	1998	1999
GDP	Np2.5tr	Np3.1tr		
	($340bn)	($372bn)		
per capita	$7,000	$7,500		
Growth	5.1%	7.0%		
Inflation	34.4%	20.6%		
Debt	$157bn	$174bn		
Def exp	Np27bn	Np29bn		
	($3.6bn)	($3.7bn)		
Def bdgt			Np20.1bn	
			($2.3bn)	
FMA (US)	$3m	$6m	$6m	$9m
$1 = new peso	7.6	7.9	8.6	
Population		95,458,000 (Chiapas region 4%)		
Age	*13–17*	*18–22*	*23–32*	
Men	5,164,000	4,874,000	8,572,000	
Women	5,023,000	4,781,000	8,592,000	

Total Armed Forces

ACTIVE 175,000

(60,000 conscripts)

Terms of service 1 year conscription (4 hours per week) by lottery

RESERVES 300,000

Army 130,000

(incl ε60,000 conscripts)

12 Mil Regions

40 Zonal Garrisons incl 1 armd, 19 mot cav, 1 mech inf, 7 arty regt, plus 3 arty, 8 inf bn • 4 armd bde (each 2 armd recce, 1 arty regt, 1 ATK gp, 1 mech inf bn) • 1 Presidential Guard bde (3 inf, 1 SF, 1 arty bn) • 1 mot inf bde (3 mot inf regt) • 2 inf bde (each 3 inf bn, 1 arty bn) • 1 AB bde (3 bn) • 1 MP, 1 engr bde • 1 SF 'corps' with 64 airmobile SF gp • AD, engr and spt units

EQUIPMENT

RECCE 40 M-8, 119 ERC-90F *Lynx*, 40 VBL, 25 MOWAG, 40 MAC-1

APC 40 HWK-11, 32 M-2A1 half-track, 40 VCR/TT, 24 DN-3, 40 DN-4 *Caballo*, 70 DN-5 *Toro*, 395 AMX-VCI, 95 BDX, 26 LAV-150 ST, some BTR-60 (reported)

TOWED ARTY 75mm: 18 M-116 pack; **105mm**: 16 M-2A1/M-3, 80 M-101, 80 M-56

SP ARTY 75mm: 5 DN-5 *Bufalo*

MOR 81mm: 1,500; **120mm**: 75 Brandt

ATGW *Milan* (incl 8 VBL)
RL 82mm: B-300
ATK GUNS 37mm: 30 M-3
AD GUNS 12.7mm: 40 M-55; 20mm: 40 Oerlikon
SAM RBS-70

Navy 37,000

(incl 1,100 Naval Aviation and 10,000 Marines)
NAVAL REGIONS Gulf 6 Pacific 11
BASES Gulf Vera Cruz (HQ), Tampico, Chetumal,
Ciudad del Carmen, Yukalpetén, Lerna, Frontera,
Coatzacoalcos, Isla Mujéres Pacific Acapulco (HQ),
Ensenada, La Paz, San Blas, Guaymas, Mazatlán,
Manzanillo, Salina Cruz, Puerto Madero, Lázaro
Cárdenas, Puerto Vallarta

PRINCIPAL AND SURFACE COMBATANTS 9
DESTROYERS 3
  2 *Ilhuicamina* (ex-*Quetzalcoatl*) (US *Gearing*) ASW
    with 1 x 8 ASROC, 2 x 3 ASTT; plus 2 x 2 127mm
    guns and 1 Bo-105 hel
  1 *Cuitlahuac* (US *Fletcher*) with 5 533mm TT, 5
    127mm guns
FRIGATES 6
  2 *Knox* with 1 x 8 ASROC, 4 x 324mm TT, 1 x 127mm
    gun, 1 x BO 105 hel
  2 *H. Galeana* (US *Bronstein*) with 1 x 8 ASROC, 2 x 3
    ASTT, 1 x 2 76mm guns
  1 *Comodoro Manuel Azueta* (US *Edsall*) (trg)
  1 *Zacatecas* (US *Lawrence/Crosley*) with 1 127mm gun

PATROL AND COASTAL COMBATANTS 106
PATROL, OFFSHORE 39
  4 *S. J. Holzinger* (ex-*Uxmal*) (imp *Uribe*) with Bo-105
    hel
  6 *Cadete Virgilio Uribe* (Sp '*Halcon*') with Bo-105 hel
  16 *Leandro Valle* (US *Auk* MSF)
  1 *Guanajuato* with 2 102mm gun
  12 D-01 (US *Admirable* MSF), 3 with hel deck
PATROL, INSHORE 47
  4 *Isla* (US *Halter*) XFPB
  31 *Quintana Roo* (UK *Azteca*) PCI
  3 *Cabo* (US *Cape Higgon*) PCI
  2 *Punta* (US *Point*) PCI
  7 *Tamiahua* (US *Polimar*)
PATROL, RIVERINE 20<, plus boats
AMPHIBIOUS 2
  2 *Panuco* (US-511) LST
SUPPORT AND MISCELLANEOUS 22
  3 AOT, 1 PCI spt, 4 log spt, 6 ocean tugs, 5 survey, 1
    Durango tpt, plus 2 other tpt

NAVAL AVIATION (1,100)
9 cbt ac, no armed hel
MR 1 sqn with 9* C-212-200M
MR HEL 12 Bo-105 (8 afloat)
TPT 1 C-212, 2 C-180, 3 C-310, 1 DHC-5, 1 FH-227, 1
  King Air 90, 1 *Learjet* 24, 1 *Commander*, 2 C-337, 2 C-
402, 2 An-32
HEL 3 Bell 47, 4 SA-319, 20 UH-1H, 20 Mi-8/17, 4 AS-
355
TRG ac 8 Cessna 152, 10 F-33C *Bonanza*, 10 L-90 *Redigo*
  hel 4 MD-500E

MARINES (10,000)
3 marine bde (each 3 bn), 1 AB bde (3 bn) • 1 Presiden-
tial Guard bn • 14 regional bn • 1 Coast def gp: 2 coast
arty bn • 1 indep sy coy
EQUIPMENT
  AAV 25 VAP-3550
  TOWED ARTY 105mm: 8 M-56
  MRL 51mm: 6 *Firos*
  MOR 100 incl 60mm, 81mm
  RCL 106mm: M-40A1
  AD GUNS 20mm: Mk 38; 40mm: Bofors

Air Force 8,000

125 cbt ac, 95 armed hel
FTR 1 sqn with 8 F-5E, 2 -F
CCT 9 sqn
  7 with 74 PC-7
  2 with 27 AT-33
ARMED HEL 1 sqn with 1 Bell 205, 27 Bell 206, 25 Bell
  212, 20 UH-1H
RECCE 1 photo sqn with 14* *Commander* 500S, 1 SA 2-
  37A, 4 C-26
TPT 5 sqn with 2 BN-2, 12 C-47, 1 C-54, 10 C-118, 9 C-
  130A, 5 *Commander* 500, 5 DC-6 *Skytrain*, 2 F-27, 5
  Boeing 727, 1 sqn with 12 IAI-201 (tpt/SAR)
HEL 4 Bell 205, 3 SA-332, 2 UH-60, 6 S-70A, 73 UH-
  1H, 20 Mi-17
PRESIDENTIAL TPT ac 1 Boeing 757, 3 Boeing 737, 1
  L-188, 3 FH-227, 2 *Merlin*, 4 *Sabreliners* hel 1 AS-332,
  2 SA-330, 2 UH-60, 2 Bell-412
LIAISON/UTL 2 *King Air*, 1 *Musketeer*, 40 Beech
  Bonanza F-33A, 10 Beech *Musketeer*
TRG ac 20 CAP-10, 20 L-90 *Redigo*, 5 T-39 *Sabreliner*
  hel 22* MD 530F (SAR/paramilitary/trg)

Paramilitary

RURAL DEFENCE MILITIA (R) 14,000

COAST GUARD
  4 *Mako* 295 PCI

Nicaragua

	1996	1997	1998	1999
GDP	Co17bn	Co19bn		
	($2.3bn)	($2.5bn)		
per capita	$1,900	$2,000		
Growth	4.5%	5.0%		

contd	1996	1997	1998	1999
Inflation	11.6%	10.0%		
Debt	$5.4bn	$6.0bn		
Def exp	Co240m	Co258m		
	($37m)	($36m)		
Def bdgt			Co314m	
			($31m)	
FMA (US)		$0.1m	$0.2m	$0.2m
$1 = Co*	8.4	9.5	10.2	
* Cordoba oro				
Population		4,574,000		
Age	*13–17*	*18–22*	*23–32*	
Men	308,000	248,000	318,000	
Women	275,000	232,000	364,000	

Total Armed Forces

ACTIVE ε17,000

Terms of service voluntary, 18–36 months

Army 15,000

Reorganisation in progress
5 Regional Comd (10 inf, 1 tk coy) • 2 mil det (2 inf bn)
• 1 lt mech bde (1 mech inf, 1 tk, 1 recce bn, 1 fd arty
gp (2 bn), 1 atk gp) • 1 comd regt (1 inf, 1 sy bn) • 1 SF
bde (3 SF bn) • 1 tpt regt (incl 1 APC bn) • 1 engr bn

EQUIPMENT
　MBT some 127 T-55 (42 op remainder in store)
　LT TK 10 PT-76 (in store)
　RECCE 20 BRDM-2
　APC 102 BTR-152 (in store), 64 BTR-60
　TOWED ARTY 122mm: 12 D-30, 100 *Grad* 1P
　　(single-tube rocket launcher); **152mm**: 30 D-20 (in
　　store)
　MRL 107mm: 33 Type-63; **122mm**: 18 BM-21
　MOR 82mm: 579; **120mm**: 24 M-43; **160mm**: 4 M-
　　160 (in store)
　ATGW AT-3 *Sagger* (12 on BRDM-2)
　RCL 82mm: B-10
　ATK GUNS 57mm: 354 ZIS-2 (90 in store); **76mm**:
　　83 Z1S-3; **100mm**: 24 M-1944
　SAM 200+ SA-7/-14/-16

Navy ε800

BASES Corinto, Puerto Cabezas, El Bluff

PATROL AND COASTAL COMBATANTS 13†
PATROL, INSHORE 13†
　2 Sov *Zhuk* PFI<, 5 *Dabur* PCI, 6 small PCI, plus boats

MINECOUNTERMEASURES 3
　3 *Yevgenya* MCI

Air Force 1,200

no cbt ac, 15 armed hel
TPT 2 An-2, 5 An-26
HEL 15 Mi-17 (tpt/armed), 1 Mi-17 (VIP)
UTL/TRG ac 1 Cessna 180, 1 Cessna-T-41D, 2 Cessna-
　U-17
ASM AT-2 *Swatter* ATGW
AD GUNS 1 air def gp, 18 ZU-23, 18 C3-*Morigla* M1

Panama

	1996	1997	1998	1999
GDP	B8bn	B9bn		
	($8.2bn)	($8.7bn)		
per capita	$6,100	$6,400		
Growth	2.4%	4.2%		
Inflation	1.3%	1.2%		
Debt	$6.9bn	$5.1bn		
Sy bdgt	B110m	B114m	B124m	
	($110m)	($114m)	($124m)	
FMA (US)				$0.1m
$1 = balboa	1.0	1.0	1.0	
Population		2,792,000		
Age	*13–17*	*18–22*	*23–32*	
Men	142,000	136,000	249,000	
Women	136,000	131,000	243,000	

Total Armed Forces

ACTIVE Nil

Paramilitary ε11,800

NATIONAL POLICE FORCE 11,000
Presidential Guard bn (-), 1 MP bn plus 8 coys, 18
Police coy, 1 SF unit (reported); no hy mil eqpt, small
arms only

NATIONAL MARITIME SERVICE ε400
BASES Amador (HQ), Balboa, Colón
　PATROL CRAFT, INSHORE 7
　2 *Panquiaco* (UK *Vosper* 31.5m), 1 *President HI*
　Remeliik PCI, 1 *General Esteban Huertas* PCI, 1 *Tres*
　de Noviembre (ex-USCG *Cape Higgon*), 2 ex-US
　MSB 5-class (plus about 10 other ex-US patrol/spt
　craft and boats)

NATIONAL AIR SERVICE 400
　TPT 1 CN-235-2A, 1 BN-2B, 1 PA-34, 3 CASA-212M
　Aviocar
　TRG 6 T-35D
　HEL 2 Bell 205, 6 Bell 212, 13 UH-1H

Foreign Forces

US 3,500: **Army** 822; 1 inf bde (1 inf bn), 1 avn bde
Navy 700 **Marines** 180 **Air Force** 1,800; 1 wg (1 C-21, 9
C-27, 1 CT-43)

Paraguay

	1996	1997	1998	1999
GDP	Pg20tr	Pg22tr		
	($8.5bn)	($8.9bn)		
per capita	$3,700	$3,800		
Growth	1.0%	2.5%		
Inflation	8.2%	6.2%		
Debt	$2.5bn	$2.3bn		
Def exp	Pg280bn	Pg310bn		
	($131m)	($134m)		
Def bdgt			Pg280bn	
			($109m)	
FMA (US)	$0.2m	$0.2m	$0.2m	$0.2m
$1 = Pg*	2,063	2,191	2,576	
* Paraguayan guarani				
Population		5,359,000		
Age	*13–17*	*18–22*	*23–32*	
Men	291,000	252,000	423,000	
Women	281,000	244,000	408,000	

Total Armed Forces

ACTIVE 20,200

(12,900 conscripts)
Terms of service 12 months **Navy** 2 years

RESERVES some 164,500

Army 14,900

(10,400 conscripts)
3 corps HQ • 9 div HQ (6 inf, 3 cav) • 9 inf regt (bn) •
3 cav regt (horse) • 3 mech cav regt • Presidential
Guard (1 inf, 1 MP bn, 1 arty bty) • 20 frontier det • 3
arty gp (bn) • 1 AD arty gp • 4 engr bn
EQUIPMENT
MBT 5 M-4A3
RECCE 8 M-8, 5 M-3, 30 EE-9 *Cascavel*
APC 10 EE-11 *Urutu*
TOWED ARTY 75mm: 20 Model 1927/1934;
  105mm: 15 M-101; 152mm: 6 Vickers 6in (coast)
MOR 81mm: 80
RCL 75mm: M-20
AD GUNS 30: 20mm: 20 Bofors; 40mm: 10 M-1A1

Navy 3,600

(incl 900 Marines, 800 Naval Aviation, Harbour and

River Guard, and ε1,900 conscripts)
BASES Asunción (Puerto Sajonia), Bahía Negra,
Ciudad Del Este

PATROL AND COASTAL COMBATANTS 15
PATROL, COASTAL 15
  2 *Paraguais* with 4 120mm guns
  2 *Nanawa* PCO with 4 40mm and 2 12.7mm guns
  1 *Itapu* PCR with 1 40mm, 6 12.7mm guns, 2 81mm
    mor
  1 *Capitan Cabral* PCR with 1 40mm, 2 20mm, 2
    12.7mm guns
  2 *Capitan Ortiz* PFC
  7 *Rodman* SS/101 PCI (plus 13 riverine boats)`

SUPPORT AND MISCELLANEOUS 6
  1 tpt, 1 *Boqueron* spt (ex-US LSM with hel deck), 1
    trg/tpt, 1 survey<, 2 LCT

MARINES (900)
(incl 200 conscripts); 2 bn

NAVAL AVIATION (800)
2 cbt ac, no armed hel
  CCT 2 AT-6G
  LIAISON 2 Cessna 150, 2 C-206, 1 C-210
  HEL 2 HB-350, 1 OH-13

Air Force 1,700

(600 conscripts); 29 cbt ac, no armed hel
  FTR/FGA 8 F-5E, 4 F-5F
  CCT 6 AT-33, 7 EMB-326, 4 T-27
  LIAISON 1 Cessna 185, 4 C-206, 2 C-402, 2 T-41
  HEL 3 HB-350, 1 UH-1B, 2 UH-1H, 4 UH-12, 4 Bell
    47G
  TPT 1 sqn with 5 C-47, 4 C-212, 3 DC-6B, 1 DHC-6
    (VIP), 1 C-131D
  TRG 6 T-6, 10 T-23, 5 T-25, 10 T-35, 1 T-41

Paramilitary 14,800

SPECIAL POLICE SERVICE 14,800
(incl 4,000 conscripts)

Peru

	1996	1997	1998	1999
GDP	NS149bn	NS167bn		
	($54bn)	($59bn)		
per capita	$4,000	$4,300		
Growth	2.6%	7.4%		
Inflation	11.5%	8.6%		
Debt	$29bn	$28bn		
Def exp	εNS2.8bn	εNS3.4bn		
	($1.1bn)	($1.3bn)		
Def bdgt			εNS2.3bn	
			($838m)	

	1996	1997	1998	1999
FMAᵃ (US)	$16m	$26m	$31m	$50m
$1 = new sol	2.5	2.7	2.8	
ᵃ MOMEP 1996 ε$15m 1997 ε$15m				

Population		25,022,000		
Age	*13–17*	*18–22*	*23–32*	
Men	1,336,000	1,260,000	2,172,000	
Women	1,324,000	1,251,000	2,164,000	

Total Armed Forces

ACTIVE 125,000

(74,500 conscripts)
Terms of service 2 years, selective

RESERVES 188,000

Army only

Army 85,000

(60,000 conscripts)
6 Mil Regions
Army tps
1 AB div (3 cdo, 1 para bn, 1 arty gp) • 1 Presidential Escort regt • 1 AD arty gp
Regional tps
3 armd div (each 2 tk, 1 armd inf bn, 1 arty gp, 1 engr bn) • 1 armd gp (3 indep armd cav, 1 fd arty, 1 AD arty, 1 engr bn) • 1 cav div (3 mech regt, 1 arty gp) • 7 inf div (each 3 inf bn, 1 arty gp) • 1 jungle div • 2 med arty gp; 2 fd arty gp • 1 indep inf bn • 1 indep engr bn • 3 hel sqn
EQUIPMENT
MBT 300 T-54/-55 (ε50 serviceable)
LT TK 110 AMX-13 (ε30 serviceable)
RECCE 60 M-8/-20, 10 M-3A1, 50 M-9A1, 15 Fiat 6616, 30 BRDM-2
APC 130 M-113, 12 BTR-60, 130 UR-416, Fiat 6614, *Casspir*, 4 *Repontec*
TOWED ARTY 105mm: 20 Model 56 pack, 130 M-101; **122mm**: 36 D-30; **130mm**: 30 M-46; **155mm**: 36 M-114
SP ARTY 155mm: 12 M-109A2, 12 Mk F3
MRL 122mm: 14 BM-21
MOR 81mm: incl some SP; **107mm**: incl some SP; **120mm**: 300 Brandt, ECIA
ATGW 400 SS-11
RCL 106mm: M40A1
AD GUNS 23mm: 80 ZSU-23-2, 35 ZSU-23-4 SP; **40mm**: 45 M-1, 80 L60/70
SAM SA-7, 236 SA-16, 10 SA-19 (2S6 SP) (8 SAM, plus twin **30mm** gun), *Javelin*
AC 13 Cessna incl 1 C-337, 1 *Queen Air* 65, 5 U-10, 3 U-17, 1 U-150, 2 U-206, 4 AN-32B
HEL 2 Bell 47G, 2 Mi-6, 26 Mi-8, 13 Mi-17, 6 SA-315, 5 SA-316, 3 SA-318, 2 *Agusta* A-109

Navy 25,000

(incl some 800 Naval Aviation, 3,000 Marines and 12,500 conscripts)
NAVAL AREAS Pacific, Lake Titicaca, Amazon River
BASES Ocean Callao, San Lorenzo Island, Paita, Talara **Lake** Puno **River** Iquitos, Puerto Maldonado
SUBMARINES 8
6 *Casma* (Ge T-209/1200) with 533mm TT (It A184 HWT) (2 in refit)
2 *Abato* with 533mm TT, 1 127mm gun
(Plus 1 *Pedrera* (US *Guppy* I) with 533mm TT (Mk 37 HWT) alongside trg only)
PRINCIPAL SURFACE COMBATANTS 7
CRUISERS 2
1 *Almirante Grau* (Nl *De Ruyter*) with 4 x 2 152mm guns, 8 Otomat SSM
1 *Aguirre* (Nl *De 7 Provincien*) with 3 SH-3D *Sea King* hel (ASW/ASUW) (Mk 46 LWT/AM-39 *Exocet*), 2 x 2 152mm guns
DESTROYERS 1 *Ferre* (UK *Daring*) with 4 x 2 MM-38 *Exocet*, 3 x 2 114mm guns, hel deck
FRIGATES 4 *Carvajal* (mod It *Lupo*) with 1 AB-212 hel (ASW OTHT), 2 x 3 ASTT; plus 8 *Otomat* Mk 2 SSM, 1 127mm gun (2 non-op)
PATROL AND COASTAL COMBATANTS 11
MISSILE CRAFT 6 *Velarde* PFM (Fr PR-72 64m) with 4 MM-38 *Exocet*
PATROL CRAFT 1 *Unanue* (ex-US *Sotoyomo*) PCC (Antarctic ops)
RIVERINE 4
2 *Marañon*
2 *Amazonas*
AMPHIBIOUS 3
3 *Paita* (US *Terrebonne Parish*) LST, capacity 395 tps, 16 tk
SUPPORT AND MISCELLANEOUS 9
3 AO, 1 AGOR, 1 AOT, 1 tpt, 2 survey, 1 ocean tug (SAR)
LAKE PATROL
4 craft
NAVAL AVIATION (some 800)
7 cbt ac, 9 armed hel
ASW/MR 4 sqn with **ac** 5 *Super King Air* B 200T, 3 EMB-111A, 1 F-27 **hel** 5 AB-212 ASW, 4 ASH-3D (ASW)
TPT 2 An-32B, 1 Y-12
LIAISON 4 Bell 206B, 6 UH-1D hel, 3 Mi-8
TRG 1 Cessna 150, 5 T-34C
ASM *Exocet* AM-39 (on SH-3 hel)
MARINES (3,000)
1 Marine bde (5 bn, 1 recce, 1 cdo coy)

EQUIPMENT
RECCE V-100
APC 15 V-200 *Chaimite*, 20 BMR-600
MOR **81mm**; **120mm** ε18
RCL **84mm**: *Carl Gustav*; **106mm**· M-40A1
AD GUNS twin 20mm SP

COASTAL DEFENCE 3 bty with 18 **155mm** how

Air Force 15,000

(2,000 conscripts); 118 cbt ac, 23 armed hel
BBR 8 *Canberra*
FGA 2 gp, 6 sqn
   3 with 28 Su-22 (incl 4* Su-22U), 18 Su-25 (incl 8* Su-25UB)
   3 with 23 Cessna A-37B
FTR 3 sqn
   1 with 10 *Mirage* 2000P, 2 -DP
   2 with 9 *Mirage* 5P, 2 -DP
   1 with 18 MiG-29 (incl 2 MiG-29UB)
ATTACK HEL 1 sqn with 23 Mi-24/-25
RECCE 1 photo-survey unit with 2 *Learjet* 25B, 2 -36A
TKR 1 Boeing KC 707-323C
TPT 3 gp, 7 sqn
   ac 17 An-32, 3 AN-72, 4 C-130A, 6 -D, 5 L-100-20, 2 DC-8-62F, 12 DHC-5, 8 DHC-6, 1 FH-227, 9 PC-6, 6 Y-12, 1 Boeing 737 **hel** 3 sqn with 8 Bell 206, 14 B-212, 5 B-214, 1 B-412, 10 Bo-105C, 5 Mi-6, 3 Mi-8, 35 Mi-17, 5 SA-316
PRESIDENTIAL FLT 1 F-28, 1 *Falcon* 20F
LIAISON ac 2 Beech 99, 3 Cessna 185, 1 Cessna 320, 15 *Queen Air* 80, 3 *King Air* 90, 1 PA-31T **hel** 8 UH-1D
TRG ac 2 Cessna 150, 25 EMB-312, 13 MB-339A, 20 T-37B/C, 15 T-41A/-D **hel** 12 Bell 47G
MISSILES
   ASM AS-30
   AAM AA-2 *Atoll*, AA-8 *Aphid*, AA-10 *Alemo*, R-550 *Magic*
   AD 3 SA-2, 6 SA-3 bn with 18 SA-2, 24 SA-3 launchers

Paramilitary 78,000

NATIONAL POLICE 77,000
General Police 43,000 **Security Police** 21,000
Technical Police 13,000
   100+ MOWAG *Roland* APC

COAST GUARD 1,000
   5 *Rio Nepena* PCC, 3 PCI, 10 riverine PCI<

RONDAS CAMPESINAS (peasant self-defence force)
perhaps 2,000 *rondas* 'gp', up to pl strength, some with small arms. Deployed mainly in emergency zone.

Opposition

SENDERO LUMINOSO (Shining Path) ε1,500
Maoist

MOVIMIENTO REVOLUCIONARIO TUPAC AMARU (MRTA) ε200
mainly urban gp

Suriname

	1996	1997	1998	1999
GDP	gld n.k.	gld n.k.		
	($315m)	($338m)		
per capita	$4,100	$4,300		
Growth	6.9%	4.7%		
Inflation	-0.8%	7.2%		
Debt	$178m	$187m		
Def exp	εgld n.k.	εgld n.k.		
	($14m)	($15m)		
Def bdgt			εgld n.k.	
			($15m)	
FMA (US)	$0.1m	$0.1m	$0.1m	$0.1m
$1 = guilder	401	401	401	
Population		415,000		
Age	*13–17*	*18–22*	*23–32*	
Men	21,000	19,000	36,000	
Women	21,000	18,000	36,000	

Total Armed Forces

ACTIVE (all services form part of the Army) ε1,800

Army 1,400

1 inf bn (4 inf coy) • 1 mech cav sqn • 1 MP 'bde' (bn)
EQUIPMENT
   RECCE 6 EE-9 *Cascavel*
   APC 9 YP-408, 15 EE-11 *Urutu*
   MOR **81mm**: 6
   RCL **106mm**: M-40A1

Navy 240

BASE Paramaribo

PATROL CRAFT, INSHORE 3
   3 S-401 (Nl 32m), plus boats

Air Force ε160

7 cbt ac, no armed hel
MPA 2 C-212-400
TPT/TRG 4* BN-2 *Defender*, 1* PC-7

LIAISON 1 Cessna U206
HEL 2 SA-319, 1 AB-205

Trinidad and Tobago

	1996	1997	1998	1999
GDP	TT$33bn	TT$37bn		
	($5.5bn)	($5.9bn)		
per capita	$9,400	$9,900		
Growth	3.1%	3.9%		
Inflation	3.4%	3.7%		
Debt	$2.2bn	$2.7bn		
Def exp	εTT$395m	εTT$520m		
	($66m)	($83m)		
Def bdgt			εTT$550m	
			($88m)	
FMA (US)		$0.1m	$0.1m	$0.1m
US$1 = TT$	6.0	6.2	6.3	
Population		1,337,000		
Age	13–17	18–22	23–32	
Men	70,000	62,000	104,000	
Women	69,000	62,000	108,000	

Total Armed Forces

ACTIVE (all services form part of the Trinidad and Tobago Defence Force) 2,600

Army 1,900

2 inf bn • 1 spt bn
EQUIPMENT
   MOR 60mm: ε40; 81mm: 6 L16A1
   RL 82mm: 13 B-300
   RCL 84mm: *Carl Gustav*

Coast Guard 700

(incl 50 Air Wing)
BASE Staubles Bay (HQ), Hart's Cut, Point Fortin, Tobago, Galeota
PATROL CRAFT, INSHORE 7 (some non-op)
   2 *Barracuda* PFI (Sw *Karlskrona* 40m)
   5 *Plymouth* PCI< (plus 13 boats and 2 auxiliary vessels)
AIR WING
   1 Cessna 310, 1 C-402, 1 C-172

Paramilitary 4,800

POLICE 4,800

Uruguay

	1996	1997	1998	1999
GDP	pU152bn	pU189bn		
	($12bn)	($13bn)		
per capita	$8,200	$8,800		
Growth	4.9%	6.0%		
Inflation	28.3%	19.8%		
Debt	$5.9bn	$5.4bn		
Def exp	εpU2.2bn	εpU2.9bn		
	($280m)	($307m)		
Def bdgt			εpU3.3bn	
			($323m)	
FMA (US)	$0.4m	$0.3m	$0.3m	$0.3m
$1 = pU*	8.0	9.4	10.2	
*Uruguayan peso				
Population		3,230,000		
Age	13–17	18–22	23–32	
Men	134,000	136,000	241,000	
Women	128,000	131,000	238,000	

Total Armed Forces

ACTIVE 25,600

Army 17,600

4 Mil Regions/div HQ • 5 inf bde (4 of 3 inf bn, 1 of 1 mech, 1 mot, 1 para bn) • 3 cav bde (10 cav bn (4 horsed, 3 mech, 2 mot, 1 armd)) • 1 arty bde (2 arty, 1 AD arty bn) • 1 engr bde (3 bn) • 3 arty, 4 cbt engr bn
EQUIPMENT
   MBT 15 T-55 (reported)
   LT TK 17 M-24, 29 M-3A1, 22 M-41A1
   RECCE 16 EE-3 *Jararaca*, 10 EE-9 *Cascavel*
   AIFV 10 BMP-1
   APC 15 M-113, 50 *Condor*, 60 OT-64 SKOT
   TOWED ARTY 75mm: 12 Bofors M-1902; 105mm:
      48 M-101A/M-102; 155mm: 5 M-114A1
   MRL 122mm: 2 RM-70
   MOR 81mm: 97; 107mm: 8 M-30; 120mm: 44
   ATGW 5 *Milan*
   RCL 57mm: 30 M-18; 106mm: 30 M-40A1
   AD GUNS 20mm: 6 M-167 *Vulcan*; 40mm: 8 L/60

Navy 5,000

(incl 280 Naval Aviation, 400 Naval Infantry, 1,600 *Prefectura Naval* (Coast Guard))
BASES Montevideo (HQ), La Paloma, Fray Bentos
FRIGATES 3
   3 *General Artigas* (Fr *Cdt Rivière*) with 2 x 3 ASTT, 1 x
      2 ASW mor, 2 100mm guns
PATROL AND COASTAL COMBATANTS 10
PATROL, INSHORE 10

2 *Colonia* PCI (US *Cape*), 3 *15 de Noviembre* PFI (Fr *Vigilante* 42m), 1 *Salto* PCI, 1 *Paysandu* PCI<, 3 other<

MINE COUNTERMEASURES 4

4 *Temerario* MSC (Ge *Kondor* II)

AMPHIBIOUS craft only

4 LCM, 2 LCVP

SUPPORT AND MISCELLANEOUS 5

1 *Presidente Rivera* AOT, 1 *Vanguardia* Salvage, 1 *Campbell* (US *Auk* MSF) PCO (Antarctic patrol/ research), 1 tug (ex-GDR *Elbe*-Class), 1 trg

NAVAL AVIATION (280)

1 cbt ac, no armed hel
   ASW 1 *Super King Air* 200T
   TRG/LIAISON 2 T-28, 2 T-34B, 2 T-34C, 2 PA-34-200T, 3 C-182
   HEL 3 Wessex Mk60, 5 Wessex HC2, 2 Bell 47G, 2 SH-34J

NAVAL INFANTRY (400)

1 bn

Air Force 3,000

33 cbt ac, no armed hel
Flying hours 120
CBT AC 2 sqn
   1 with 10 A-37B, 6 T-33A, 1 with 5 IA-58B)
SURVEY 1 EMB-110B1
SAR 1 sqn with 2 Bell 212, 3 UH-1H hel, 6 *Wessex* HC2
TPT 3 sqn with 3 C-212 (tpt/SAR), 3 EMB-110C, 1 F-27, 3 C-130B, 1 Cessna 310 (VIP), 1 Cessna 206
LIAISON 2 Cessna 182, 2 *Queen Air* 80, 5 U-17, 1 T-34A
TRG *12 T-34A/B, 5 T-41D, 5 PC-7U

Forces Abroad

UN AND PEACEKEEPING

ANGOLA (UNOMA): 6 incl 3 obs. **EGYPT** (MFO): 60. **GEORGIA** (UNOMIG): 3 obs. **INDIA/PAKISTAN** (UNMOGIP): 3 obs. **IRAQ/KUWAIT** (UNIKOM): 6 Obs. **TAJIKISTAN** (UNMOT): 6 obs. **WESTERN SAHARA** (MINURSO): 13 obs

Paramilitary 920

GUARDIA DE GRANADEROS 450

GUARDIA DE CORACEROS 470

COAST GUARD (1,600)

Prefectura Naval (PNN) is part of the Navy

Venezuela

	1996	1997	1998	1999
GDP	Bs29bn	Bs43bn		
	($81bn)	($88bn)		
per capita	$8,100	$8,500		
Growth	-0.4%	5.1%		
Inflation	99.9%	50.0%		
Debt	$36bn	$32bn		
Def exp	Bs325bn	Bs470bn		
	($779m)	($962m)		
Def bdgt			Bs685bn	Bs859bn
			($1,315m)	($1,544m)
FMA (US)	$1m	$1m	$1m	$1m
$1=bolivar	417	489	521	
Population		23,296,000		
Age	*13–17*	*18–22*	*23–32*	
Men	1,219,000	1,135,000	1,961,000	
Women	1,174,000	1,097,000	1,908,000	

Total Armed Forces

ACTIVE 79,000

(incl National Guard and ε31,000 conscripts)
Terms of service 30 months selective, varies by region for all services

RESERVES ε8,000

Army

Army 34,000

(incl 27,000 conscripts)
6 inf div • 1 armd bde • 1 cav bde • 7 inf bde (18 inf, 1 mech inf, 4 fd arty bn) • 1 AB bde • 2 Ranger bde (1 with 4 bn, 1 with 2 bn) • 1 avn regt
RESERVES ε6 inf, 1 armd, 1 arty bn
EQUIPMENT
   MBT 70 AMX-30
   LT TK 75 M-18, 36 AMX-13, 80 *Scorpion* 90
   RECCE 10 AML-60/-90, 30 M-8
   APC 25 AMX-VCI, 100 V-100, 30 V-150, 100 *Dragoon* (some with **90mm** gun), 35 EE-11 *Urutu*
   TOWED ARTY 105mm: 40 Model 56, 40 M-101; **155mm**: 12 M-114
   SP ARTY 155mm: 5 M-109, 10 Mk F3
   MRL 160mm: 20 LAR SP
   MOR 81mm: 165; **120mm**: 65 Brandt
   ATGW AT-4, AS-11, 24 *Mapats*
   RCL 84mm: *Carl Gustav*; **106mm**: 175 M-40A1
   SURV RASIT (veh, arty)
   AC 3 IAI-202, 2 Cessna 182, 2 C-206, 2 C-207
   ATTACK HEL 5 A-109 (atk)
   TPT HEL 4 AS-61A, 3 Bell 205, 6 UH-1H
   LIAISON 2 Bell 206

Navy 15,000

(incl 1,000 Naval Aviation, 5,000 Marines, 1,000 Coast Guard and ε4,000 conscripts)
NAVAL COMMANDS Fleet, Marines, Naval Avn, Coast Guard, Fluvial (River Forces)
NAVAL FLEET SQN submarine, frigate, patrol, amph, service
BASES Main bases Caracas (HQ), Puerto Cabello (submarine, frigate, amph and service sqn), Punto Fijo (patrol sqn) **Minor bases** Puerto de Hierro, Puerto La Cruz, El Amparo (HQ Arauca River), Maracaibo, La Guaira, Ciudad Bolivar (HQ Fluvial Forces)

SUBMARINES 2

2 *Sabalo* (Ge T-209/1300) with 533mm TT (SST-4 HWT)

FRIGATES 6

6 *Mariscal Sucre* (It *Lupo*) with 1 AB-212 hel (ASW/OTHT), 2 x 3 ASTT (A-244S LWT); plus 8 *Teseo* SSM, 1 127mm gun, 1 x 8 *Aspide* SAM

PATROL AND COASTAL COMBATANTS 6

MISSILE CRAFT 6
3 *Constitución* PFM (UK Vosper 37m), with 2 *Teseo*
3 *Constitución* PFI with 4 *Harpoon* SSM

AMPHIBIOUS 4

4 *Capana* LST (Sov *Alligator*), capacity 200 tps, 12 tk
Plus craft: 2 LCU (river comd), 12 LCVP

SUPPORT AND MISCELLANEOUS 5

1 log spt, 1 trg, 1 *Punta Brava* AGHS, 2 survey

NAVAL AVIATION (1,000)

7 cbt ac, 8 armed hel
ASW 1 hel sqn (afloat) with 8 AB-212
MR 1 sqn with 4 C-212-200 MPA, 3 C-212-400
TPT 2 C-212, 1 DHC-7, 1 *Rockwell Commander* 680
LIAISON 1 Cessna 310, 1 C-402, 1 *King Air* 90, 3 C-212-400
HEL 2 Bell 412

MARINES (5,000)

4 inf bn • 1 arty bn (3 fd, 1 AD bty) • 1 amph veh bn • 1 river patrol, 1 engr, 2 para/cdo unit
EQUIPMENT
AAV 11 LVTP-7 (to be mod to -7A1)
APC 25 EE-11 *Urutu*, 10 *Fuchs/Transportpanzer* 1
TOWED ARTY 105mm: 18 Model 56
AD GUNS 40mm: 6 M-42 twin SP

COAST GUARD (1,000)

BASE La Guaira; operates under Naval Command and Control, but organisationally separate
PATROL, OFFSHORE 3
2 *Almirante Clemente* (It FF type)
1 *Miguel Rodriguez* (ex-US ocean tug)

PATROL, INSHORE 6
2 *Petrel* (USCG *Point*-class) PCI<
4 riverine PCI<
plus 39 river patrol craft and boats

Air Force 7,000

(some conscripts); 116 cbt ac, 27 armed hel
Flying hours 155
FTR/FGA 6 air gp
1 with 15 CF-5A/B, 7 NF-5A/B
1 with 2 *Mirage* IIIEV, 5 *Mirage* 50EV
2 with 23 F-16A/B
2 with 20 EMB-312
RECCE 15* OV-10A
ECM 3 *Falcon* 20DC
ARMED HEL 1 air gp with 10 SA-316, 12 UH-1D, 5 UH-1H
TPT ac 7 C-123, 5 C-130H, 8 G-222, 2 HS-748, 2 B-707 (tkr) **hel** 2 Bell 214, 4 Bell 412, 8 AS-332B, 2 UH-1N, 18 Mi-8/17
PRESIDENTIAL FLT 1 Boeing 737, 1 *Gulfstream* III, 1 *Gulfstream* IV, 1 *Learjet* 24D **hel** 1 Bell 412
LIAISON 9 Cessna 182, 1 *Citation* I, 1 *Citation* II, 2 *Queen Air* 65, 5 *Queen Air* 80, 5 *Super King Air* 200, 9 SA-316B *Alouette* III
TRG 1 air gp: 12* EMB-312, 20 T-34, 17* T-2D, 12 SF-260E
MISSILES
AAM R-530 *Magic*, AIM-9L *Sidewinder*, AIM-9P *Sidewinder*
ASM *Exocet*
AD GUNS 20mm: some AML S530 SP; **35mm**; **40mm**: 114: Bofors L/70 towed, Otobreda 40L70 towed
SAM 10 *Roland*, RBS-70

National Guard (*Fuerzas Armadas de Cooperación*) 23,000

(internal sy, customs)
8 regional comd
EQUIPMENT
20 UR-416 AIFV, 24 Fiat-6614 APC, 100 **60mm** mor, 50 **81mm** mor **ac** 1 *Baron*, 1 BN-2A, 2 Cessna 185, 5 -U206, 4 IAI-201, 1 *King Air* 90, 1 *King Air* 200C, 2 *Queen Air* 80, 6 M-28 *Skytruck* **hel** 4 A-109, 20 Bell 206, 2 Bell 212
PATROL CRAFT, INSHORE 52 boats

Forces Abroad

UN AND PEACEKEEPING
IRAQ/KUWAIT (UNIKOM): 2 Obs. **WESTERN SAHARA** (MINURSO): 3 Obs

MILITARY DEVELOPMENTS

Hopes for stability in the region raised by Laurent Kabila's sweeping 1997 victory in the **Democratic Republic of the Congo (DROC)**, and what then appeared to be an axis of politico-military cooperation from Eritrea through Uganda, Rwanda and the DROC to the Atlantic coast, were soon dashed. A border war between **Eritrea** and **Ethiopia** broke out in May 1998; attempts at peace talks in **Sudan** failed to progress and President Yoweri Musaveni continued to be plagued by armed insurgents in northern **Uganda**. In the DROC itself, Kabila is faced with a rebellion by his former allies, the Banyamulenge (ethnic Tutsi in DROC) who are determined to remove him from power. This rebellion appears to have support from outside the country. During 1998, major new conflicts have broken out across Sub-Saharan Africa. In addition to the border war between Eritrea and Ethiopia, which by mid-June 1998 had spilled into Sudan, there has been an armed insurgency in the Casamance region of **Senegal** from early 1998 and an armed forces mutiny in **Guinea-Bissau** in June 1998 brought in the armed forces of Senegal and **Guinea** to support the Guinea-Bissau government. These developments join the long list of continuing armed conflicts, involving more than a quarter of all states in the region, to which, in many cases, no end seems in sight. Despite formal peace agreements and cease-fires in the internal conflicts of **Angola, Liberia, Central African Republic (CAR), Chad, Republic of Congo-Brazzaville** and DROC, localised, but often intensive, conflict continues. Armed groups still battle for control in southern **Somalia**; there seems no chance of a formal political process being successful. In Angola, the *União Nacional para Independencia Total de Angola* (UNITA) seemed, in early 1998, at last ready to demobilise those of its armed groups not to be integrated with government forces, in accordance with the 1994 Lusaka Accords, but the process was always delicate and liable to reverse. Clashes between UNITA armed groups and government forces increased in mid-1998. **Kenya**, the **Comoros** and **Equatorial Guinea** were among countries experiencing violent clashes between government security forces and minority political, ethnic and criminal groups. In **Sierra Leone**, 1998 brought an end to the military rebellion and restoration of the democratically elected government. In July 1998, the armed forces were disbanded, with about 1,000 of their troops incorporated into a new 5,000-strong force. However, the Revolutionary United Front (RUF) guerrillas with whom the Army formed an alliance after the coup, are continuing armed opposition and are thought to number 500–800.

The two countries which could be the economic heavyweights of the region, **Nigeria** and **South Africa**, remain focused on internal problems and, despite the key role played by Nigeria in defeating the junta in Sierra Leone, their influence remains well below its full potential. With the death of General Sani Abacha in June 1998, prospects for a more democratic and publicly accountable government in Nigeria seemed enhanced. However, there are severe challenges to the re-establishment of civil authority and, by mid-1998, there was a danger that the country could fracture along ethnic lines in the absence of unifying political leadership. The South African National Defence Force (SANDF) is undergoing reorganisation in which numbers will be cut from the 1997 level of around 80,000 by over 24,000 between 1998 and 2001, but, as indicated in the budgetary provisions outlined below, a programme of equipment modernisation is under way. Internal security threats place the most immediate demands on the SANDF. Since 1997, it has deployed over 6,000 soldiers daily in support of the South African Police Service (SAPS) and has taken over responsibility for border security from the police.

PEACEKEEPING FORCES

UN Peacekeeping Operations (PKO) in the region are now confined to the residual operation of the United Nations Observer Mission in Angola (UNOMA) and, since April 1998, the United Nations Mission in the Central African Republic (MINURCA), which took over when the French-inspired *Mission Interafricaine de Surveillance des Accords de Bangui* (MISAB) withdrew. Forces of the West African Cease-fire Monitoring Group (ECOMOG) are engaged in Sierra Leone and it retains a residual force in Liberia. Efforts continue to organise an African-led peacekeeping organisation and standing force to respond to contingencies. In May 1998, NATO announced that there were to be regular information exchanges on African security, involving mainly the US, France, the UK, and Belgium. There are also increased efforts to support African peacekeeping forces, mainly through the US-sponsored African Crisis Response Initiative (ACRI), the French Reinforcement of African Peacekeeping (RECAMP) initiative and British efforts in East and Southern Africa.

DEFENCE SPENDING

In 1997, regional defence expenditure of some $8.8bn showed a marginal real increase over 1996 and accounted for around 3.3% of regional gross domestic product (GDP), according to *The Military Balance* estimates. The direct military costs of widespread internal conflict added at least $800m, or around 10%, to expenditure. South Africa accounts for over a quarter of all regional defence spending, followed by Nigeria, with over 20%, after taking into account the real costs of military government and internal security. South Africa's defence spending continued to decline in 1997 (in contrast to police expenditure), but elsewhere in Southern Africa and in East Africa, defence spending continued to rise. In West Africa, apart from Nigeria, and in Central Africa, reliable information on military spending is difficult to obtain, but existing evidence suggests an upward trend.

Measuring military expenditure in the region continues to be very difficult because of a lack of transparency in government accounting, the heavy involvement of paramilitary forces in internal security and the off-budget funding of much military activity, including armed opposition groups and mercenaries. In these circumstances, it is impossible to judge whether spending is at an appropriate level, or effectively allocated. Estimates of regional defence and security spending vary widely. For example, *The Military Balance* estimates that defence and security accounted for some 3.3% of regional GDP in 1997, whereas the International Monetary Fund (IMF) figure is 1.9% for this region. No African country reported 1996 military expenditures to the UN under the Reporting of Military Expenditures programme. Of the 44 countries in the region, only Ethiopia, **Mauritius**, **Namibia**, **Seychelles**, South Africa and **Tanzania** reported as required on arms transfers, military holdings and domestic procurement to the 1996 UN Register of Conventional Arms. The IMF's latest audit of government finances, published in late 1997, gave 1996 figures on the military budgets of only **Burundi**, **Madagascar**, Mauritius, **Tunisia** and **Zambia** out of 22 countries surveyed.

Bilateral security assistance conducted by the US, France and the UK focuses on improving military skills through low-cost training programmes. France's military presence in Africa continues to be cut back, while its military assistance, in the form of advisers and equipment grants, continues at modest levels. In 1998, some 513 military advisers were posted to the region (compared to 645 in 1996 and 578 in 1997), while equipment grants amount to some $30m in 1998 ($30m in 1997). French military personnel stationed in Africa are being reduced from 7,900 to 5,500 over a three-year period, with cuts at the Djibouti military base from some 3,200 to 2,600.

Operating costs for Djibouti were FF1.4bn ($210m) in 1997, compared to an overall spend of just over FF3bn ($445m) for the French standing military presence in Africa. The US International Military Education and Training (IMET) programme has been allocated some $8m in 1998 and the same in 1999. The US Foreign Military Financing (FMF) programme is providing equipment funding for ACRI of $10m in 1998 and $5m in 1999. Additionally, $5m is provided in 1998 and 1999 for East African countries. Under the ACRI programme, the US is also spending $20m in 1998 and $15m in 1999 to train African forces in peacekeeping, with the object of establishing at least eight battalions of 600–800 soldiers able to respond to peacekeeping needs at short notice. The US was also a major supplier of equipment grants to ECOMOG forces in Liberia.

The parts played by other external forces in the region are less obviously constructive. China seeks political influence, access to raw materials and markets for its low-cost weaponry, particularly in the conflict zones of Sudan and Central Africa. Russia seeks markets for arms (notably in Angola) on a regional scale, as do several other East European countries. Private military companies are also playing an increasing role in the armed conflict of the region, often in the employ of governments; Sierra Leone is one example where a private company has been operating intermittently over the past three years.

1998 DEFENCE BUDGETS

South Africa's defence spending has declined by about 40% in real terms since 1989, when the defence budget stood at R17bn (in constant 1997 rands). The 1997 outturn was R10.7bn ($2.3bn). Over the same period, defence as a proportion of GDP has dropped from 4.5% to 1.6%. During 1997, Pretoria faced further pressure to cut defence spending. The 1997 budget was set at R9.6bn ($2.1bn), but, shortly after the budget authorisation, the government proposed cuts of R700m, which were successfully resisted by the Ministry of Defence. Instead, an 8% salary increase was approved in a supplementary allocation to the 1997 budget and carried forward into 1998, but, at the same time, the decision was taken to reduce the numbers of serving personnel from current levels of around 95,500 to 76,600 by 2001. The primary purpose of the cuts is to enable an increase in the level of equipment funding to some 30% of the defence budget, from the present level of around 8%. Salaries currently account for around 57% of the budget and operating expenses some 35%. South Africa's major indigenous weapons programme is the *Rooivalk* attack helicopter. The Air Force has contracted orders for 12 of these for delivery in late 1999 or early 2000. The *Cheetah* combat aircraft upgrade programme, contracted with Israel in 1988, included the integration of the *Raptor* 1 and 2 stand-off glide bombs. This is completed apart from the delayed acquisition and integration of a new air-to-air missile now under development. The Army has ordered the upgraded anti-tank *Ingwe* missile for man-portable and vehicle-mounted application.

A modernisation programme for the SANDF has been approved in principle by the government and includes the acquisition of four to six new corvette warships, four submarines, some 38–50 combat aircraft with 24 supporting trainers, six naval and 60–108 tactical helicopters, and 100–150 main battle tanks (MBTs). The whole programme has been estimated to cost over R25bn ($5.4bn at 1997 exchange rates), which reports suggest will be funded by supplementary one-off allocations to the defence budget. The government has made clear to prospective international suppliers that it requires direct and indirect industrial offsets as well as financing and foreign direct investment commitments at least equal to the value of the equipment contracts. The government issued its Request For Proposals for international tender in October 1997 and by December had drawn up its short list of preferred suppliers.

South Africa's 1998 defence budget amounts to R10bn ($1.7bn), excluding the salary increase authorised in 1997. This will bring the total to some R10.4bn. Salaries account for 58%, while the equipment allocation in the Special Defence Account is cut by over a third. In US dollar terms, the decline is over 50% due to rand depreciation. Arms export revenues assume an increasing significance to the local arms industry in the face of reducing levels of government procurement. They rose in 1997 by R500m to R1.3bn ($282m).

SANDF's increased role in supporting the civil authority has put more pressure on budgets. Under budget rules, the Department of Defence can only claim funding for primary roles; aid to the civil power is categorised as a secondary role. SAPS funding has increased from R9.4bn in 1994 to R13.1bn in 1997 and R13.7bn in 1998. It will reach R14.5bn in 1999 and R15.2bn in 2000 under 1998 plans.

Table 30 **South Africa's defence budget by programme 1995, 1997–2000**					
(Rm *[US$m]*)	**1995**	**1997**	**1998**	**1999**	**2000**
Command and Control	368 *[101]*	n.k. *[n.k.]*	458 *[78]*	474 *[81]*	475 *[81]*
Land Defence	3,980 *[1,097]*	3,992 *[866]*	3,971 *[676]*	4,034 *[687]*	4,090 *[696]*
Air Defence	1,753 *[483]*	2,041 *[443]*	1,919 *[327]*	1,956 *[333]*	1,960 *[334]*
Maritime Defence	778 *[215]*	808 *[175]*	845 *[144]*	896 *[153]*	907 *[154]*
Medical Support	739 *[204]*	813 *[176]*	918 *[156]*	965 *[164]*	973 *[166]*
General Support	367 *[101]*	n.k. *[n.k.]*	635 *[108]*	629 *[107]*	620 *[105]*
Special Defence Account and other	3,535 *[975]*	1,925 *[418]*	1,212 *[206]*	1,533 *[261]*	1,963 *[334]*
Total defence budget	11,521 *[3,176]*	9,579 *[2,079]*	9,959 *[1,695]*	1,0487 *[1,785]*	10,987 *[1,870]*
Final outturn	11,600 *[3,198]*	10,716 *[2,326]*	10,970 *[1,867]*	n.k. *[n.k.]*	n.k. *[n.k.]*
US$ exchange rate	3.6	4.6	5.9	5.9	5.9

Elsewhere in Southern Africa, defence spending has continued to rise during 1998 in **Botswana** and Namibia which are involved in a border dispute over Kasikili-Sedudu and Sintungu islands in the Caprivi strip of the Linyanti-Chobe river. Botswana's 1998 security budget is P1,380m ($323m), taking 11.5% of government spending, compared to P902m in 1997. The Botswana Defence Force accounts for about two-thirds of this. Namibia's 1998 defence budget is N$443m ($89m) compared to N$416m in 1997. The Angolan government has budgeted $380m for security in 1998 (about 10% of government spending). Actual outlays will be higher if the conflict with UNITA continues. However, spending on security appears to be declining in **Mozambique**, where security accounted for 19.4% of government recurrent spending in 1997, divided equally between the armed forces and the police. The 1998 security allocation has been cut to 17.3% of recurrent government spending (excluding equipment and infrastructure), of which defence takes M459bn ($40m). **Zimbabwe's** 1997 defence allocation of Z$5.4bn ($456m) covers an 18-month period to December 1998. In December 1997, the government approved a long-withheld disbursement of Z$2.5bn ($210m) to war veterans. There have been reports of acute budgetary squeeze with the army forced to furlough more than half its personnel in early 1998.

In East Africa, military spending continues to grow in Uganda, where the 1998 budget is 26% up on 1997 at USh175bn ($153m), and in Tanzania, where the combined defence and security (police) allocation of Sh204bn ($311m) accounts for 23% of the government budget. In the Horn of Africa, Sudan's civil war and spill-over armed conflict with neighbouring countries continues to drain resources, with reports indicating that up to 80% of government spending goes towards funding the war.

ARMS SALES

Arms sales to the region are hard to measure as the majority of transactions involve unreported light weapons and ammunition shipments. The most significant deliveries in 1997 were Russian MiG 23 combat aircraft, Mi 17 helicopters and heavy artillery to Angola in September 1997. Botswana has ordered 20 SK-105 light tanks from Austria for delivery in late 1998, having been prevented by the German government from securing second-hand *Leopard* 1 MBTs from Belgium. The deal follows Botswana's recent acquisition of 13 F-5 fighters from Canada, delivered in 1996–97, 36 *Scorpion* light tanks and 12 105mm L118 guns from the UK, and 155mm towed artillery from Israel. There were reports in August 1998 that Ethiopia ordered 10 second-hand MiG-21s from Romania, upgraded by Israel.

Light weapons and ordnance are supplied by regional industries as well as external sources. In addition, there is a large trade in recycled weaponry from past conflict zones for personal use as well as use by armed groups outside state control. While some of this trade is between governments and subject to export licensing and public accountability, much is unofficial or escapes government scrutiny and goes unreported. Under such conditions, it becomes difficult to distinguish between legitimate and illegal (unlicensed or subject to UN or unilateral embargo) transactions, particularly in conflict zones.

In 1997, South Africa exported military equipment to Congo-Brazzaville, **Togo**, Eritrea, DROC, Uganda and **Rwanda**, after the embargo on Rwanda was lifted by Pretoria in July 1997. Illicit transfers by private South African suppliers to rebel forces in Burundi and Angola have also been reported in 1997–98. While Russia remains the main arms supplier to the Angolan government forces, UNITA opposition forces continue to receive arms from other East European sources through African conduits, notably Togo. Zimbabwe Defence Industries is reported to have supplied large quantities of arms and equipment (funded by Harare) to Kabila's Alliance of Democratic Forces. Zimbabwe is also reported to be supplying Uganda and the Sudan Peoples' Liberation Army (SPLA). Belgian supplies for the operation of the small-arms ammunition factory at Eldoret in Kenya are now resumed. The Belgian government had withheld licences after fears that the factory would be used to supply ammunition to the troubled areas of Central Africa. Last year, Chad was reported to be an important conduit for Chinese arms sales to Sudan, DROC and the CAR, while 1998 reports indicate that Tanzania is also a channel for Chinese arms sales to Burundi government forces as well as Hutu rebels from Rwanda and Burundi based in Kenya. Romania is the latest East European arms supplier to figure in the regional arms trade, having delivered light weapons to Rwanda via Yemen in February–April 1997.

Table 31 Arms orders and deliveries, Sub-Saharan Africa, 1996–1998

Supplier	Classification	Designation	Units	Order Date	Delivery Date	Comment
Angola						
UK	tpt	C-130	6	1996	1997	First of 6 ex-RAF delivered in Nov 1997
Ukr	hel	Mi-24B	2	1996	1996	Ex-Ukr Army
RF	hel	Mi-17		1997	1997	
RF	FGA	MiG-23		1997	1997	
Botswana						
Ca	FGA	F-5	13	1996	1996	Ex-CAF; deliveries 1996–97
Indo	tpt	CN-212	2	1994	1996	
UK	APC	*Scorpion*	36	1995	1996	
A	lt tk	SK-105	20	1998	1998	Option on further 20
UK	arty	105mm L-118	12	1995	1996	

Supplier	Classification	Designation	Units	Order Date	Delivery Date	Comment
R	MRL	122mm	20	1995	1996	
RSA	trg	MB-326	6	1996	1997	Ex-SAAF
Cameroon						
Il	arty	155mm	4	1996	1997	
RSA	FGA	*Impala*	2	1996	1997	
Congo						
RSA	APC	*Mamba*	18	1996	1997	
DROC						
Cz	FGA	L-39	3	1997	1997	Acquired during civil war
Bel	arty	BM-21	6	1996	1997	
Eritrea						
It	trg	MB-339C	6	1996	1997	Last delivered Oct 1997
RF	hel	Mi-24	4	1995	1996	
RF	hel	Mi-17	4	1995	1996	
PRC	tpt	Y-11	4	1995	1996	
Il	PCI			1996	1997	Fast patrol boats
Ethiopia						
US	tpt	C-130B	4	1995	1998	Ex-USAF
R	ftr	MiG-21	10	1998		Upgraded by Il
Mauritius						
Chl	OPV	*Vigilant*-class	1	1994	1996	Ca design; for Coast Guard
Fr	hel	AS-555	1	1995	1997	
Niger						
LAR	tpt	An-26	1	1996	1997	Aid to replace crashed C-130
Rwanda						
RSA	APC	RG-31 *Nyala*	6	1995	1996	
Senegal						
Fr	LAV	AML-90	10	1997	1998	
Sierra Leone						
Slvk	APC	OT-64	10	1995	1996	
PRC	PFI	*Haizhui*	1	1995	1997	Replacement for *Shanghai II* boats
RSA						
Domestic	hel	*Rooivalk*	12	1996	1999	
US	tpt	C-130	5	1995	1997	7 C-130s also upgraded
Domestic	PGM	*Raptor* 1		1985	1998	Stand-off glide bomb
CH	trg	PC-7	60	1993	1995	Deliveries to 1997
Domestic	APC	*Mamba*	586	1993	1998	Deliveries 1993–98
Domestic	arty	LIW 35 DPG		1998		Twin 35mm gun completed first trials
Domestic	APC	*Rooikat*	19	1996	1997	
Rwanda						
Slvk	MRL	122mm	5	1996	1997	Type 70 122 MRL
RSA	APC	RG31	4	1997	1997	
Sudan						
PRC	FGA	F-7	6	1995	1996	Further deliveries reported in early 1998
PRC	mor	82 & 120mm	100	1995	1996	
Ukr	AIFV	BMP-2	6	1995	1996	
Bel	MBT	T-55	9	1995	1996	
Bel	hel	Mi-24B	6	1995	1996	
Togo						
Bg	arty	122mm	6	1996	1997	
Pl	APC	BWP-2	20	1996	1997	
Uganda						
RSA		*Chubby*		1998		Mine clearing vehicle
Zimbabwe						
US	tpt	C-130	2	1995	1996	
It	trg	SF-260F	6	1997	1998	

Dollar GDP figures in Sub-Saharan Africa are usually based on African Development Bank estimates. In several cases, the dollar GDP values do not reflect the exchange rates shown in the country entry.

Angola

	1996	1997	1998	1999
GDP	ε$7.0bn	ε$7.7bn		
per capita	$1,300	$1,400		
Growth	7.2%	6.5%		
Inflation	4,145%	111.2%		
Debt	$10.6bn	$11.0bn		
Def exp	ε$450m	ε$658m		
Def bdgt			$380m	
FMA[a] (Fr)	$0.02m	$0.02m	$0.05m	
(US)	$0.1m	$0.2m	$0.2m	$0.2m
$1 = kwanza				
	ε32,000	ε266,000	ε257,000	

[a] UNAVEM III **1996** $344m. UNOMA **1997** $135m

Population		11,700,000	
(Ovimbundu 37%, Kimbundu 25%, Bakongo 13%)			
Age	*13–17*	*18–22*	*23–32*
Men	637,000	538,000	815,000
Women	639,000	542,000	832,000

Total Armed Forces

ACTIVE ε114,000

A unified national army, including UNITA troops, is to form with a str of ε90,000. As of early May 1998, some 11,000 UNITA soldiers had been integrated into the Army, whilst a further 34,000 had been demobilised. The integration process has been concluded.

Army ε106,000

35 regts (armd and inf – str vary)

EQUIPMENT†
MBT 100 T-54/-55, ε150 T-62, ε50 T-72
AIFV 50+ BMP-1, ε100 BMP-2
RECCE some 40+ BRDM-2
APC 100 BTR-60/-152
TOWED ARTY 300: incl **76mm**: M-1942 (ZIS-3); **85mm**: D-44; **122mm**: D-30; **130mm**: M-46
ASLT GUNS 100mm: SU-100
MRL 122mm: 50 BM-21, 40 RM-70; **240mm**: some BM-24
MOR 82mm: 250; **120mm**: 40+ M-43
ATGW AT-3 *Sagger*
RCL 500: **82mm**: B-10; **107mm**: B-11
AD GUNS 200+: **14.5mm**: ZPU-4; **23mm**: ZU-23-2, 20 ZSU-23-4 SP; **37mm**: M-1939; **57mm**: S-60 towed, 40 ZSU-57-2 SP
SAM SA-7/-14

Navy ε1,500–2,000

BASES Luanda (HQ), Lobito, Namibe (not usually occupied)
PATROL, INSHORE 7†
4 *Mandume* Type 31.6m PCI, 3 *Patrulheiro* PCI
MINE COUNTERMEASURES 1†
1 Sov *Yevgenya* MHC
AMPHIBIOUS 1†
1 Sov *Polnochny* LSM, capacity 100 tps, 6 tk
Plus craft

COASTAL DEFENCE
SS-C-1 *Sepal* at Luanda

Air Force/Air Defence 6,000†

45 cbt ac, 28 armed hel
FGA 18 MiG-23, 9 Su-22, 4 Su-25
FTR 4 MiG-21 MF/bis
CCT/RECCE 10* PC-7/9
MR 2 EMB-111, 1 F-27MPA, 1 *King Air* B-200B
ATTACK HEL 15 Mi-25/35, 5 SA-365M (guns), 6 SA-342 (HOT), 2 Mi-24B
TPT 5 Am-2, 4 An-26, 6 BN-2, 8 C-212, 4 PC-6B, 2 L-100-20, 6 C-130
HEL 8 AS-565, 30 IAR-316, 6 Mi-8/17
TRG 3 Cessna 172, 6 Yak-11
AD 5 SAM bn†, 10 bty with 40 SA-2, 12 SA-3, 25 SA-6, 15 SA-8, 20 SA-9, 10 SA-13
MISSILES
  ASM HOT, AT-2 *Swatter*
  AAM AA-2 *Atoll*

Forces Abroad

DROC: ε2,000 tps

Paramilitary 15,000

RAPID-REACTION POLICE 15,000

Opposition

UNITA (Union for the Total Independence of Angola)
Some 11,000 tps have been integrated into the national army. UNITA claims to have completed the demobilisation process, but an ε25–30,000 fully equipped tps plus spt militia are reported.
FLEC (Front for the Liberation of the Cabinda Enclave) ε600 (claims 5,000)
small arms only

Foreign Forces

UN (UNOMA): 661 tps; 92 mil obs from 30 countries

Benin

	1996	1997	1998	1999
GDP	fr1.1tr	fr1.3tr		
	($2.1bn)	($2.2bn)		
per capita	$1,800	$1,800		
Growth	5.5%	5.8%		
Inflation	4.9%	4.1%		
Debt	$1.6bn	$1.6bn		
Def exp	εfr14bn	εfr16bn		
	($26m)	($27m)		
Def bdgt			εfr17bn	
			($28m)	
FMA (Fr)	$1.0m	$1.0m	$1.0m	
(US)	$0.3m	$0.4m	$0.4m	$0.4m
$1 = CFA fr	512	584	608	
Population		5,965,000		
Age	*13–17*	*18–22*	*23–32*	
Men	352,000	285,000	408,000	
Women	362,000	300,000	443,000	

Total Armed Forces

ACTIVE ε4,800

Terms of service conscription (selective), 18 months

Army 4,500

3 inf, 1 AB/cdo, 1 engr bn, 1 armd sqn, 1 arty bty
EQUIPMENT
  LT TK 20 PT-76 (op status uncertain)
  RECCE 9 M-8, 14 BRDM-2, 10 VBL
  TOWED ARTY 105mm: 4 M-101, 12 L-118
  MOR 81mm
  RL 89mm: LRAC

Navy† ε150

BASE Cotonou
PATROL, INSHORE 1
  1 *Patriote* PFI (Fr 38m)<, 4 Sov *Zhuk*< PFI (non-op)

Air Force† 150

no cbt ac
AC 2 An-26, 2 C-47, 1 *Commander* 500B, 2 Do-128, 1
  Boeing 707-320 (VIP), 1 F-28 (VIP), 1 DHC-6
HEL 2 AS-350B, 1 SE-3130

Paramilitary 2,500

GENDARMERIE 2,500
4 mobile coy

Botswana

	1996	1997	1998	1999
GDP	P14.6bn	P18.0bn		
	($3.4bn)	($3.7bn)		
per capita	$5,400	$5,700		
Growth	7.0%	6.6%		
Inflation	10.3%	8.5%		
Debt	$613m	$550m		
Def exp	P760m	P879m		
	($229m)	($241m)		
Def bdgt			P868m	
			($222m)	
FMA (US)	$0.5m	$0.4m	$0.5m	$0.5m
$1 = pula	3.32	3.65	3.91	
Population		1,614,000		
Age	*13–17*	*18–22*	*23–32*	
Men	98,000	83,000	125,000	
Women	100,000	84,000	130,000	

Total Armed Forces

ACTIVE 9,000

Army 8,500 (to be 10,000)

2 inf, 1 arty bde: 4 inf bn, 1 armd recce, 2 fd arty, 2 AD
arty, 1 engr regt, 1 cdo unit

EQUIPMENT
  LT TK 36 *Scorpion* (incl variants), 30 SK-105
    Kuerassier
  RECCE 12 V-150 *Commando* (some with **90mm** gun),
    RAM-V
  APC 30 BTR-60 (15 serviceable)
  TOWED ARTY 105mm: 36 lt, 4 Model 56 pack;
    155mm: Soltam (reported)
  MOR 81mm: 10; **120mm:** 6 M-43
  ATGW 6 TOW (some SP on V-150)
  RL 73mm: RPG-7
  RCL 84mm: 88 *Carl Gustav*
  AD GUNS 20mm: 7 M-167
  SAM 12 SA-7, 10 SA-16, 5 *Javelin*

Air Wing 500

40 cbt ac, no armed hel
FTR/FGA 12 F-5A, 3 F-5B
TPT 1 sqn with 2 CN-235, 2 *Skyvan* 3M, 1 BAe 125-800,
  2 CN-212 (VIP), 1 *Gulfstream* IV, 11* BN-2 *Defender*
TRG 3 sqn
  2 with 2 Cessna 152, 7* PC-7
  1 with 7*† BAC-167 Mk 90
HEL 1 sqn with 2 AS-350L, 5 Bell 412

Paramilitary 1,000

POLICE MOBILE UNIT 1,000
(org in territorial coy)

Burkina Faso

	1996	1997	1998	1999
GDP	fr1.7tr	fr1.8tr		
	($2.8bn)	($3.0bn)		
per capita	$900	$900		
Growth	6.2%	5.5%		
Inflation	6.2%	2.1%		
Debt	$1.3bn	$1.3bn		
Def exp	εfr34bn	εfr39bn		
	($67m)	($67m)		
Def bdgt			εfr45bn	
			($74m)	
FMA (Fr)	$1.1m	$1.0m	$1.0m	
$1 = CFA fr	512	584	608	
Population		11,467,000		
Age	*13–17*	*18–22*	*23–32*	
Men	661,000	538,000	806,000	
Women	639,000	528,000	828,000	

Total Armed Forces

ACTIVE 10,000
(incl *Gendarmerie*)

Army 5,600

6 Mil Regions • 5 inf 'regt': HQ, 3 'bn' (each 1 coy of 5 pl) • 1 AB 'regt': HQ, 1 'bn', 2 coy • 1 tk 'bn': 2 pl • 1 arty 'bn': 2 tp • 1 engr 'bn'
EQUIPMENT
    RECCE 15 AML-60/-90, 24 EE-9 *Cascavel*, 10 M-8, 4 M-20, 30 *Ferret*
    APC 13 M-3
    TOWED ARTY 105mm: 8 M-101; **122mm**: 6
    MRL 107mm: PRC Type-63
    MOR 81mm: Brandt
    RL 89mm: LRAC, M-20
    RCL 75mm: PRC Type-52
    AD GUNS 14.5mm: 30 ZPU
    SAM SA-7

Air Force 200

5 cbt ac, no armed hel
TPT 1 *Beech Super King*, 1 *Commander* 500B, 2 HS-748, 2 N-262, 1 Boeing 727 (VIP)
LIAISON 2 Cessna 150/172, 1 SA-316B, 1 AS-350, 3 Mi-8/17
TRG 5* SF-260W/WL

Forces Abroad

UN AND PEACEKEEPING
CAR (MINURCA): 126 tps

Paramilitary

GENDARMERIE 4,200
SECURITY COMPANY (CRG) 250
PEOPLE'S MILITIA (R) 45,000 trained

Burundi

	1996	1997	1998	1999
GDP	fr312bn	fr370bn		
	($1.0bn)	($1.1bn)		
per capita	$600	$600		
Growth	-8.4%	4.4%		
Inflation	12.0%	31.2%		
Debt	$1.1bn	$1.1bn		
Def exp	εfr15bn	εfr21bn		
	($50m)	($60m)		
Def bdgt			fr27bn	
			($65m)	
FMA (US)	$0.1m	$0.1m	$0.1m	
(Fr)	$1.0m			
$1 = franc	303	352	412	
Population		ε6,860,000 (Hutu 85%, Tutsi 14%)		
Age	*13–17*	*18–22*	*23–32*	
Men	411,000	332,000	514,000	
Women	375,000	305,000	478,000	

Total Armed Forces

ACTIVE ε30–43,500
(incl *Gendarmerie*)

Army ε30-40,000

5 inf bn • 2 lt armd 'bn' (sqn), 1 arty bn • 1 engr bn • some indep inf coy • 1 AD bty
RESERVES
    10 bn (reported)
EQUIPMENT
    RECCE 18 AML (6-60, 12-90), 7 Shorland, 30 BRDM-2
    APC 9 Panhard M-3, 20 BTR-40
    TOWED ARTY 122mm: 18 D-30
    MRL 122mm: 12 BM-21
    MOR 82mm: M-43; **120mm**
    RL 83mm: *Blindicide*

RCL 75mm: 15 PRC Type-52
AD GUNS 150: **14.5mm**: 15 ZPU-4; **23mm**: ZU-23; **37mm**: Type-54
SAM SA-7

AIR WING (100)

4 cbt ac, no armed hel
TRG 4* SF-260W/TP
TP 2 DC-3
HEL 3 SA-316B, 2 Mi-8

Paramilitary

GENDARMERIE ε3,500 (incl ε50 Marine Police)

BASE Bujumbura
3 *Huchan* (PRC Type 026) PHT† plus 1 LCT, 1 spt, 4 boats

Opposition

FORCES FOR THE DEFENCE OF DEMOCRACY (FDD) ε3–4,000
HUTU PEOPLE'S LIBERATION PARTY (PALIPEHUTU) armed wing (FNL) ε2–3,000

Cameroon

	1996	1997	1998	1999
GDP	fr4.5bn	fr4.8bn		
	($8.9bn)	($9.0bn)		
per capita	$2,100	$2,200		
Growth	5.0%	5.2%		
Inflation	4.3%	2.0%		
Debt	$9.5bn	$9.2bn		
Def exp	εfr114bn	εfr140bn		
	($223m)	($240m)		
Def bdgt			εfr155bn	
			($255m)	
FMA (US)	$0.1m	$0.1m	$0.1m	
(Fr)	$1.3m	$1.6m	$1.5m	
$1 = CFA fr	512	584	608	
Population		14,677,000		
Age	*13–17*	*18–22*	*23–32*	
Men	824,000	701,000	1,049,000	
Women	822,000	703,000	1,067,000	

Total Armed Forces

ACTIVE ε22,100
(incl *Gendarmerie*)

Army 11,500

8 Mil Regions each 1 inf bn under comd • Presidential

Guard: 1 guard, 1 armd recce bn, 3 inf coy • 1 AB/cdo bn • 1 arty bn (5 bty) • 5 inf bn (1 trg) • 1 AA bn (6 bty) • 1 engr bn

EQUIPMENT

RECCE 8 M-8, *Ferret*, 8 V-150 *Commando* (**20mm** gun), 5 VBL
AIFV 14 V-150 *Commando* (**90mm** gun)
APC 21 V-150 *Commando*, 12 M-3 half-track
TOWED ARTY **75mm**: 6 M-116 pack; **105mm**: 16 M-101; **130mm**: 12 Type-59
MRL **122mm**: 20 BM-21
MOR **81mm** (some SP); **120mm**: 16 Brandt
ATGW *Milan*
RL **89mm**: LRAC
RCL **57mm**: 13 PRC Type-52; **106mm**: 40 M-40A2
AD GUNS **14.5mm**: 18 PRC Type-58; **35mm**: 18 GDF-002; **37mm**: 18 PRC Type-63

Navy ε1,300

BASES Douala (HQ), Limbe, Kribi
PATROL AND COASTAL COMBATANTS 30
MISSILE CRAFT 1 *Bakassi* (Fr P-48) PFM with 2 x 4 MM-40 *Exocet* SSM
PATROL, INSHORE 3
1 *L'Audacieux* (Fr P-48) PFI, 1 *Bizerte* (Fr PR-48) PCI†, 1 *Quartier* PCI
PATROL, RIVERINE 26
20 US *Swift*-38†, 6 *Simonneau*†
AMPHIBIOUS craft only
2 LCM

Air Force 300

15 cbt ac, 4 armed hel
1 composite sqn, 1 Presidential Fleet
FGA 4† *Alpha Jet*, 5 CM-170, 6 MB-326
MR 2 Do-128D-6
ATTACK HEL 4 SA-342L (with HOT)
TPT ac 3 C-130H/-H-30, 1 DHC-4, 4 DHC-5D, 1 IAI-201, 2 PA-23, 1 *Gulfstream* III, 1 Do-128, 1 Boeing 707 **hel** 3 Bell 206, 3 SE-3130, 1 SA-318, 3 SA-319, 2 AS-332, 1 SA-365

Paramilitary

GENDARMERIE 9,000

10 regional groups; about 10 US *Swift*-38 (see Navy)

Cape Verde

	1996	1997	1998	1999
GDP	E18bn	E21bn		
	($213m)	($224m)		
per capita	$2,100	$2,100		

contd	1996	1997	1998	1999
Growth	3.0%	3.0%		
Inflation	5.9%	8.9%		
Debt	$211m	$200m		
Def exp	εE310m	εE350m		
	($4m)	($4m)		
Def bdgt			εE380m	
			($4m)	
FMA (US)	$0.1m	$0.1m	$0.1m	$0.1m
(Fr)	$0.2m	$0.1m		
$1 = escudo	83	93	98	
Population		449,000		
Age	*13–17*	*18–22*	*23–32*	
Men	26,000	22,000	36,000	
Women	27,000	24,000	40,000	

Total Armed Forces

ACTIVE ε1,100

Terms of service conscription (selective)

Army 1,000

2 inf bn gp
EQUIPMENT
 RECCE 10 BRDM-2
 TOWED ARTY 75mm: 12; 76mm: 12
 MOR 82mm: 12; 120mm: 6 M-1943
 RL 89mm: 3.5in
 AD GUNS 14.5mm: 18 ZPU-1; 23mm: 12 ZU-23
 SAM 50 SA-7

Coast Guard ε50

1 *Zhuk* PCI<, 1 *Espadarte* PCI<

Air Force under 100

no cbt ac
MR 1 Do-228

Central African Republic

	1996	1997	1998	1999
GDP	fr545bn	fr572bn		
	($1.0bn)	($1.0bn)		
per capita	$1,200	$1,200		
Growth	-2.8%	4.6%		
Inflation	4.4%	0.6%		
Debt	$927m	$919m		
Def exp	εfr15bn	εfr23bn		
	($30m)	($39m)		
Def bdgt			εfr23bn	
			($38m)	

contd	1996	1997	1998	1999
FMA[a] (US)	$0.1m	$0.2m	$0.2m	$0.1m
(Fr)	$1.8m	$2.0m	$2.0m	
$1 = CFA fr	512	584	608	

[a] MISAB 1997 $31m

Population		3,681,000		
Age	*13–17*	*18–22*	*23–32*	
Men	196,000	169,000	278,000	
Women	198,000	172,000	275,000	

Total Armed Forces

ACTIVE 4,950

(incl *Gendarmerie*)
Terms of service conscription (selective), 2 years; reserve
obligation thereafter, term n.k.

Army 2,500

1 Republican Guard regt (2 bn) • 1 territorial defence
regt (bn) • 1 combined arms regt (1 mech, 1 inf bn) • 1
spt/HQ regt • 1 Presidential Guard bn
EQUIPMENT†
 MBT 4 T-55
 RECCE 10 *Ferret*
 APC 4 BTR-152, some 10 VAB, 25+ ACMAT
 MOR 81mm; 120mm: 12 M-1943
 RL 89mm: LRAC
 RCL 106mm: 14 M-40
 RIVER PATROL CRAFT 9<

Air Force 150

no cbt ac, no armed hel
TPT 1 Cessna 337, 1 *Mystère Falcon* 20, 1 *Caravelle*
LIAISON 6 AL-60, 6 MH-1521
HEL 1 AS-350, 1 SE-3130

Paramilitary

GENDARMERIE 2,300
3 regional legions, 8 'bde'

Foreign Forces

UN (MINURCA): 1,345 tps from 10 countries

Chad

	1996	1997	1998	1999
GDP	fr568bn	fr609bn		
	($1.0bn)	($1.0bn)		
per capita	$800	$800		
Growth	3.0%	8.6%		

contd	1996	1997	1998	1999
Inflation	11.3%	5.6%		
Debt	$997m	$1,011m		
Def exp	εfr20bn	εfr25bn		
	($39m)	($43m)		
Def bdgt			εfr27bn	
			($44m)	
FMA (Fr)	$4.0m	$2.0m	$2.0m	
(US)		$0.03m	$0.1m	$0.1m
$1 = CFA fr	512	584	608	
Population		6,991,000		
Age	*13–17*	*18–22*	*23–32*	
Men	371,000	307,000	487,000	
Women	370,000	309,000	496,000	

Total Armed Forces

ACTIVE ε30,350

(incl Republican Guard)
Terms of service conscription authorised

Army ε25,000

(being re-organised)
7 Mil Regions
EQUIPMENT
  MBT 60 T-55
  AFV 4 ERC-90, some 50 AML-60/-90, 9 V-150 with
    90mm, some EE-9 *Cascavel*
  TOWED ARTY 105mm: 5 M-2
  MOR 81mm; 120mm: AM-50
  ATGW *Milan*
  RL 89mm: LRAC
  RCL 106mm: M-40A1; **112mm**: APILAS
  AD GUNS 20mm, 30mm

Air Force 350

4 cbt ac, no armed hel
TPT ac 3 C-130, 1 C-212, 1 An-26 **hel** 2 SA-316
LIAISON 2 PC-6B, 5 Reims-Cessna FTB 337
TRG 2* PC-7, 2* SF-260W

Forces Abroad

UN AND PEACEKEEPING
CAR (MINURCA): 126 tps

Paramilitary 4,500 active

REPUBLICAN GUARD 5,000
GENDARMERIE 4,500

Opposition

WESTERN ARMED FORCES str n.k.

Foreign Forces

FRANCE 800: 2 inf coy; 1 AML sqn(-); 1 C-160, 3 F-ICT, 2 F-ICR

Congo

	1996	1997	1998	1999
GDP	fr1.2tr	fr1.3tr		
	($2.8bn)	($2.9bn)		
per capita	$2,000	$2,000		
Growth	5.9%	0.3%		
Inflation	10.6%	13.1%		
Debt	$5.2bn	$4.7bn		
Def exp	εfr28bn	εfr43bn		
	($55m)	($74m)		
Def bdgt			εfr37bn	
			($61m)	
FMA (US)	$0.2m	$0.1m		
(Fr)	$1.0m	$1.0m		
$1 = CFA fr	512	584	608	
Population		2,952,000		
Age	*13–17*	*18–22*	*23–32*	
Men	168,000	138,000	218,000	
Women	159,000	131,000	210,000	

Total Armed Forces

ACTIVE ε10,000

Army 8,000

2 armd bn • 2 inf bn gp (each with lt tk tp, 76mm gun bty) • 1 inf bn • 1 arty gp (how, MRL) • 1 engr bn • 1 AB/cdo bn
EQUIPMENT†
  MBT 25 T-54/-55, 15 PRC Type-59 (some T-34 in
    store)
  LT TK 10 PRC Type-62, 3 PT-76
  RECCE 25 BRDM-1/-2
  APC M-3, 50 BTR (30 -60, 20 -152)
  TOWED ARTY 76mm: M-1942; **100mm**: 10 M-1944;
    122mm: 10 D-30; **130mm**: 5 M-46; **152mm**: some
    D-20
  MRL 122mm: 8 BM-21; **140mm**: BM-14-16
  MOR 82mm; 120mm: 10 M-43
  RCL 57mm: M-18
  ATK GUNS 57mm: 5 M-1943
  AD GUNS 14.5mm: ZPU-2/-4; **23mm**: ZSU-23-4 SP;
    37mm: 28 M-1939; **57mm**: S-60; **100mm**: KS-19

Navy† ε800

BASE Pointe Noire
PATROL AND COASTAL COMBATANTS ε6
PATROL, INSHORE 6
  3 *Marien N'gouabi* PFI (Sp *Barcelo* 33m)†
  3 Sov *Zhuk* PFI<†
PATROL, RIVERINE n.k.
  boats only

Air Force† 1,200

12 cbt ac, no armed hel
FGA 12 MiG-21
TPT 5 An-24, 1 An-26, 1 Boeing 727, 1 N-2501
TRG 4 L-39
HEL 2 SA-316, 2 SA-318, 1 SA-365, 2 Mi-8
MISSILES
AAM AA-2 *Atoll*

Forces Abroad

UN AND PEACEKEEPING
ANGOLA (UNOMA): 2 obs

Paramilitary 2,000 active

GENDARMERIE 2,000
20 coy
PEOPLE'S MILITIA 3,000
being absorbed into national Army
PRESIDENTIAL GUARD
(forming)

Côte D'Ivoire

	1996	1997	1998	1999
GDP	fr5.5tr	fr6.0tr		
	($10.7bn)	($11.7bn)		
per capita	$1,500	$1,600		
Growth	6.5%	7.0%		
Inflation	2.5%	5.2%		
Debt	$19bn	$21bn		
Def exp	εfr48bn	εfr59bn		
	($94m)	($101m)		
Def bdgt			εfr70bn	
			($115m)	
FMA (US)	$0.2m	$0.2m	$0.2m	$0.2m
(Fr)	$2.5m	$2.1m	$2.0m	
$1 = CFA fr	512	584	608	
Population		15,967,000		
Age	*13–17*	*18–22*	*23–32*	
Men	943,000	745,000	1,093,000	
Women	941,000	748,000	1,084,000	

Total Armed Forces

ACTIVE ε13,900
(incl Presidential Guard, *Gendarmerie*)
Terms of service conscription (selective), 6 months

RESERVES 12,000

Army 6,800

4 Mil Regions • 1 armd, 3 inf bn, 1 arty gp • 1 AB, 1
AA, 1 engr coy
EQUIPMENT
  LT TK 5 AMX-13
  RECCE 7 ERC-90 *Sagaie*, 16 AML-60/-90, 10 *Mamba*
  APC 16 M-3, 13 VAB
  TOWED ARTY 105mm: 4 M-1950
  MOR 81mm; 120mm: 16 AM-50
  RL 89mm: LRAC
  RCL 106mm: M-40A1
  AD GUNS 20mm: 16, incl 6 M-3 VDA SP; **40mm**: 5
  L/60

Navy ε900

BASE Locodjo (Abidjan)
PATROL AND COASTAL COMBATANTS 4
MISSILE CRAFT 2 *L'Ardent* (Fr *Auroux* 40m) with 4
  SS 12M SSM
PATROL, INSHORE 2 *Le Vigilant* (Fr SFCN 47m) PCI
AMPHIBIOUS 1
  1 *L'Eléphant* (Fr *Batral*) LSM, capacity 140 tps, 7 tk,
  hel deck, plus some 8 craft

Air Force 700

5† cbt ac, no armed hel
FGA 1 sqn with 5† *Alpha Jet*
TPT 1 hel sqn with 1 SA-318, 1 SA-319, 1 SA-330, 4 SA
  365C
PRESIDENTIAL FLT ac 1 F-28, 1 *Gulfstream* IV, 3
  Fokker 100 **hel** 1 SA-330
TRG 3 Beech F-33C, 2 Reims Cessna 150H
LIAISON 1 Cessna 421, 1 *Super King Air* 200

Forces Abroad

UN AND PEACEKEEPING
CAR (MINURCA): 233 tps

Paramilitary

PRESIDENTIAL GUARD 1,100

GENDARMERIE 4,400
VAB APC, 4 patrol boats
MILITIA 1,500

Foreign Forces

FRANCE 500: 1 marine inf bn; 1 AS-555 hel

Democratic Republic of Congo

	1996	1997	1998	1999
GDP	$6.0bn	$5.8bn		
per capita	$500	$500		
Growth	0.9%	-5.7%		
Inflation	659%	176%		
Debt	$13bn	$15bn		
Def exp	ε$170m	ε$308m		
Def bdgt[a]			ε$250m	
FMA (US)				$0.1m
$1 = new zaire[b]				
	ε50,000	ε94,000	ε138,000	

[a] Defence outlays **January–June 1998** $135m
[b] Congolese franc introduced in July 1998: CF1 =
US$1.43 (CF1 = NZ100,000)

Population		47,742,000	
Age	*13–17*	*18–22*	*23–32*
Men	2,822,000	2,260,000	3,307,000
Women	2,795,000	2,256,000	3,336,000

Total Armed Forces

ACTIVE ε50,000

Army ε50,000

10 inf, 1 Presidential Guard bde
1 armd bde (forming)
EQUIPMENT†
MBT 20 PRC Type-59 (being refurbished), some 40
  PRC Type-62
RECCE† 60 AML (30 -60, 30 -90)
APC 12 M-113, 12 YW-531, 60 Panhard M-3, some
  Casspir
TOWED ARTY 75mm: 30 M-116 pack; **85mm**: 20
  Type-56; **122mm**: 20 M-1938/D-30, 15 Type-60;
  130mm: 8 Type-59
MRL 107mm: 20 Type 63; **122mm**: 10 BM-21
MOR 81mm; 107mm: M-30; **120mm**: 50 Brandt
RCL 57mm: M-18; **75mm**: M-20; **106mm**: M-40A1
AD GUNS 14.5mm: ZPU-4; **37mm**: 40 M-1939/
  Type 63; **40mm**: L/60
SAM SA-7

Navy 90†

BASES Coast Banana **River** Boma, Matadi, Kinshasa
Lake Tanganyika (4 boats) Kalémié
PATROL AND COASTAL COMBATANTS 7

PATROL, INSHORE 7
5 PRC *Shanghai* II PFI
2 *Swiftships*<, plus about 6 armed boats

Paramilitary

NATIONAL POLICE incl Rapid Intervention Police
(National and Provincial forces)

Foreign Forces

ANGOLA: ε2,000. **UGANDA**: ε500. **ZIMBABWE**: ε600

Djibouti

	1996	1997	1998	1999
GDP	fr68bn	fr71bn		
	($384m)	($402m)		
per capita	$900	$900		
Growth	-5.1%	1.0%		
Inflation	4.0%	3.7%		
Debt	$241m	$248m		
Def exp	εfr3.7bn	εfr3.6bn		
	($21m)	($20m)		
Def bdgt			εfr3.5bn	
			($20m)	
FMA (US)	$0.2m	$0.2m	$0.1m	$0.1m
(Fr)	$1.2m	$1.1m	$1.0m	
$1 = franc	178	178	178	

Population		708,000 (Somali 60%, Afar 35%)	
Age	*13–17*	*18–22*	*23–32*
Men	38,000	32,000	52,000
Women	37,000	33,000	56,000

Total Armed Forces

ACTIVE ε9,600
(incl *Gendarmerie*)

Army ε8,000

3 Comd (North, Central, South) • 1 inf bn, incl mor,
ATK pl • 1 arty bty • 1 armd sqn • 1 border cdo bn • 1
AB coy • 1 spt bn
EQUIPMENT
RECCE 15 VBL, 4 AML-60†
APC 12 BTR-60 (op status uncertain)
TOWED ARTY 122mm: 6 D-30
MOR 81mm: 25; **120mm**: 20 Brandt
RL 73mm; 89mm: LRAC
RCL 106mm: 16 M-40A1
AD GUNS 20mm: 5 M-693 SP; **23mm**: 5 ZU-23;
  40mm: 5 L/70

Navy ε200

BASE Djibouti
PATROL CRAFT, INSHORE 7
5 *Sawari* PCI<, 2 *Moussa Ali* PCI<, plus boats

Air Force 200

no cbt ac or armed hel
TPT 2 C-212, 2 N-2501F, 2 Cessna U206G, 1 *Socata* 235GT
HEL 3 AS-355, 1 AS-350; Mi-8, Mi-24 hel from **Eth**

Paramilitary ε3,000 active

GENDARMERIE (Ministry of Defence) 1,200
1 bn, 1 patrol boat
NATIONAL SECURITY FORCE (Ministry of Interior)
ε3,000

Foreign Forces

FRANCE 1,500: incl 1 marine inf (-); 1 Foreign Legion
regt (-), 1 sqn: **ac** 6 *Mirage* F-1C (plus 4 in store), 1 C-
160 **hel** 3 SA-319, 2 SA-330

Equatorial Guinea

	1996	1997	1998	1999
GDP	fr140bn	fr225bn		
	($230m)	($385m)		
per capita	$1,300	$2,400		
Growth	29%	76%		
Inflation	6.0%	4.9%		
Debt	$282m	$291m		
Def exp	εfr1.2bn	εfr3bn		
	($2.3m)	($5.1m)		
Def bdgt			εfr3.0bn	
			($5.0m)	
FMA (Fr)	$0.2m	$0.1m	$0.1m	
$1 = CFA fr	512	584	608	
Population		501,000		
Age	13–17	18–22	23–32	
Men	26,000	21,000	36,000	
Women	26,000	22,000	36,000	

Total Armed Forces

ACTIVE 1,320

Army 1,100

3 inf bn
EQUIPMENT
RECCE 6 BRDM-2

APC 10 BTR-152

Navy† 120

BASES Malabo (Santa Isabel), Bata
PATROL CRAFT, INSHORE 2 PCI<

Air Force 100

no cbt ac or armed hel
TPT ac 1 Yak-40, 3 C-212, 1 Cessna-337 **hel** 2 SA-316

Paramilitary

GUARDIA CIVIL
2 coy
COAST GUARD
1 PCI<

Eritrea

	1996	1997	1998	1999
GDP	ε$714m	ε$780m		
per capita	$400	$400		
Growth	6.8%	7.0%		
Inflation	9.3%	3.2%		
Debt	ε$46m	n.k.		
Def exp	ε$60m	ε$65m		
Def bdgt			ε$65m	
FMA (US)	$4.3m	$0.4m	$0.4m	$0.4m
$ = nakfa	6.4	7.2	7.2	
Population	ε3,889,000			

(Tigrinya 50%, Tigre and Kunama 40%, Afar 4%,
Saho 3%)

Age	13–17	18–22	23–32
Men	231,000	193,000	294,000
Women	229,000	192,000	292,000

Total Armed Forces

ACTIVE ε47,100 (ε20,000 conscripts)
Terms of service 18 months (6 month mil trg)
RESERVES ε120,000 (reported)
Eritrea became independent from Ethiopia on 27 April 1993.
Total holdings of army assets n.k.

Army ε46,000

5 div (4 inf 1 cdo)
EQUIPMENT
MBT T-54/-55
RECCE BRDM-2
AIFV/APC BMP-1, BTR-60

TOWED ARTY **85mm**: D-44; **122mm**: D-30; **130mm**: M-46
MRL 122mm: BM-21
MOR 120mm; 160mm
RL 73mm: RPG-7
ATGW AT-3 *Sagger*

Navy 1,100

BASES Massawa (HQ), Assab, Dahlak
FRIGATES 1
1 *Zerai Deres* (Sov *Petya* II) with 2 ASW RL, 5 406mm TT†
PATROL AND COASTAL COMBATANTS 12
TORPEDO CRAFT 1 *Mol* PFT† with 4 533mm TT
PATROL, INSHORE 11
1 Mol PFT, 2 Sov Zhuk<, 4 *Super Dvora* PCF<, 1 *Osa* II PFM, 3 *Swiftships* PCI
AMPHIBIOUS 8
3 LCT (1 *Fredic* and 2 *Chamo* (Ministry of Transport)), 1 *Polnocny* LSM, 4 LCM
SUPPORT AND MISCELLANEOUS 1
1 AOT

Air Force

15† cbt ac
FTR/FGA 2† MiG-23, 8† MiG-21
TPT 3 Y-12, 1 IAI-1125
TRG 6 L-90 *Redigo*, 5* MB-339CE
HEL 4 Mi-17

Ethiopia

	1996	1997	1998	1999
GDP	EB38bn	EB42bn		
	($6.1bn)	($6.5bn)		
per capita	$500	$500		
Growth	10.6%	5.3%		
Inflation	0.9%	-6.4%		
Debt	$10bn	$10bn		
Def exp	EB790m	εEB900m		
	($124m)	($139m)		
Def bdgt			εEB890m	
			($131m)	
FMA (US)	$7.3m	$0.3m	$0.5m	$0.6m
$1 = birr	6.35	6.47	6.78	
Population	ε55,000,000			

(Oromo 40%, Amhara and Tigrean 32%, Sidamo 9%, Shankella 6%, Somali 6%, Afar 4%)

Age	*13–17*	*18–22*	*23–32*
Men	3,571,000	2,903,000	4,380,000
Women	3,437,000	2,768,000	4,216,000

Total Armed Forces

ACTIVE ε120,000

The Ethiopian armed forces were formed following Eritrea's declaration of independence in April 1993. Extensive demobilisation of former members of the Tigray People's Liberation Front (TPLF) has taken place, while efforts to introduce a 'national balance' are being made involving recruitment from other ethnic groups. The armed forces are still in transition. Ethiopia auctioned off its naval assets in Sep 1996. Reports indicate that large quantities of eqpt are in preservation. Numbers in service should be treated with caution.

Army ε100,000

Being re-org to consist of 3 Mil Regions each with corps HQ (each corps 2 divs, 1 reinforced mech bde); strategic reserve div of 6 bde will be located at Addis Ababa
MBT ε350 T-54/-55, T-62
RECCE/AIFV/APC ε200, incl BRDM, BMP, BTR-60/-152
TOWED ARTY **76mm**: ZIS-3; **85mm**: D-44; **122mm**: D-30/M-30; **130mm**: M-46
MRL BM-21
MOR **81mm**: M-1/M-29; **82mm**: M-1937; **120mm**: M-1938
ATGW AT-3 *Sagger*
RCL **82mm**: B-10; **107mm**: B-11
AD GUNS **23mm**: ZU-23, ZSU-23-4 SP; **37mm**: M-1939; **57mm**: S-60
SAM 20 SA-2, 30 SA-3, 300 SA-7, SA-9

Air Force

† 63 cbt ac, 24 armed hel
Most of the Air Force is grounded. Air Force activity is believed to be limited to re-org, trg and maint. Types and numbers of ac are assessed as follows:
FGA 40 MiG-21MF, 18 MiG-23BN, 5 MiG-27
TPT 4 C-130B, 6 An-12, 2 DH-6, 1 Yak-40 (VIP), 2 Y-12
TRG 10 L-39, 10 SF-260
ATTACK HEL 24 Mi-24
TPT HEL 22 Mi-8

Gabon

	1996	1997	1998	1999
GDP	fr2.9tr	fr3.5tr		
	($5.6bn)	($6.0bn)		
per capita	$5,300	$5,500		
Growth	3.1%	4.5%		
Inflation	5.1%	3.5%		
Debt	$4.2bn	$3.9bn		
Def exp	εfr57bn	εfr67bn		
	($111m)	($115m)		

contd	1996	1997	1998	1999
Def bdgt			εfr73bn	
			($120m)	
FMA (Fr)	$1.2m	$1.0m	$1.0m	
(US)				$0.05m
$1 = CFA fr	512	584	608	
Population		1,431,000		
Age	*13–17*	*18–22*	*23–32*	
Men	69,000	56,000	93,000	
Women	70,000	58,000	97,000	

Total Armed Forces

ACTIVE ε4,700

Army 3,200

Presidential Guard bn gp (1 recce/armd, 3 inf coy, arty, AA bty), under direct Presidential control
8 inf, 1 AB/cdo, 1 engr coy

EQUIPMENT
   RECCE 14 EE-9 *Cascavel*, 24 AML-60/-90, 6 ERC-90 *Sagaie*, 12 EE-3 *Jararaca*, 14 VBL
   AIFV 12 EE-11 *Urutu* with **20mm** gun
   APC 9 V-150 *Commando*, Panhard M-3, 12 VXB-170
   TOWED ARTY 105mm: 4 M-101
   MRL 140mm: 8 *Teruel*
   MORS 81mm: 35; **120mm**: 4 Brandt
   ATGW 4 *Milan*
   RL 89mm: LRAC
   RCL 106mm: M40A1
   AD GUNS 20mm: 4 ERC-20 SP; **23mm**: 24 ZU-23-2; **37mm**: 10 M-1939; **40mm**: 3 L/70

Navy ε500

BASE Port Gentil (HQ)
PATROL AND COASTAL COMBATANTS 3
MISSILE CRAFT 1 *General Nazaire Boulingu* PFM (Fr 42m) with 4 SS 12M SSM
PATROL, COASTAL 2 *General Ba'Oumar* (Fr P-400 55m)
AMPHIBIOUS 2
   2 *President Omar Bongo* (Fr *Batral*) LST, capacity 140 tps, 7 tk; plus craft: 1 LCM

Air Force 1,000

16 cbt ac, 5 armed hel
FGA 9 *Mirage* 5 (2 -G, 4 -GII, 3 -DG)
MR 1 EMB-111
TPT 1 C-130H, 3 L-100-30, 1 EMB-110, 2 YS-11A, 1 CN-235
HELICOPTERS
   ATTACK 5 SA-342

   TPT 3 SA-330C/-H
   LIAISON 3 SA-316/-319
PRESIDENTIAL GUARD
   CCT 4 CM-170, 3 T-34
   TPT ac 1 ATR-42F, 1 EMB-110, 1 *Falcon* 900 **hel** 1 AS-332

Forces Abroad

UN AND PEACEKEEPING
CAR (MINURCA): 125 tps

Paramilitary 4,800

COAST GUARD ε2,800
boats only
GENDARMERIE 2,000
3 'bde', 11 coy, 2 armd sqn, air unit with 1 AS-355, 2 AS-350

Foreign Forces

FRANCE 600: 1 marine inf bn **ac** 1 C-160 **hel** 1 AS-555

The Gambia

	1996	1997	1998	1999
GDP	D3.7bn	D4.0bn		
	($374m)	($396m)		
per capita	$1,100	$1,100		
Growth	3.2%	3.8%		
Inflation	5.5%	2.9%		
Debt	$452m	$470m		
Def exp	εD143m	εD150m		
	($15m)	($15m)		
Def bdgt			εD156m	
			($15m)	
$1 = dalasi	9.8	10.2	10.1	
Population		1,168,000		
Age	*13–17*	*18–22*	*23–32*	
Men	63,000	52,000	79,000	
Women	63,000	51,000	79,000	

Total Armed Forces

ACTIVE 800

Gambian National Army 800

Presidential Guard (reported) • 2 inf bn • engr sqn

MARINE UNIT (about 70)

BASE Banjul
PATROL CRAFT, INSHORE 5

 2 *Gonjur* (PRC *Shanghai* II) PFI, 3 PFI<, boats

Ghana

	1996	1997	1998	1999
GDP	C10.6tr	C14.0tr		
	($8.5bn)	($8.9bn)		
per capita	$2,200	$2,200		
Growth	5.2%	3.0%		
Inflation	34.0%	27.9%		
Debt	$6.2bn	$6.4bn		
Def exp[a]	εC197bn	εC275bn		
	($120m)	($134m)		
Def bdgt		C95bn	C133bn	
		($46m)	($58m)	
FMA (US)	$0.3m	$0.2m	$0.3m	$0.4m
$1 = cedi	1,637	2,050	2,300	

[a] Defence and security budget including police

Population		18,899,000		
Age	*13–17*	*18–22*	*23–32*	
Men	1,116,000	921,000	1,373,000	
Women	1,110,000	919,000	1,385,000	

Total Armed Forces

ACTIVE 7,000

Army 5,000

2 Comd HQ • 2 bde (6 inf bn (incl 1 UNIFIL, 1
ECOMOG), spt unit) • 1 Presidential Guard, 1 trg bn •
1 recce regt (3 sqn) • 1 arty 'regt' (1 arty, 2 mor bty) • 1
AB force (incl 1 para coy) • 1 SF bn • 1 fd engr regt
(bn)

EQUIPMENT
 RECCE 3 EE-9 *Cascavel*
 AIFV 50 MOWAG *Piranha*
 TOWED ARTY 122mm: 6 D-30
 MOR 81mm: 50; **120mm**: 28 Tampella
 RCL 84mm: 50 *Carl Gustav*
 AD GUNS 14.5mm: 4 ZPU-2, ZPU-4; **23mm**: 4 ZU-
 23-2
 SAM SA-7

Navy 1,000

COMMANDS Western and **Eastern**
BASES HQ Western Sekondi **HQ Eastern** Tema
PATROL AND COASTAL COMBATANTS 4
PATROL, COASTAL 2 *Achimota* (Ge *Lürssen* 57m)
 PFC
PATROL, INSHORE 2 *Dzata* (Ge *Lürssen* 45m) PCI

Air Force 1,000

17 cbt ac, no armed hel
TPT 5 Fokker (4 F-27, 1 F-28 (VIP)); 1 C-212, 6 *Skyvan*
HEL 4 AB-212 (1 VIP, 3 utl), 2 Mi-2, 4 SA-319
TRG 12* L-29, 2* MB 339F, 3* MB-326K

Forces Abroad

UN AND PEACEKEEPING

ANGOLA (UNOMA): 3 obs. **CROATIA** (UNMOP): 2
obs. **FYROM** (UNPREDEP): 1 obs. **LEBANON**
(UNIFIL): 644; 1 inf bn. **IRAQ/KUWAIT** (UNIKOM): 6
obs. **SIERRA LEONE** (ECOMOG): ε1,000. **TAJIKIS-
TAN** (UNMOT): 4 obs. **WESTERN SAHARA**
(MINURSO): 13 incl 6 obs

Guinea

	1996	1997	1998	1999
GDP	fr3.5tr	fr3.7tr		
	($3.0bn)	($3.2bn)		
per capita	$800	$900		
Growth	4.6%	4.7%		
Inflation	4.7%	5.2%		
Debt	$3.2bn	$3.2bn		
Def exp	εfr56bn	εfr59bn		
	($57m)	($54m)		
Def bdg			εfr65bn	
			($55m)	
FMA (US)	$0.04m	$0.2m	$0.2m	$0.2m
(Fr)	$1.3m	$1.1m	$1.1m	
$1 = franc	1,004	1,100	1,185	

Population		7,224,000		
Age	*13–17*	*18–22*	*23–32*	
Men	410,000	339,000	509,000	
Women	418,000	343,000	516,000	

Total Armed Forces

ACTIVE 9,700

(perhaps 7,500 conscripts)
Terms of service conscription, 2 years

Army 8,500

1 armd bn • 1 arty bn • 1 cdo bn • 1 engr bn • 5 inf bn
• 1 AD bn • 1 SF bn

EQUIPMENT†
 MBT 30 T-34, 8 T-54
 LT TK 20 PT-76
 RECCE 25 BRDM-1/-2, 2 AML-90
 APC 40 BTR (16 -40, 10 -50, 8 -60, 6 -152)
 TOWED ARTY 76mm: 8 M-1942; **85mm**: 6 D-44;
 122mm: 12 M-1931/37

MOR **82mm**: M-43; **120mm**: 20 M-1938/43
RCL **82mm**: B-10
ATK GUNS **57mm**: M-1943
AD GUNS **30mm**: twin M-53; **37mm**: 8 M-1939;
  57mm: 12 S-60, PRC Type-59; **100mm**: 4 KS-19
SAM SA-7

Navy 400

BASES Conakry, Kakanda
PATROL AND COASTAL COMBATANTS 7
  PATROL, INSHORE 7
  Some 2 Sov *Bogomol* PFI (1 prob non-op), 2 Sov
  Zhuk, 1 US *Swiftships 77*, 2 other PCI<

Air Force† 800

8 cbt ac, no armed hel
FGA 4 MiG-17F, 4 MiG-21
TPT 4 An-14, 1 An-24
TRG 2 MiG-15UTI
HEL 1 IAR-330, 1 Mi-8, 1 SA-316B, 1 SA-330, 1 SA-
  342K
MISSILES
  AAM AA-2 *Atoll*

Forces Abroad

GUINEA-BISSAU: some 400
UN AND PEACEKEEPING
WESTERN SAHARA (MINURSO): 3 obs

Paramilitary 2,600 active

PEOPLE'S MILITIA 7,000
GENDARMERIE 1,000
REPUBLICAN GUARD 1,600

Guinea-Bissau

	1996	1997	1998	1999
GDP	$281m	$301m		
per capita	$900	$900		
Growth	4.6%	5.1%		
Inflation	65.6%	16.8%		
Debt	$937m	$921m		
Def exp	ε$8m	ε$8m		
Def bdgt			ε$8m	
FMA (Fr)	$0.1m	$0.1m	$0.1m	
(US)	$0.1m	$0.1m	$0.1m	$0.1m
$1 = CFA fr			608	
Population		1,152,000		
Age	*13–17*	*18–22*	*23–32*	
Men	65,000	57,000	89,000	
Women	63,000	53,000	84,000	

Total Armed Forces

ACTIVE (all services, incl *Gendarmerie*, form part of the armed forces) ε9,250
Terms of service conscription (selective)
A revolt by dissident army tps is currently being quelled by tps from Senegal and Guinea. Manpower and equipment totals should be treated with caution.

Army 6,800

1 armd 'bn' (sqn) • 5 inf, 1 arty bn • 1 recce, 1 engr coy
EQUIPMENT
  MBT 10 T-34
  LT TK 20 PT-76
  RECCE 10 BRDM-2
  APC 35 BTR-40/-60/-152, 20 PRC Type-56
  TOWED ARTY 85mm: 8 D-44; **122mm**: 18 M-1938/
    D-30
  MOR 82mm: M-43; **120mm**: 8 M-1943
  RL 89mm: M-20
  RCL 75mm: PRC Type-52; **82mm**: B-10
  AD GUNS 23mm: 18 ZU-23; **37mm**: 6 M-1939;
    57mm: 10 S-60
  SAM SA-7

Navy ε350

BASE Bissau
PATROL AND COASTAL COMBATANTS 8
PATROL, INSHORE 8
  2 *Alfeite* PCC<, 1 ex-Ge *Kondor* I PCI†, 1 Sov
  Bogomol†, 1 Indian SDB Mk III PCI, some 3 PCI†<
  (incl 1 customs service)
AMPHIBIOUS I
  1 LCM

Air Force 100

3 cbt ac, no armed hel
FTR/FGA 3 MiG-17
HEL 1 SA-318, 2 SA-319

Forces Abroad

UN AND PEACEKEEPING
ANGOLA (UNOMA): 2 obs

Paramilitary

GENDARMERIE 2,000

Foreign Forces

ε2,400 tps incl Sen (ε2,000), Gui (400)

Kenya

	1996	1997	1998	1999
GDP	sh518bn	sh576bn		
	($9.5bn)	($9.8bn)		
per capita	$1,400	$1,400		
Growth	4.2%	1.3%		
Inflation	6.4%	12.0%		
Debt	$6.9bn	$6.8bn		
Def exp	εsh12.1bn	εsh13.8bn		
	($212m)	($235m)		
Def bdgt			εsh13.0bn	
			($216m)	
FMA (US)	$0.3m	$0.3m	$0.4m	$0.4m
$1 = shilling	57	59	60	
Population	29,946,000 (Kikuyu ε22–32%)			
Age	13–17	18–22	23–32	
Men	1,919,000	1,614,000	2,306,000	
Women	1,913,000	1,617,000	2,328,000	

Total Armed Forces

ACTIVE 24,200

Army 20,500

1 armd bde (3 armd bn) • 2 inf bde (1 with 2, 1 with 3 inf bn) • 1 indep inf bn • 1 arty bde (2 bn) • 1 AD arty bn • 1 engr bde • 2 engr bn • 1 AB bn • 1 indep air cav bn

EQUIPMENT
MBT 76 Vickers Mk 3
RECCE 72 AML-60/-90, 12 Ferret, 8 Shorland
APC 52 UR-416, 10 Panhard M-3 (in store)
TOWED ARTY 105mm: 40 lt, 8 pack
MOR 81mm: 50; 120mm: 12 Brandt
ATGW 40 Milan, 14 Swingfire
RCL 84mm: 80 Carl Gustav
AD GUNS 20mm: 50 TCM-20, 11 Oerlikon; 40mm: 13 L/70

Navy 1,200

BASE Mombasa
PATROL AND COASTAL COMBATANTS 8
MISSILE CRAFT 6
2 Nyayo (UK Vosper 57m) PFM with 4 Ottomat SSM, 1 Mamba, 3 Madaraka (UK Brooke Marine 37m/32m), PFM with 4 Gabriel II SSM
PATROL, OFFSHORE 1 Gondam
PATROL, INSHORE 1 Simba with 2 40mm gun
AMPHIBIOUS 2
2 Galana LCM
SUPPORT AND MISCELLANEOUS 1
1 tug

Air Force 2,500

30 cbt ac, 34 armed hel
FGA 10 F-5 (8 -E, 2 -F)
TPT 7 DHC-5D, 6 Do-28D-2, 1 PA-31, 3 DHC-8, 1 Fokker 70 (VIP)
ATTACK HEL 11 Hughes 500MD (with TOW), 8 Hughes 500ME, 15 Hughes 500M
TPT HEL 9 IAR-330, 3 SA-330, 1 SA-342
TRG 12 Bulldog 103/127, 8* Hawk Mk 52, 12* Tucano, **hel** 2 Hughes 500D
MISSILES
ASM AGM-65 Maverick, TOW
AAM AIM-9 Sidewinder

Forces Abroad

UN AND PEACEKEEPING
ANGOLA (UNOMA): 3 obs. **CROATIA** (UNMOP): 1 obs. **FYROM** (UNPREDEP): 2 obs. **IRAQ/KUWAIT** (UNIKOM): 4 obs. **SIERRA LEONE** (UNOMSIL): 2 obs. **WESTERN SAHARA** (MINURSO): 8 obs

Paramilitary 5,000

POLICE GENERAL SERVICE UNIT 5,000
AIR WING ac 7 Cessna lt **hel** 3 Bell (1 206L, 2 47G)
POLICE NAVAL SQN/CUSTOMS about 5 PCI< (2 Lake Victoria), some 12 boats

Lesotho

	1996	1997	1998	1999
GDP	M3.7bn	M4.1bn		
	($637m)	($697m)		
per capita	$2,100	$2,300		
Growth	13.1%	7.2%		
Inflation	8.9%	8.9%		
Debt	$654m	$600m		
Def exp	M137m	M148m		
	($32m)	($34m)		
Def bdgt			M170m	
			($34m)	
FMA (US)	$0.07m	$0.08m	$0.08m	$0.08m
$1 = maloti	4.3	4.6	5.0	
Population		2,131,000		
Age	13–17	18–22	23–32	
Men	123,000	105,000	158,000	
Women	121,000	105,000	160,000	

Total Armed Forces

ACTIVE 2,000

Army 2,000

7 inf coy • 1 spt coy (incl recce/AB, 81mm mor) • 1 air sqn

EQUIPMENT

RECCE 10 Il *Ramta*, 8 Shorland, AML-90
MOR 81mm: some
RCL 106mm: M-40
AC 3 C-212 *Aviocar* 300, 1 Cessna 182Q
HEL 2 Bo-105 CBS, 1 Bell 47G, 1 Bell 412 SP, 1 Bell 412EP

Liberia

	1996	1997	1998	1999
GDP	ε$1.1bn	ε$1.1bn		
per capita	$1,000	$1,000		
Growth	ε2.7%	ε4.0%		
Inflation	ε10%	ε11%		
Debt	$2.1bn	$2.0bn		
Def exp	ε$45m	ε$45m		
Def bdgt			ε$34m	
FMAᵃ (US)	$15m			$0.1m
US$1 = L$	1.0	1.0	1.0	

ᵃ UNOMIL **1996** $34m **1997** $19m
ECOMOG **1994–97** ε$30m annually

Population	ε3,400,000			
(Americo-Liberians 5%)				
Age	*13–17*	*18–22*	*23–32*	
Men	161,000	131,000	179,000	
Women	156,000	125,000	169,000	

Total Armed Forces

ACTIVE some 14,000 reported

On 19 August 1995, the warring factions signed a peace accord. Under a transitional plan negotiated in 1996 between the principal armed factions, it was agreed to disarm and demobilise all militias. Implementation of the plan is now complete, with most ECOMOG forces being withdrawn. Nga continues to maintain a garrison of some 5,000 tps. Unified armed forces are to form with a strength of some 5,000.

Madagascar

	1996	1997	1998	1999
GDP	fr16tr	fr18tr		
	($4.4bn)	($4.6bn)		
per capita	$600	$700		
Growth	2.0%	3.7%		
Inflation	19.8%	4.5%		
Debt	$4.2bn	$4.1bn		
Def exp	εfr150bn	εfr190bn		
	($37m)	($37m)		

contd	1996	1997	1998	1999
Def bdgt			εfr220bn	
			($44m)	
FMA (US)	$0.1m	$0.1m	$0.1m	$0.1m
(Fr)	$1.5m	$1.2m	$1.2m	
$1 = franc	4,061	5,091	5,020	
Population		14,694,000		
Age	*13–17*	*18–22*	*23–32*	
Men	847,000	701,000	1,062,000	
Women	825,000	687,000	1,055,000	

Total Armed Forces

ACTIVE some 21,000

Terms of service conscription (incl for civil purposes), 18 months

Army some 20,000

2 bn gp • 1 engr regt

EQUIPMENT

LT TK 12 PT-76
RECCE 8 M-8, ε20 M-3A1, 10 *Ferret*, ε35 BRDM-2
APC ε30 M-3A1 half-track
TOWED ARTY 76mm: 12 ZIS-3; 105mm: some M-101; 122mm: 12 D-30
MOR 82mm: M-37; 120mm: 8 M-43
RL 89mm: LRAC
RCL 106mm: M-40A1
AD GUNS 14.5mm: 50 ZPU-4; 37mm: 20 Type-55

Navy† 500

(incl some 100 Marines)
BASES Diégo-Suarez, Tamatave, Fort Dauphin, Tuléar, Majunga
PATROL CRAFT 1
 1 *Malaika* (Fr PR48m) PCI†
AMPHIBIOUS 3
 1 *Toky* (Fr *Batram*) LSM, capacity 30 tps, 4 tk plus craft: 1 LCT (Fr *Edic*), 1 LCA
SUPPORT AND MISCELLANEOUS 1
 1 tpt/trg

Air Force 500

12 cbt ac, no armed hel
FGA 1 sqn with 4 MiG-17F, 8 MiG-21FL
TPT 4 An-26, 1 BN-2, 2 C-212, 2 Yak-40 (VIP)
HEL 1 sqn with 6 Mi-8
LIAISON 1 Cessna 310, 2 Cessna 337, 1 PA-23
TRG 4 Cessna 172

Paramilitary 7,500

GENDARMERIE 7,500
incl maritime police with some 5 PCI<

patrol), 1 *Skyvan* 3M, 4 Cessna **hel** 2 AS-365

Malawi

	1996	1997	1998	1999
GDP	K34bn	K37bn		
	($1.9bn)	($2.1bn)		
per capita	$800	$800		
Growth	10.4%	6.6%		
Inflation	37.7%	7.2%		
Debt	$2.3bn	$2.3bn		
Def exp	εK360m	εK420m		
	($24m)	($23m)		
Def bdgt			εK650m	
			($25m)	
FMA (US)	$0.2m	$0.2m	$0.3m	$0.3m
FMA (ROC)		$2.0m		
$1 = kwacha	15.3	18.0	25.5	
Population		10,273,000		
Age	*13–17*	*18–22*	*23–32*	
Men	611,000	493,000	738,000	
Women	605,000	494,000	774,000	

Total Armed Forces

ACTIVE (all services form part of the Army) 5,000

Army 5,000

2 bde HQ, 3 inf, 1 spt, 1 AB bn

EQUIPMENT (less than 50% serviceability)
  RECCE 20 *Fox*, 8 *Ferret*, 12 *Eland*
  TOWED ARTY 105mm: 9 lt
  MOR 81mm: 8 L16
  SAM 15 *Blowpipe*

MARITIME WING (220)
BASE Monkey Bay (Lake Nyasa)
  PATROL CRAFT 2
  1 *Kasungu* PCI†, 1 *Namacurra* PCI<, some boats
AMPHIBIOUS
  1 LCU

AIR WING (80)
no cbt ac, no armed hel
  TPT AC 1 sqn with 3 Do-228, 1 Do-28D, 1 *King Air*
  C90, 1 HS-125-800
  TPT HEL 2 SA-330F, 1 AS-365N

Paramilitary 1,000

MOBILE POLICE FORCE (MPF) 1,000
8 Shorland armd car **ac** 3 BN-2T *Defender* (border

Mali

	1996	1997	1998	1999
GDP	fr1.3tr	fr1.4tr		
	($2.3bn)	($2.5bn)		
per capita	$600	$600		
Growth	4.0%	6.7%		
Inflation	6.5%	2.8%		
Debt	$3.0bn	$3.0bn		
Def exp	εfr21bn	εfr25bn		
	($41m)	($43m)		
Def bdgt			εfr27bn	
			($44m)	
FMA (US)	$0.2m	$0.2m	$0.3m	$0.3m
(Fr)	$0.7m	$1.0m	$1.0m	
$1 = CFA fr	512	584	608	
Population		10,858,000 (Tuareg 6–10%)		
Age	*13–17*	*18–22*	*23–32*	
Men	601,000	490,000	733,000	
Women	624,000	511,000	774,000	

Total Armed Forces

ACTIVE (all services form part of the Army) about 7,350
Terms of service conscription (incl for civil purposes), 2 years (selective)

Army about 7,350

2 tk • 4 inf • 1 AB, 2 arty, 1 engr, 1 SF bn • 2 AD, 1 SAM bty

EQUIPMENT†
  MBT 21 T-34, T-54/-55 reported
  LT TK 18 Type-62
  RECCE 20 BRDM-2
  APC 30 BTR-40, 10 BTR-60, 10 BTR-152
  TOWED ARTY 85mm: 6 D-44; 100mm: 6 M-1944;
    122mm: 8 D-30; 130mm: M-46 reported
  MRL 122mm: 2 BM-21
  MOR 82mm: M-43; 120mm: 30 M-43
  AD GUNS 37mm: 6 M-1939; 57mm: 6 S-60
  SAM 12 SA-3

NAVY† (about 50)
BASES Bamako, Mopti, Segou, Timbuktu
PATROL CRAFT, RIVERINE 3<

AIR FORCE (400)
16† cbt ac, no armed hel
FGA 5 MiG-17F
FTR 11 MiG-21
TPT 2 An-24, 1 An-26
TRG 6 L-29, 1 MiG-15UTI, 4 Yak-11, 2 Yak-18

HEL 1 Mi-8, 1 AS-350

Forces Abroad

UN AND PEACEKEEPING
ANGOLA (UNOMA): 3 obs. CAR (MINURCA): 125 tps

Paramilitary 4,800

GENDARMERIE 1,800
8 coy
REPUBLICAN GUARD 2,000
MILITIA 3,000
NATIONAL POLICE 1,000

Mauritius

	1996	1997	1998	1999
GDP	R77bn	R86bn		
	($4.0bn)	($4.2bn)		
per capita	$14,100	$15,100		
Growth	4.7%	5.6%		
Inflation	6.5%	6.9%		
Debt	$1.8bn	$1.8bn		
Def exp	εR1.8bn	εR1.9bn		
	($92m)	($87m)		
Def bdgt			R351m	
			($15m)	
FMA (US)		$0.02m	$0.05m	$0.05m
$1 = rupee	18.0	20.6	23.1	
Population		1,168,000		
Age	*13–17*	*18–22*	*23–32*	
Men	53,000	54,000	101,000	
Women	52,000	53,000	102,000	

Total Armed Forces

ACTIVE Nil

Paramilitary ε1,800

SPECIAL MOBILE FORCE 1,300
6 rifle, 2 mob, 1 engr coy, spt tp
  APC 10 VAB
  MOR 81mm: 2
  RL 89mm: 4 LRAC

COAST GUARD ε500
  PATROL CRAFT 13
  1 *Vigilant* (Ca *Guardian* design) OPV, capability for 1 hel

9 *Marlin* (Ind *Mandovi*) PCI
1 SDB-3 PFI
2 Sov *Zhuk* PCI<, plus 26 boats
MR 1 Do-228-101, 1 BN-2T *Defender*, 3 SA-316B

POLICE AIR WING
  2 *Alouette* III

Mozambique

	1996	1997	1998	1999
GDP	M14tr	M17tr		
	($1.7bn)	($1.9bn)		
per capita	$900	$1,000		
Growth	6.4%	8.0%		
Inflation	44.6%	16.5%		
Debt	$5.8bn	$7.0bn		
Def exp	M704bn	M830bn		
	($62m)	($72m)		
Def bdgt			M459bn	
			($40m)	
FMA (US)	$0.2m	$0.2m	$0.2m	$0.2m
$1 = metical	11,294	11,544	11,495	
Population		18,755,000		
Age	*13–17*	*18–22*	*23–32*	
Men	1,085,000	902,000	1,381,000	
Women	1,098,000	918,000	1,419,000	

Total Armed Forces

ACTIVE ε5,100–6,100
Terms of service conscription, 2-3 years

Army ε4–5,000 (to be 12–15,000)

5 inf, 3 SF, 1 log bn • 1 engr coy
EQUIPMENT† (ε10% or less serviceability)
  MBT some 80 T-54/-55 (300+ T-34, T-54/-55 non-op)
  RECCE 30 BRDM-1/-2
  AIFV 40 BMP-1
  APC 150+ BTR-60, 100 BTR-152
  TOWED ARTY 100+: 76mm: M-1942; 85mm: 150+: D-44, D-48, Type-56; 100mm: 24 M-1944; 105mm: M-101; 122mm: M-1938, D-30; 130mm: 24 M-46; 152mm: 20 D-1
  MRL 122mm: 30 BM-21
  MOR 82mm: M-43; 120mm: M-43
  RCL 75mm; 82mm: B-10; 107mm: B-11
  AD GUNS 400: 20mm: M-55; 23mm: 90 ZU-23-2; 37mm: 100 M-1939; 57mm: 90: S-60 towed, ZSU-57-2 SP
  SAM SA-7

Navy 100

Sub-Saharan Africa

BASES Maputo (HQ), Beira, Nacala, Pemba, Inhambane **Ocean** Quelimane **Lake Nyasa** Metangula
PATROL AND COASTAL COMBATANTS 3
   PATROL, INSHORE 3 PCI< (non-op) Lake Malawi

Air Force 1,000

(incl AD units); no cbt ac, 4† armed hel
TPT 1 sqn with 5 An-26, 2 C-212, 4 PA-32 *Cherokee*
TRG 1 Cessna 182, 7 ZLIN-326
HEL
   ATTACK 4† Mi-24
   TPT 5 Mi-8
   AD SAM †SA-2, 10 SA-3

Namibia

	1996	1997	1998	1999
GDP	N$14bn	N$15bn		
	($2.4bn)	($2.6bn)		
per capita	$4,600	$4,800		
Growth	3.0%	4.0%		
Inflation	8.0%	6.9%		
Debt	$64m	$107m		
Def exp	N$312m	N$416m		
	($73m)	($90m)		
Def bdgt			N$443m	
			($89m)	
FMA (US)	$0.2m	$0.2m	$0.2m	$0.2m
US$1 = N$	4.3	4.6	5.0	
Population		1,787,000		
Age	*13–17*	*18–22*	*23–32*	
Men	105,000	87,000	132,000	
Women	103,000	86,000	131,000	

Total Armed Forces

ACTIVE 9,000

Army 9,000

5 inf bn • 1 cbt spt bde with 1 arty, 1 AD, 1 ATK regt

EQUIPMENT
   MBT some T-34, T-54/-55 (serviceability doubtful)
   RECCE BRDM-2
   APC some *Casspir, Wolf*, BTR-152
   MRL 122mm: 5 BM-21
   MOR 81mm; **82mm**
   RCL 82mm: B-10
   ATK GUNS 57mm; **76mm**: M-1942 (ZIS-3)
   AD GUNS 14.5mm: 50 ZPU-4; **23mm**: 15 *Zumlac* (ZU-23-2) SP
   SAM SA-7

AIR WING
   ac 1 *Falcon* 900, 1 *Learjet* 36, 6 Cessna 337./02-A **hel** 4 SA-319 *Alouette*

Coast Guard ε100

(fishery protection, part of the Ministry of Fisheries)
BASE Walvis Bay
PATROL CRAFT 3
   1 *Osprey*, 1 *Oryx*, 1 *Cuito Cuanavale* PCO
   1 Cessna, 1 hel

Forces Abroad

UN AND PEACEKEEPING
ANGOLA (UNOMA): 140 tps

Niger

	1996	1997	1998	1999
GDP	fr860bn	fr922bn		
	($1.6bn)	($1.6bn)		
per capita	$800	$800		
Growth	3.3%	3.5%		
Inflation	5.3%	4.5%		
Debt	$1.6bn	$1.6bn		
Def exp	εfr11bn	εfr13bn		
	($21m)	($22m)		
Def bdgt			εfr13bn	
			($23m)	
FMA (US)	$0.01m			
(Fr)	$1.9m	$1.1m	$1.1m	
(LAR)		$4.0m		
$1 = CFA fr	512	584	608	
Population		9,687,000 (Tuareg 8–10%)		
Age	*13–17*	*18–22*	*23–32*	
Men	558,000	450,000	661,000	
Women	562,000	457,000	685,000	

Total Armed Forces

ACTIVE 5,300
Terms of service selective conscription (2 years)

Army 5,200

3 Mil Districts • 4 armd recce sqn • 7 inf, 2 AB, 1 engr coy
EQUIPMENT
   RECCE 90 AML-90, 35 AML-60/20, 7 VBL
   APC 22 M-3
   MOR 81mm: 19 Brandt; **82mm**: 17; **120mm**: 4 Brandt
   RL 89mm: 36 LRAC

RCL **75mm**: 6 M-20; **106mm**: 8 M-40
ATK GUNS 85mm; 90mm
AD GUNS 20mm: 39 incl 10 M-3 VDA SP

Air Force 100

no cbt ac or armed hel
TPT 1 C-130H, 1 Do-28, 1 Do-228, 1 Boeing 737-200
(VIP), 1 An-26
LIAISON 2 Cessna 337D

Paramilitary 5,400

GENDARMERIE 1,400

REPUBLICAN GUARD 2,500

NATIONAL POLICE 1,500

Nigeria

	1996	1997	1998	1999
GDP	ε$45bn	ε$49bn		
per capita	$1,200	$1,300		
Growth	4.6%	5.1%		
Inflation	29.2%	20.0%		
Debt	$31bn	$35bn		
Def exp	ε$1.9bn	ε$2.0bn		
Def bdgt			εN19.5bn	
			($891m)	
$1 = nairaᵃ	21.9	21.9	21.9	

ᵃ Market rate **1998** $1 = N85

Population	ε110,000,000

(*North* Hausa and Fulani *South-west* Yoruba *South-east* Ibo; these tribes make up ε65% of population)

Age	13–17	18–22	23–32
Men	7,133,000	6,088,000	9,086,000
Women	7,141,000	6,186,000	9,449,000

Total Armed Forces

ACTIVE 77,000

RESERVES
planned, none org

Army 62,000

1 armd div (2 armd bde) • 1 composite div (1 mot inf,
1 amph bde, 1 AB bn) • 2 mech div (each 1 mech, 1
mot inf bde) • 1 Presidential Guard bde (2 bn) • 1 AD
bde • each div 1 arty, 1 engr bde, 1 recce bn
EQUIPMENT
MBT 50 T-55†, 150 Vickers Mk 3
LT TK 140 *Scorpion*
RECCE ε120 AML-60, 60 AML-90, 55 *Fox*, 75 EE-9

Cascavel, 72 VBL (reported)
APC 10 *Saracen*, 300 Steyr 4K-7FA, 70 MOWAG
Piranha, EE-11 *Urutu* (reported)
TOWED ARTY **105mm**: 200 M-56; **122mm**: 200 D-
30/-74; **130mm**: 7 M-46; **155mm**: 24 FH-77B (in
store)
SP ARTY **155mm**: 27 *Palmaria*
MRL **122mm**: 11 APR-21
MOR **81mm**: 200; **82mm**: 100; **120mm**: 30+
RCL **84mm**: *Carl Gustav*; **106mm**: M-40A1
AD GUNS **20mm**: some 60; **23mm**: ZU-23, 30 ZSU-
23-4 SP; **40mm**: L/60
SAM 48 *Blowpipe*, 16 *Roland*
SURV RASIT (veh, arty)

Navy 5,500

(incl Coast Guard)
BASES Lagos, HQ Western Comd Apapa **HQ
Eastern Comd** Calabar **Akwa Ibom state** Warri, Port
Harcourt, Ibaka
FRIGATES 1
  1 *Aradu* (Ge MEKO 360)† with 1 *Lynx* hel, 2 x 3
  ASTT; plus 8 *Otomat* SSM, 1 127mm gun
PATROL AND COASTAL COMBATANTS 35
CORVETTES 1† *Erinomi* (UK Vosper Mk 9) with 1 x 3
  Seacat, 1 76mm gun, 1 x 2 ASW mor† (plus 1 non-op)
MISSILE CRAFT 4
  2 *Ekpe* (Ge Lürssen 57m) PFM with 4 *Otomat* SSM
  (non-op)
  2† *Ayam* (Fr *Combattante*) PFM with 2 x 2 MM-38
  Exocet SSM
PATROL, INSHORE 30
  4 *Makurdi* (UK *Brooke Marine* 33m) (non-op)
  6 *Simmoneau* 500
  5 *Van Mill*
  some 15 PCI<
MINE COUNTERMEASURES 2
  2 *Ohue* (mod It *Lerici*) MCC (non-op)
AMPHIBIOUS 1
  1 *Ambe* (Ge) LST (1 non-op), capacity 220 tps 5 tk
SUPPORT AND MISCELLANEOUS 5
  1 *Lana* AGHS, 3 tugs, 1 nav trg

NAVAL AVIATION
HEL 2† *Lynx* Mk 89 MR/SAR

Air Force 9,500

91† cbt ac, 15† armed hel
FGA/FTR 3 sqn
  1 with 19 *Alpha Jet* (FGA/trg)
  1 with 6† MiG-21MF, 4† MiG-21U, 12† MiG-21B/FR
  1 with 15† *Jaguar* (12 -SN, 3 -BN)
ARMED HEL †15 Bo-105D
TPT 2 sqn with 5 C-130H, 3 -H-30, 17 Do-128-6, 2 Do-
228 (VIP), 5 G-222

PRESIDENTIAL FLT **ac** 1 Boeing 727, 1 *Falcon*, 2
Gulfstream, 1 BAe 125-700, 1 BAe 125-1000 **hel** 4 AS-
332, 2 SA-330
TRG ac† 23* L-39MS, 12* MB-339AN, 59 Air *Beetle* **hel**
14 Hughes 300
AAM AA-2 *Atoll*

Forces Abroad

UN AND PEACEKEEPING
ANGOLA (UNOMA): 4 obs. CROATIA (UNMOP): 1
obs. FYROM (UNPREDEP): 1 obs. IRAQ/KUWAIT
(UNIKOM): 5 obs. LIBERIA (ECOMOG): ε5,000.
SIERRA LEONE: ε9,000. TAJIKISTAN (UNMOT): 8
obs. WESTERN SAHARA (MINURSO): 5 obs

Paramilitary

COAST GUARD
incl in Navy
PORT SECURITY POLICE ε2,000
about 60 boats and some 5 hovercraft
SECURITY AND CIVIL DEFENCE CORPS (Ministry
of Internal Affairs)
POLICE UR-416, 70 AT-105 *Saxon*† APC **ac** 1 Cessna
500, 3 Piper (2 *Navajo*, 1 *Chieftain*) **hel** 4 Bell (2 -
212, 2 -222)

Rwanda

	1996	1997	1998	1999
GDP	fr427bn	fr562bn		
	($1.4bn)	($1.9bn)		
per capita	$500	$500		
Growth	12.0%	10.9%		
Inflation	17.0%	11.0%		
Debt	$1.0bn	$1.1bn		
Def exp	εfr29bn	εfr31bn		
	($95m)	($103m)		
Def bdgt			εfr39bn	
			($112m)	
FMA (US)	$0.2m	$0.4m	$0.3m	$0.3m
$1 = franc	307	302	348	
Population	ε8,309,000 (Hutu 80%, Tutsi 19%)			
Age	*13–17*	*18–22*	*23–32*	
Men	526,000	424,000	612,000	
Women	542,000	440,000	640,000	

Total Armed Forces

ACTIVE ε30–47,000 (all services, incl *Gendarmerie*, form
part of the Army)

Army ε30–40,000

6 inf bde, 1 mech inf regt
EQUIPMENT
MBT 12 T-54/-55
RECCE AML-245, 15 AML-60, AML-90, 16 VBL
APC some BTR, Panhard, 6 RG-31 *Nyala*
TOWED ARTY 105mm†; 122mm: 6
MOR 81mm: 8; 120mm
AD GUNS 14.5mm; 23mm; 37mm
SAM SA-7
HEL 6 Mi-24 (reported)

Paramilitary 7,000

GENDARMERIE 7,000

Opposition

ε7,000 former govt tps dispersed in DROC. Some have
returned to Rwanda with associated *Interahamwe*
militia. Equipped with small arms and lt mor only.

Senegal

	1996	1997	1998	1999
GDP	fr2.5tr	fr2.7tr		
	($4.3bn)	($4.5bn)		
per capita	$1,700	$1,800		
Growth	5.7%	5.2%		
Inflation	2.9%	1.8%		
Debt	$3.7bn	$3.6bn		
Def exp	fr38bn	fr41bn		
	($74m)	($71m)		
Def bdgt			fr40bn	
			($66m)	
FMA (US)	$0.6m	$0.7m	$0.7m	$0.7m
(Fr)	$2.8m	$2.1m	$1.8m	
$1 = CFA fr	512	584	608	
Population	9,199,000			

(Wolof 36%, Fulani 17%, Serer 17%, Toucouleur 9%,
Mandingo 9%, Diola 9%, of which 30–60% in
Casamance)

Age	*13–17*	*18–22*	*23–32*
Men	559,000	455,000	664,000
Women	553,000	452,000	670,000

Total Armed Forces

ACTIVE 11,000
Terms of service conscription, 2 years selective

RESERVES n.k.

Army 10,000 (3,500 conscripts)

7 Mil Zone HQ • 4 armd bn • 1 engr bn • 6 inf bn • 1 Presidential Guard (horsed) • 1 arty bn • 3 construction coy • 1 cdo bn • 1 AB bn • 1 engr bn

EQUIPMENT
RECCE 10 M-8, 4 M-20, 30 AML-60, 27 AML-90
APC some 16 Panhard M-3, 12 M-3 half-track
TOWED ARTY 18: **75mm**: 6 M-116 pack; **105mm**: 6 M-101/HM-2; **155mm**: ε6 Fr Model-50
MOR 81mm: 8 Brandt; **120mm**: 8 Brandt
ATGW 4 *Milan*
RL 89mm: 31 LRAC
AD GUNS 20mm: 21 M-693; **40mm**: 12 L/60

Navy 600

BASES Dakar, Casamance
PATROL AND COASTAL COMBATANTS 10
PATROL, COASTAL 2
    1 *Fouta* (Dk *Osprey*) PCC
    1 *Njambuur* (Fr SFCN 59m) PFC
PATROL, INSHORE 8
    3 *Saint Louis* (Fr 48m) PCI, 3 *Senegal* II PFI<, 2 *Alioune Samb* PCI<
AMPHIBIOUS craft only
    1 LCT

Air Force 400

8 cbt ac, no armed hel
MR/SAR 1 EMB-111
TPT 1 sqn with 6 F-27-400M, 1 Boeing 727-200 (VIP), 1 DHC-6 *Twin Otter*
HEL 2 SA-318C, 2 SA-330, 1 SA-341H
TRG 4* CM-170, 4* R-235 *Guerrier*, 2 *Rallye* 160, 2 R-235A

Forces Abroad

GUINEA-BISSAU: ε2,000

UN AND PEACEKEEPING
ANGOLA (UNOMA): 4 obs. **CAR** (MINURCA): 129 tps. **IRAQ/KUWAIT** (UNIKOM): 5 obs

Paramilitary ε5,800

GENDARMERIE ε5,800
12 VXB-170 APC
CUSTOMS
2 PCI<, boats

Opposition

CASAMANCE MOVEMENT OF DEMOCRATIC FORCES 2–3,000 eqpt with lt wpns

Foreign Forces

FRANCE 1,300: 1 marine inf bn; **ac** 1 *Atlantic*, 1 C-160 **hel** 1 SA-319

Seychelles

	1996	1997	1998	1999
GDP	SR2.5bn	SR2.6bn		
	($342m)	($355m)		
per capita	$4,000	$4,100		
Growth	1.5%	2.0%		
Inflation	-1.0%	0.6%		
Debt	$148m	$147m		
Def exp	SR52m	SR51m		
	($11m)	($10m)		
Def bdgt			εSR54m	
			($10m)	
FMA (US)	$0.03m	$0.08m	$0.08m	$0.08m
$1 = rupee	5.0	5.0	5.2	
Population		73,000		
Age	*13–17*	*18–22*	*23–32*	
Men	4,000	4,000	7,000	
Women	4,000	4,000	7,000	

Total Armed Forces

ACTIVE (all services, incl Coast Guard, form part of the Army) 400

Army 200

1 inf coy
1 sy unit
EQUIPMENT†
    RECCE 6 BRDM-2
    MOR 82mm: 6 M-43
    RL RPG-7
    AD GUNS 14.5mm: ZPU-2/-4; **37mm**: M-1939
    SAM 10 SA-7

Paramilitary 250 active

NATIONAL GUARD 250

COAST GUARD (200)
(incl 20 Air Wing and ε80 Marines)
BASE Port Victoria
PATROL, INSHORE 4
1 *Andromache* (It *Pichiotti* 42m) PFI, 1 *Gemini* PCI, 2 *Zhuk* PFI< (1 non-op)

AIR WING (20)
No cbt ac, no armed hel

MR 1 BN-2 *Defender*
TPT 1 Reims-Cessna F-406/*Caravan* 11
TRG 1 Cessna 152

Sierra Leone

	1996	1997	1998	1999
GDP	ε$776m	ε$752m		
per capita	$700	$600		
Growth	4.9%	-5.0%		
Inflation	23.2%	7.4%		
Debt	$1.2bn	$1.2bn		
Def exp	ε$46m	ε$48m		
Def bdgt			$9m	
FMA (US)	$0.13m			
$1 = leone	921	968	905	
Population	ε5,104,000			
Age	*13–17*	*18–22*	*23–32*	
Men	274,000	230,000	356,000	
Women	273,000	229,000	360,000	

Total Armed Forces

ACTIVE n.k.

Following the civil war of May–June 1997, restoration of the legitimate government of President Kabbah was achieved on 10 March 1998 by ECOWAS forces. Fighting by remnants of the AFRC and RUF with an est str of 2–4,000 is confined to the eastern border area. The army has disbanded and a new National Army is to form with a strength of some 5,000.

EQUIPMENT

MOR 81mm: 3; 82mm: 2; 120mm: 2
RCL 84mm: *Carl Gustav*
AD GUNS 12.7mm: 4; 14.5mm: 3
SAM SA-7
HEL 1 Mi-24

Navy ε200

BASE Freetown
PATROL AND COASTAL COMBATANTS 6
2 PRC *Shanghai* II PFI, 1 *Swiftship* 32m† PFI, 2 CAT 900S PC<, 1 *Fairy Marine Tracker* II

Foreign Forces

UN AND PEACEKEEPING
UN (UNOMSIL): 14 mil obs from 5 countries.
ECOMOG: tps from **Gha** ε1,000, **Nga** ε9,000 reported

Somali Republic

	1996	1997	1998	1999
GDP	ε$825m	n.k.		
per capita	$800	$800		
Growth	ε-1.0%	n.k.		
Inflation	ε17%	n.k.		
Debt	$2.6bn	$2.5bn		
Def exp	ε$40m	ε$40m		
Def bdgt			ε$40m	
$1 = shilling[a]	2,620	2,620	2,620	

[a] Market rate June **1997** $1 = 8,000 shillings

Population	ε6,000,000 (Somali 85%)		
Age	*13–17*	*18–22*	*23–32*
Men	567,000	460,000	667,000
Women	565,000	456,000	672,000

Total Armed Forces

ACTIVE Nil

Following the 1991 revolution, no national armed forces have yet been formed. The Somali National Movement has declared northern Somalia the independent 'Republic of Somaliland', while insurgent groups compete for local supremacy in the south. Heavy military equipment is in poor repair or inoperable.

Clan/Movement Groupings

'SOMALILAND' (northern Somalia) (Total armed forces reported as some 12,900)
UNITED SOMALI FRONT clan Issa **leader** Abdurahman Dualeh Ali
SOMALI DEMOCRATIC ALLIANCE clan Gadabursi
SOMALI NATIONAL MOVEMENT 5–6,000 **clan** Issaq, 3 factions (Tur, Dhegaweyne, Kahin)
UNITED SOMALI PARTY clan Midigan/Tumaal **leader** Ahmed Guure Adan

SOMALIA
SOMALI SALVATION DEMOCRATIC FRONT 3,000 **clan** Darod **leaders** Abdullah Yusuf Ahmed
UNITED SOMALI CONGRESS clan Hawiye **sub-clan** Habr Gidir **leader** Hussein Mohamed Aideed/ Osman Atto
Ali Mahdi Faction 10,000(-) **clan** Abgal **leader** Mohammed Ali Mahdi
SOMALI NATIONAL FRONT 2–3,000 **clan** Darod **sub-clan** Marehan **leader** General Omar Hagi Mohammed Hersi
SOMALI DEMOCRATIC MOVEMENT clan Rahenwein/Dighil
SOMALI PATRIOTIC MOVEMENT 2–3,000 **clan** Darod **leader** Ahmed Omar Jess

South Africa

	1996	1997	1998	1999
GDP	R543bn	R595bn		
	($126bn)	($129bn)		
per capita	$5,500	$5,700		
Growth	3.1%	1.7%		
Inflation	7.4%	8.5%		
Debt	$64bn	$67bn		
Def exp	R11.0bn	R10.7bn		
	($2.6bn)	($2.3bn)		
Def bdgt			R11.0bn	R11.5bn
			($2.3bn)	($2.3bn)
FMA (US)	$0.5m	$0.7m	$0.8m	$0.8m
$1 = rand	4.3	4.6	5.9	
Population		39,100,000		
Age	*13–17*	*18–22*	*23–32*	
Men	2,440,000	2,198,000	3,584,000	
Women	2,408,000	2,181,000	3,583,000	

Total Armed Forces

ACTIVE 82,400

(incl 1,400 MoD staff, 6,000 South African Military Health Service; ε12,100 women)
Terms of service voluntary service in 3 categories (full career, up to 10 yrs, up to 6 yrs)
Up to 35,000 personnel from non-statutory forces, incl MK, plus some 11,500 from the Homelands, were to be absorbed into the new South African National Defence Force (SANDF). Only 28,000 did so, of whom 16,600 are now SANDF members. The remainder resigned. The process is complete.

RESERVES 61,000

Army 55,600 Navy 3,900 Air Force 1,100 Medical Service (SAMHS) 400

Army 58,600

(11,100 White, 41,900 Black, 5,600 Coloured/Asian; 8,400 women)

FULL-TIME FORCE (FTF)

9 regional comd (each consists of HQ and a number of group HQ, but no tps which are provided when necessary by FTF and PTF units)
18 group HQ
1 mech inf bde HQ (designated units 1 tk, 1 armd car, 2 mech inf bn, 4 inf, 1 arty, 1 AD, 1 engr bn)
1 AB bde (1 AB bn, AB trg school)
1 SF bde (2 bn)

RESERVES

PART-TIME FORCE (PTF)(55,600)

1 div (3 bde each 1 tk, 1 armd car, 2 mech inf, 1 SP arty, 1 AD, 1 engr bn)
div tps incl: 1 armd car, 1 mech inf, 1 mot inf, 1 arty, 1

MRL, 1 AD bn
some 183 inf bn home-defence units

EQUIPMENT

MBT some 124 *Olifant* 1A/-B
RECCE 118 *Eland*-90 (in store), 188 *Rooikat*-76
AIFV 1,200 *Ratel*-20
APC 429 *Casspir*, 545 *Mamba*
TOWED ARTY 75 G-2; **155mm**: 45 G-5
SP ARTY 155mm: 41 G-6
MRL 127mm: 16 *Bateleur* (40 tube), 72 *Valkiri* (24 tube); **120mm**: 36
MOR 81mm: 1,190 (incl some SP)
ATGW ZT-3 *Swift* (52 SP), *Milan*
RL 92mm: FT-5
RCL 106mm: 100 M-40A1 (some SP)
AD GUNS 20mm: 84 *Ystervark* SP; **23mm**: 36 *Zumlac* (ZU-23-2) SP; **35mm**: 99 GDF Mk1/3, 48 GDF Mk5
SAM SA-7/-14
SURV *Green Archer* (mor), *Cymbeline* (mor)

Navy 5,500

(ε400 women)
NAVAL HQ Pretoria, Flag Officer Fleet Simons Town
FLOTILLAS submarine, strike, MCM
BASES Simon's Town, Durban (Salisbury Island)

SUBMARINES 3

3 *Maria van Riebeek* (Mod Fr *Daphné*) with 550mm TT (2 in refit, 1 test bed)

PATROL AND COASTAL COMBATANTS 8

MISSILE CRAFT 8 *Warrior* (Il *Reshef*) with 6–8 *Skerpioen* (Il *Gabriel*) SSM (incl 2 in reserve and 2 in refit)

MINE COUNTERMEASURES 8

4 *Kimberley* (UK *Ton*) MSC (incl 1 in refit) plus 2 in reserve
4 *River* (Ge *Navors*) MHC (incl 2 in refit)

SUPPORT AND MISCELLANEOUS 41

1 *Drakensberg* AO with 2 hel and extempore amph capability (perhaps 60 tps and 2 small landing craft – in maintenance)
1 *Outeniqua* AO with similar capability as *Drakensberg* (in maintenance)
1 AGHS
1 diving spt
1 Antarctic tpt with 2 hel (operated by Ministry of Environmental Affairs)
6 LCU
3 tugs
27 harbour patrol

Air Force 10,900

(800 women); 116 cbt ac, ε14+ armed hel
2 Territorial Area Comd, log, trg comds

Flying hours 160
FTR/FGA 2 sqn
    1 sqn with 36 *Cheetah* C
    1 sqn with 33 *Impala* Mk2
TPT/TKR/EW 1 sqn with 5 Boeing 707-320 (EW/tkr)
TPT 5 sqn
    1 with 4 *Super King Air* 300, 11 Cessna-208 *Caravan*, 1
      PC-12
    1 (VIP) with 5 HS-125, 4 *Super King Air* 200, 1 *King Air*
      300, 2 *Citation* II, 2 *Falcon* 50, 1 *Falcon* 900
    1 with 11 C-47 TP
    1 with 12 C-130
    1 with 4 CASA-212, 1 CASA-235
LIAISON/FAC 14 Cessna 185A/D/E, 1 PC-12
HEL 4 sqn with 56 SA-316/-319 *Alouette* III, 41 *Oryx*
    (some armed), 9 BK-117, 1 SA-365 (VIP)
TRG COMD 5 schools
    12* *Cheetah* D, 35 *Impala* Mk1, 58 PC-7
UAV *Seeker*, *Scout*
MISSILES
    ASM AS-11/-20/-30
    AAM R-530, R-550 *Magic*, AIM-9 *Sidewinder*, V-3C
      Darter, R-*Darter*, V-3A/B *Kukri*, *Python* 3
GROUND DEFENCE
RADAR 2 Air Control Sectors, 3 fixed and some mob
    radars
SAM 2 wg (2 sqn each), SA-8/-9/-13

South African Military Health Service (SAMHS) 6,000

(2,500 women); a separate service within the SANDF. 9
regional med comd

Paramilitary

SOUTH AFRICAN POLICE SERVICE 129,300 (Public
Order Police some 8,200) has been demilitarised and
is no longer considered a paramilitary force
    AIR WING
      ac 1 Cessna 402, 1 Beech 400, 8 PC-6 **hel** 2 BK-117,
      15 Bo-105 CBS, 5 *Hughes* 500D/E
    MARINE WING
      20 PC

    COAST GUARD
    3 PCI, 3 anti-pollution

Sudan

	1996	1997	1998	1999
GDP	ε$7.0bn	ε$7.5bn		
per capita	$1,300	$1,300		
Growth	4.0%	5.5%		
Inflation	114%	32%		

contd	1996	1997	1998	1999
Debt	$17bn	$17.7bn		
Def exp	ε$404m	ε$418m		
Def bdgt			ε$300m	
$1 = pound	1,251	1,554	1,613	
Population	ε31,339,000			

(Muslim 70% *mainly in North;* Christian 10%
mainly in South; African 52% *mainly in South;* Arab
39% *mainly in North*)

Age	13–17	18–22	23–32
Men	1,837,000	1,547,000	2,327,000
Women	1,755,000	1,478,000	2,238,000

Total Armed Forces

ACTIVE 94,700
(ε20,000 conscripts)
Terms of service conscription (males 18–30), 3 years

Army ε90,000

(ε20,000 conscripts)
1 armd div • 1 recce bde • 6 inf div (regional comd) •
10+ arty bde (incl AD) • 1 AB div (incl 1 SF bde) • 3
arty regt • 1 mech inf bde • 1 engr div • 1 border gd
div • 24 inf bde
EQUIPMENT
    MBT 250 T-54/-55, 20 M-60A3, 10+ ORC Type-59
    LT TK 70 PRC Type-62
    RECCE 6 AML-90, 90 *Saladin*, 80 *Ferret*, 60 BRDM-1/-
      2
    AIFV 6 BMP-2
    APC 90 BTR-50/-152, 80 OT-62/-64, 36 M-113, 100
      V-100/-150, 120 *Walid*
    TOWED ARTY 600 incl: **85mm**: D-44; **105mm**: M-
      101 pack, Model 56 pack; **122mm**: D-74, M-1938,
      Type-54/D-30; **130mm**: M-46/PRC Type 59-1
    SP ARTY 155mm: 6 AMX Mk F-3
    MRL 107mm: 400 Type-63; **122mm**: 30 BM-21
    MOR 81mm: 120; **82mm**; **120mm**: 12 M-43, 24 AM-
      49
    ATGW 4 *Swingfire*
    RCL 106mm: 40 M-40A1
    ATK GUNS 40 incl: **76mm**: M-1942; **100mm**: M-
      1944
    AD GUNS 425 incl: **14.5mm**; **20mm**: M-167 towed,
      M-163 SP; **23mm**: ZU-23-2; **37mm**: M-1939/Type-
      63, Type-55; **57mm**: Type-59
    SAM SA-7
    SURV RASIT (veh, arty)

Navy ε1,700

BASES Port Sudan (HQ), Flamingo Bay (Red Sea),
Khartoum (Nile)

PATROL AND COASTAL COMBATANTS 7
PATROL, INSHORE 3 *Kadir* PCI< (1 non-op)
PATROL, RIVERINE 4 PCI<, about 12 armed boats
AMPHIBIOUS craft only
some 7 *Sobat* (FRY DTK-221) LCT (used for transporting stores)

Air Force 3,000

(incl Air Defence); 51† cbt ac, 9 armed hel
FGA 9 F-5 (7 -E, 2 -F), 9 PRC J-5 (MiG-17), 9 PRC J-6 (MiG-19), 6 F-7 (MiG-21)
FTR 6 MiG-23, PRC J-6 (MiG-19)
TPT 4 An-24, 4 C-130H, 4 C-212, 3 DHC-5D, 6 EMB-110P, 1 F-27, 2 *Falcon* 20/50
HEL 11 AB-412, 8 IAR/SA-330, 4 Mi-4, 8 Mi-8, 4* Mi-24B, 5* Mi-35
TRG incl 4* MiG-15UTI, 4* MiG-21U, 2* JJ-5, 2* JJ-6, 10 PT-6A
AD 5 bty SA-2 SAM (18 launchers)
AAM AA-2 *Atoll*

Paramilitary 15,000

POPULAR DEFENCE FORCE 15,000 active
85,000 reserve; mil wg of National Islamic Front; org in bn of 1,000

Opposition

NATIONAL DEMOCRATIC ALLIANCE
coalition of many groups, of which the main forces are:

SUDANESE PEOPLE'S LIBERATION ARMY
(SPLA) 20–30,000
four factions, each org in bn, operating mainly in southern Sudan; some captured T-54/-55 tks, BM-21 MRL and arty pieces, but mainly small arms plus **60mm** and **120mm** mor, **14.5mm** AA, SA-7 SAM
SUDAN ALLIANCE FORCES ε500
based in Eritrea, operate in border area
BEJA CONGRESS FORCES ε500
operates on Eritrean border
NEW SUDAN BRIGADE ε2,000
operates on Ethiopian and Eritrean borders

Foreign Forces

IRAN: some mil advisers

Tanzania

	1996	1997	1998	1999
GDP	sh3.8tr	sh4.4tr		
	($3.4bn)	($3.6bn)		
per capita	$700	$700		
Growth	4.5%	4.1%		
Inflation	21.0%	16.1%		
Debt	$7.4bn	$7.3bn		
Def exp	εsh65bn	εsh75bn		
	($112m)	($123m)		
Def bdgt			sh71bn	
			($107m)	
FMA (US)	$0.1m		$0.2m	$0.2m
$1 = shilling	580	612	656	
Population		31,098,000		
Age	*13–17*	*18–22*	*23–32*	
Men	1,794,000	1,448,000	2,165,000	
Women	1,859,000	1,524,000	2,323,000	

Total Armed Forces

ACTIVE ε34,000
Terms of service incl civil duties, 2 years
RESERVES 80,000

Army 30,000+

5 inf bde • 1 tk bde • 2 arty bn • 2 AD arty bn • 2 mor bn • 2 ATK bn • 1 engr regt (bn)
EQUIPMENT†
MBT 30 PRC Type-59 (15 op), 35 T-54 (all non-op)
LT TK 30 PRC Type-62, 40 *Scorpion*
RECCE 40 BRDM-2
APC 66 BTR-40/-152, 30 PRC Type-56
TOWED ARTY **76mm**: 45 ZIS-3; **85mm**: 80 PRC Type-56; **122mm**: 20 D-30, 100 PRC Type-54-1; **130mm**: 40 PRC Type-59-1
MRL **122mm**: 58 BM-21
MOR **82mm**: 350 M-43; **120mm**: 50 M-43
RCL **75mm**: 540 PRC Type-52

Navy† ε1,000

BASES Dar es Salaam, Zanzibar, Mwanza (Lake Victoria – 4 boats)
PATROL AND COASTAL COMBATANTS 13
TORPEDO CRAFT 2 PRC *Huchuan* PHT< with 2 533mm TT
PATROL, INSHORE 11
8 PRC *Shanghai* II PFI (6 non-op)
3 *Thornycroft* PC<
AMPHIBIOUS 2
2 *Yunnan* LCU

Air Defence Command 3,000

(incl ε2,000 AD tps); 19 cbt act, no armed hel

FTR 3 sqn with 3 PRC J-5 (MiG-17), 10 J-6 (MiG-19), 6 J-7 (MiG-21)

TPT 1 sqn with 3 DHC-5D, 1 PRC Y-5, 2 CH Y-12, 3 HS-748, 2 F-28, 1 HS-125-700

HEL 4 AB-205

LIAISON ac 5 Cessna 310, 2 Cessna 404, 1 Cessna 206 **hel** 6 Bell 206B

TRG 2 MiG-15UTI, 5 PA-28

AD GUNS 14.5mm: 40† ZPU-2/-4; **23mm:** 40 ZU-23; **37mm:** 120 PRC Type-55

SAM† 20 SA-3, 20 SA-6, 120 SA-7

Paramilitary 1,400 active

POLICE FIELD FORCE 1,400

18 sub-units incl Police Marine Unit
  MARINE UNIT (100)
    boats only
  AIR WING
    ac 1 Cessna U-206 **hel** 2 AB-206A, 2 Bell 206L, 2 Bell 47G

Togo

	1996	1997	1998	1999
GDP	fr742bn	fr817bn		
	($1.2bn)	($1.4bn)		
per capita	$1,300	$1,300		
Growth	5.9%	4.8%		
Inflation	5.6%	7.0%		
Debt	$1.5bn	$1.4bn		
Def exp	εfr14bn	εfr17bn		
	($28m)	($29m)		
Def bdgt			εfr19bn	
			($31m)	
FMA (Fr)	$1.0m	$1.0m	$1.0m	
(US)		$0.03m	$0.04m	$0.05m
$1 = CFA fr	512	584	608	
Population		4,707,000		
Age	*13–17*	*18–22*	*23–32*	
Men	276,000	214,000	315,000	
Women	280,000	226,000	343,000	

Total Armed Forces

ACTIVE some 6,950

Terms of service conscription, 2 years (selective)

Army 6,500

2 inf regt
  1 with 1 mech bn, 1 mot bn

1 with 2 armd sqn, 3 inf coy; spt units (trg)
1 Presidential Guard regt: 2 bn (1 cdo), 2 coy
1 para cdo regt: 3 coy
1 spt regt: 1 fd arty, 2 AD arty bty; 1 log/tpt/engr bn

EQUIPMENT

MBT 2 T-54/-55

LT TK 9 *Scorpion*

RECCE 6 M-8, 3 M-20, 10 AML (3 -60, 7 -90), 36 EE-9 *Cascavel*, 2 VBL

APC 4 M-3A1 half-track, 30 UR-416

TOWED ARTY 105mm: 4 HM-2

MOR 82mm: 20 M-43

RCL 57mm: 5 ZIS-2; **75mm:** 12 PRC Type-52/-56; **82mm:** 10 PRC Type-65

AD GUNS 14.5mm: 38 ZPU-4; **37mm:** 5 M-39

Navy ε200

(incl Marine Infantry unit)

BASE Lomé

PATROL CRAFT, INSHORE 2

  2 *Kara* (Fr *Esterel*) PFI<

Air Force †250

15 cbt ac, no armed hel

FGA 4 *Alpha Jet*, 4 EMB-326G

TPT 2 *Baron*, 2 DHC-5D, 1 Do-27, 1 F-28-1000 (VIP), 1 Boeing 707 (VIP), 2 Reims-Cessna 337

HEL 1 AS-332, 2 SA-315, 1 SA-319, 1 SA-330

TRG 4* CM-170, 3* TB-30

Forces Abroad

UN AND PEACEKEEPING

CAR (MINURCA): 126 tps

Paramilitary 750

GENDARMERIE (Ministry of Interior) 750

1 trg school, 2 reg sections, 1 mob sqn

Uganda

	1996	1997	1998	1999
GDP	Ush6.7tr	Ush7.4tr		
	($6.4bn)	($6.8bn)		
per capita	$1,600	$1,700		
Growth	7.0%	5.0%		
Inflation	5.0%	7.2%		
Debt	$3.7bn	$3.6bn		
Def exp	Ush160bn	Ush180bn		
	($153m)	($166m)		
Def bdgt			Ush175bn	
			($153m)	

contd	1996	1997	1998	1999
FMA (US)	$4.2m	$0.3m	$0.4m	$0.4m
$1 = shilling	1,046	1,083	1,145	
Population		21,019,000		
Age	13–17	18–22	23–32	
Men	1,183,000	1,013,000	1,455,000	
Women	1,190,000	1,017,000	1,600,000	

Total Armed Forces

ACTIVE ε30–40,000

Ugandan People's Defence Force ε30–40,000

4 div (1 with 5, 1 with 3, 2 with 2 bde)

EQUIPMENT†
- **MBT** 50 T-54/-55
- **LT TK** ε20 PT-76
- **APC** 20 BTR-60, 4 OT-64 SKOT, 10(+) *Mamba*, some *Buffel*
- **TOWED ARTY 76mm**: 60 M-1942; **122mm**: 20 M-1938; **130mm**: ε12; **155mm** (reported)
- **MRL 122mm**: BM-21
- **MOR 81mm**: L 16; **82mm**: M-43; **120mm**: 60 Soltam
- **ATGW** 40 AT-3 *Sagger*
- **AD GUNS 14.5mm**: ZPU-1/-2/-4; **23mm**: 20 ZU-23; **37mm**: 20 M-1939
- **SAM** SA-7
- **AVN** 4 cbt ac†, 2 armed hel
- **TRG** 3†* L-39, 1 SF*-260
- **TPT HEL** 1 Bell 206, 1 Bell 412, 4 Mi-17, 2* Mi-24
- **TPT/LIAISON HEL** 1 AS-202 *Bravo*, 1 *Gulfstream* III

Forces Abroad

DROC: ε500

Paramilitary ε600 active

BORDER DEFENCE UNIT ε600
- small arms

POLICE AIR WING
- **hel** 2 Bell 206, 2 Bell 212

MARINES (ε400)
- 8 riverine patrol craft<, plus boats

Opposition

LORD'S RESISTANCE ARMY ε2,000
(ε1,000 in Uganda, remainder in Sudan)
ALLIED DEMOCRATIC FORCES ε500–1,000

Zambia

	1996	1997	1998	1999
GDP	K4.0tr ($3.2bn)	K5.2tr ($3.4bn)		
per capita	$900	$900		
Growth	5.0%	4.6%		
Inflation	43.1%	23.9%		
Debt	$7.1bn	$7.2bn		
Def exp	εK71bn ($59m)	εK83bn ($59m)		
Def bdgt			εK99bn ($61m)	
FMA (US)	$0.1m	$0.2m	$0.2m	$0.2m
(PRC)		$2.0m		
$1 = kwacha	1,204	1,400	1,630	
Population		9,825,000		
Age	13–17	18–22	23–32	
Men	593,000	483,000	710,000	
Women	584,000	482,000	741,000	

Total Armed Forces

ACTIVE 21,600

Army 20,000

(incl 3,000 reserves)
3 bde HQ • 1 arty regt • 9 inf bn (3 reserve) • 1 engr bn • 1 armd regt (incl 1 armd recce bn)

EQUIPMENT
- **MBT** 10 T-54/-55, 20 PRC Type-59
- **LT TK** 30 PT-76
- **RECCE** 88 BRDM-1/-2
- **APC** 13 BTR-60
- **TOWED ARTY 76mm**: 35 M-1942; **105mm**: 18 Model 56 pack; **122mm**: 25 D-30; **130mm**: 18 M-46
- **MRL 122mm**: 50 BM-21
- **MOR 81mm**: 55; **82mm**: 24; **120mm**: 14
- **ATGW** AT-3 *Sagger*
- **RCL 57mm**: 12 M-18; **75mm**: M-20; **84mm**: *Carl Gustav*
- **AD GUNS 20mm**: 50 M-55 triple; **37mm**: 40 M-1939; **57mm**: 55 S-60; **85mm**: 16 KS-12
- **SAM** SA-7

Air Force 1,600

63† cbt ac, some armed hel
FGA 1 sqn with 12 J-6 (MiG-19)†
FTR 1 sqn with 12 MiG-21 MF†
TPT 1 sqn with 4 An-26, 4 C-47, 3 DHC-4, 4 DHC-5D
VIP 1 fleet with 1 HS-748, 3 Yak-40
LIAISON 7 Do-28, 2 Y-12
TRG 2*-F5T, 2* MiG-21U†, 12* *Galeb* G-2, 15* MB-326GB, 8* SF-260MZ

HEL 1 sqn with 4 AB-205A, 5 AB-212, 12 Mi-8
LIAISON HEL 12 AB-47G
MISSILES
  ASM AT-3 *Sagger*
  SAM 1 bn; 3 bty: SA-3 *Goa*

Forces Abroad

UN AND PEACEKEEPING
ANGOLA (UNOMA): 11 incl 3 obs plus. SIERRA
LEONE (UNOMSIL): 2 obs

Paramilitary 1,400

POLICE MOBILE UNIT (PMU) 700
1 bn of 4 coy
POLICE PARAMILITARY UNIT (PPMU) 700
1 bn of 3 coy

Zimbabwe

	1996	1997	1998	1999
GDP	Z$86bn	Z$104bn		
	($6.1bn)	($6.4bn)		
per capita	$2,200	$2,300		
Growth	8.1%	4.2%		
Inflation	21.4%	18.0%		
Debt	$5.0bn	$5.2bn		
Def exp	Z$2.3bn	Z$3.6bn		
	($237m)	($304m)		
Def bdgt[a]			Z$5.4bn	
			($471m)	
FMA (US)	$0.2m	$0.3m	$0.4m	$0.3m
US$1 = Z$	9.9	11.9	16.0	

[a] 18-month funding to 31 December 1998

Population	11,814,000		
Age	*13–17*	*18–22*	*23–32*
Men	753,000	613,000	950,000
Women	746,000	611,000	950,000

Total Armed Forces

ACTIVE ε39,000

Army ε35,000

5 bde HQ • 1 Mech, 1 Presidential Guard bde •
1 armd sqn • 15 inf bn (incl 2 guard, 1 mech, 1 cdo, 1
para) • 2 fd arty regt • 1 AD regt • 1 engr regt
EQUIPMENT
  MBT 22 PRC Type-59, 10 PRC Type-69
  RECCE 90 EE-9 *Cascavel* (**90mm** gun)
  APC 30 PRC Type-63 (YW-531), UR-416, 75 *Croco-
    dile*, 23 ACMAT
  TOWED ARTY 122mm: 12 PRC Type-60, 4 PRC
    Type-54
  MRL 107mm: 18 PRC Type-63; **122mm**: 52 RM-70
  MOR 81mm/82mm 502; **120mm**: 14 M-43
  AD GUNS 215 incl **14.5mm**: ZPU-1/-2/-4; **23mm**:
    ZU-23; **37mm**: M-1939
  SAM 17 SA-7

Air Force 4,000

62 cbt ac, 24 armed hel
Flying hours 100
FGA 2 sqn
  1 with 11 *Hunters* (9 FGA-90, 1 -F80, 1 T-81)
  1 with 6 *Hawk* Mk 60 and 5 *Hawk* Mk 60A
FTR 1 sqn with 12 PRC F-7 (MiG-21)
RECCE 1 sqn with 15* Reims-Cessna 337 *Lynx*
TRG/RECCE/LIAISON 1 sqn with 22 SF-260 *Genet* (9
  -C, 6* -F, 5* -W, 2* TP)
TPT 1 sqn with 6 BN-2, 11 C-212-200 (1 VIP)
HEL 1 sqn with 24 SA-319 (armed/liaison), 1 sqn with
  10 AB-412, 4 AS-532UL (VIP)

Forces Abroad

DROC: ε600

UN AND PEACEKEEPING
ANGOLA (UNOMA): 7 incl 3 obs plus 22 civ pol

Paramilitary 21,800

ZIMBABWE REPUBLIC POLICE FORCE 19,500
(incl Air Wg)
POLICE SUPPORT UNIT 2,300

The international arms trade grew by some 12% in 1997, bringing real growth between 1995 and 1997 to some 36% according to *The Military Balance* estimates. By contrast, from 1992 to 1994 there was a decline in real value to levels last seen in the early-to-mid 1970s. Much of the recent growth reflects the surge of orders from the Gulf States after the Gulf War. Arms deliveries to East Asia have doubled in value since 1994, reaching a peak in 1997 as a result of delivery to Taiwan of large numbers of combat aircraft from the US and France. Similar levels of growth are evident in the smaller regional markets of southern Asia, Latin America and Sub-Saharan Africa.

Arms Deliveries

The US delivered arms and military services worth almost $21bn in 1997, raising its share of the international market to 45%. Foreign Military Sales (FMS), which are administered by the Department of Defense, were valued at some $18bn, compared to $12.5bn in 1996. US deliveries to developing countries were worth $11.7bn during the year, while deliveries to NATO countries, Japan, Australia, New Zealand and other West European countries were worth over $6bn. Deliveries to developing countries of Direct Commercial Exports (DCE), which involve direct firm–government transactions, were worth $1.1bn in 1997. DCE to OECD countries, together with Excess Defense Articles (EDA) and Emergency Drawdown transfers, totaled some $1.7bn. US aerospace exports, mainly combat aircraft deliveries, accounted for $10.3bn of US military exports in 1997.

Among other leading country suppliers, the UK, France and Israel increased the value of their defence exports in 1997. French exports rose by 26%, mainly as a result of combat aircraft deliveries to Taiwan and Qatar and increasing exports of missile and land systems. In contrast, Russia's military exports declined in 1997 to some $2.5bn, compared to $3.6bn in 1996. This fall was partly due to the Asian economic crisis, which caused China and Indonesia, in particular, to cancel or delay deliveries, and partly because of the increasing competition Russia is facing from Ukraine and Belarus.

Saudi Arabia's $11bn defence imports in 1997 were again the largest of any single country in value terms, mainly because of combat aircraft deliveries. During the year, Saudi Arabia took delivery of 36 *Tornado* bombers and 20 *Hawk* trainers from the UK and 16 F-15s from the US. Taiwan was a clear second to Saudi Arabia, taking delivery of weapons and equipment worth over $7bn, mainly 60 F-16s from the US and some 20 *Mirage* 2000s from France. Deliveries to Saudi Arabia and Taiwan accounted for 39% of the world arms market in 1997. Other major arms importers in 1997 included: the UK, Finland and Switzerland in Europe; Egypt, Iran, Kuwait, Israel and Qatar in the Middle East; and Japan, India and Thailand in Asia.

Order data since 1992 suggests that the value of deliveries may fall from 1997 levels over the next two years, then begin to rise again at the turn of the century. The top five suppliers (US, UK, France, Russia and Israel) appear to be becoming less dominant. It remains difficult to identify orders placed with second-tier country suppliers such as China, Belarus and several countries which do not belong to the Wassenaar Arrangement and are not subject to its notification requirements.

A primary source for 1997 data is Richard F. Grimmett, *Conventional Arms Transfers to Developing Nations 1990–1997* (Washington DC: Congressional Research Service (CRS), July 1998). Historical arms trade data are often sourced from *World Military Expenditures and Arms Transfers 1996* (Washington DC: US Arms Control and Disarmament Agency (ACDA), July 1997). Where cited figures differ from those of ACDA and CRS, it is because *The Military Balance* uses figures supplied by national governments and defence industries.

Table 32 Country suppliers to the international arms trade, 1992–1997

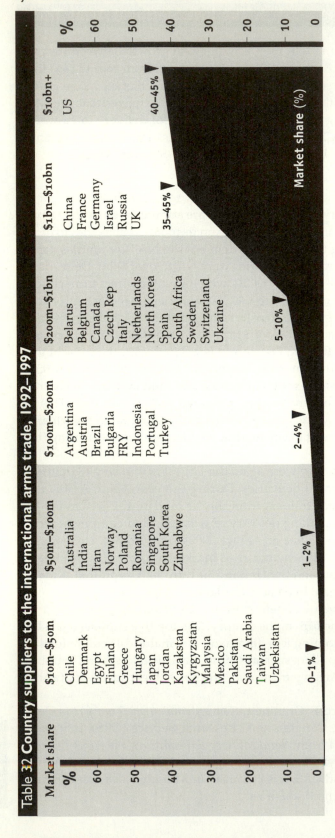

$10m–$50m	$50m–$100m	$100m–$200m	$200m–$1bn	$1bn–$10bn	$10bn+
Chile	Australia	Argentina	Belarus	China	US
Denmark	India	Austria	Belgium	France	
Egypt	Iran	Brazil	Canada	Germany	
Finland	Norway	Bulgaria	Czech Rep	Israel	
Greece	Poland	FRY	Italy	Russia	
Hungary	Romania	Indonesia	Netherlands	UK	
Japan	Singapore	Portugal	North Korea		
Jordan	South Korea	Turkey	Spain		
Kazakstan	Zimbabwe		South Africa		
Kyrgyzstan			Sweden		
Malaysia			Switzerland		
Mexico			Ukraine		
Pakistan					
Saudi Arabia					
Taiwan					
Uzbekistan					
Market share
0–1%	1–2%	2–4%	5–10%	35–45%	40–45%

Table 33 Value of arms deliveries and market share, 1987, 1992–1997

(constant 1997 US$m)

	Total	USSR/Russia	%	Warsaw Pact excl. USSR	%	US	%	UK	%	France	%	Germany	%	Total Western Europe	%	China	%	Israel	%	Others	%
1987	88,542	31,186	35.2	5,507	6.2	23,624	26.7	7,359	8.3	7,969	9.0	2,159	2.4	22,099	25.0	2,566	2.9	1,460	1.6	2,101	2.4
1992	37,453	2,806	7.5	n.a.	n.a.	14,811	39.5	5,532	14.8	4,610	12.3	1,877	5.0	14,948	39.9	1,231	3.3	1,648	4.4	2,010	5.4
1993	37,075	3,390	9.1	n.a.	n.a.	16,625	44.8	5,106	13.8	3,199	8.6	1,629	4.4	12,051	32.5	1,199	3.2	1,606	4.3	2,202	5.9
1994	33,992	2,906	8.5	n.a.	n.a.	14,393	42.3	4,960	14.6	3,580	10.5	1,501	4.4	12,285	36.1	772	2.3	1,481	4.4	2,156	6.3
1995	38,718	3,687	9.5	n.a.	n.a.	16,271	42.0	7,776	20.1	3,970	10.3	1,442	3.7	14,778	38.2	657	1.7	1,293	3.3	2,032	5.2
1996	41,397	3,583	8.7	n.a.	n.a.	17,731	42.8	8,156	19.7	5,871	14.2	685	1.7	16,679	40.3	609	1.5	1,356	3.3	1,439	3.5
1997	46,317	2,500	5.4	n.a.	n.a.	20,860	45.0	8,553	18.5	7,419	16.0	751	1.6	18,475	39.9	1,000	2.2	1,521	3.3	1,961	4.2

Table 34 Deliveries by other major arms suppliers, 1987, 1992–1997

(constant 1997 US$m)

	Italy	Sweden	Canada	Brazil	South Africa	Ukraine	Czech Republic	Belarus
1987	978	1013	978	877	209	n.a.	906	n.a.
1992	415	942	1347	202	169	n.a.	167	n.a.
1993	383	540	820	110	238	313	183	n.k.
1994	365	573	782	203	246	209	209	n.k.
1995	355	514	305	209	284	209	161	177
1996	209	653	466	52	190	209	120	204
1997	300	481	339	52	294	500	183	388

Table 35 Arms deliveries to South Asia, 1987, 1992–1997

(constant 1997 US$m)

	India	Pakistan	Afghanistan	Bangladesh	Sri Lanka
1987	4,050	459	1890	68	68
1992	729	505	n.k.	45	5
1993	295	602	5	32	22
1994	334	310	22	32	107
1995	469	522	21	63	167
1996	522	428	63	73	209
1997	500	469	104	83	261

Table 36 Arms deliveries to NATO and West Europe, 1987, 1992–1997

(constant 1997 US$m)

	Intra-West Europe	West Europe exports to US	US exports to West Europe	Intra-US/ Canada/ West Europe	Turkey imports	Total	US balance with West Europe
1987	6,326	1,485	5,215	1,147	1,620	15,793	3,730
1992	5,385	898	2,920	730	1,122	11,056	2,023
1993	4,184	766	3,025	887	1,312	10,173	2,259
1994	4,139	588	3,025	782	1,177	9,711	2,436
1995	3,687	522	3,233	608	956	9,006	2,712
1996	2,973	720	3,651	750	1,252	9,324	2,931
1997	2,931	730	4,276	774	626	9,371	3,546

Table 37 Identified arms orders, 1992–1997

(US$bn)

	Total	US	%	UK	%	France	%	Russia	%	Israel	%	Top 5	%	Other	%
1992	50.6	23.4	46.2	9.3	18.4	8.6	17.0	1.6	3.2	1.4	2.8	44.3	87.5	6.3	12.5
1993	59.2	33.0	55.7	10.6	17.9	6.9	11.7	1.8	3.0	1.8	3.0	54.1	91.4	5.1	8.6
1994	44.2	17.0	38.5	7.0	15.8	8.7	19.7	4.4	10.0	1.0	2.3	38.1	86.2	6.1	13.8
1995	45.2	19.1	42.3	7.8	17.3	7.4	16.4	2.4	5.3	1.0	2.2	37.7	83.4	7.5	16.6
1996	35.2	10.8	30.7	8.1	23.0	2.9	8.2	3.4	9.7	1.2	3.4	26.4	75.0	8.8	25.0
1997	42.6	16.4	38.5	8.9	20.9	5.1	12.0	3.2	7.5	1.9	4.5	35.5	83.3	7.1	16.7

Analyses and Tables

Table 38 Regional distribution of international arms deliveries, 1987, 1992–1997

(constant 1997 US$m)

	NATO and W. Europe	%	Eastern Europe	%	USSR/CIS	%	Middle East & N. Africa	%	East Asia	%	South Asia	%	Latin America	%	Sub-Saharan Africa	%	Australasia	%
1987	15,793	17.8	7,162	8.1	1,890	2.1	33,232	37.5	10,531	11.9	6,534	7.4	5,319	6.0	6,791	7.7	1,289	1.5
1992	11,056	29.5	261	0.7	104	0.3	16,346	43.6	6,433	17.2	1,284	3.4	943	2.5	600	1.6	427	1.1
1993	10,173	27.4	1,476	4.0	104	0.3	15,110	40.8	7,045	19.0	956	2.6	789	2.1	617	1.7	804	2.2
1994	9,711	28.6	1,356	4.0	96	0.3	12,394	36.5	7,401	21.8	805	2.4	808	2.4	972	2.9	450	1.3
1995	9,006	23.3	871	2.2	365	0.9	15,004	38.8	9,048	23.4	1,241	3.2	1,606	4.1	575	1.5	1,001	2.6
1996	9,324	22.5	1,252	3.0	313	0.8	14,911	36.0	10,818	26.1	1,460	3.5	1,773	4.3	782	1.9	763	1.8
1997	9,371	20.2	834	1.8	417	0.9	15,629	33.7	14,693	31.7	1,669	3.6	1,982	4.3	991	2.1	730	1.6

Table 39 Arms deliveries to the Middle East and North Africa, 1987, 1992–1997

(constant 1997 US$m)

	Saudi Arabia	Iraq	Iran	Egypt	Israel	Syria	UAE	Kuwait	Libya	Algeria
1987	9,728	7965	2,295	2,430	3,105	2,700	189	270	810	945
1992	10,815	n.k.	953	1,234	898	427	382	1094	90	156
1993	8,728	n.k.	1,203	1,531	1,203	295	503	1012	83	136
1994	7,769	n.k.	417	1,283	641	147	428	864	83	150
1995	9,032	n.k.	522	1,982	626	177	913	939	83	240
1996	9,439	n.k.	417	1,669	939	94	678	1081	83	261
1997	11,001	n.k.	800	1,100	600	104	626	700	104	469

Table 40 Arms deliveries to East Asia, 1987, 1992–1997

(constant 1997 US$m)

	Japan	Taiwan	ROK	DPRK	Vietnam	China	Thailand	Malaysia	Singapore	Indonesia	Myanmar	Philippines
1987	1,620	1,972	945	567	2,565	877	581	95	418	351	27	95
1992	1,347	924	1,252	33	21	1,458	415	146	247	56	168	157
1993	2,809	1,093	1,384	5	21	629	153	295	142	98	142	66
1994	2,338	1,069	1,497	96	86	278	417	908	246	53	107	96
1995	2,399	1,252	1,565	104	209	756	1,147	782	209	177	146	94
1996	2,161	1,773	1,669	104	261	1,565	730	469	522	730	261	104
1997	2,190	7,261	1,565	104	261	469	600	417	469	417	313	156

THE NEED FOR CHANGE

All NATO governments are now confronted by the problem of the escalating cost of defence procurement. This has serious consequences for their ability to equip their armed forces with weapons of the right type and quality. This difficulty is compounded by the governments' reluctance to allow full play to transnational defence industry mergers and acquisitions (M&A) and their failure to exploit the full benefits of cooperative procurement.

There is now an opportunity for NATO's fragmented defence industries to consolidate as a transatlantic supply base featuring the most competent US and European firms in competition to meet NATO's future equipment needs. A transatlantic structure would entail barrier-free access to NATO's internal defence market for any defence company, or consortium, located and owned in a NATO country. For this to happen, NATO governments need to take two measures. First, they should lift national restrictions on ownership of defence companies to allow a transatlantic defence industry structure to evolve. Second, a NATO procurement organisation is needed to generate an inclusive system of cooperative weapons acquisition.

Some transatlantic defence firms already combine the virtues of unified management with markets and production plants in both Europe and the US. But they are far outnumbered by firms with a predominantly national focus. In Europe, the ubiquitous joint venture has been promoted by both governments and industry as the only acceptable structure for transnational industrial cooperation, to the detriment of industrial efficiency. The European joint venture served its purpose during the Cold War as a political and economic compromise but it resulted in second-best outcomes in terms of cost and quality. European defence firms should now be free to acquire full control of, merge with, or be acquired by, other European or US companies under market conditions. Joint ventures, accompanied by minority equity stakes, are inadequate for the purpose of bringing about the greater degree of efficiency and flexibility required by the present global trading environment and the pace of technological change. As the scope for further national consolidation has largely run its course, a 'Fortress Europe' mentality is serving only to preserve existing shortcomings in European defence industries at an increasing political and economic cost, while inhibiting further access to US defence markets.

It is not in US interests for a Fortress Europe policy to prevail. The US government is faced with a sharply falling number of domestic prime contractors, reducing competition and forcing up costs of procurement. Globalisation strategies pursued by US firms already reflect a marked bias towards the European market. US defence companies invest heavily in direct sales to European governments as well as being major suppliers of intermediate products to European companies. European governments spend some $50bn annually on defence equipment including spares and support – about half US government spending. At present, the US takes only about 10% (worth about $5bn in 1997) of this part of the defence market because of European preferential purchasing policies. Under truly competitive market conditions, the US share could be expected to grow. US sales into Europe's intermediate market for sub-systems and components (many of which are incorporated into final products for export outside the NATO region) are also about $5bn. Many European firms currently benefit from access to US intermediate markets in the same way. In 1997, the value of this market to European companies was some $6.1bn, compared to $730m for direct sales to the US government. (In 1998 the latter figure is likely to increase to around $1.3bn as a result of the takeover of the US company Tracor by the UK's GEC). NATO governments should exploit the transatlantic industrial structure already in place at the sub-system and component level for the procurement of complete weapon systems.

Since the Cold War, the governments of all NATO countries with defence industrial capabilities face a common set of challenges in regard to equipment procurement and industry regulation which should have unified rather than divided them. However, it is industry rather governments that have made the running on both national and transnational consolidation with very little policy direction. A frequent perception is that 'market forces ' have driven defence industrial restructuring since the Cold War. The 'market forces' have been, in effect, governments, which determine the scale and structure of domestic arms markets through contract allocation, usually as single buyers. Domestic defence markets do not in any way resemble consumer or industrial markets, where there are many buyers and suppliers, and where the term 'market forces' properly applies. Governments have, deliberately or by default, stifled competition in three ways.

- By giving primacy to national autonomy thus reducing competition, and thereby driving up costs and inhibiting innovation. Governments justify these extra costs on the grounds that their national base for key strategic defence and dual-use technologies should be maintained.
- By preventing firms from achieving greater specialisation in defence sectors through transnational consolidation, which is their best protection against being swallowed up by national conglomerates.
- By supporting joint ventures rather than allocating contracts to more efficient firms with a single management structure.

In the face of these these governmental barriers, consolidation has lost its momentum.

REMOVING THE BARRIERS TO TRANSATLANTIC DEFENCE INDUSTRIES

To revive the impetus towards cooperative procurement, NATO governments need first to remove the legal restrictions on foreign ownership of defence firms. These can prevent or deter transatlantic M&A both in Europe and in the US. Transatlantic M&A are also effectively ruled out where state-owned industries are involved, as in France, Italy and Spain, and where the defence firm is a subsidiary of a much larger civil enterprise, as in Germany where Daimler-Benz Aerospace (DASA) forms a small part of the former Daimler-Benz, shortly to be Daimler-Chrysler, or where family interests hold a large part of the equity as is often the case in Germany. Governments with state-owned industries need to make firm commitments to privatisation together with firm schedules. The slow pace of privatisation in France since the government programme was announced in 1993 has undoubtedly stalled the momentum of European transnational consolidation. The experience of UK industry, which took a decade to reach efficient performance levels following the privatisation programme the 1980s, may influence the French government, which has shown a clear preference for transnational joint ventures rather than equity-based transactions. Since genuine efficiencies are impossible under joint venture arrangements, the French government should expedite the complete privatisation of Thomson-CSF (whose restructuring was approved in 1998 with the government retaining a 43% stake), Aerospatiale, Dassault, DCN and GIAT. In Germany, DASA needs to be demerged from Daimler-Benz, the more so now that the latter is taking control of the US automotive company Chrysler, which has already sold its specialist defence business.

Removing the legal and structural obstacles to transatlantic M&A is not in itself a sufficient measure to lift the trade barriers in European and transatlantic defence markets. At present, transnational M&As between defence firms reflect short to medium term strategies for penetrating protected internal markets rather than efficiency criteria. To ensure that such transatlantic companies are not the subjects of discrimination, governments with large protected internal defence markets (US, France, UK, Germany, and Italy) should formally and unambiguously open their procurement to international competition. At the same time they should take measures to keep the costs of competitive tendering to a minimum, since bureaucratic requirements often, and deliberately, add substantially to bidding costs and deter potential foreign competitors. The fact that US firms have avoided M&A in Europe is evidence both of the difficulty of acquiring majority control of European defence prime-contractors and of the discrimination that foreign ownership entails in European defence markets. Among the Europeans, only British firms have succeeded in acquiring and merging with major US defence contractors. (Allison was taken over by Rolls-Royce in 1995, Tracor by GEC in 1998, and Lucas merged with Varity in 1996.)

Technology transfer and intellectual property rights (IPR) issues also raise barriers against transnational M&A, particularly where governments own, or jointly own, the IPR. The US protects its IPR by insisting on non-disclosure (firewalls) by those companies taken over or merged with a foreign concern. The same issues complicate the functioning of many European joint ventures. As transatlantic companies mature, technology transfers and IPR issues are likely to become less sensitive, particularly if cooperative procurement becomes the norm across the range of conventional weapons. Certain weapons systems and technologies, however, will remain sensitive and under national control, but this should not be allowed to retard the momentum of transatlantic industrial consolidation.

THE ORGANISATION OF PROCUREMENT IN NATO MEMBER STATES

The largest obstacle to the development of an effective NATO system of equipment procurement supplied by transnational defence industries lies in the organisation of procurement in NATO member states. Current organisations and practices reflect national priorities, among which the potential for cooperative equipment procurement and production on a NATO scale is underdeveloped. The governments of the major producer countries (US, France, UK, Germany and Italy) have currently three choices. They can continue to buy from protected national sources at a considerable incremental cost compared to a properly managed cooperative venture. This option may be attractive for a small number of strategic, highly specialised programmes. In the case of many major conventional weapon systems, neither the European nor US governments can in future, at a reasonable cost, sustain purely national programmes. Or they can cooperate in a joint international procurement programme supplied primarily from national industry under a joint venture. European collaborative programmes have undoubtedly served their purpose in establishing the building-blocks for joint procurement and industrial rationalisation, but they typically suffer from a range of management, technical, schedule and cost problems inherent in a compromise arrangement and epitomised in the partner-nation insistence on the principle of *juste retour* in determining the allocation of work country-by-country. This has meant that the value of orders placed by governments has been matched by the industrial work placed in the country of that government at levels all the way down the supply chain, irrespective of the economic logic of that arrangement. Moreover, joint European programmes have not always suited the needs of the smaller NATO member states. Misguided policies to use European collaborative programmes as a vehicle for developing the defence industries of smaller NATO countries have added to the costs for all partners. As a result, the countries with smaller defence industries have alternated between buying direct from foreign sources of supply and joining a cooperative programme and thus having to meet a share of the bill for the full costs of development and production. The third option is the least favoured by all the larger NATO member states: they can buy direct from abroad, usually from the US or another NATO country. While this option has its attractions when short-term considerations are paramount, it does not address the underlying NATO requirement for an effective, cooperative system for procuring weapons.

None of these options are likely to provide NATO's armed forces with the equipment they need in the future at the most reasonable cost. The way forward for NATO should lie in a further evolution in the organisation of cooperative defence procurement. Transatlantic defence industries now offer governments a fourth choice in the way weapons are purchased – one that will require a radical reform of national procurement policy and practice. Reform will challenge deep-rooted national privileges and prejudices in governments, the armed forces, procurement agencies and industry. In particular, two countries, the US and France, and one organisation, NATO, have the power to block or advance the evolution of collective NATO procurement and transatlantic defence industries. There will be those in the US who will continue to argue for self-sufficiency. NATO, never a powerful forum, through the Conference of National Armaments Directors, (CNAD), in matters of weapons procurement, may continue to leave the initiative to the Europeans through the Western European Armaments Group (WEAG), and in the future, possibly, the European Commission. There will be those in France who will persist in the justification of state-controlled defence monopolies in a European defence market and industry led by France.

PROGRESS IN THE REORGANISATION OF EUROPEAN PROCUREMENT

In the absence of any NATO-led initiative, the lead in European inter-governmental policy coordination has been taken by the Western European Union (though WEAG) and increasingly, albeit indirectly, the European Commission. The latter is formally denied legal competence in matters relating to defence procurement and industry under Article 223 of the 1958 Treaty of Rome. There was an unsuccessful attempt to overturn this article during the European Union Amsterdam Inter-Governmental Conference of 1996–1997. There are now two new procurement organisations, both created in November 1996, that form the building blocks for a European-only armaments agency. The UK and Italy joined France and Germany in the creation of the Joint Armaments Co-operation Organisation (JACO) or OCCAR in French (*Organisme Conjoint de Cooperation en matière d'Armement*). Soon after, the ten WEU member countries formed the Western European Armaments Organisation (WEAO), which also includes Norway, Denmark and Turkey. A condition for qualifying for JACO membership is that member states must have a major equipment programme (in development or production) on which they are ready to cooperate with other JACO members. Apart from the four founding partners, several nations have applied to join, or are signalling interest. Among these are the Netherlands, Spain and Sweden – countries with the largest equipment requirements and industrial supply capabilities outside the JACO grouping. The focus of WEAO is on defence research, rather than on development and production as in the case of JACO. For countries currently unwilling or unable to participate in the current generation of major collaborative programmes, and therefore excluded from JACO, the rationale for the WEAO is that it presents the opportunity to join in the research leading up to the next generation of weapons and military equipment.

The promise of JACO lies in its organisational and financial reforms. If the programme-by-programme *juste* retour is abandoned, JACO has potential to bring about a sea change in

European procurement. Three major problems have resulted from the operation of the *juste retour* principle.

- Arrangements for industrial participation, particularly for the production phase, have resulted in expensive excess capacity that has worked against economies of scale and pushed programme costs up significantly.
- Complex industrial arrangements, put in place at the outset of a programme, have often been compromised by reductions in orders placed by particular governments, upsetting the equitable distribution of the industrial work and arousing considerable resentment on the part of the losers.
- Companies that hold a comparative advantage over those with which they are obliged to cooperate resent the free technology transfers that inevitably result. This has often led to a breakdown in communications at the working level and delays in programme schedules.

The new feature of JACO is that the industrial division of labour is determined over a longer time-scale and across several different programmes. Participation is to be determined on the basis of proven industrial competence, not the putative claims of sub-contractors seeking technology transfer and market entry. JACO represents an advance in terms of European cooperative procurement, but its potential is limited given the absence of the US and an equivalent organisation to manage NATO-wide programmes on a similar, collective basis.

For these reasons, the future evolution of JACO might take several forms. The organisation could develop on existing lines with participation effectively restricted to the major supplier countries. This would deter the formation of a pan-European Armaments Agency. Non-member countries would face the same choices in regard to equipment supply as they currently encounter. JACO could develop into a European Armaments Agency within the WEU and conceivably within the European Commission. In this event it would inevitably adopt a European preferential purchasing policy (already the practice of some partners and reinforcing the Fortress Europe mentality), and might compromise access to advanced US technology and US defence markets. Or, in the event of NATO and US initiatives, it is even possible that JACO might act as a spur to increasing transatlantic equipment collaboration. NATO planners are currently studying ways to improve NATO-wide equipment cooperation and coordination with the US and Canada, which might be facilitated by the emergence of a JACO able to speak with a single voice on major European requirements.

The creation of JACO is not yet contributing towards the objective of consolidating European defence industries. This is because of continuing divisions among its partners on fundamental issues of procurement policy and privatisation. In particular, the UK opposes France's vision of a protected European supply chain, while France is wary of the UK's greater presence in the US defence market and well-established links with US industry. Germany is also increasingly disenchanted with a Franco-German defence industrial axis dominated by France. From the industrial perspective, there are few incentives for engaging in costly transnational M&A in a European defence market still fettered by national trade barriers. The impasse could be broken by greater commitment from the US and NATO to cooperative procurement and a change in France's industrial policy.

ADVANCING ARMAMENTS COOPERATION IN NATO

To make a transatlantic industrial structure work, NATO governments also need to reform radically the way they procure weapons. There should be a joint NATO Armaments Agency whose responsibilities go beyond those of the CNAD and, in Europe, of JACO. At the same time an obstacle to closer international cooperation is the large number of procurement organisations (currently 21) in the US representing different Services within the US Department of Defense. Before a new agency could be set up there is also a need for stronger institutional links than JACO currently provides between the major procurement organisations in European defence ministries. This must, in particular, involve the UK's Procurement Executive, France's *Délégation Génerale pour l'Armement (DGA)*, and Germany's *Bundesamt fur Wehrtechnik und Beschaffung (BWB)*. The role of a joint armaments agency should be to address fundamental issues relating to the next generation of conventional weapon systems.

Most importantly, it would need to identify a common set of requirements, harmonise entry-into-service and establish agreed equipment performance targets around which design specifications could be written. If agreement could be reached based on platform requirements based on the highest common factor, partner nations would be free, at their own expense, to customise equipment thereafter if they wished. The paucity of new development programmes means that NATO partners have every opportunity to resolve differences on the timing and specification of the next generation of conventional weapons systems. There is no reason why most future military aircraft, unmanned aerial vehicles (UAVs), warships, armoured fighting vehicles, artillery and tactical missiles should not be cooperatively procured within NATO. Research and development could be managed to avoid costly duplication of effort – a perennial feature of both European and US procurement, and also to ensure competition in the prototype and user trial phases if necessary. Production could be single or multiple-source, depending on competition issues.

The allocation of contracts could be determined through competitive tendering in all phases, research, development, production and in-service. Transatlantic firms and consortia would form the supply base. The distribution of labour should depend on specialisation and comparative advantage. Having more than one prototype design through most of the development phase and more than one source of supply in the production phase should offset concerns over the market power of any dominant firms. Concerns that one nation or firm might attain dominant positions in a particular sector could be allayed by ensuring that contracts within one sector were allocated to as many firms or consortia as was possible without compromising technical standards or efficiency. As a precedent, NATO's Family of Weapons concept of the 1980s sought to achieve an effective division of labour in the air-to-air missile sector. Under this scheme, the US developed the medium-range variant (which became AMRAAM) and the UK the short-range variant (ASRAAM), although the US later withdrew its commitment for the British missile. Like JACO, there would be no guaranteed *juste retour* on a programme-by-programme basis. Instead, governments of countries with a highly developed defence industrial base, as well as those with lesser capabilities, might expect to obtain work in their country in one or more product phases, from research through to in-service repair, maintenance and overhaul, and upgrades, depending on their proven competence. The management of offsets would, like *juste retour* arrangements, be planned over several programmes rather than a single programme. Managing the division of labour of major programmes collectively by equipment groupings in sectors, sub-sectors and life-cycle phase should promote the horizontal integration of a competitive, transatlantic supply base, while inhibiting any further vertical integration on a national scale.

RECENT DEVELOPMENTS

The most recent moves by NATO governments give little indication of impending change on a collective front. The US government blocked the attempt by Lockheed Martin to acquire Northrop Grumman (the first major case of government intervention in the restructuring process since the Cold War). The companies abandoned the transaction in July 1998, leaving Northrop-Grumman a possible party for a transatlantic M&A. As a result of its Strategic Defence Review (SDR), announced in July 1998, the UK is streamlining its procurement organisation and procedures in order to take account of the pace of technological change and industrial consolidation. This change has opened further differences between the UK and other Europeans. Some of these differences are addressed in the inter-governmental 'Letter of Intent' on European defence industrial consolidation signed by the UK together with France, Germany, Italy, Spain and Sweden in July 1998, shortly after the release of the SDR. Later in July, the French government announced the acquisition by the state-owned Aerospatiale of the defence interests (missiles and space) of Matra, part of the Lagardère group. This transaction is also seen as initiating the partial privatisation of Aerospatiale, as Lagardère is to take a share of 30–33%, and up to a further 20% is to be sold on the stock market, leaving the French government with a share of 46–48%. In September 1998, NATO's CNAD is due to report the results of a year's study of cooperative arms procurement.

As long as the policy emphasis in some countries remains predominantly on sustaining protected national defence industries, there is small chance of these initiatives breaking the stalemate in trans-European and transatlantic industrial consolidation. However, some governments seem unable to keep up with the pace of technological development and rising costs. This prevents them from seizing oppertunities that are available . The Joint Strike Fighter looks set to be the most substantive transatlantic cooperative programme over the next decade. It already has two full partners, the US and UK, and Denmark, Netherlands and Norway have joined as a single associate partner (in addition Canada and Italy have observer status). This could be a model for other transatlantic programmes such as the Tactical Reconnaissance Armoured Vehicle Combat Requirement (TRACER), a light tank needed for NATO's new missions, which is currently confined to the US and UK.

CONCLUSION

The process of defence industrial restructuring in both the US and Europe since the Cold War has resulted largely in the consolidation of national industries with a degree of market power which sustains over-capacity while inhibiting competition, raising equipment prices and threatening technical innovation. In a period of reducing demand for defence equipment, NATO governments have a real opportunity turn the course of defence industrial consolidation to their advantage. Action is needed to remove legal and trade barriers to transatlantic M&A and to create a NATO organisation to manage cooperative procurement. These steps should be backed by policies that focus on three objectives:

• Creating and maintaining competition throughout the supply chain;
• Creating conditions to encourage greater specialisation in a transatlantic defence industry thereby reducing the role of conglomerates; and:
• Phasing out joint ventures and favouring firms with single management.

The costs of failing to overcome the formidable political obstacles and sectional interests to achieve such a level of armaments cooperation are likely to be high, not only in economic terms, but also in military terms. Effective transatlantic cooperation in armaments procurement is essential to ensure that NATO armed forces are properly equipped for the missions that will face them over the coming years.

Analyses and Tables

Table 41 Major defence companies in NATO member states and Sweden
listed under country of ownership

Space	Military Aircraft	Military Helicopters	Aero-engines	Missiles	Electronics
US					
■ Lockheed Martin	■ Lockheed Martin	■ Boeing	■ GE	■ Raytheon	■ Raytheon *
■ Boeing	■ Boeing	■ Textron Bell ‡	■ UTC Pratt	■ Lockheed Martin	■ Northrop Grumman
■ Raytheon	■ Northrop	■ UTC Sikorsky	& Whitney ‡	■ Boeing	■ Boeing
■ TRW	Grumman		■ Allied-Signal	■ Northrop	■ Lockheed Martin ‡
■ Loral Space Systems	■ Raytheon			Grumman	■ ITT
					■ General Dynamics * & ‡
					■ GTE
					■ Honeywell
					■ Harris
					■ TRW
					■ Litton * & ‡
					■ Allied-Signal
					■ Motorola
					■ Rockwell
					■ EG&G
					■ Orbital Sciences
Canada					
	■ Bombadier *		■ Bombadier Shorts *		■ CAE *
					■ Spar Aerospace
UK					
■ GEC	■ BAe	■ GKN Westland	■ Rolls-Royce *	■ BAe	■ GEC Marconi *
■ BAe				■ GEC Marconi	■ BAe
					■ Smiths Industries *
					■ Cobham *
					■ Racal
					■ Meggitt
					■ Ultra *
France					
■ Aerospatiale	■ Aerospatiale	■ Aerospatiale	■ SNECMA	■ Aerospatiale	■ Thomson-CSF †
■ Alcatel	■ Dassault		■ Labinal Turbomeca	■ Lagardere Matra	■ Dassault Electonique
■ Lagardere Matra				■ Thomson-CSF	■ Lagardere Matra
					■ Alcatel
					■ CNM SFIM
					■ CSEE

Space	Military Aircraft	Military Helicopters	Aero-engines	Missiles	Electronics
Germany					
■DASA	■DASA	■DASA	■DASA	■DASA	■DASA
				■Diehl	■Diehl
					■ELG
					■Rohde & Schwarz
					■Carl Zeiss
					■Liebherr
					■Renk
					■LITEF
					■EEL
Italy					
■Finmeccannica	■Finmeccannica	■Finmeccannica	■Fiat	■Finmeccannica	■Finmeccannica
	■Aermacchi		■Finmeccannica		
Sweden					
	■Saab		■Volvo	■Saab	■Celsius
					■Ericsson
Netherlands					
	■Stork Fokker				
Spain					
	■CASA	■CASA			■ENOSA
					■Indra

Warships	Submarines	Armoured Fighting Vehicles	Artillery & Ordnance	Utilities and other major sub-contractors
US				
■Newport News	■Newport News	■General Dynamics	■Carlyle United Defense	■Lucas Varity *
■Litton	■General Dynamics	■United Defense		■Sunstrand
■General Dynamics		■Textron	■Alliant Techsystems	■Allied-Signal *
■Avondale			■Honeywell	■UTC Hamilton Standard
■NASSCO		■AM General	■Olin	■Dyncorp
		■General Motors ‡	■Textron	■Carlyle Aerostructures
		■Oskosh	■Lockheed Martin	■Rohr
		■Stewart & Stevenson	■Primex	■Coltec Industries
			■Chamberlain	■BF Goodrich
			■Cordant Technologies	■GenCorp
				■Parker Hannifin
				■Cordant Technologies

Analyses and Tables

Warships	Submarines	Armoured Fighting Vehicles	Artillery & Ordnance	Utilities and other major sub-contractors
Canada				
St John Shipbuilding				CAE
				Bristol
UK				
GEC Yarrow	GEC VSEL	GKN	BAe	TI Dowty *
Vosper		Vickers	Hunting	Lucas Varity *
		Alvis †	GEC VSEL	Doughty Hanson
				Chemring
				Cobham *
				Babcock
France				
DCN	DCN	GIAT	GIAT	SAGEM
Alstom †		Citroen Panhard	Thomson-CSF Brandt	Intertechnique
			SNPE	Labinal
			Societe Alsetex	
			Arcane	
Germany				
Thyssen-Krupp	Preussag HDW	Wegmann Krauss Maffei	Diehl	ZF Luftfahrttechnik
		Rheinmetall/MaK	Rheinmetall	Liebherr
		Thyssen/KUKA	Liebherr	LITEF
		MAN	Dynamit Nobel	Renk
			Buck Werke	EEL
			KUKA	
			MEN	
			Wegmann	
Italy				
Fincantieri	Fincantieri	Finmeccannica	Finmeccannica	
		Fiat	Borletti	
			BPD	
			Fiocchi Munizione	
Netherlands				
RGS	RDM			
Sweden				
Celsius	Celsius		Celsius	Celsius

Warships	Submarines	Armoured Fighting Vehicles	Artillery & Ordnance	Utilities and other major sub-contractors

Spain

■Bazan	■Bazan	■Santa Barbara	■Santa Barbara	
			■UEE	
			■Barreiros Hermanos	
			■Expal	
			■FAEX	

Key

*	Company with Transatlantic Merger or Acquisition
†	Company with Transnational European Merger or Acquisition
‡	Company with Canadian Merger or Acquisition

Note: Companies are those listed as top defence manufacturing contractors by national governments.

IT and service companies are not included.

Peacekeeping Operations

UNITED NATIONS

On 1 August 1998, the United Nations was maintaining 15 peacekeeping operations around the world. These missions involve the deployment of 14,537 troops world-wide from 76 countries. The leading troop suppliers to the UN's 1998 peacekeeping activities are shown below. The UN peacekeeping budget for the year to 30 June 1998 was $1.3 billion. For the year to 30 June 1999, the latest budgetary projection is between $900 million and $1bn. Arrears in payments of contributions to the UN peacekeeping budget amounted to $1.5bn at 30 June 1998, of which the US owed 63% and Russia 9%.

Table 42 Average strength and cost of UN peacekeeping forces, 1991–1998

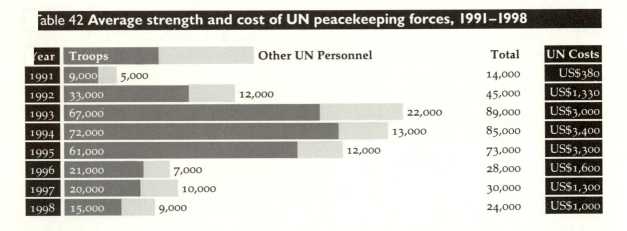

Year	Troops	Other UN Personnel	Total	UN Costs
1991	9,000	5,000	14,000	US$380
1992	33,000	12,000	45,000	US$1,330
1993	67,000	22,000	89,000	US$3,000
1994	72,000	13,000	85,000	US$3,400
1995	61,000	12,000	73,000	US$3,300
1996	21,000	7,000	28,000	US$1,600
1997	20,000	10,000	30,000	US$1,300
1998	15,000	9,000	24,000	US$1,000

Table 43 Leading troop contributors to UN operations (as at 30 June 1998)

Country	Strength	Country	Strength	Country	Strength
Poland	1,048	Norway	729	USA	622
Bangladesh	886	Ireland	726	Fiji	602
Austria	795	Argentina	696	United Kingdom	393
Ghana	789	France	677	India	297
Finland	777	Nepal	649	Canada	292

Table 44 Leading financial contributors to UN operations, 1998

(US$m)	Assessment	%	Arrears		Assessment	%	Arrears
US	288	31.5	966	Brazil	3	0.3	13
Japan	160	17.6	19	Netherlands	15	1.6	—
Germany	86	9.5	10	Australia	13	1.5	—
France	71	7.8	22	Sweden	10	1.1	—
UK	56	6.1	—	Belgium	10	1.1	—
Russia	33	3.6	129	ROK	2	0.2	1
Italy	48	5.3	7	Sub-total	844	92.4	1,168
Canada	26	2.8	—	Other	69	7.6	360
Spain	23	2.5	1	Total	913	100.0	1,528

United Nations Truce Supervision Organisation (UNTSO)

Mission UNTSO was established in 1948 to assist the Mediator and Truce Commission supervise the truce in Palestine. Since then, UNTSO has performed various tasks, including supervising the General Armistice Agreements of 1949 and the cease-fire in the Suez Canal area and the Golan Heights following the Arab–Israeli Six Day War of June 1967. UNTSO assists and cooperates with the UN Disengagement Observer Force (UNDOF) on the Golan Heights in the Israeli–Syrian sector, and with the UN Interim Force in Lebanon (UNIFIL) in the Israeli–Lebanese sector. UNTSO also has a presence in the Egyptian–Israeli sector in the Sinai, and maintains offices in Beirut and Damascus.

Headquarters Government House, Jerusalem.

Strength 153 Military Observers.

Contributors Arg, Aus, A, Be, Ca, Chl, PRC, Da, Ea, SF, Fr, Irl, It, Nl, NZ, No, RF, Swe, CH, US.

Cost *1996* $27m *1997* $27m *1998* $27m. Total cost to June 1998: $532m.

United Nations Disengagement Observer Force (UNDOF)

Mission UNDOF was established in 1974 after the 1973 Middle East war to maintain the cease-fire between Israel and Syria; supervise the disengagement of Israeli and Syrian forces; and supervise the areas of separation and limitation, as provided in the Agreement on Disengagement of 31 May 1974. The situation in the Israeli–Syrian sector has remained quiet and there have been no serious incidents.

Location Syrian Golan Heights.

Headquarters Damascus.

Strength 1,045 troops, assisted by 80 military observers from UNSTO's Observer Group Golan and supported by international and locally recruited civilian staff.

Contributors A, Ca, J, Pl, Slvk.

Cost *1996* $32m *1997* $38m *1998* $35m. Total cost to June 1998: $716m.

United Nations Interim Force in Lebanon (UNIFIL)

Mission UNIFIL was established in March 1978 to confirm the withdrawal of Israeli forces from southern Lebanon; restore international peace and security; and help the Lebanese government maintain effective authority in the area. UNIFIL has, however, been prevented from fully implementing its mandate. Israeli forces continue to occupy parts of southern Lebanon, where they and their local auxiliary in turn remain targets for attack by groups resisting the occupation.

Location Southern Lebanon.

Headquarters Naqoura.

Current Strength 4,473 troops assisted by 60 military observers from UNSTO's Observer Group Lebanon.

Contributors Fji, SF, Fr, Gha, Irl, It, N, No, Pl.

Cost *1996* $135m *1997* $121m *1998* $143m. Total cost to to June 1998: $2,826m.

United Nations Iraq–Kuwait Observer Force (UNIKOM)

Mission UNIKOM was established in April 1991 as part of the cease-fire arrangement at the end of the Gulf War to monitor the Iraq–Kuwait border area in the Khor Abdullah and demilitarised zones. The demilitarised zone extends 10km into Iraq and 5km into Kuwait from the agreed boundary between the two countries. UNIKOM's function is to deter violations of the inter-state boundary by direct action, and observe and report hostile or potentially hostile actions. Kuwait pays two-thirds of the costs.

Analyses and Tables

Location Iraqi–Kuwaiti border area.
Headquarters Umm Qasr, Iraq.
Strength 904 troops, assisted by 194 military observers and supported by 200 international and locally recruited civilian staff.
Contributors Units from Bng (infantry); Observers from Arg, A, Bng, Ca, PRC, Da, Fji, SF, Fr, Ge, Gha, Gr, Hu, Ind, Indo, Irl, It, Kya, Mal, Nga, Pak, Pl, R, RF, Sen, Sgp, Swe, Th, Tu, UK, Ury, US, Ve.
Cost *1996* $62m *1997* $50m *1998* $52m. Total cost to June 1998: $415m.

United Nations Peacekeeping Force in Cyprus (UNFICYP)

Mission UNFICYP was established in March 1964 to prevent a recurrence of fighting between the Greek Cypriot and Turkish Cypriot communities and to help restore and maintain law and order and peaceful conditions. Following a *de facto* cease-fire on 16 August 1974, UNFICYP's mandate was expanded to include supervising the cease-fire and maintaining a buffer zone between the lines of the Cyprus National Guard and the Turkish and Turkish Cypriot forces.
Location Cyprus.
Headquarters Nicosia.
Strength 1,244 troops, assisted by 35 civilian police and 330 international and locally recruited staff.
Contributors Arg, Aus, A, Ca, SF, Hu, Irl, Nl, Slvn, UK.
Cost *1996* $44m *1997* $46m *1998* $45m (including voluntary contributions by Cyprus of one-third of the total cost and by Greece of $7m) Total cost to June 1998: $928m.

United Nations Military Observer Group in India and Pakistan (UNMOGIP)

Mission UNMOGIP was established in January 1949 to supervise the cease-fire between India and Pakistan in the state of Jammu and Kashmir. Following the 1972 India–Pakistan agreement defining a Line of Control in Kashmir, India claimed that UNMOGIP's mandate had lapsed. Pakistan, however, did not agree. Consequently, the UN Secretary-General has declared that UNMOGIP's mission can only be terminated by the UN Security Council. In the absence of such a decision, UNMOGIP has been maintained with the same mandate and functions.
Location The cease-fire line between India and Pakistan in the state of Jammu and Kashmir.
Headquarters Rawalpindi (November–April); Srinagar (May–October).
Strength 45 military observers, supported by international and locally recruited police.
Contributors Be, Chl, Da, SF, It, ROK, Swe, Ury.
Cost *1996* $7m *1997* $7m *1998* $8m. Total cost to June 1998: $115m.

United Nations Observer Mission in Angola (UNOMA)

Mission On 1 July 1997, UNOMA took over from the United Nations Angola Verification Mission (UNAVEM) III to continue the process of restoring peace on the basis of the accords signed on 31 May 1991, the Lusaka Protocol signed on 20 November 1994, and relevant Security Council resolutions. The main objectives of UNOMA are to:
* provide mediation for the Angolan parties in completing the peace process;
* monitor the normalisation of the state administration throughout the country;
* assist in resolving and managing any conflicts that may arise;
* monitor and verify the integration of the forces of the *União Nacional para a Independência Total de Angola* (UNITA) into the government structure;
* promote a climate of confidence by maintaining a presence in major population areas and areas of tension.

Although UNOMA's last military forces were scheduled to have departed by the end of November 1997, on 12 January 1998 the Security Council approved retaining a task force of four infantry companies. The mandate of UNOMA was extended until 31 August 1998.

Location Angola.

Headquarters Luanda.

Strength 661 troops, assisted by 92 military observers and 403 civilian police monitors.

Contributors Arg, Bng, Br, Bg, RC, Et, Fr, Gam, Gha, GuB, Hu, HKJ, Ind, Kya, Mal, RMM, Nba, Nga, No, NZ, Pak, Pl, Po, R, RF, Sen, Slvk, Sp, Swe, Tz, Ukr, Ury Z, Zw; others provide military observers.

Cost UNAVEM III *1996* $344m; UNOMA *1997* $135m *1998* $46m. Total cost to June 1998: $1,079m.

United Nations Mission for the Referendum in Western Sahara (MINURSO)

Mission MINURSO was established in April 1991 in accordance with 'the settlement proposals', as accepted by Morocco and the *Frente Popular para la Liberación de Saguia el-Hamra y de Río de Oro* (POLISARIO) on 30 August 1988 to:

- monitor a cease-fire;
- verify the reduction of Moroccan troops in the territory;
- monitor the confinement of Moroccan and POLISARIO troops to designated locations, and ensure the release of all Western Saharan political prisoners or detainees;
- oversee the exchange of prisoners of war;
- implement the repatriation programme;
- identify and register qualified voters;
- organise and ensure a free referendum and proclaim the results.

In its limited deployment, MINURSO's primary function was restricted to complementing the identification process; verifying the cease-fire and cessation of hostilities; and monitoring local police and ensuring security and order at identification and registration sites. In May 1996, in the absence of any meaningful progress towards completing the settlement plan, the Security Council suspended the identification process, authorised the withdrawal of the civilian police component – except for a small number of officers to maintain contacts with the authorities on both sides – and decided to reduce the strength of MINURSO's military component by 20%.

Location Western Sahara.

Headquarters Laayoune.

Strength 161 troops, assisted by 80 civilian police monitors and 202 military observers, and supported by international and locally recruited staff.

Contributors Arg, A, Bng, Ca, PRC, Et, ElS, Fr, Gha, Gr, Gui, Hr, Irl, It, Kya, Mal, Nga, Pak, Pl, Por, ROK, RF, Swe, Ury, US, Ve.

Civilian personnel provided by Ca, Et, Gha, Ind, Mal, Pak, Po, Swe.

Cost *1996* $59m *1997* $29m *1998* $23m. Total cost to June 1998: $314m.

United Nations Preventive Deployment Force (UNPREDEP)

Mission UNPREDEP was established on 31 March 1995 to replace UNPROFOR in the former Yugoslav Republic of Macedonia (FYROM). UNPREDEP's mandate is to monitor and report any developments in the border areas that could undermine confidence and stability in FYROM and threaten its territory. Effective on 1 February 1996, following the termination of the mandates of the UN Confidence-Restoration Operation in Croatia (UNCRO), the UN Protection Force (UNPROFOR) in Bosnia-Herzegovina and the UN Peace Forces Headquarters (UNPF-HQ), UNPREDEP became an independent mission, reporting directly to the UN Secretariat in New York. As a result of fighting in Kosovo, the Security Council voted on 21 July 1998 to increase the size of UNPREDEP to 1,050 personnel.

Location FYROM.
Headquarters Skopje.
Strength 736 troops, assisted by 34 military observers and 26 civilian police, and supported by international and locally recruited staff.
Contributors Arg, Bng, Be, Br, Ca, Cz, Da, Et, SF, Gha, Indo, Irl, HKJ, Kya, N, NZ, Nga, No, Pak, Pl, Por, RF, Swe, CH, Tu, Ukr, US.
Cost *1996* $50m *1997* $45m *1998* $21m. Total cost to June 1998: $155m.

United Nations Mission of Observers in Prevlaka (UNMOP)

Mission United Nations military observers have been deployed in the strategically important Prevlaka peninsula of Croatia since October 1992, when the Security Council authorised UNPROFOR to assume responsibility for monitoring the area's demilitarisation. Following UNPROFOR's restructuring in March 1995, those functions were carried out by UNCRO. With the termination of UNCRO's mandate in January 1996, the Security Council authorised UN military observers as UNMOP to continue monitoring the demilitarisation of the peninsula for three months, to be extended for a further three months if the Secretary-General reported this would continue to help decrease tension. UNMOP is under the command and direction of a Chief Military Observer, who reports directly to the UN Secretariat in New York.
Location Prevlaka peninsula, Croatia.
Headquarters Dubrovnik.
Strength 24 military observers, supported by international and locally recruited staff.
Contributors Arg, Be, Br, Ca, Cz, Et, SF, Gha, Indo, Irl, HKJ, Kya, N, NZ, Nga, No, Pak, Pl, Por, RF, Swe, CH, Ukr.
Cost *1996* $118m *1997* $190m *1998* $190m. Total cost to June 1998: $308m.

United Nations Observer Mission in Georgia (UNOMIG)

Mission UNOMIG was originally established to verify compliance with the 27 July 1993 cease-fire agreement between the government of Georgia and the Abkhaz authorities with special attention to the situation in the city of Sukhumi; to investigate reports of cease-fire violations; and to attempt to resolve such incidents with the parties involved. Following the signing in May 1994 of the Agreement on a Cease-fire and Separation of Forces by the Georgian and Abkhaz parties, UNOMIG's tasks are to:

- monitor and verify the implementation of the Agreement;
- observe the operation of the peacekeeping force of the Commonwealth of Independent States (CIS);
- verify that troops do not remain in or re-enter the security zone and that heavy military equipment does not remain and is not re-introduced into the security zone or the restricted weapons zone;
- monitor the storage areas for heavy military equipment withdrawn from the security zone and restricted weapons zone;
- monitor the withdrawal of Georgian troops from the Kodori valley to locations beyond the frontiers of Abkhazia;
- patrol the Kodori valley regularly;
- investigate reported or alleged violations of the Agreement and attempt to resolve such incidents.

Location Georgia.
Headquarters Sukhumi.
Strength 83 military observers, supported by locally recruited staff.

Contributors Alb, A, Bng, Cz, Da, Et, Ge, Gr, Hu, Indo, HKJ, ROK, Pak, Pl, RF, Swe, CH, UK, Ury, US.
Cost *1996* $16m *1997* $18m *1998* $19m. Total cost to June 1998: $65m.

United Nations Mission of Observers in Tajikistan (UNMOT)

Mission UNMOT was established in December 1994 to assist a Joint Commission – composed of representatives of the Tajik government and the Tajik opposition – to monitor the implementation of the Agreement on a Temporary Cease-fire and the Cessation of Other Hostile Acts on the Tajik–Afghan Border and within Tajikistan. Since the June 1997 peace accord its tasks are to:
* monitor the implementation of the Agreement of National Reconciliation and Peace Establishment of 27 June 1997 and the cessation of other hostile acts on the Tajik–Afghan border and within the country;
* investigate alleged violations of the agreement and report them;
* provide liaison with the mission of the Organisation for Security and Cooperation in Europe (OSCE), with the collective peacekeeping forces of the CIS in Tajikistan and with the border forces;
* provide support for the UN Secretary-General's Special Envoy;
* provide political liaison and coordination services to facilitate expeditious humanitarian assistance by the international community.
Location Tajikistan.
Headquarters Dushanbe.
Strength 74 military observers, supported by locally recruited staff.
Contributors A, Bng, Bg, Cz, Da, Gha, Indo, HKJ, N, Nga, Pl, CH, Ukr, Ury.
Cost *1996* $7m *1997* $8m *1998* $8m. Total cost to June 1998: $27m.

United Nations Mission in the Central African Republic (MINURCA)

Mission MINURCA was established on 15 April 1998 to:
* maintain security and stability in the area surrounding Bangui;
* supervise the final disposition of weapons;
* assist in efforts to train a national police force;
* provide advice and technical assistance for national elections;
* ensure the safety and freedom of movement of United Nations personnel and property.
MINURCA replaced the Mission Interafricaine de Surveillance des Accords de Bangui (MISAB).
Location Central African Republic.
Headquarters Bangui.
Strength 1,345 troops, 20 civilian police.
Contributors Bn, BF, Ca, Cha, CI, Et, Fr, Gbn, Por, RMM, Sen, Tg.
Cost *1998* $29m. Total cost to June 1998: $23m.

United Nations Civilian Police Support Group (UNPSG)

Mission UNPSG was established on 16 January 1998 to monitor the performance of the Croatian police with respect to the return of displaced persons. The UNPSG has stationed police monitors in the main Croatian police headquarters and at 20 Croatian police stations in the Danube region. It also maintains three mobile patrols. UNPSGs original mandate was for nine months but the group may be terminated before that should its mission be deemed complete.
Location Eastern Slavonia, Baranja and Western Sirmium (Croatia).
Headquarters Vukovar and Zagreb.

Analyses and Tables

Strength 177 civilian police, assisted by 31 troops and supported by international and locally recruited staff.
Contributors Arg, A, CH, Da, Et, Fji, HF, Indo, Irl, HKJ, Kya, L, N, Nga, No, Pl, RF, Swe, Tn, Ukr, US.
Cost *1998* $8m. Total cost to June 1998: $3m.

United Nations Observer Mission in Sierra Leone (UNOMSIL)

Mission UNOMSIL was established in July 1998 to observe the disarmament, demobilisation and reintegration of ex-combatants, and to monitor the military and security situation within Sierra Leone. The original mandate of UNOMSIL is scheduled to end after a six month period.
Location Sierra Leone.
Headquarters Freetown.
Authorised Strength 70 military observers, accompanied by a medical unit and assisted by international and locally recruited civilian staff. (As of 1 August, 14 and 1 civilian police.)
Contributors PRC, Et, Ind, Kya, Kgz, NZ, Pak, RF, UK, Z.
Cost *1998* $18m.

OTHER MISSIONS

A number of peacekeeping missions are currently under way which are not under UN control. The major operations are shown below. Not shown are those of very brief duration or those that are covered under the regional text and country section concerned (for example ECOMOG in Liberia and Sierra Leone, and MOMEP in Ecuador and Peru). The OSCE conducts a number of observer missions in areas of conflict – for example, Chechnya and Nagorno-Karabakh – which fluctuate in size and contributors. The OSCE also undertakes a number of important security-related non-military missions, such as supervising elections and conflict mediation (as in Tajikistan). There are nine long-term missions deployed in Bosnia-Herzegovina, Croatia, Estonia, Georgia, Latvia, Moldova, Skopje, Tajikistan and Ukraine. A small number of military observers are participating in these missions, but no armed forces formations are involved. While the OSCE describes these missions as long term, their mandates vary from three to six months (renewable).

NATO Stabilisation Force (SFOR) II for Bosnia and Herzegovina

Mission SFOR II was established on 20 June 1998 to follow on from SFOR I. Its mission is to continue to support implementation of the 1995 General Framework Agreement for Peace in Bosnia and Herzegovina and respond to the resolutions of the United Nation's Security Council. No date has been set for the end of the mandate. SFOR's principal tasks remain:

- to maintain the Zone of Separation (ZOS) and keep it free from armed groups, ensuring heavy weapons remain in approved storage areas, and freedom of movement exists throughout the country for SFOR and civilian agencies. SFOR is to promote freedom of movement across the Inter Entity Boundary Line (IEBL) for all citizens of Bosnia and Herzegovina, but cannot be expected to guarantee the freedom of movement of individuals throughout Bosnia and Herzegovina or forcibly return refugees. By successfully accomplishing these principal military tasks, SFOR will contribute to a secure environment within which civilian agencies can continue to undertake economic development, reconstruction, establish political institutions, and create an overall climate of reconciliation for the people of Bosnia and Herzegovina;
- to maintain control of the airspace over Bosnia and Herzegovina and of the movement of military traffic over key ground routes;
- to continue to use Joint Military Commissions;

- to give selective support to international organisations in their humanitarian missions;
- to assist in observing and preventing interference with the movement of civilian populations, refugees and displaced persons, and respond appropriately to deliberate violence;
- to assist in monitoring the clearance of minefields and obstacles.

Location Bosnia-Herzegovina with supporting elements in Croatia and bases in Italy and Hungary. A maritime component is at sea in the Adriatic with a naval unit based ashore at Split.

Headquarters

- The Commander of SFOR (COMSFOR) has a headquarters in Sarajevo and commands three divisions with their headquarters based in Mostar, Tuzla and Banja Luka.
- The Commander of the SFOR Air Component is the NATO Commander Allied Air Forces Southern Europe who exercises his operational control through his Combined Air Operations Centre (CAOC) at Vincenza, Italy.
- The SFOR Naval Component is commanded by NATO's Commander Allied Naval Forces Southern Europe. This component comprises ships from several nations which are formed into task forces and are available or can be called upon for support.
- NATO's Commander Allied Striking Forces Southern Europe commands carrier-based aviation and amphibious forces in the region, which are not an integral part of SFOR, but are earmarked to support it if needed.

Strength up to 33,200 (up to 27,055 NATO forces and 6,110 from non-NATO countries).

Contributors

NATO Be, Ca, Fr, Ge, Gr, It, Lu, Nl, Po, Sp, Tu, UK, US. Iceland, which has no armed forces, is contributing civilian medical personnel.

Non-NATO A, Alb, Bg, Cz, Et, Ea, Hu, HKJ, Lat, L, Mal, Mor, Pl, R, RF, Slvk (civilian personnel only), Ukr.

Cost *1996*ε $5bn (IFOR) *1997*ε $4bn *1998*ε $4bn. Total cost to June 1998: ε$11bn.

NUCLEAR WEAPONS

Strategic Arms Reduction Treaty (START)

While the inspection process under the Strategic Arms Reduction Treaty (START) I is proceeding satisfactorily, the progress to entry-into-force of START II is stalled. The US Congress ratified the treaty in 1996, but the Russian *Duma* has yet to approve ratification. The reasons for the delay are political rather than military. There are strong military and economic reasons for Russia to ratify the treaty and move quickly to negotiate on further reductions under a START III. Russia cannot, given present economic conditions, maintain parity with the US under the allowed START I levels. It would even have difficulty in maintaining parity at the reduced levels of 3,000 to 3,500 warheads under START II, particularly as only single warhead missiles will be allowed under this treaty. Russia would have to build up its inventory of single warhead missiles (SS-27) to reach the permitted levels. This factor was taken into account in the March 1997 US–Russia Presidential Summit declarations and confirmed in a document signed by both governments in September 1997; both sides agreed to commit themselves to START III negotiations once Russia has ratified START II.

The number of strategic delivery vehicles declared by Russia and the US under their Memorandum of Understanding under START I, and by Belarus, Kazakstan and Ukraine under the terms of the Lisbon Protocols to the treaty are shown below (as at 1 January 1998).

Table 45 **Aggregate numbers of strategic offensive delivery vehicles**			
(as at 1 January 1998)	**ICBM**	**SLBM**	**Bombers**
US	701	464	321
Russia	756	648	80
Belarus	0	0	0
Kazakstan	0	0	0
Ukraine	66[1]	0	44
Totals	**1,523**	**1,112**	**445**

Note: [1]There are no warheads with these missiles.

Other Nuclear Developments

The nuclear tests by India and Pakistan have been a serious set back to progress in nuclear disarmament, particularly for the Comprehensive Nuclear Test Ban Treaty (CTBT). However, more states have come forward to sign and ratify the treaty; as at 31 July 1998, 150 states had signed and 17 had ratified. The treaty does not come into force until 44 states with nuclear capabilities, named in the treaty, have ratified it. Of the 44, only India, North Korea and Pakistan have not signed, but by 31 July 1998 only nine had ratified. All five permanent members of the UN Security Council have signed, but to date only France and the UK have ratified.

A positive development is that the long-awaited negotiations on the Fissile Material Cut Off Treaty (FMCT) can now start. In August 1998, all 60 members of the Conference on Disarmament (CD) in Geneva, including India and Pakistan, reached consensus on setting up a committee to negotiate the treaty beginning at the autumn 1998 session of the CD.

BIOLOGICAL WEAPONS CONVENTION

Efforts to agree a legally binding compliance and verification protocol for the Biological Weapons Convention (BWC) continue. The *Ad Hoc* Group of states party to the convention, which was set up to draft the protocol, held its eleventh session in Geneva from 22 June to 10 July 1998. The Group is working on a rolling text in which the key issues are:

- *Declarations* under which members of the Convention will provide data on specified facilities that have potential for use in a biological weapons (BW) programme. Such facilities could include, for example, veterinary vaccine production facilities where special equipment is required to handle potentially lethal pathogens.
- *On-site measures* which include visits or inspections, some of which are pre-planned and others are undertaken at short notice to specified types of facilities that have a BW capability. The Group is also engaged in drafting procedures for field investigations of alleged use of BW or other major breaches of the Convention.
- *Conducting exchanges of materials, equipment and scientific and technological information* on biological agents and toxins for peaceful purposes (as called for under Article X of the BWC) and ensuring that measures being devised do not hinder non-military economic or technological development.

There are other important issues taxing the negotiators in the Group such as definitions, listing of human pathogens and protecting the confidentiality of information exchanged during visits and inspections. There are many aspects of the rolling text yet to be agreed by the 50–60 Convention members participating in the discussions and agreement on a text is unlikely in 1998. The last of three meetings of the *Ad Hoc* Group in 1998 was due to be held from 28 September to 16 October.

CHEMICAL WEAPONS CONVENTION

As at 14 August 1998, 114 states were members of the Chemical Weapons Convention (CWC). All five permanent members of the UN Security Council have now joined – the last to do so being Russia which deposited its ratification on 5 November 1998. The organisation overseeing the implementation of the CWC, the Organisation for the Prohibition of Chemical Weapons (OPCW), is now in full swing. It has a great deal of work dealing with the declarations required of member states of past and present CW programmes (if any), their chemical industries and their defensive programmes. More states declared past or present programmes than expected; nine states had made such declarations by 14 August 1998. This has placed a heavy inspection and oversight burden on the OPCW that has hindered their routine activities to some degree. The biggest destruction tasks by far are those which Russia and the US have to complete within the next decade.

ANTI-PERSONNEL LAND-MINES

The 'Convention on the Prohibition of the Use, Stockpiling, Production and Transfer of Anti-Personnel Mines and on their Destruction' (ICBL) opened for signature on 3 December 1997. By 18 August 1998, 31 of the 129 signatories had ratified the Convention. Among the signatories are former anti-personnel land-mine (APL) producers including the Czech Republic, Italy, France, Germany, the United Kingdom and Hungary.

A number of important APL producers and users have not signed the Convention on the basis that they consider the responsible use of mines to be a legitimate means of self-defence. These include Belarus, China, Cuba, India, Egypt, Iran, Iraq, Israel, Libya, North Korea, Russia, South Korea, Syria, Turkey, United States and Yugoslavia (Serbia and Montenegro).

The principal US objections to the ICBL are:

- the lack of an adequate transition period;
- the prohibition of mixed munitions, combining anti-tank mines with anti-personnel sub-munitions that self-destruct after a short time.

However, the US has stated its intention to end the use of APL outside Korea by 2003.

UN Weaponry Convention

The amended Protocol II of the Convention on Prohibitions or Restrictions on the Use of Certain Conventional Weapons that may be deemed to be Excessively Injurious or to have Indiscriminate Effects (UN Weaponry Convention) is to enter into force on the 3 December 1998. The Review Conference (September 1995–May 1996) adopted the protocol amendments on 3 May 1996. By 18 August 1998, 24 of the 72 states parties to the Convention had adopted the amended protocol. The principal purposes of the amendments are to:

- apply the Convention to internal as well as international conflicts;
- ban undetectable (plastic) mines and mines which explode on electro-magnetic detection;
- introduce a set of criteria for self-destructing or self-deactivating remotely delivered mines;
- introduce more rigorous standards for marking minefields.

Under amended Protocol II, states have nine years in which to replace existing stocks with land-mines built to the newly agreed specification. Protocol II also prohibits the transfer of prescribed land-mines to states that are not bound by the amended protocol and to non-state groups. The Protocol applies to all types of land-mines not only anti-personnel mines (which are banned for those countries that belong to the ICBL). Future review conferences are to be held more frequently with the next scheduled for no later than 2001.

UN REGISTER OF CONVENTIONAL ARMS

By mid-August 1998, 86 governments had submitted responses to the UN Arms Register of Conventional Arms covering 1997 deliveries of weapons in the seven prescribed categories[1]. This was two more than at the same stage in 1997. Of those reporting their arms imports and exports for 1997, 15 had not done so in the previous year, including Jordan, Qatar and Libya. This is encouraging as Arab League members were under pressure from Egypt to not report unless the Register was expanded to include weapons of mass destruction. The other 12 were Benin, Cameroon, Niger, Belize, Jamaica, Venezuela, Bhutan, Micronesia, Philippines, Tajikistan, San Marino and the Solomon Islands. Thirteen countries not reporting by mid-August 1998, which had responded by the same period in 1997, included Russia and China. Also missing in 1998 (as at 16 August 1998) were responses from the Dominican Republic, Ecuador, Grenada, Honduras, Indonesia, Latvia, Madagascar, Marshall Islands, Mexico, Trinidad and Tobago and Namibia.

---

[1] The categories are main battle tanks, armoured combat vehicles, large calibre artillery (100mm and above), combat aircraft, attack helicopters (with an integrated fire control system), warships (750 tonnes or over) and missiles and missile launchers with a range of 25 kilometres and over (excluding surface-to-air missiles).

Table 46 International comparisons of defence expenditure and military manpower in 1985, 1996 and 1997

(1997 constant prices)	Defence Expenditure US$m			US$ per capita			% of GDP			Numbers in Armed Forces (000)		Estimated Reservists (000)	Para-military (000)
	1985	1996	1997	1985	1996	1997	1985	1996	1997	1985	1997	1997	1997
Canada	11,147	8,624	7,757	439	304	270	2.2	1.4	1.3	83.0	61.6	28.7	11.1
US	367,711	277,254	272,955	1,537	1,044	1,018	6.5	3.6	3.4	2,151.6	1,447.6	1,711.7	85.7
NATO Europe													
Belgium	5,863	4,333	3,769	595	430	373	3.0	1.8	1.6	91.6	44.5	144.2	n.a.
Denmark	2,978	3,152	2,816	582	603	538	2.2	1.9	1.7	29.6	32.9	70.5	n.a.
France	46,522	47,401	41,545	843	812	708	4.0	3.3	3.0	464.3	380.8	292.5	92.3
Germany	50,220	39,828	33,416	662	491	412	3.2	1.8	1.6	478.0	347.1	315.0	n.a.
Greece	3,317	5,700	5,552	334	543	526	7.0	4.7	4.6	201.5	162.3	291.0	4.0
Iceland	n.a.	n.a.	n.a.	n.a.	n.a.	n.a.	n.a.	n.a.	n.a.	n.a.	n.a.	n.a.	0.1
Italy	24,471	23,947	21,837	428	414	377	2.3	2.1	1.9	385.1	325.2	484.0	255.7
Luxembourg	91	145	129	248	353	313	0.9	0.9	0.8	0.7	0.8	n.a	0.6
Netherlands	8,470	8,022	6,888	585	517	442	3.1	2.2	1.9	105.5	57.2	75.0	3.6
Norway	2,948	3,754	3,336	710	859	760	3.1	2.6	2.3	37.0	33.6	234.0	0.7
Portugal	1,746	2,657	2,559	171	269	259	3.1	2.8	2.6	73.0	59.3	210.9	40.9
Spain	10,731	8,802	7,671	278	225	196	2.4	1.7	1.4	320.0	197.5	431.9	75.8
Turkey	3,269	7,674	8,110	65	125	131	4.5	4.3	4.2	630.0	639.0	378.7	182.2
United Kingdom	45,408	35,266	35,736	803	604	611	5.2	3.0	2.8	327.1	213.8	320.8	n.a.
Subtotal NATO Europe	206,033	190,681	173,363	450	446	403	3.1	2.4	2.2	3,143.4	2,494.0	3,248.5	655.8
Total NATO	584,891	476,559	454,076	517	474	433	3.3	2.4	2.2	5,378.0	4,003.2	4,988.9	752.6
Non-NATO Europe													
Albania	269	103	94	91	29	26	5.3	6.7	6.7	40.4	54.0	155.0	13.5
Armenia	n.a.	125	138	n.a.	33	37	n.a.	7.7	8.9	n.a.	60.0	300.0	1.0
Austria	1,839	2,098	1,786	243	262	222	1.2	1.0	0.8	54.7	45.5	100.7	n.a.
Azerbaijan	n.a.	133	146	n.a.	18	19	n.a.	5.3	4.0	n.a.	66.7	560.0	40.0
Belarus	n.a.	501	381	n.a.	48	37	n.a.	4.1	2.9	n.a.	81.8	289.5	8.0
Bosnia-Herzegovina	n.a.	255	327	n.a.	58	74	n.a.	5.0	5.0	n.a.	40.0	100.0	n.a.
Bulgaria	2,331	373	339	276	45	41	14.0	3.3	3.4	148.5	101.5	303.0	34.0
Croatia	n.a.	1,308	1,147	n.a.	278	244	n.a.	6.8	5.7	n.a.	58.0	220.0	40.0
Cyprus	124	487	505	186	580	594	3.6	5.8	5.8	10.0	10.0	88.0	0.5
Czech Republic	n.a.	1,176	987	n.a.	114	96	n.a.	2.7	2.2	n.a.	61.7	240.0	5.6
Czechoslovakia	3,338	n.a.	n.a.	214	n.a.	n.a.	8.2	n.a.	n.a.	203.3	n.a.	n.a.	n.a.
Estonia	n.a.	110	119	n.a.	75	81	n.a.	2.5	2.5	n.a.	3.5	14.0	2.8
Finland	2,139	2,255	1,956	436	440	381	2.8	2.0	1.7	36.5	31.0	500.0	3.4
FYROM	n.a.	122	132	n.a.	54	58	n.a.	9.2	10.2	n.a.	15.4	100.0	7.5
Georgia	n.a.	110	109	n.a.	21	20	n.a.	3.3	2.9	n.a.	33.2	250.0	n.k.
Hungary	3,380	713	666	317	70	66	7.2	1.6	1.4	106.0	49.1	186.4	14.1
Ireland	456	757	767	128	209	210	1.8	1.1	1.0	13.7	12.7	15.6	n.a.
Latvia	n.a.	139	156	n.a.	56	63	n.a.	4.5	4.6	n.a.	4.5	16.6	3.6
Lithuania	n.a.	128	135	n.a.	34	36	n.a.	4.3	4.4	n.a.	5.3	11.0	4.8

(1997 constant prices)

	Defence Expenditure US$m			US$ per capita			% of GDP			Numbers in Armed Forces (000)		Estimated Reservists (000)	Para-military (000)
	1985	1996	1997	1985	1996	1997	1985	1996	1997	1985	1997	1997	1997
Malta	23	34	31	64	92	82	1.4	1.0	0.9	0.8	2.0	n.a.	n.a.
Moldova	n.a.	48	53	n.a.	11	12	n.a.	4.2	4.4	n.a.	11.0	66.0	3.4
Poland	8,202	3,730	3,073	220	97	79	8.1	3.4	2.3	319.0	241.8	406.0	23.4
Romania	1,987	762	793	87	33	35	4.5	2.3	2.3	189.5	227.0	427.0	79.1
Slovakia	n.a.	469	414	n.a.	87	77	n.a.	2.4	2.1	n.a.	41.2	20.0	4.0
Slovenia	n.a.	231	310	n.a.	115	154	n.a.	1.4	1.7	n.a.	9.6	53.0	4.5
Sweden	4,546	6,501	5,481	544	737	619	3.3	3.0	2.4	65.7	53.4	570.0	35.6
Switzerland	2,749	4,672	3,837	426	662	544	2.1	1.8	1.5	20.0	26.3	390.0	n.a.
Ukraine	n.a.	1,286	1,324	n.a.	25	26	n.a.	2.8	2.7	n.a.	387.4	1,000.0	36.0
FRY (Serbia-Montenegro)	4,759	1,502	1,489	204	142	140	3.8	8.7	7.8	241.0	114.2	400.0	30.0
Total	**36,142**	**30,129**	**26,693**	**246**	**158**	**146**	**4.8**	**3.8**	**3.7**	**1,449.1**	**1,847.5**	**6,781.8**	**394.8**
Russia	n.a.	73,990	64,000	n.a.	502	435	n.a.	6.5	5.8	n.a.	1,240.0	2,400.0	583.0
Soviet Union	343,616	n.a.	n.a.	1,232	n.a.	n.a.	16.1	n.a.	n.a.	5,300.0	n.a.	n.a.	n.a.

Middle East and North Africa

	1985	1996	1997	1985	1996	1997	1985	1996	1997	1985	1997	1997	1997
Algeria	1,357	1,840	2,114	62	65	73	1.7	4.0	4.6	170.0	124.0	150.0	146.2
Bahrain	215	295	364	516	504	608	3.5	5.4	6.5	2.8	11.0	n.a.	9.9
Egypt	3,679	2,742	2,743	76	46	45	7.2	4.5	4.3	445.0	450.0	254.0	230.0
Gaza and Jericho	n.a.	n.a.	n.a.	n.a.	n.a.	n.a.	n.a.	n.a.	n.a.	n.a.	n.a.	n.a.	35.0
Iran	20,258	3,442	4,695	454	52	68	36.0	5.0	6.6	305.0	518.0	350.0	350.0
Iraq	18,328	1,277	1,250	1,153	59	56	25.9	8.3	7.4	520.0	387.5	650.0	55.4
Israel	7,196	11,202	11,143	1,700	1,943	1,917	21.2	11.8	11.5	142.0	175.0	430.0	6.1
Jordan	857	461	496	245	101	105	15.9	6.4	6.4	70.3	104.1	35.0	30.0
Kuwait	2,558	3,973	3,618	1,496	1,897	1,681	9.1	12.5	11.4	12.0	15.3	23.7	5.0
Lebanon	285	494	676	107	121	163	9.0	3.7	4.5	17.4	55.1	n.a.	18.5
Libya	1,923	1,327	1,250	511	237	215	6.2	5.1	4.7	73.0	65.0	40.0	0.5
Mauritania	74	27	24	44	12	10	6.5	2.5	2.2	8.5	15.7	n.a.	5.0
Morocco	913	1,431	1,386	42	51	48	5.4	3.8	4.2	149.0	196.3	150.0	42.0
Oman	3,072	1,957	1,815	1,920	997	887	20.8	12.5	10.9	2.5	43.5	n.a.	4.4
Qatar	427	772	1,346	1,357	1,391	2,380	6.0	8.9	13.7	6.0	11.8	n.a.	n.a.
Saudi Arabia	25,585	17,730	18,151	2,217	1,075	1,071	19.6	12.7	12.4	62.5	162.5	n.a.	15.5
Syria	4,961	2,132	2,217	472	144	145	16.4	6.4	6.3	402.5	320.0	500.0	8.0
Tunisia	594	406	334	83	44	35	5.0	2.0	1.8	35.1	35.0	n.a.	12.0
UAE	2,910	2,115	2,424	2,078	903	978	7.6	5.2	5.5	43.0	64.5	n.a.	1.0
Yemen	696	369	403	69	23	24	9.9	7.2	7.0	64.1	66.3	40.0	80.0
Total	**95,890**	**53,992**	**56,451**	**768**	**509**	**553**	**12.3**	**6.7**	**6.9**	**2,530.7**	**2,820.5**	**2,622.7**	**1,054.4**

Central and Southern Asia

	1985	1996	1997	1985	1996	1997	1985	1996	1997	1985	1997	1997	1997
Afghanistan	409	208	209	23	10	10	8.7	13.6	12.5	47.0	429.0	n.a.	n.a.
Bangladesh	356	554	593	4	4	5	1.4	1.7	1.9	91.3	121.0	n.a.	49.7

(1997 constant prices)

	Defence Expenditure US$m			US$ per capita			% of GDP			Numbers in Armed Forces (000)		Estimated Reservists (000)	Para-military (000)
	1985	1996	1997	1985	1996	1997	1985	1996	1997	1985	1997	1997	1997
India	8,921	12,079	12,805	12	13	13	3.0	3.3	3.3	1,260.0	1,145.0	528.4	1088.0
Kazakhstan	n.a.	552	503	n.a.	34	31	n.a.	2.8	2.3	n.a.	35.1	n.a.	34.5
Kyrgyzstan	n.a.	50	45	n.a.	11	10	n.a.	3.0	2.5	n.a.	12.2	57.0	5.0
Nepal	51	39	42	3	2	2	1.5	0.9	0.9	25.0	46.0	n.a.	40.0
Pakistan	2,957	3,652	3,503	31	27	26	6.9	5.9	5.8	482.8	587.0	513.0	247.0
Sri Lanka	325	887	898	21	49	49	3.8	6.3	6.1	21.6	117.0	4.2	110.2
Tajikistan	n.a.	118	132	n.a.	19	22	n.a.	11.0	12.1	n.a.	9.0	n.a.	1.2
Turkmenistan	n.a.	141	107	n.a.	31	23	n.a.	2.8	2.7	n.a.	18.0	n.a.	n.k.
Uzbekistan	n.a.	441	447	n.a.	19	19	n.a.	3.9	3.9	n.a.	70.0	n.a.	16.0
Total	13,019	18,722	19,283	15	20	19	4.2	5.0	4.9	1,927.7	2,589.3	1,102.6	1,591.6

East Asia and Australasia

	1985	1996	1997	1985	1996	1997	1985	1996	1997	1985	1997	1997	1997
Australia	7,755	8,755	8,501	492	474	456	3.4	2.3	2.2	70.4	57.4	33.7	1.0
Brunei	292	344	353	1,304	1,138	1,141	6.0	6.7	6.7	4.1	5.0	0.7	4.1
Cambodia	n.a.	185	254	n.a.	19	25	n.a.	5.7	7.3	35.0	140.5	n.a.	220.0
China	28,273	36,176	36,551	27	30	30	7.9	5.7	5.7	3,900.0	2,840.0	1,200.0	800.0
Fiji	20	49	48	29	63	61	1.2	2.6	2.6	2.7	3.6	6.0	n.a.
Indonesia	3,334	4,797	4,812	21	24	24	2.8	2.1	2.2	278.1	284.0	400.0	200.0
Japan	30,612	45,502	40,891	254	362	325	1.0	1.0	1.0	243.0	235.6	46.7	12.0
Korea, North	5,919	5,559	5,409	290	254	246	23.0	27.2	27.0	838.0	1,055.0	4,700.0	189.0
Korea, South	8,962	16,172	14,732	218	358	320	5.1	3.7	3.3	598.0	672.0	4,500.0	4.5
Laos	78	79	63	22	16	12	7.8	4.9	3.9	53.7	29.0	n.a.	100.0
Malaysia	2,513	3,695	3,377	161	176	157	5.6	4.2	3.7	110.0	111.5	37.8	20.1
Mongolia	49	15	18	26	6	8	9.0	1.4	2.0	33.0	9.0	137.0	5.9
Myanmar	1,252	2,012	2,167	34	42	45	5.1	7.6	7.7	186.0	429.0	n.a.	85.3
New Zealand	920	1,022	901	283	287	251	2.9	1.8	1.6	12.4	9.6	7.0	n.a.
Papua New Guinea	51	80	63	15	18	14	1.5	1.5	1.2	3.2	4.3	n.a.	n.a.
Philippines	675	1,520	1,422	12	21	20	1.4	2.0	1.7	114.8	110.5	131.0	42.5
Singapore	1,692	4,129	4,122	661	1,382	1,360	6.7	4.6	4.3	55.0	70.0	263.8	108.0
Taiwan	9,171	13,868	13,657	473	651	634	7.0	4.8	4.7	444.0	376.0	1,657.5	26.7
Thailand	2,669	4,393	3,248	52	72	52	5.0	2.6	2.1	235.3	266.0	200.0	71.0
Vietnam	3,418	970	990	55	13	13	19.4	4.0	4.1	1,027.0	492.0	3,000.0	65.0
Total	107,656	149,324	141,580	233	270	260	6.4	4.8	4.7	8,243.7	7,200.0	16,321.1	1,955.0

Caribbean, Central and Latin America

Caribbean

	1985	1996	1997	1985	1996	1997	1985	1996	1997	1985	1997	1997	1997
Antigua and Barbuda	3	4	3	41	52	39	0.5	0.6	0.5	0.1	0.2	0.1	n.a.
Bahamas	14	22	22	59	83	82	0.5	0.7	0.6	0.5	0.9	n.a.	2.3
Barbados	16	14	14	74	51	49	0.9	0.6	0.6	1.0	0.6	0.4	n.a.
Cuba	2,275	715	720	225	65	65	9.6	5.4	5.2	161.5	60.0	39.0	19.0

| (1997 constant prices) | Defence Expenditure | | | | | | | | | Numbers in Armed Forces (000) | | Estimated Reservists (000) | Para-military (000) |
| | US$m | | | US$ per capita | | | % of GDP | | | | | | |
	1985	1996	1997	1985	1996	1997	1985	1996	1997	1985	1997	1997	1997
Dominican Republic	73	116	120	11	15	15	1.1	1.2	1.2	22.2	24.5	n.a.	15.0
Haiti	44	102	99	7	14	14	1.5	5.4	5.2	6.9	n.a.	n.a.	5.5
Jamaica	28	28	29	13	11	11	0.9	0.5	0.6	2.1	3.3	1.0	0.2
Trinidad and Tobago	104	67	83	88	51	63	1.4	1.2	1.4	2.1	2.1	n.a.	4.8
Central America													
Belize	6	15	16	34	68	69	1.4	2.5	2.6	0.6	1.1	0.7	n.a.
Costa Rica	41	53	59	16	15	17	0.7	0.6	0.7	n.a.	n.a.	n.a.	7.0
El Salvador	359	149	176	75	26	30	4.4	1.7	1.9	41.7	28.4	15.0	12.0
Guatemala	167	211	182	21	19	16	1.8	1.8	1.5	31.7	40.7	35.0	9.8
Honduras	103	100	101	23	16	16	2.1	2.2	2.1	16.6	18.8	60.0	5.5
Mexico	1,768	3,629	3,664	22	39	39	0.7	1.0	1.0	129.1	175.0	300.0	15.0
Nicaragua	314	37	36	96	9	8	17.4	1.6	1.4	62.9	17.0	n.a.	n.a.
Panama	128	112	114	59	42	41	2.0	1.3	1.3	12.0	n.a.	n.a.	11.8
South America													
Argentina	5,157	4,644	4,687	169	134	134	3.8	1.8	1.7	108.0	73.0	375.0	31.2
Bolivia	181	159	155	28	19	18	2.0	2.2	2.0	27.6	33.5	n.a.	37.1
Brazil	3,347	14,248	13,944	25	87	84	0.8	2.4	2.3	276.0	314.7	1115.0	385.6
Chile	1,769	2,038	2,148	147	141	147	7.8	2.8	2.8	101.0	94.3	50.0	31.2
Colombia	604	2,562	3,068	21	72	85	1.6	3.5	4.0	66.2	146.3	60.7	87.0
Ecuador	405	625	692	43	52	57	1.8	3.5	3.5	42.5	57.1	100.0	0.3
Guyana	45	7	7	57	9	9	6.8	1.0	1.0	6.6	1.6	1.5	1.5
Paraguay	85	134	134	23	26	26	1.3	1.5	1.5	14.4	20.2	164.5	14.8
Peru	913	1,135	1,276	49	47	52	4.5	2.1	2.2	128.0	125.0	188.0	78.0
Suriname	12	14	15	30	35	36	2.4	4.4	4.4	2.0	1.8	n.a.	n.a.
Uruguay	340	286	307	113	89	96	3.5	2.3	2.3	31.9	25.6	n.a.	0.5
Venezuela	1,174	796	962	68	36	42	2.1	1.0	1.1	49.0	56.0	8.0	23.0
Total	19,474	32,022	32,832	58	47	49	3.0	2.0	2.0	1,344.2	1,321.6	2,513.9	798.0
Sub-Saharan Africa													
Horn Of Africa													
Djibouti	46	21	20	106	32	30	7.9	5.4	5.0	3.0	9.6	n.a.	3.0
Eritrea	n.a.	61	65	n.a.	17	17	n.a.	8.4	8.3	n.a.	46.0	n.a.	n.a.
Ethiopia	636	127	139	15	2	3	17.9	2.0	2.1	217.0	120.0	n.a.	n.a.
Somali Republic	66	41	40	12	7	7	6.2	4.8	4.8	62.7	225.0	n.a.	n.a.
Sudan	152	412	418	7	14	14	3.2	5.8	5.6	56.6	79.7	n.a.	15.0
Central Africa													
Burundi	50	52	60	11	8	9	3.0	5.1	5.7	5.2	18.5	n.a.	3.5
Cameroon	226	228	240	22	16	17	1.4	2.5	2.9	7.3	13.1	n.a.	9.0
Cape Verde	5	4	4	16	9	9	0.9	1.8	1.7	7.7	1.1	n.a.	0.5

(1997 constant prices)

	Defence Expenditure US$m			US$ per capita			% of GDP			Numbers in Armed Forces (000)		Estimated Reservists (000)	Para-military (000)
	1985	1996	1997	1985	1996	1997	1985	1996	1997	1985	1997	1997	1997
Central African Republic	25	31	39	10	9	11	1.4	3.1	4.0	2.3	2.7	n.a.	2.3
Chad	53	40	43	11	6	6	2.9	4.0	4.1	12.2	25.4	n.a.	9.5
Congo	80	56	74	43	20	26	1.9	1.9	2.5	8.7	10.0	n.a.	5.0
DROC	115	174	308	4	4	7	1.5	2.8	5.3	48.0	40.0	n.a.	37.0
Equatorial Guinea	4	2	5	11	5	10	2.0	1.0	1.3	2.2	1.3	n.a.	0.3
Gabon	113	114	115	113	84	83	1.8	2.0	1.9	2.4	4.7	n.a.	4.8
Rwanda	47	97	103	8	12	13	1.9	6.8	5.5	5.2	55.0	n.a.	7.0
East Africa													
Kenya	365	216	235	18	8	8	3.1	2.2	2.4	13.7	24.2	n.a.	5.0
Madagascar	77	38	37	8	3	3	2.0	0.9	0.8	21.1	21.0	n.a.	7.5
Mauritius	3	94	87	4	82	75	0.3	2.3	2.1	1.0	n.a.	n.a.	1.8
Seychelles	11	11	10	175	150	141	2.1	3.1	2.9	1.2	0.2	n.a.	0.3
Tanzania	199	114	123	9	4	4	4.4	3.3	3.4	40.4	34.6	80.0	1.4
Uganda	75	156	166	5	8	8	1.8	2.4	2.4	20.0	55.0	n.a.	1.5
West Africa													
Benin	30	27	27	7	5	5	1.1	1.2	1.3	4.5	4.8	n.a.	2.5
Burkina Faso	48	68	67	6	6	6	1.1	2.4	2.2	4.0	5.8	n.a.	4.2
Côte d'Ivoire	108	96	101	11	6	7	0.8	0.9	0.9	13.2	8.4	12.0	7.0
Gambia, The	3	15	15	4	14	13	1.5	3.9	3.7	0.5	0.8	n.a.	n.a.
Ghana	90	123	134	7	7	7	1.0	1.4	1.5	15.1	7.0	n.a.	1.0
Guinea	74	58	51	12	8	7	1.8	1.9	1.6	9.9	9.7	n.a.	9.6
Guinea Bissau	16	9	8	18	8	7	5.7	3.0	2.6	8.6	7.3	n.a.	2.0
Liberia	40	46	45	18	15	14	2.4	4.1	3.9	6.8	22.0	n.a.	n.a.
Mali	43	42	43	6	4	4	1.4	1.8	1.7	4.9	7.4	n.a.	7.8
Niger	17	22	22	3	2	2	0.5	1.4	1.4	2.2	5.3	n.a.	5.4
Nigeria	1,069	1,913	1,965	11	18	18	3.4	4.1	4.0	94.0	77.0	n.a.	30.0
Senegal	90	76	71	14	9	8	1.1	1.7	1.6	10.1	13.4	n.k.	4.0
Sierra Leone	7	47	52	2	10	10	1.0	5.9	6.9	3.1	15.0	n.a.	0.8
Togo	27	29	29	9	6	6	1.3	2.5	2.1	3.6	7.0	n.a.	0.8
Southern Africa													
Angola	921	460	658	105	42	58	15.1	6.5	8.8	49.5	110.5	n.a.	15.0
Botswana	53	234	241	49	153	153	1.1	6.7	6.5	4.0	7.5	n.a.	1.0
Lesotho	66	33	32	42	16	15	4.6	5.0	4.6	2.0	2.0	n.a.	n.a.
Malawi	30	24	23	4	2	2	1.0	1.2	1.1	5.3	5.0	n.a.	1.0
Mozambique	340	64	72	25	4	5	8.5	3.7	3.9	15.8	6.1	n.a.	n.a.
Namibia	n.a.	74	89	n.a.	44	51	n.a.	3.0	3.5	n.a.	5.8	n.a.	0.1
South Africa	4,091	2,804	2,326	122	74	60	2.7	2.2	1.8	106.4	79.4	386.0	138.0
Zambia	57	60	59	8	6	6	1.1	1.8	1.7	16.2	21.6	n.a.	1.4
Zimbabwe	242	242	304	29	21	26	3.1	3.9	4.7	41.0	39.0	n.a.	21.8
Total	**9,810**	**8,650**	**8,763**	**27**	**22**	**23**	**3.1**	**3.2**	**3.3**	**958.5**	**1,254.7**	**478.0**	**367.8**

Global Totals (1997 constant prices)

	Defence Expenditure US$m			US$ per capita			% of GDP			Numbers in Armed Forces (000)		Estimated Reservists (000)	Para-military (000)
	1985	1996	1997	1985	1996	1997	1985	1996	1997	1985	1997	1997	1997
NATO	584,891	476,559	454,076	517 / 965	474 / 713	433 / 639	3.3 / 4.7	2.4 / 3.0	2.2 / 2.8	5,378.0	4,003.2	4,988.9	752.6
Non-NATO Europe	36,142	30,129	26,693	246 / n.a.	158 / 133	146 / 108	4.8 / n.a.	3.8 / 2.4	3.7 / 2.0	1,449.1	1,847.5	6,781.8	394.8
Russia	n.a.	73,990	64,000	n.a.	502	435	n.a.	6.5	5.8	n.a.	1,240.0	2,400.0	583.0
Soviet Union	343,616	n.a.	n.a.	1,232	n.a.	n.a.	16.1	n.a.	n.a.	5,300.0	n.a.	n.a.	n.a.
Middle East and North Africa	95,890	53,992	56,451	768 / 458	509 / 185	553 / 188	12.3 / 15.1	6.7 / 8.2	6.9 / 8.1	2,530.7	2,820.5	2,622.7	1,054.4
Central and South Asia	13,019	18,722	19,283	15 / 11	20 / 14	19 / 14	4.2 / n.a.	5.0 / 3.6	4.9 / 3.6	1,927.7	2,589.3	1,102.6	1,591.6
East Asia and Australasia	107,656	149,324	141,580	233 / 67	270 / 82	260 / 72	6.4 / 2.3	4.8 / 1.9	4.7 / 2.1	8,243.7	7,200.0	16,321.1	1,955.0
Caribbean, Central and Latin America	19,474	32,022	32,832	58 / 50	47 / 55	49 / 67	3.0 / 1.9	2.0 / 1.7	2.0 / 2.0	1,344.2	1,321.6	2,513.9	798.0
Sub-Saharan Africa	9,810	8,650	8,763	27 / 23	22 / 15	23 / 15	3.1 / 3.3	3.2 / 2.7	3.3 / 2.7	958.5	1,254.7	478.0	367.8
Global totals	1,210,499	843,387	803,678	387 / 293	249 / 156	240 / 139	6.7 / 5.2	4.3 / 2.9	4.2 / 2.7	27,131.9	22,276.7	37,209.0	7,497.1

Note

Under *Defence Expenditure per capita* and *Defence Expenditure as a proportion of GDP*, the top figure is the arithmetic mean of individual country values, and the bottom number is the arithmetic mean of the sum of regional and global totals.

Table 47 **Warships** *Aircraft carriers, cruisers and destroyers*

This table provides a list of major surface combatants with a displacement of 2,000 tons and above (excluding ships specifically designed for amphibious operations). When a warship has been acquired from another country, the original class name is listed in the remarks column. Definitions of the types of principal surface combatants shown are on pp. 7–8.

Aircraft Carriers

Class name	Displacement (tons)	No. in service	Countries operating	Aircraft (average)	Missile launchers	Remarks
Chakri Naruebet	11,500	1	Th	12	8 LCHR *Sea Sparrow* SAM 3 Matra *Sadral* SAM	Built in Sp, not fully op
Clemenceau	27,300	1	Fr	39	2 *Crotale* SAM	Unit 2 (Foch) also has 2 Matra PDMS
Enterprise	75,700	1	US	56	3 x 8 *Sea Sparrow*	
Garibaldi	10,100	1	It	18	4 *Oto Melara* SSM 2 x 8 *Albatross* SAM	
Invincible	20,600	3	UK	20	1 x 2 *Sea Dart* SAM	
Kennedy	60,100	1	US	80	3 x 8 *Sea Sparrow* SAM	Reserve status, but fully op
Kitty Hawk	60,100	2	US	80	3 x 8 *Sea Sparrow* SAM	Kennedy reserve status, but fully op
Kuznetzov	55,000	1	RF	35	12 SS-NN-19 SSM 4 SA-N-9 SAM 8 CADS-N-1 SAM/gun	
Minas Gerais	17,500	1	Br	15	2 x 2 *Mistral* SAM	Ex-UK *Colossus*-class
Nimitz	73,000	8	US	80	3 x 8 *Sea Sparrow* SAM	Nuclear-powered
Principe de Asturias	17,100	1	Sp	20	0	
Viraat	23,900	1	Ind	20	2 x 4 *Seacat* SAM	Ex-UK *Hermes*-class; capacity for 32 ac

Class name	Displacement (Tons)	No. in service	Countries operating	Missile launchers	Torpedo tubes	Main guns	Remarks
Aguirre	12,000	1	Pe	0	0	4 152mm	Ex-Nl *De Ruyter*-class
Almirante Grau	12,100	1	Pe	8 *Otomat* SSM	0	8 152mm	Ex-Nl *De Ruyter*-class
California	8,700	2	US	2 x 4 *Harpoon* SSM 7 *Standard* SAM 8 ASROC ASW	4 324mm	2 127mm	Nuclear-powered
Jeanne d'Arc	10,000	1	Fr	6 *Exocet* SSM	0	4 100mm	4 *Alouette 3 / Dauphin* hel
Kara	9,000	2	RF	2 x 2 SA-N-3 SAM 6 SA-N-6 SAM 2 SA-N-4 SAM 2 x 4 SA-N-14 SSM/ASW	4 or 10 533mm	4 76mm	1 KA-25 hel

Cruisers

Class name	Displacement (Tons)	No. in service	Countries operating	Missile launchers	Torpedo tubes	Main guns	Remarks
Kirov	20,000	2	RF	20 SS-N-19 SSM, 12 SA-N-6 SAM, 2 SA-N-4 SAM, 2 SA-N-9 SAM, 6 CADS-N-1 SAM/gun, 2 SS-N-14 ASW	SS-N-15, 10 533mm	2 130mm, 2 100mm	SS-N-15 fired from TT not fitted to unit 1; nuclear-powered
Kynda	4,400	1	RF	8 SSN-3B SSM, 2 SAN-1 SAM	6 533mm	4 76mm	
Slava	10,000	3	RF	16 SS-N-12 SSM, 8 SA-N-6 SAM, 2 SA-N-4 SAM	10 533mm	2 130mm	Fourth unit nearly complete
Ticonderoga (CG-47 to 51)	9,000	5	US	8 Harpoon SSM, 4 ASROC ASW, 68 Standard SAM	6 324mm	2 127mm	*Aegis*-fitted
Ticonderoga (CG-52 to 73)	9,000	22	US	61 Tomahawk SLCM, 68 Standard SAM, 4 ASROC ASW	6 324mm	2 127mm	*Aegis*-fitted
Udaloy	7,000	9	RF	8 SA-N-9 SAM, 2 SS-N-14 SSM/ASW	8 533mm	2 100mm	2 KA-27 hel
Vittorio Veneto	9,000	1	It	4 Oto Melara SSM, 2 SM-1-ER SAM, 6 ASROC ASW	6 324mm	8 76mm	6 AB-212 hel

Destroyers

Class name	Displacement (Tons)	No. in service	Countries operating	Missile launchers	Torpedo tubes	Main guns	Remarks
Alamgir	2,500	2	Pak	6 SSM, 8 ASROC ASW	6 324mm	2 127mm	Ex-US *Gearing* hel deck
Almirante Brown	3,000	4	Arg	8 Exocet SSM, 8 Aspide SAM	6 324mm	1 127mm	Ex-Ge MEKO 360 2 SA-319B hel
Arleigh Burke	8,500	24	US	59 Tomahawk SLCM, 8 Harpoon SSM, 2M-2MR SAM, ASROC ASW	6 324mm	1 127mm	VLS for combination of *Tomahawk*, SM-2 MR and ASROC; SH-60B hel; *Aegis*-fitted
Audace	4,000	2	It	8 Oto Melara SSM, 1 SM-1ER SAM	6 324mm	1 127mm	2 AB 212 hel
Birmingham	3,500	12	UK	2 Sea Dart SAM	6 324mm	1 114mm	1 *Lynx* hel
Blanco Encalada	6,000	2	Chl	4 Exocet SSM, 2 Barak 1 SAM	6 324mm	2 114mm	Ex-UK *County*; 2 Super Puma hel
Cassard	4,500	2	Fr	8 Exocet SSM, 1 Standard SAM	2 ECAN L-5	1 100mm	

Class name	Displacement (Tons)	No. in service	Countries operating	Missile launchers	Torpedo tubes	Main guns	Remarks
Chien Yang	3,000	7	ROC	10 SM-1MR SAM, 8 ASROC ASW	6 324mm	1 76mm	Ex-US Gearing
Chung Buk	3,000	4	ROK	8 Harpoon SSM (5 of the class) 8 ASROC ASW (2 of the class)	6 324mm	4 or 6 127mm	Ex-US Gearing; 6 with SA-316B hel
Cuitlahuac	2,500	1	Mex	0	5 533mm	5 127mm	Ex-US Fletcher
Delhi	6,200	1	Ind	16 SS-N-25 SSM 1 SAN-7 SAM	6 324mm	1 100mm	
El Fateh	2,000	1	Et	0	5 533mm	4 114mm	Ex-UK Z
Ferre	3,000	1	Pe	8 Exocet SSM	0	6 114mm	Ex-UK Daring
Fu Yang	3,000	6	ROC	6 with 5 Hsiung Feng 1 SSM 1 with 8 ASROC ASW 4 Sidewinder SAM	6 324mm	2 or 4 127mm	Ex-US Gearing; 5 with MD-500 hel
Hatakaze	5,000	2	J	8 Harpoon SSM 1 SM-1MR SAM 8 ASROC ASW	6 324mm	2 127mm	
Hercules	3,500	2	Arg	4 Exocet SSM 2 Sea Dart SAM	6 324mm	1 114mm	Ex-UK Type 42
Illuicamina	3,000	2	Mex	8 ASROC ASW	6 324mm	4 127mm	Ex-US Gearing
Iroquois	5,000	4	Ca	1 Mk41 VLS SAM	6 324mm	1 76mm	Carries 2 CH-124 hel
Kashin	4,000	2	RF	4 SSN-2C SSM 2 SAN-SAM	6 533mm	4 76mm	
Kidd	8,000	2	US	8 Harpoon SSM 1 SM-2MR SAM 16 ASROC ASW	6 324mm	2 127mm	Carries 2 LAMPS hel
Kilic Ali Pasa	3,000	2	Tu	8 Harpoon (2 unit) 8 ASROC (1 unit)	6 324mm	4 127mm	Ex-US Gearing
Kimon	3,000	4	Gr	4 Harpoon SSM 8 ASROC ASW	6 324mm	4 127mm	Ex-US Adams
Komsomolets Ukrainyy	4,000	2	RF	4 SA-N-1 SAM	5 533mm	4 76mm	Kashin
Kongo	8,000	4	J	8 Harpoon SSM 2 SM-2MR SAM and ASROC ASW	3 324mm	1 127mm	
Kun Yang	2,500	3	ROC	5 HF-1 SSM	6 324mm	2 127mm	Ex-US Fletcher
Luda	3,500	15	PRC	6 HY-2 SSM 8 Crotale SAM	6 324mm	4 130mm	
Luda (Mod)	3,500	1	PRC	8 CSS-N-2 SSM on unit 1 8 C-801 SSM on unit 2	6 324mm	4 130mm	
Luhu	4,000	2	PRC	8 C-801 SSM, 8 Crotale SAM	6 324mm	2 100mm	
Luigi Durand de la Penne	4,500	2	It	8 Oto Melara/Tesco SSM 1 SM-1MR SAM	6 324mm	1 127mm	Ex-Animoso; carries 2 AB-312 hel

Analyses and **Tables**

Class name	Displacement (Tons)	No. in service	Countries operating	Missile launchers	Torpedo tubes	Main guns	Remarks
Lütjens	4,000	3	Ge	1 SM-1MR *Harpoon* SSM/SAM 8 ASROC ASW	6 324mm	2 127mm	Ex-US *Charles F. Adams*; temporarily non-op
Muntenia	5,000	1	R	8 SS-N-2C SSM 1 SA-N-5 SAM	6 533mm	4 76mm	Ex-*Muntenia*; carries 1 *Alouette 3* hel
Perth	4,000	3	Aus	1 SM-1MR SAM/*Harpoon*	6 324mm	2 127mm	Ex-US *Adams*
Po Yang	3,000	2	ROC	5 or 6 HF1 SSM 4 *Sea Chapparal*/ *Sidewinder* SAM	6 324mm	4 127mm	Ex-US *Sumner*
Prat	6,000	2	Chl	2 *Seaslug* SAM 4 *Exocet* SSM	6 324mm	2 114mm	Ex-UK *County*; carries 1 Bell 206B hel
Rajput	3,500	5	Ind	4 SS-N-2C SSM 4 SA-N-1 SAM	5 533mm	2 76mm	Ex-Sov *Kashin*
Sergipe	3,000	2	Br	0	6 324mm	6 127mm	Ex-US *Sumner*
Sovremennyy	7,000	11	RF	8 SS-N-22 SSM 1 SA-N-7 SAM	4 533mm	2 130mm	Carries 1 KA25/27 hel
Spruance		31	US	7 with 8 Mk44 *Tomahawk* SLCM 24 with 1 VLS Mk41 *Tomahawk* SLCM 7 with 8 ASROC ASW 8 *Harpoon* SSM 8 *Sea Sparrow* SAM	0	2 127mm	1 LAMPS hel
Suffren	5,500	2	Fr	4 *Exocet* SAM 2 *Mascura* SAM 1 *Malafon* ASW	4 ECAN L5	2 100mm	
Tachikaze	3,900	3	J	1 SM-1MR SAM 8 ASROC	6 324mm	2 127mm	
Tromp	4,000	2	Nl	1 SM-1MR SAM 2 4 *Harpoon*	6 324mm	2 120mm	1 *Lynx* hel
Van Heemskerck	3,700	2	Nl	8 *Harpoon* SSM 1 SM-1MR SAM	4 324mm	1 *Goalkeeper*	
Warszawa	4,000	1	Pl	4 SS-N-2C SSM 4 SA-N-1 SAM	5 533mm	4 76mm	Ex-Sov Mod *Kashin*

Table 48 Conventional Armed Forces in Europe (CFE) Treaty

Manpower and Treaty Limited Equipment: current holdings and CFE limits on the forces of the Treaty members

Current holdings are derived from data declared as of 1 January 1998 and so may differ from *The Military Balance* listings

	Manpower		Tanks[1]		ACV[1]		Artillery[1]		Attack Helicopters		Combat Aircraft[2]	
	Holding	Limit	Holding	Limit	Holding	Limit	Holding	Limit	Holding	Limit	Holding	Limit
Budapest/Tashkent Group												
Armenia	60,000	60,000	102	220	218	220	225	285	7	50	6	100
Azerbaijan	69,941	70,000	270	220	557	220	301	285	15	50	48	100
Belarus	83,518	100,000	1,778	1,800	2,520	2,600	1,529	1,615	64	80	250	294
Bulgaria	92,955	104,000	1,475	1,475	1,985	2,000	1,744	1,750	43	67	234	235
Czech Republic	58,343	93,333	948	957	1,238	1,367	767	767	36	50	122	230
Georgia	30,000	40,000	79	220	111	220	107	285	3	50	7	100
Hungary	43,286	100,000	835	835	1,316	1,700	840	840	59	108	138	180
Moldova	11,063	20,000	0	210	209	210	154	250	0	50	0	50
Poland	225,690	234,000	1,727	1,730	1,440	2,150	1,580	1,610	105	130	306	460
Romania	219,639	230,000	1,375	1,373	2,095	2,100	1,435	1,475	16	120	362	430
Russia[a]	748,776	1,450,000	5,559	6,400	9,841	11,480	5,999	6,415	805	890	2,868	3,416
Slovakia	45,483	46,667	478	478	683	683	382	383	19	25	113	115
Ukraine	335,231	450,000	4,014	4,080	4,902	5,050	3,749	4,040	290	330	966	1,090
North Atlantic Treaty Group												
Belgium	38,873	70,000	155	334	539	1,099	243	320	46	46	137	232
Canada[b]	0	10,660	0	77	0	277	0	38	0	90	0	90
Denmark	30,520	39,000	327	353	286	316	503	553	12	12	77	106
France	285,763	325,000	1,210	1,306	3,672	3,820	1,107	1,292	303	396	619	800
Germany	268,481	345,000	3,135	4,166	2,500	3,446	2,059	2,705	204	306	532	900
Greece	158,621	158,621	1,735	1,735	2,306	2,534	1,887	1,878	20	30	503	650
Italy	250,692	315,000	1,313	1,348	2,924	3,339	1,758	1,955	134	139	542	650
Netherlands	38,288	80,000	697	743	624	1,080	405	607	12	50	180	230
Norway	19,300	32,000	170	170	165	225	216	527	0	0	73	100
Portugal	38,417	75,000	187	300	354	430	340	450	0	26	101	160
Spain	160,372	300,000	688	794	1,187	1,588	1,154	1,310	28	90	198	310
Turkey[a]	527,670	530,000	2,542	2,795	2,529	3,120	2,839	3,523	26	103	388	750
UK	223,322	260,000	505	1,015	2,449	3,176	431	636	271	371	550	900
US	102,670	250,000	927	4,006	1,809	5,372	497	2,492	138	431	218	784

Notes

[1] Includes TLE with land-based maritime forces (Marines, Naval Infantry etc.)
[2] Does not include land-based maritime aircraft for which a separate limit has been set

[a] Manpower and TLE is for that in the Atlantic to the Urals (ATTU) zone only
[b] Canada has now withdrawn all its TLE from the ATTU

Table 49 Small arms and light weapons

This table describes a representative selection of military equipment in the categories defined in 'Report of Governmental Experts on Small Arms', A/52/298, United Nations, 27 August 1997. The entries are listed by country of origin (far-left column). Countries in square brackets no longer produce. The index of country abbreviations is on pp. 317–18.

Definitions
Sub-Machine Gun A small calibre weapon, generally 9mm or less, used as a close quarter infantry assault weapon but not normally capable of sustained fire.

Light Machine Gun A small calibre weapon, generally 7.62mm or less, used as an infantry assault weapon at ranges up to 600m but may act as a medium machine gun in a sustained fire role (1,000m plus) when fitted with a heavy barrel.

Heavy Machine Gun Generally of .50 in or 12.7mm in calibre, providing sustained fire to a range of some 1,500m and capable of being used in a ground or anti-air role.

Recoilless Rifle (RCL) A light portable weapon providing heavy fire power to infantry units and used chiefly in an anti-tank role at ranges up to 1,500m.

Rocket Launcher (RL) Smaller and lighter than the RCL, this weapon is portable by one man and is used primarily in an anti-tank role, firing its projectiles at lower muzzle velocities to a much reduced range, usually no more than 300m.

Notes
Weight Except where a warhead forms an integral part of a weapon system, figures in kg are for unloaded equipment.

Ammo (Ammunition) Figures represent total magazine holdings unless specified otherwise.

Effective Range/Altitude Ranges given are the maximum distance, under best conditions, at which a target could be engaged. In some cases it has not been possible to give a figure due to the absence of relevant information.

	Calibre (mm)	Designation	Weight (kg)	Effective range (m)	Ammo	Other producers • Remarks
Rifles						
A	5.56	Steyr AUG	3.8	–	30/42	Aus, Mal
Be	7.62	FN FAL	4.455	600	20	Arg, [A], [Aus], Br, [Ca], Ind, [Il], [Mex], [RSA], [UK], Ve
	5.56	FN FNC	4.01	450	30	Indo, Swe
CH	7.62	SG510-4	4.25	–	20	
	7.62	SG542	3.55	600	20/30	Chl
	5.56	SG540	3.26	–	20/30	Chl
Cz	7.62	Model 58	3.14	400	30	
Fr	5.56	FAMAS G2	3.8	450	30	
Ge	7.62	G3	4.4	400	20	Fr, Gr, Ir, Mex, My, [No], Pak, Por, Sau, [Swe], Tu, UK
	5.56	HK33	3.9	–	25/30	Th, UK
Il	5.56	*Galil*	3.95	–	35/50	Cr, RSA
	7.62	*Galil*	4.0	–	25	
It	7.62	BM 59	4.6	600	20	Indo, Mor
	5.56	AR70	3.8	–	30	
RF	7.62	SKS	3.85	400	10	PRC, DPRK, [FRY]
	7.62	AK-47	4.3	–	30	Bg
	7.62	AKM	3.14	300	30	PRC, Et, SF, Hu, Irq, DPRK, Pl, R, FRY
	5.45	AK-74	3.3	–	30	Bg, [Hu], Pl, R
UK	5.56	L85A1 (SA-80)	3.8	–	30	
US	0.30	M1 Carbine	2.36	300	15/30	
	7.62	M14	5.1	–	20	
	5.56	M16	3.1	400	20/30	Ca, [ROK], [Pi], [Sgp]
	5.56	M4 Carbine	2.52	360	20/30	
Sub-Machine Guns						
Cz	9	Model 23	3.27	–	24/40	
	7.65	Model 61 *Skorpion*	1.28			FRY
Da	9	*Madsen*	3.2	–	32	Br
Ge	9	MP5	2.55	–	15/30	Gr, Ir, Mex, Pak, Tu, UK
Il	9	*Uzi*	3.5	–	20/25/32	PRC, Cr, [RSA] • Production not licenced in PRC, Cr.
It	9	Model 12	3	–	20/32/40	Br, Indo
PRC	7.62	Type 79	1.9	–	20	
Swe	9	m/45	3.9	–	36	Et
UK	9	L2A3 (*Sterling*)	2.72	–	10/15/34	[Ca], Ind
US	9	Model 10 (*Ingram*)	2.84	–	32	

	Calibre (mm)	Designation	Weight (kg)	Effective range (m)	Ammo	Other producers • Remarks

Light Machine Guns

	Calibre (mm)	Designation	Weight (kg)	Effective range (m)	Ammo	Other producers • Remarks
A	5.56	AUG LSW	4.9	–	30/42	**Aus, Mal**
Be	7.62	FN MAG	11.65	1,500	belt	**Arg, Et, Ind, UK, US**
	5.56	FN *Minimi*	7.1	Up to 1,000	200-round belt or 30-round mag	**Aus, US**
Cz	7.62	Model 68	8.67	1,000–1,500	belt 50/250	
Fr	7.62	N AAT mle F1	9.97	1,200	belt	
Ge	7.62	HK 21	7.92	1,200	belt 20/80	**Por**
	7.62	HK 21A1	8.3	–	belt	**Gr**
	5.56	HK 13	6.0	400	25	
	7.62	MG3	11.05	800–2,200	belt	**Gr, Ir, Pak, [Sp], Tu**
PRC	7.62	Type 67	15.6	800–1,000	belt/drum 250/50	
RF	7.62	RP-46	13.0	800	250-round belt	
	7.62	RPD	7.1	800	100-round belt	**PRC, Et, [DPRK]**
	7.62	RPK	5.0	800	30/40/75	**Bg, Irq, R**
	5.45	RPK-74	4.6	460	30/40/45	**Bg, PRC, R**
RSA	7.62	SS77	9.6	–	belt	
UK	7.62	L4A4 (*Bren*)	8.68	–	30	**Ind**
	5.56	L86A1 LSW	5.4	–	30	
US	7.62	M60E3	8.8	1,100	belt	

Heavy Machine Guns

	Calibre (mm)	Designation	Weight (kg)	Effective range (m)	Ammo	Other producers • Remarks
Be	.50 in	M2 HB/QCB	36.0	1,500	belt	
PRC	12.7	Type 77	56.1	1,500	60-round belt	
	12.7	Type 85	41.0	1,500	60-round belt	
RF	12.7	DShK-38 & Model 38/46	35.7	1,500	belt	**PRC, Ir, Pak, R**
	12.7	NSV	25	2,000	belt	**Bg, Ind, Pl, FRY**

Grenade Launchers

	Calibre (mm)	Designation	Weight (kg)	Effective range (m)	Ammo	Other producers • Remarks
Cr	40	RGB-1	1.46	300	single shot	Mounted under fore-stock of AK-series assault rifles
Ge	40	HK69A1	2.62	350	single shot	
	40	HK79	1.5	350	single shot	Add-on launcher fitting all G3 rifles
Pl	40	PALLAD	2.3	430	single shot	Add-on launcher fitting AKM rifles
PRC	35	Type W87	12	600	6/9/12	
R	40	AGA-40	23.0	1,300	10	
RF	30	AGS-17	18.0	800–1,700	29	**PRC, Irq**
	40	GP-25	1.5	400	single shot	**Bg** • Add-on launcher for AKM/AK-74 rifles
RSA	40	MGL Mark 1	5.3	400	6	**Cr** (production reported as unauthorised and unlicenced)
Sgp	40	40AGL	33.0	2,200	belt	**Indo**
Sp	40	LAG 40 SB-M1	34.0	1,500	32-round belt	
US	40	M203	1.36	350	single shot	**Et, ROK**
	40	M79	2.72	350	single shot	**ROK**
	40	MK 19 Mod 3	35.3	1,500	32/48 belt	**ROK**

	Diameter/ calibre (mm)	Designation	Weight (kg)	Effective range (m)	Crew	Other producers • Remarks

Rocket Launchers (RL)

	Diameter/ calibre (mm)	Designation	Weight (kg)	Effective range (m)	Crew	Other producers • Remarks
Fr	70	*Wasp*	3.0	400	1	Single shot, disposable
	112	APILAS	4.7	330	1	As above
FRY	44	M80	6.6	200	2	
	90	M79	6.2	350–600	1	**Cr, FYROM** • Prepacked rocket and combustion chamber
Ge	60	*Panzerfaust* 3	12.0	300–400	1	Reusable firing/sighting device
Il	82	B-300	3.5	400	1	

Diameter/calibre (mm)		Designation	Weight (kg)	Effective range (m)	Crew	Other producers • Remarks
PRC	62	Type 70-1	3.21	150	1	Over-the-shoulder fired
	80	Type PF89	3.7	300–400	1	Single shot, disposable
RF	40	RPG-2	2.83	150	1	PRC • No longer produced
	40	RPG-7	6.9	300–500	1	Bg, PRC, Et, Ir, Irq, Pak, R
	64	RPG-18	2.7	200	1	Cz • Disposable launcher
	72.5	RPG-22	2.7	250	1	Bg
	105	RPG-27	7.6	200	1	
	105.2	RPG-29	11.5	450	1	Portable, shoulder fired
RSA	92	FT-5	5.9	400	1	
SF	55	M-55	8.5	200	1	
Sgp	75	*Armbrust*	6.3	300	1	Disposable launcher
Sp	88.9	M65	6.0	300–450	1	
	90	C90 (M3)	5.0	300	1	Disposable launcher
Swe	84	AT-4	7.5	300	1	US • Disposable launcher
UK	94	LAW 80	10.0	500	1	Disposable launcher
US	66	M72A5	3.45	220	1	No, FRY • Disposable launcher
	89 (3.5in)	M20	5.5	110	1	Br • Length is assembled 2-piece tube

Recoilless Launcher (RCL)

Br	57	M18A1	18.2	1,800–4,500	2	Shoulder/ground-mount fired
RF	73	SPG-9	45.0	1,300–4,500	4	Bg, Ir, R • Carried by 2 men
Swe	84	M3 *Carl Gustav*	8.5	700–1,100	2	Ind

Anti-Tank Guided Weapon

Arg	102	*Mathogo*	11.3	2–3,000	1	Wire-guided
Fr	160	*Eryx*	12.0	600	1	
Int	133	*Milan*	12.62	2,000	2	Ind • SACLOS, wire-guided
PRC	120	*Red Arrow 8*	24.5	3,000	2	Pak • SACLOS, wire-guided
RF	125	AT-3 *Sagger*	10.9	3,000	3	Bg, Ir, R, ROC, FRY • Wire-guided. Can be switched between MCLOS and SACLOS modes
	120	AT-4 *Fagot*	22.5	2,500	2–3	Bg • SACLOS, wire-guided
	135	AT-5 *Spandrel*	22.5	4,000	2–3	Bg, Ind, Slvk • SACLOS, wire-guided
	94	AT-7 *Saxhorn*	10.0	1,000	2	Bg • SACLOS, wire-guided
Swe	150	RBS-56 *Bill*	38.0	2,200	2	SACLOS, laser beam rider msl
US	–	*Dragon* II	15.4	1,500	1	CLOS, wire-guided
	127	*Javelin*	22.3	2,000	2	Fire-and-forget

Calibre (mm)		Designation	Total weight (kg)	Maximum range (m)	Crew	Other producers • Remarks

Mortars

Arg	60	MC 1-60 FMK-2	5.68	1,356	2–3	No longer produced
	60	MA 1-60 FMK-1	8.0	2,200	2–3	No longer produced
	60	MS 1-60 FMK-3	15.57	3,000	3–4	No longer produced
	81	LR FMK-2	42.0	4,000	3–4	No longer produced
A	60	C6	4.3	1,600	2–3	
	81	M8-111	35.6	5,800	3–4	
Be	60	NR 493	22.1	1,800	2–3	
	81	NR 475 A1	43.0	5,500	3–4	
CH	60	Model 87	7.6	1,000	2–3	
	81	Model 1972	45.5	4,100	3–4	
Chl	60	*Commando*	7.7	1,050	2–3	
Cr	60	M84	34.0	5,000	3–4	
Fr	60	*Commando*	8.1	1,050	2–3	
	81	MO 81 LC	39.2	4,140	3–4	Pak
FRY	50	M-8	7.3	480	2–3	
	60	M-70	7.8	1,632	2–3	
	60	M-57	19.85	1,700	2–3	
	60	M-90	32.6	5,208	2–3	

Calibre (mm)	Designation	Total weight (kg)	Maximum range (m)	Crew	Other producers • Remarks
81	M-68	41.5	5,000	3–4	
82	M-69A	45.0	6,050	3–4	
81	M-69B	47.6	5,400	3–4	
Il 52	IMI	7.9	420	2	
60	C-08	16.3	2,550	2–3	
81	Soltam	44.0	5,000	3–4	
Ind 51	E1	6.1	850	2	Copy of UK 2in
81	E1	40.6	5,000	3–4	
Ir 60	Hadid	17.5	2,550	2–3	Probably copy of Il Soltam
81	Hadid	50.5	4,900	3–4	Probably copy of Il Soltam
Irq 60	Al-Jaleel	22.0	2,500	2–3	
82	Al-Jaleel	63.0	4,900	3–4	
It 81	Breda	43.0	5,000	3–4	
Por 60	M/965	15.5	1,820	2–3	No longer produced
PRC 60	Type M-83A	14.7	2,655	2–3	
60	Type 63-1	11.5	1,550	2–3	**Et, Pak**
82	Type 67	35.0	3,040	3–4	
RF 82	M-36	57.3	3,100	3–4	No longer produced
82	M-37	56.0	3,040	3–4	**Bg, Et**
82	M-41	52.0	3,040	3–4	No longer produced
82	2B14 Podnos	41.88	4,270	3–4	**Bg**
ROK 60	KM 181	19.5	3,590	2	
RSA 60	M4	7.6	2,050	2–3	
SF 60	Vammas	16.0	2,600	3	
81	Vammas	40.0	5,900	3–4	
Sp 60	Model L	12.0	1,975	2–3	
81	Model LN	43.0	4,215	3–4	
Swe 81	m/29	60.0	2,600	3–4	No longer produced
Tu 60	Commando	8.4	1,700	2–3	
81	UT-1	71.2	5,900	3–4	
UK 51	L10A1	6.3	800	2	
81	L16A2	38.1	5,800	3–4	**J, US**
US 60	M2	19.07	1,816	2–3	No longer produced
60	M19	21.03	e1,800	2–3	No longer produced
81	M29	52.2	3,600	3–4	No longer produced

Surface-to-Air Missiles (Portable SAM)

	Designation	Length (m)	Weight (kg)	Max effective range (m)	Max effective altitude (m)	Other producers • Remarks
Fr	Mistral	2.0	24.0	5,000–6,000	3,000	Man portable or vehicle mounted, disposable
PRC	QW-1	1.532	16.5	5,000	4,000	**Pak** • Man portable, single round, disposable
	HN-5	1.44	16.0	4,400	2,500	**DPRK, Pak** • As above
RF	SA-18	1.708	18.0	5,200	3,000	Man portable, single round, reusable launch tube
	SA-16	1.7	18.7	5,200	2,000–3,000	**Bg, DPRK** • As above
	SA-14	1.5	16.0	4,500	3,000	**Bg** • As above
	SA-7	1.49	9.2	4,200	2,300	**Bg, PRC, Cr, Cz, Et, Pl, R, Slvn, FRY** • As above
Swe	RBS-70	1.745	16.5	7,000	4,000	Man portable, single round, disposable launch tube
UK	Starstreak	1.397	16.82	7,000	–	Man portable or vehicle mounted, disposable launch tube
	Starburst	1.394	23.7	4,000	–	As above
	Javelin	1.39	24.3	5,500	3,000	Man portable, disposable launch tube. No longer produced
	Blowpipe	1.40	20.7	3,500	2,500	As above
US	Stinger	1.52	20.7	4,800	3,800	**European Group (Ge, Gr, Nl, Tu)** • Man portable, single round, disposable launch tube

Table 50 **Armed Helicopters** *key characteristics*

Armed helicopters include attack helicopters equipped with integrated fire-control and aiming systems and combat support helicopters which are equipped with a variety of self defence and area suppression weapons. The data in this table are based on manufacturers' information which usually gives optimum capabilities. Abbreviations are listed on pp. 319–20.

Designation	Roles	Armament (major items)	Cruising Speed (km/hr)	Combat Radius (km)
A-109	AP•ATGW•obs	8 x TOW	230	167
A-129	AP•ATGW	8 x TOW	200	100
AB-212 ASW	ASW•ASUW	2 x Mk46 torp	156	122
AB-412 *Griffon*	AP•ATGW•obs	8 x TOW	226	197
AH-1 *Cobra*	Aslt•AP•ATGW•obs	8 x TOW	191	149
AH-6	AP•ATGW	4 x TOW	186	60
AH-64D *Apache*	AP•ATGW•aslt	16 x *Hellfire*; 30mm can	274	250
AS-332F *Super Puma*	ASUW	2 x *Exocet*	240	350
AS-350L2 *Ecureuil*	AP•ATGW	8 x TOW	204	143
AS-355 *Ecureuil 2*	AP•ATGW	4 x HOT	186	198
AS-365 *Dauphin*	ASUW	4 x AS-15 TT	234	76
AS-565 *Panther*	ASW•ASUW	4 x AS-15 TT	222	250
AUH-76	AP•ATGW	16 x *Hellfire*	232	141
Bell 406 CS	AP•ATGW	4 x TOW	204	139
BO-105	AP•ATGW	6 x HOT	204	130
Gazela	AP•aslt	4 x AT-3	218	217
EH-101 *Merlin*	ASW	4 x torp	278	500
Ka-25 *Hormone*	ASW	2 x torp	195	200
Ka-27 *Helix*	ASW	2 x torp	250	250
Ka-50 *Hokum*	AP•ATGW	12 x AT-12	300	260
Lynx AH-7	AP•ATGW	8 x TOW	213	90
Lynx HAS-3/HMA 8	ASW•ASUW	4 x *Sea Skua*; 2 x *Stingray* torp	177	75
MD-500	AP•ATGW	4 x TOW	186	73
MD-530	AP•ATGW	4 TOW	202	68
MH-6	AP•ATGW	4 x TOW	186	73
Mi-8 *Hip*	AP•ATGW	192 x rkt	189	60
Mi-14 *Haze*	ASW	2 x torp	184	271
Mi-17 *Hip*	AP•ATGW	4 x AT-6 rkt	202	90
Mi-24 *Hind*	AP•ATGW	8 x AT-6 rkt	248	80
MI-28 *Havoc*	AP•ATGW	16 x AT-9; 40 x C-8/C-13 rkt	250	200
OH-58D *Kiowa Warrior*	AP•ATGW•obs	4 x *Hellfire*	204	400
Rooivalk	AP•ATGW	Can; 4 x ZT-35	277	350
S-70A	ATGW	16 x *Hellfire*	225	129
SA-315B *Lama*	AP•ATGW•obs	4 x AS-11	161	130
SA-319 *Alouette*	AP•ATGW•obs	4 x AS-11	155	137
SA-321 *Super Frelon*	ASW•ASUW	2 x *Exocet*	208	143
SA-341 *Gazelle*	AP•ATGW•obs	4 x HOT	222	167
SA-342L *Gazelle*	AP•ATGW•obs	4 x HOT	218	187
Sea King HAS 5/6	ASW	2 x *Stingray* torp	207	200
SH-2G *Seasprite*	ASW	2 x Mk46/50 torp	222	200
SH-3	ASW	4 x Mk46 torp	220	250
SH-60B/F *Sea Hawk*	ASW	3 x Mk46/50 torp	224	280
Tiger/Tigre	ATGW	4 x HOT	230	360

Table 51 Designations of aircraft and helicopters

Notes

1 [Square brackets] indicate the type from which a variant was derived: 'Q-5 … [MiG-19]' indicates that the design of the Q-5 was based on that of the MiG-19.

2 (Parentheses) indicate an alternative name by which an aircraft is known, sometimes in another version: 'L-188 … *Electra* (P-3 *Orion*)' shows that in another version the Lockheed Type 188 *Electra* is known as the P-3 *Orion*.

3 Names given in 'quotation marks' are NATO reporting names, e.g., 'Su-27… "*Flanker*"'.

4 When no information is listed under 'Country of origin' or 'Maker', the primary reference given under 'Name/ designation' should be looked up under 'Type'.

5 For country abbreviations, see 'Index of Countries and Territories' (pp. 317–18).

Type	Name/ designation	Country of origin•Maker
Aircraft		
A-1	AMX	Br/It•AMX
A-1B	AMX	Br/It•AMX
A-3	*Skywarrior*	US•Douglas
A-4	*Skyhawk*	US•MD
A-5	*Fantan*	PRC•Nanchang
A-6	*Intruder*	US•Grumman
A-7	*Corsair II*	US•LTV
A-10	*Thunderbolt*	US•Fairchild
A-36	*Halcón* (C-101)	
A-37	*Dragonfly*	US•Cessna
AC-47	(C-47)	
AC-130	(C-130)	
Air Beetle		Nga•AIEP
Airtourer		NZ•Victa
AJ-37	(J-37)	
Alizé		Fr•Breguet
Alpha Jet		Fr/Ge•Dassault–Breguet/Dornier
AM-3	*Bosbok* (C-4M)	It•Aermacchi
An-2	'Colt'	Ukr•Antonov
An-12	'Cub'	Ukr•Antonov
An-14	'Clod'	Ukr•Antonov
An-22	'Cock'	Ukr•Antonov
An-24	'Coke'	Ukr•Antonov
An-26	'Curl'	Ukr•Antonov
An-28	'Cash'	Ukr•Antonov
An-30	'Clank'	Ukr•Antonov
An-32	'Cline'	Ukr•Antonov
An-124	'Condor'	Ukr•Antonov
Andover	[HS-748]	
AS-202	*Bravo*	CH•FFA
AT-3		ROC•AIDC
AT-6	(T-6)	
AT-11		US•Beech
AT-26	EMB-326	
AT-33	(T-33)	
Atlantic	(*Atlantique*)	Fr•Dassault–Breguet
AU-23	*Peacemaker*[PC-6B]	US•Fairchild
AV-8	*Harrier* II	US/UK•MD/BAe
Aztec	PA-23	US•Piper
B-1	*Lancer*	US•Rockwell
B-2	*Spirit*	US•Northrop Grumman
B-52	*Stratofortress*	US•Boeing
B-65	*Queen Air*	US•Beech
BAC-167	*Strikemaster*	UK•BAe
BAe-146		UK•BAe
BAe-748	(HS-748)	UK•BAe
Baron	(T-42)	
Be-6	'Madge'	RF•Beriev
Be-12	'Mail' (*Tchaika*)	RF•Beriev

Type	Name/ designation	Country of origin•Maker
Beech 50	*Twin Bonanza*	US•Beech
Beech 95	*Travel Air*	US•Beech
BN-2	*Islander, Defender, Trislander*	UK•Britten-Norman
Boeing 707		US•Boeing
Boeing 727		US•Boeing
Boeing 737		US•Boeing
Boeing 747		US•Boeing
Bonanza		US•Beech
Bronco	(OV-10)	
Bulldog		UK•BAe
C-1		J•Kawasaki
C-2	*Greyhound*	US•Grumman
C-4M	*Kudu* (AM-3)	RSA•Atlas
C-5	*Galaxy*	US•Lockheed
C-7	DHC-7	
C-9	*Nightingale* (DC-9)	
C-12	*Super King Air* (*Huron*)	US•Beech
C-17	*Globemaster III*	US•McDonnell Douglas
C-18	[Boeing 707]	
C-20	(*Gulfstream III*)	
C-21	(*Learjet*)	
C-22	(Boeing 727)	
C-23	(*Sherpa*)	UK•Short
C-26	*Expediter/Merlin*	US•Fairchild
C-42	(Neiva *Regente*)	Br•Embraer
C-45	*Expeditor*	US•Beech
C-46	*Commando*	US•Curtis
C-47	DC-3 (*Dakota*) (C-117 *Skytrain*)	US•Douglas
C-54	*Skymaster* (DC-4)	US•Douglas
C-91	HS-748	
C-93	HS-125	
C-95	EMB-110	
C-97	EMB-121	
C-101	*Aviojet*	Sp•CASA
C-115	DHC-5	Ca•De Havilland
C-117	(C-47)	
C-118	*Liftmaster* (DC-6)	
C-123	*Provider*	US•Fairchild
C-127	(Do-27)	Sp•CASA
C-130	*Hercules* (L-100)	US•Lockheed
C-131	Convair 440	US•Convair
C-135	[Boeing 707]	
C-137	[Boeing 707]	
C-140	(*Jetstar*)	US•Lockheed
C-141	*Starlifter*	US•Lockheed
C-160		Fr/Ge•Transall
C-212	*Aviocar*	Sp•CASA
C-235		Sp•CASA
CA-25	*Winjeel*	Aus•Commonwealth

Type	Name/ designation	Country of origin • Maker
Canberra		UK•BAe
CAP-10		Fr•Mudry
CAP-20		Fr•Mudry
CAP-230		Fr•Mudry
Caravelle	SE-210	Fr•Aérospatiale
CC-109	(Convair 440)	US•Convair
CC-115	DHC-5	
CC-117	(Falcon 20)	
CC-132	(DHC-7)	
CC-137	(Boeing 707)	
CC-138	(DHC-6)	
CC-144	CL-600/-601	Ca•Canadair
CF-18	F/A-18	
CF-116	F-5	
Cheetah	[*Mirage* III]	RSA•Atlas
Cherokee	PA-28	US•Piper
Cheyenne	PA-31T [*Navajo*]	US•Piper
Chieftain	PA-31-350 [*Navajo*]	US•Piper
Ching-Kuo		ROC•AIDC
Citabria		US•Champion
Citation	(T-47)	US•Cessna
CJ-6	[*Yak-18*]	PRC•Nanchang
CL-44		Ca•Canadair
CL-215		Ca•Canadair
CL-601	*Challenger*	Ca•Canadair
CM-170	*Magister* [*Tzukit*]	Fr•Aérospatiale
CM-175	*Zéphyr*	Fr•Aérospatiale
CN-235		Sp/Indo•CASA/IPTN
Cochise	T-42	
Comanche	PA-24	US•Piper
Commander	Aero-/TurboCommander	US•Rockwell
Commodore	MS-893	Fr•Aérospatiale
CP-3	P-3 *Orion*	
CP-121	S-2	
CP-140	*Aurora* (P-3 *Orion*)	US•Lockheed
	Acturas	
CT-4	*Airtrainer*	NZ•Victa
CT-39	*Sabreliner*	US•Rockwell
CT-114	CL-41 *Tutor*	Ca•Canadair
CT-133	*Silver Star* [T-33]	Ca•Canadair
CT-134	*Musketeer*	
Dagger	(*Nesher*)	
Dakota		US•Piper
Dakota	(C-47)	
DC-3	(C-47)	US•Douglas
DC-4	(C-54)	US•Douglas
DC-6	(C-118)	US•Douglas
DC-7		US•Douglas
DC-8		US•Douglas
DC-9		US•MD
Deepak	(HPT-32)	
Defender	BN-2	
DHC-3	*Otter*	Ca•DHC
DHC-4	*Caribou*	Ca•DHC
DHC-5	*Buffalo*	Ca•DHC
DHC-6	*Twin Otter*, CC-138	Ca•DHC
DHC-7	*Dash-7* (*Ranger*, CC-132)	Ca•DHC
DHC-8		Ca•DHC
Dimona	H-36	Ge•Hoffman
Do-27	(C-127)	Ge•Dornier
Do-28	*Skyservant*	Ge•Dornier
Do-128		Ge•Dornier
Do-228		Ge•Dornier
E-2	*Hawkeye*	US•Grumman

Type	Name/ designation	Country of origin • Maker
E-3	*Sentry*	US•Boeing
E-4	[Boeing 747]	US•Boeing
E-6	[Boeing 707]	
E-26	T-35A (*Tamiz*)	Chl•Enear
EA-3	[A-3]	
EA-6	*Prowler* [A-6]	
EC-130	[C-130]	
EC-135	[Boeing 707]	
EF-11	*Raven*	US•General Dynamic
Electra	(L-188)	
EMB-110	*Bandeirante*	
EMB-111	*Maritime Bandeirante*	Br•Embraer
EMB-120	*Brasilia*	Br•Embraer
EMB-121	*Xingu*	Br•Embraer
EMB-312	*Tucano*	Br•Embraer
EMB-326	*Xavante* (MB-326)	Br•Embraer
EMB-810	[*Seneca*]	Br•Embraer
EP-3	(P-3 *Orion*)	
Etendard		Fr•Dassault
EV-1	(OV-1)	
F-1	[T-2]	J•Mitsubishi
F-4	*Phantom*	US•MD
F-5	-A/-B *Freedom Fighter*	
	-E/-F *Tiger* II	US•Northrop
F-5T	JJ-5	PRC•Shenyang
F-6	J-6	
F-7	J-7	
F-8	J-8	
F-8	*Crusader*	US•Republic
F-14	*Tomcat*	US•Grumman
F-15	*Eagle*	US•MD
F-16	*Fighting Falcon*	US•GD
F-18	[F/A-18], *Hornet*	
F-21	*Kfir*	Il•IAI
F-27	*Friendship*	Nl•Fokker
F-28	*Fellowship*	Nl•Fokker
F-35	*Draken*	Swe•SAAB
F-104	*Starfighter*	US•Lockheed
F-111	EF-111	US•GD
F-117	*Nighthawk*	US•Lockheed
F-172	(Cessna 172)	Fr/US•Reims-Cessna
F/A-18	*Hornet*	US•MD
Falcon	*Mystère-Falcon*	
FB-111	(F-111)	
FH-227	(F-27)	US•Fairchild-Hiller
Firefly	(T-67M)	UK• Slingsby
Flamingo	MBB-233	Ge•MBB
FT-5	JJ-5	PRC•CAC
FT-6	JJ-6	
FTB-337	[Cessna 337]	
G-91		It•Aeritalia
G-222		It•Aeritalia
Galaxy	C-5	
Galeb		FRY•SOKO
Genet	SF-260W	
GU-25	(Falcon 20)	
Guerrier	R-235	
Gulfstream		US•Gulfstream Aviation
Gumhuria	(Bücker 181)	Et•Heliopolis
H-5	[Il-28]	PRC•Harbin
H-6	[Tu-16]	PRC•Xian
H-36	*Dimona*	
Halcón	[C-101]	
Harrier	(AV-8)	UK•BAe

Type	Name/designation	Country of origin•Maker
Hawk		UK•BAe
HC-130	(C-130)	
HF-24	Marut	Ind•HAL
HFB-320	Hansajet	Ge•Hamburger FB
HJ-5	(H-5)	
HJT-16	Kiran	Ind•HAL
HPT-32	Deepak	Ind•HAL
HS-125	(Dominie)	UK•BAe
HS-748	[Andover]	UK•BAe
HT-2		Ind•HAL
HU-16	Albatross	US•Grumman
HU-25	(Falcon 20)	
Hunter		UK•BAe
HZ-5	(H-5)	
IA-35	Huanquero	Arg•FMA
IA-50	Guaraní	Arg•FMA
IA-58	Pucará	Arg•FMA
IA-63	Pampa	Arg•FMA
IAI-201/-202	Arava	Il•IAI
IAI-1124	Westwind, Seascan	Il•IAI
IAI-1125	Astra	Il • IAI
IAR-28		R•IAR
IAR-93	Orao	FRY/R•SOKO/IAR
Il-14	'Crate'	RF•Ilyushin
Il-18	'Coot'	RF•Ilyushin
Il-20	(Il-18)	
Il-28	'Beagle'	RF•Ilyushin
Il-38	'May'	RF•Ilyushin
Il-62	'Classic'	RF•Ilyushin
Il-76	'Candid' (tpt), 'Mainstay' (AEW), 'Midas' (tkr)	RF•Ilyushin
Impala	[MB-326]	RSA•Atlas
Islander	BN-2	
J-2	[MiG-15]	PRC•
J-5	[MiG-17F]	PRC•Shenyang
J-6	[MiG-19]	PRC•Shenyang
J-7	[MiG-21]	PRC•Xian
J-8	[Sov Ye-142]	PRC•Shenyang
J-32	Lansen	Swe•SAAB
J-35	Draken	Swe•SAAB
J-37	Viggen	Swe•SAAB
JA-37	(J-37)	
Jaguar		Fr/UK•SEPECAT
JAS-39	Gripen	Swe•SAAB
Jastreb		FRY•SOKO
Jet Provost		UK•BAe
Jetstream		UK•BAe
JJ-6	(J-6)	
JZ-6	(J-6)	
K-8		PRC/Pak•NAMC/PAC
KA-3	[A-3]	
KA-6	[A-6]	
KC-10	Extender [DC-10]	US•MD
KC-130	[C-130]	
KC-135	[Boeing 707]	
KE-3A	[Boeing 707]	
Kfir		Il•IAI
King Air		US•Beech
Kiran	HJT-16	
Kraguj		FRY•SOKO
Kudu	C-4M	
L-4	Cub	
L-18	Super Cub	US•Piper
L-19	O-1	

Type	Name/designation	Country of origin•Maker
L-21	Super Cub	US•Piper
L-29	Delfin	Cz•Aero
L-39	Albatros	Cz•Aero
L-70	Vinka	SF•Valmet
L-90TP	Redigo	SF•Valmet
L-100	C-130 (civil version)	
L-188	Electra (P-3 Orion)	US•Lockheed
L-410	Turbolet	Cz•LET
L-1011	Tristar	US•Lockheed
LAC52	YAK52	RF•Aerostar
Learjet	(C-21)	US•Gates
LR-1	(MU-2)	J•Mitsubishi
M-28	Skytruck	Pl•MIELEC
Magister	CM-170	
Marut	HF-24	
Mashshaq	MFI-17	Pak/Swe•PAC/SAAB
Matador	(AV-8)	
MB-326		It•Aermacchi
MB-339	(Veltro)	It•Aermacchi
MBB-233	Flamingo	
MC-130	(C-130)	
Mercurius	(HS-125)	
Merlin		US•Fairchild
Mescalero	T-41	
Metro		US•Fairchild
MFI-15	Safari	Swe•SAAB
MFI-17	Supporter (T-17)	Swe•SAAB
MH-1521	Broussard	Fr•Max Holste
MiG-15	'Midget' trg	RF•MiG
MiG-17	'Fresco'	RF•MiG
MiG-19	'Farmer'	RF•MiG
MiG-21	'Fishbed'	RF•MiG
MiG-23	'Flogger'	RF•MiG
MiG-25	'Foxbat'	RF•MiG
MiG-27	'Flogger D'	RF•MiG
MiG-29	'Fulcrum'	RF•MiG
MiG-31	'Foxhound'	RF•MiG
Mirage		Fr•Dassault
Missionmaster	N-22	
Mohawk	OV-1	
MS-760	Paris	Fr•Aérospatiale
MS-893	Commodore	
MU-2	LR-1	J•Mitsubishi
Musketeer	Beech 24	US•Beech
Mya-4	'Bison'	RF•Myasishchev
Mystère-Falcon		Fr•Dassault
N-22	Floatmaster, Missionmaster	Aus•GAF
N-24	Searchmaster B/L	Aus•GAF
N-262	Frégate	Fr•Aérospatiale
N-2501	Noratlas	Fr•Aérospatiale
Navajo	PA-31	US•Piper
NC-212	C-212	Sp/Indo•CASA/Nurtanio
NC-235	C-235	Sp/Indo•CASA/Nurtanio
Nesher	[Mirage III]	Il•IAI
NF-5	(F-5)	
Nightingale	(DC-9)	
Nimrod		UK•BAe
Nomad		Aus•GAF
O-1	Bird Dog	US•Cessna
O-2	(Cessna 337 Skymaster)	US•Cessna
OA-4	(A-4)	
OA-37	Dragonfly	

Type	Name/designation	Country of origin•Maker
Orao	IAR-93	
Ouragan		Fr•Dassault
OV-1	*Mohawk*	US•Rockwell
OV-10	*Bronco*	US•Rockwell
P-2J	[SP-2]	J•Kawasaki
P-3		CH•Pilatus
P-3	*Orion*	US•Lockheed
P-92		It•Teenam
P-95	EMB-110	
P-149		It•Piaggio
P-166		It•Piaggio
P-180	*Avanti*	It•Piaggio
PA-18	*Super Cub*	US•Piper
PA-23	*Aztec*	US•Piper
PA-24	*Comanche*	US•Piper
PA-28	*Cherokee*	US•Piper
PA-31	*Navajo*	US•Piper
PA-32	*Cherokee Six*	US•Piper
PA-34	*Seneca*	US•Piper
PA-44	*Seminole*	US•Piper
PBY-5	*Catalina*	US•Consolidated
PC-6	*Porter*	CH•Pilatus
PC-6A/B	*Turbo Porter*	CH•Pilatus
PC-7	*Turbo Trainer*	CH•Pilatus
PC-9		CH•Pilatus
PC-12		CH•Pilatus
PD-808		It•Piaggio
Pillán	T-35	
PL-1	*Chien Shou*	ROC•AIDC
PLZ M-28	[An-28]	Pl•PZL
Porter	PC-6	
PS-5	[SH-5]	PRC•HAMC
PT-6	[CJ-6]	PRC•Nanchang
PZL M-28	M-28 [An-28]	Pl•PZL
PZL-104	*Wilga*	Pl•PZL
PZL-130	*Orlik*	Pl•PZL
Q-5	'Fantan' [MiG-19]	PRC•Nanchang
Queen Air	(U-8)	
R-160		Fr•Socata
R-235	*Guerrier*	Fr•Socata
RC-21	(C-21, *Learjet*)	
RC-47	(C-47)	
RC-95	(EMB-110)	
RC-135	[Boeing 707]	
RF-4	(F-4)	
RF-5	(F-5)	
RF-35	(F-35)	
RF-104	(F-104)	
RG-8A		US•Schweizer
RT-26	(EMB-326)	
RT-33	(T-33)	
RU-21	(*King Air*)	
RV-1	(OV-1)	
S-2	*Tracker*	US•Grumman
S-3	*Viking*	US•Lockheed
S-208		It•SIAI
S-211		It•SIAI
SA 2-37A		US•Schweizer
Sabreliner	(CT-39)	US•Rockwell
Safari	MFI-15	
Safir	SAAB-91 (SK-50)	Swe•SAAB
SC-7	*Skyvan*	UK•Short
SE-210	*Caravelle*	
Sea Harrier	(*Harrier*)	

Type	Name/designation	Country of origin•Maker
Seascan	IAI-1124	
Searchmaster	N-24 B/L	
Seneca	PA-34 (EMB-810)	US•Piper
Sentry	(O-2)	US•Summit
SF-37	(J-37)	
SF-260	(SF-260W *Warrior*)	It•SIAI
SH-37	(J-37)	
Sherpa	Short 330, C-23	UK•Short
Short 330	(*Sherpa*)	UK•Short
Sierra 200	(*Musketeer*)	
SK-35	(J-35)	Swe•SAAB
SK-37	(J-37)	
SK-50	(*Safir*)	
SK-60	(SAAB-105)	Swe•SAAB
SK-61	(*Bulldog*)	
Skyvan		UK•Short
SM-90		RF•Technoavia
SM-1019		It•SIAI
SP-2H	*Neptune*	US•Lockheed
SR-71	*Blackbird*	US•Lockheed
Su-7	'Fitter A'	RF•Sukhoi
Su-15	'Flagon'	RF•Sukhoi
Su-17/-20/-22	'Fitter'	RF•Sukhoi
Su-24	'Fencer'	RF•Sukhoi
Su-25	'Frogfoot'	RF•Sukhoi
Su-27	'Flanker'	RF•Sukhoi
Su-29		RF•Sukhoi
Super		Fr•Dassault
Shrike Aerocommander		US•Rockwell
Super Galeb		FRY•SOKO
T-1		J•Fuji
T-1A	*Jayhawk*	US•Beech
T-2	*Buckeye*	US•Rockwell
T-2		J•Mitsubishi
T-3		J•Fuji
T-17	(*Supporter, MFI-17*)	Swe•SAAB
T-23	*Uirapurú*	Br•Aerotec
T-25	Neiva *Universal*	Br•Embraer
T-26	EMB-326	
T-27	*Tucano*	Br•Embraer
T-28	*Trojan*	US•North American
T-33	*Shooting Star*	US•Lockheed
T-34	*Mentor*	US•Beech
T-35	*Pillán* [PA-28]	Chl•Enaer
T-36	(C-101)	
T-37	(A-37)	
T-38	*Talon*	US•Northrop
T-39	(*Sabreliner*)	US•Rockwell
T-41	*Mescalero* (Cessna 172)	US•Cessna
T-42	*Cochise* (*Baron*)	US•Beech
T-43	(Boeing 737)	
T-44	(*King Air*)	
T-47	(*Citation*)	
T-67M	(*Firefly*)	UK • Slingsby
T-400	(T-1A)	US•Beech
TB-20	*Trinidad*	Fr•Aérospatiale
TB-21	*Trinidad*	Fr•Socata
TB-30	*Epsilon*	Fr•Aérospatiale
TB-200	*Tobago*	Fr•Socata
TBM-700		Fr•Socata
TC-45	(C-45, trg)	
TCH-1		ROC•AIDC
Texan	T-6	

Type	Name/ designation	Country of origin•Maker
TL-1	(KM-2)	J•Fuji
Tornado		UK/Ge/It•Panavia
TR-1	[U-2]	US•Lockheed
Travel Air	Beech 95	
Trident		UK•BAe
Trislander	BN-2	
Tristar	L-1011	
TS-8	*Bies*	Pl•PZL
TS-11	*Iskra*	Pl•PZL
Tu-16	'Badger'	RF•Tupolev
Tu-22	'Blinder'	RF•Tupolev
Tu-26	'Backfire', (Tu-22M)	RF•Tupolev
Tu-28	'Fiddler'	RF•Tupolev
Tu-95	'Bear'	RF•Tupolev
Tu-126	'Moss'	RF•Tupolev
Tu-134	'Crusty'	RF•Tupolev
Tu-142	'Bear F'	RF•Tupolev
Tu-154	'Careless'	RF•Tupolev
Tu-160	'Blackjack'	RF•Tupolev
Turbo Porter	PC-6A/B	
Twin Bonanza	Beech 50	
Twin Otter	DHC-6	
Tzukit	[CM-170]	Il•IAI
U-2		US•Lockheed
U-3	(Cessna 310)	US•Cessna
U-4	*Gulfstream IV*	US•Gulfstream Aviation
U-7	(L-18)	
U-8	(Twin Bonanza/Queen Air)	US•Beech
U-9	(EMB-121)	
U-10	*Super Courier*	US•Helio
U-17	(Cessna 180, 185)	US•Cessna
U-21	(King Air)	
U-36	(Learjet)	
U-42	(C-42)	
U-93	(HS-125)	
U-125	BAe 125-800	UK•BAe
UC-12	(King Air)	
UP-2J	(P-2J)	
US-1		J•Shin Meiwa
US-2A	(S-2A, tpt)	
US-3	(S-3, tpt)	
UTVA-66		FRY•UTVA
UTVA-75		FRY•UTVA
UV-18	(DHC-6)	
V-400	*Fantrainer 400*	Ge•VFW
V-600	*Fantrainer 600*	Ge•VFW
Vampire	DH-100	
VC-4	*Gulfstream I*	
VC-10		UK•BAe
VC-11	*Gulfstream II*	
VC-91	(HS-748)	
VC-93	(HS-125)	
VC-97	(EMB-120)	
VC-130	(C-130)	
VFW-614		Ge•VFW
Vinka	L-70	
VU-9	(EMB-121)	
VU-93	(HS-125)	
WC-130	[C-130]	
WC-135	[Boeing 707]	US•Boeing
Westwind	IAI-1124	
Winjeel	CA-25	
Xavante	EMB-326	
Xingu	EMB-121	

Type	Name/ designation	Country of origin•Maker
Y-5	[An-2]	PRC•Hua Bei
Y-7	[An-24]	PRC•Xian
Y-8	[An-12]	PRC•Shaanxi
Y-12		PRC•Harbin
Yak-11	'Moose'	RF•Yakovlev
Yak-18	'Max'	RF•Yakovlev
Yak-28	'Firebar' ('Brewer')	RF•Yakovlev
Yak-38	'Forger'	RF•Yakovlev
Yak-40	'Codling'	RF•Yakovlev
YS-11		J•Nihon
Z-43		Cz•Zlin
Z-226		Cz•Zlin
Z-326		Cz•Zlin
Z-526		Cz•Zlin
Zéphyr	CM-175	

Helicopters

Type	Name/ designation	Country of origin•Maker
A-109	*Hirundo*	It•Agusta
A-129	*Mangusta*	It•Agusta
AB-...	(Bell 204/205/206/ 212/214, etc.)	It/US•Agusta/Bell
AH-1	*Cobra/Sea Cobra*	US•Bell
AH-6	(Hughes 500/530)	US•MD
AH-64	*Apache*	US•Hughes
Alouette II	SA-318, SE-3130	Fr•Aérospatiale
Alouette III	SA-316, SA-319	Fr•Aérospatiale
AS-61	(SH-3)	US/It•Sikorsky/Agusta
AS-332	*Super Puma*	Fr•Aérospatiale
AS-350	*Ecureuil*	Fr•Aérospatiale
AS-355	*Ecureuil II*	Fr•Aérospatiale
AS-365	*Dauphin*	Fr•Aérospatiale
AS-532	*Super Puma*	Fr•Aérospatiale
AS532 UL	*Cougar*	Fr•Eurocopter
AS-550	*Fennec*	Fr•Aérospatiale
AS-565	*Panthar*	Fr•Eurocopter
ASH-3	(Sea King)	It/US•Agusta/Sikorsky
AUH-76	(S-76)	
Bell 47		US•Bell
Bell 204		US•Bell
Bell 205		US•Bell
Bell 206		US•Bell
Bell 212		US•Bell
Bell 214		US•Bell
Bell 406		US•Bell
Bell 412		US•Bell
Bo-105	(NBo-105)	Ge•MBB
CH-3	(SH-3)	
CH-34	*Choctaw*	US•Sikorsky
CH-46	*Sea Knight*	US•Boeing-Vertol
CH-47	*Chinook*	US•Boeing-Vertol
CH-53	*Stallion (Sea Stallion)*	US•Sikorsky
CH-54	*Tarhe*	US•Sikorsky
CH-113	(CH-46)	
CH-124	SH-3	
CH-139	Bell 206	
CH-146	Bell 412	Ca•Bell
CH-147	CH-47	
Cheetah	[SA-315]	Ind•HAL
Chetak	[SA-319]	Ind•HAL
Commando	(SH-3)	UK/US•Westland/Sikorsky
EH-60	(UH-60)	
EH-101		UK/It•Westland/Agusta

Type	Name/designation	Country of origin•Maker
F-28F		US•Enstrom
FH-1100	(OH-5)	US•Fairchild-Hiller
Gazela	(SA-342)	Fr/FRY•Aérospatiale/SOKO
Gazelle	SA-341/-342	
H-34	(S-58)	
H-76	S-76	
HA-15	Bo-105	
HB-315	*Gavião* (SA-315)	Br/Fr•Helibras Aérospatiale
HB-350	*Esquilo* (AS-350)	Br/Fr•Helibras Aérospatiale
HD-16	SA-319	
HH-3	(SH-3)	
HH-34	(CH-34)	
HH-53	(CH-53)	
HH-65	(AS-365)	Fr•Eurocopter
Hkp-2	*Alouette* II/SE-3130	
Hkp-3	AB-204	
Hkp-4	KV-107	
Hkp-5	Hughes 300	
Hkp-6	AB-206	
Hkp-9	Bo-105	
Hkp-10	AS-332	
HR-12	OH-58	
HSS-1	(S-58)	
HSS-2	(SH-3)	
HT-17	CH-47	
HT-21	AS-332	
HU-1	(UH-1)	J/US•Fuji/Bell
HU-8	UH-1B	
HU-10	UH-1H	
HU-18	AB-212	
Hughes 269		US•MD
Hughes 300		US•MD
Hughes 369		US•MD
Hughes 500/520	*Defender*	US•MD
IAR-316/-330	(SA-316/-330)	R/Fr•IAR/Aérospatiale
Ka-25	'Hormone'	RF•Kamov
Ka-27	'Helix'	RF•Kamov
Ka-50	*Hokum*	RF•Kamov
KH-4	(Bell 47)	J/US•Kawasaki/ Bell
KH-300	(Hughes 269)	J/US•Kawasaki/MD
KH-500	(Hughes 369)	J/US•Kawasaki/MD
Kiowa	OH-58	
KV-107	[CH-46]	J/US•Kawasaki/Vertol
Lynx		UK•Westland
MD-500/530	*Defender*	US•McDonnell Douglas
MH-6	(AH-6)	
MH-53	(CH-53)	
Mi-1	'Hare'	RF•Mil
Mi-2	'Hoplite'	RF•Mil
Mi-4	'Hound'	RF•Mil
Mi-6	'Hook'	RF•Mil
Mi-8	'Hip'	RF•Mil
Mi-14	'Haze'	RF•Mil
Mi-17	'Hip'	RF•Mil
Mi-24	'Hind'	RF•Mil
Mi-25	'Hind'	RF•Mil
Mi-26	'Halo'	RF•Mil
Mi-28	'Havoc'	RF•Mil
Mi-35	(Mi-25)	
NAS-332	AS-332	Indo/Fr•Nurtanio/Aérospatiale
NB-412	Bell 412	Indo/US•Nurtanio/Bell
NBo-105	Bo-105	Indo/Ge•Nurtanio/MBB
NH-300	(Hughes 300)	It/US•Nardi/MD
NSA-330	(SA-330)	Indo/Fr•Nurtanio/Aérospatiale
OH-6	*Cayuse* (Hughes 369)	US•MD
OH-13	(Bell 47G)	
OH-23	*Raven*	US•Hiller
OH-58	*Kiowa* (Bell 206)	
OH-58D	(Bell 406)	
Oryx	(SA-330)	
PAH-1	(Bo-105)	
Partizan	(*Gazela*, armed)	
PZL-W3	*Sokol*	Pl•Swidnik
RH-53	(CH-53)	
S-55	(*Whirlwind*)	US•Sikorsky
S-58	(*Wessex*)	US•Sikorsky
S-61	SH-3	
S-65	CH-53	
S-70	UH-60	US•Sikorsky
S-76		US•Sikorsky
S-80	CH-53	
SA-315	*Lama* [*Alouette* II]	Fr•Aérospatiale
SA-316	*Alouette* III (SA-319)	Fr•Aérospatiale
SA-318	*Alouette* II (SE-3130)	Fr•Aérospatiale
SA-319	*Alouette* III (SA-316)	Fr•Aérospatiale
SA-321	*Super Frelon*	Fr•Aérospatiale
SA-330	*Puma*	Fr•Aérospatiale
SA-341/-342	*Gazelle*	Fr•Aérospatiale
SA-360	*Dauphin*	Fr•Aérospatiale
SA-365	*Dauphin* II (SA-360)	
Scout	(*Wasp*)	UK•Westland
SE-316	(SA-316)	
SE-3130	(SA-318)	
Sea King	[SH-3]	UK•Westland
SH-2	*Sea Sprite*	US•Kaman
SH-3	(*Sea King*)	US•Sikorsky
SH-34	(S-58)	
SH-57	Bell 206	
SH-60	*Sea Hawk* (UH-60)	
Sioux	(Bell 47)	UK•Westland
TH-50	Esquilo (AS-550)	
TH-55	Hughes 269	
TH-57	*Sea Ranger* (Bell 206)	
TH-67	Creek (Bell 206B-3)	Ca•Bell
UH-1	*Iroquois* (Bell 204/205/212)	
UH-12	(OH-23)	US•Hiller
UH-13	(Bell 47J)	
UH-19	(S-55)	
UH-34T	(S-58T)	
UH-46	(CH-46)	
UH-60	*Black Hawk* (SH-60)	US•Sikorsky
VH-4	(Bell 206)	
VH-60	(S-70)	
Wasp	(*Scout*)	UK•Westland
Wessex	(S-58)	US/UK•Sikorsky/Westland
Whirlwind	(S-55)	US/UK•Sikorsky/Westland
Z-5	[Mi-4]	PRC•Harbin
Z-6	[Z-5]	PRC•Harbin
Z-8	[SA-321]	PRC•Changhe
Z-9	[SA-365]	PRC•Harbin

Index of Countries and Territories

Index of **Country Abbreviations**

A	Austria	Ga	Georgia	Pan	Panama
AB	Antigua and Barbuda	Gam	Gambia, The	Pe	Peru
Afg	Afghanistan	Gbn	Gabon	Pi	Philippines
Ag	Algeria	Ge	Germany	Pl	Poland
Alb	Albania	Gha	Ghana	PNG	Papua New Guinea
Ang	Angola	Gr	Greece	Por	Portugal
Arg	Argentina	Gua	Guatemala	PRC	China, People's Republic of
Arm	Armenia	GuB	Guinea-Bissau	Py	Paraguay
Aus	Australia	Gui	Guinea		
Az	Azerbaijan	Guy	Guyana	Q	Qatar
		GzJ	Palestinian Autonomous		
Bds	Barbados		Areas of Gaza and Jericho	R	Romania
Be	Belgium			RC	Congo
Bel	Belarus	HKJ	Jordan	RF	Russia
BF	Burkina Faso	Hr	Honduras	RH	Haiti
Bg	Bulgaria	Hu	Hungary	RIM	Mauritania
BiH	Bosnia-Herzegovina			RL	Lebanon
Bn	Benin	Icl	Iceland	RMM	Mali
Bng	Bangladesh	Il	Israel	ROC	Taiwan
Bol	Bolivia	Ind	India	ROK	Korea, Republic of
Br	Brazil	Indo	Indonesia		(South)
Brn	Bahrain	Ir	Iran	RSA	South Africa
Bru	Brunei	Irl	Ireland	Rwa	Rwanda
Btwa	Botswana	Irq	Iraq		
Bu	Burundi	It	Italy	Sau	Saudi Arabia
Bze	Belize			Sdn	Sudan
		J	Japan	Sen	Senegal
C	Cuba	Ja	Jamaica	Sey	Seychelles
Ca	Canada			SF	Finland
Cam	Cambodia	Kaz	Kazakstan	Sgp	Singapore
CAR	Central African Republic	Kgz	Kyrgyzstan	Ska	Sri Lanka
CH	Switzerland	Kwt	Kuwait	SL	Sierra Leone
Cha	Chad	Kya	Kenya	Slvk	Slovakia
Chl	Chile			Slvn	Slovenia
CI	Côte d'Ivoire	L	Lithuania	Sme	Suriname
Co	Colombia	Lao	Laos	Sp	Spain
Cr	Croatia	LAR	Libya	SR	Somali Republic
CR	Costa Rica	Lat	Latvia	Swe	Sweden
Crn	Cameroon	Lb	Liberia	Syr	Syria
CV	Cape Verde	Ls	Lesotho		
Cy	Cyprus	Lu	Luxembourg	Tg	Togo
Cz	Czech Republic			Th	Thailand
		M	Malta	Tjk	Tajikistan
Da	Denmark	Mal	Malaysia	Tkm	Turkmenistan
Dj	Djibouti	Mdg	Madagascar	Tn	Tunisia
DROC	Democratic Republic of	Mex	Mexico	TT	Trinidad and Tobago
	Congo	Mgl	Mongolia	Tu	Turkey
DPRK	Korea, Democratic People's	Mlw	Malawi	Tz	Tanzania
	Republic of (North)	Mol	Moldova		
DR	Dominican Republic	Mor	Morocco	UAE	United Arab Emirates
		Moz	Mozambique	Uga	Uganda
Ea	Estonia	Ms	Mauritius	UK	United Kingdom
Ec	Ecuador	My	Myanmar (Burma)	Ukr	Ukraine
EG	Equatorial Guinea			Ury	Uruguay
ElS	El Salvador	N	Nepal	US	United States
Er	Eritrea	Nba	Namibia	Uz	Uzbekistan
Et	Egypt	Nga	Nigeria		
Eth	Ethiopia	Ngr	Niger	Ve	Venezuela
		Nic	Nicaragua	Vn	Vietnam
Fji	Fiji	Nl	Netherlands		
Fr	France	No	Norway	Ye	Yemen, Republic of
FRY	Federal Republic of	NZ	New Zealand		
	Yugoslavia			Z	Zambia
	(Serbia-Montenegro)	O	Oman	Zw	Zimbabwe
FYROM	Former Yugoslav				
	Republic of Macedonia	Pak	Pakistan		

See 'Index of Countries and Territories' (pp. 317–18) for country abbreviations

<	under 100 tonnes
–	part of unit is detached/less than
+	unit reinforced/more than
*	training aircraft considered combat-capable
†	serviceability in doubt
ε	estimated
' '	unit with overstated title/ship class nickname
AAA	anti-aircraft artillery
AAM/R	air-to-air missile/refuelling
AAV	amphibious armoured vehicle
AAW	anti-air warfare
AB(D)	airborne (division)
ABM	anti-ballistic missile
about	the total could be higher
ac	aircraft
ACM	advanced cruise missile
ACV	air cushion vehicle/vessel/ armoured combat vehicle
AD	air defence
adj	adjusted
AE	auxiliary, ammunition carrier
AEW	airborne early warning
AF	stores ship with RAS
AFB/S	Air Force Base/Station
AG	misc auxiliary
AGHS	hydrographic survey vessel
AGI	intelligence collection vessel
AGM	air-to-ground missile
AGOR	oceanographic research vessel
AGOS	ocean surveillance vessel
AH	hospital ship
AIFV	armoured infantry fighting vehicle
AIP	air-independent propulsion
AK	cargo ship
AKR	fast sealift ship
ALARM	air-launched anti-radiation missile
ALCM	air-launched cruise missile
amph	amphibious/amphibian
AMRAAM	advanced medium-range air-to-air missile
AO/T	tanker(s) with/without RAS capability
AOE	auxiliary, fuel and ammu-nition, RAS capability
AP	armed for anti-personnel attack
APC	armoured personnel carrier
APL	anti-personnel land-mine
AR	repair ship
ARG	amphibious ready group
ARM	anti-radiation (radar) missile
armd	armoured
ARS	salvage ship
arty	artillery
AR(R)V	armoured recovery (and repair) vehicle
AS	submarine depot ship
aslt	assault
ASM	air-to-surface missile
ASR	submarine rescue craft
ASROC	anti-submarine rocket
ASTT/W	anti-submarine TT/warfare

ASUW	anti-surface-unit warfare
AT	tug
ATACMS	army tactical missile system
ATBM	anti-tactical ballistic missile
ATGW	anti-tank guided weapon
ATK	anti-tank
avn	aviation
AWACS	airborne warning and control system
BB	battleship
bbr	bomber
bde	brigade
bdgt	budget
BG	battle group
BMD	ballistic missile defence
bn	battalion/billion
BOFI	Bofors Optronic Fire control Instrument
bty	battery
cal	calibration
CALCM	conventional air-launched cruise missile
can	cannon
CAS	close air support
casevac	casualty evacuation
CASM	conventionally armed stand-off missiles
Cat	category
cav	cavalry
cbt	combat
CBU	cluster bomb unit
CC	cruiser
CCT	combat-capable trainer
cdo	commando
CET	combat engineer tractor
CFE	Conventional Armed Forces in Europe
CG/H/N	SAM cruiser/with helicopters/nuclear-fuelled
cgo	freight aircraft
civ pol	civilian police
CLOS	command to line of sight
CMDS	command ship
comb	combined/combination
comd	command
comms	communications
CONUS	continental United States
coy	company
CV/N/V/S	aircraft carrier/nuclear-fuelled/V/STOL and hel
CVBG	carrier battle group
CW	chemical warfare/weapons
DD/G/H	destroyer/with area SAM/ with hel
DDS	dry dock shelter
def	defence
defn	definition
det	detachment
div	division
DMS	defence mobilisation ship
ECM	electronic countermeasures
Econ aid	economic aid with a military use
ECR	electronic combat and reconnaissance
EDA	Excess Defense Articles (US)
EEZ	exclusive economic zone
ELINT	electronic intelligence
elm	element
EmDA	Emergency Drawdown Authority (US)

engr	engineer
EOD	explosive ordnance disposal
eqpt	equipment
ESM	electronic support measures
est	estimate(d)
EW	electronic warfare
excl	excludes/excluding
exp	expenditure
FAC	forward air control
fd	field
FF/G/H	frigate/with area SAM/with helicopter
FGA	fighter, ground-attack
flo-flo	float-on, float-off
flt	flight
FMA/F/S	Foreign Military Assistance/ Financing/Sales
FPS	fleet patrol ship
FROG	Free Rocket Over Ground
ftr	fighter (aircraft)
FW	fixed-wing
FY	fiscal year
GA	group army
gd	guard
GDP	gross domestic product
GNP	gross national product
gp	group
GS	General Service (UK)
GW	guided weapon
HACV	heavy armoured combat vehicle
HARM	high-speed anti-radiation missile
hel	helicopter
HMMWV	high-mobility multipurpose wheeled vehicle
HOT	High-subsonic Optically Teleguided
how	howitzer
HS	Home Service (UK)
HWT	heavy-weight torpedo
hy	heavy
ICBM	intercontinental ballistic missile
IMET	International Military Education and Training
imp	improved
incl	includes/including
indep	independent
inf	infantry
IRBM	intermediate-range ballistic missile
JSTARS	joint strategic airborne reconnaissance system
KT	kiloton
LACV	light armoured combat vehicle
LAMPS	light airborne multi-purpose system
LANTIRN	low-altitude navigation and targeting infra-red system night
LASH	cargo ship barge
LAW	light anti-tank weapon
LCA	landing craft, assault
LCAC	landing craft, air cushion
LCC	amphibious command ship
LCH/M/T/ U/VP	landing craft, heavy/ mechanised/tank/utility/ vehicles and personnel
LGB	laser-guided bomb

Index of **Abbreviations**

LHA	landing ship, assault	nm	nautical mile	SOC	special operations capable
LKA	assault cargo ship	NMP	net material product	some	up to
log	logistic	nuc	nuclear	Sov	Soviet
LPD/H	landing platform, dock/ helicopter	obs	observation	SP	self-propelled
		OCU	operational conversion unit(s)	spt	support
LSD/H/ M/T	landing ship, dock/heavy/ medium/ tank	off	official	sqn	squadron
		O&M	operations and maintenance	SRAM	short-range attack missile
lt	light	OOA	out of area	SRBM	short-range ballistic missile
LWT	light-weight torpedo	OOV	objects of verification	SS(C/I)	submarine (coastal/inshore)
maint	maintenance	op/ops	operational/operations	SSB/N	ballistic-missile submarine/ nuclear-fuelled
MBT	main battle tank	OPV	offshore patrol vessel		
MCC/I/O	mine countermeasures vessel, coastal/inshore/offshore	org	organised/organisation	SSGN	SSN with dedicated non- ballistic missile launchers
		OTH/-B	over-the-horizon/backscatter (radar)		
MCDV	maritime coastal defence vessel			SSM	surface-to-surface missile
		OTHR/T	over-the-horizon radar/ targeting	SSN	nuclear-fuelled submarine
MCLOS	manual CLOS			START	Strategic Arms Reduction Talks/Treaty
MCM/CS	mine countermeasures/ command and support ship	PAAMS	principal anti-air missile system		
				STO(V)L	short take-off and (vertical) landing
		para	paratroop/parachute		
MD	Military District	pax	passenger/passenger transport aircraft	str	strength
mech	mechanised			SUGW	surface-to-underwater GW
med	medium			SURV	surveillance
MEF/B/U	Marine Expeditionary Force/ Brigade/Unit (US)	PCC/I/ O/R/H	patrol craft, coastal/inshore/ offshore/riverine/harbour	SWATH	small waterplane area twin hulled (vessel)
		PDMS	point defence missile system		
MG	machine gun	pdr	pounder	sy	security
MHC/I/O	minehunter, coastal/inshore/ offshore	PFC/I/O	fast patrol craft, coastal/ inshore/offshore	t	tonnes
				TA	Territorial Army (UK)
mil	military	PFM/T	fast patrol craft, SSM/torpedo	tac	tactical
MIRV	multiple independently targetable re-entry vehicle	PGG	patrol craft with SSM	TACS	auxiliary crane ship
		PHM/T	hydrofoil, SSM/torpedo	T-AFS	combat stores ship
misc	miscellaneous	PKO	peacekeeping operation	TAGOS	towed array AGOS
MIUW	mobile inshore undersea warfare	pl	platoon	T-AH	hospital ship
		POMCUS	prepositioning of materiel configured to unit sets	T-AOT	transport oiler
Mk	mark (model number)			T-AVB	maintenance aviation support ship
ML	minelayer	PPP	purchasing-power parity		
MLRS	multiple launch rocket system	PSC	principal surface combatant	TASM	tactical air-to-surface missile
mob	mobilisation/mobile	publ	public	TD	tank division
mod	modified/modification	RAPID	Reorganised Army Plains Infantry Division	tempy	temporary
mor	mortar			tk	tank
mot	motorised/motor	RAM	Rolling Airframe Missile	tkr	tanker
MP	Military Police	RAS	replenishment at sea	TLE	treaty-limited equipment (CFE)
MPA	maritime patrol aircraft	RCL	recoilless launcher		
MPS	marine prepositioning squadron	R&D	research and development	TMD	theater missile defense (US)
		recce	reconnaissance	TOW	Tube-launched Optically- tracked Wire-guided missile
MR	maritime reconnaissance/ motor rifle	regt	regiment		
		rkt	rocket		
MRAAM	medium-range air-to-air missile	RL	rocket launcher	torp	torpedo
		ro-ro	roll-on, roll-off	tp	troop
MRBM	medium-range ballistic missile	RPV	remotely piloted vehicle	tpt	transport
		RRC	rapid-reaction corps	tr	trillion
MRD	motor rifle division	RV	re-entry vehicle	trg	training
MRL	multiple rocket launcher	SACLOS	semi-automatic CLOS	TT	torpedo tube
MRR	motor rifle regiment	SAM	surface-to-air missile	UAV	unmanned aerial vehicle
MRV	multiple re-entry vehicle	SAR	search and rescue	UN	United Nations
MSA	minesweeper, auxiliary	SDV	swimmer delivery vehicles	URG	under way replenishment group
MSC	military sealift command	SEAL	sea–air–land		
MSC/I/ O/R	minesweeper, coastal/ inshore/offshore/riverine	SES	surface-effect ship	USGW	underwater-to-surface GW
		SEWS	satellite early-warning system	utl	utility
msl	missile	SF	Special Forces	UUGW	underwater-to- underwater GW
MT	megaton	SIGINT	signals intelligence		
mtn	mountain	sigs	signals	veh	vehicle
n.a.	not applicable	SLAM	stand-off land attack missile	VIP	very important person
Narcs	narcotics (funding for anti- drug operations)	SLBM	submarine-launched ballistic missile	VLS	vertical launch system
				V(/S)TOL	vertical(/short) take-off and landing
NASAMS	Norwegian Advanced SAM System	SLCM	sea-launched cruise missile		
				wg	wing
NBC	nuclear, biological and chemical	SLEP	service life extension programme	WMD	weapon(s) of mass destruction
NCO	non-commissioned officer	SMAW	shoulder-launched multi- purpose assault weapon	wpn	weapon
n.k.	not known			XFPB	extra-fast patrol boat